GRAFFITI. FROM A TO Z

RAFFITI. DE A À Z | GRAFFITI. VON A BIS Z | GRAFFITI. VAN A TOT Z

Godefriduskaai 22
2000 Antwerp
Belgium
Tel: +32 3 226 66 73
Fax: +32 3 226 53 65
www.booqs.be
info@booqs.be

ISBN: 978-94-60650-246
WD: D/2009/11978/025
(Q037)

Texts: Cristian Campos
Photography: Itzel Valle Padilla, www.itzelvalle.tk
Art direction: Mireia Casanovas Soley
Design and layout coordination:
Emma Termes Parera
Layout: Esperanza Escudero
Translation: Cillero & de Motta

Editorial project:

maomao publications
Via Laietana, 32, 4.º, of. 104
08003 Barcelona, Spain
Tel.: +34 932 688 088
Fax: +34 933 174 208
maomao@maomaopublications.com
www.maomaopublications.com

Printed in China

CONTENTS

Global graffiti. From Tokyo to Barcelona via Mexico

The art world is regularly hit by typhoons with some devastating consequences. In the late 1970s, punk demonstrated that there was no need to be able to read music to get up on stage with a guitar hanging around your neck. Prior to this, at the turn of the century, avant-garde art had ridiculed the ideas of beauty traditionally associated with classical art, opting instead for abstraction and irrationality. Cult of ugliness was imposed on architecture, literature, comics... The main message of all these revolutionary movements was quite simple: 'anyone can do it'. But the real punk movement in art was not twentieth-century avant-garde art, but graffiti. Graffiti is the ultimate democratisation of art, the appropriation of public space by completely anonymous youths armed only with a spray can. Even Duchamp depended on the acquiescence of a gallery and a receptive art critic to be able to exhibit his work. A street artist does not ask for anyone's permission, he only needs spray, a template and a wall far enough away from the nearest police station. Graffiti IS revolutionary, and for this same reason it is illegal. It has seized the monopoly on 'good taste in art' owned by barely a thousand people worldwide who decide – for a none-too-small fee – who is an artist, what is art and how much it is worth.

Graffiti originated in the late 1960s and early 1970s on a wall somewhere in New York. Although some say it was in Philadelphia. Since then, its progress has been unstoppable. Today, the term graffiti refers only to one specific technique – that of spray-painting – in the varied genre of street art. Templates, stickers and posters have extended the possibilities of this genre almost infinitely. This book is a comprehensive catalogue of the latest street art trends in cities like Mexico City, Barcelona and Tokyo. Divided into four chapters, the collection comprises over 400 photographs of works by some of the leading contemporary street artists, but also by dozens of anonymous artists who are willing to play with genre boundaries and to invent new forms, colours and mediums for their art.

Because urban art has not stopped evolving since it arrived to stay nearly 40 years ago, whether on the streets or in the pages of a book like this one.

Le graffiti dans le monde. De Tokyo à Barcelone, en passant par Mexico

Le monde de l'art est périodiquement frappé par des typhons aux conséquences dévastatrices. À la fin des années 70, le punk a démontré qu'il n'était pas nécessaire de savoir lire une partition pour monter sur scène avec une guitare en bandoulière. Auparavant, au début du siècle, les avant-gardes artistiques avaient ridiculisé les idées de beauté traditionnellement associées à l'art classique et avaient opté pour l'abstraction et l'irrationalité. Le « goût pour le laid » s'est imposé dans l'architecture, la littérature, la bande dessinée... Le message principal de tous ces mouvements révolutionnaires était assez simple : « n'importe qui peut le faire ».
Mais le véritable punk de l'art, ce ne sont pas les avant-gardes artistiques du XXème siècle, mais le graffiti. Le graffiti suppose la démocratisation définitive de l'art, l'appropriation de l'espace public par des jeunes totalement anonymes, avec pour seule arme un marqueur. Même Duchamp dépendait de l'approbation d'un galeriste et d'un critique d'art réceptif pour pouvoir exposer son œuvre. Un artiste de rue ne demande l'autorisation à personne, il ne dépend de personne : il n'a besoin que d'une bombe de peinture, d'un pochoir et d'un mur suffisamment éloigné du policier le plus proche. Le graffiti est RÉELLEMENT révolutionnaire, c'est pour cela qu'il est illégal : il a ravi le monopole du « bon

GRAFFITI. FROM A TO Z

GRAFFITI. DE A À Z I GRAFFITI. VON A BIS Z I GRAFFITI. VAN A TOT Z

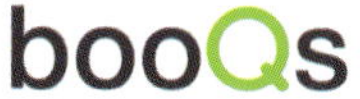

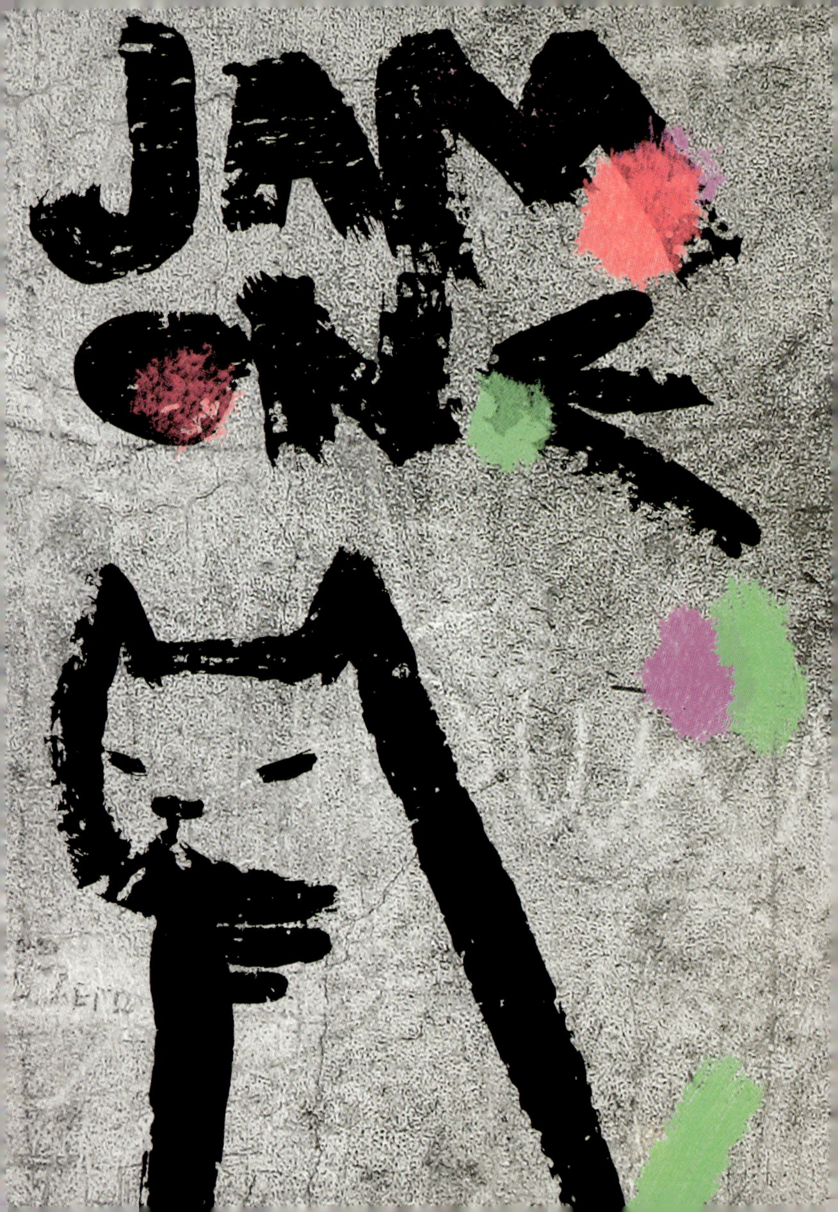
JAM

goût artistique » aux quelques 1 000 personnes dans le monde entier qui décident, pour un prix loin d'être dérisoire, qui est un artiste, ce qui est de l'art et combien vaut cet art.
Le graffiti est né à la fin des années 60, début des années 70 sur un mur de New York. D'autres affirment que c'était à Philadelphie. Dès lors, sa progression a été imparable. Aujourd'hui, le mot graffiti fait uniquement référence à une technique en particulier, parmi toutes celles formant ce que l'on appelle l'art urbain, il s'agit de la peinture à la bombe. Pochoirs, autocollants et affiches ont élargi les possibilités du genre presque à l'infini.
Ce livre est un catalogue approfondi des dernières tendances dans le domaine de l'art urbain dans des villes telles que Mexico, Barcelone et Tokyo. Divisé en quatre chapitres, il comporte plus de 400 photographies des œuvres de quelques-uns des artistes urbains contemporains les plus remarquables, mais également de dizaines d'artistes anonymes disposés à jouer avec les limites du genre et à inventer de nouvelles formes, couleurs et supports pour leur art.
Parce que l'art urbain n'a cessé d'évoluer depuis son arrivée, il y a environ 40 ans, bien décidé à durer, que ce soit dans les rues ou dans les pages d'un livre comme celui-ci.

Graffiti weltweit – Von Tokio über Mexiko nach Barcelona

Die Welt der Kunst wird in regelmäßigen Abständen von Unwettern mit verheerenden Folgen heimgesucht. Ende der siebziger Jahre zeigte die Punk-Bewegung, dass man keineswegs in der Lage sein musste, Noten zu lesen, um sich mit einer Gitarre um den Hals auf eine Bühne zu stellen. Zuvor hatten Anfang des letzten Jahrhunderts die avantgardistischen Kunstströmungen die traditionell der klassischen Kunst zugeschriebenen Schönheitsideale lächerlich gemacht und Abstraktion und Irrationalität propagiert. Der „Hässlichkeitskult" eroberte die Architektur, die Literatur, den Comic... Die wichtigste Message all dieser revolutionären Bewegungen war wirklich einfach: „Jeder kann es".

Die echten Punks der Kunstszene sind jedoch nicht die avantgardistischen Kunstbewegungen des 20. Jahrhunderts, sondern Graffiti. Graffiti bedeutet die endgültige Demokratisierung der Kunst, die Beschlagnahmung des öffentlichen Raums durch anonyme Jugendliche, die allesamt mit einem Filzstift bewaffnet sind. Sogar Duchamp war abhängig von der Zustimmung eines Galeristen und eines offen eingestellten Kunstkritikers, um seine Werke ausstellen zu dürfen. Ein Straßenkünstler bittet niemanden um Erlaubnis und ist von niemandem abhängig. Er braucht lediglich eine Spraydose, eine Schablone und eine Wand, die weit genug von der nächsten Polizeistation entfernt ist. Graffiti IST revolutionär und daher illegal: diese Ausdrucksform hat den rund 1000 Personen weltweit, die für einen keineswegs bescheidenen Preis darüber entscheiden, wer sich Künstler nennen darf, was Kunst ist und wie viel diese Kunst wert ist, das Monopol des „guten Kunstgeschmacks“ entrissen.

Graffiti entstand Ende der sechziger bis Anfang der siebziger Jahre auf einer Wand in New York. Anderswo heißt es, es sei in Philadelphia gewesen. Seit damals war seine Entwicklung unaufhaltsam. Heute bezeichnet der Begriff Graffiti ausschließlich eine bestimmte Technik innerhalb der so genannten urbanen Kunst, nämlich die Malerei mit Farbspray. Schablonen, Sticker und Plakate haben die Möglichkeiten dieser Kunstform beinahe bis ins Unendliche gesteigert.

Der vorliegende Band ist ein umfassender Katalog der neuesten Trends der urbanen Kunst in Städten wie z. B. Mexiko-City, Barcelona und Tokio. In vier Kapiteln zeigt er über 400 Fotos von Werken einiger der berühmtesten zeitgenössischen urbanen Künstler sowie von Dutzenden anonymen Kreativen, die mit den Grenzen des Genres spielen und für ihre Kunst neue Formen, Farben und Flächen erfinden.

Die urbane Kunst hat sich seit ihrer Entstehung vor fast 40 Jahren stetig weiterentwickelt, um einen bleibenden Eindruck zu hinterlassen, sei es auf der Straße oder auf den Seiten dieses Buches.

Graffiti wereldwijd. Van Tokio naar Barcelona via Mexico

De kunstwereld wordt regelmatig geteisterd door wervelstormen met verwoestende gevolgen. Aan het eind van de jaren zeventig liet de punk zien dat het niet nodig was om een notenbalk te kunnen lezen om met een gitaar om de nek op het toneel te gaan staan. Vroeger, aan het begin van de eeuw, hadden avant-gardekunstenaars de schoonheidsideeën die traditioneel in verband werden gebracht met de klassieke kunst belachelijk gemaakt en gekozen voor abstractie en irrationaliteit. Lelijkheid als vorm van kunst kreeg de overhand in de architectuur, literatuur, stripverhalen... De belangrijkste boodschap van al deze revolutionaire bewegingen was nogal eenvoudig: "iedereen kan het".

Maar de ware punk van de kunst zijn niet de avant-gardekunstenaars van de twintigste eeuw, maar de graffiti. Graffiti is de definitieve democratisering van de kunst, de toe-eigening van de openbare ruimte door volledig anonieme knullen die uitsluitend gewapend zijn met een viltstift. Zelfs Duchamp was afhankelijk van de goedkeuring van een galeriehouder en van een ontvankelijke kunstcriticus om zijn werk te kunnen tentoonstellen. De straatkunstenaar vraagt niemand om toestemming, is van niemand afhankelijk: het enige wat hij nodig heeft is een spuitbus, een sjabloon en een muur die zich ver genoeg van de dichtstbij zijnde politie bevindt. Graffiti zijn WEL revolutionair, en dus illegaal: deze kunstvorm heeft het alleenrecht van de "goede artistieke smaak" ontnomen van de amper duizend personen die overal ter wereld, tegen een geenszins billijke prijs, beslissen over wie kunstenaar is, wat kunst is en hoeveel die kunst kost. Graffiti zijn ontstaan aan het eind van de jaren zestig en begin jaren zeventig op een muur in New York. Anderen zeggen dat het in Philadelphia was. Sindsdien is de ontwikkeling ervan niet meer te stuiten. Tegenwoordig verwijst het woord graffiti slechts naar een bepaalde techniek van de diverse technieken waaruit de zogenaamde straatkunst of urban art bestaat, namelijk naar de muurschilderingen aangebracht met spuitbus. Sjablonen, stickers en posters hebben de mogelijkheden van het genre oneindig uitgebreid.

Dit boek is een uitvoerige catalogus van de laatste trends op het gebied van straatkunst in steden zoals Mexico-stad, Barcelona en Tokio. Het boek is verdeeld in vier hoofdstukken en bevat meer dan 400 foto's van werken van sommige van de opvallendste hedendaagse straatkunstenaars, maar ook van tientallen anonieme artiesten die bereid zijn om de grenzen van het genre te overschrijden en nieuwe vormen, kleuren en ondergronden voor hun kunst te verzinnen.

Omdat straatkunst alsmaar in ontwikkeling is sinds zij bijna veertig jaar geleden is ontstaan om niet meer te verdwijnen uit de straten of uit de pagina's van een boek zoals dit.

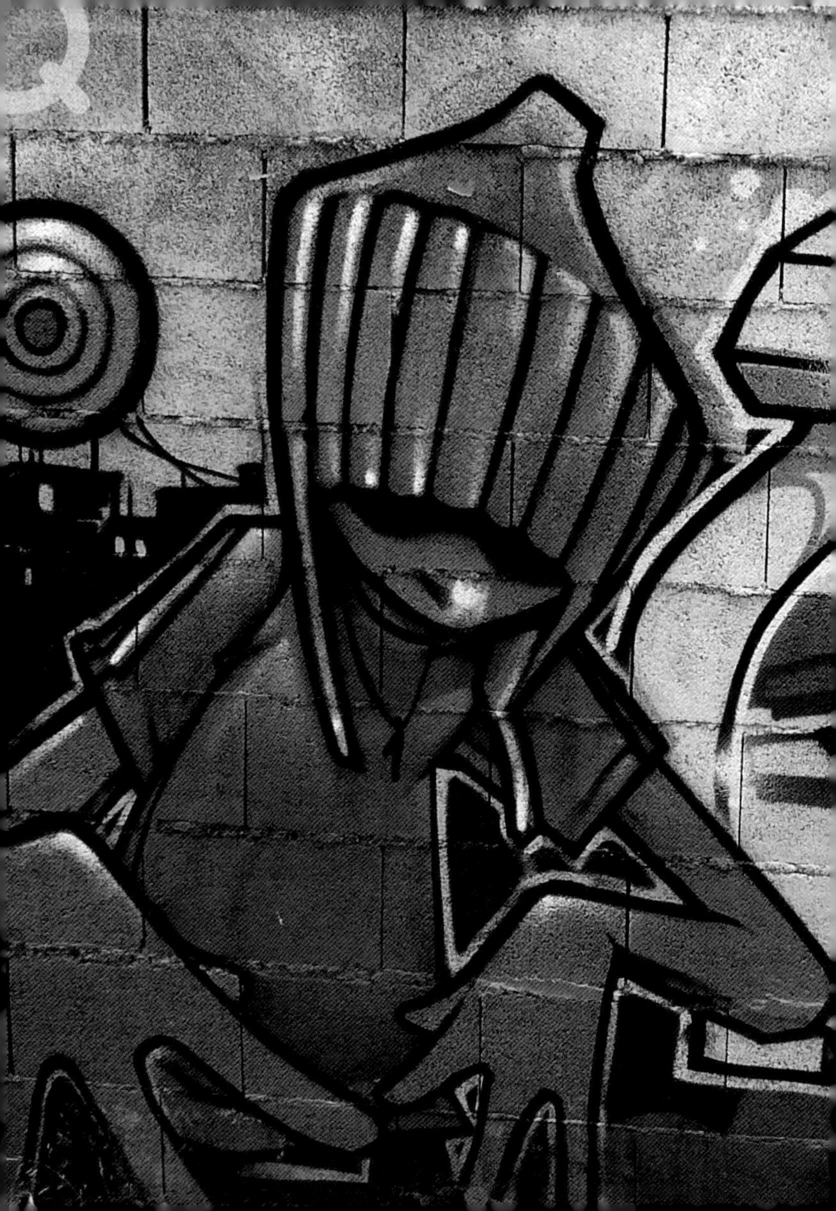

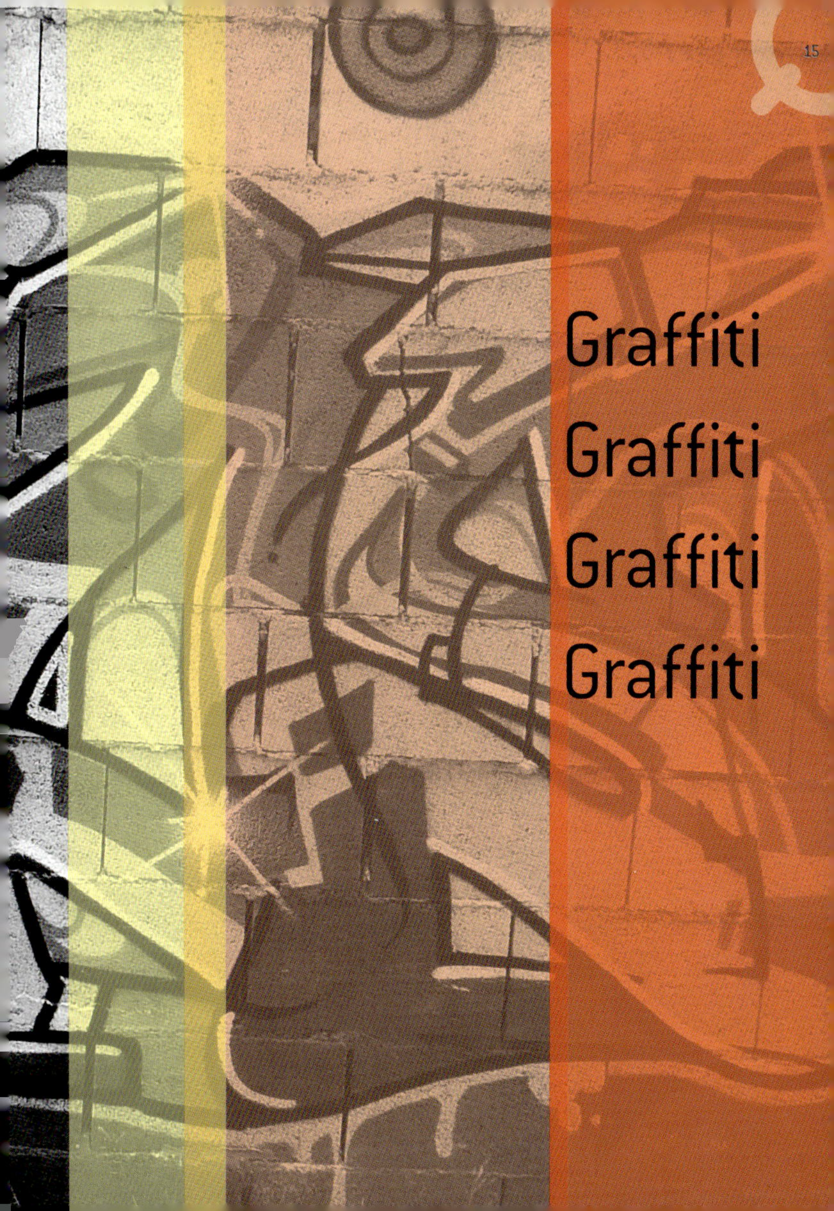

Graffiti
Graffiti
Graffiti
Graffiti

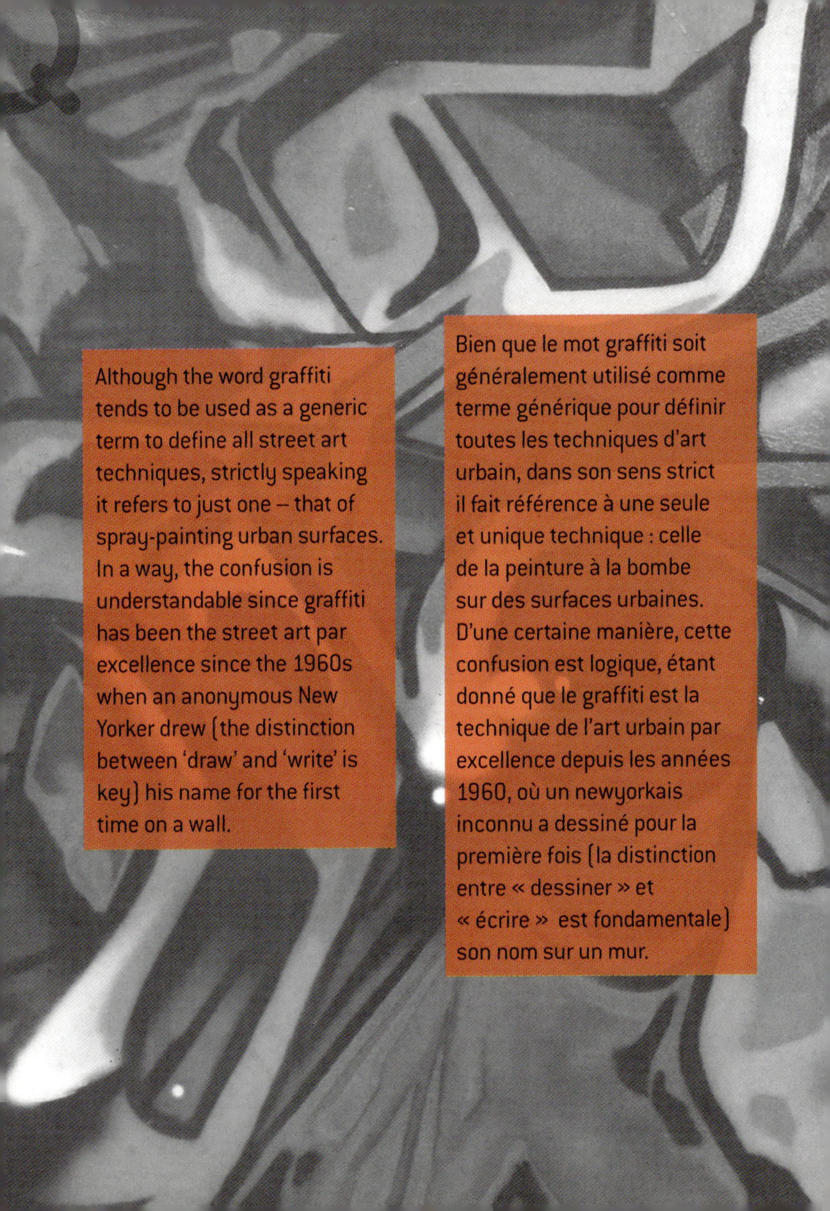

Although the word graffiti tends to be used as a generic term to define all street art techniques, strictly speaking it refers to just one – that of spray-painting urban surfaces. In a way, the confusion is understandable since graffiti has been the street art par excellence since the 1960s when an anonymous New Yorker drew (the distinction between 'draw' and 'write' is key) his name for the first time on a wall.

Bien que le mot graffiti soit généralement utilisé comme terme générique pour définir toutes les techniques d'art urbain, dans son sens strict il fait référence à une seule et unique technique : celle de la peinture à la bombe sur des surfaces urbaines. D'une certaine manière, cette confusion est logique, étant donné que le graffiti est la technique de l'art urbain par excellence depuis les années 1960, où un newyorkais inconnu a dessiné pour la première fois (la distinction entre « dessiner » et « écrire » est fondamentale) son nom sur un mur.

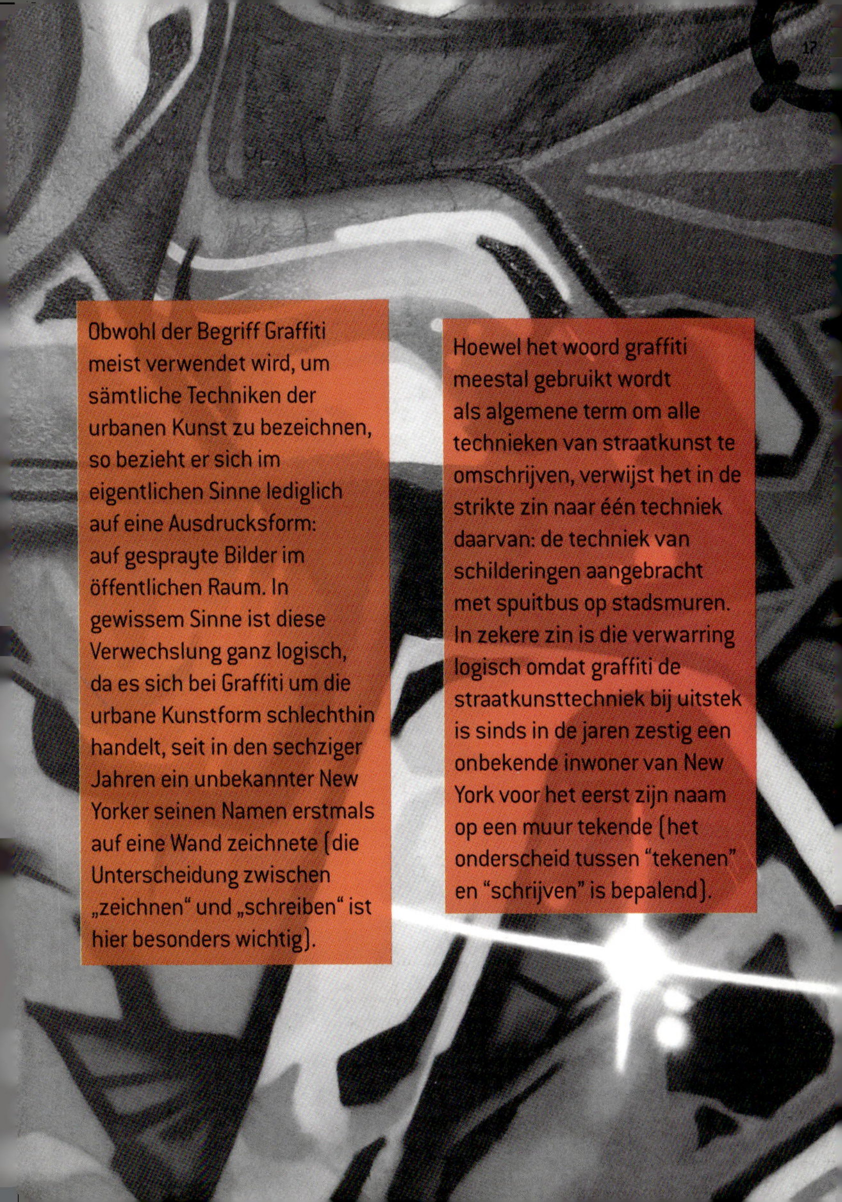

Obwohl der Begriff Graffiti meist verwendet wird, um sämtliche Techniken der urbanen Kunst zu bezeichnen, so bezieht er sich im eigentlichen Sinne lediglich auf eine Ausdrucksform: auf gesprayte Bilder im öffentlichen Raum. In gewissem Sinne ist diese Verwechslung ganz logisch, da es sich bei Graffiti um die urbane Kunstform schlechthin handelt, seit in den sechziger Jahren ein unbekannter New Yorker seinen Namen erstmals auf eine Wand zeichnete (die Unterscheidung zwischen „zeichnen“ und „schreiben“ ist hier besonders wichtig).

Hoewel het woord graffiti meestal gebruikt wordt als algemene term om alle technieken van straatkunst te omschrijven, verwijst het in de strikte zin naar één techniek daarvan: de techniek van schilderingen aangebracht met spuitbus op stadsmuren. In zekere zin is die verwarring logisch omdat graffiti de straatkunsttechniek bij uitstek is sinds in de jaren zestig een onbekende inwoner van New York voor het eerst zijn naam op een muur tekende (het onderscheid tussen “tekenen” en “schrijven” is bepalend).

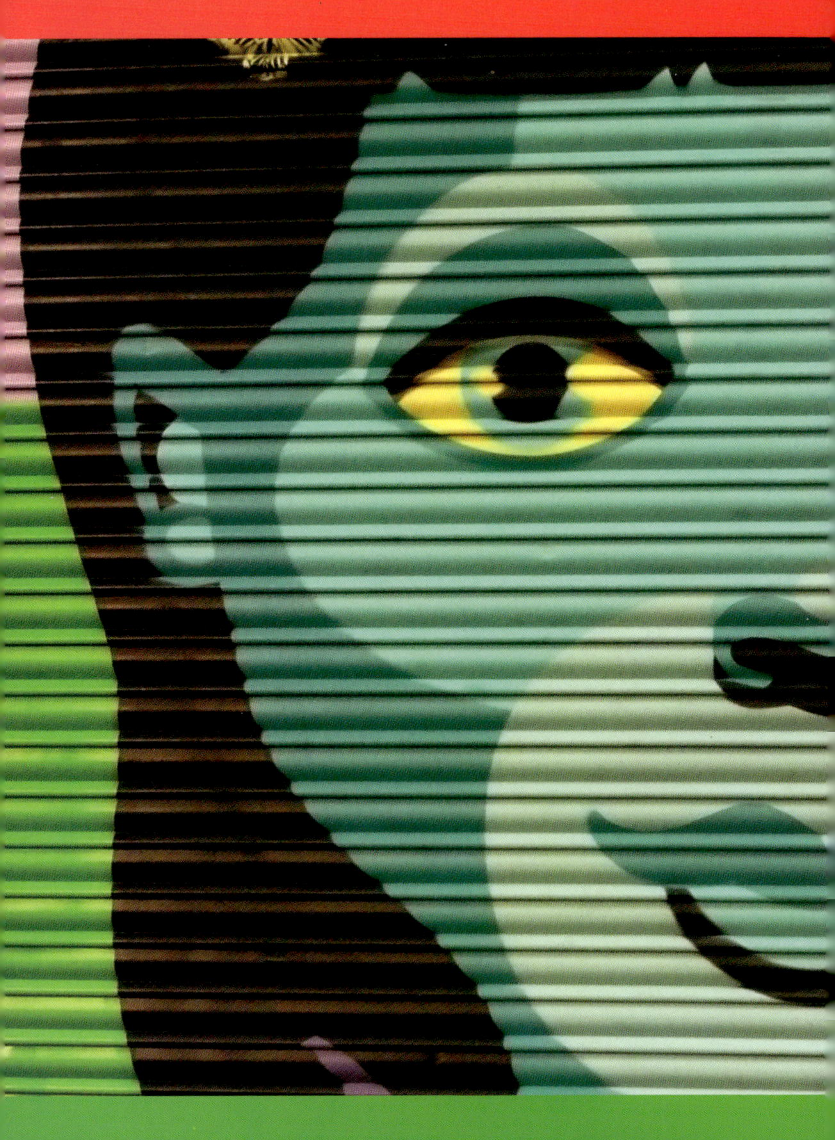

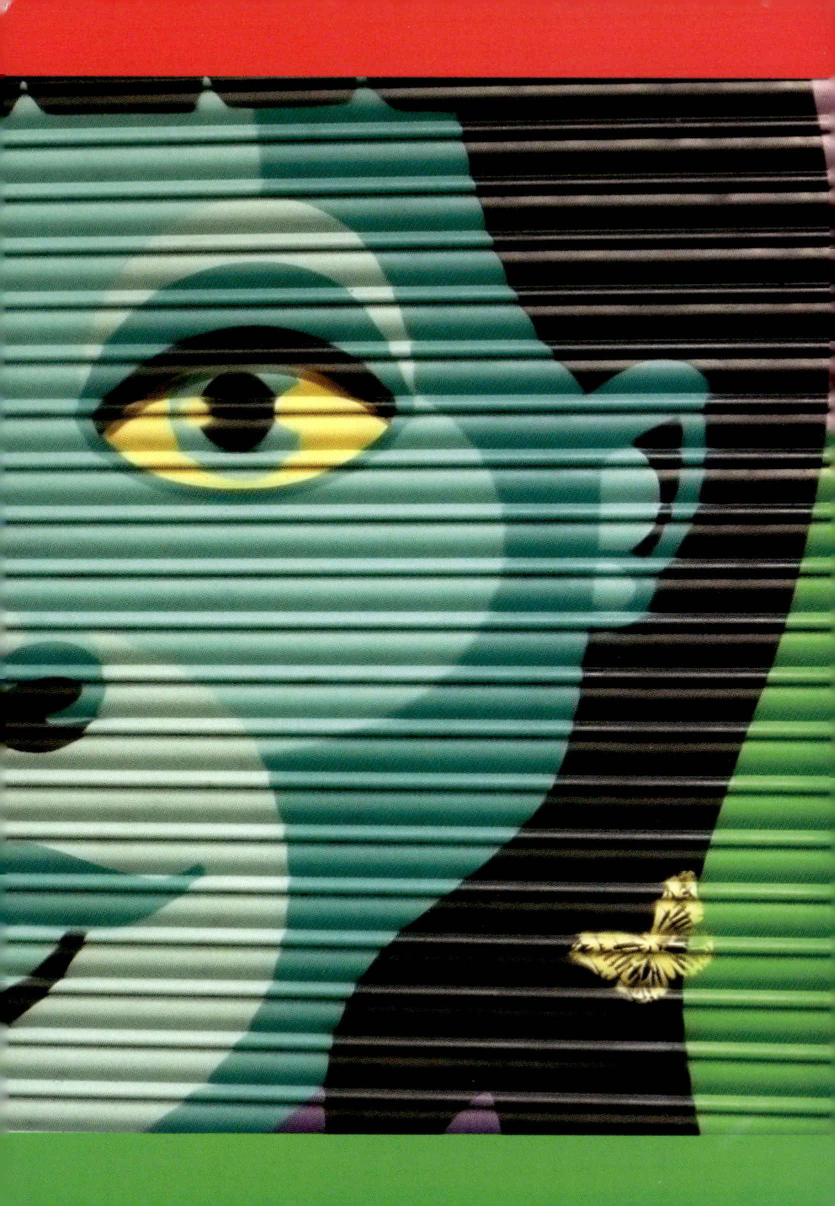

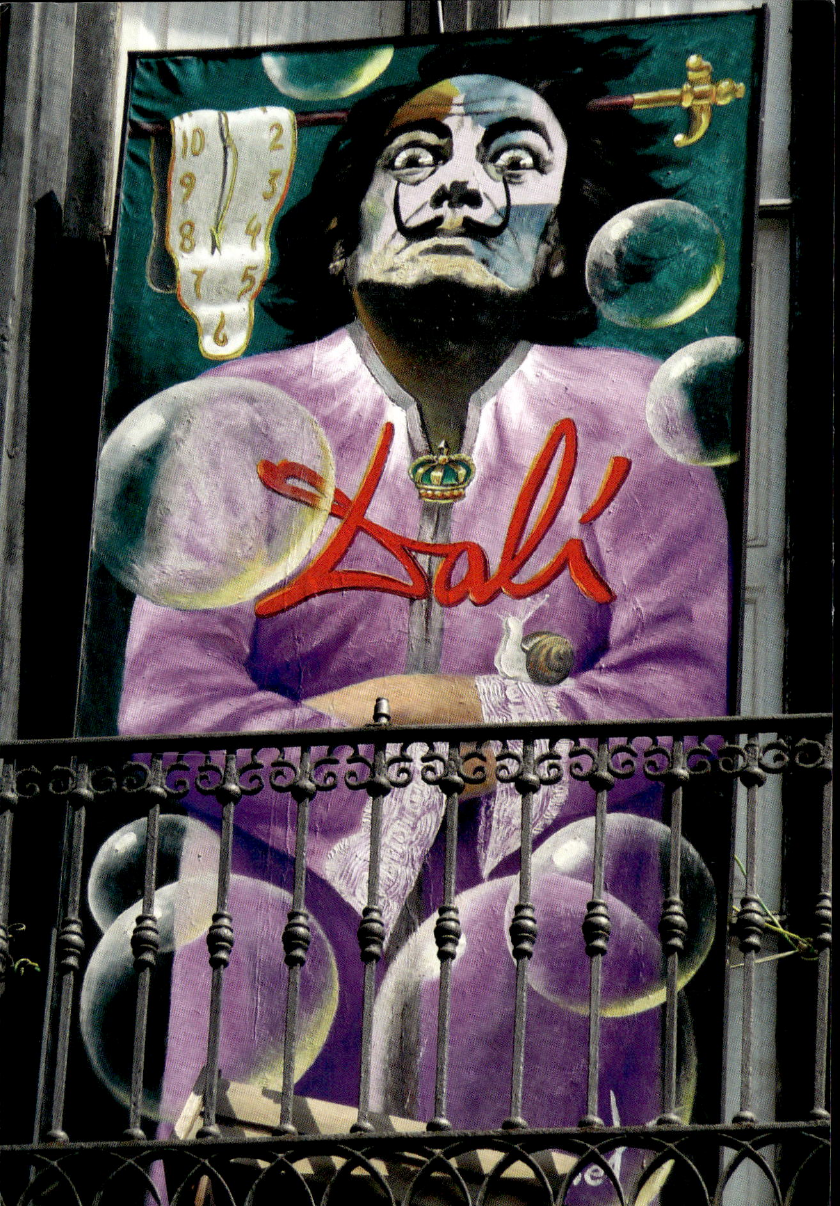
Dalí

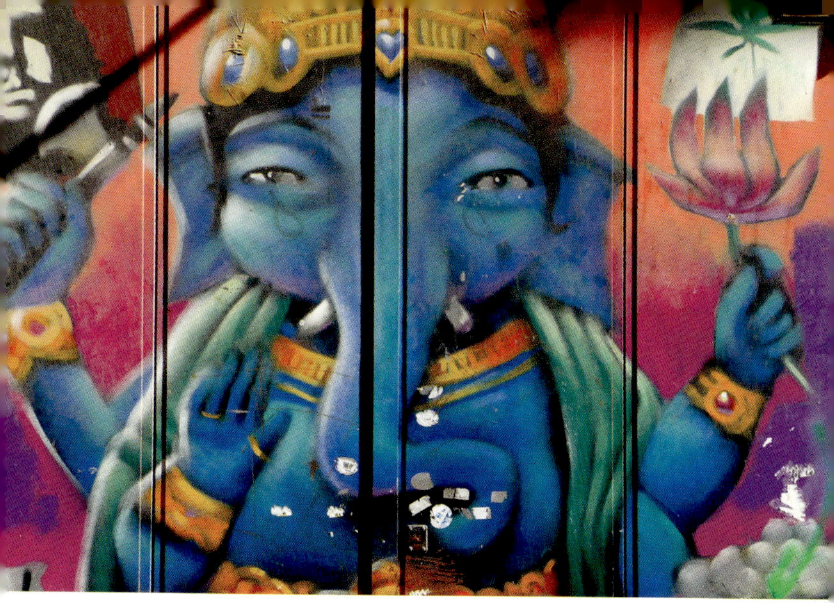

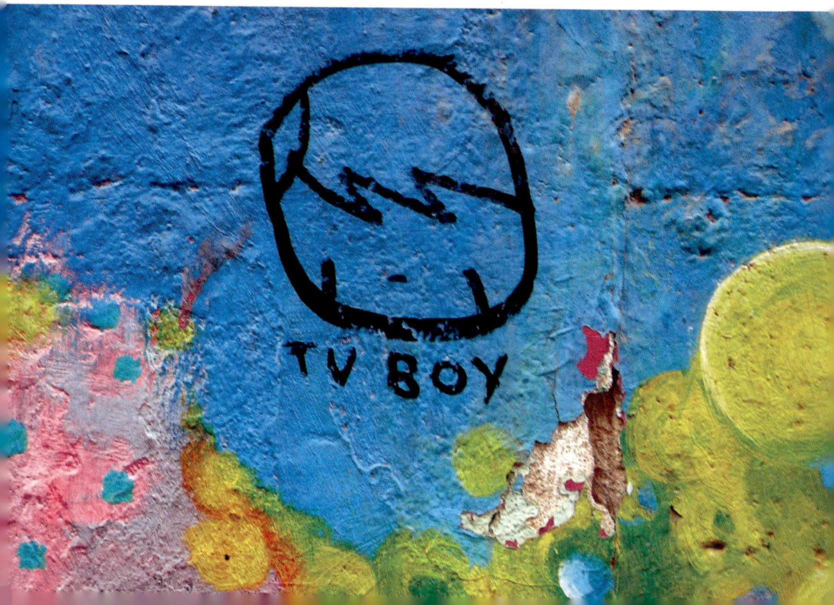

TV BOY

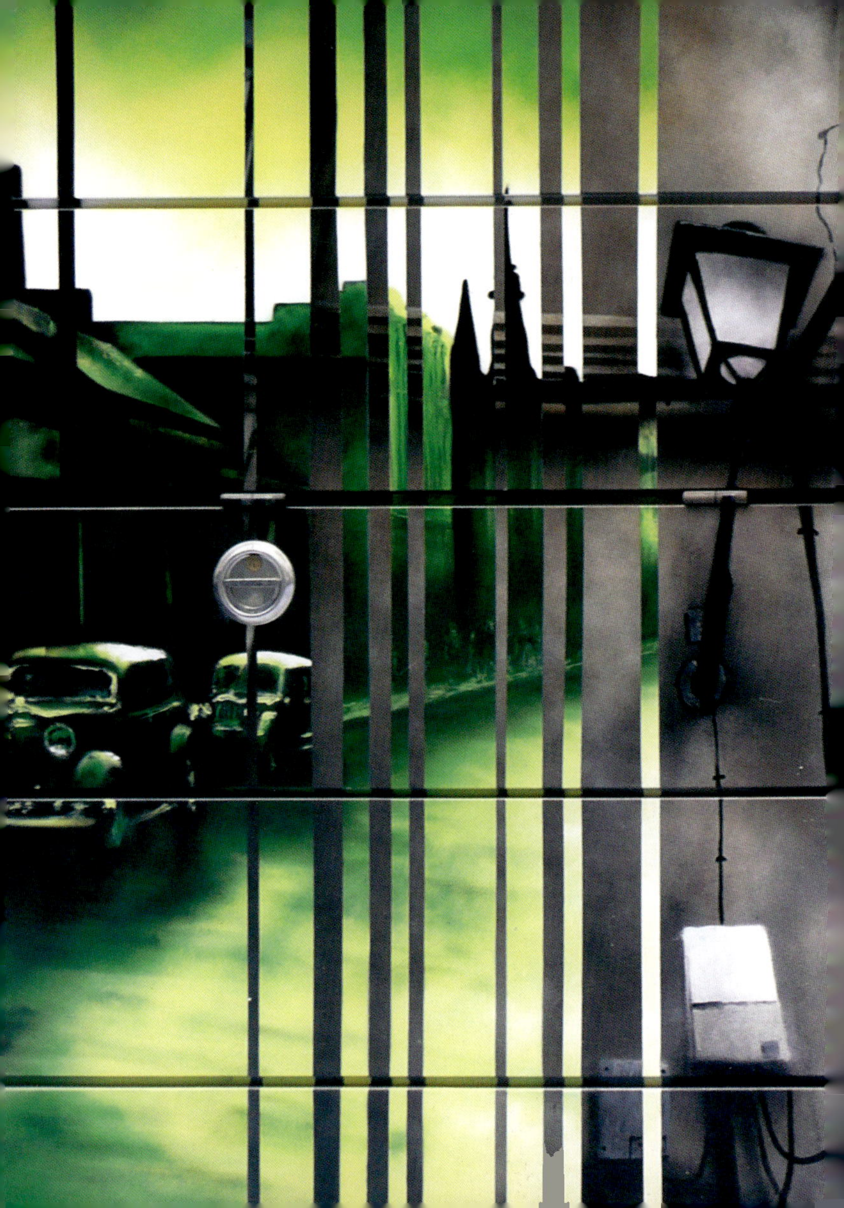

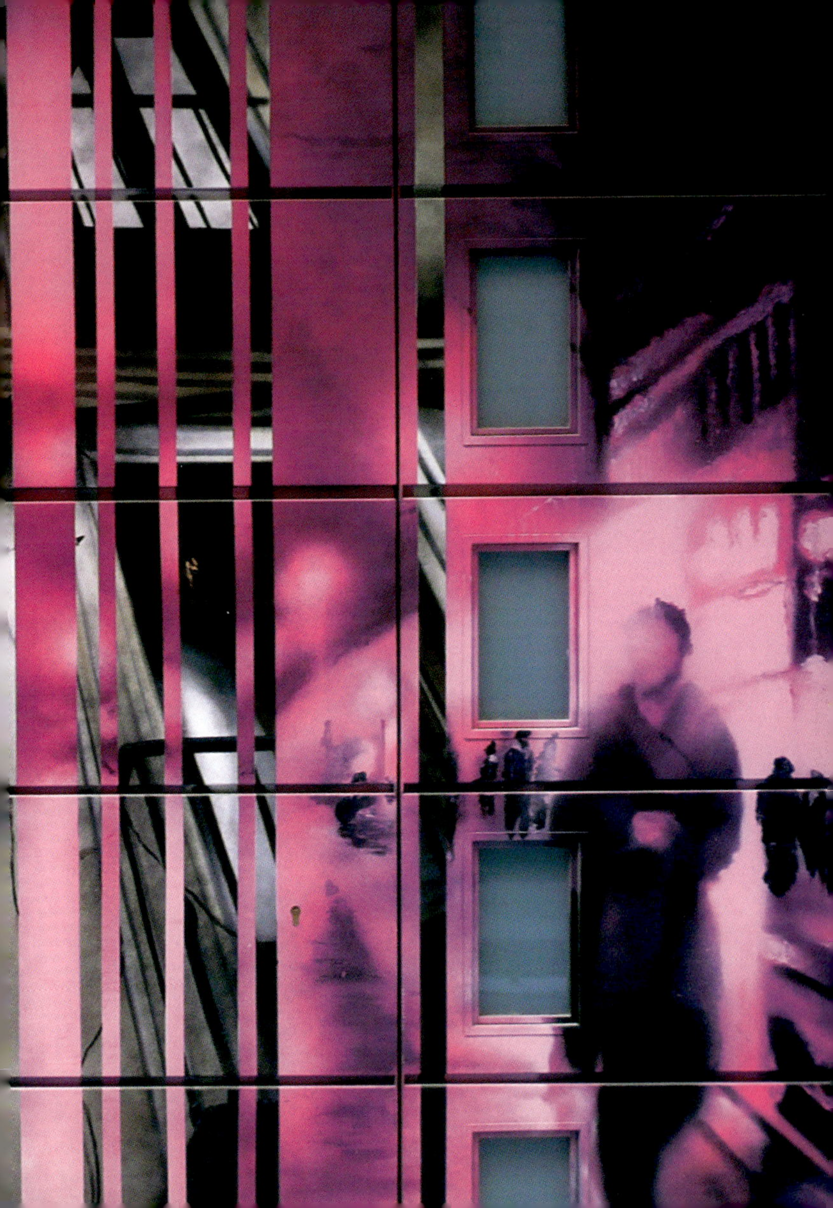

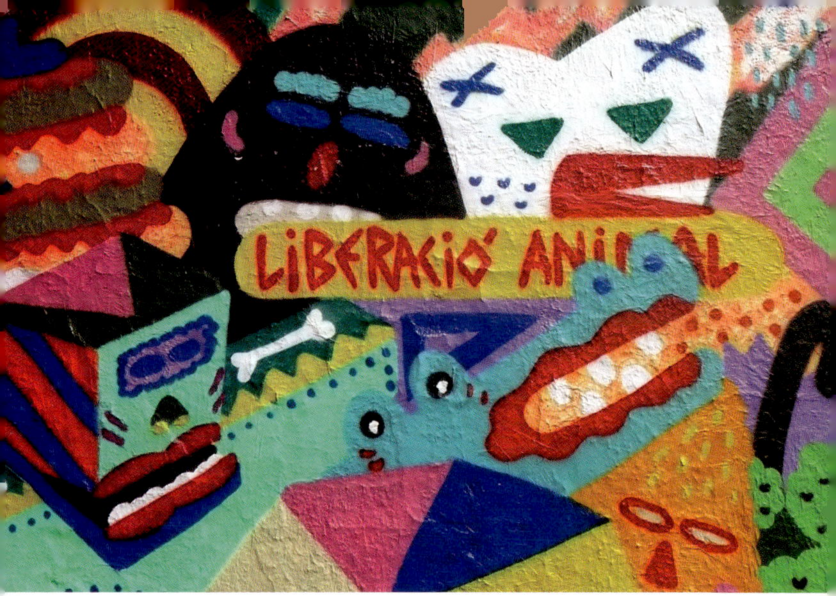

LIBERACIÓ ANI
YO
DE
MAYOR
Y
YO DE

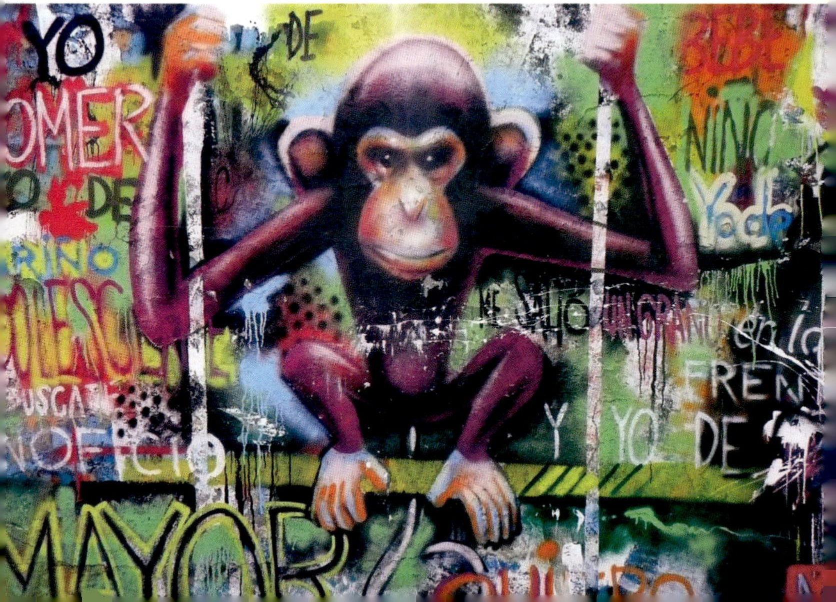

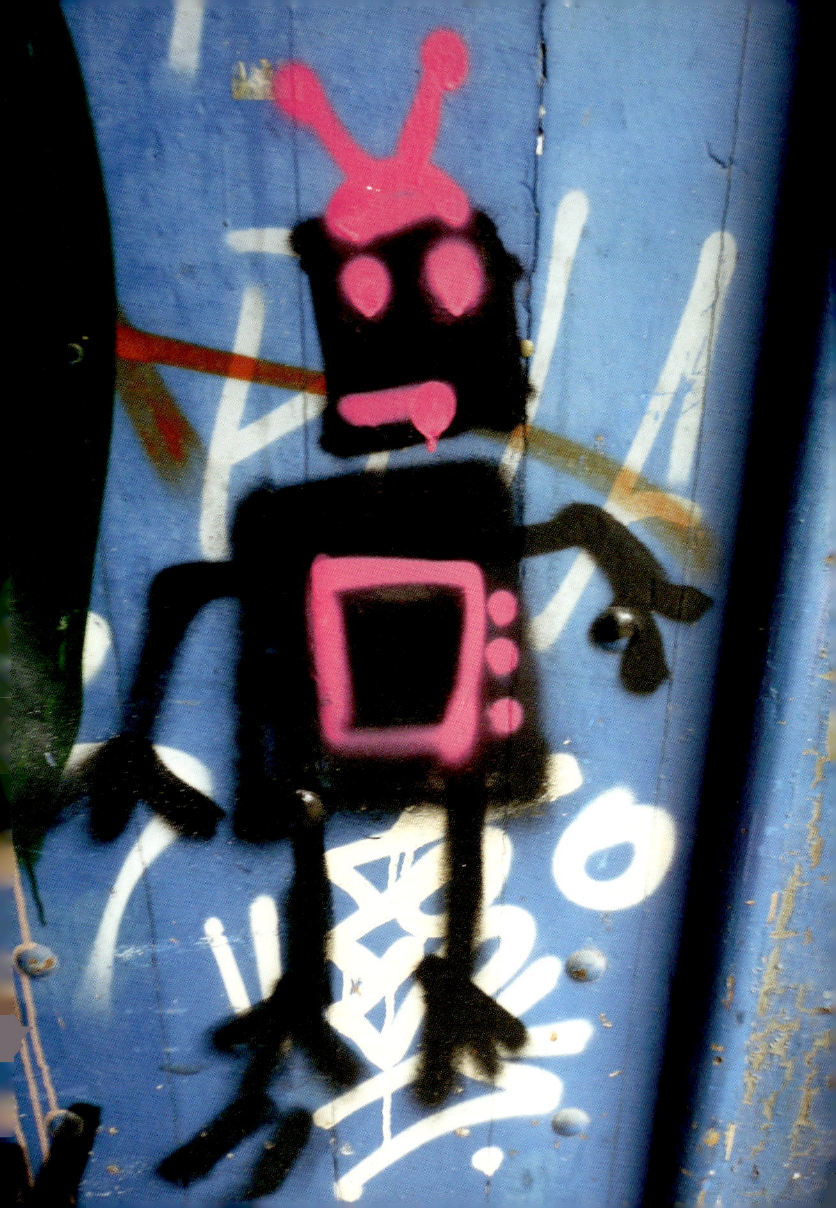

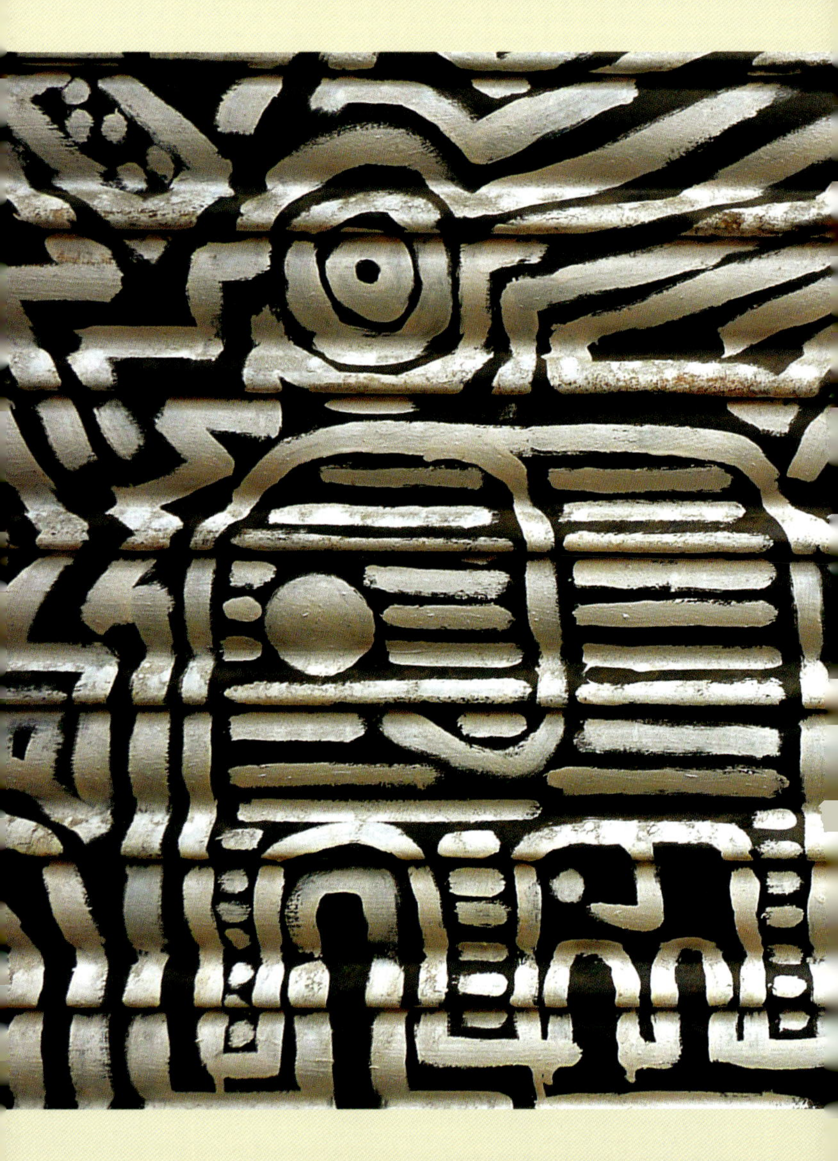

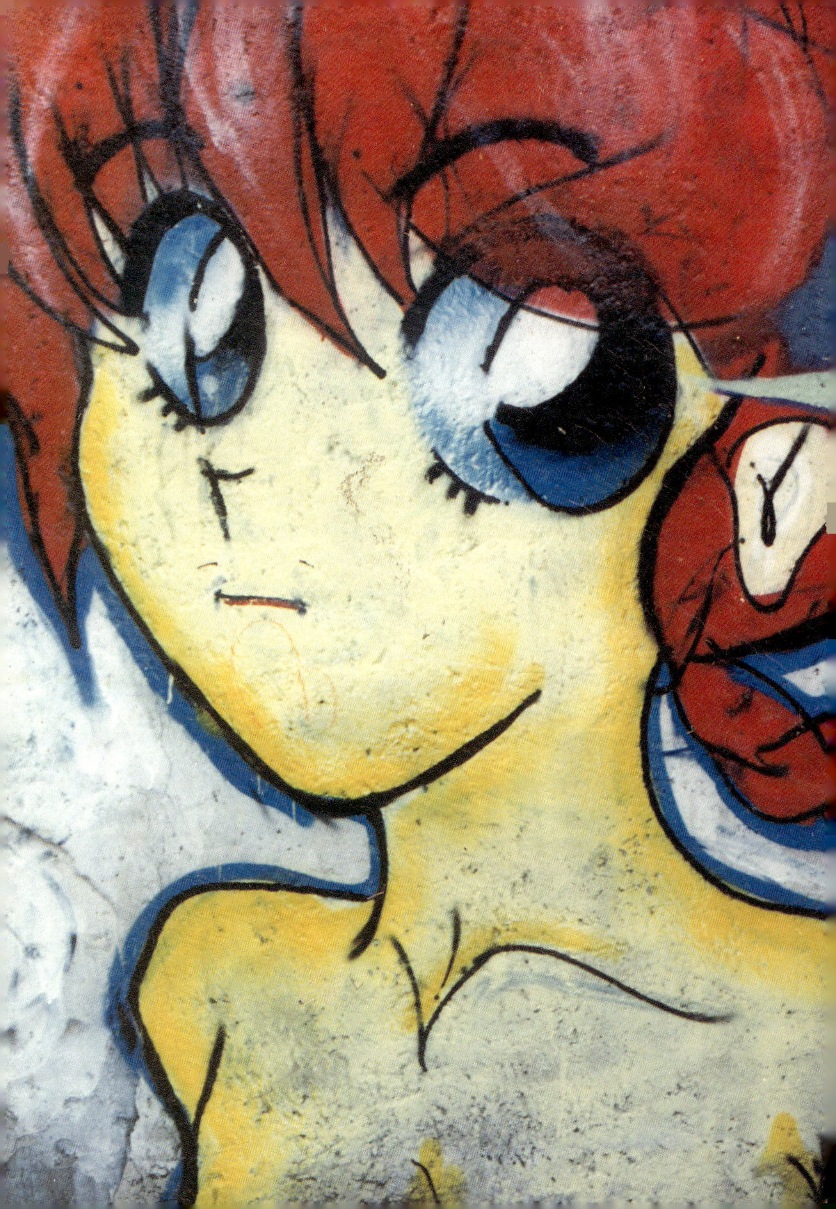

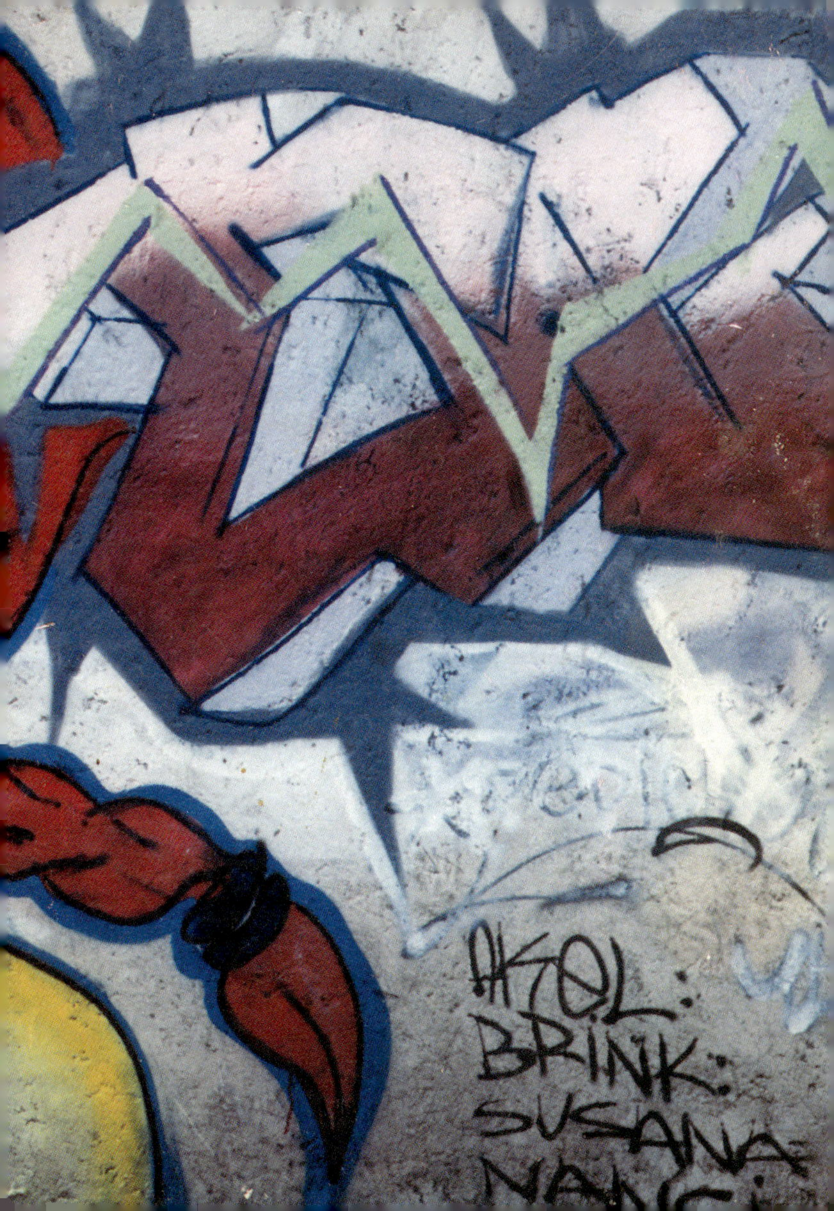
AKEL:
BRINK:
SUSANA:

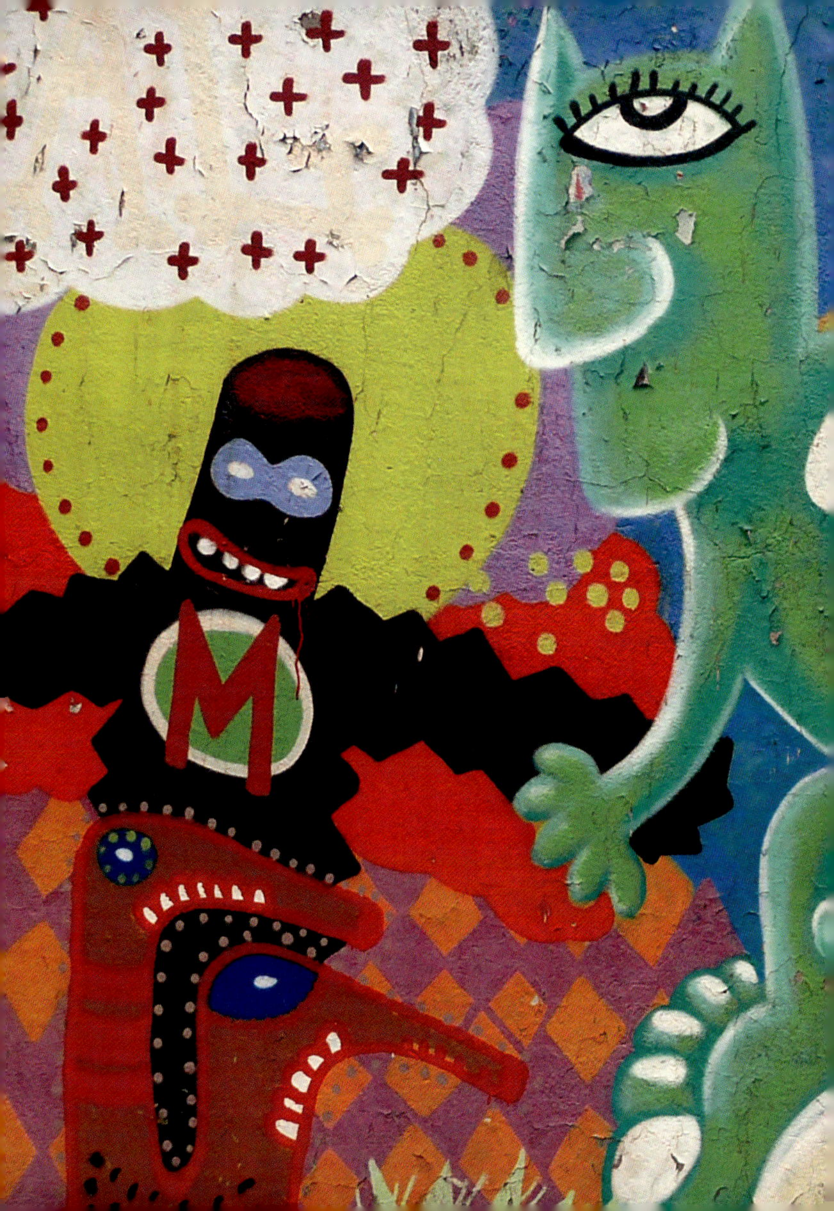
M

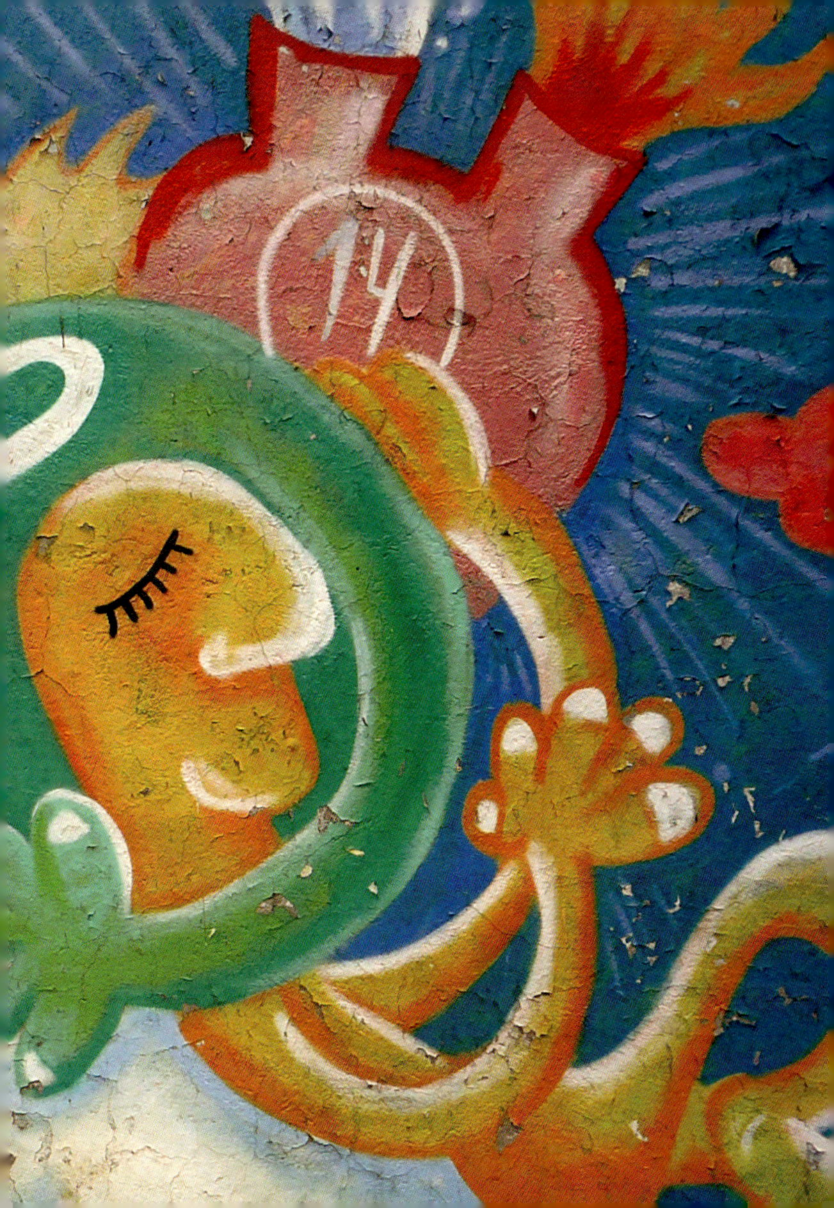
14

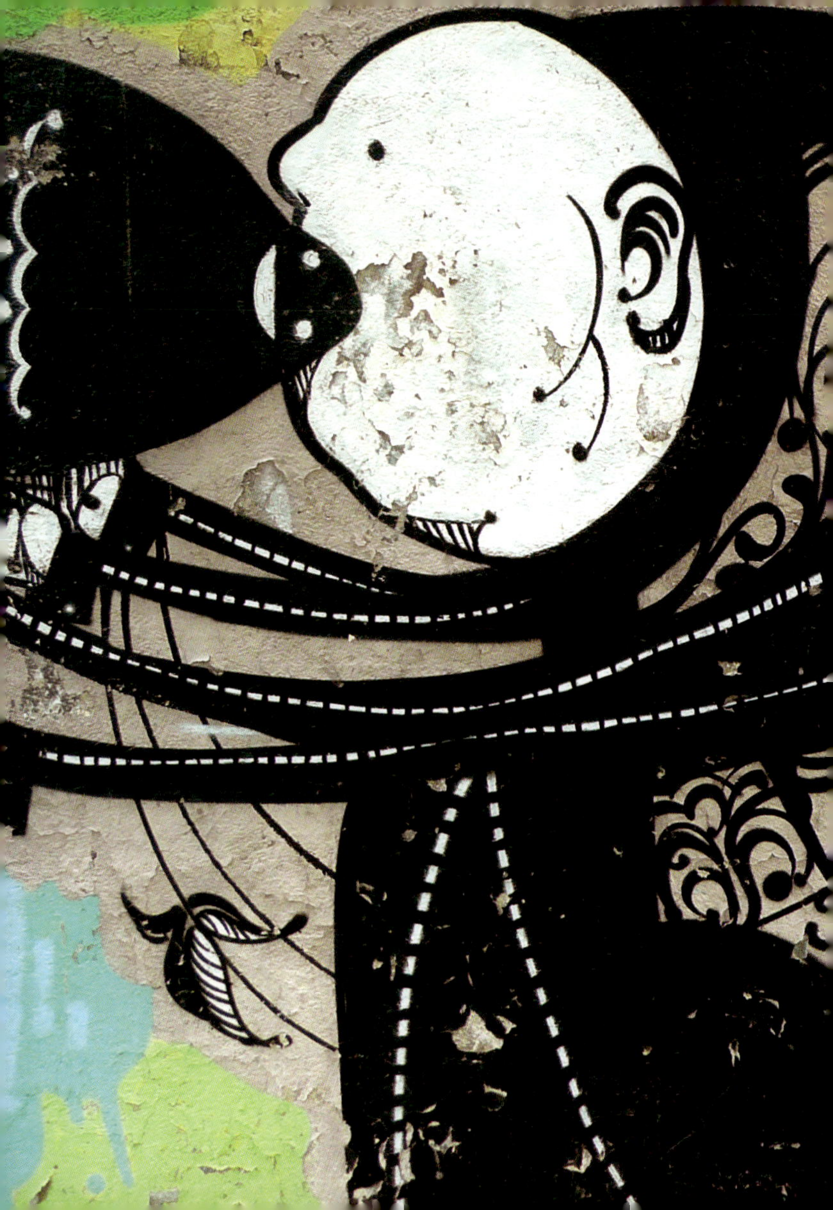

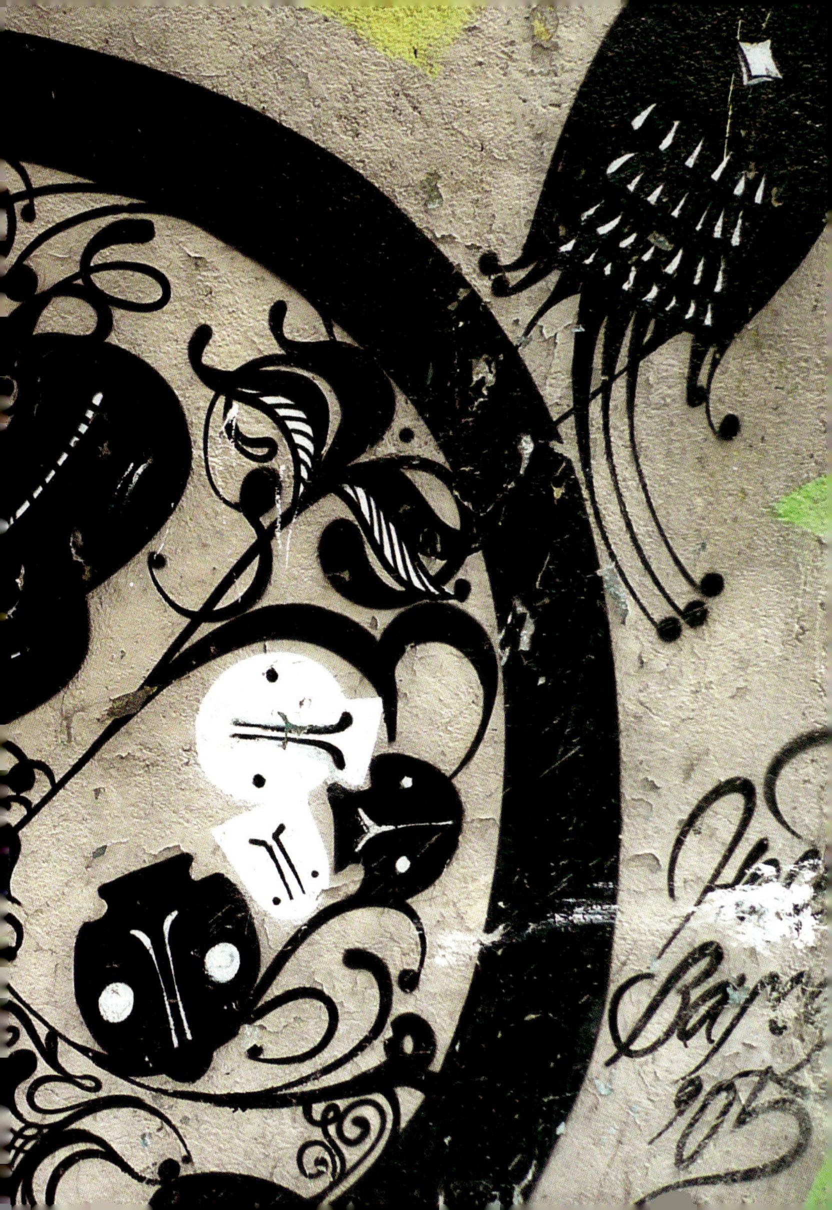

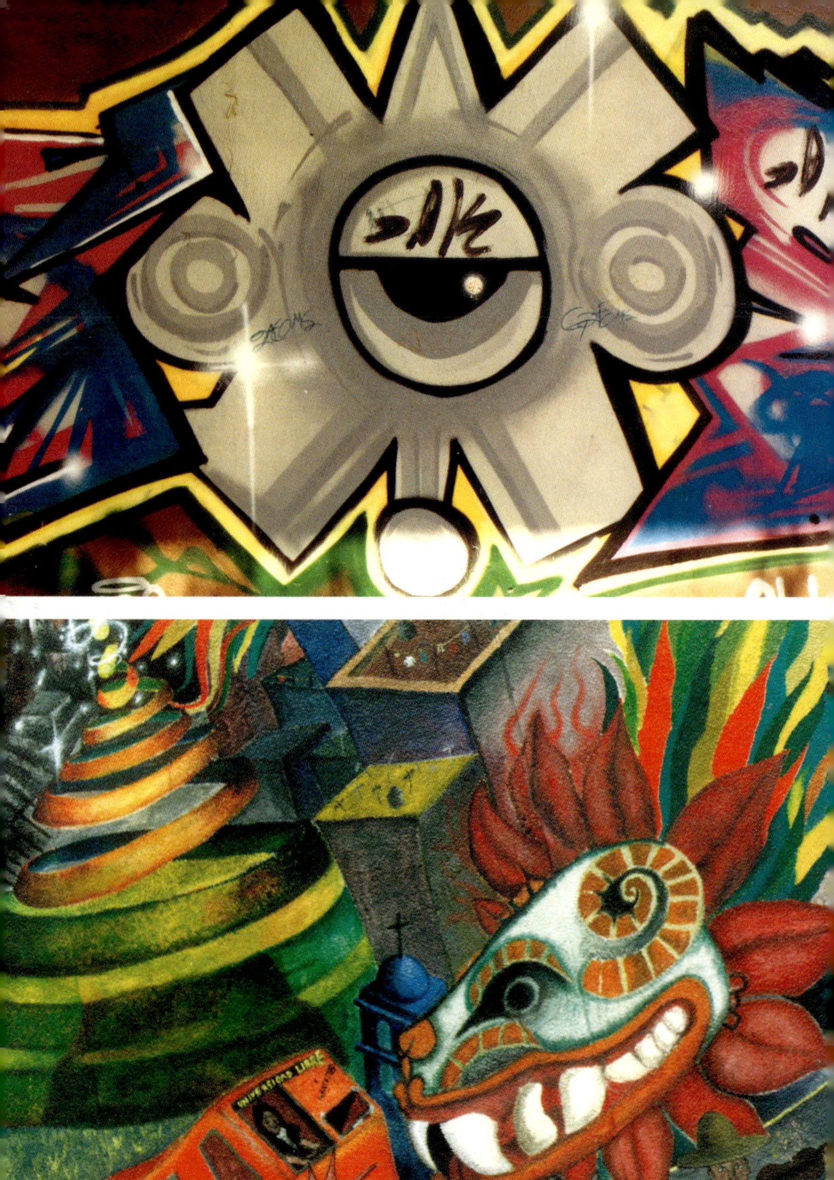
UNIVERSIDAD LIBRE

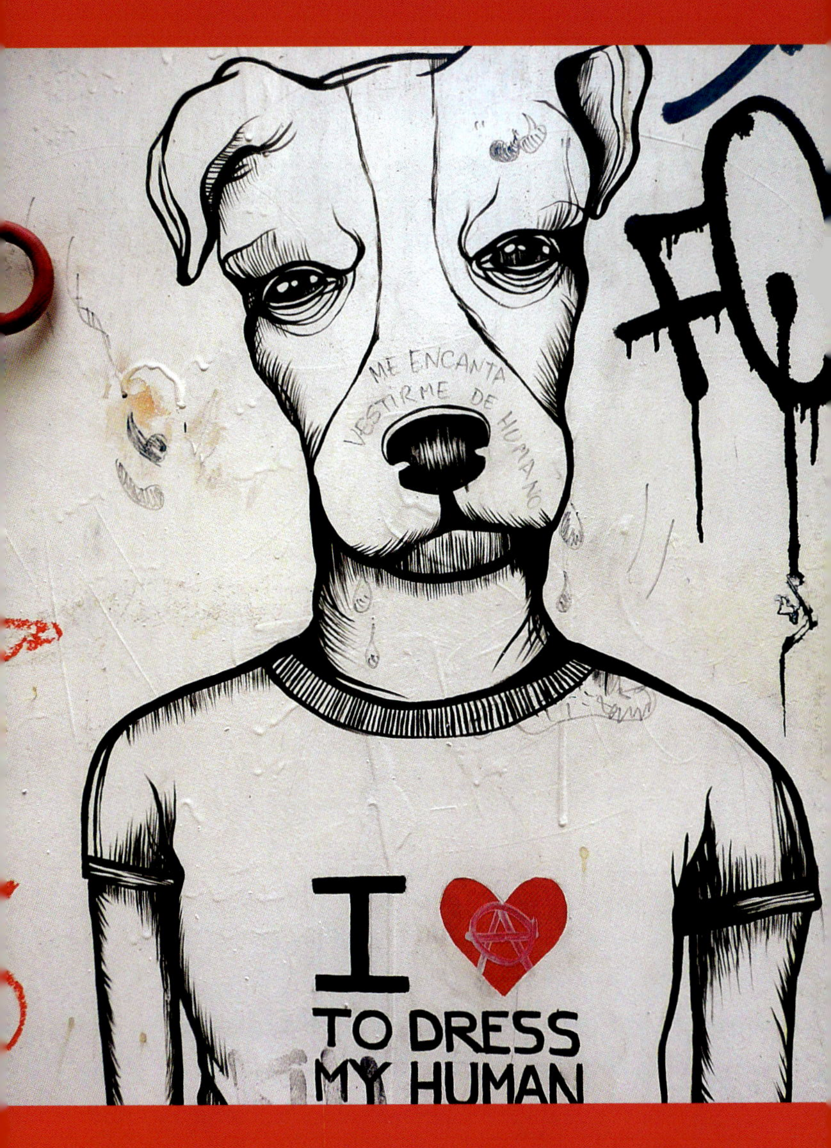
ME ENCANTA
VESTIRME DE HUMANO
I
TO DRESS
MY HUMAN

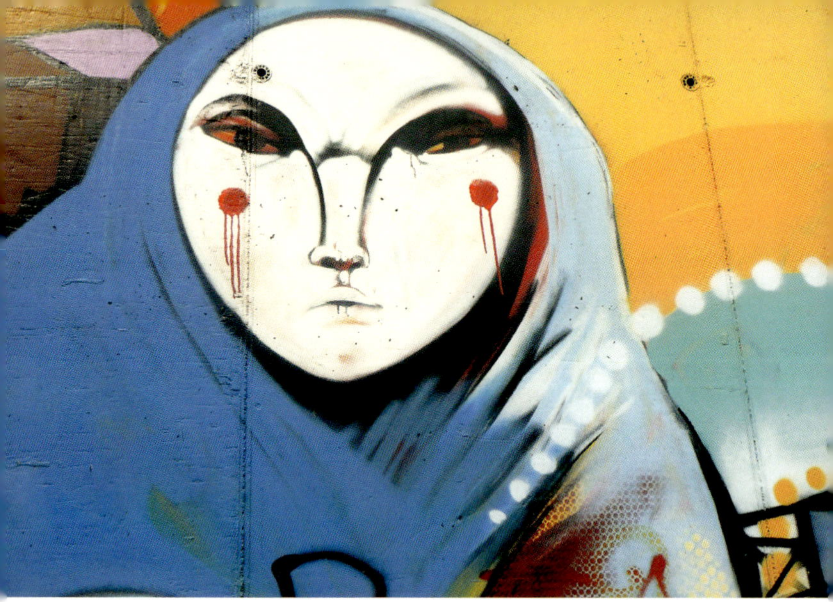

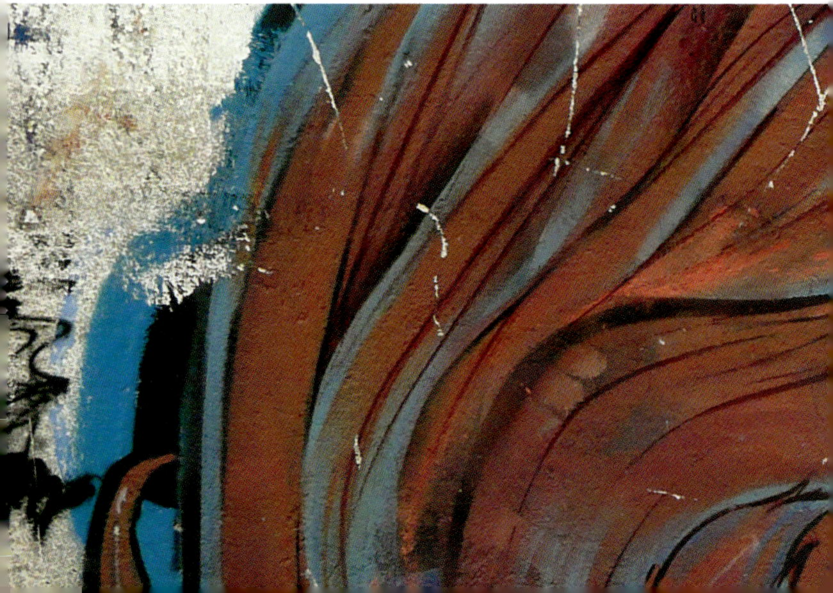

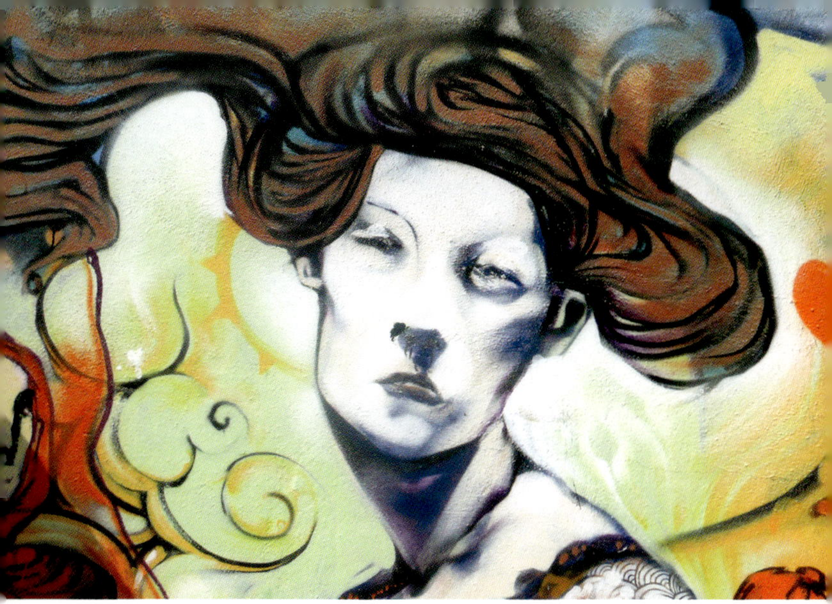

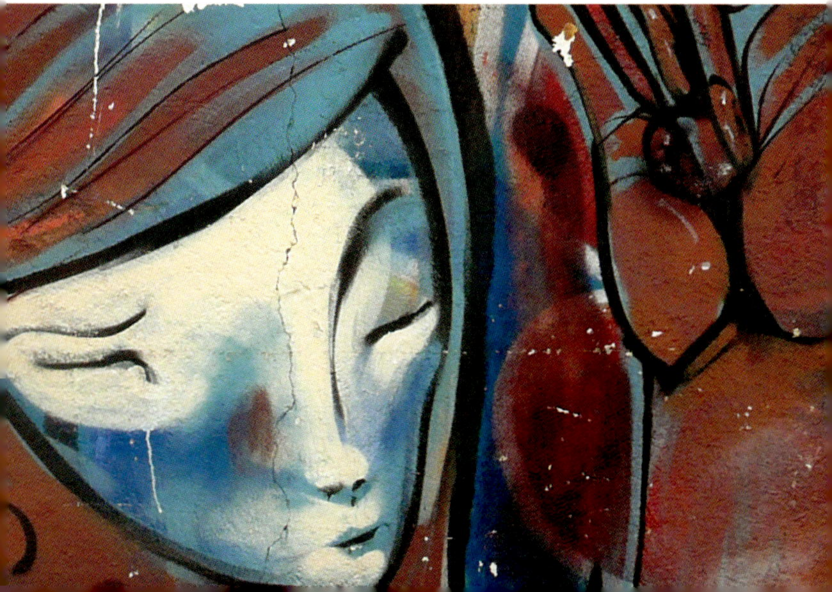

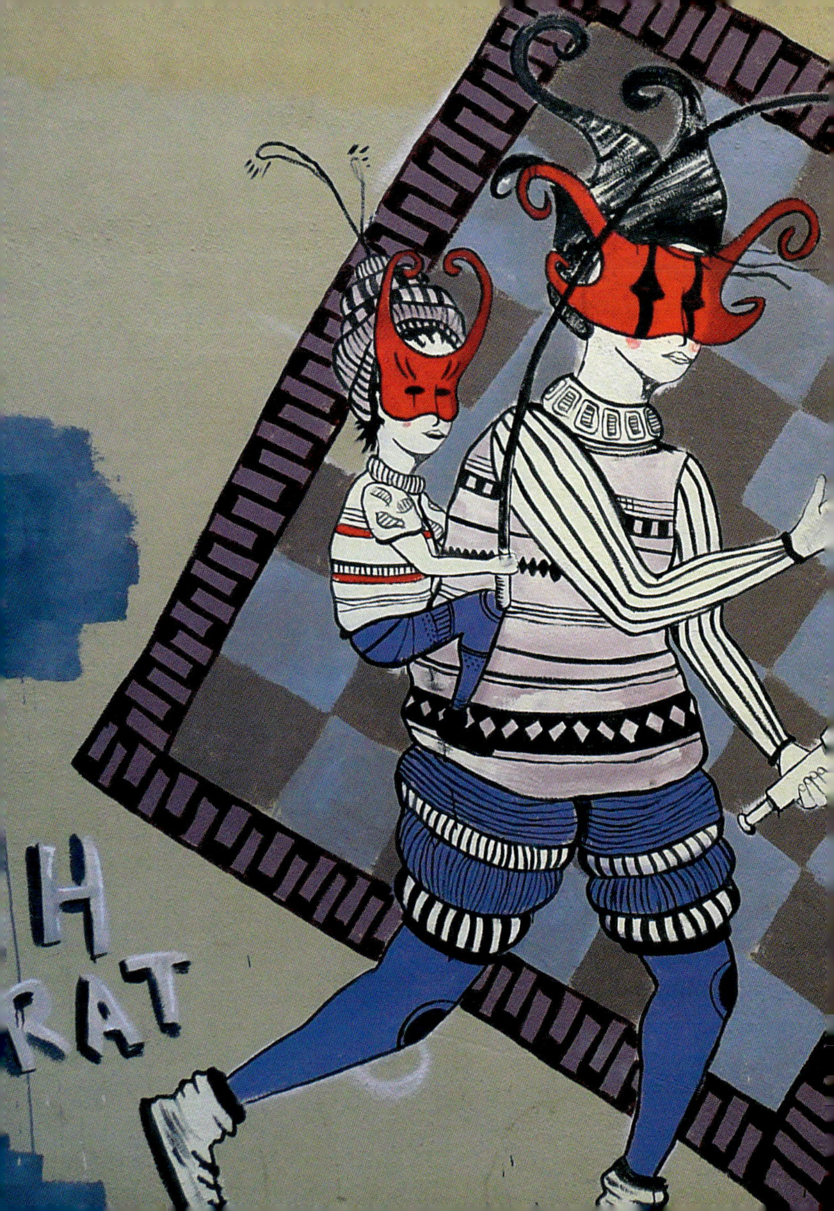
H
RAT

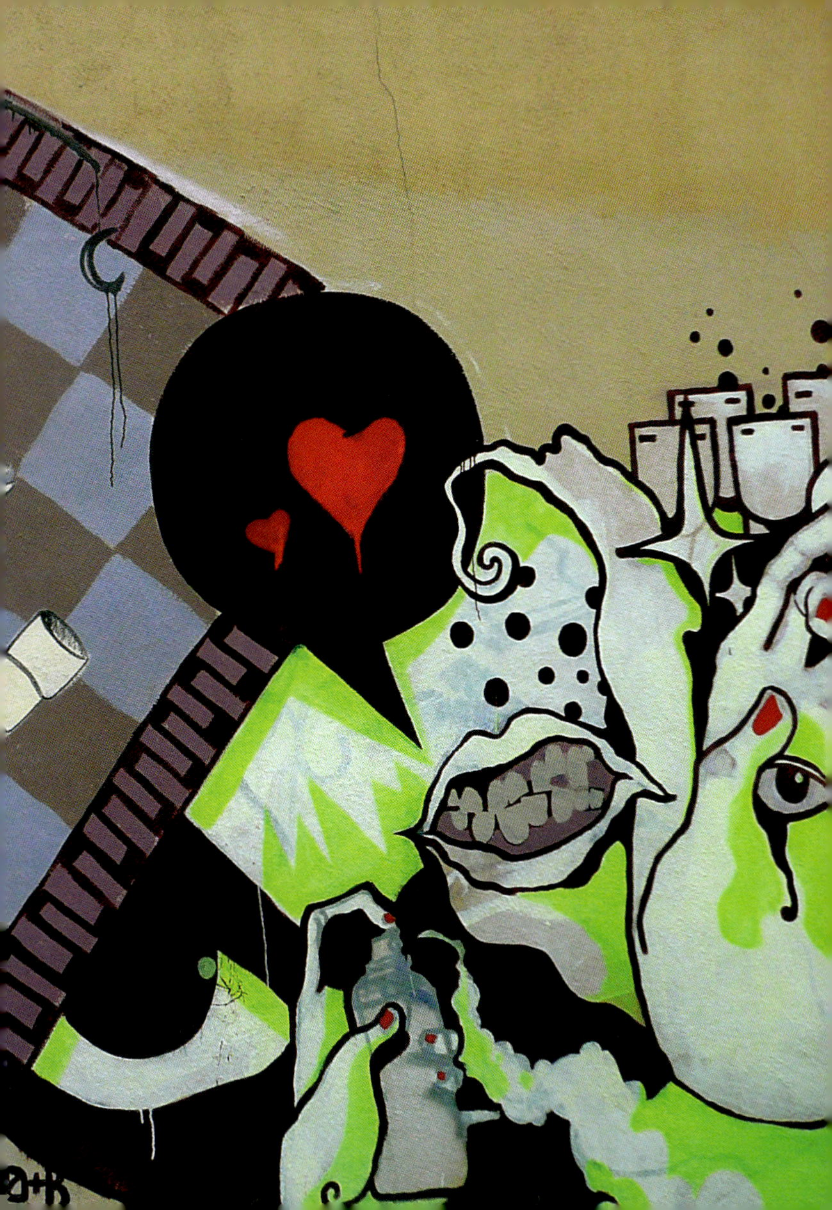

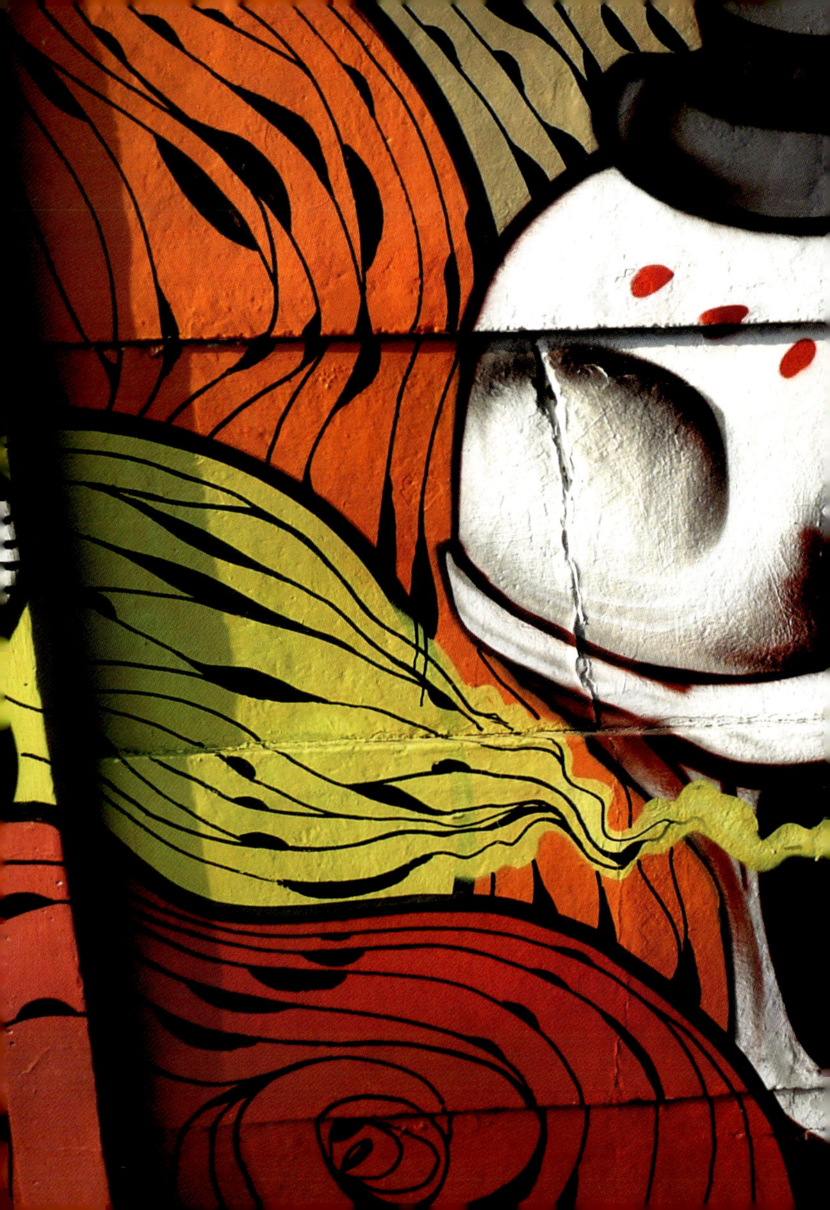

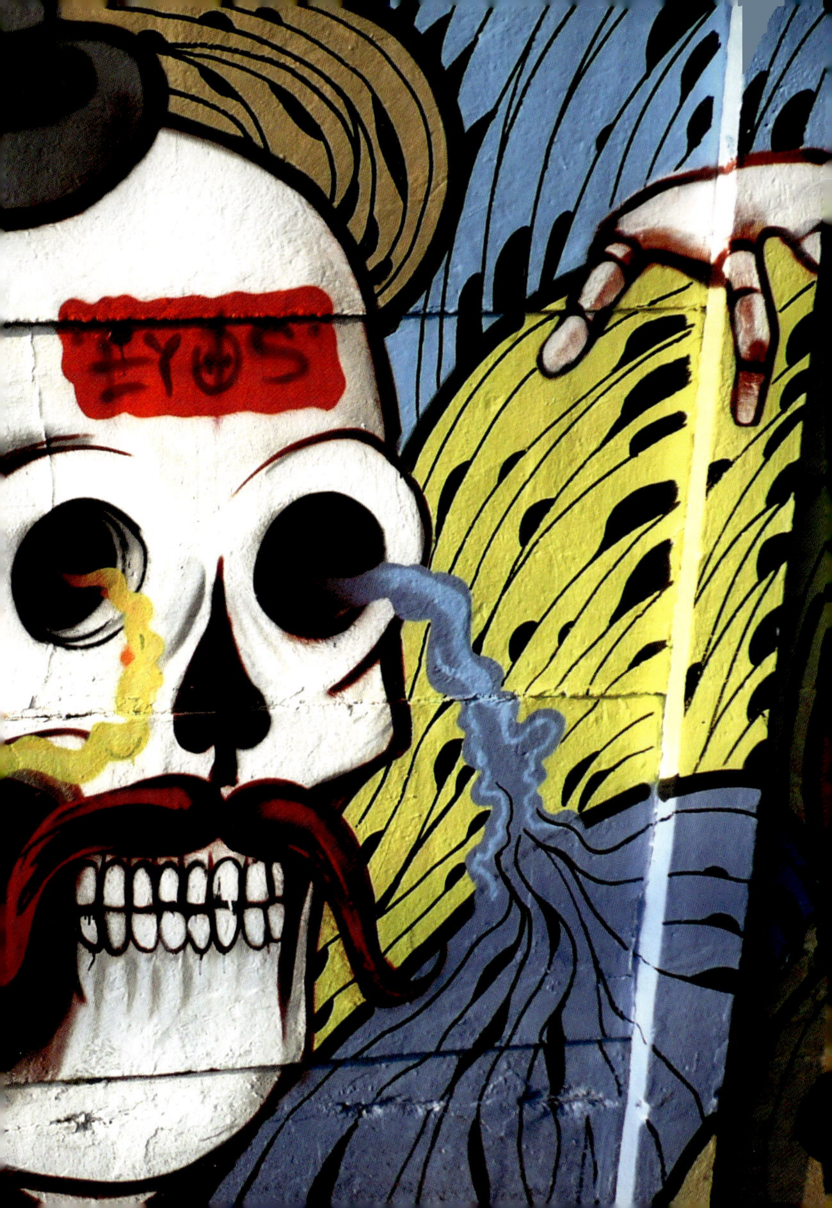

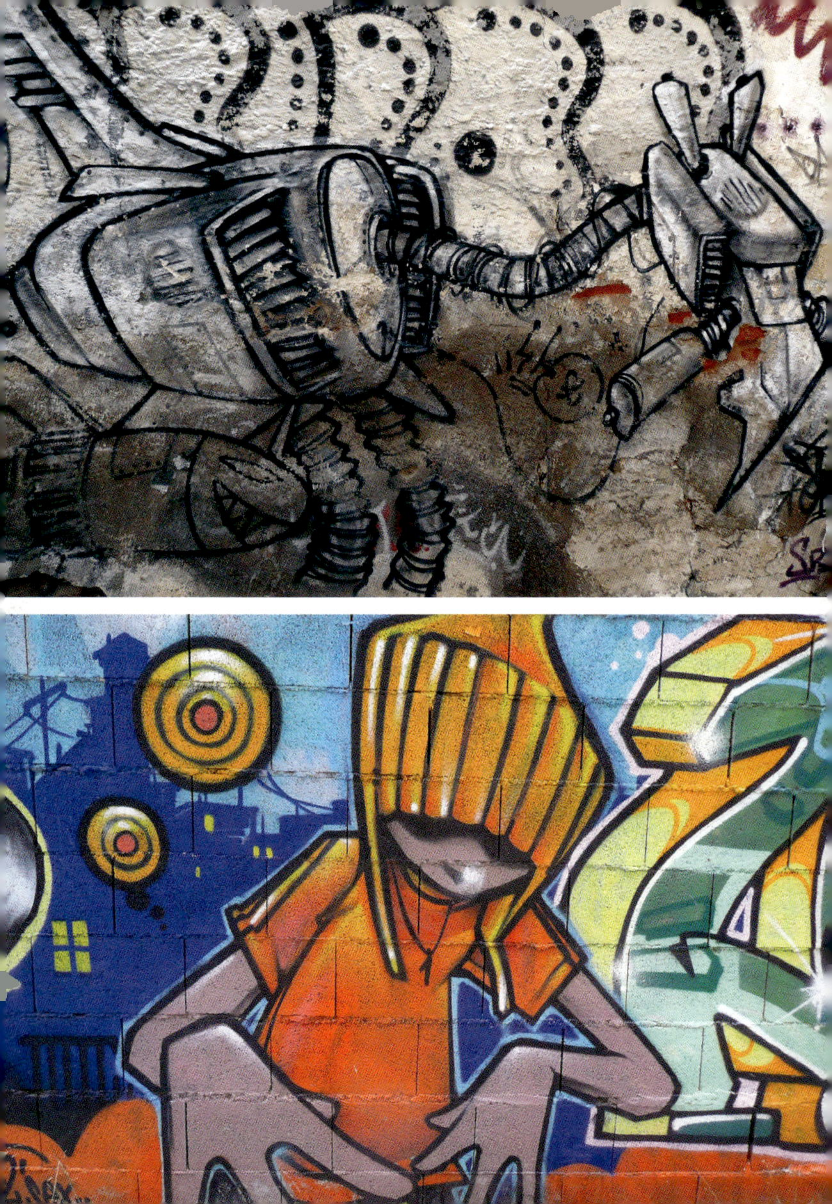

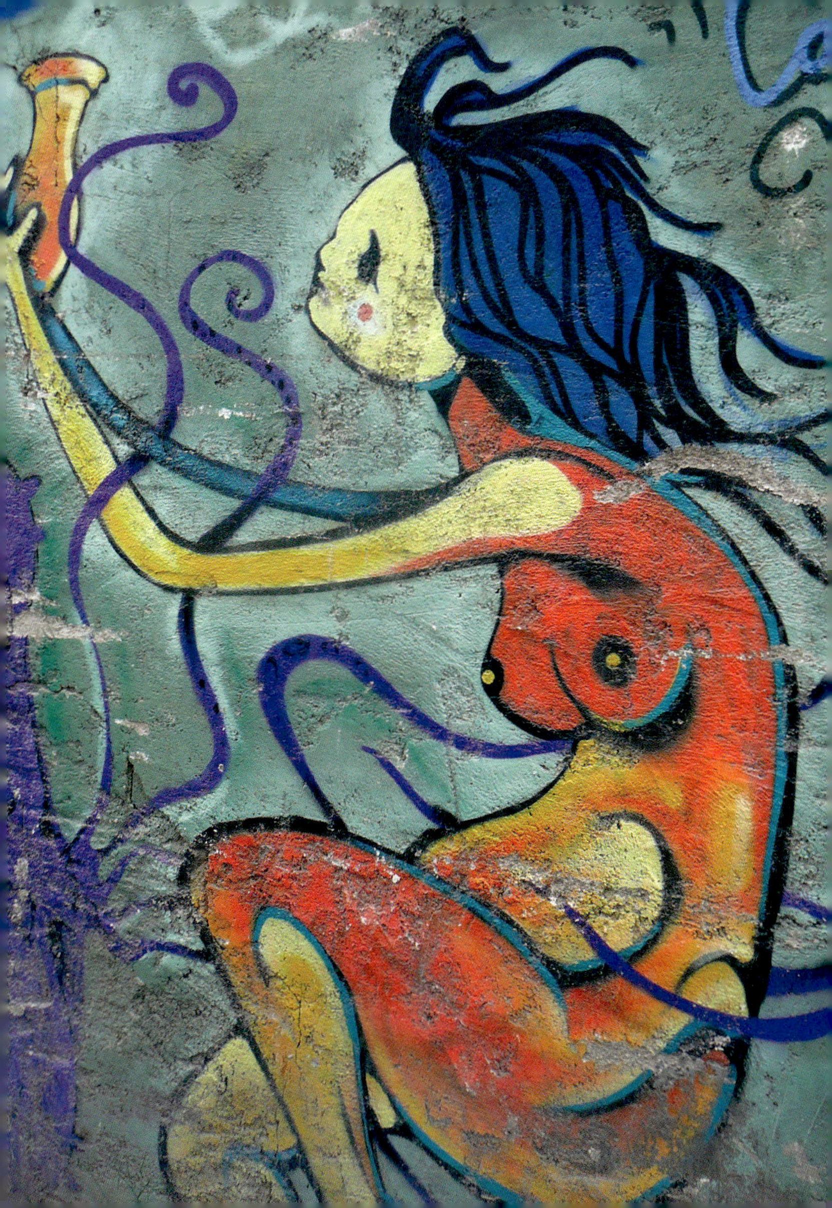

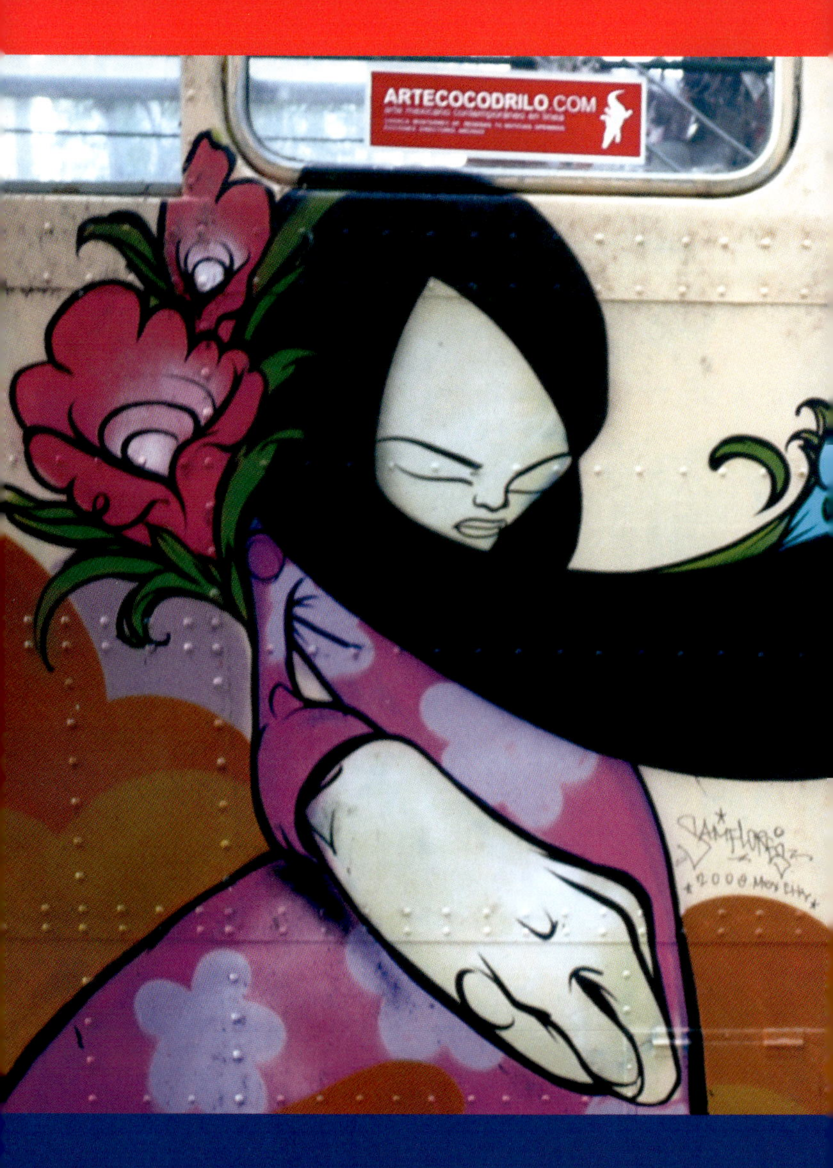
ARTECOCODRILO.COM

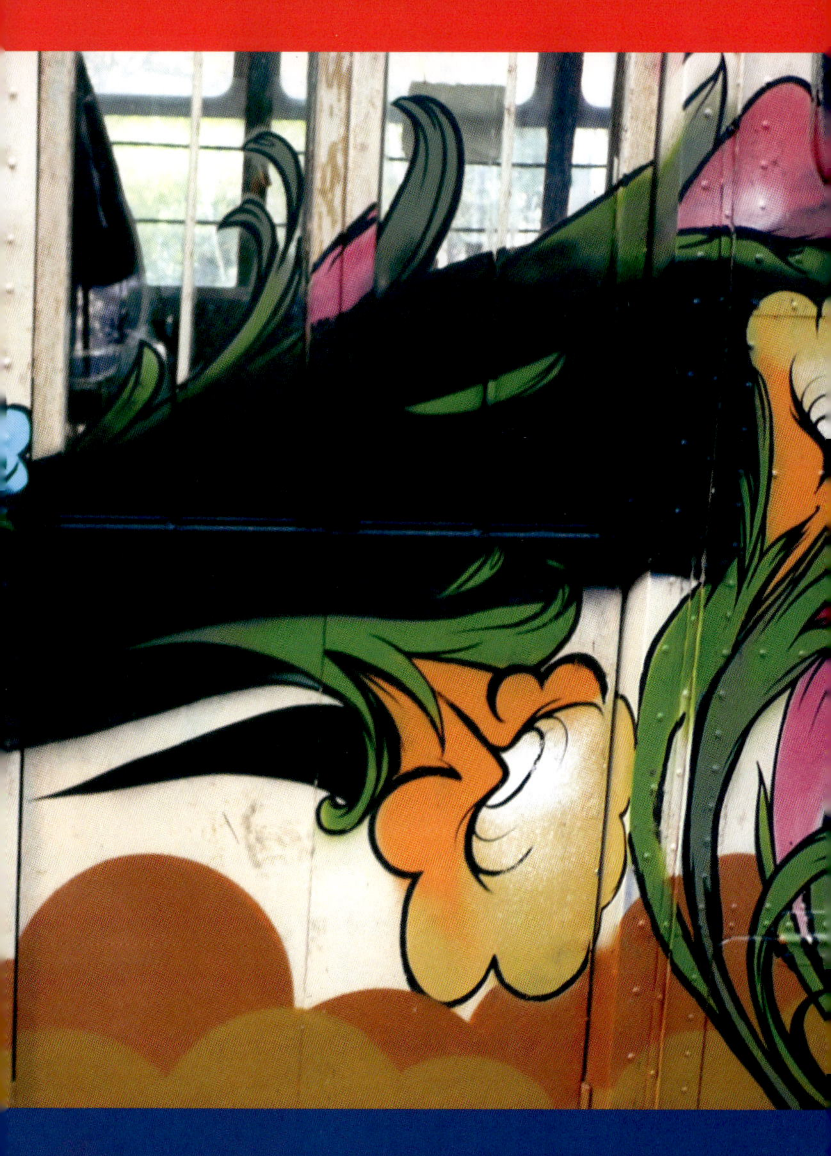

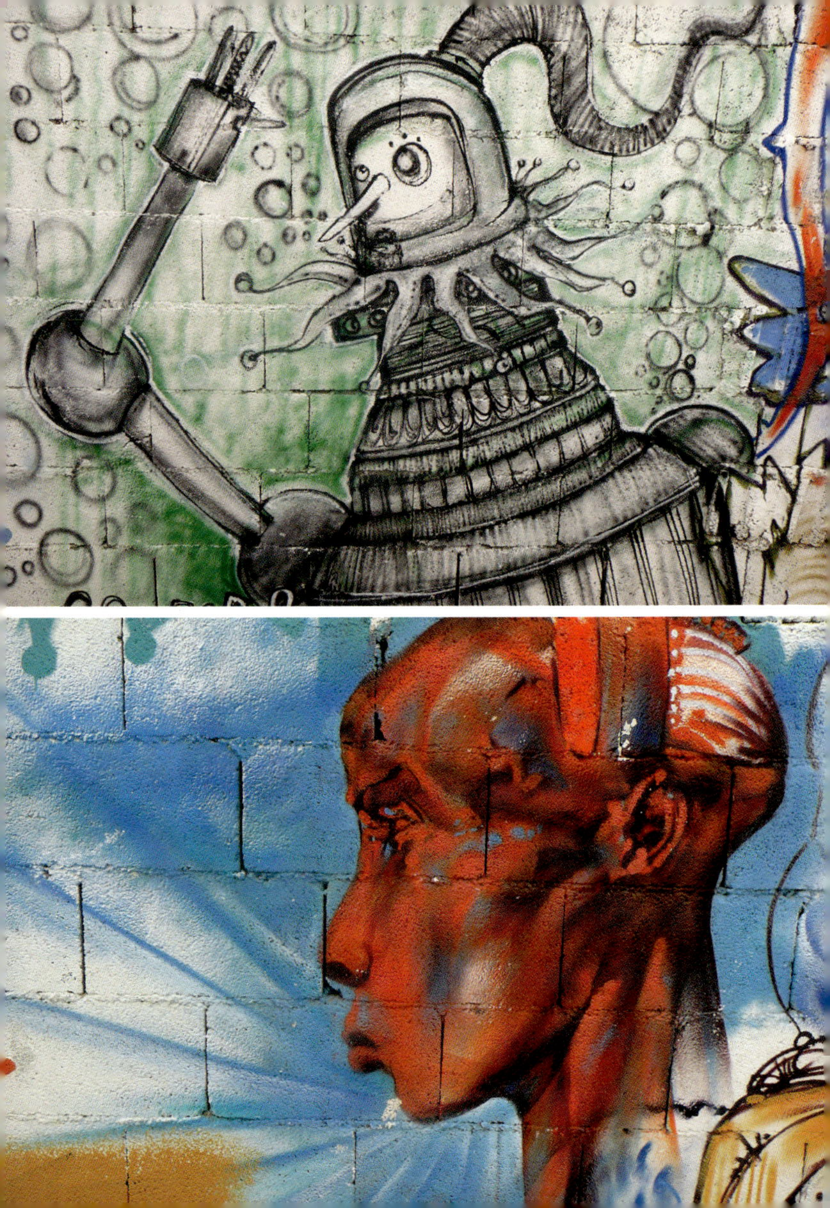

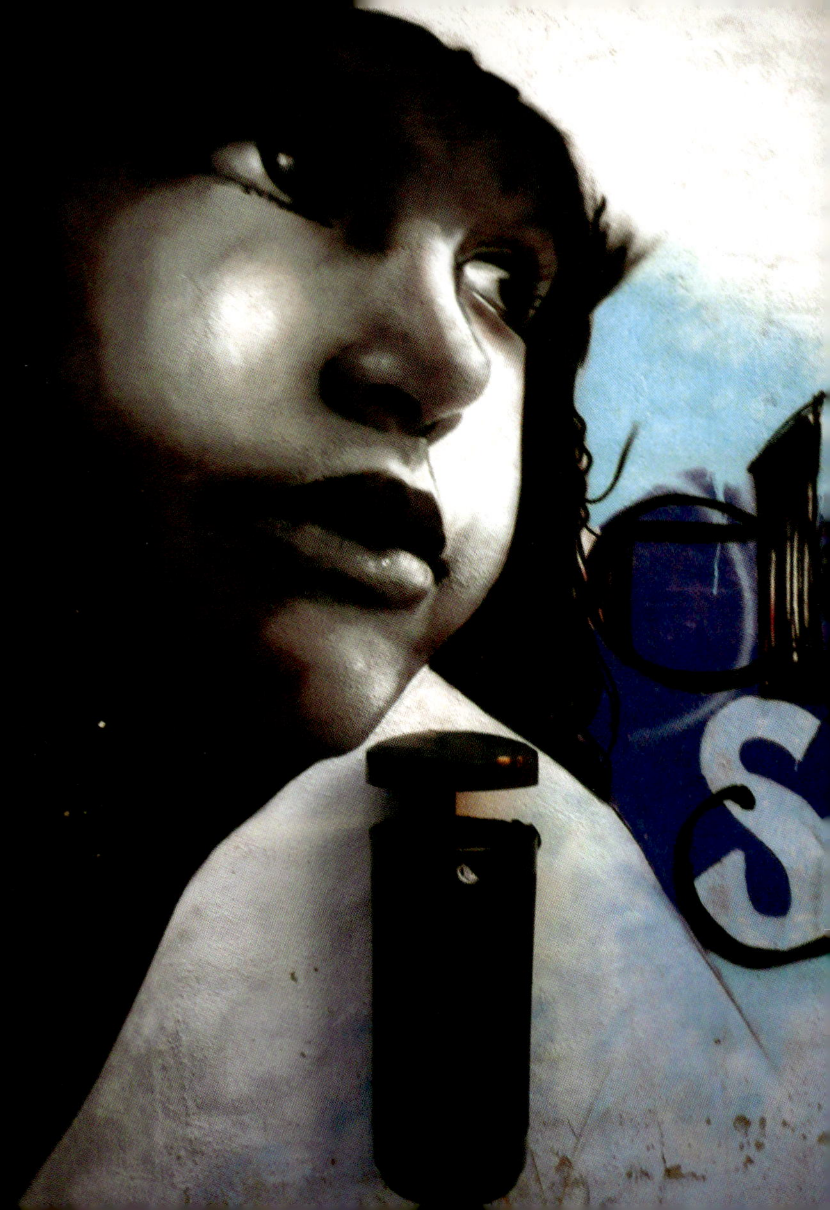

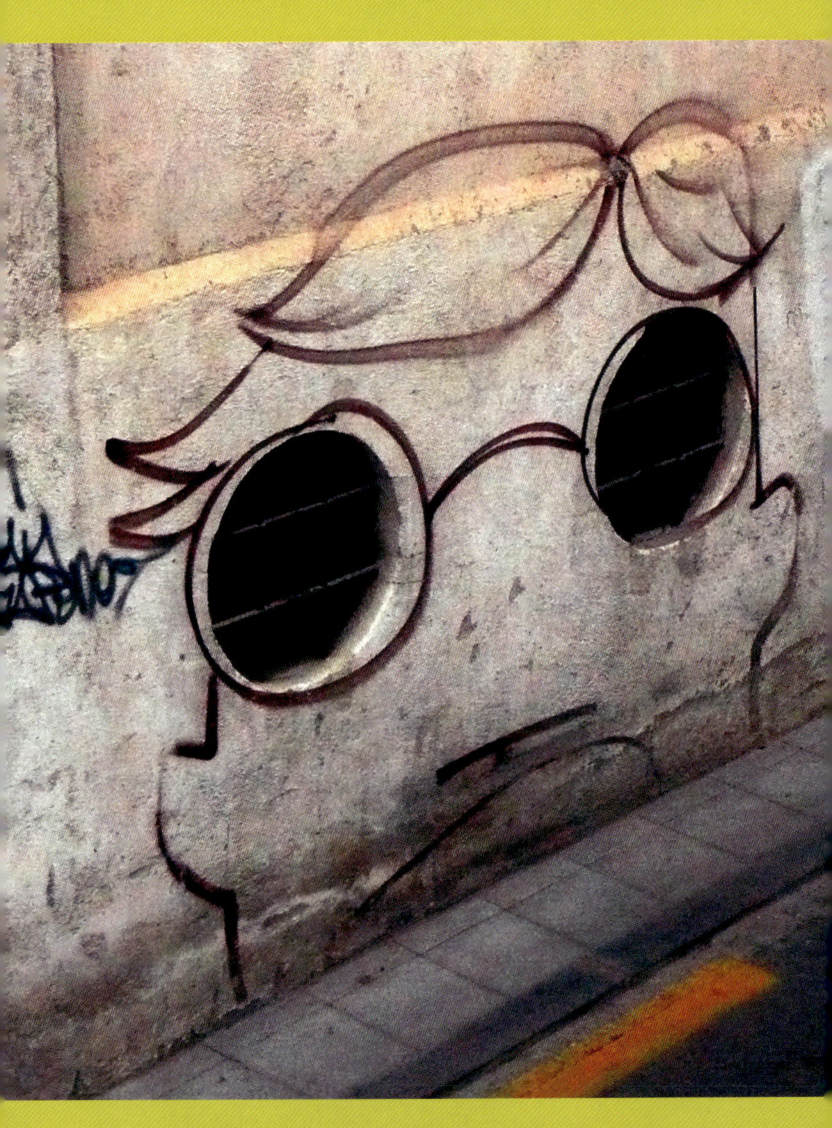

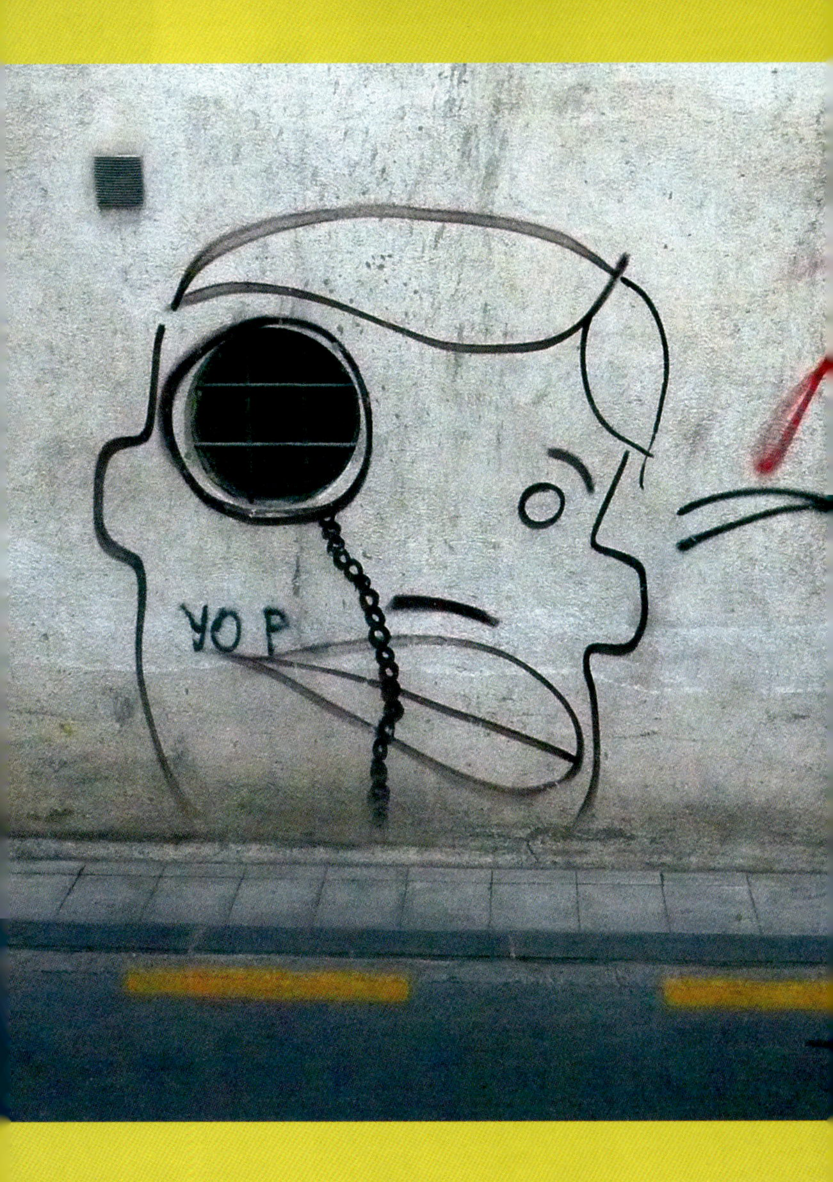
YO P

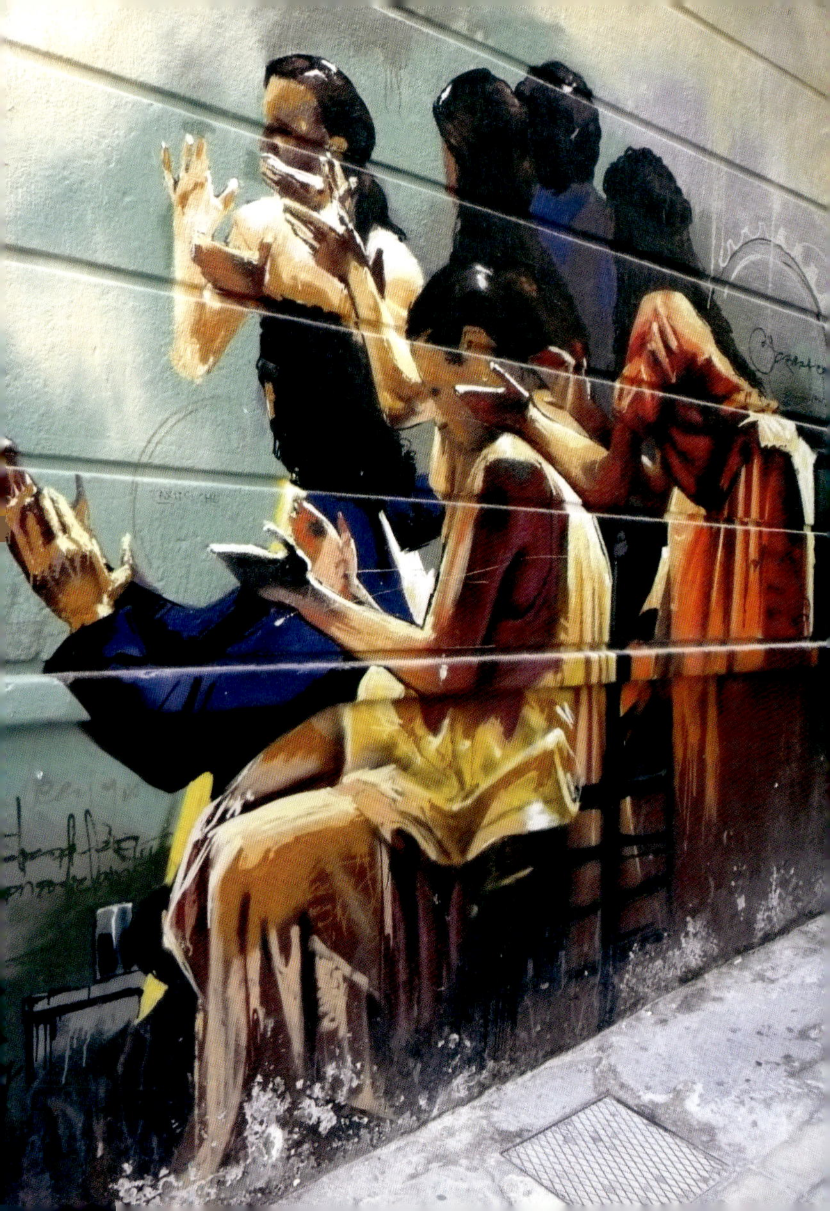

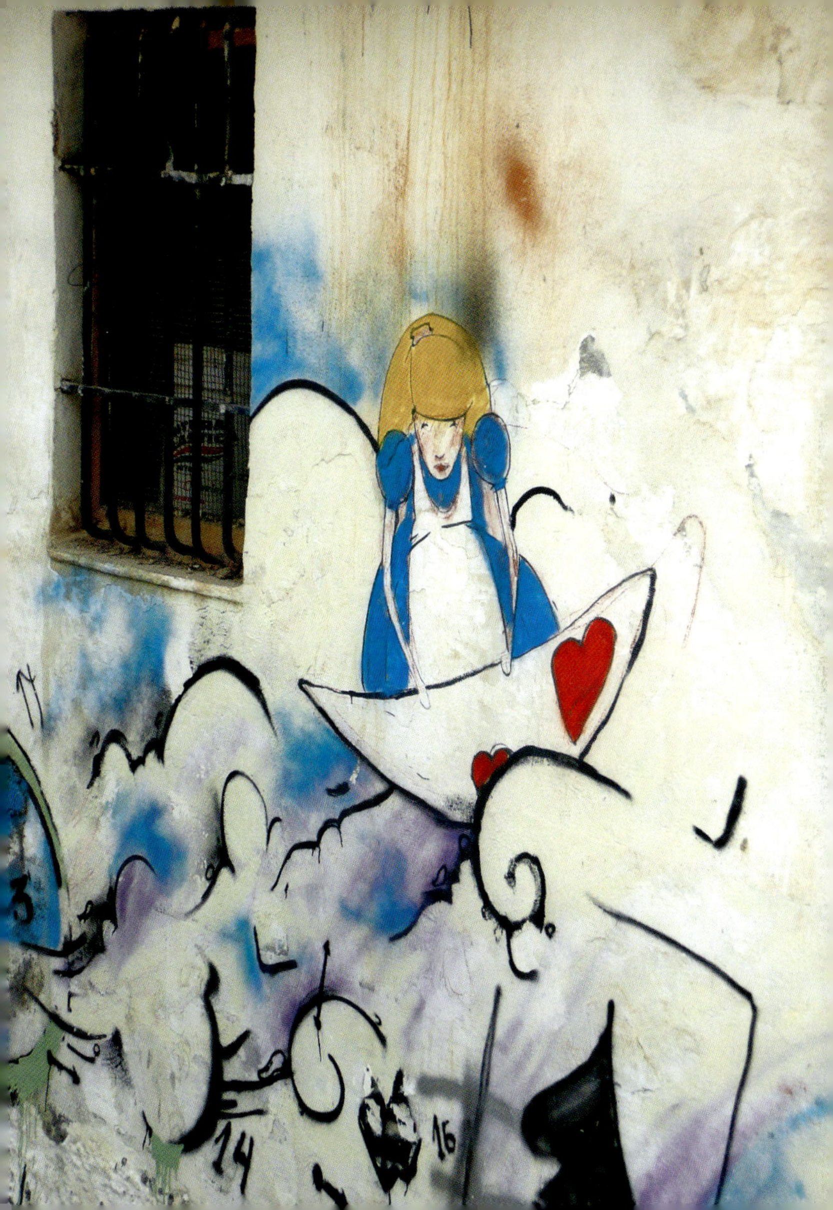

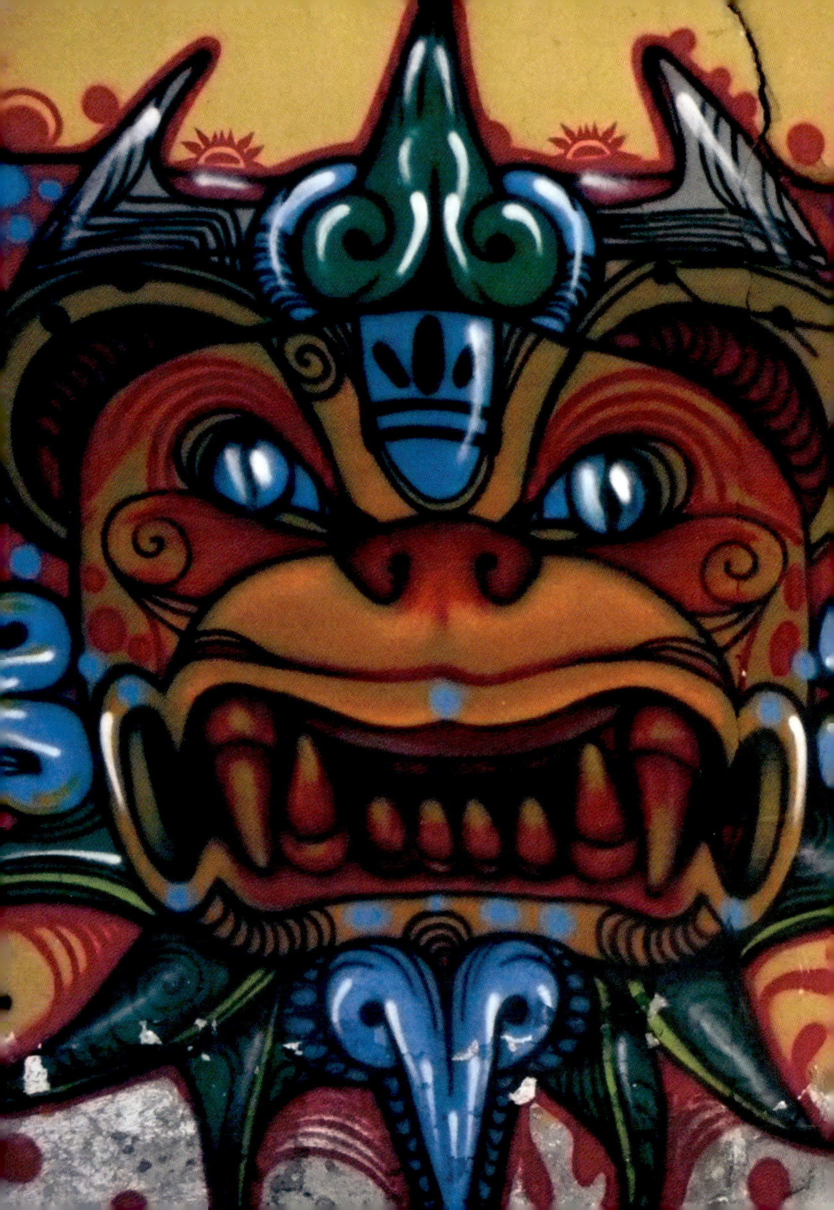

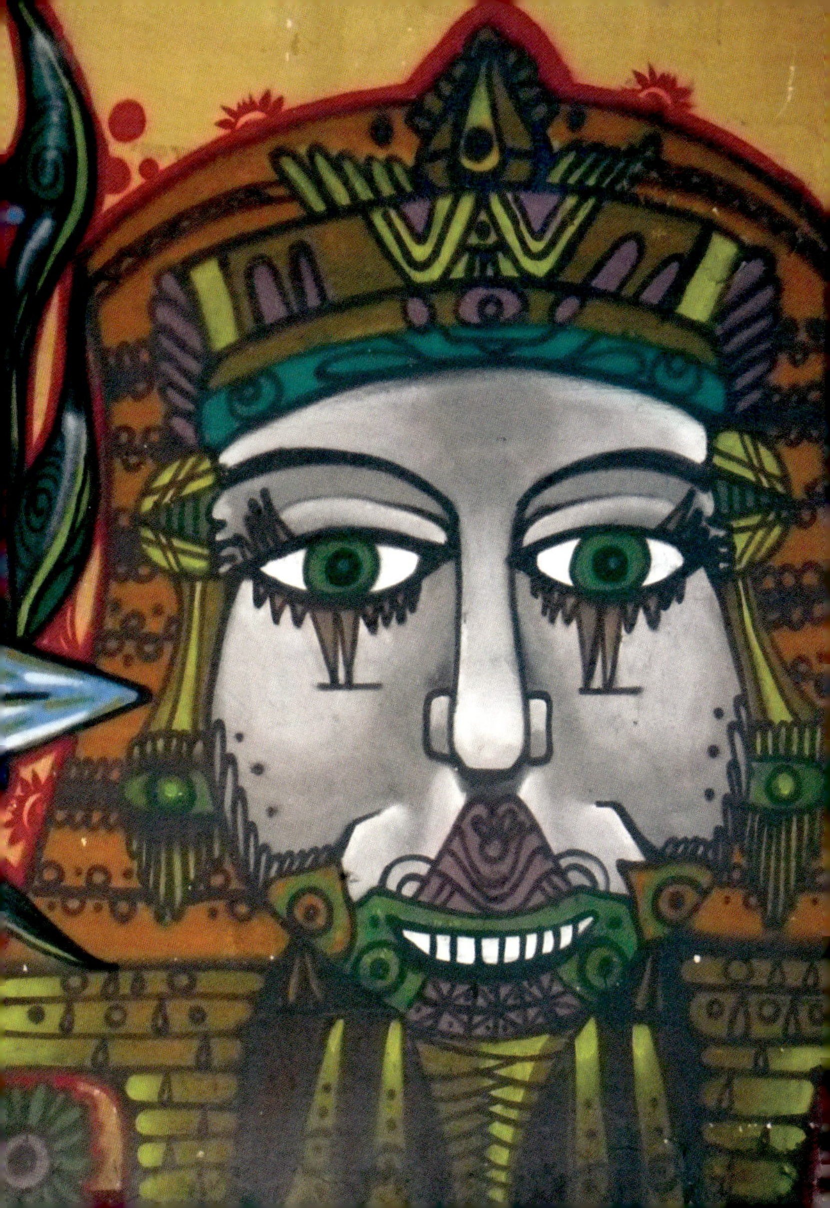

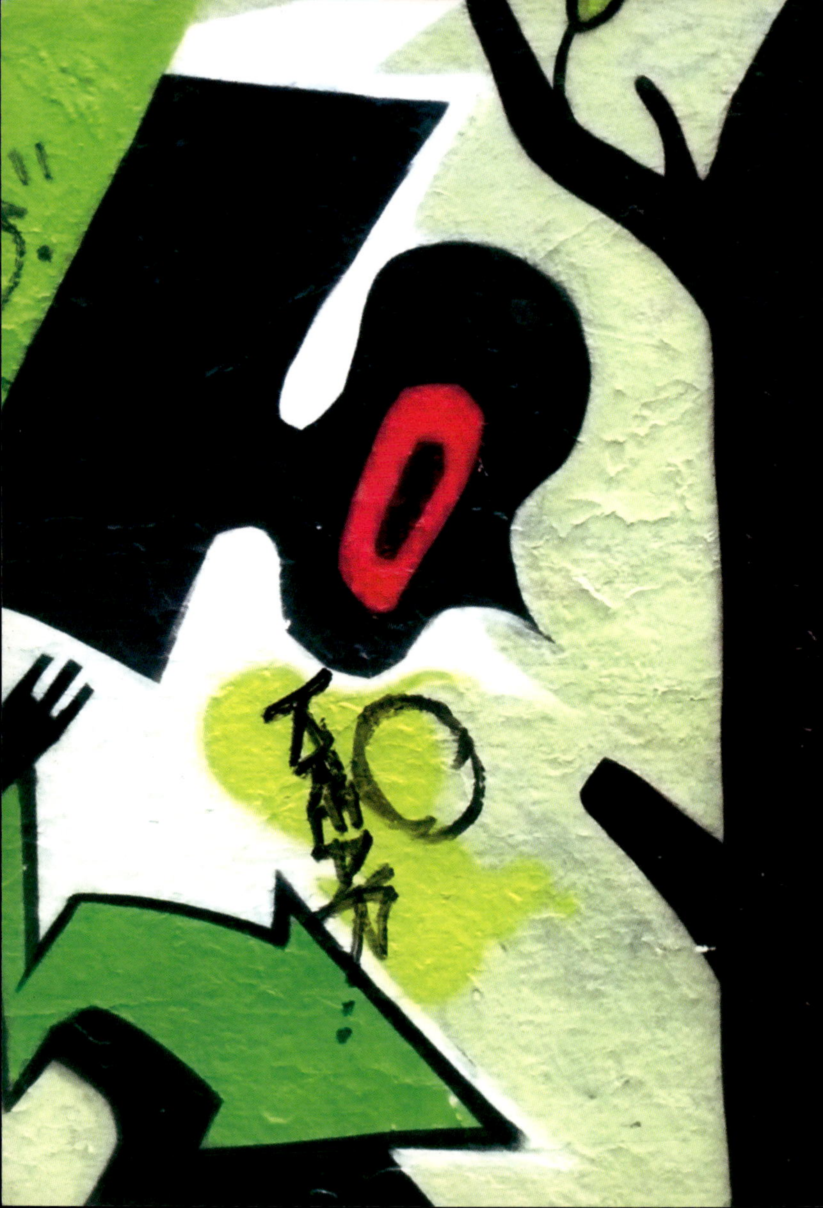

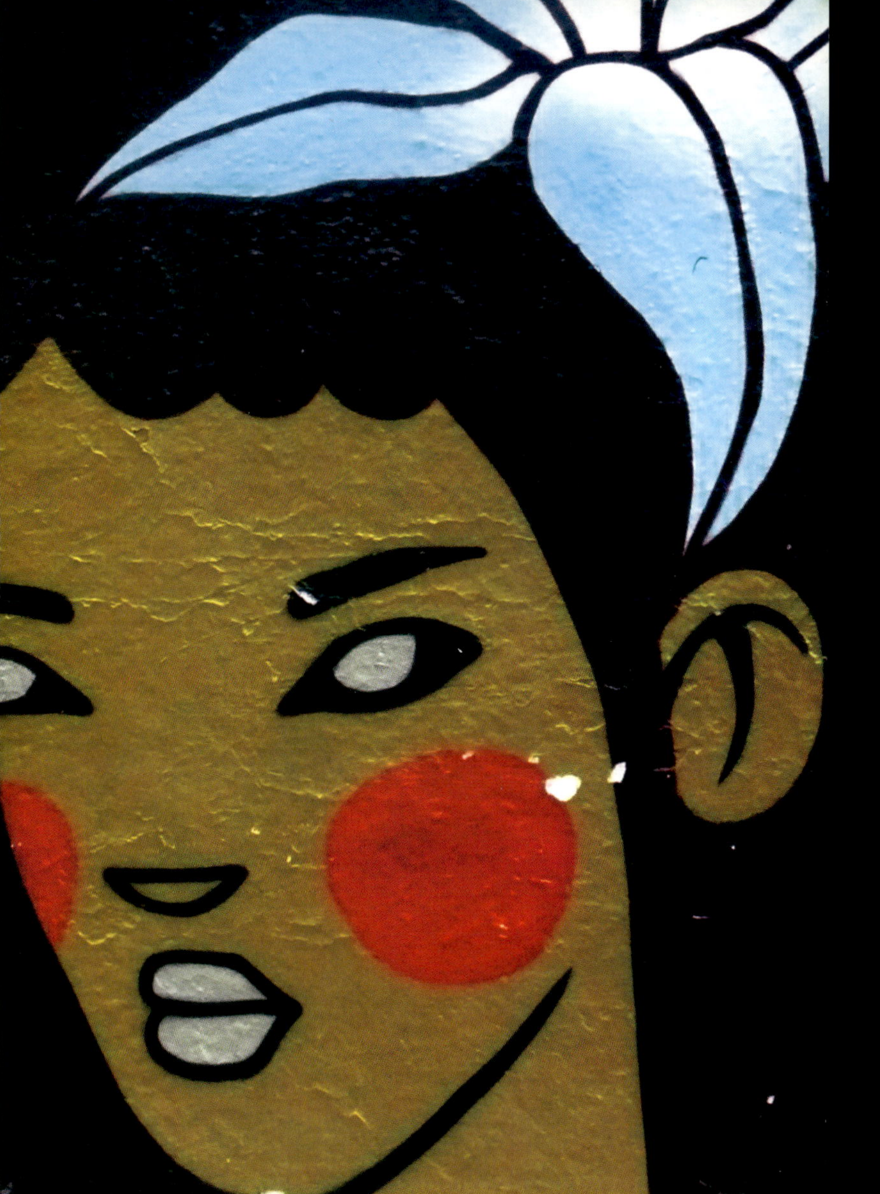

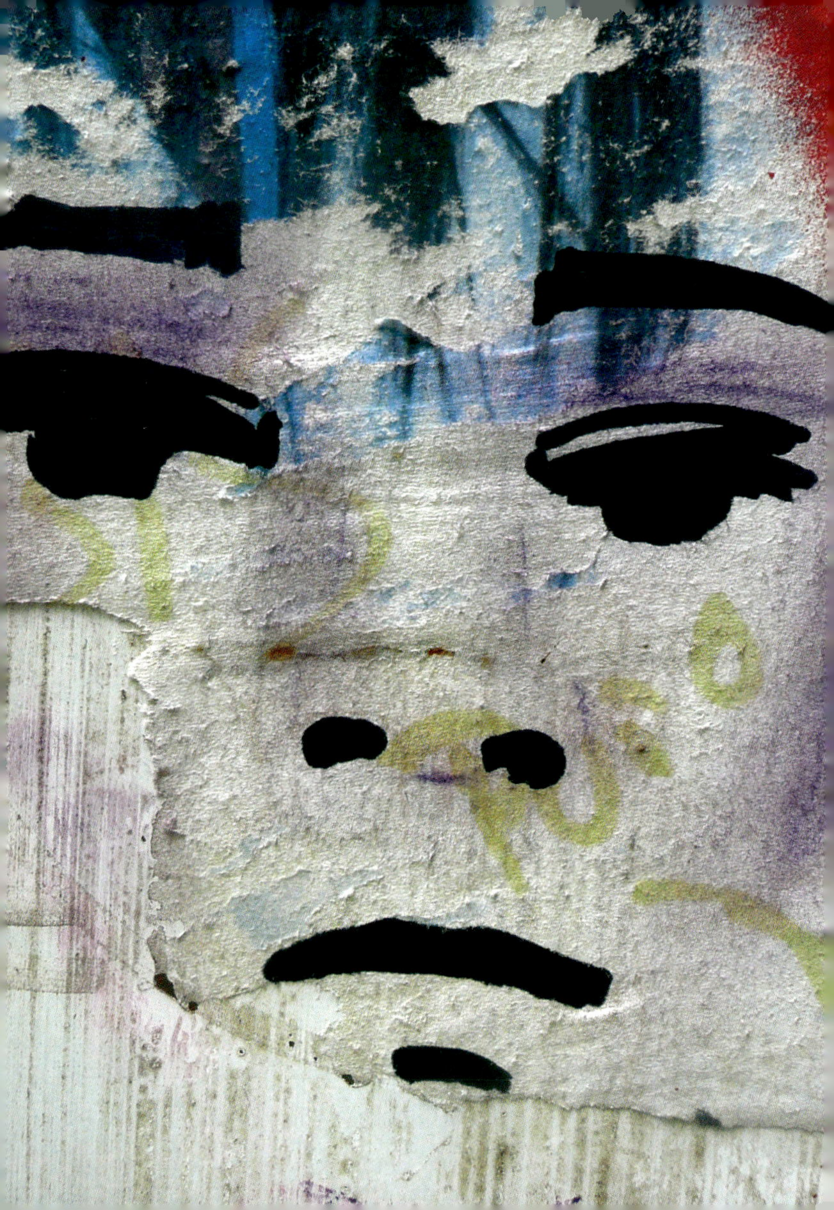

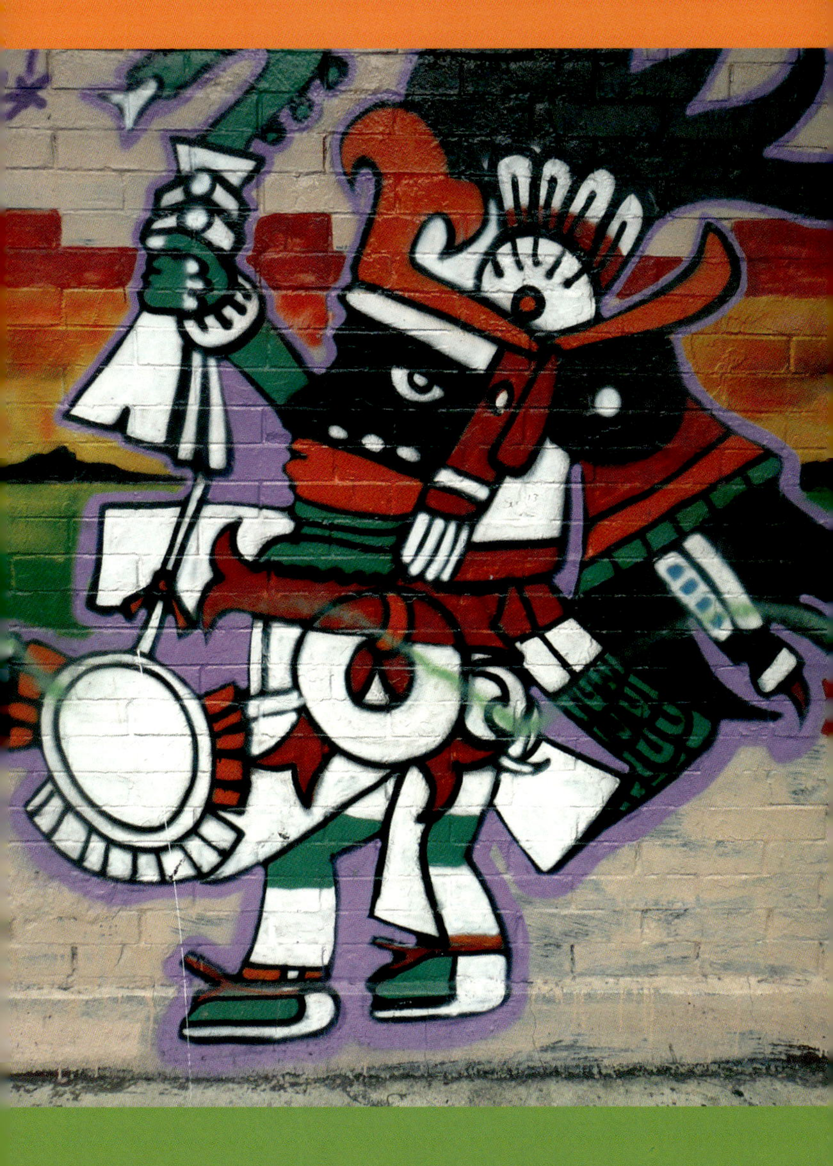

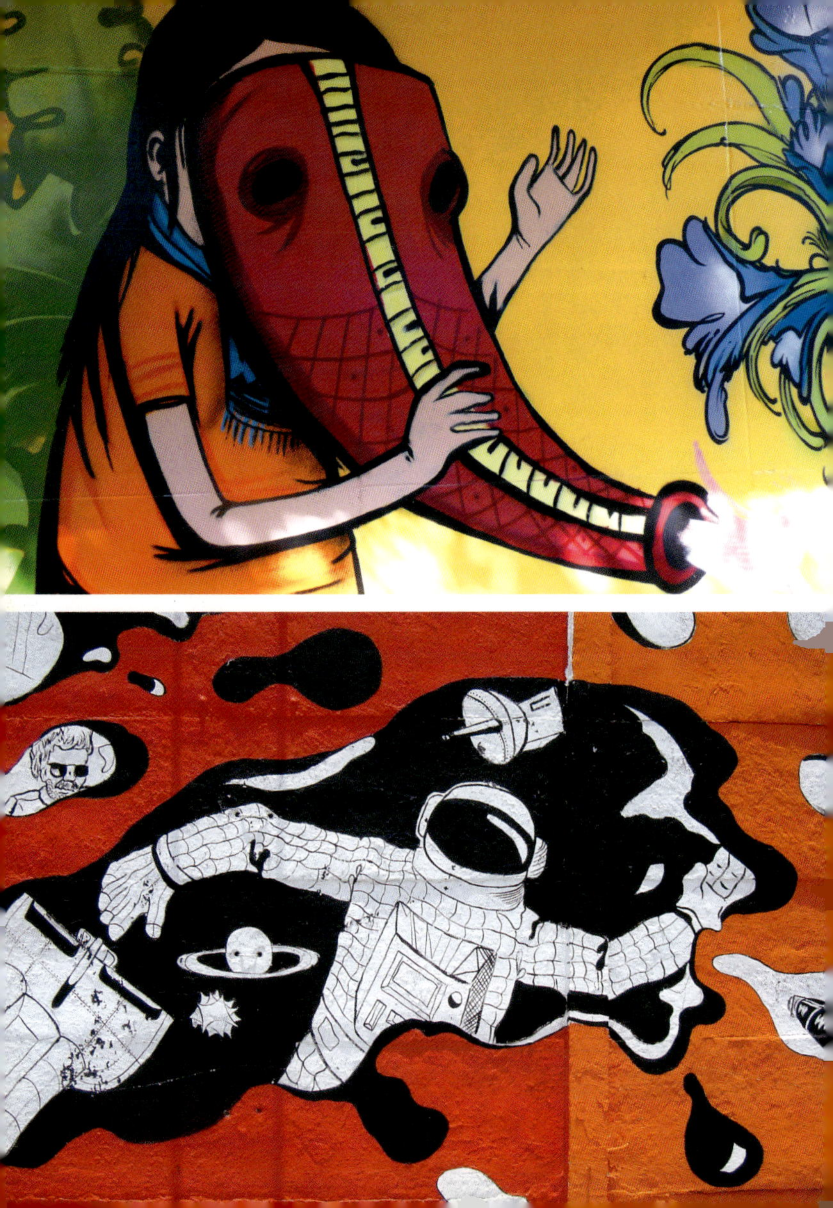

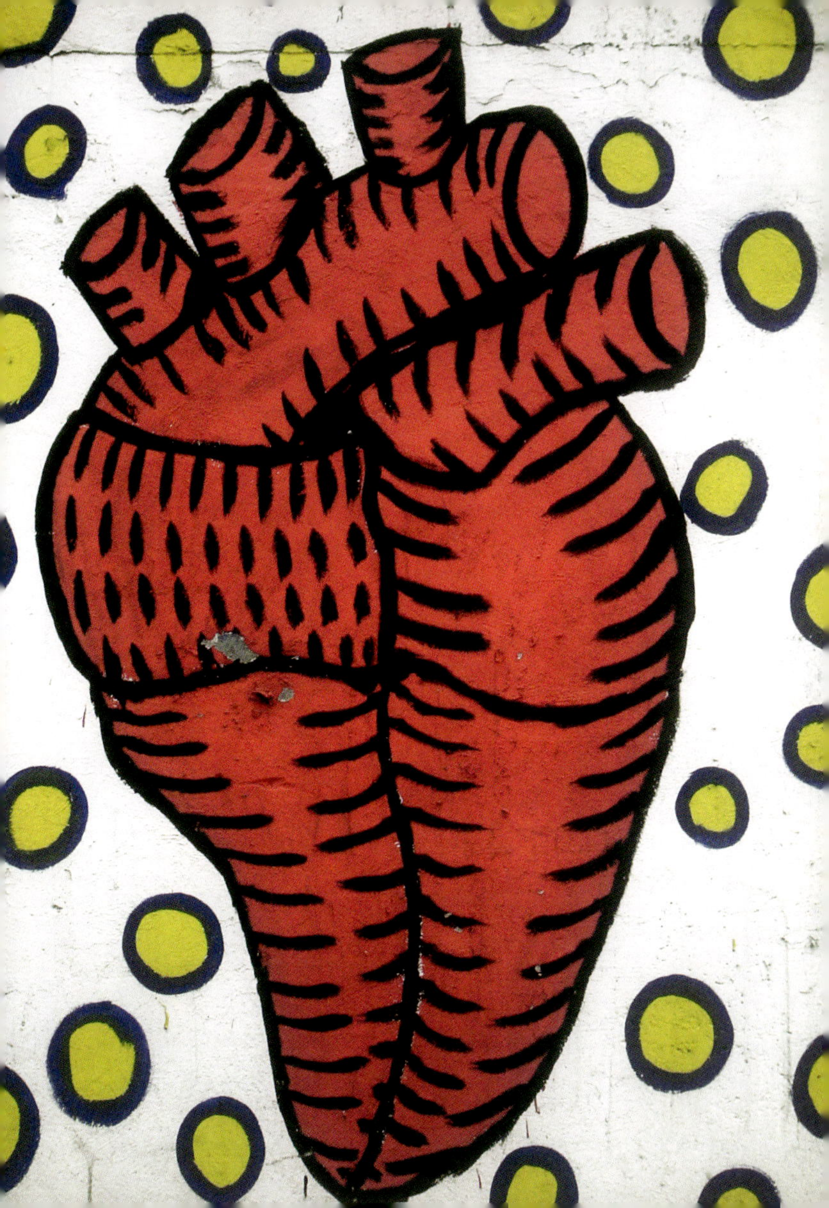

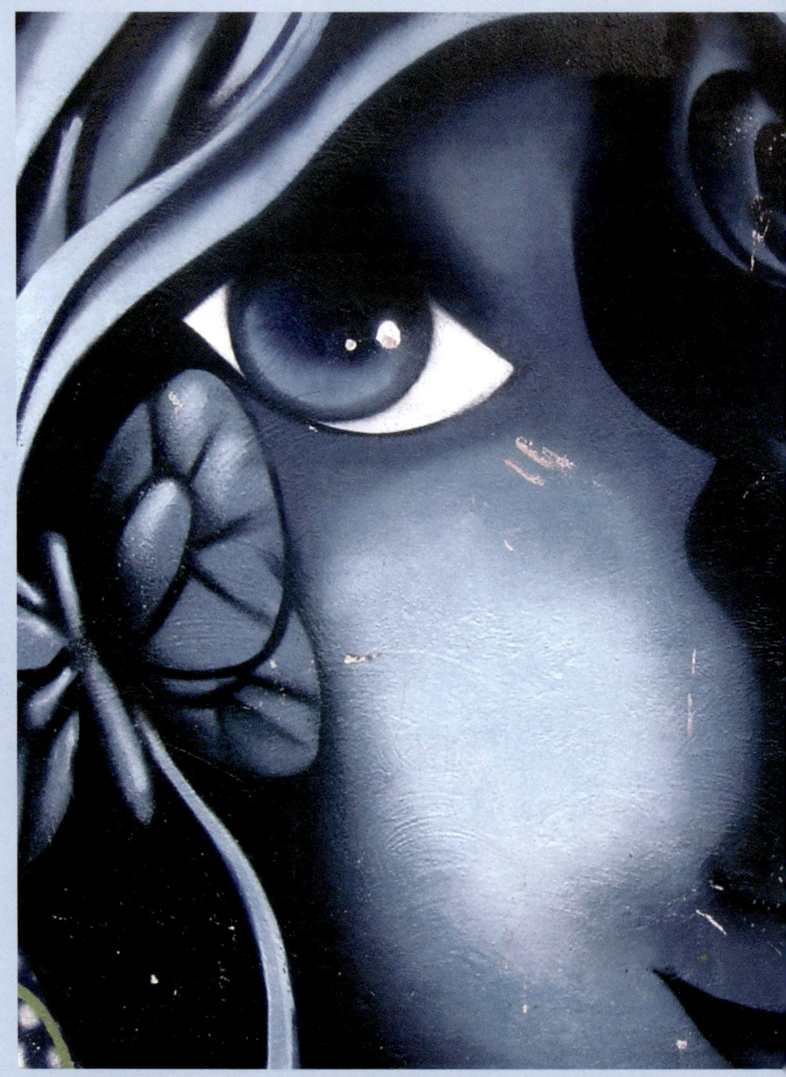

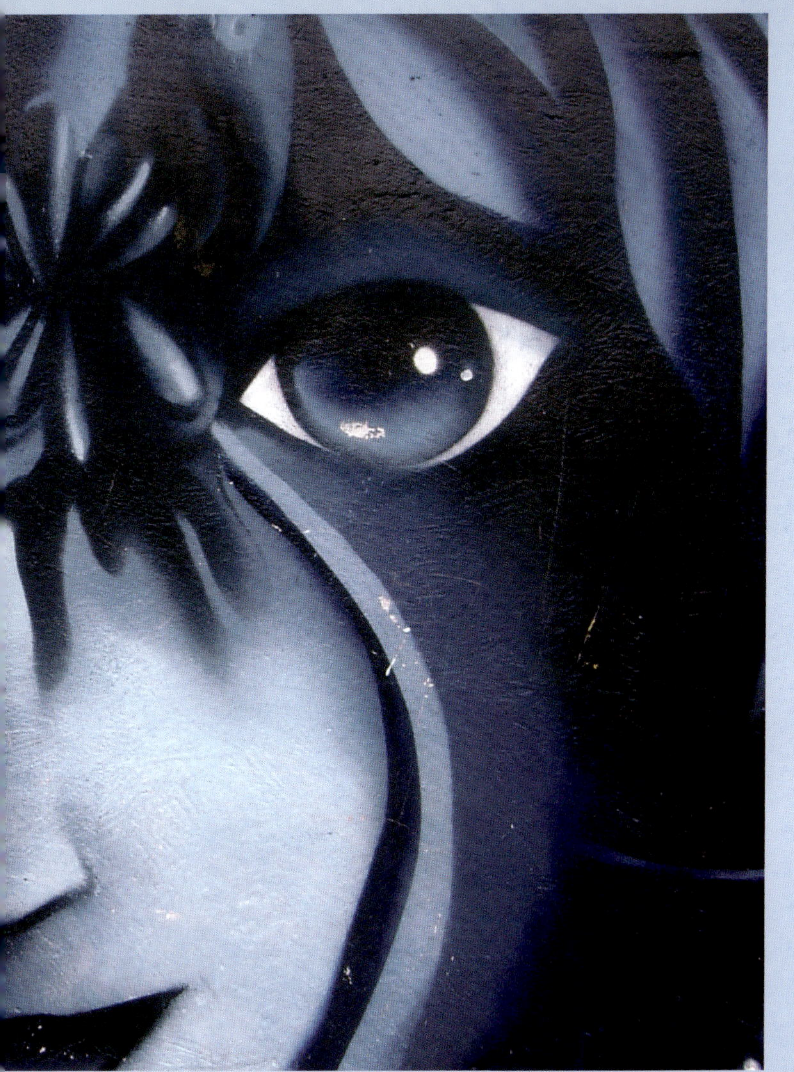

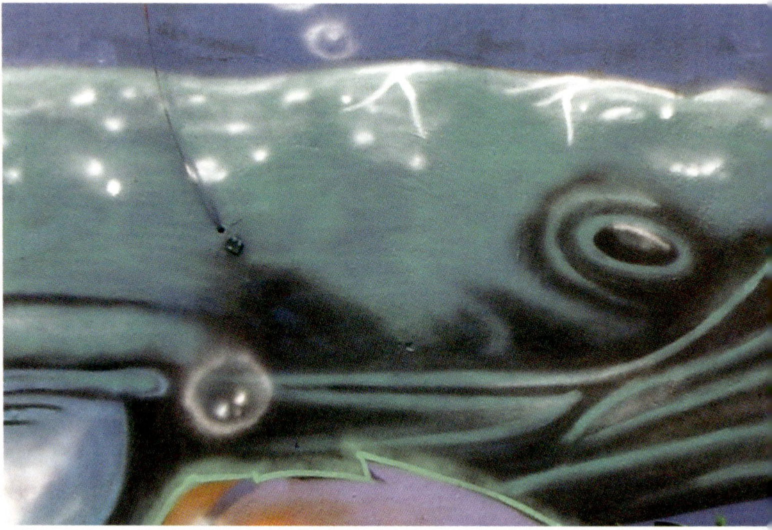

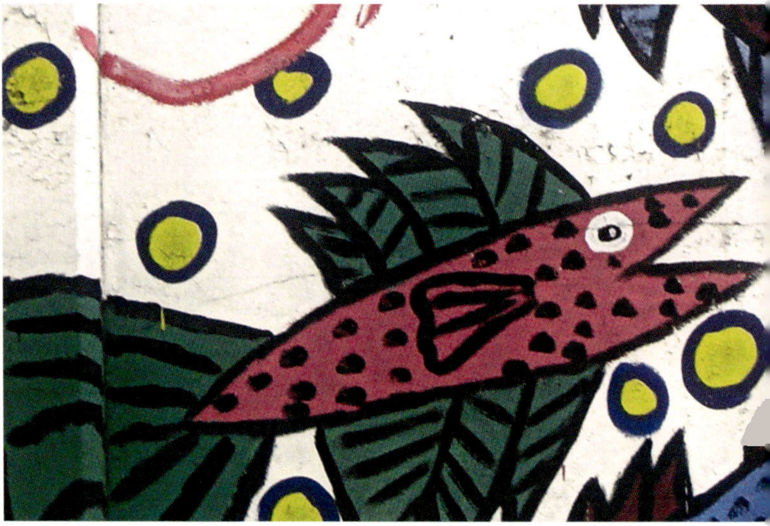

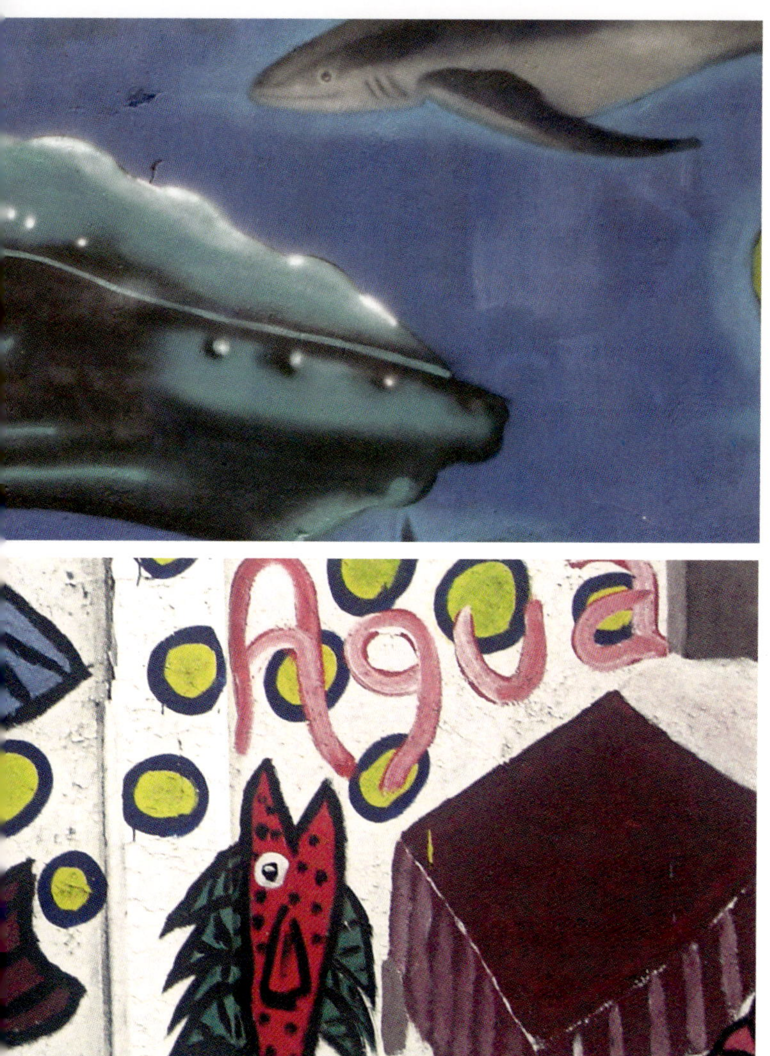

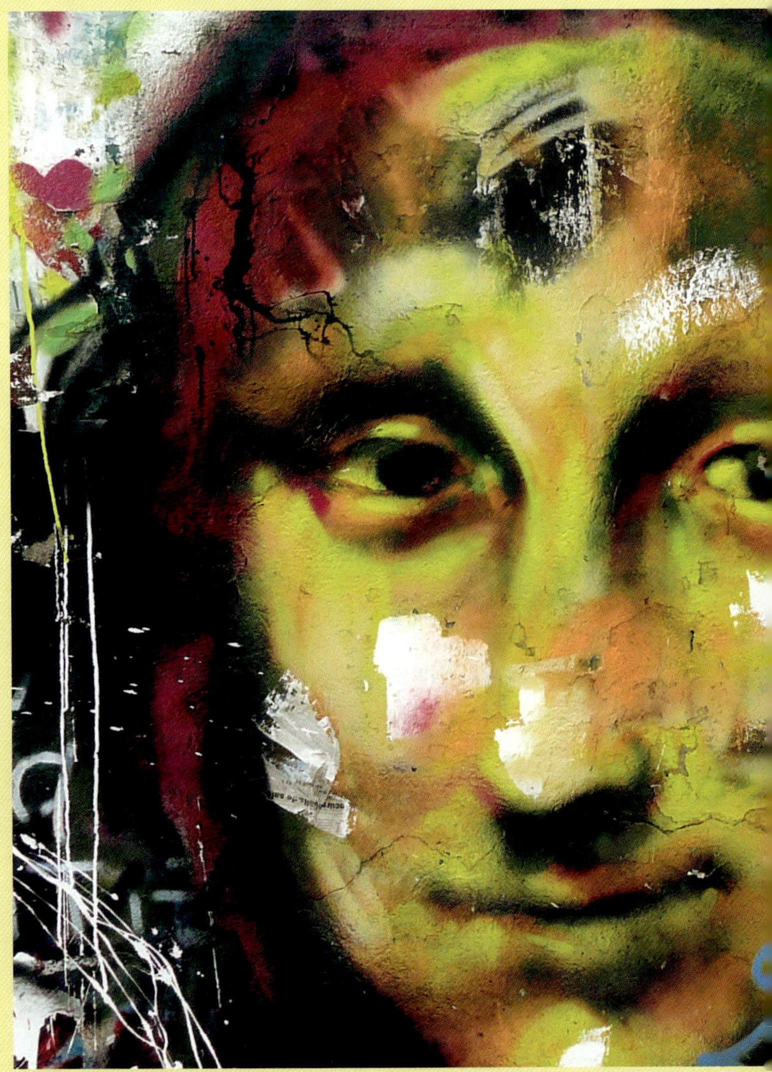

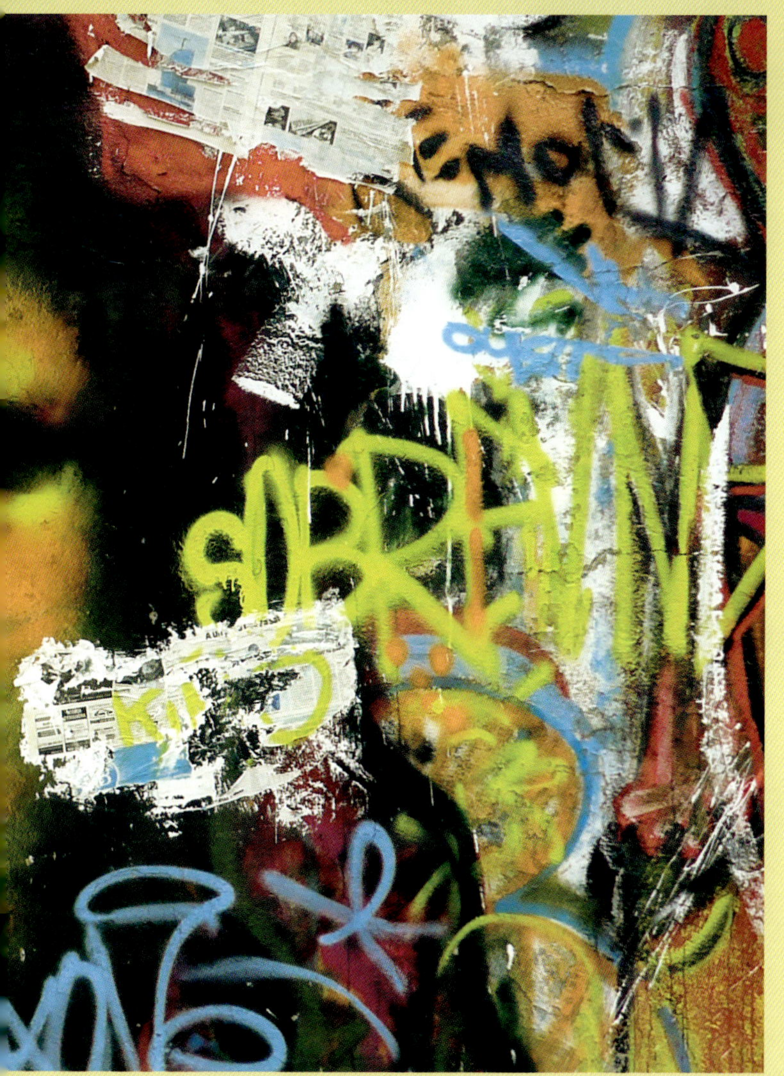

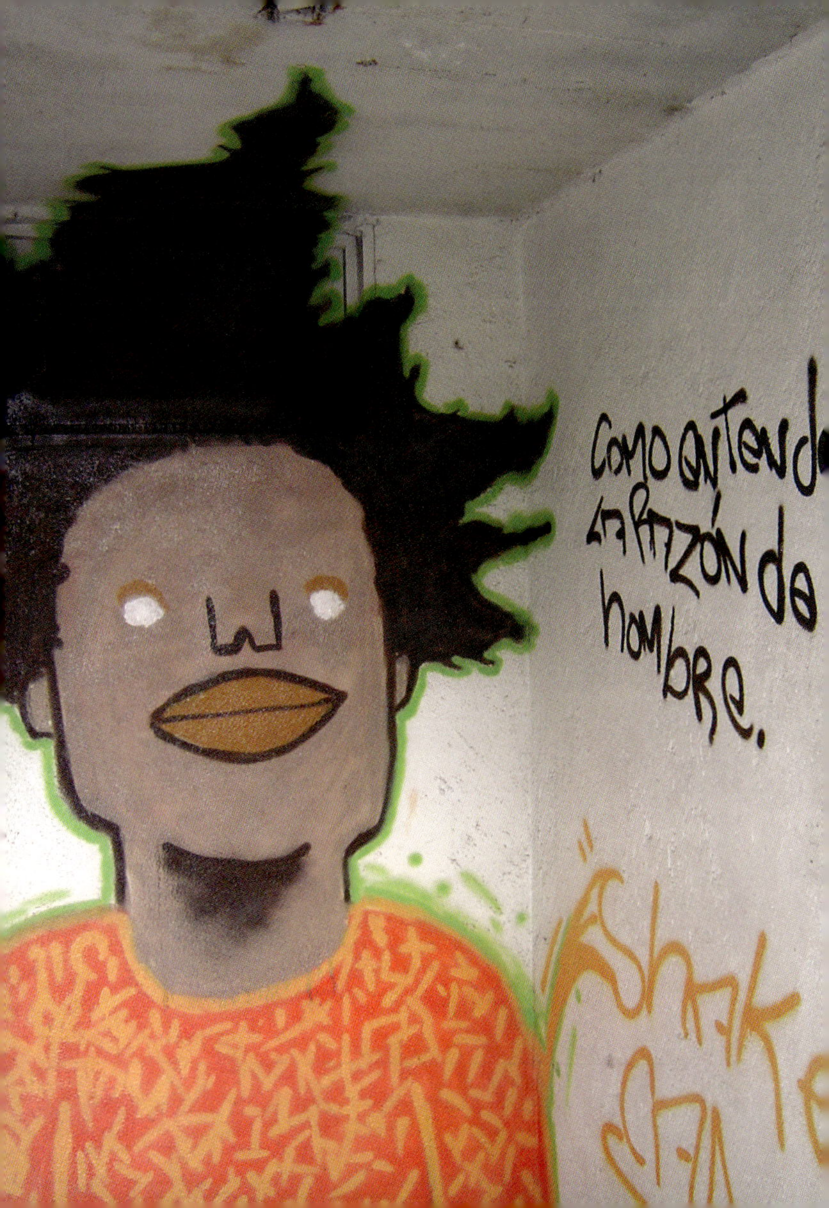
Como entende
la razón de
hombre.

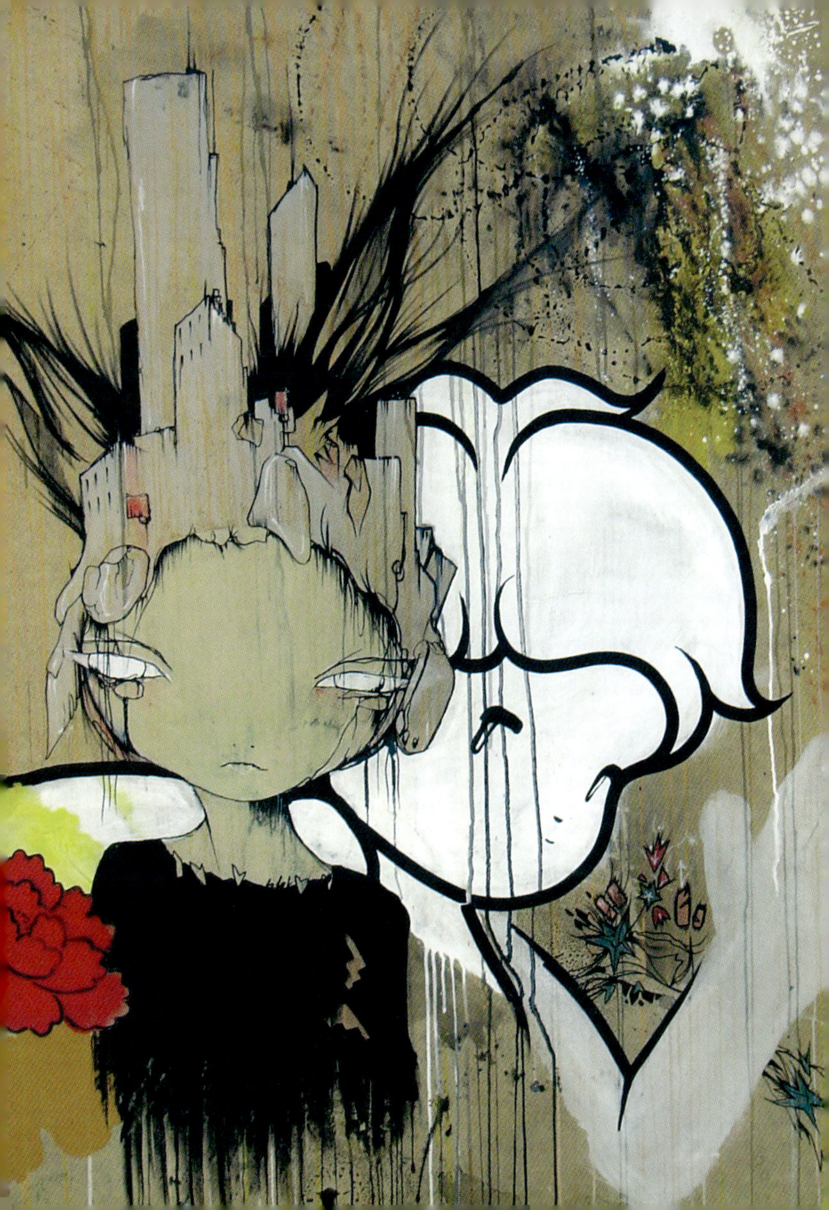

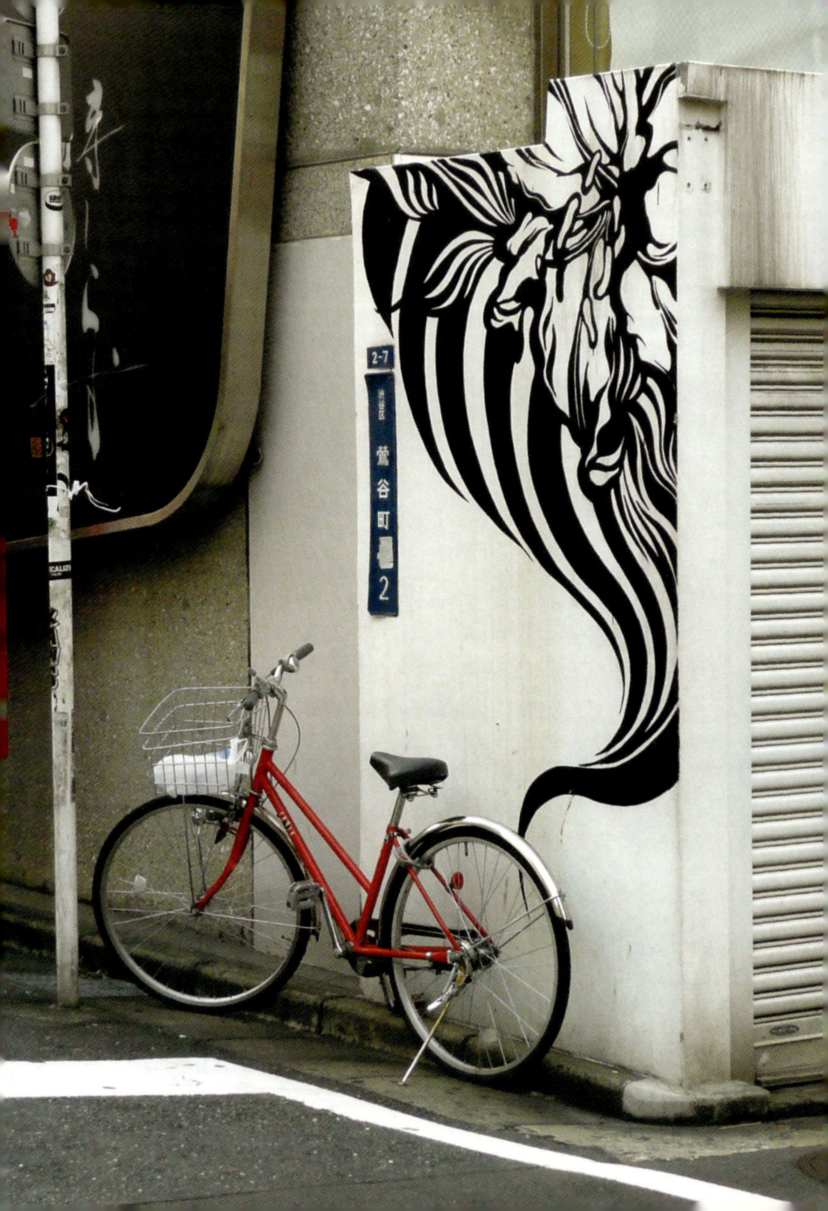
2-7
鶯谷町
2

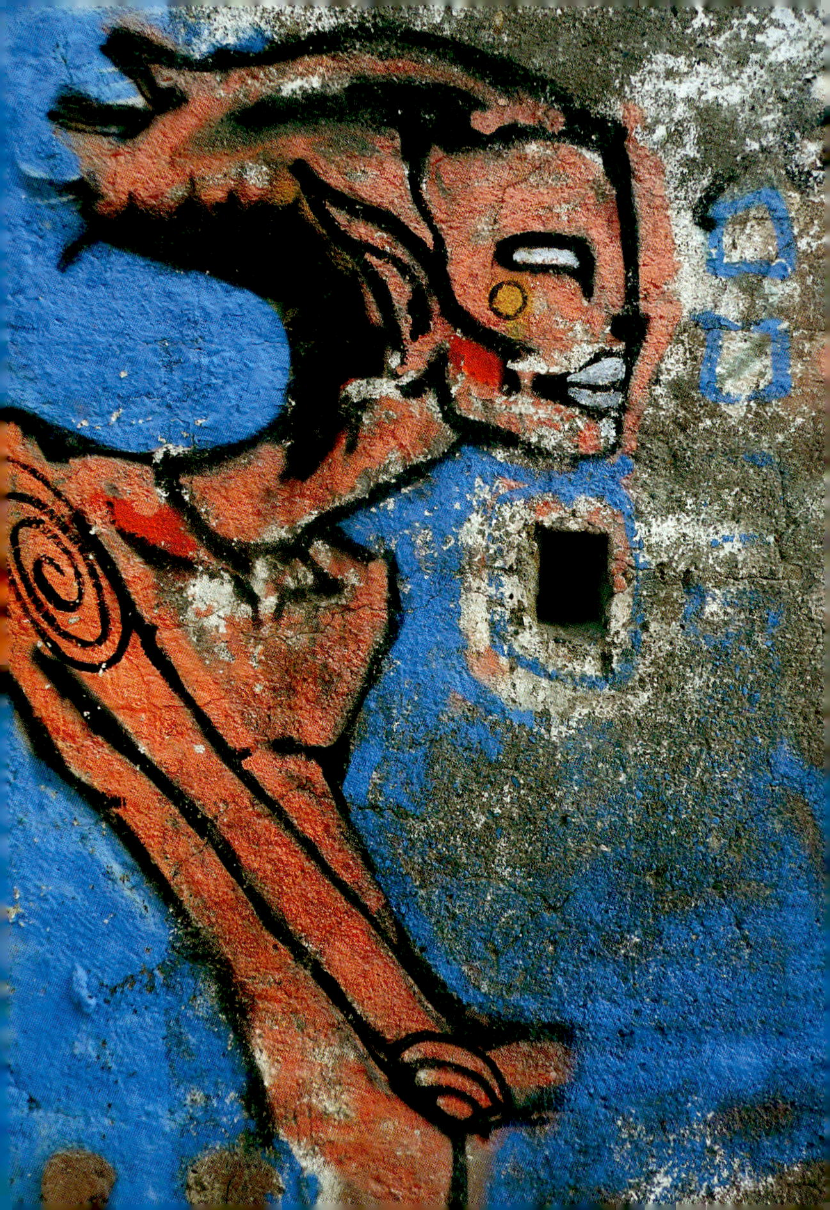

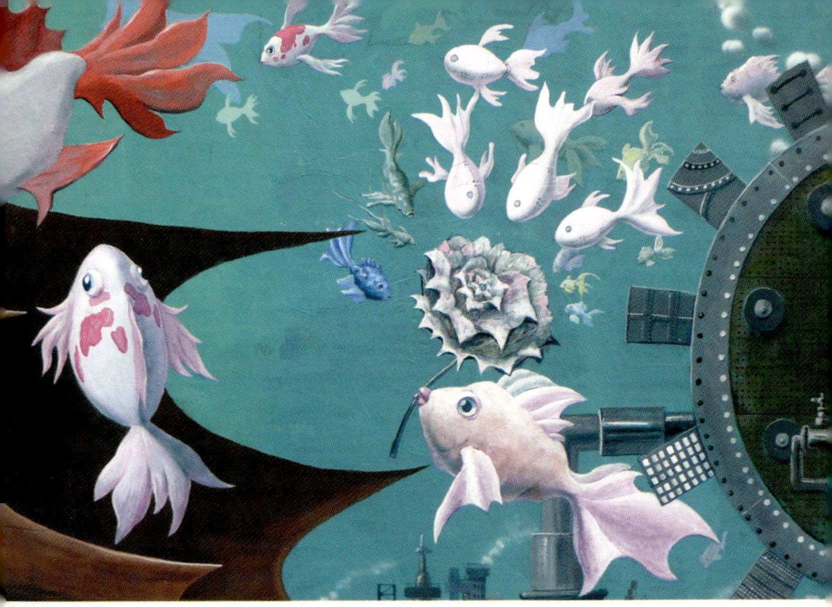

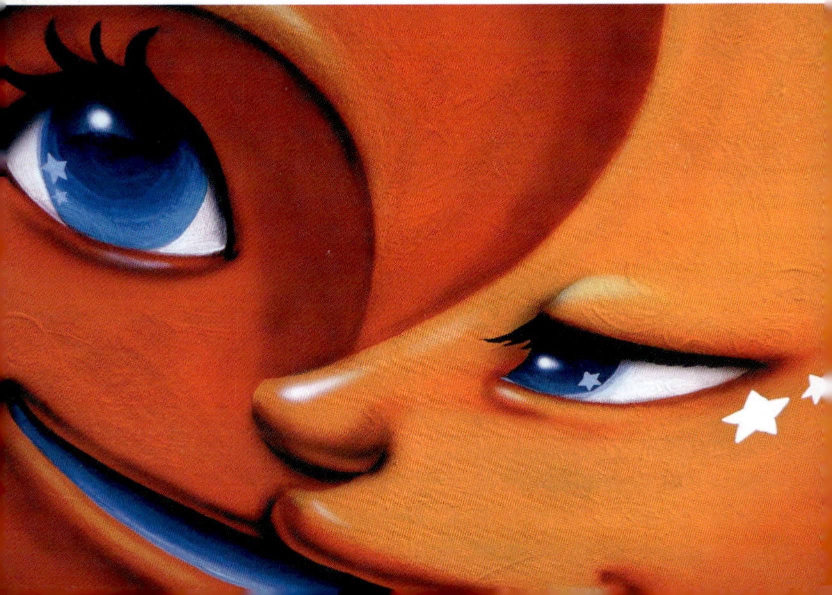

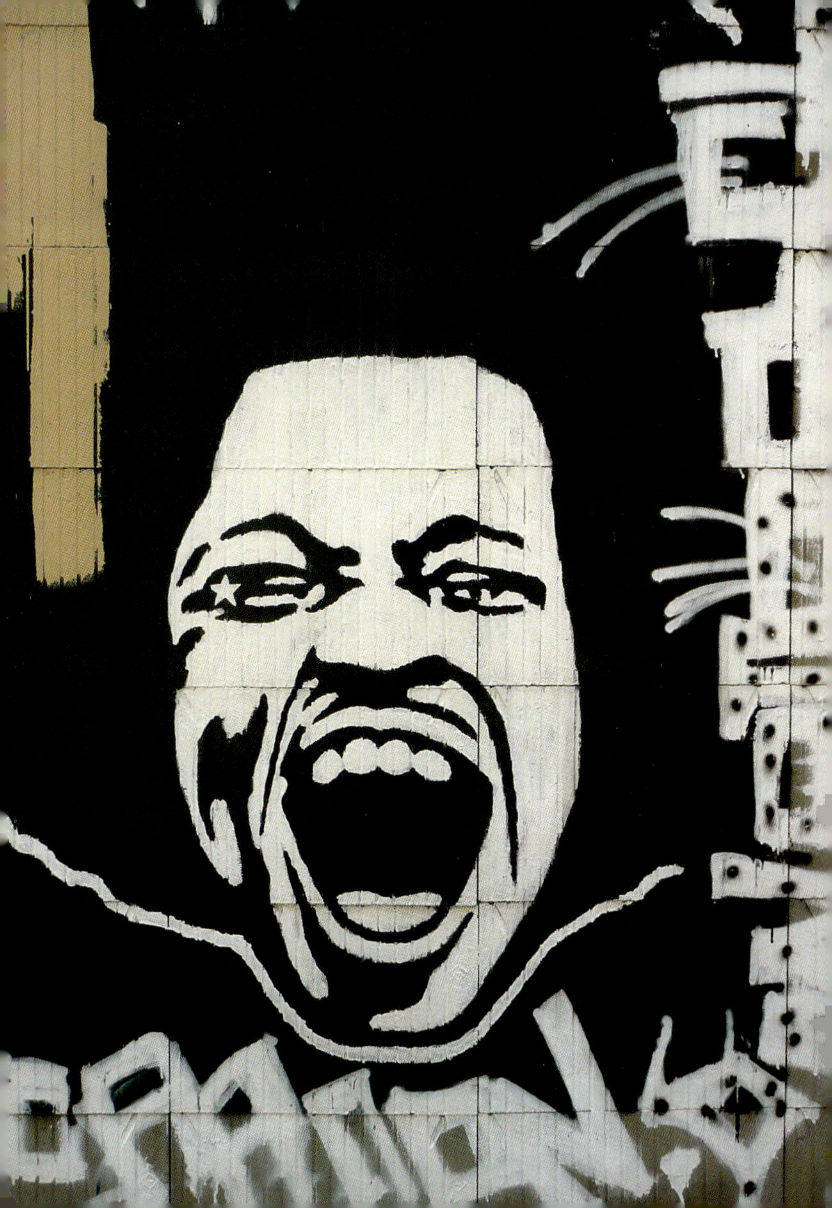

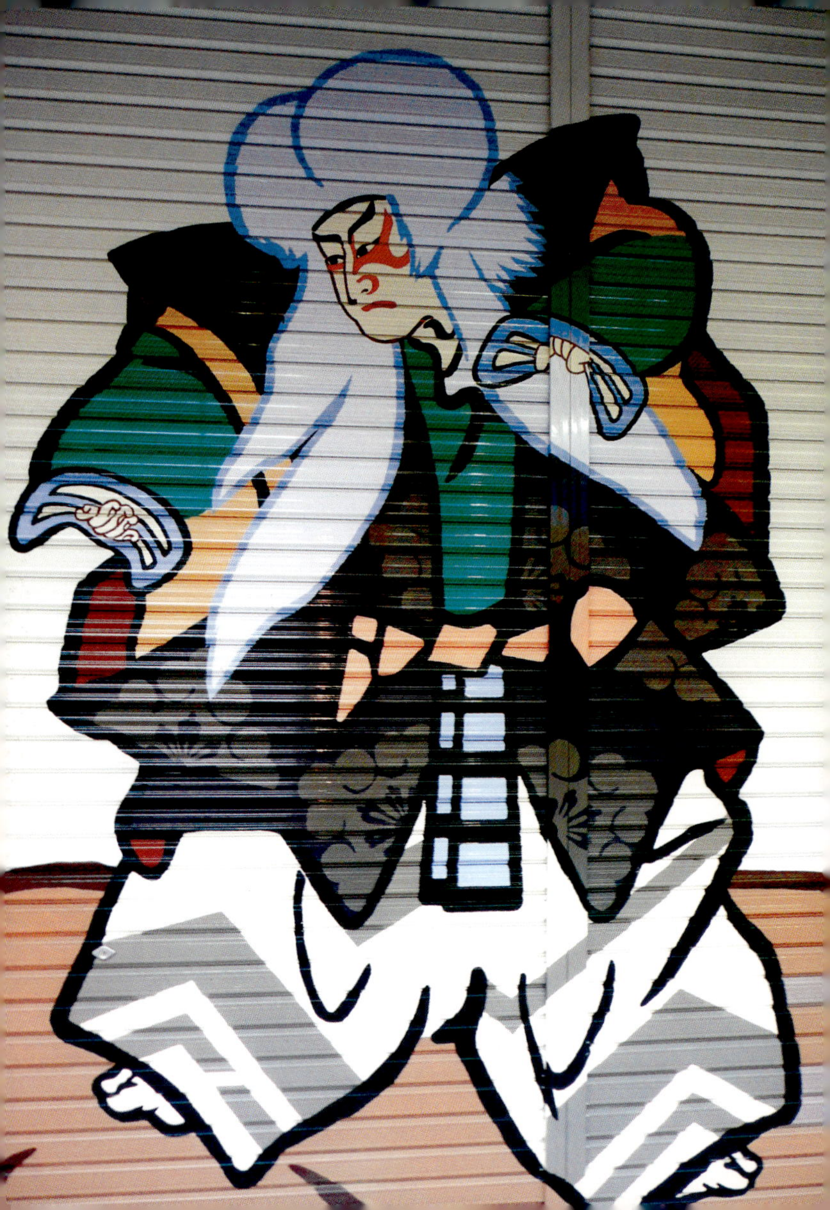

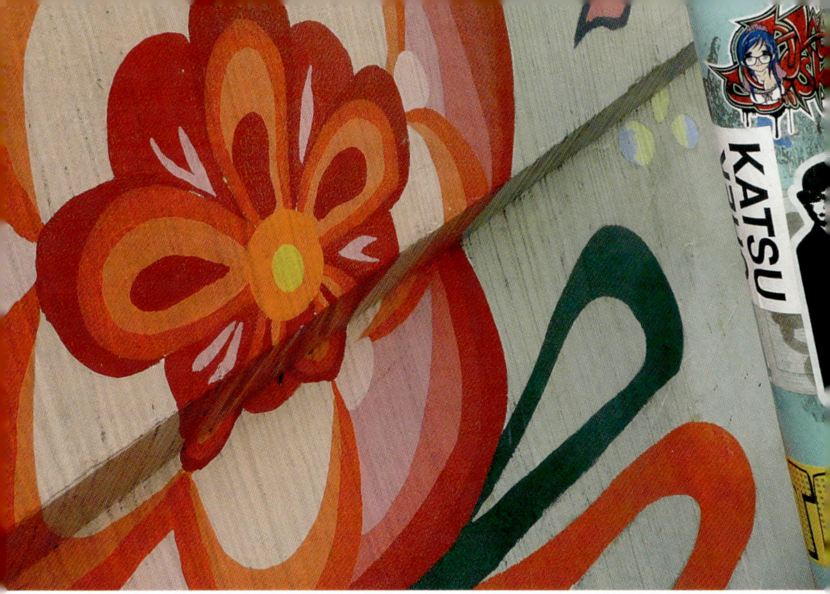

KATSU

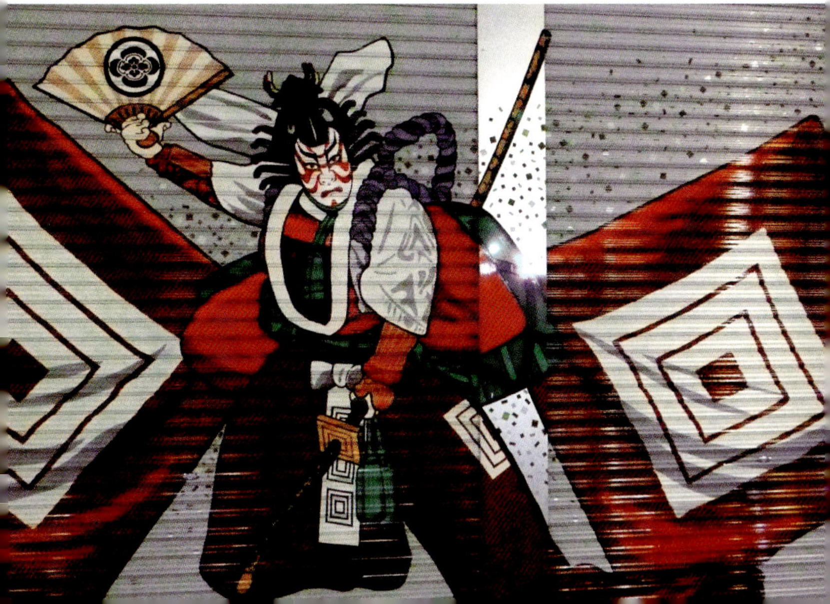

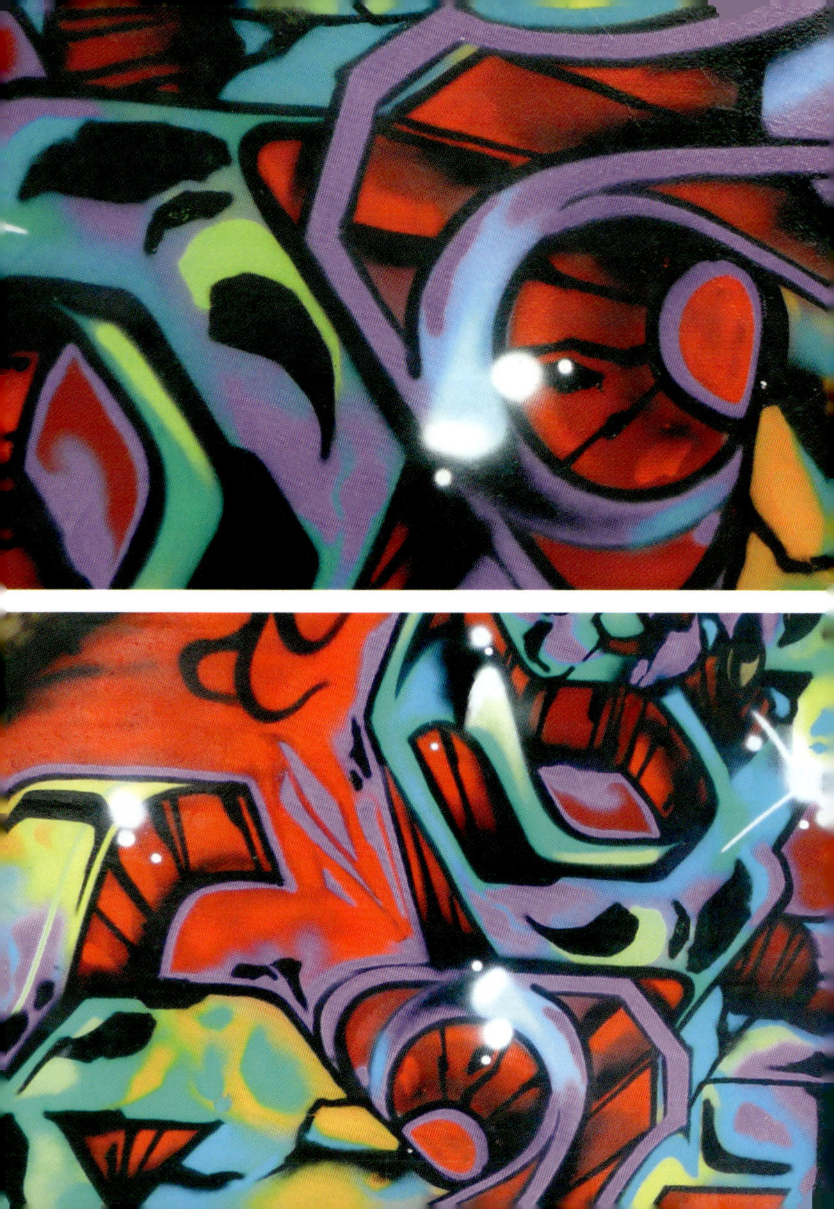

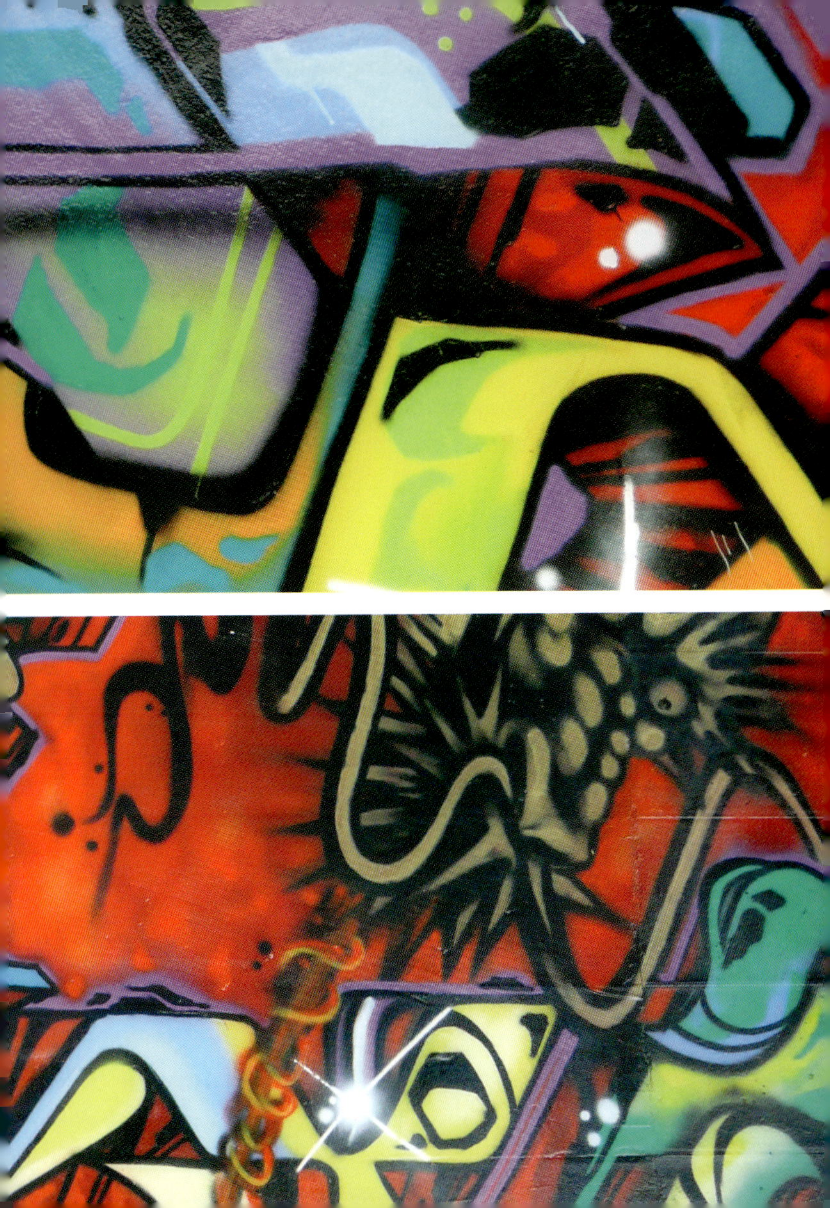

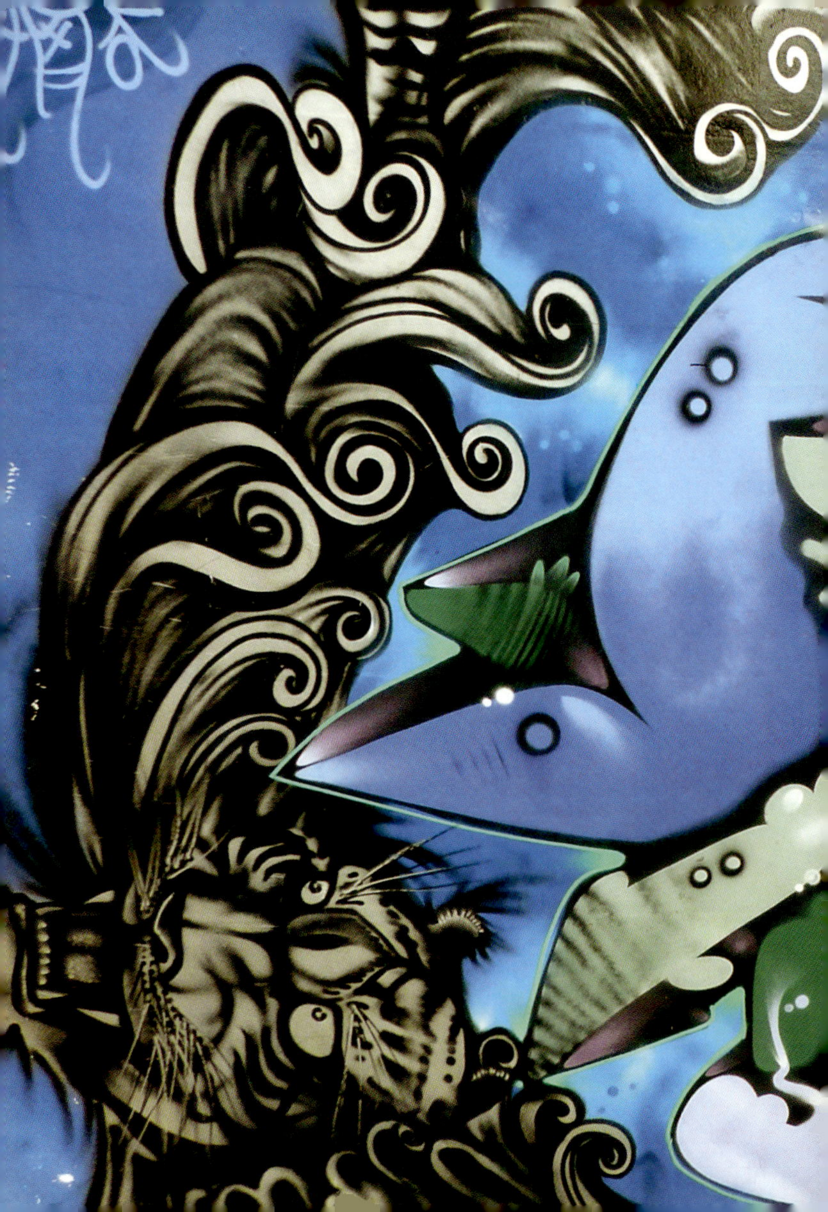

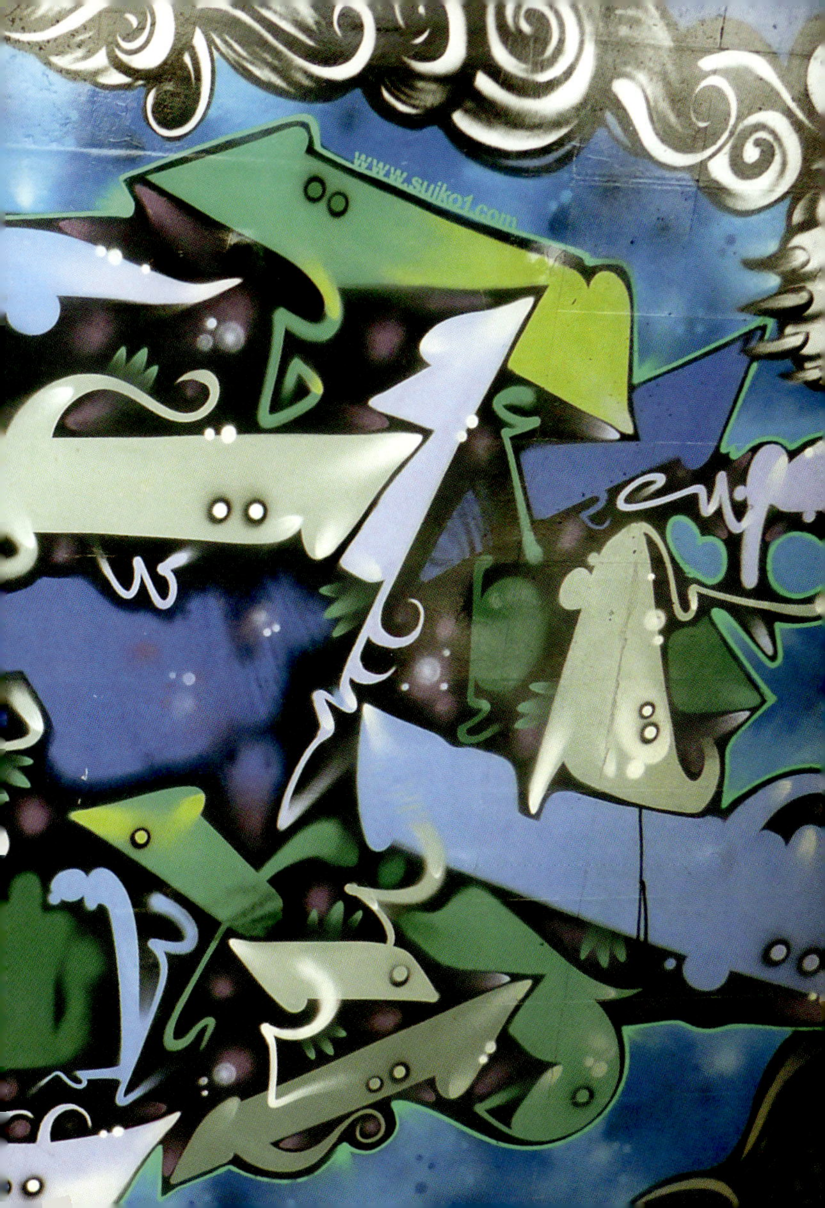
www.suiko1.com

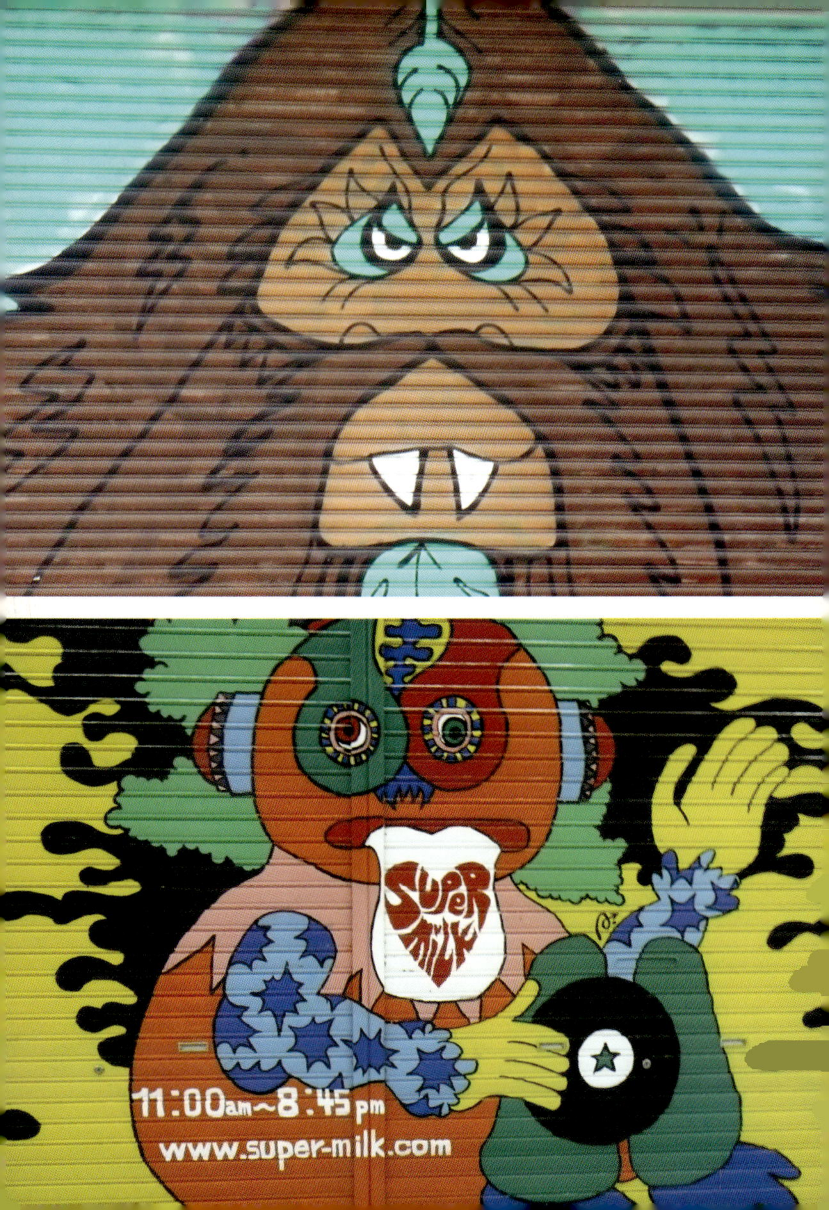
SUPER MILK
11:00am~8:45pm
www.super-milk.com

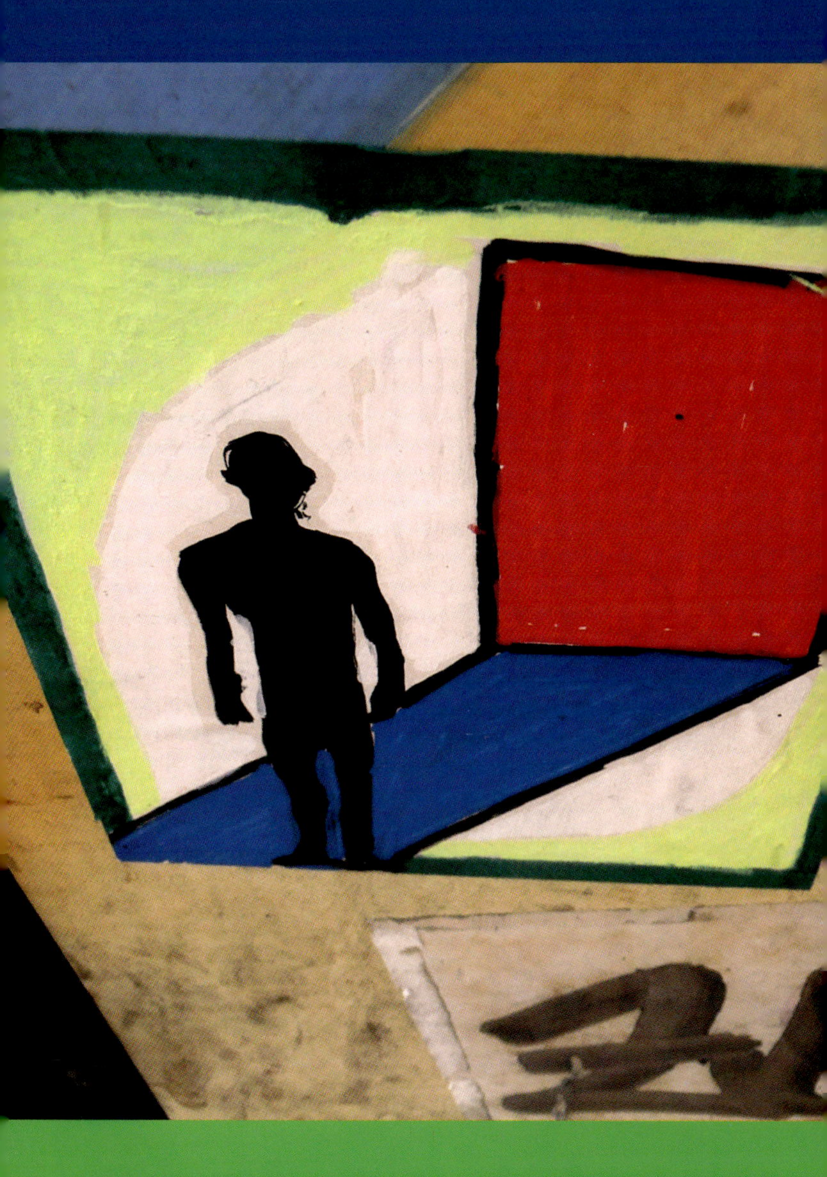

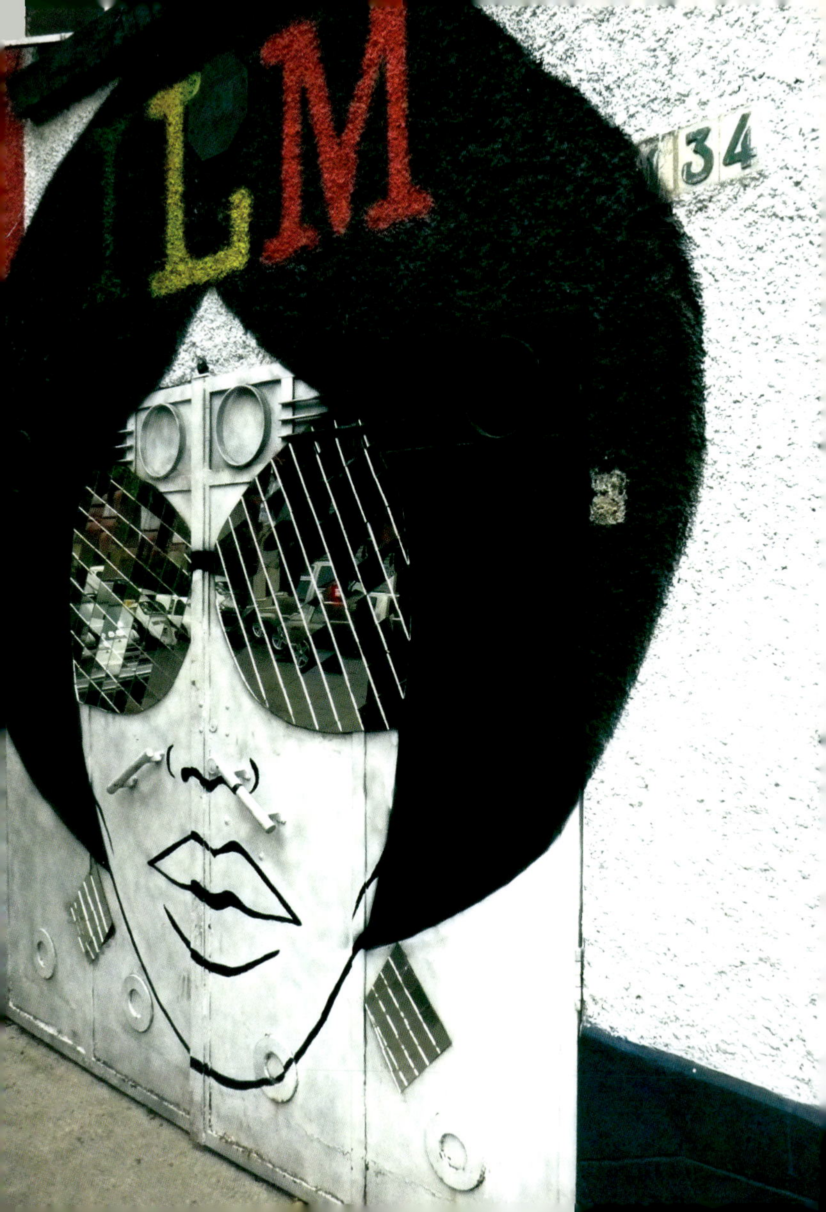
LM
34

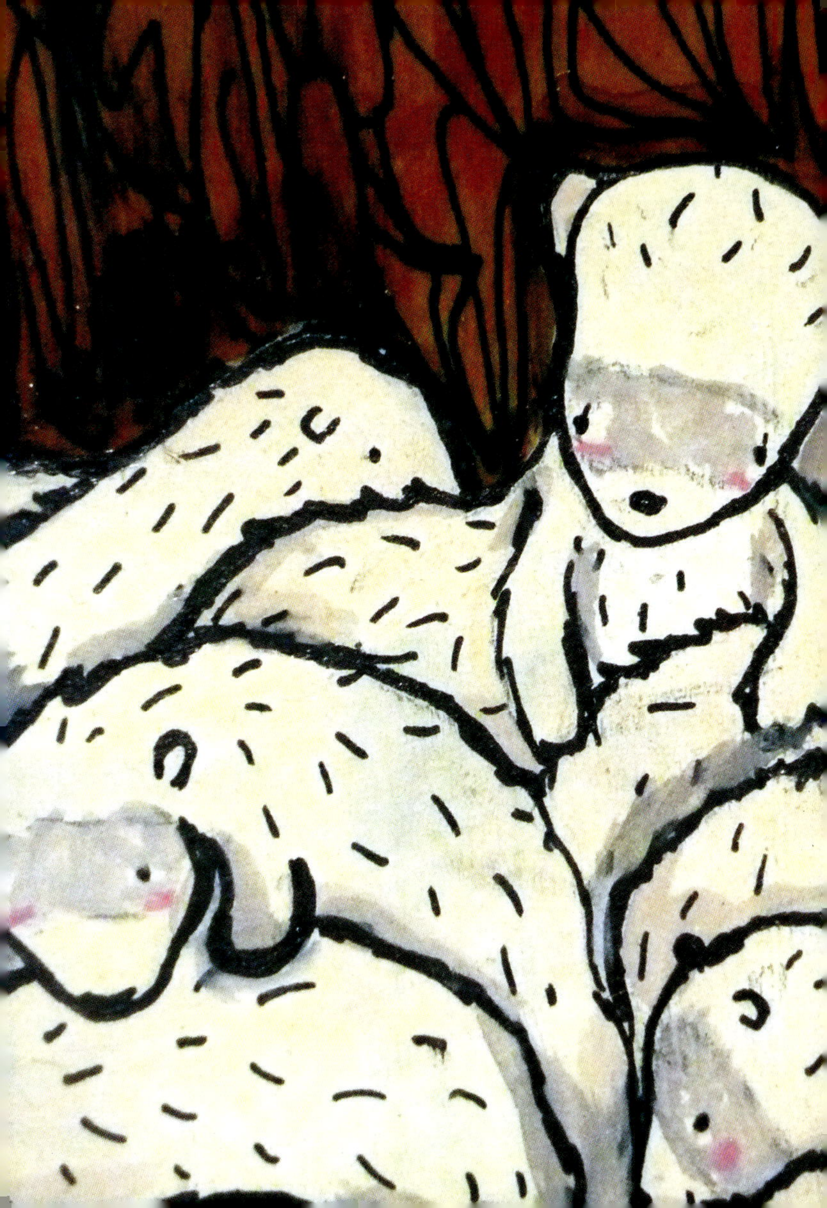

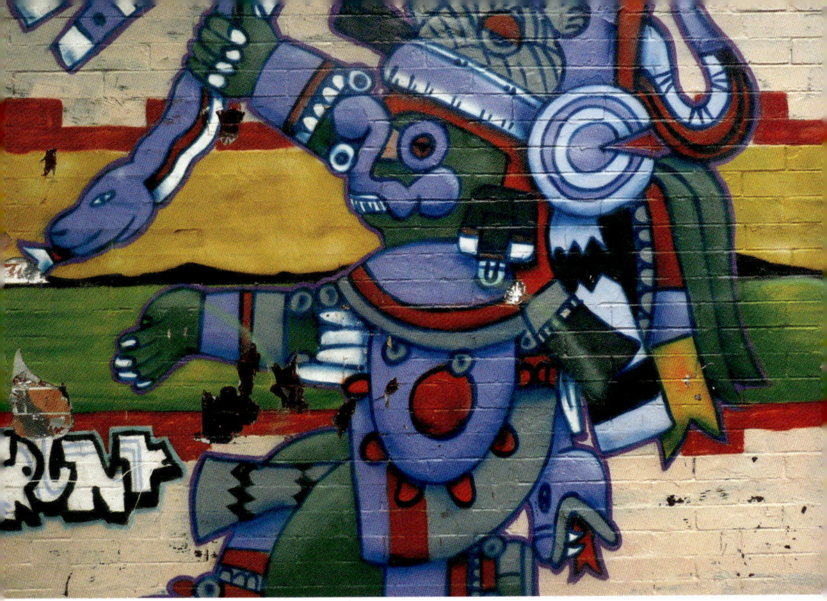

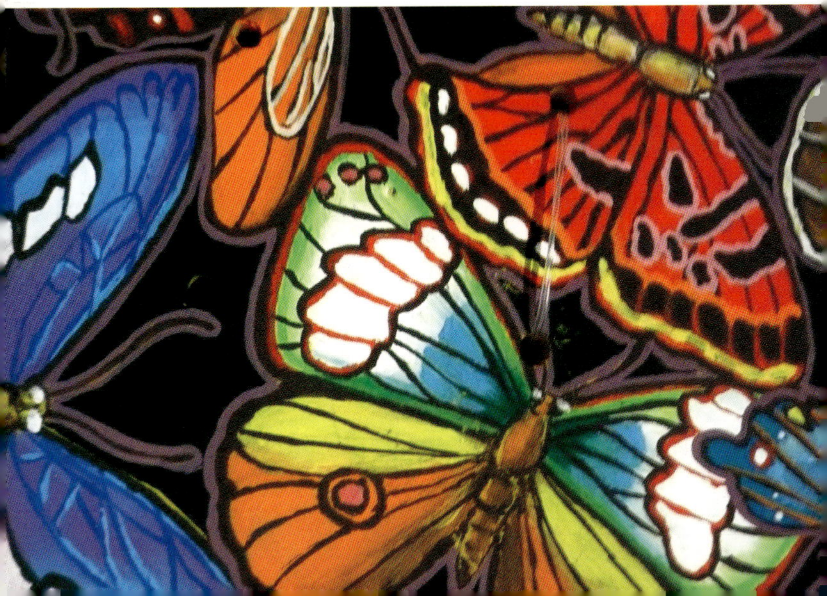

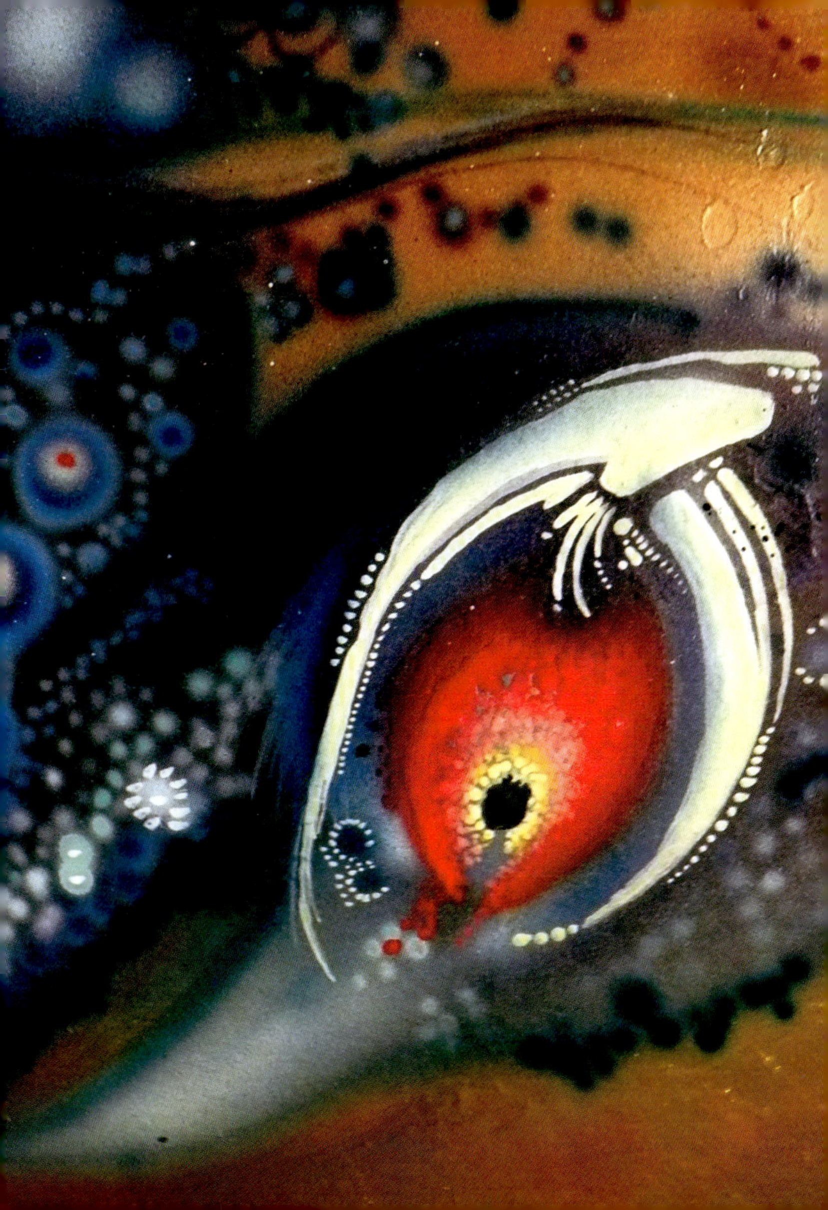

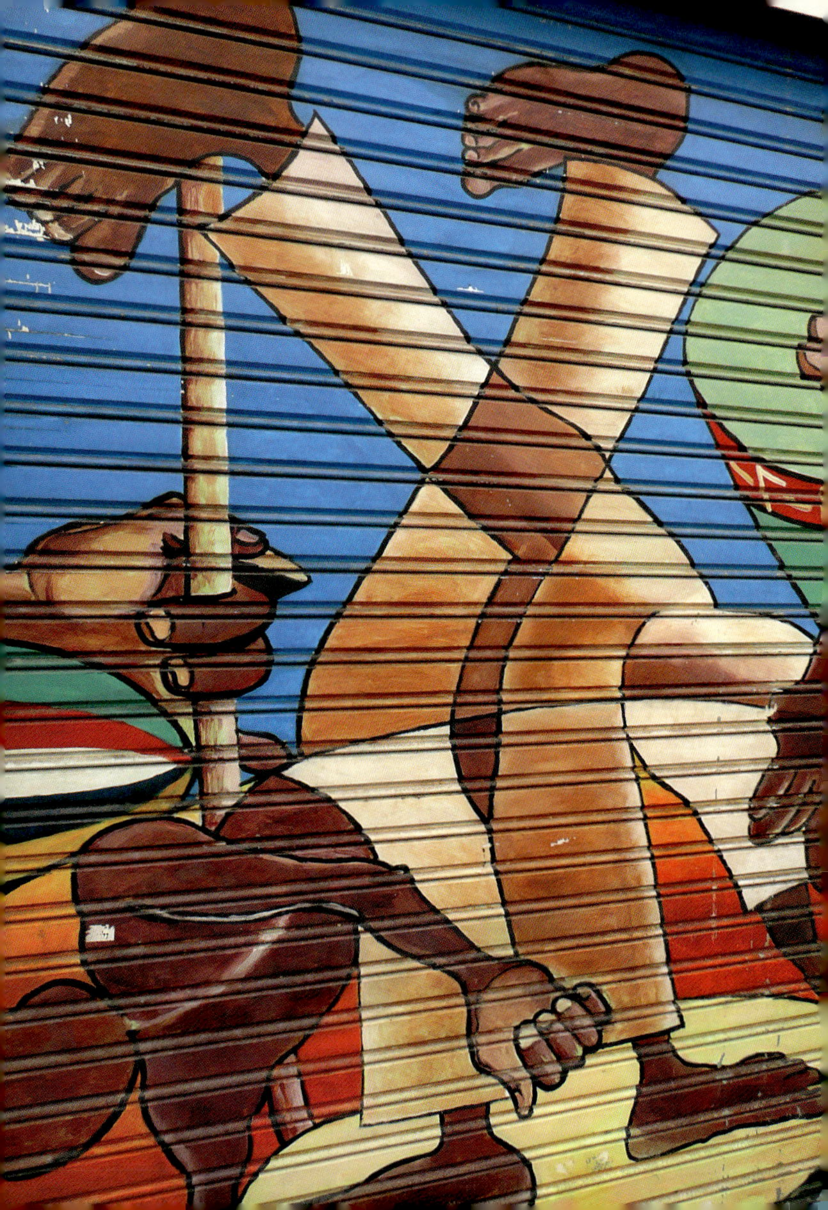

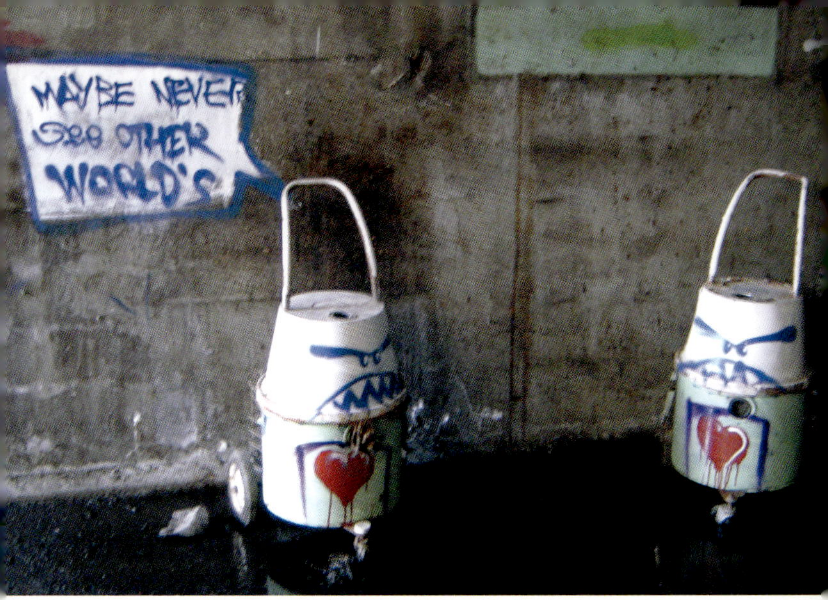

MAYBE NEVER SEE OTHER WORLD'S

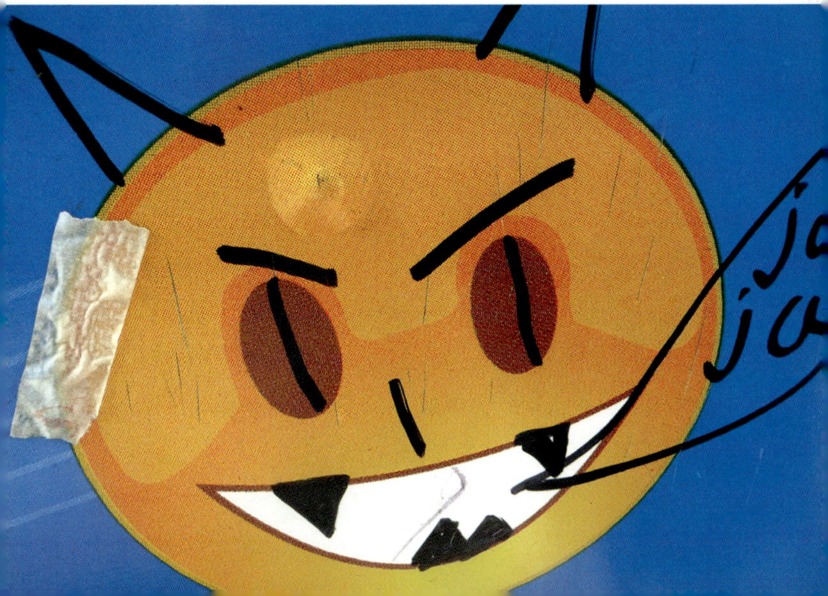

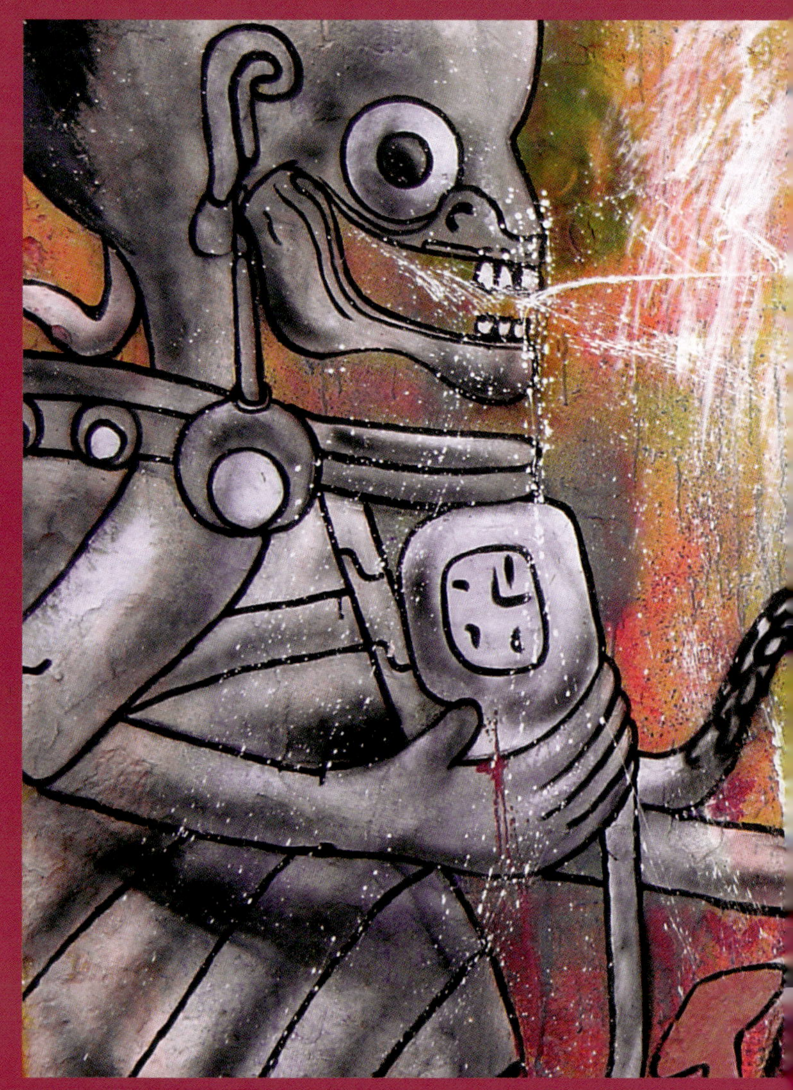

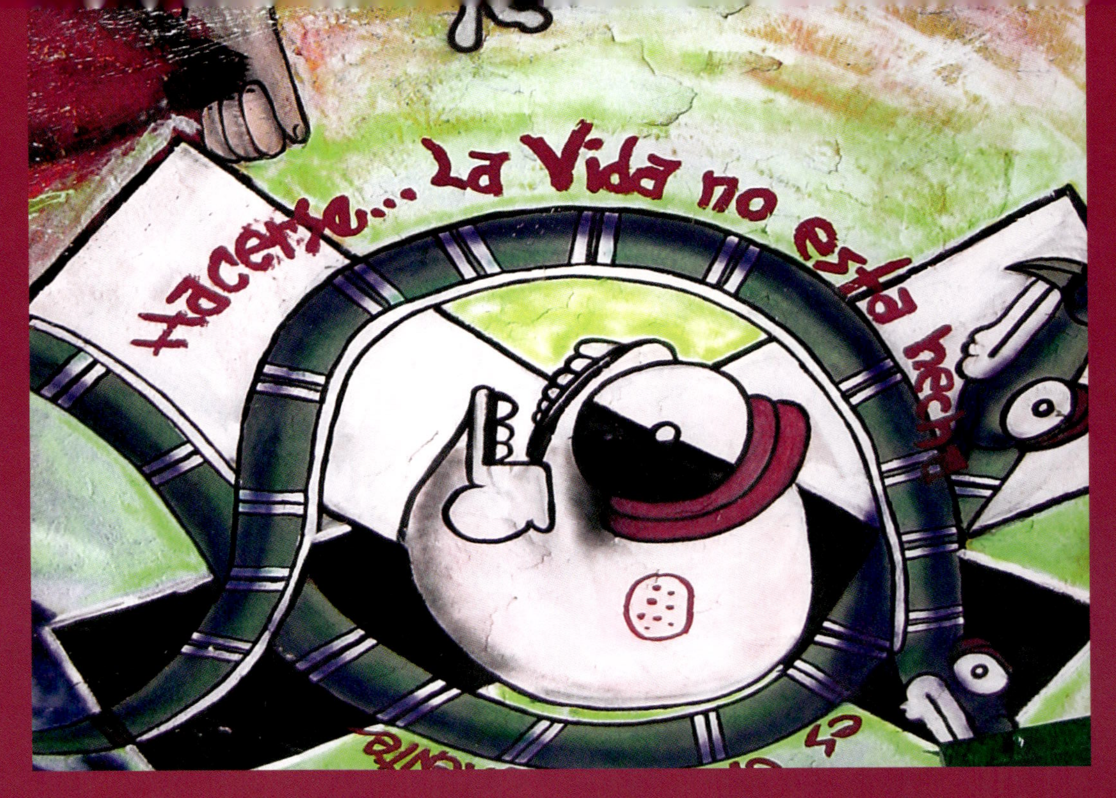
Hacerte... La Vida no esta hecha

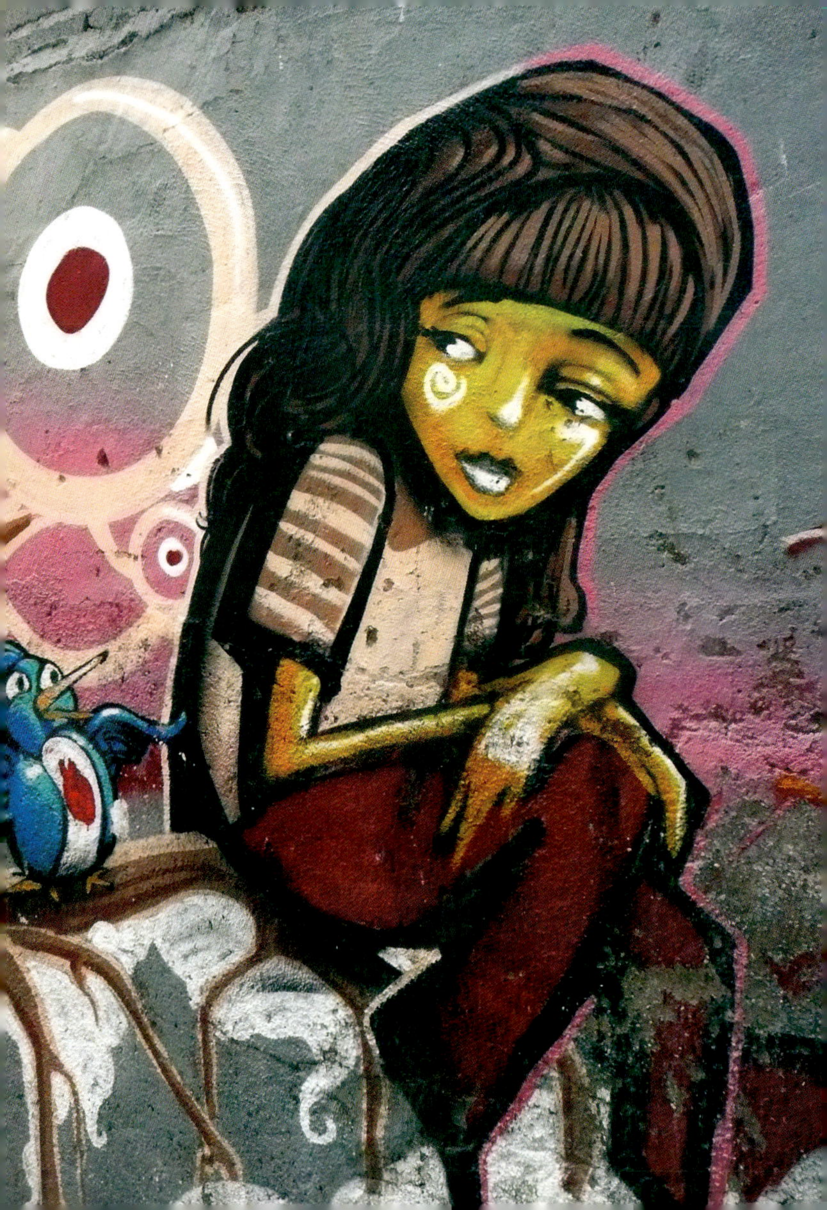

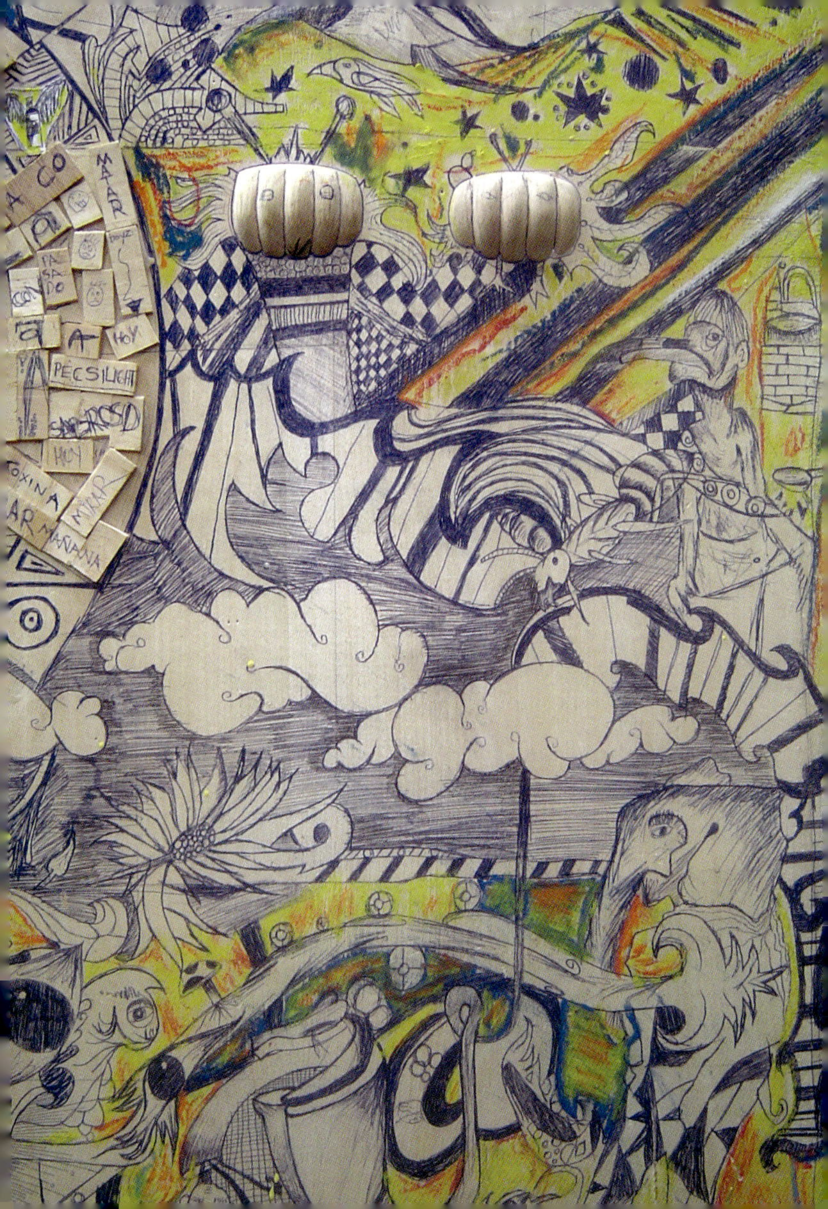

MATAR
PASADO
HOY
PECSILIGHT
HOY
TOXINA
MAÑANA

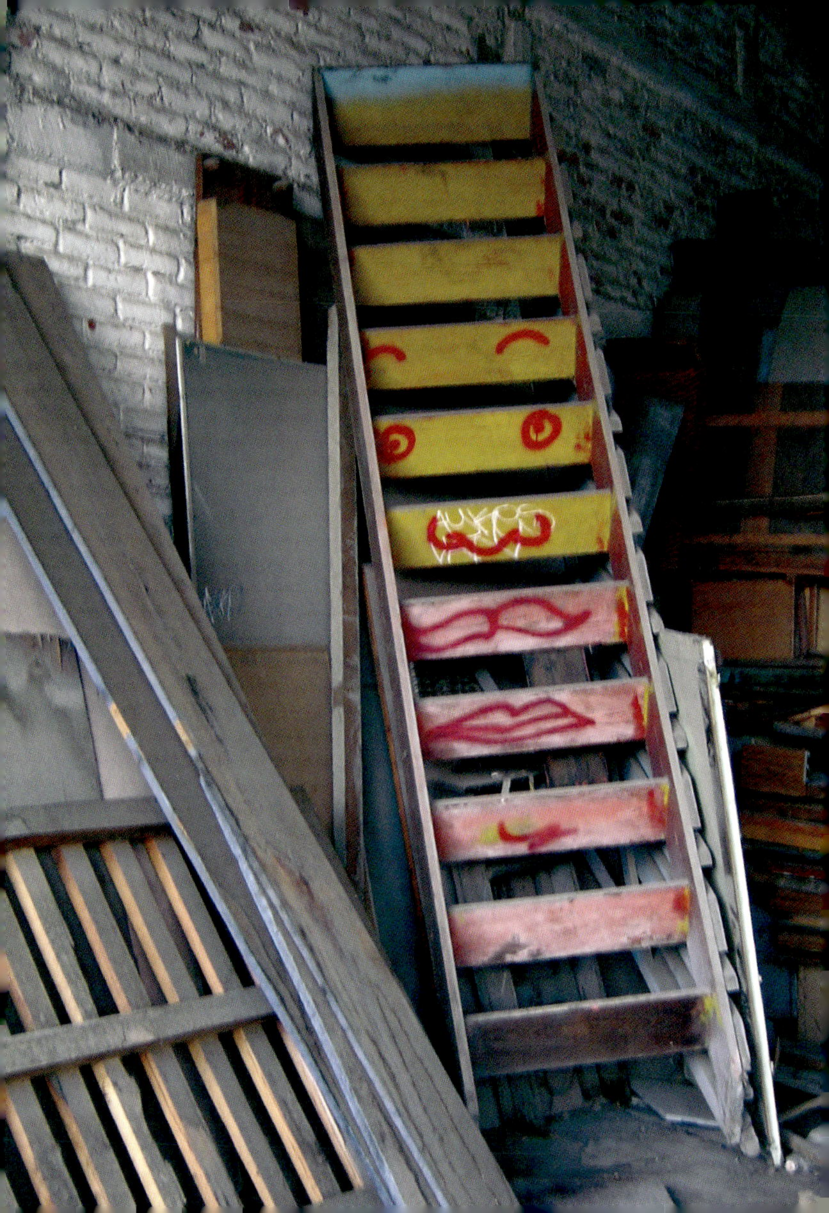

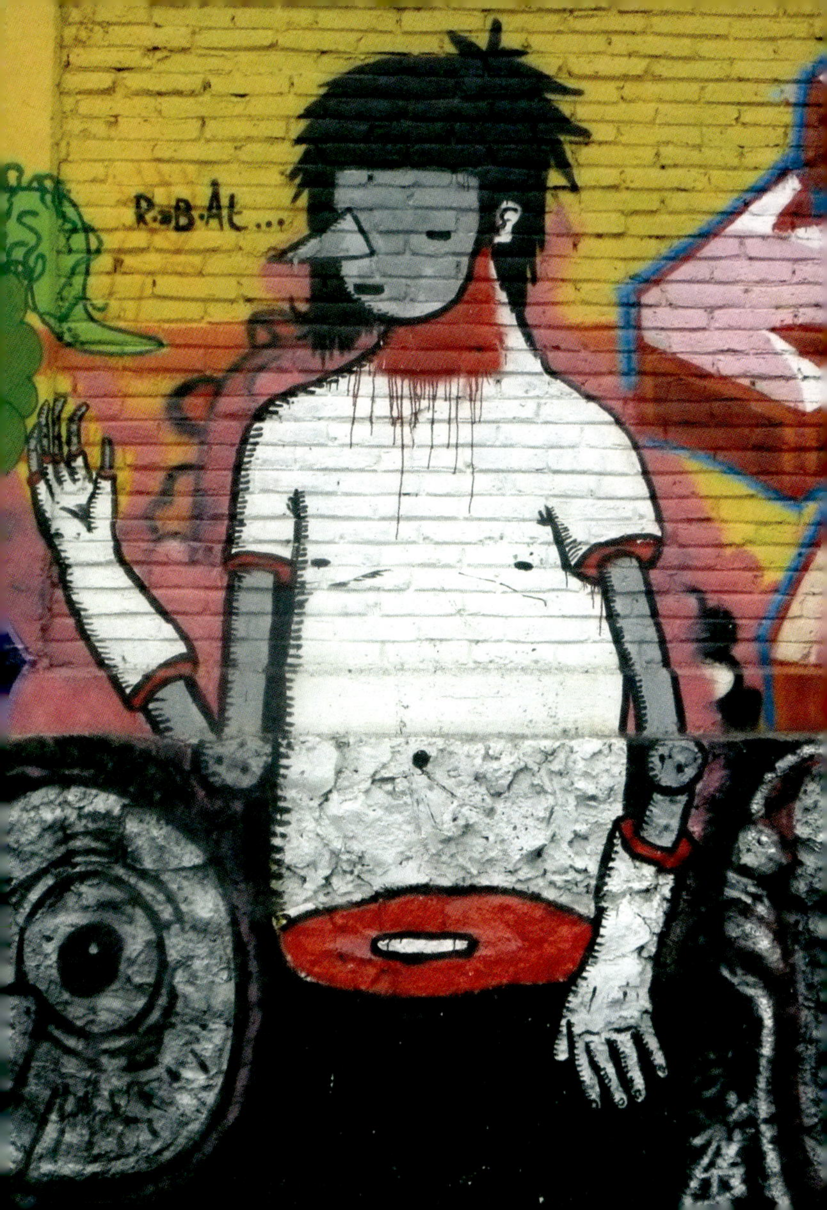
R.B.ÅL...

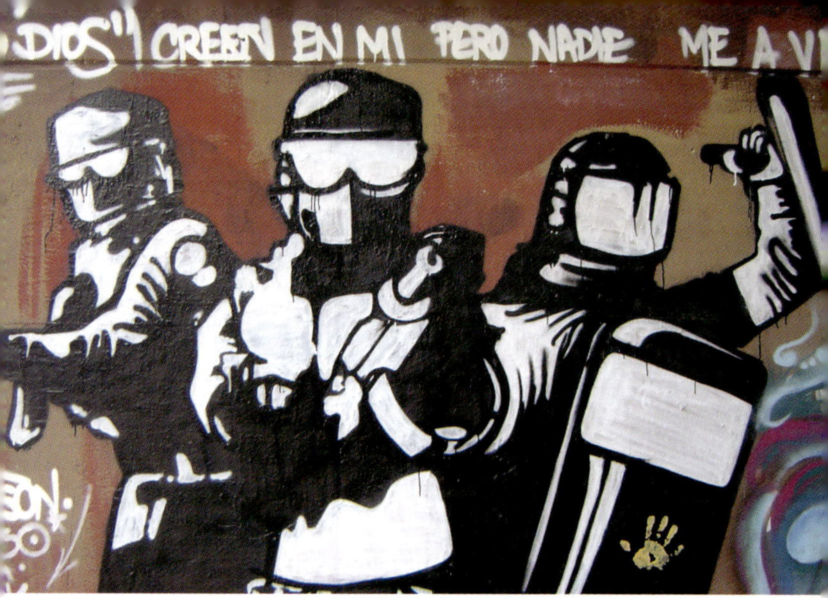
DIOS" CREEN EN MI PERO NADIE ME A

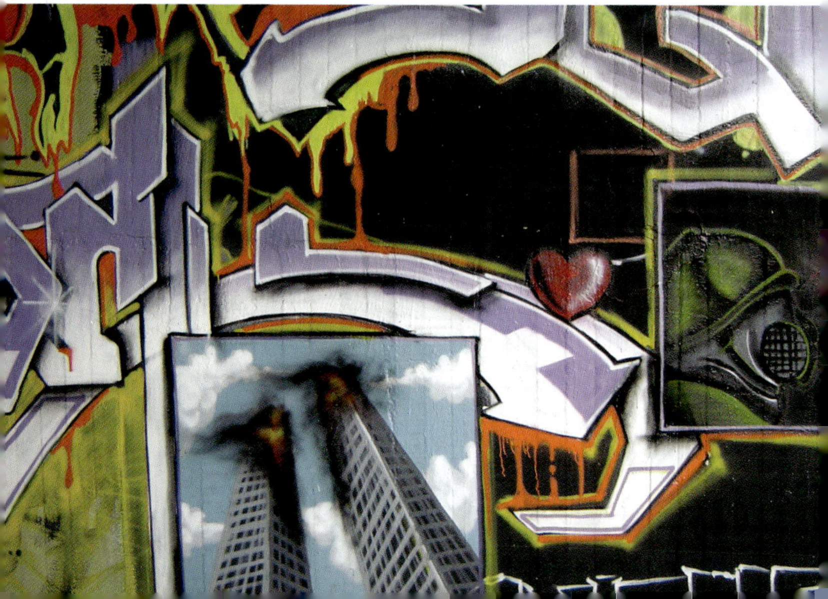

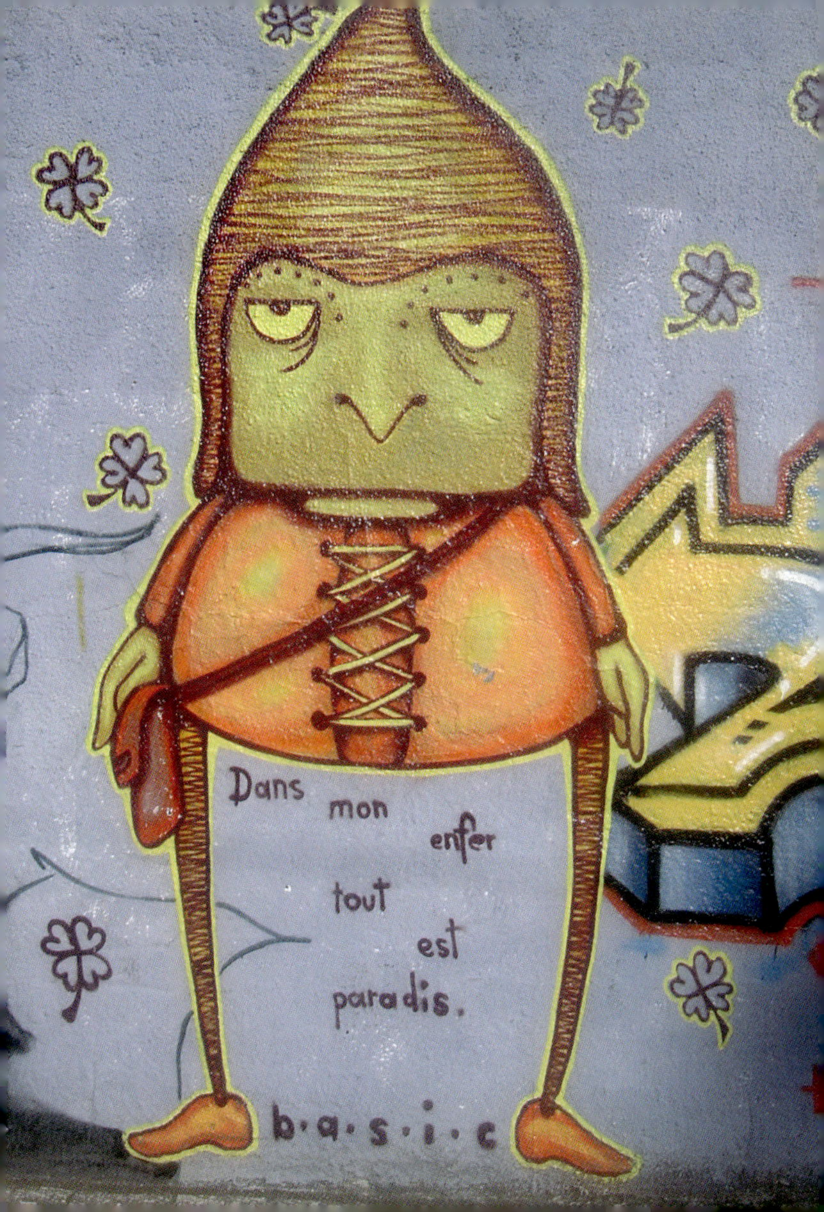
Dans mon enfer tout est paradis.
b·a·s·i·c

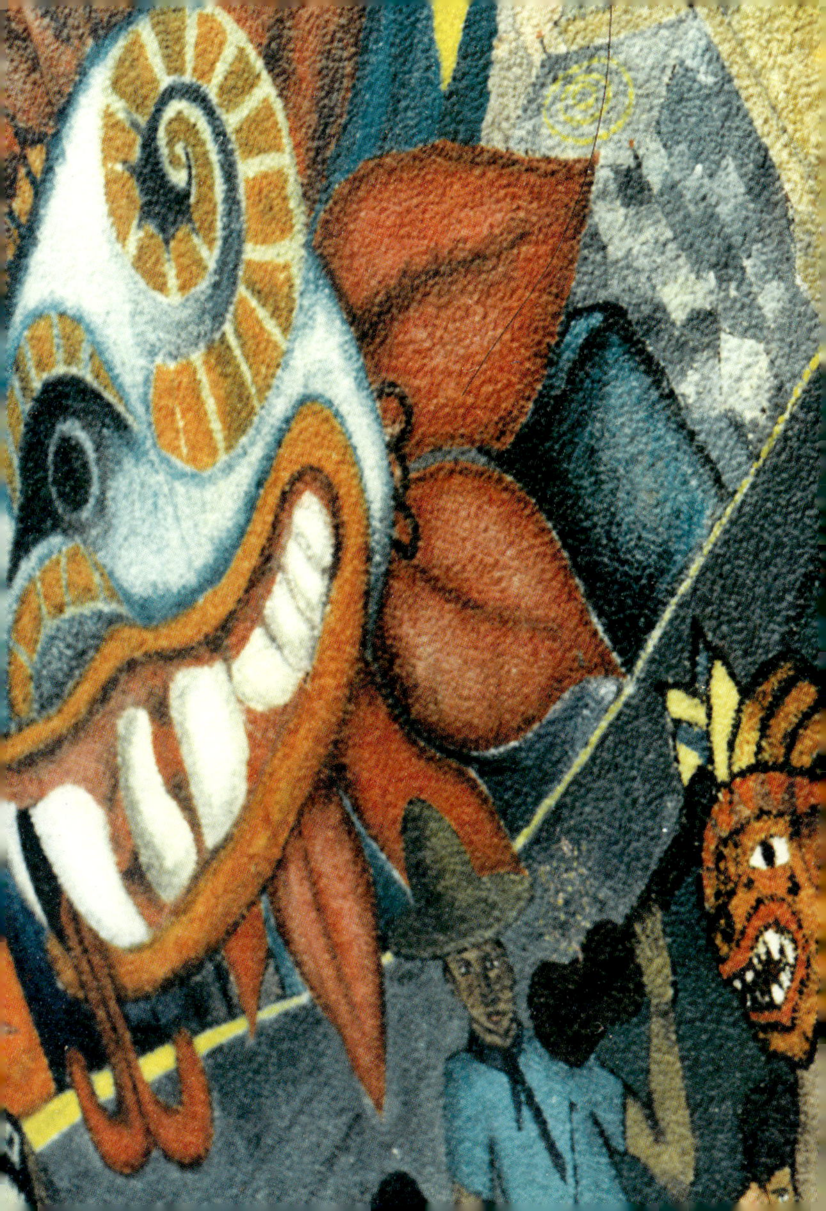

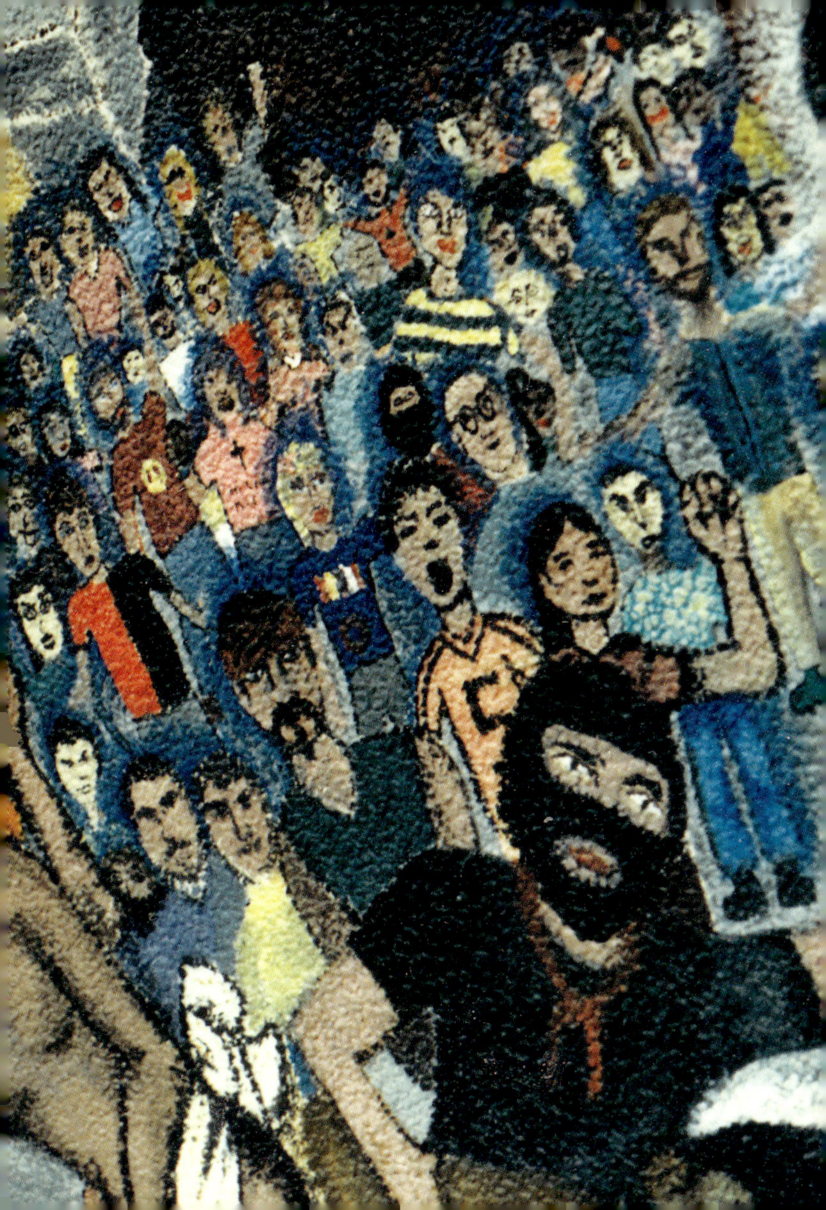

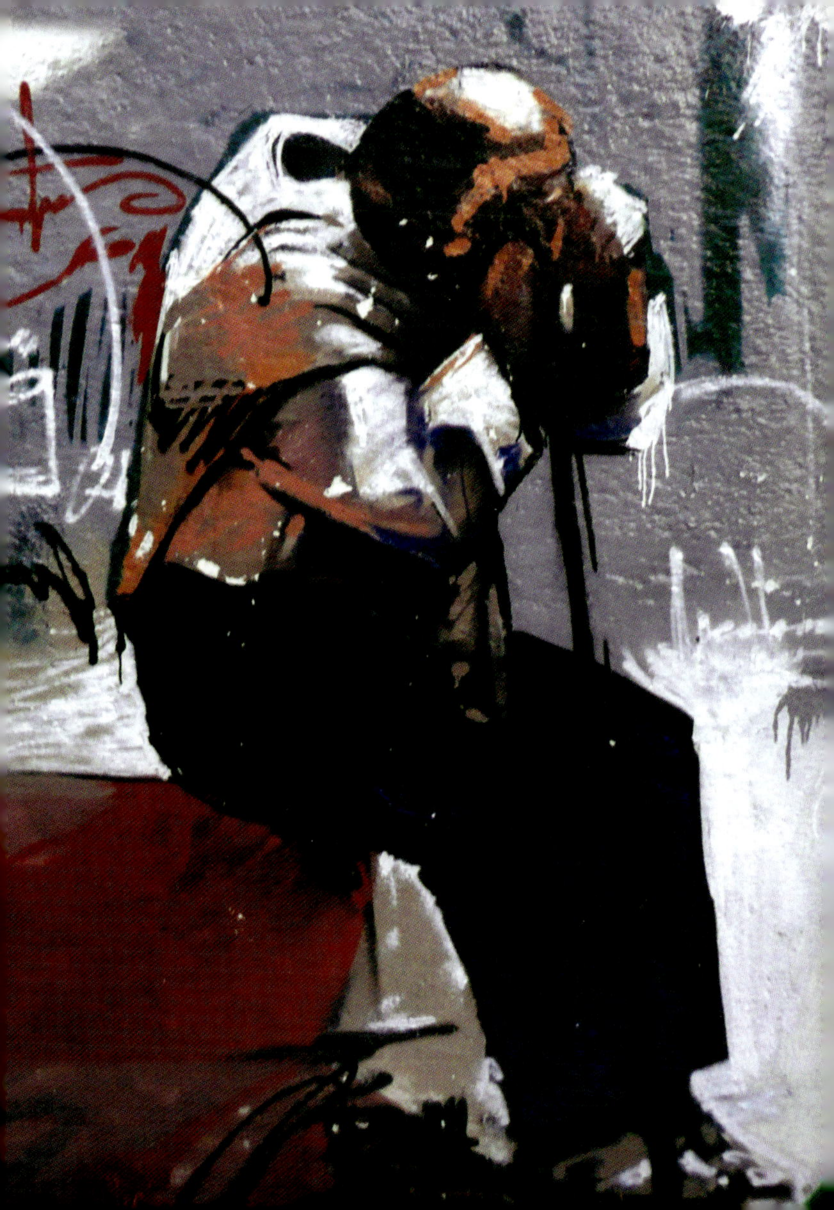

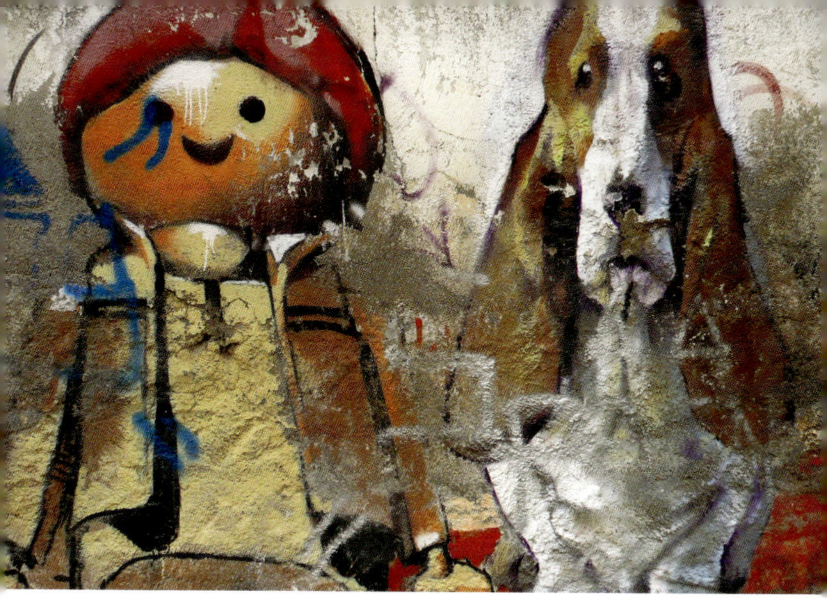

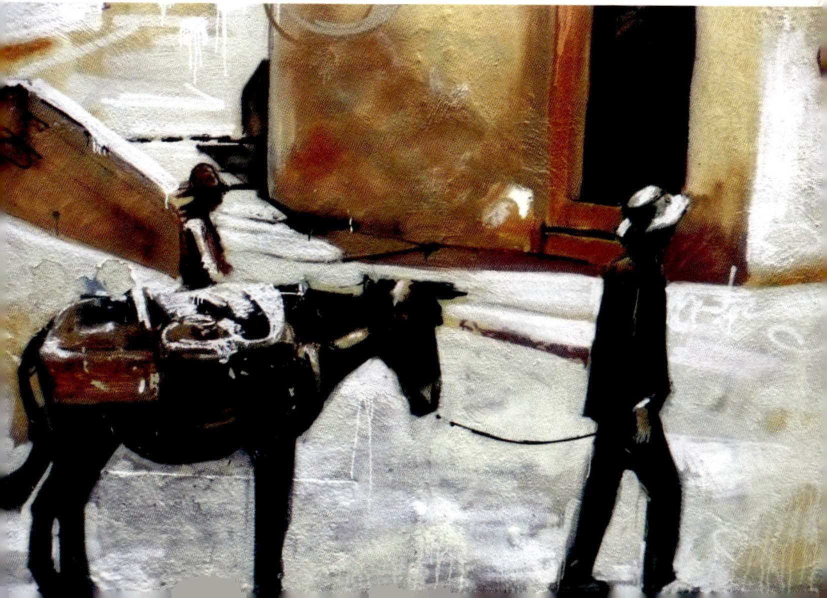

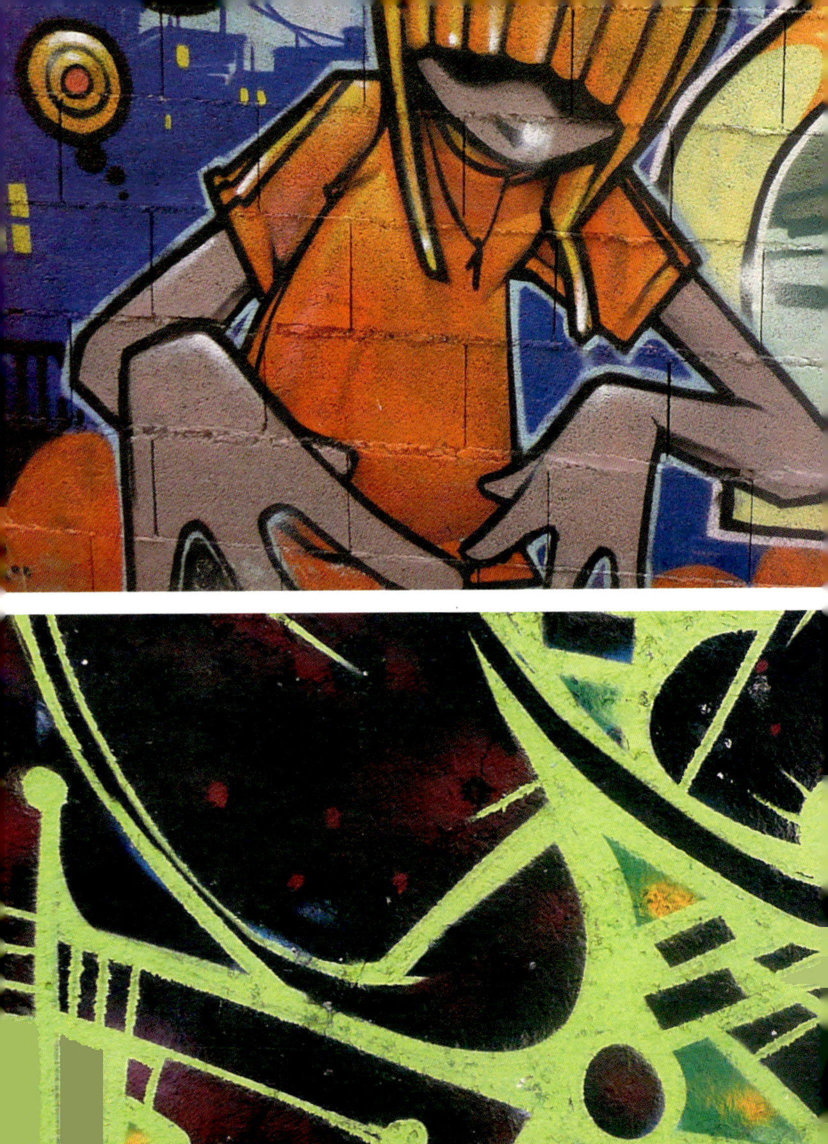

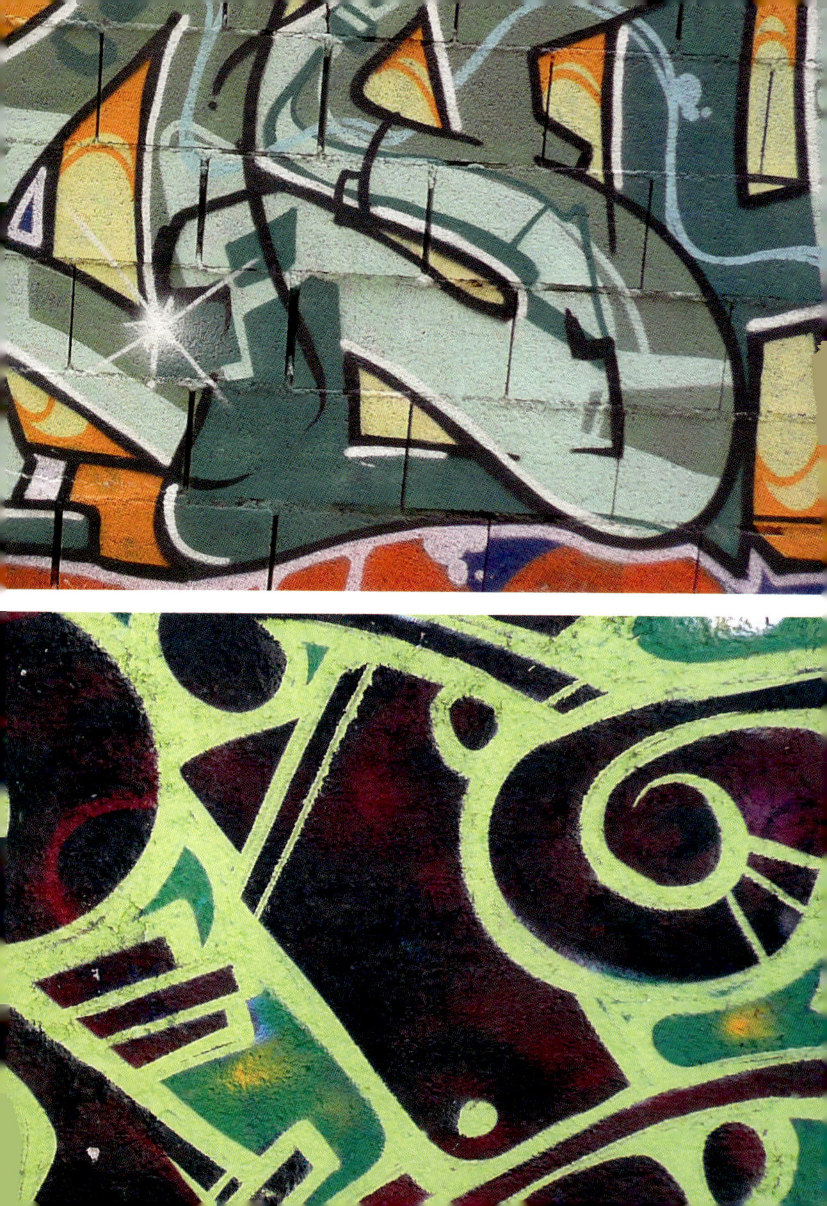

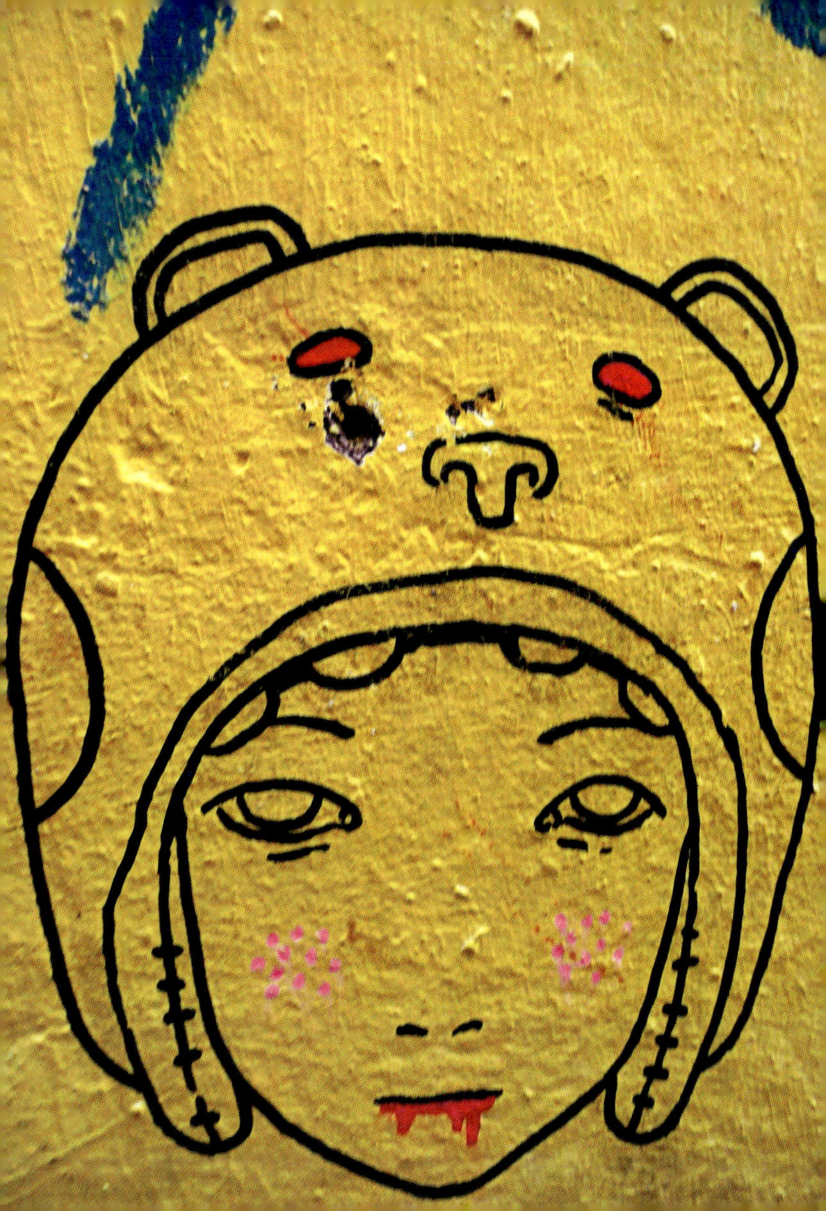

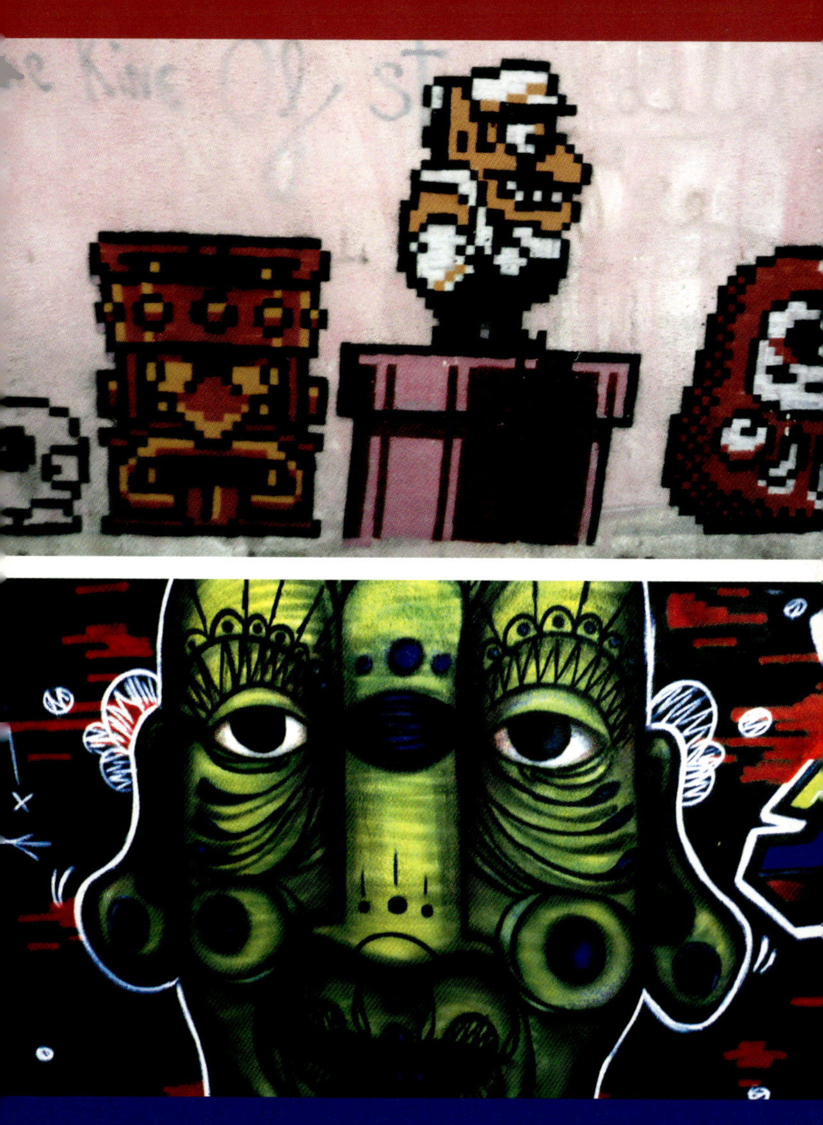

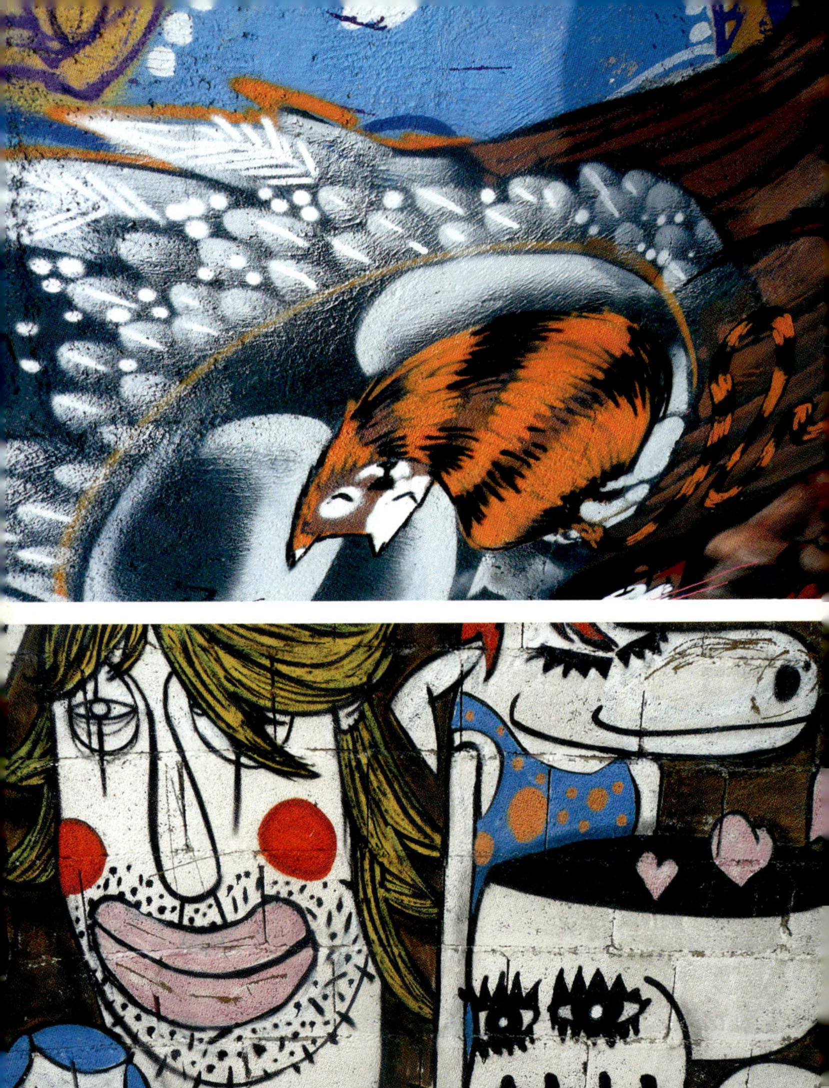

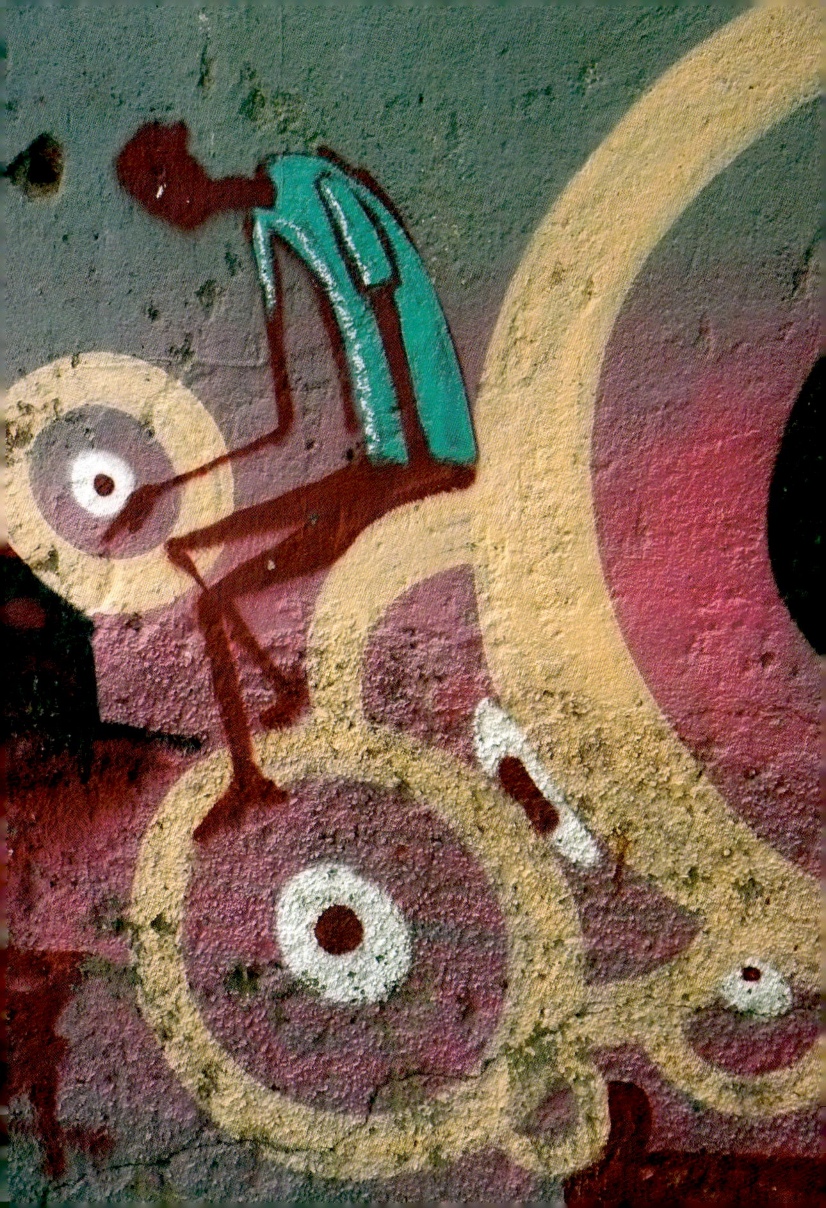

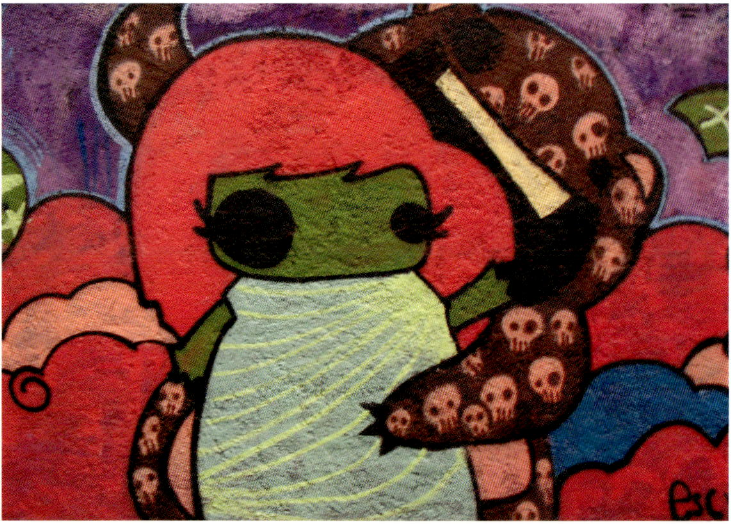

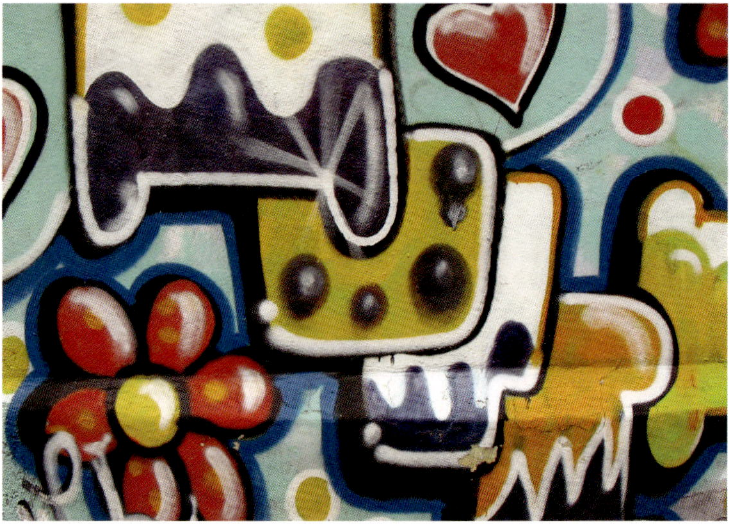

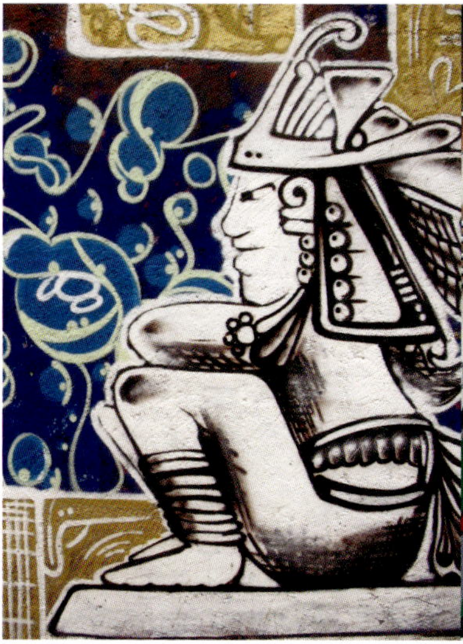

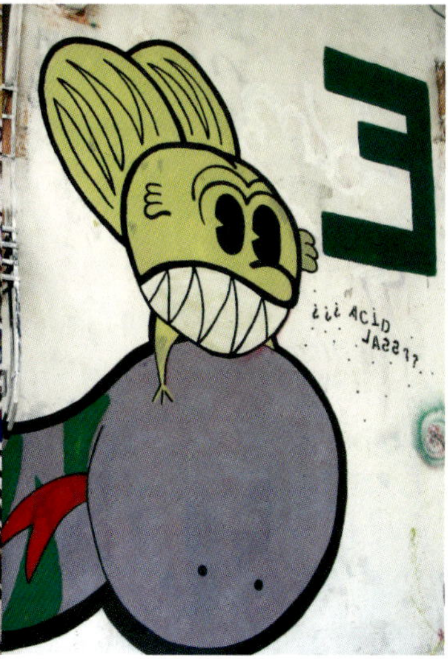

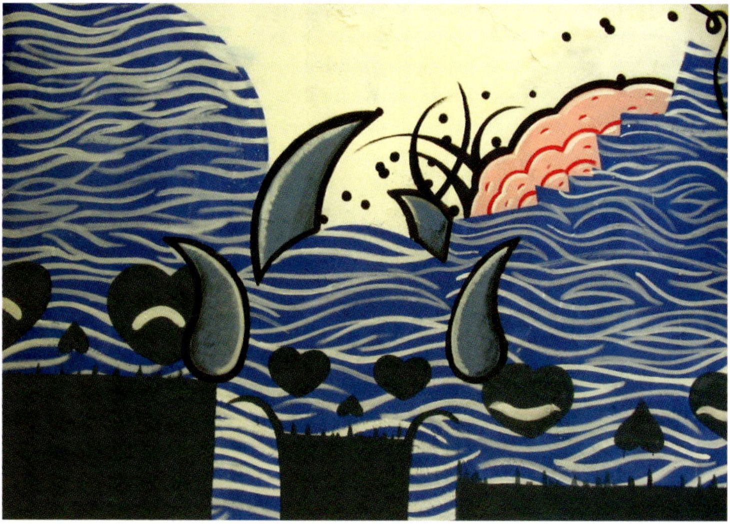

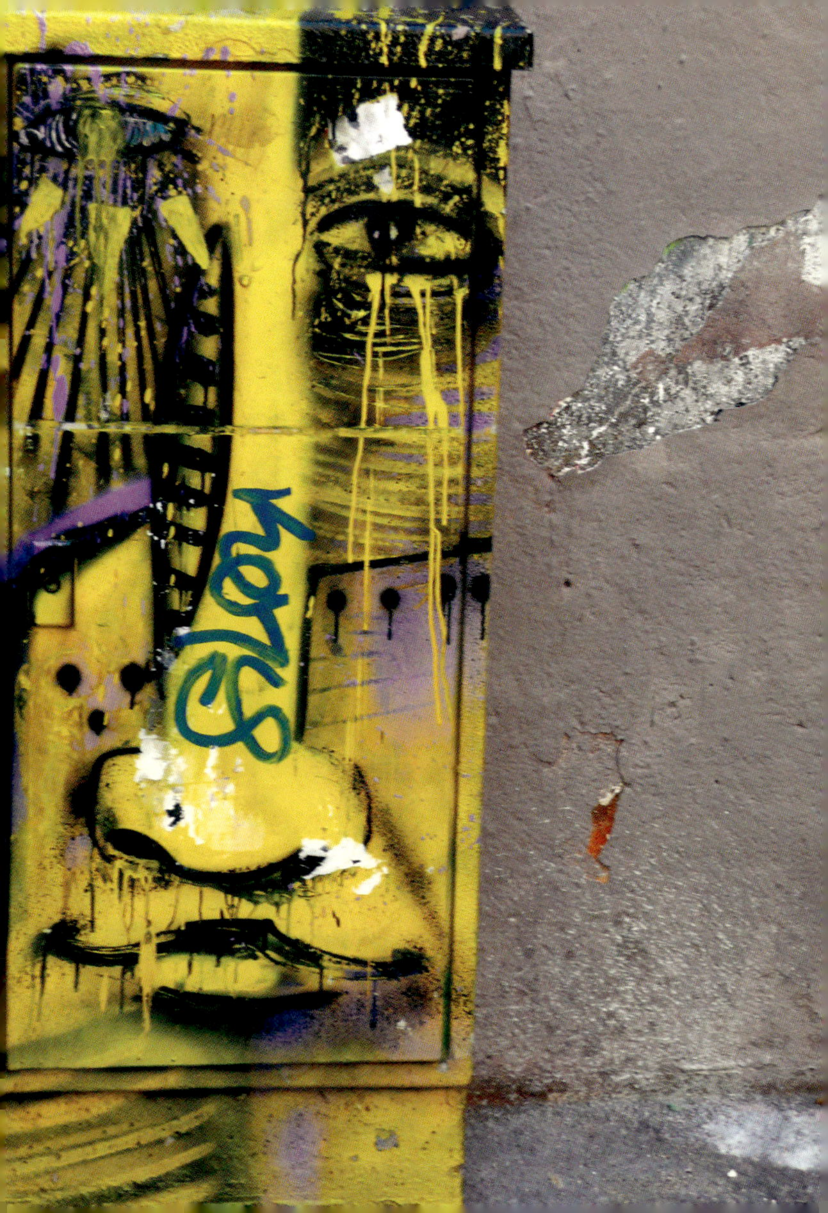

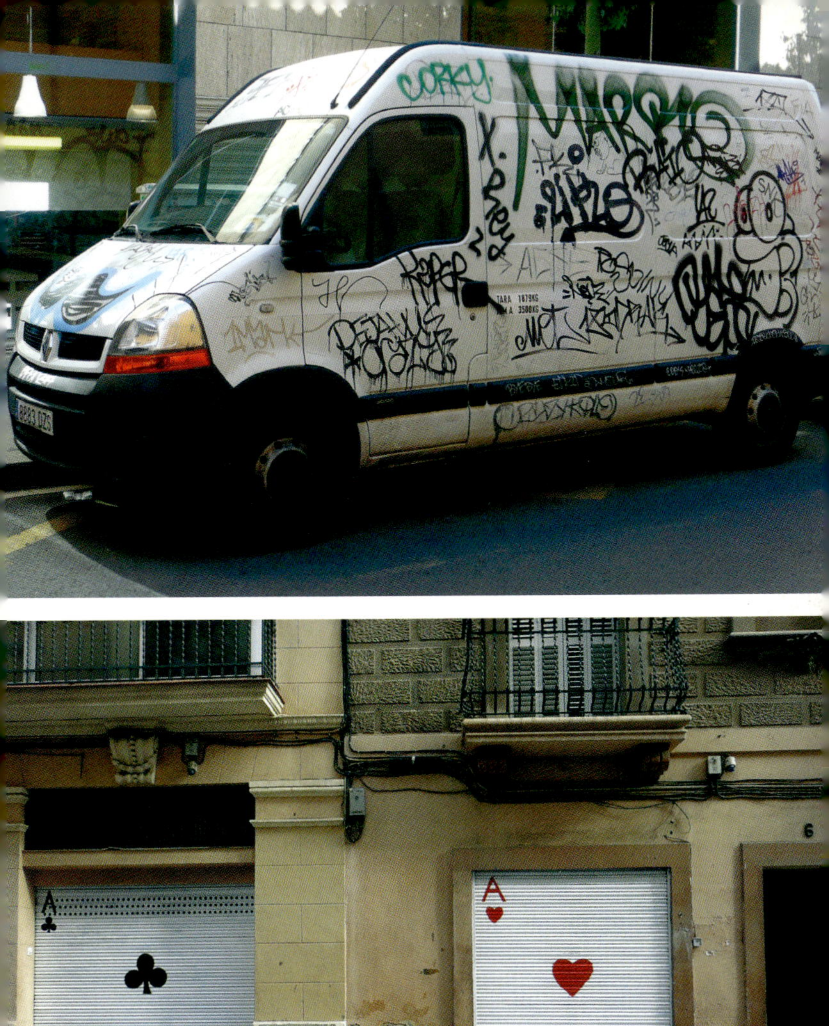
CORKY
TARA 1879KG

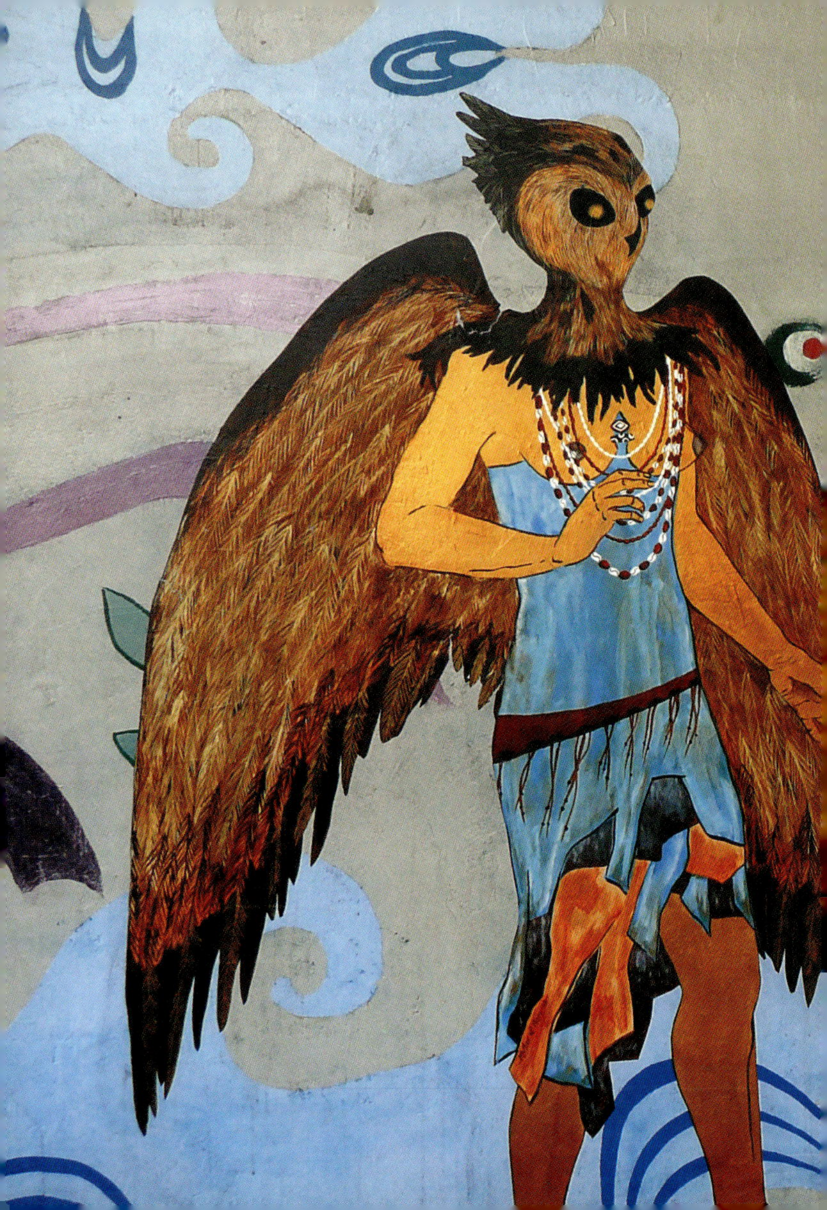

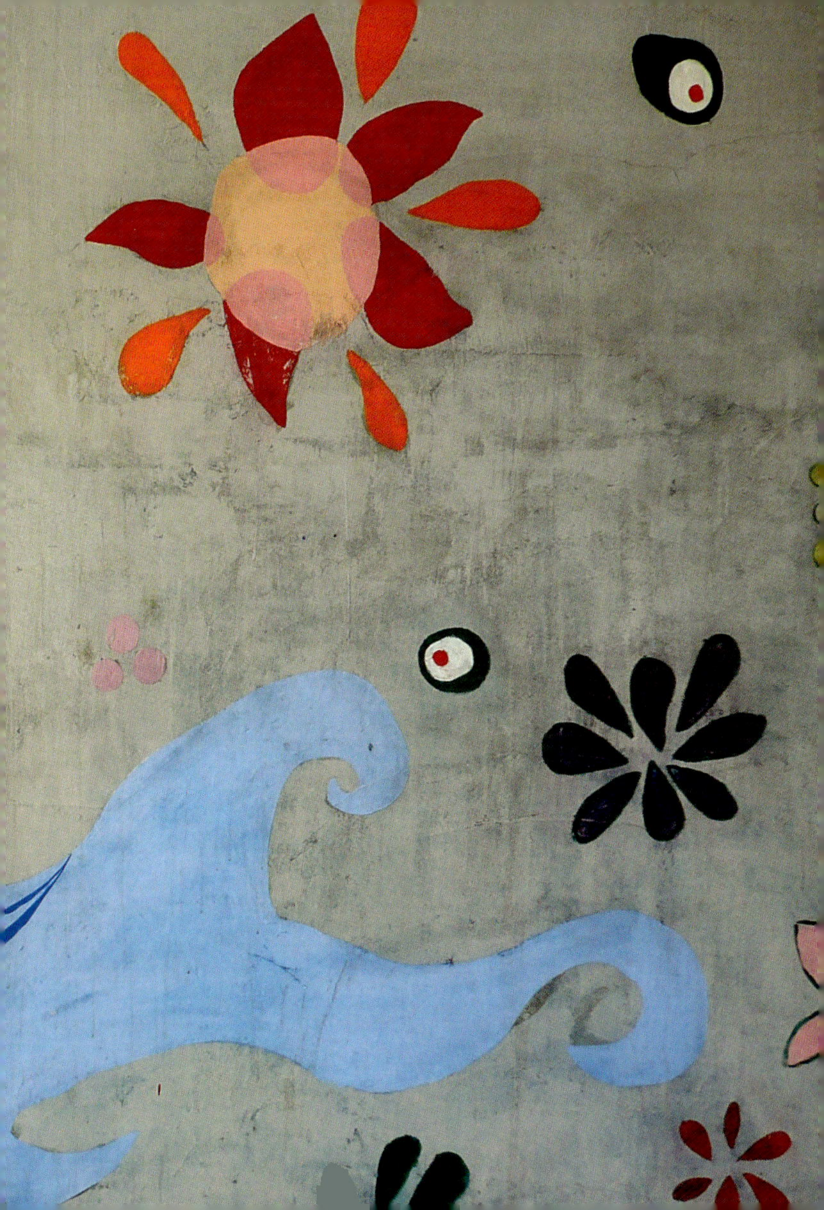

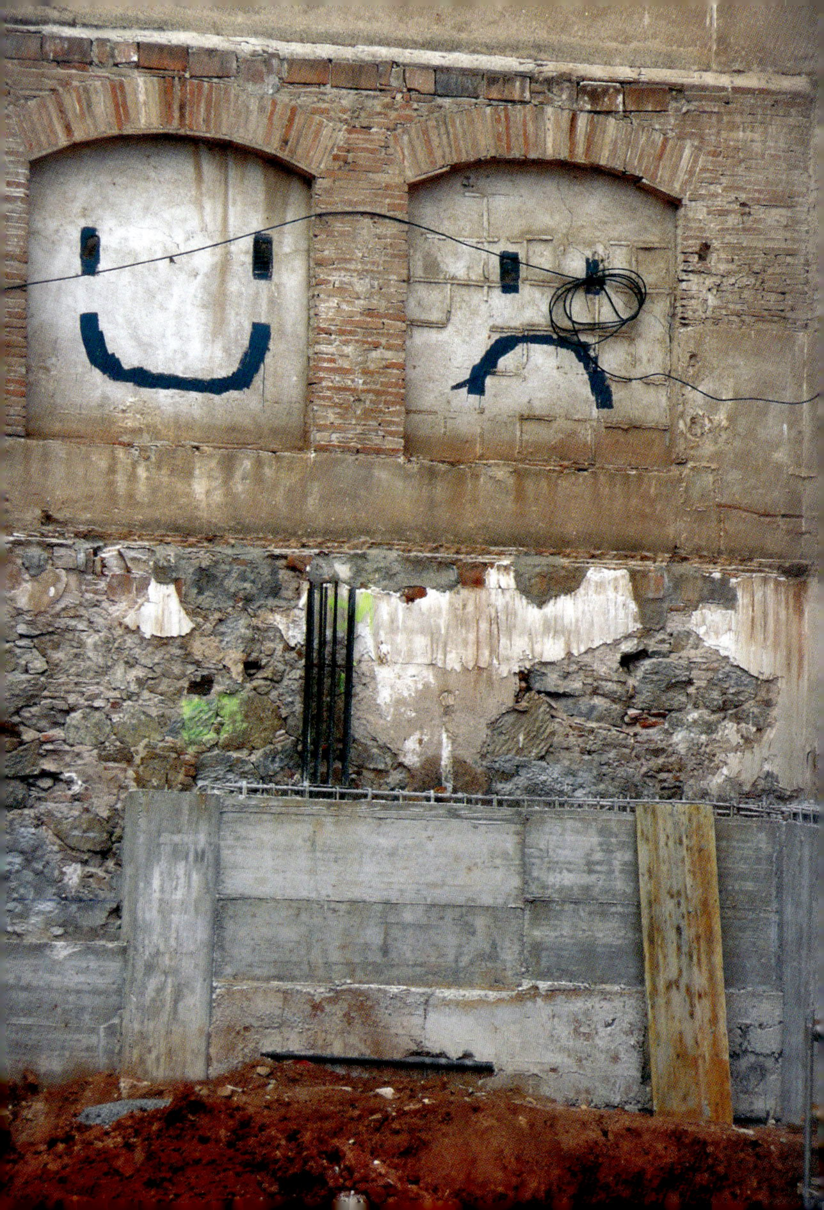

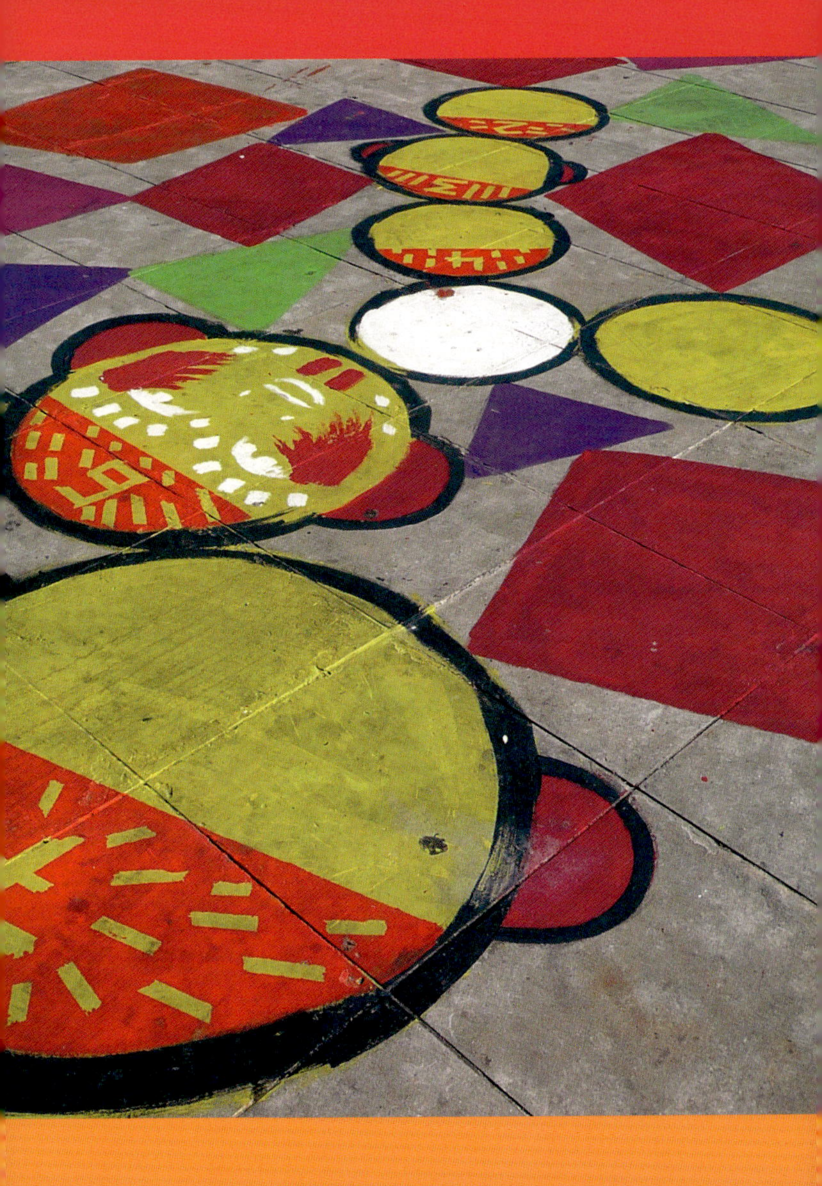

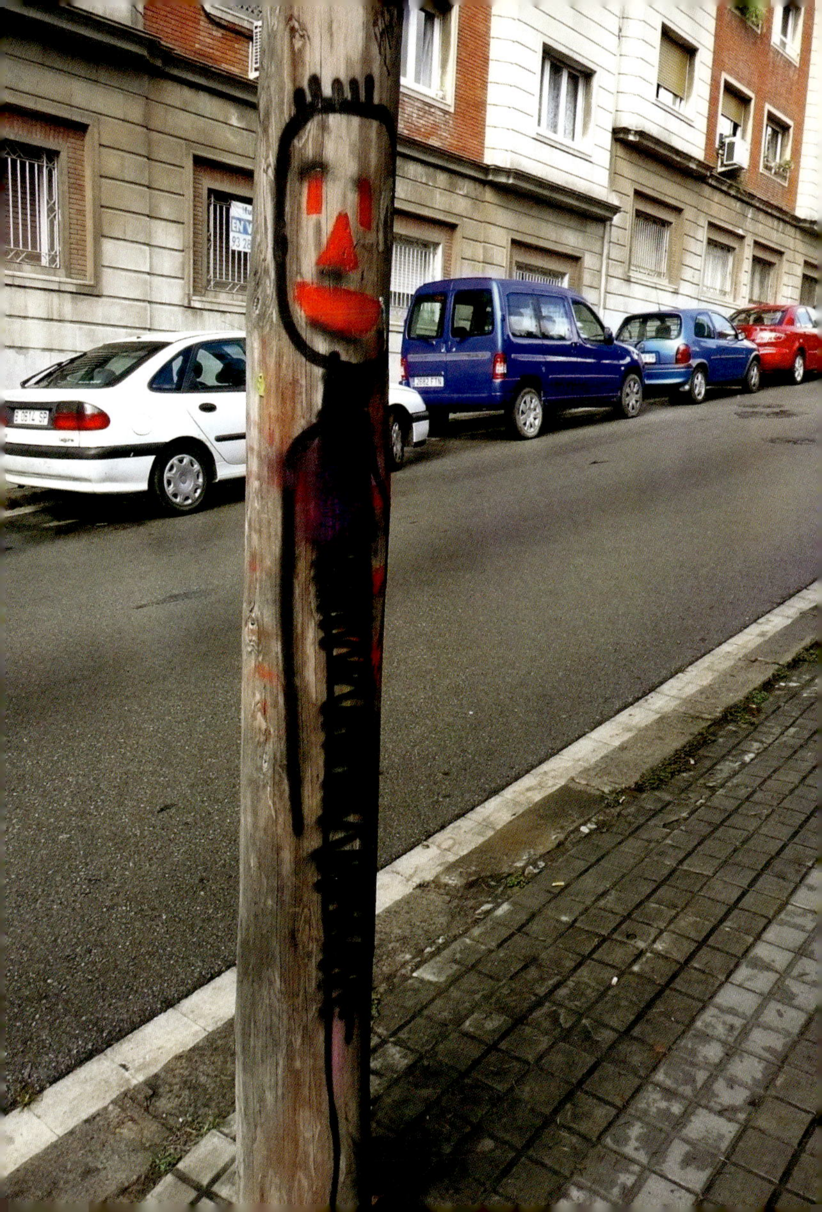

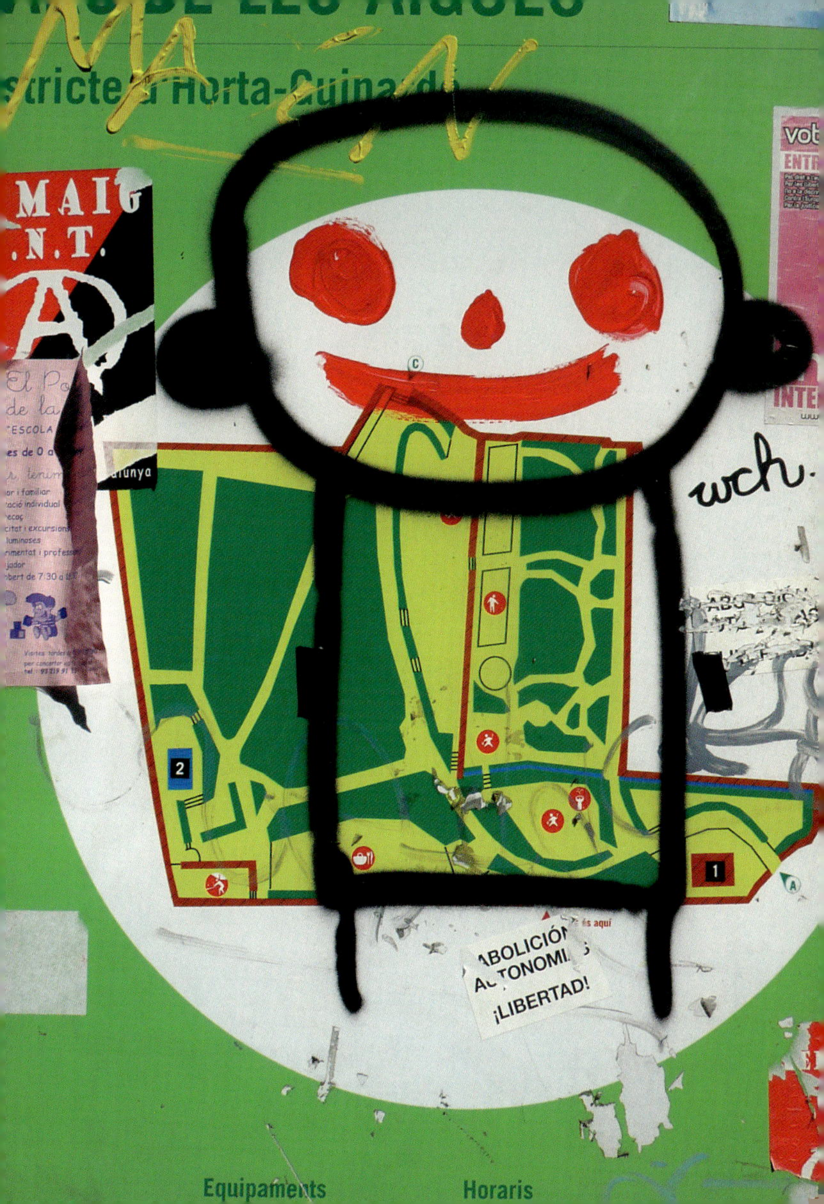
stricte d'Horta-Guinardó
MAIG
.N.T.
ABOLICIÓN
AUTONOMIAS
¡LIBERTAD!
wch.
Equipaments
Horaris

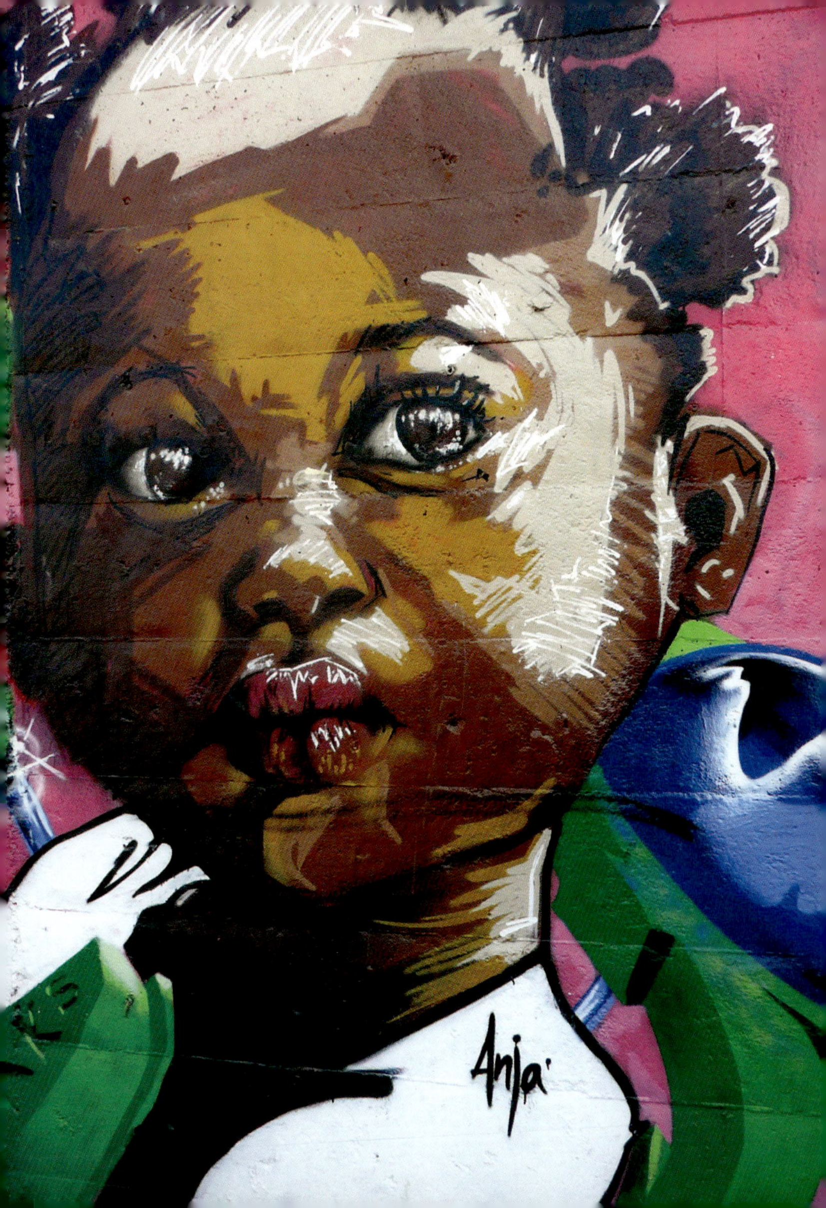
Anja

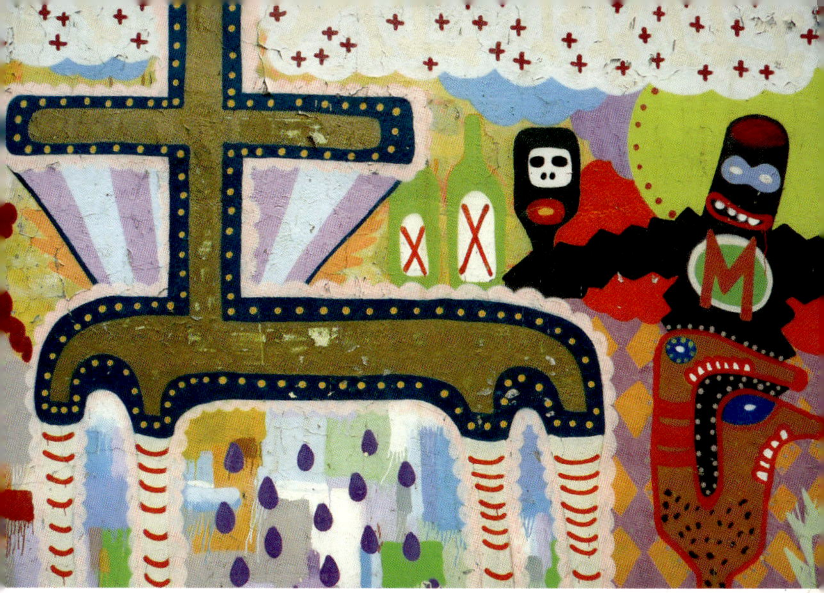

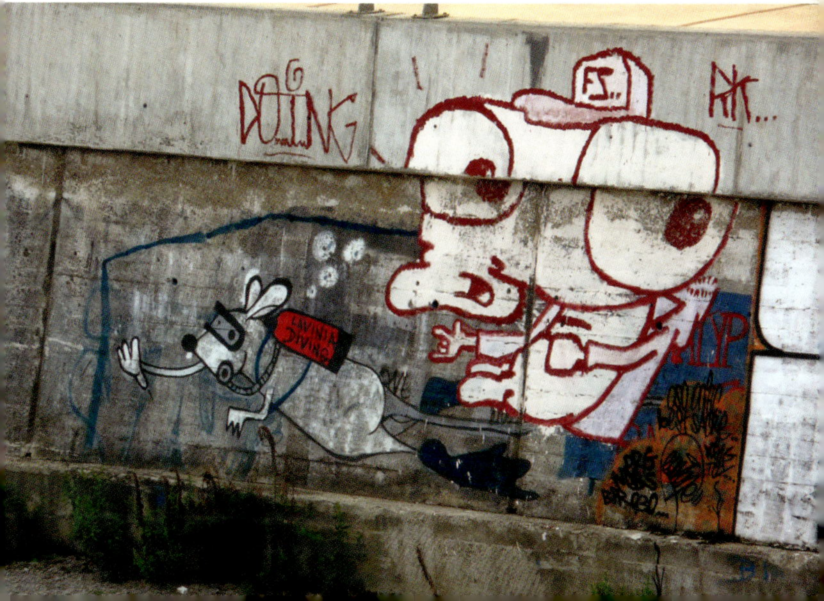

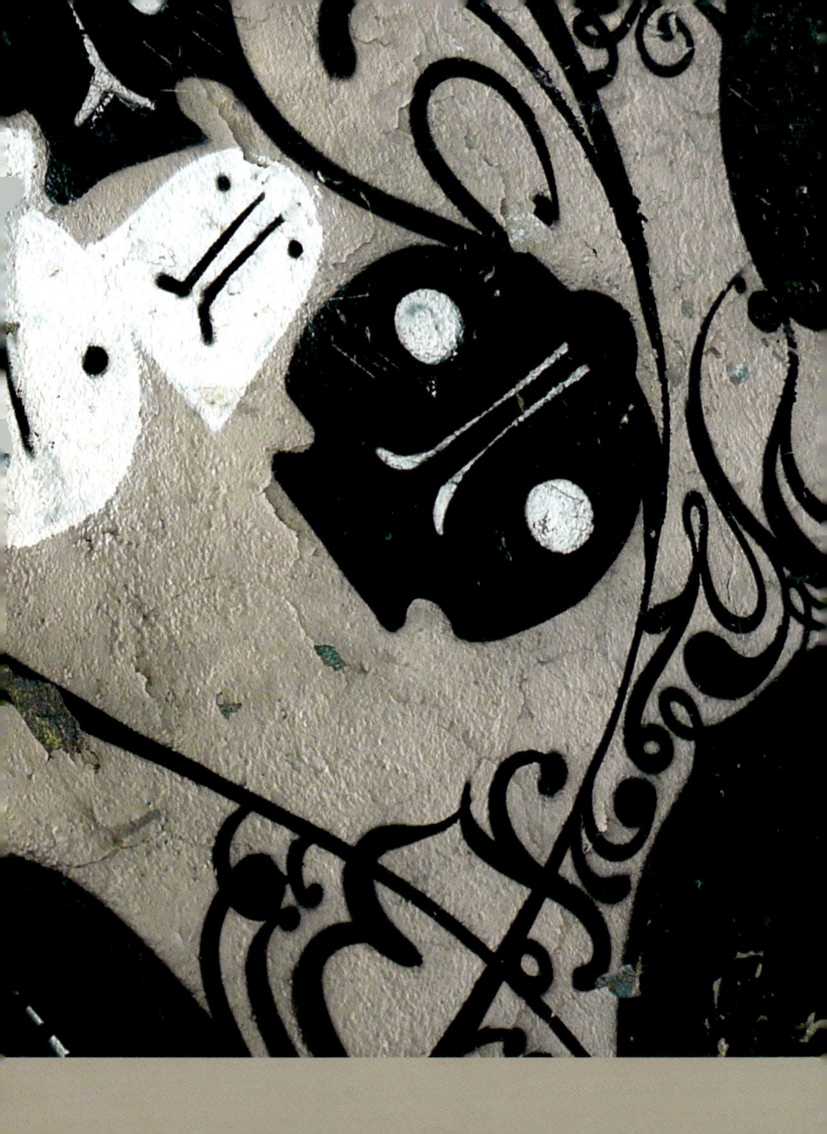

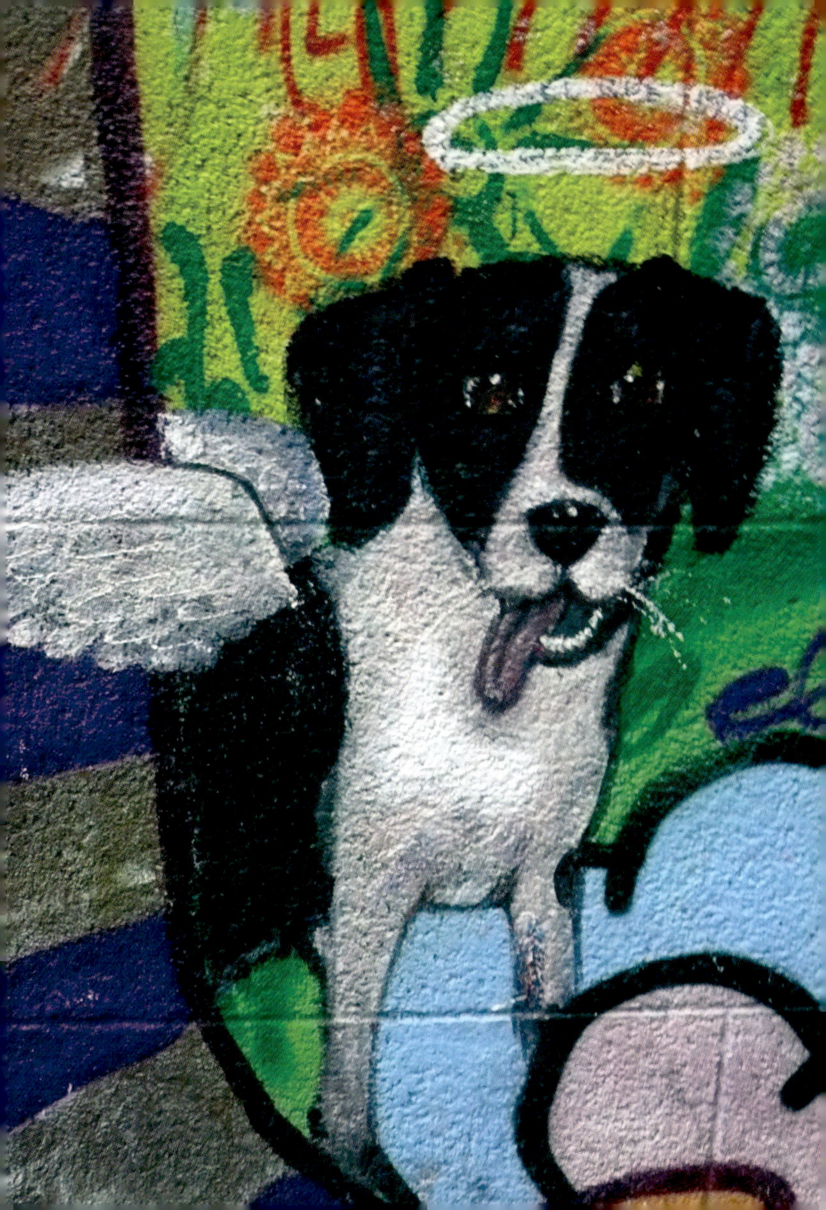

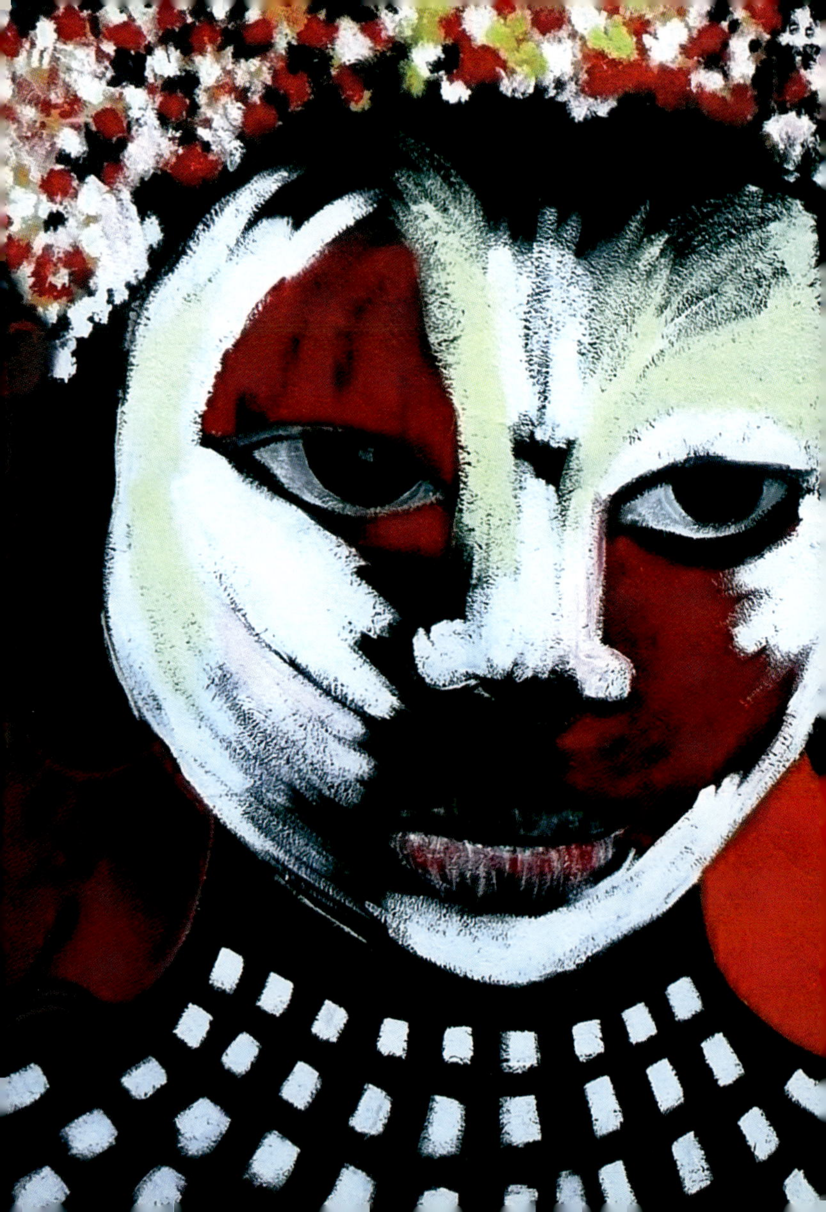

BE
AUTY
FREE

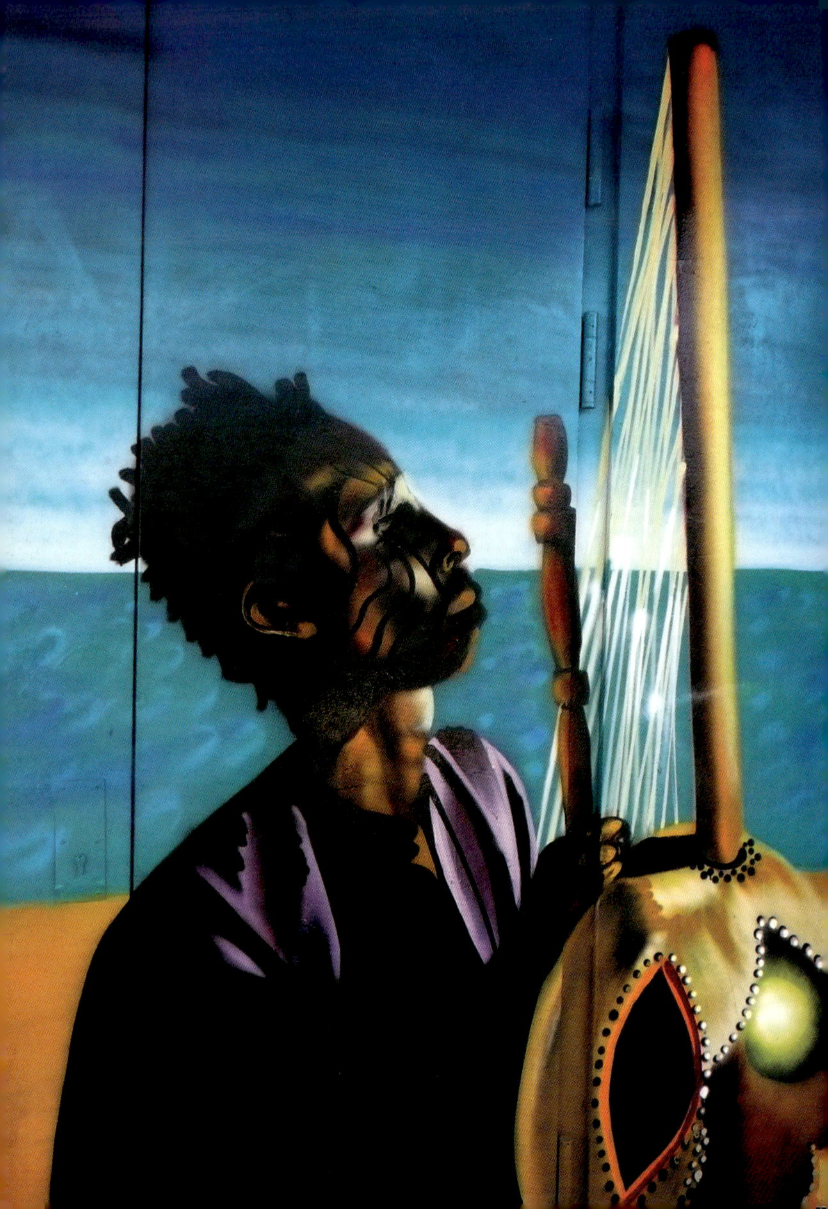

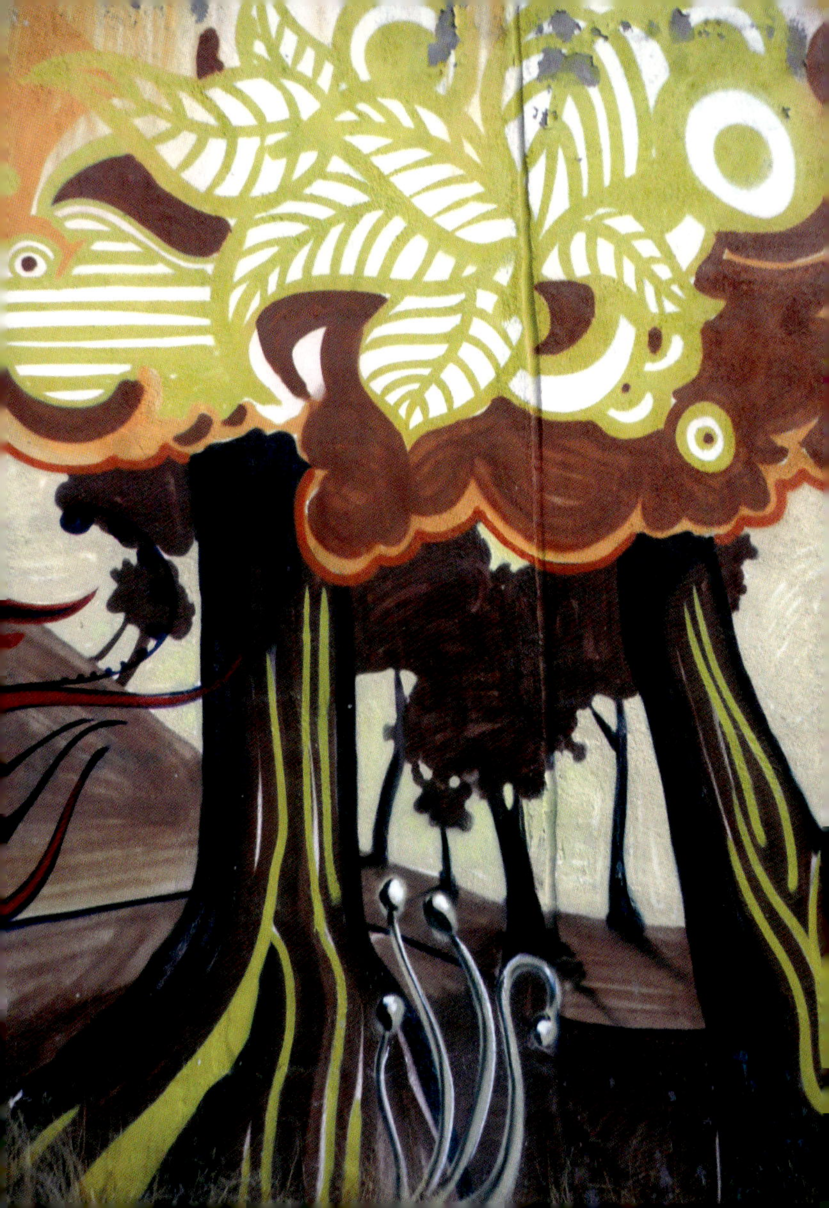

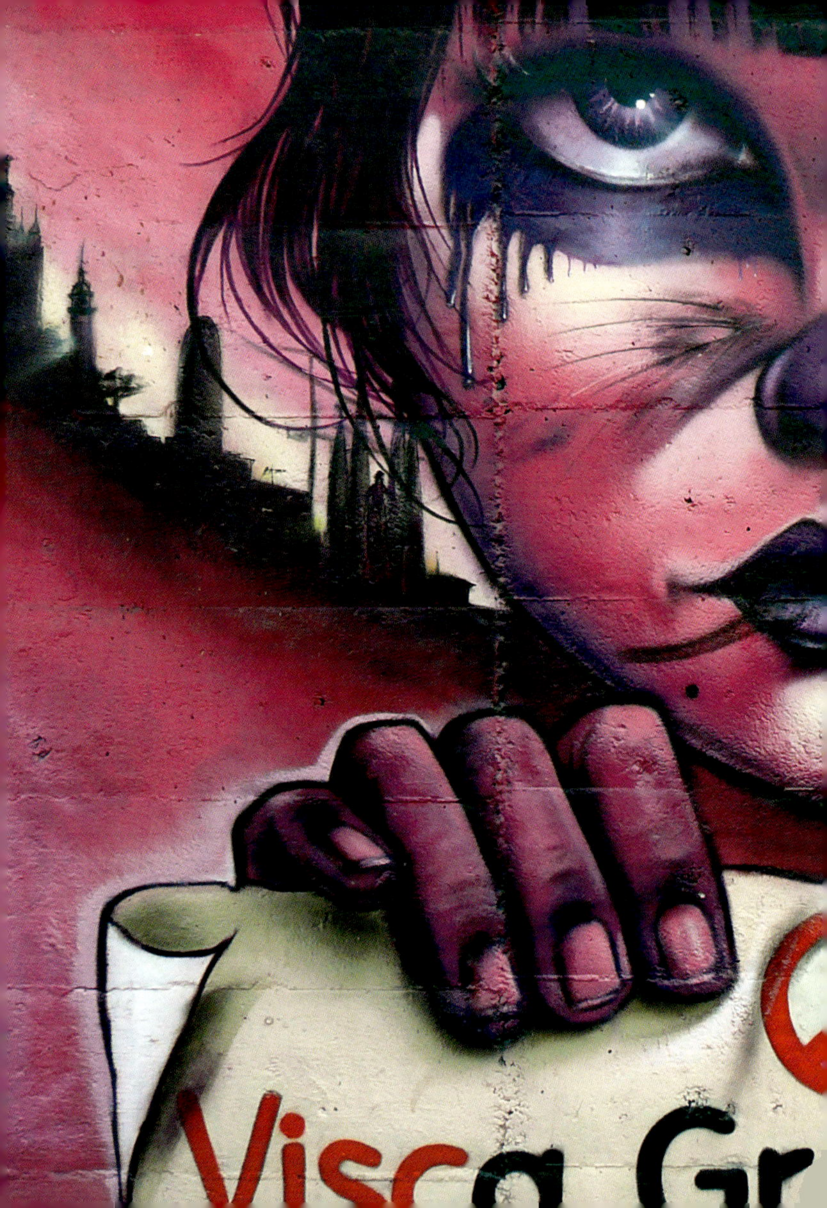
Visca Gr

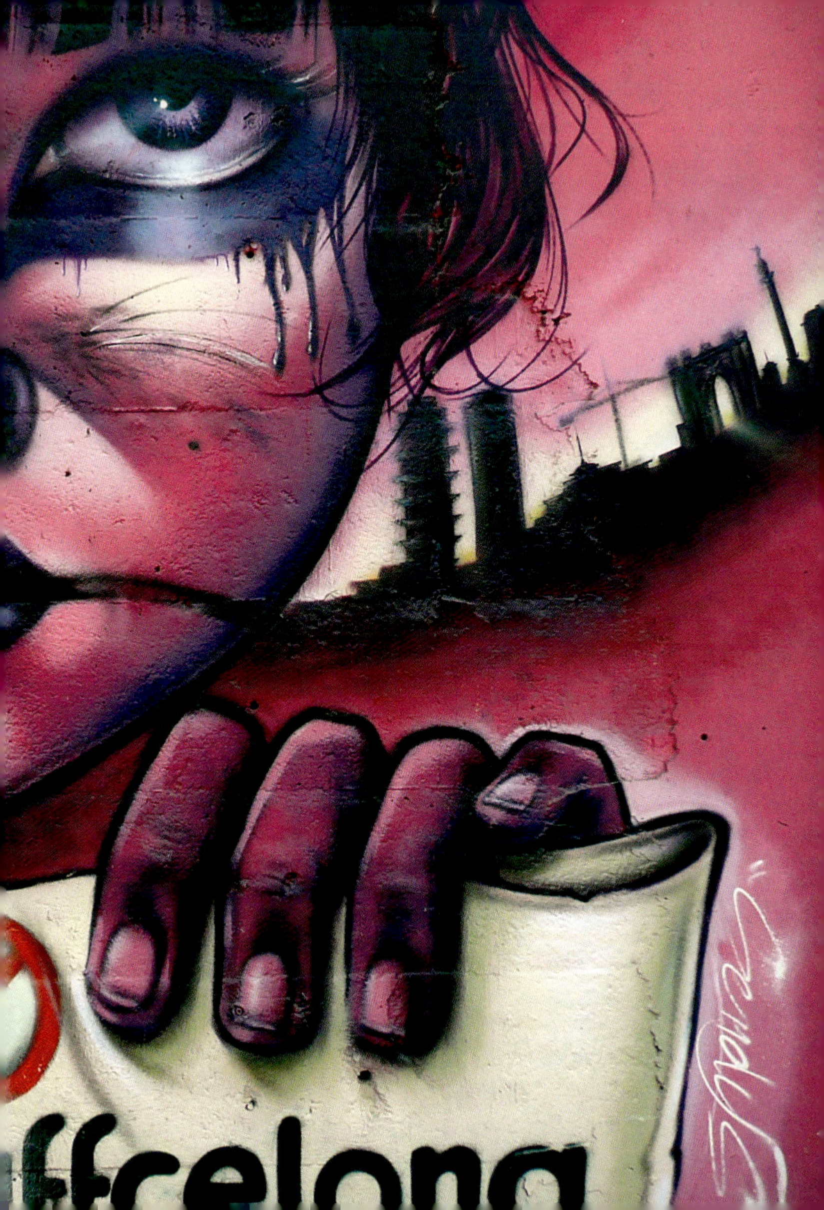

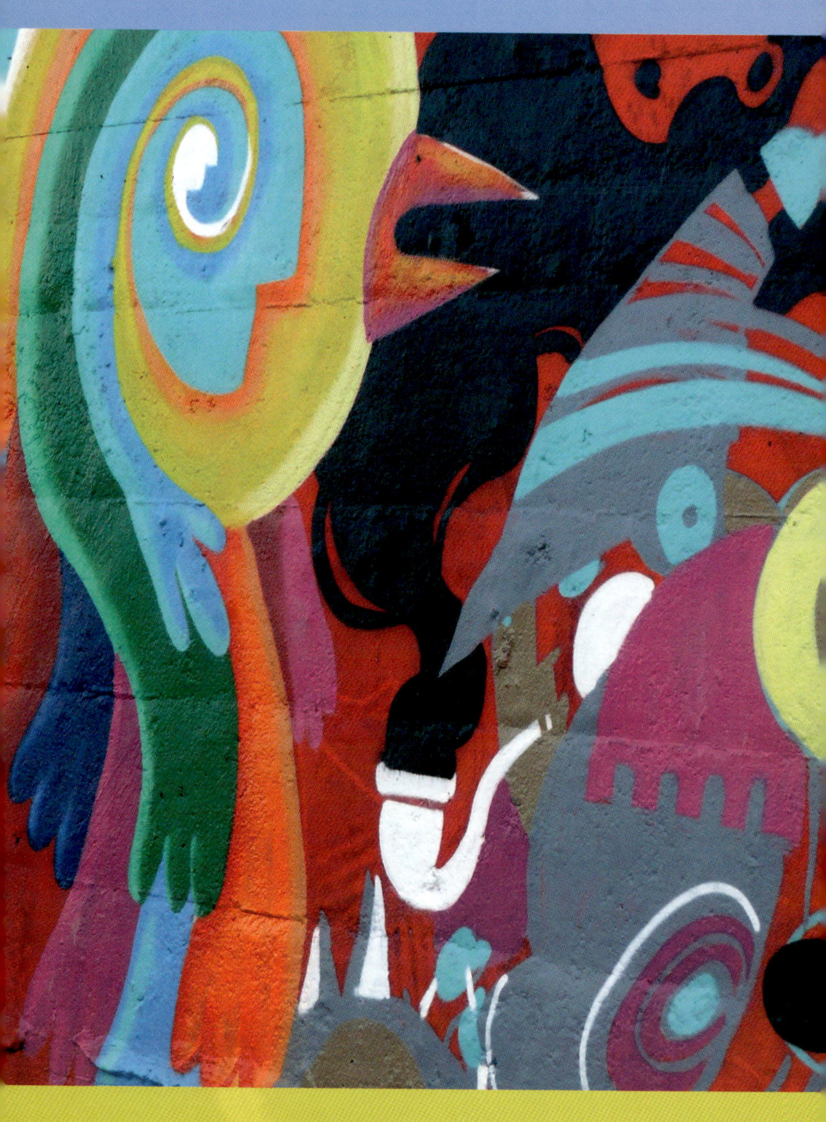

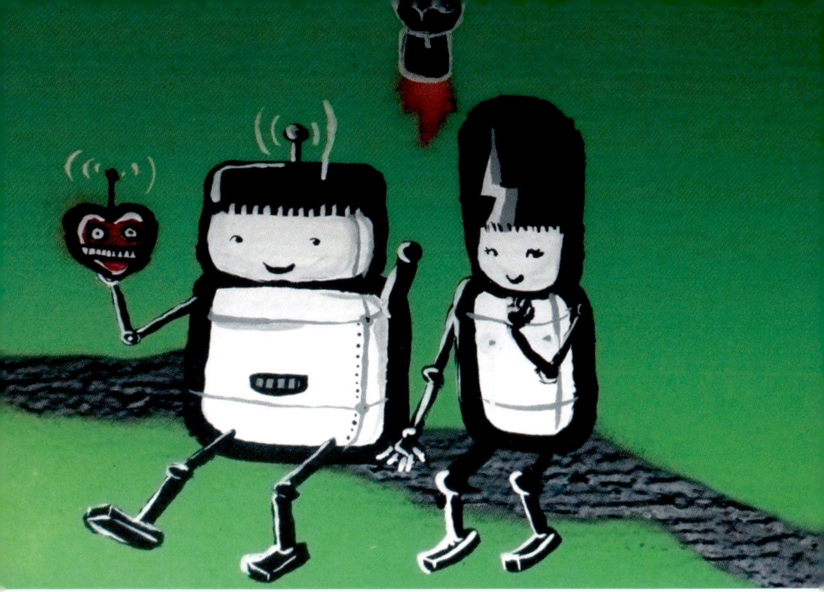

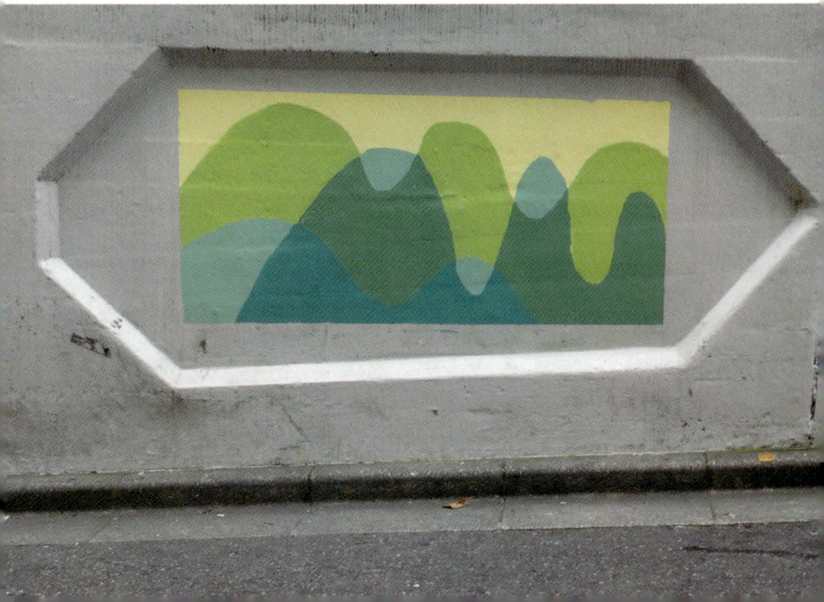

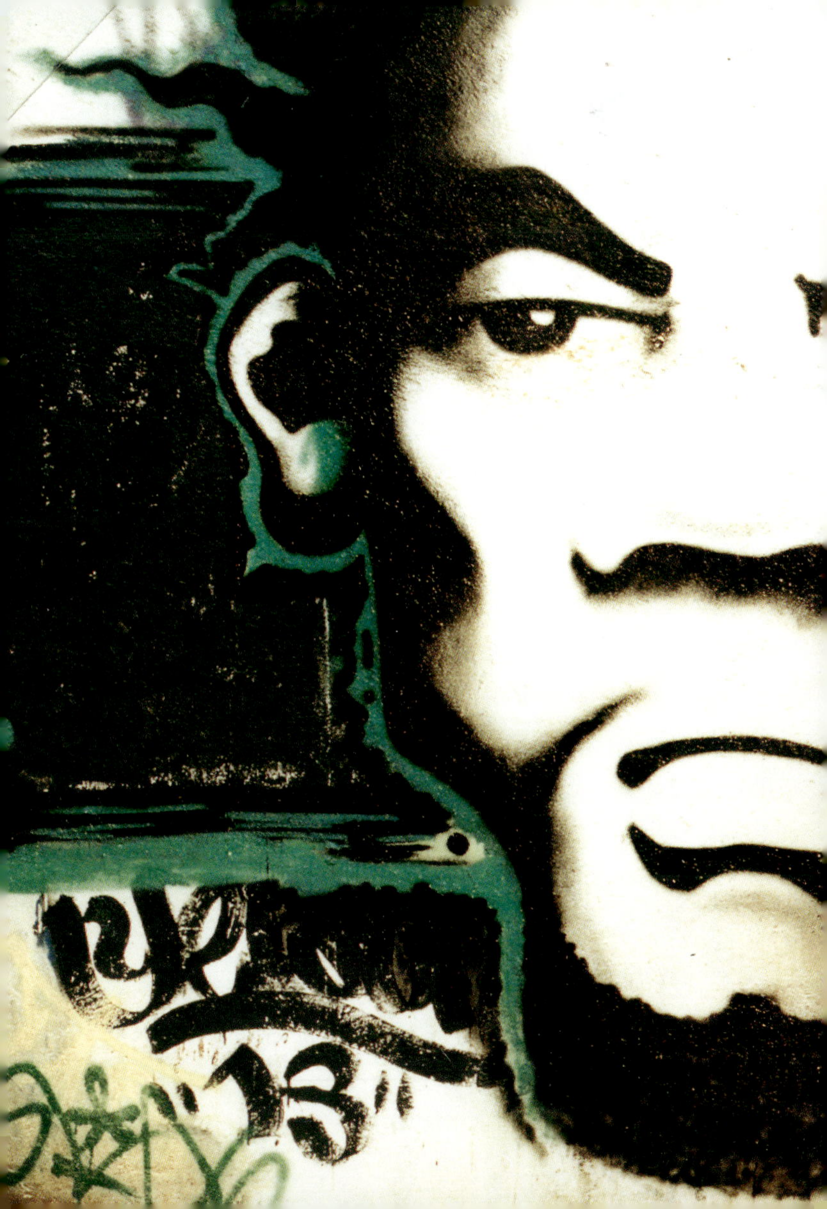

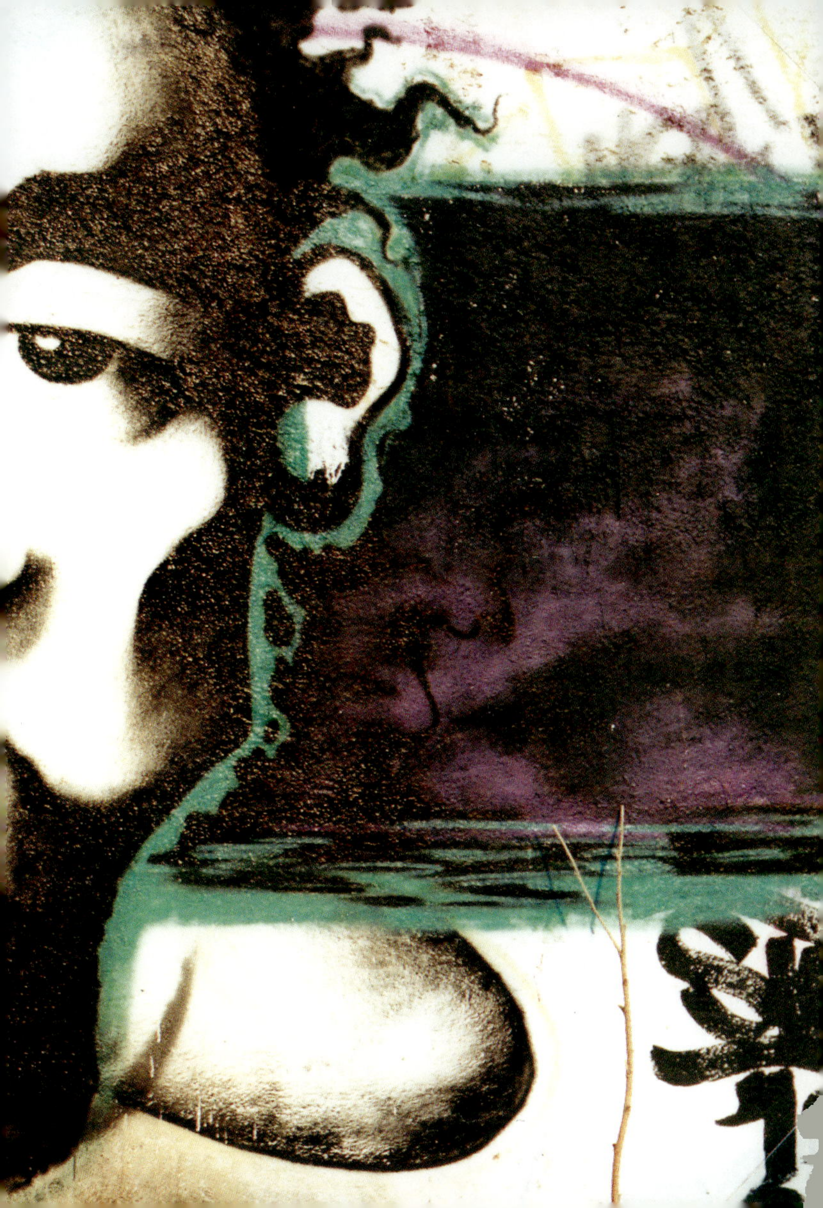

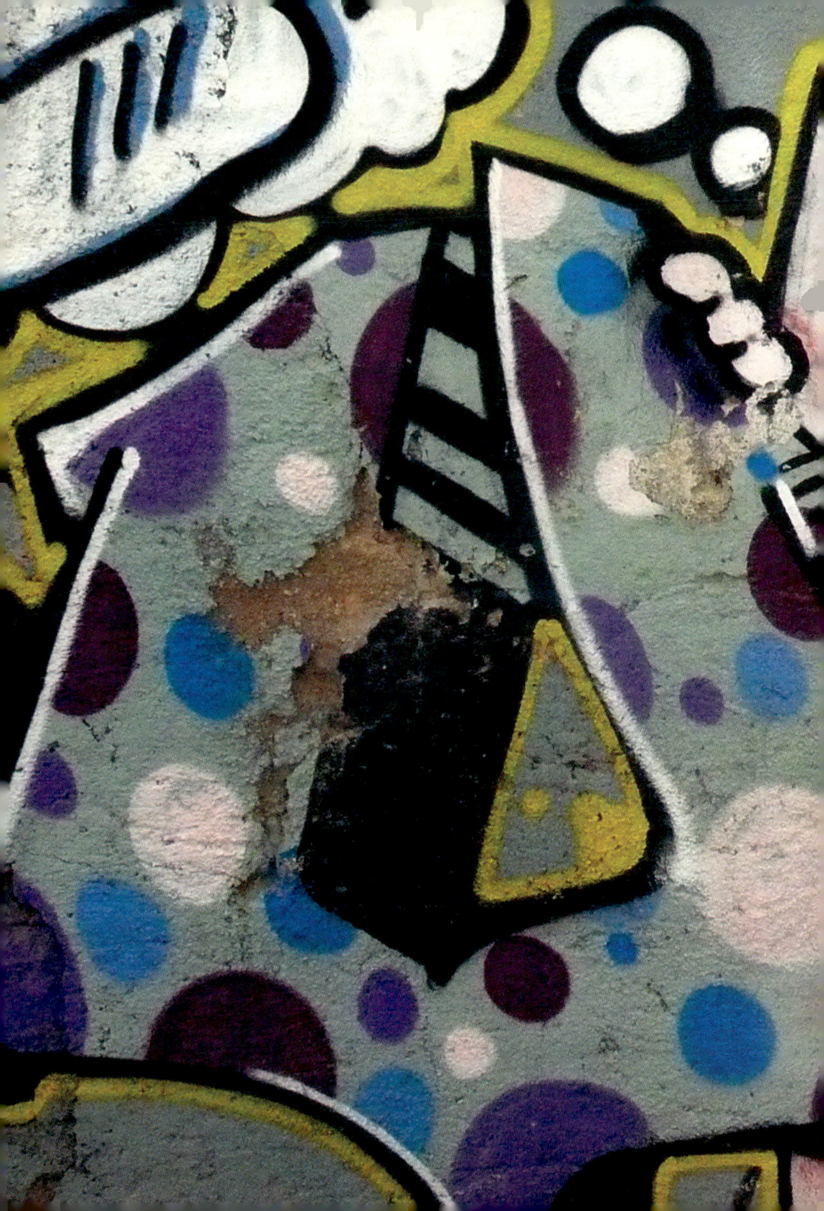

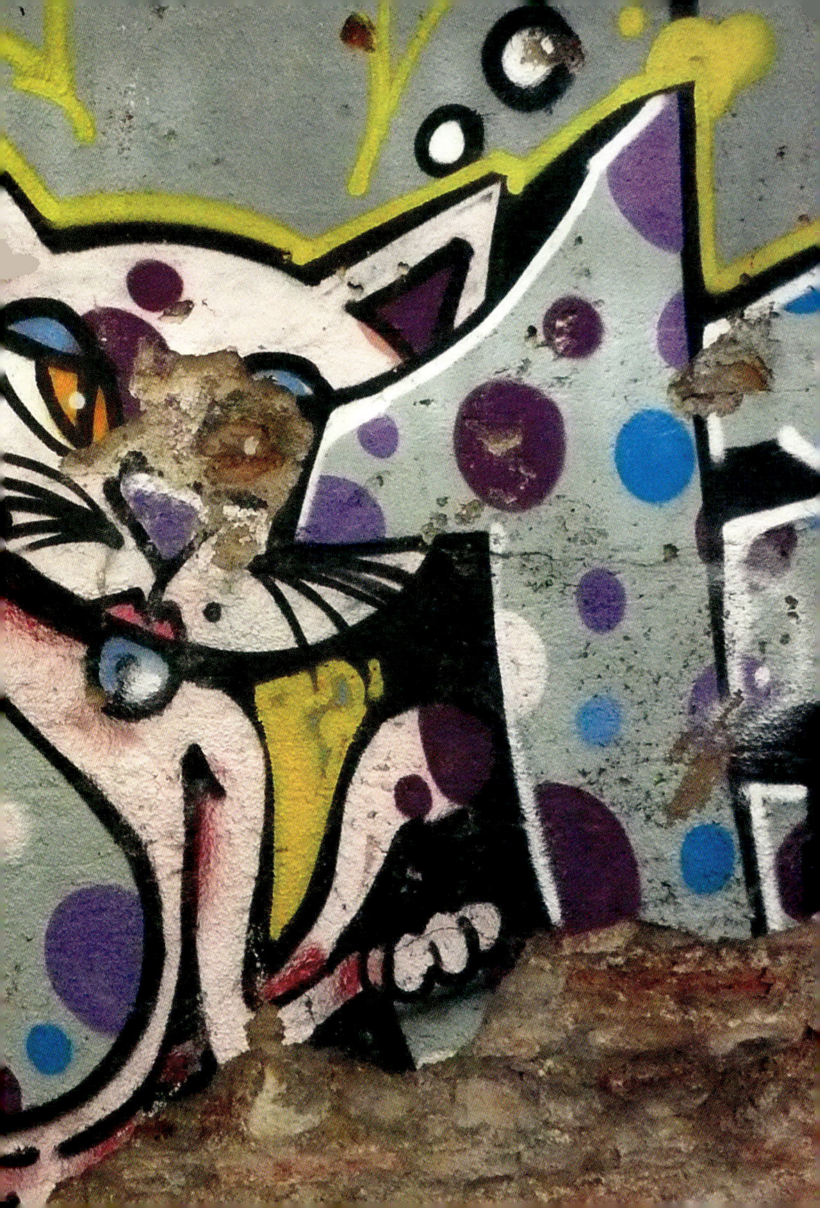

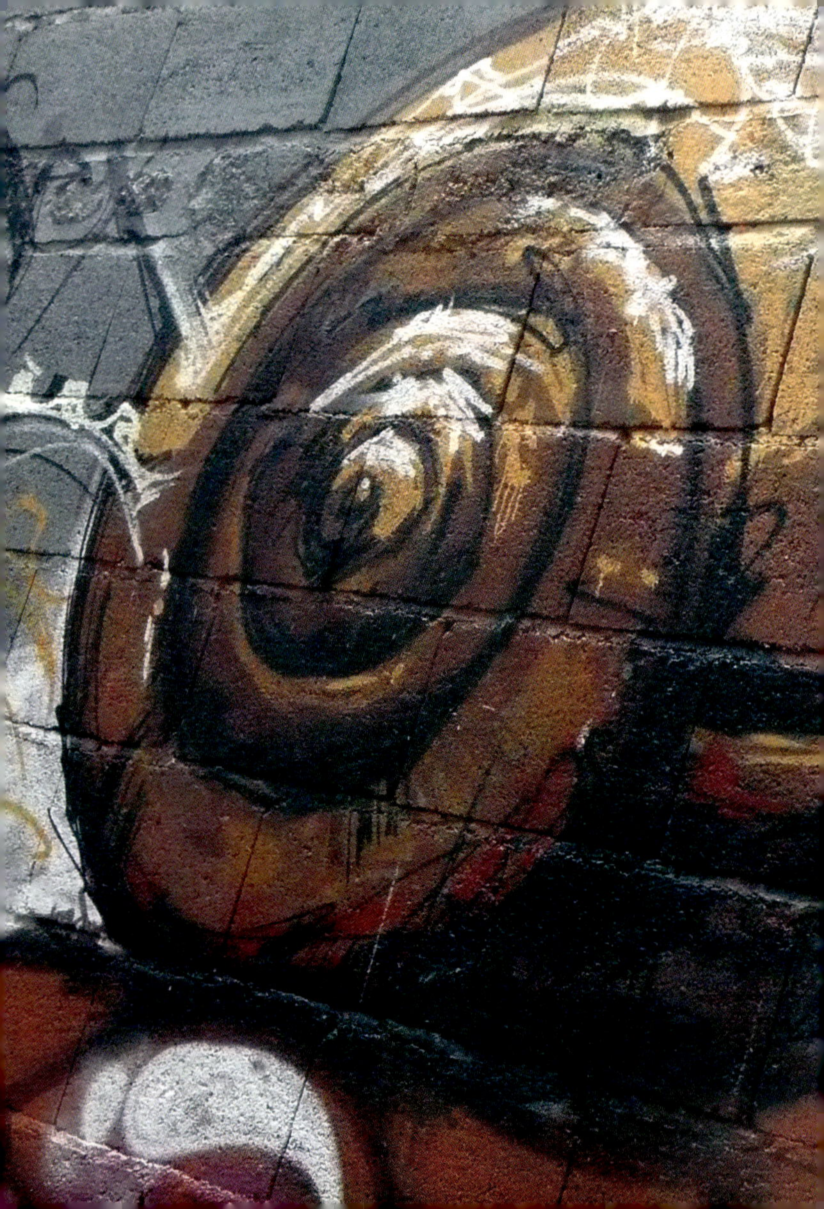

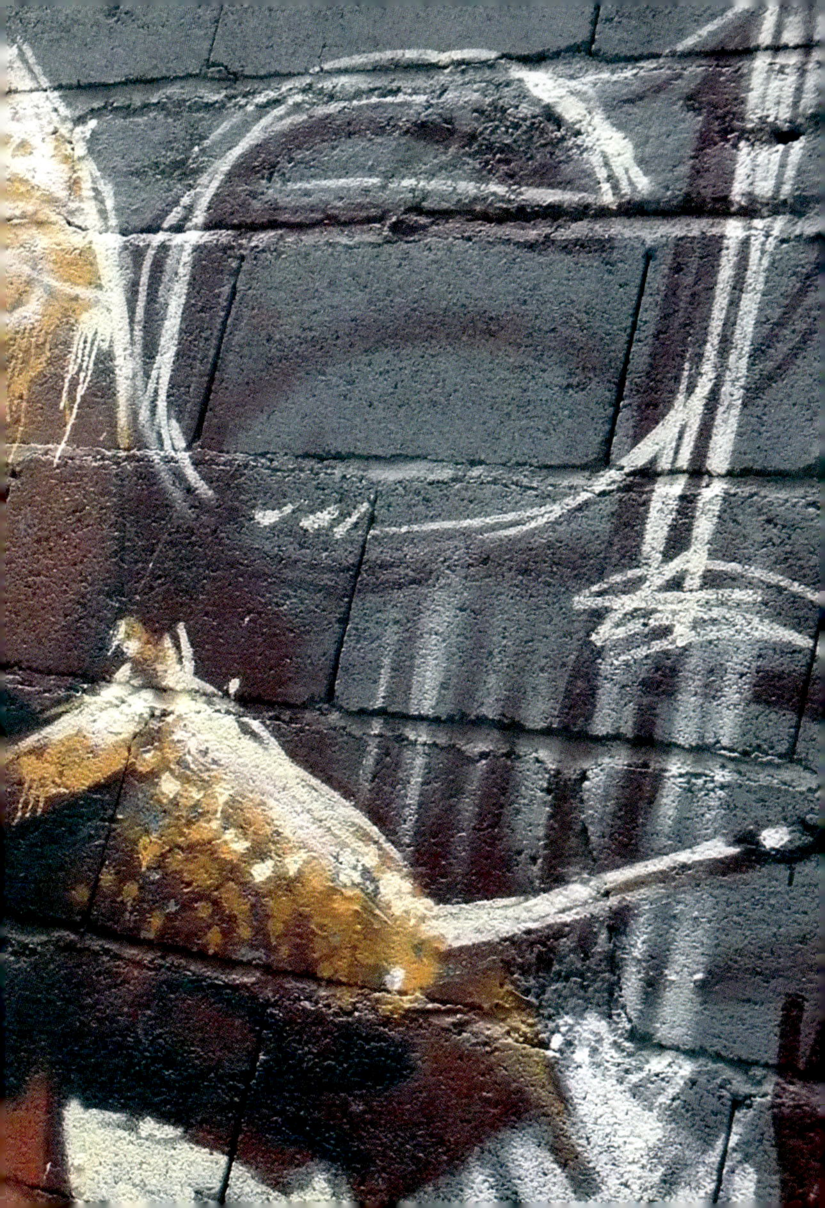

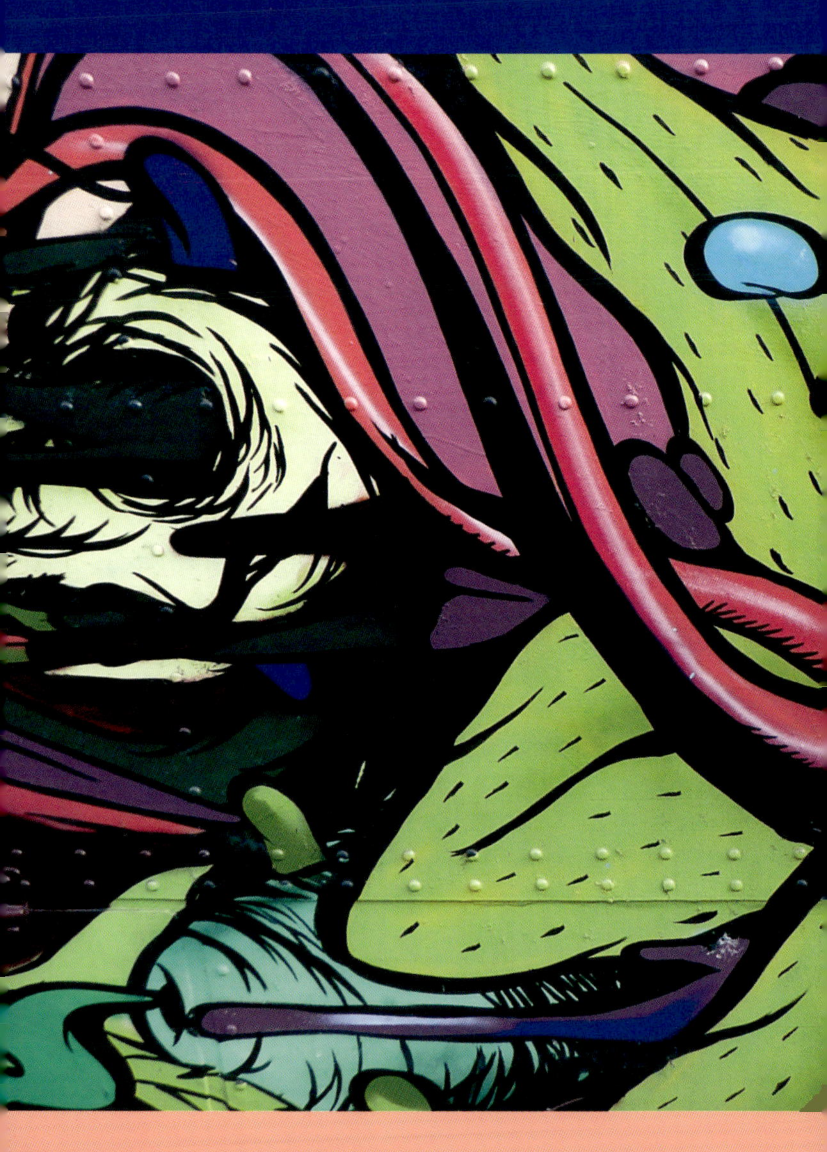

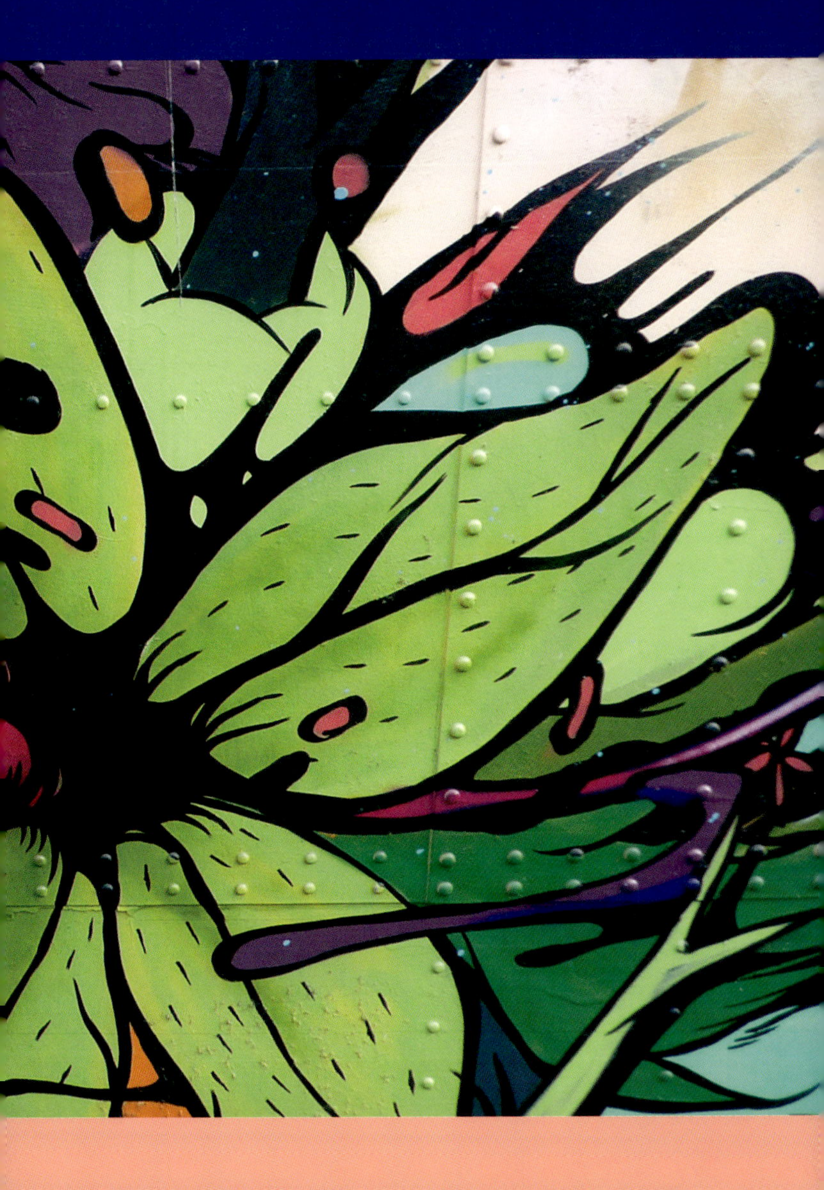

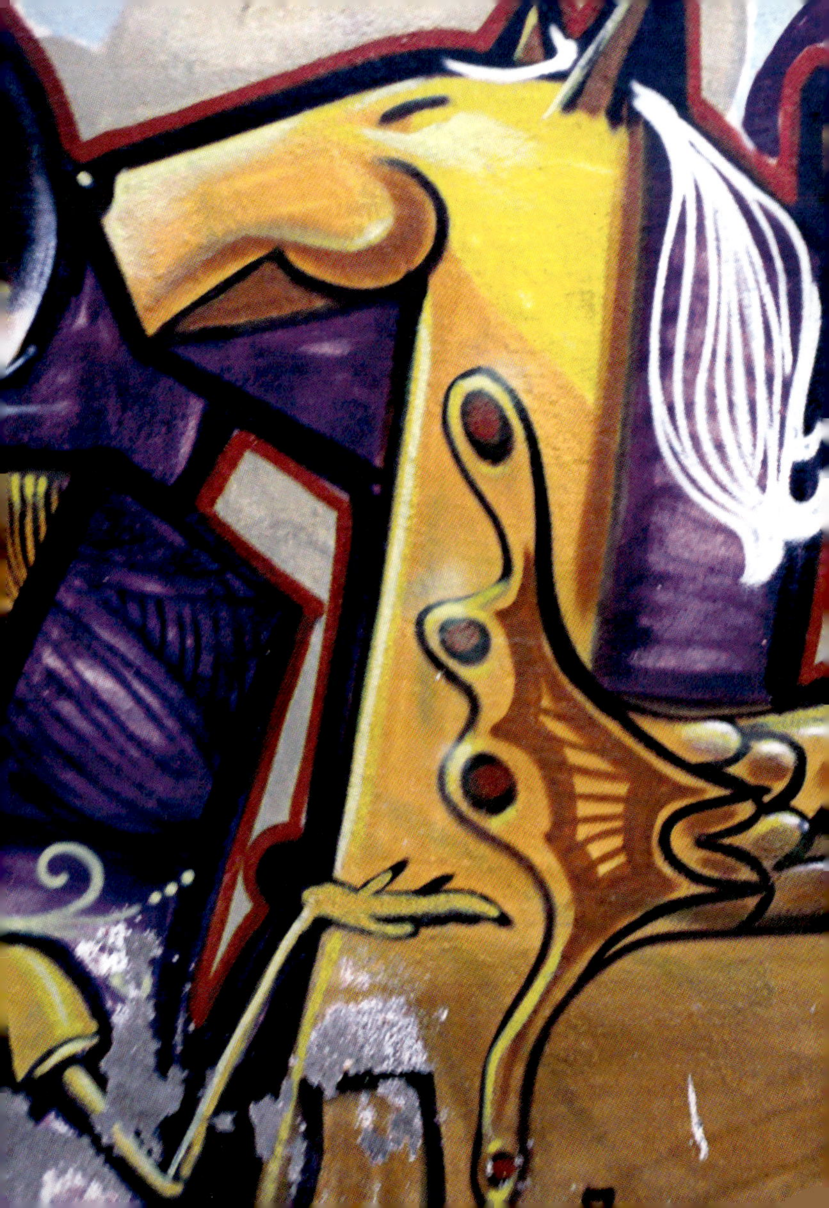

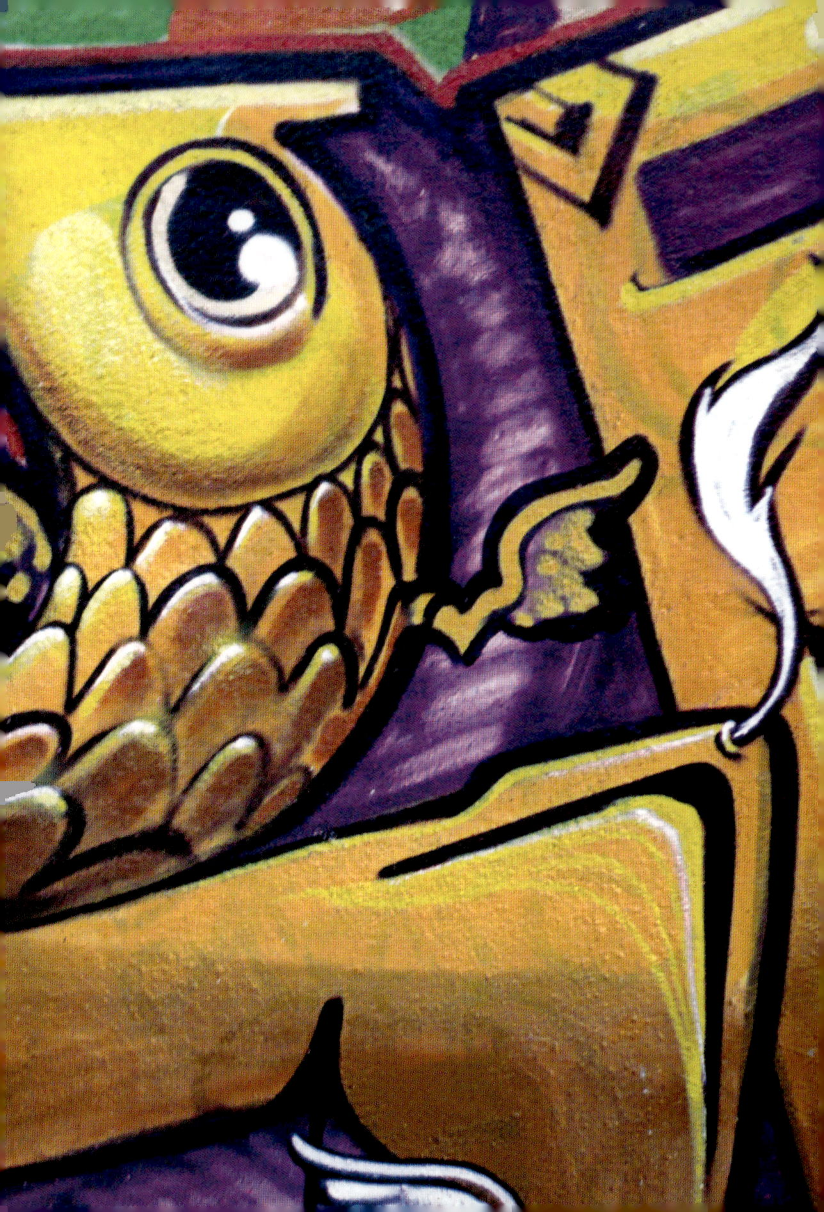

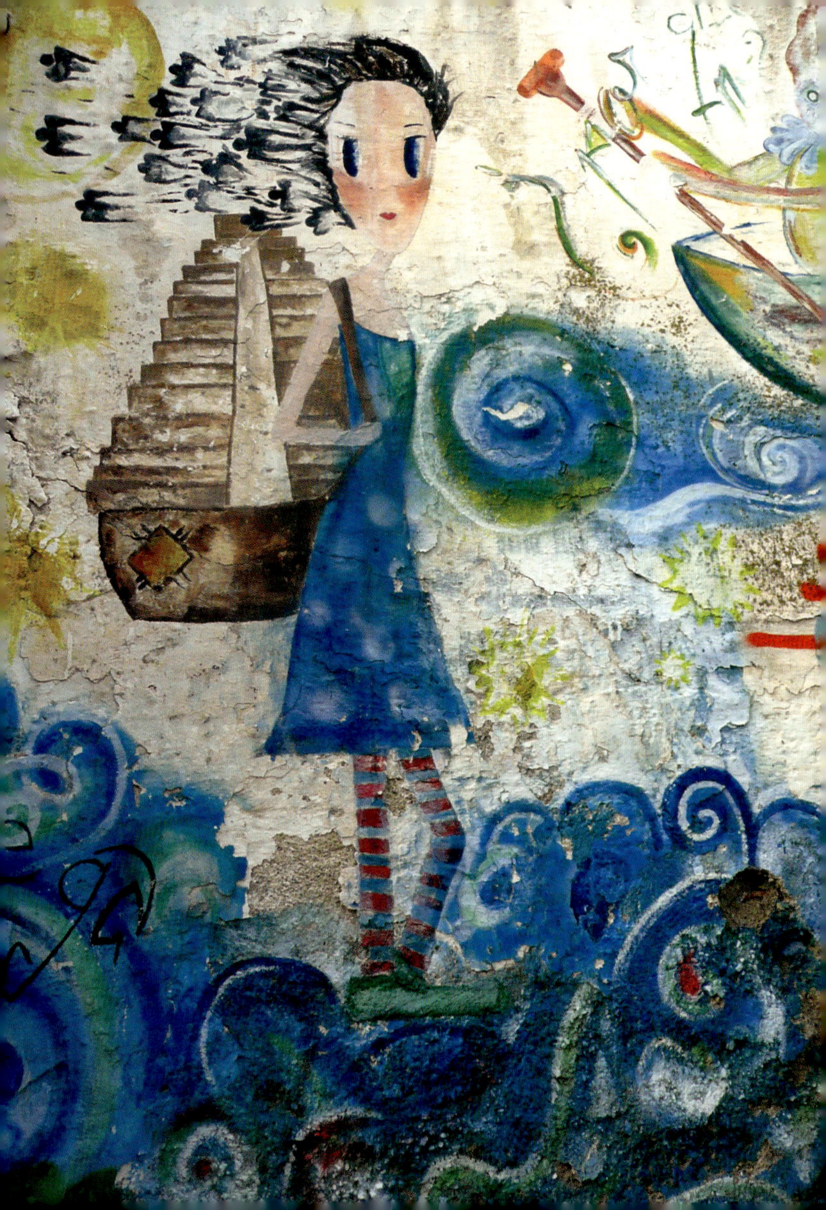

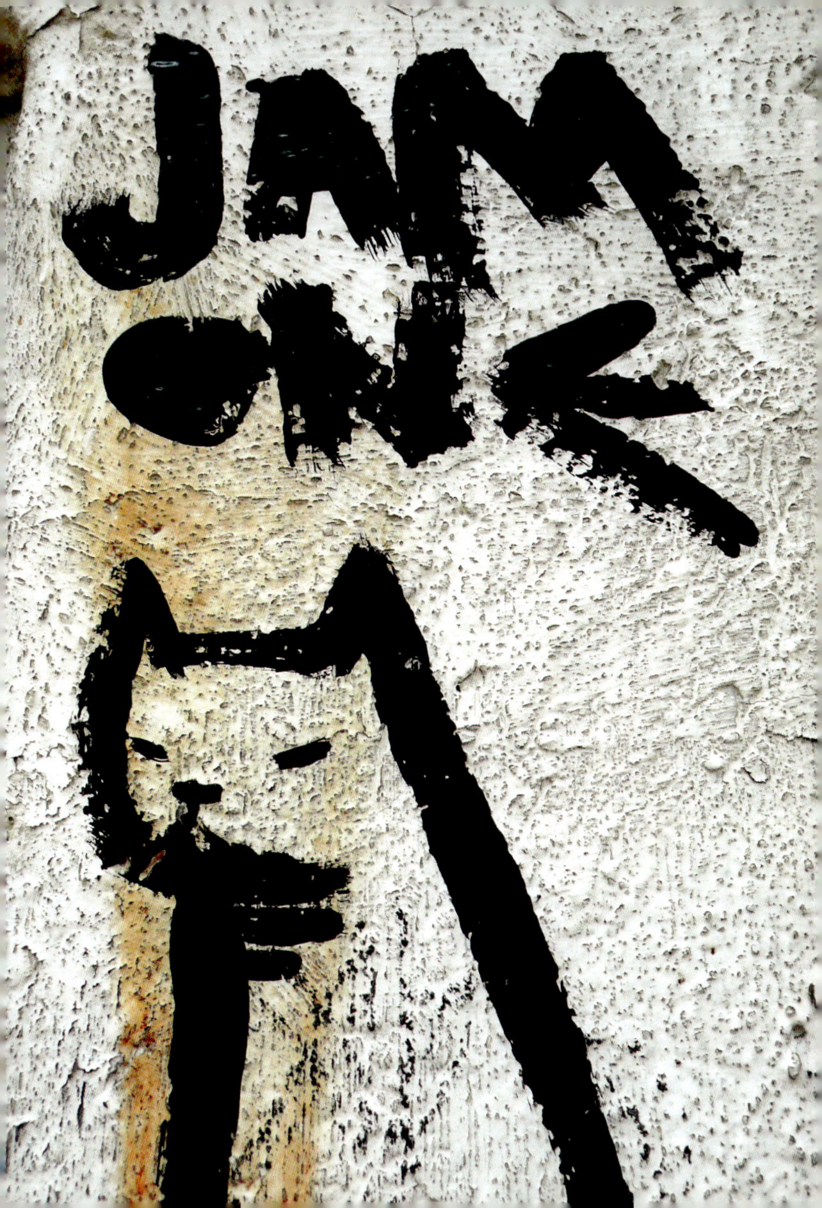
JAM

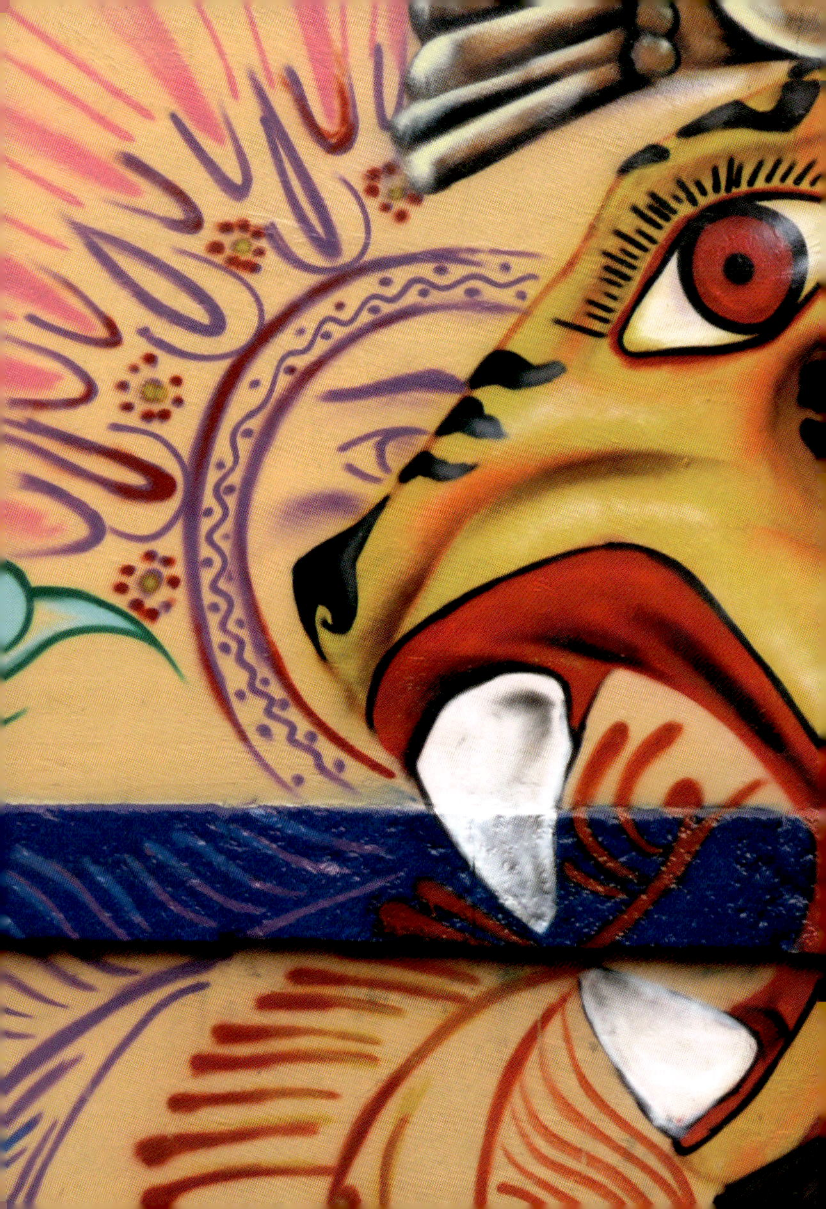

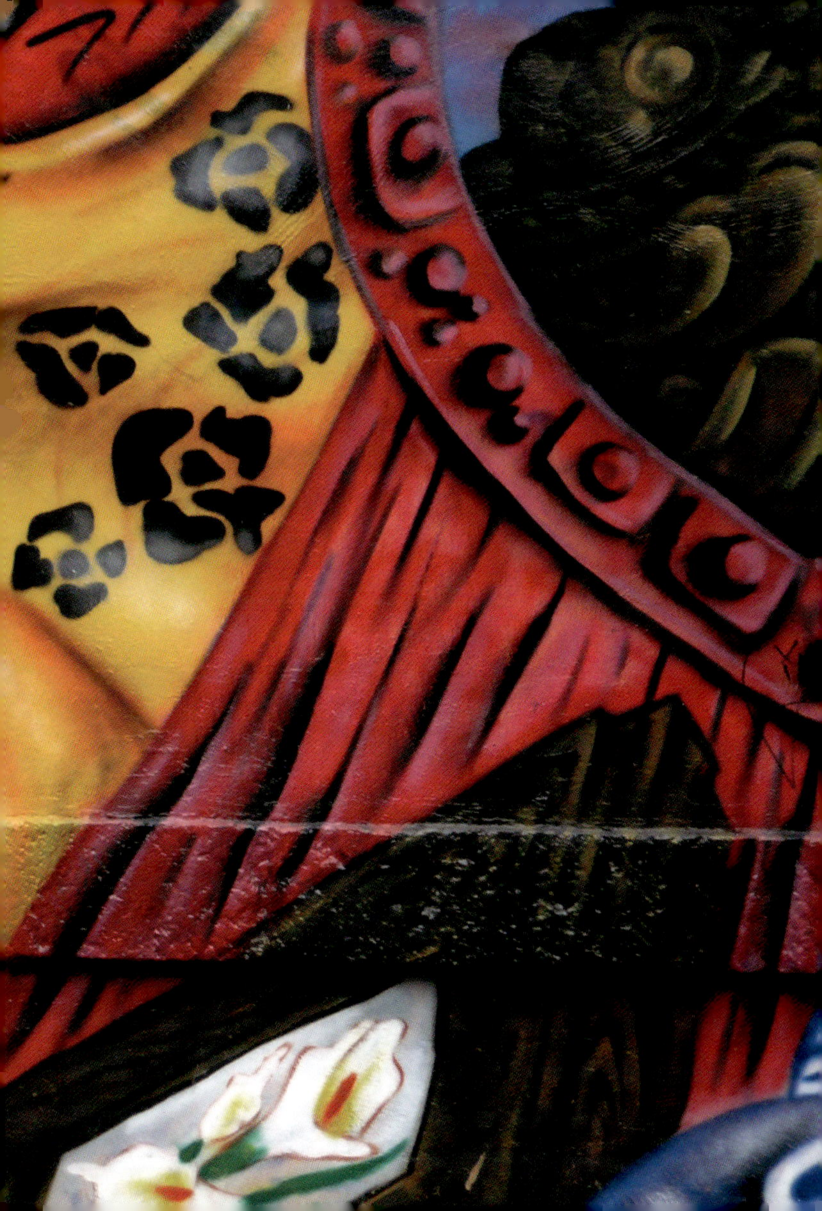

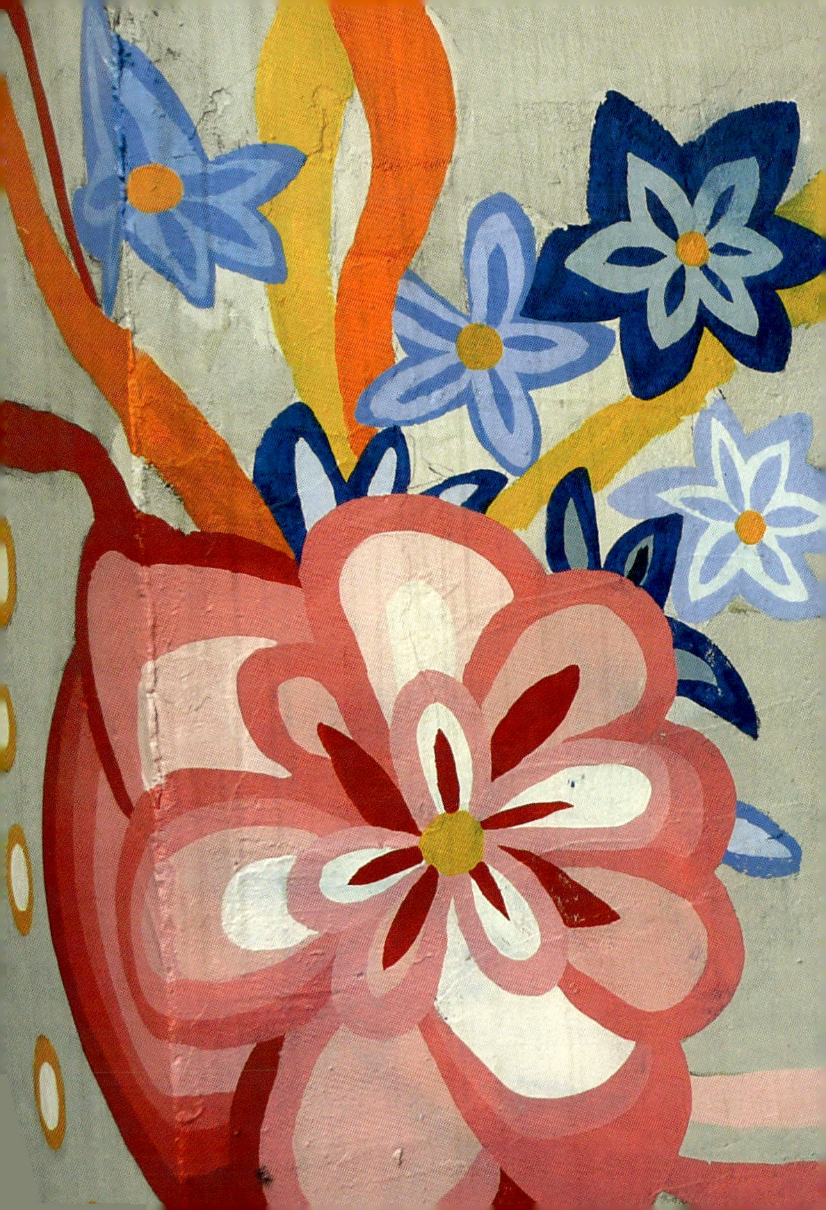

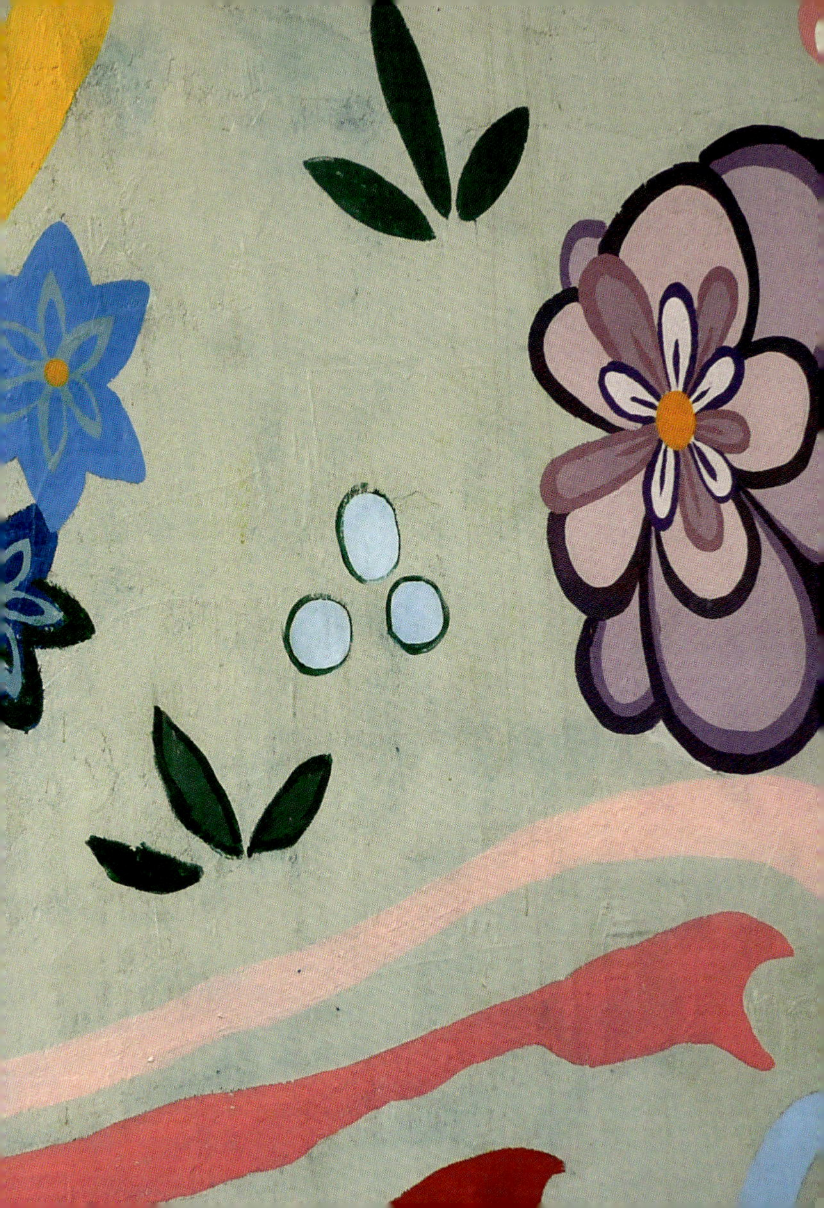

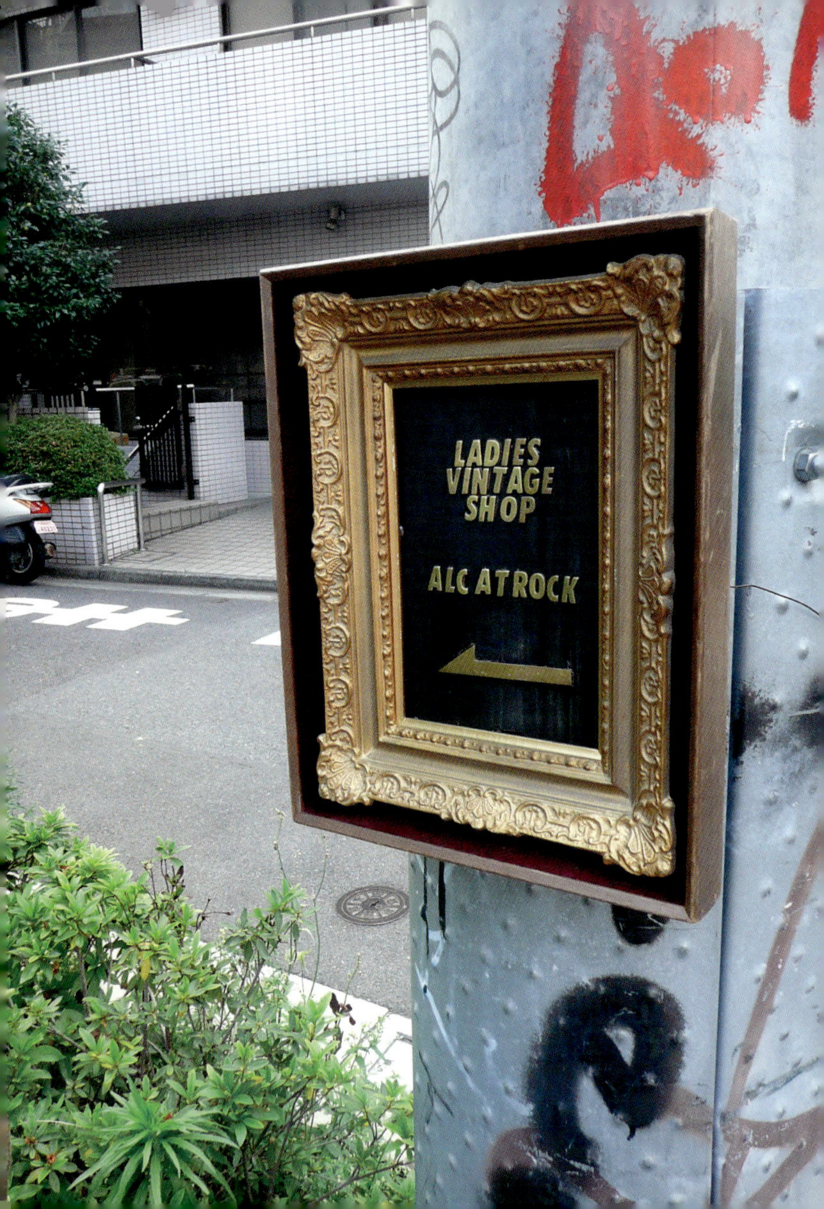
LADIES
VINTAGE
SHOP
ALC ATROCK

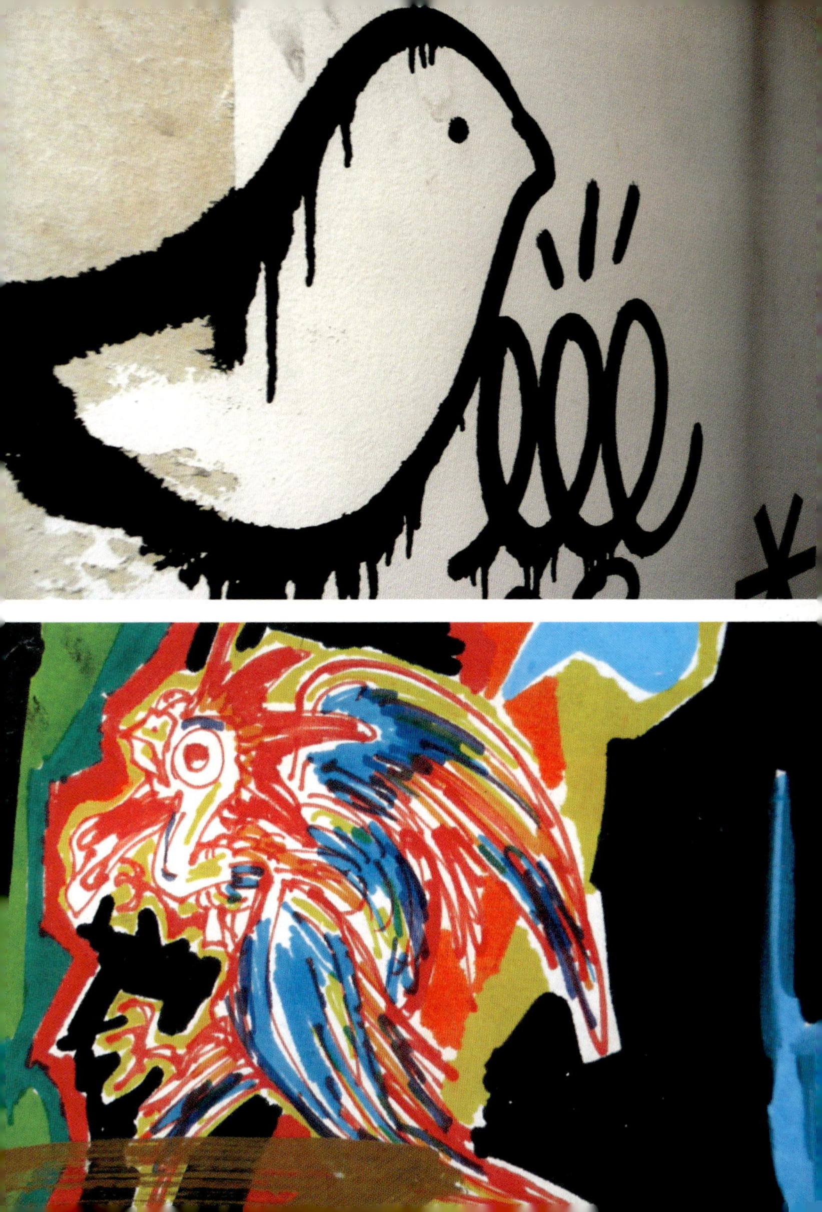

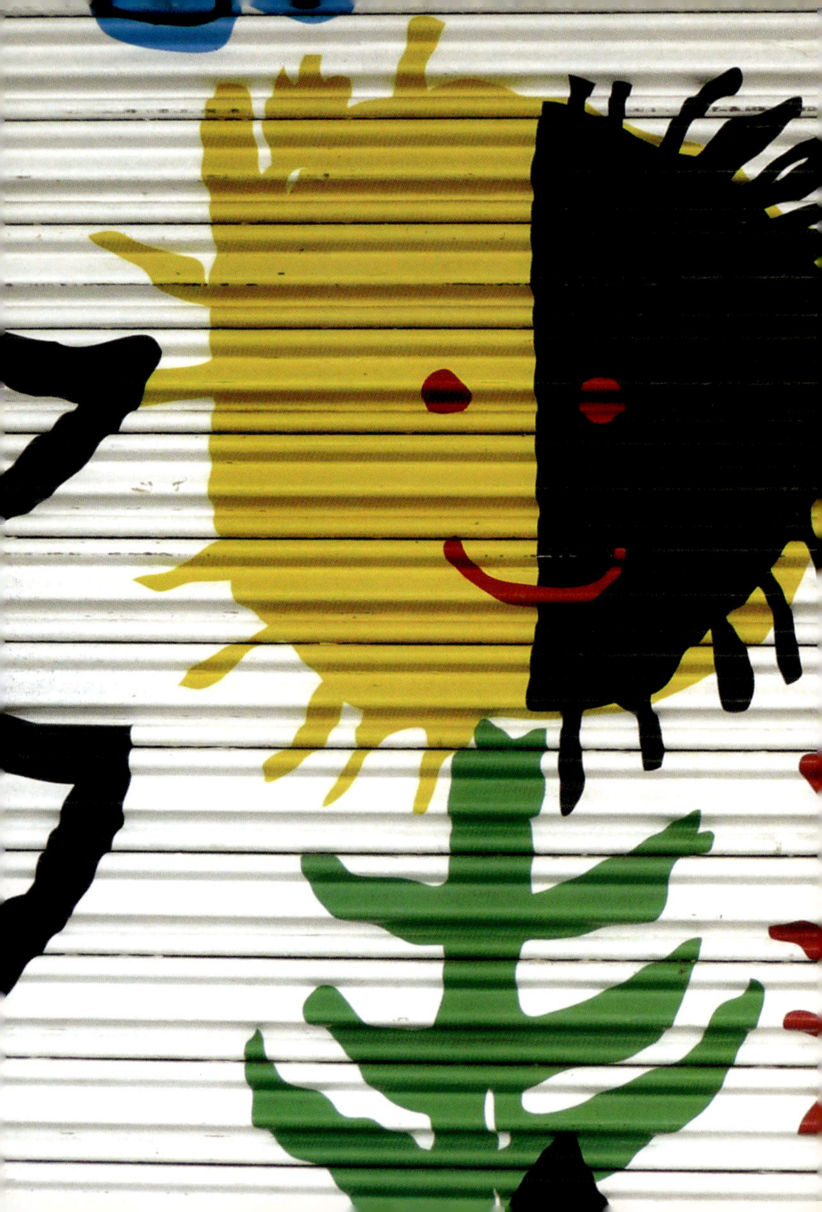

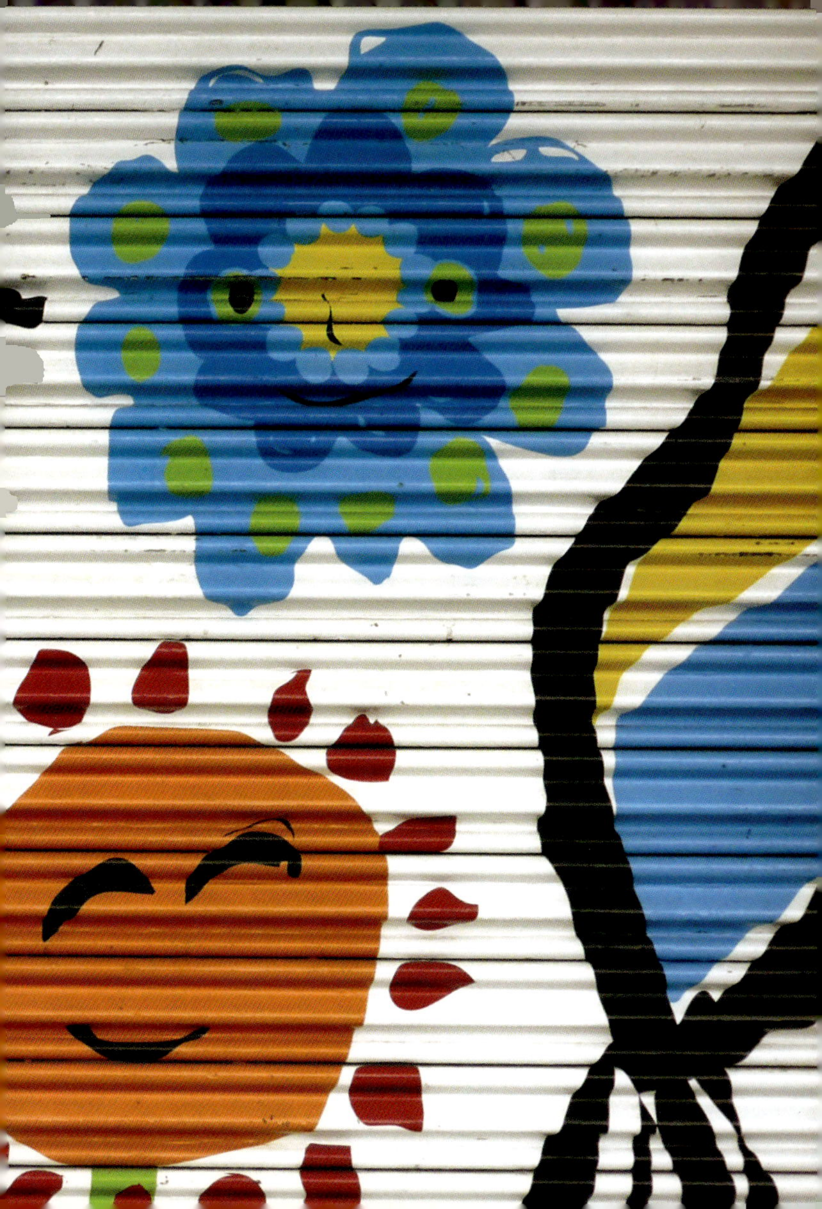

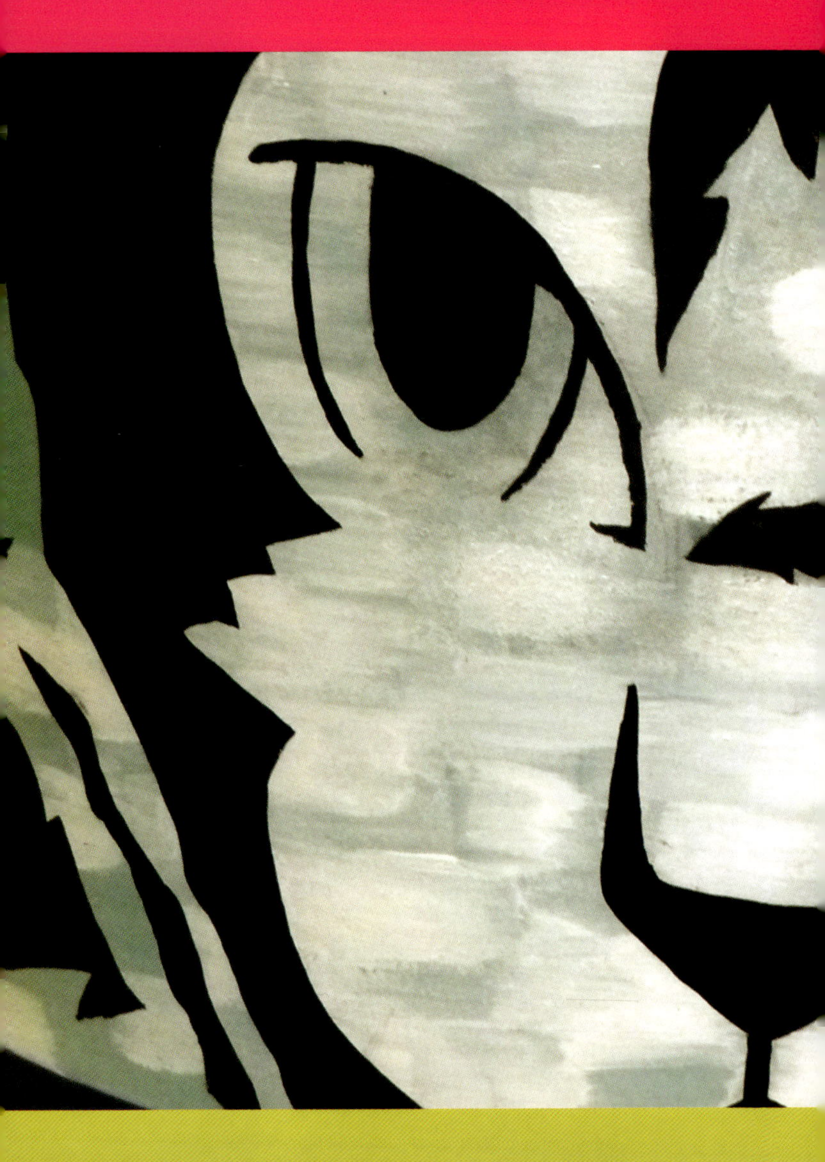

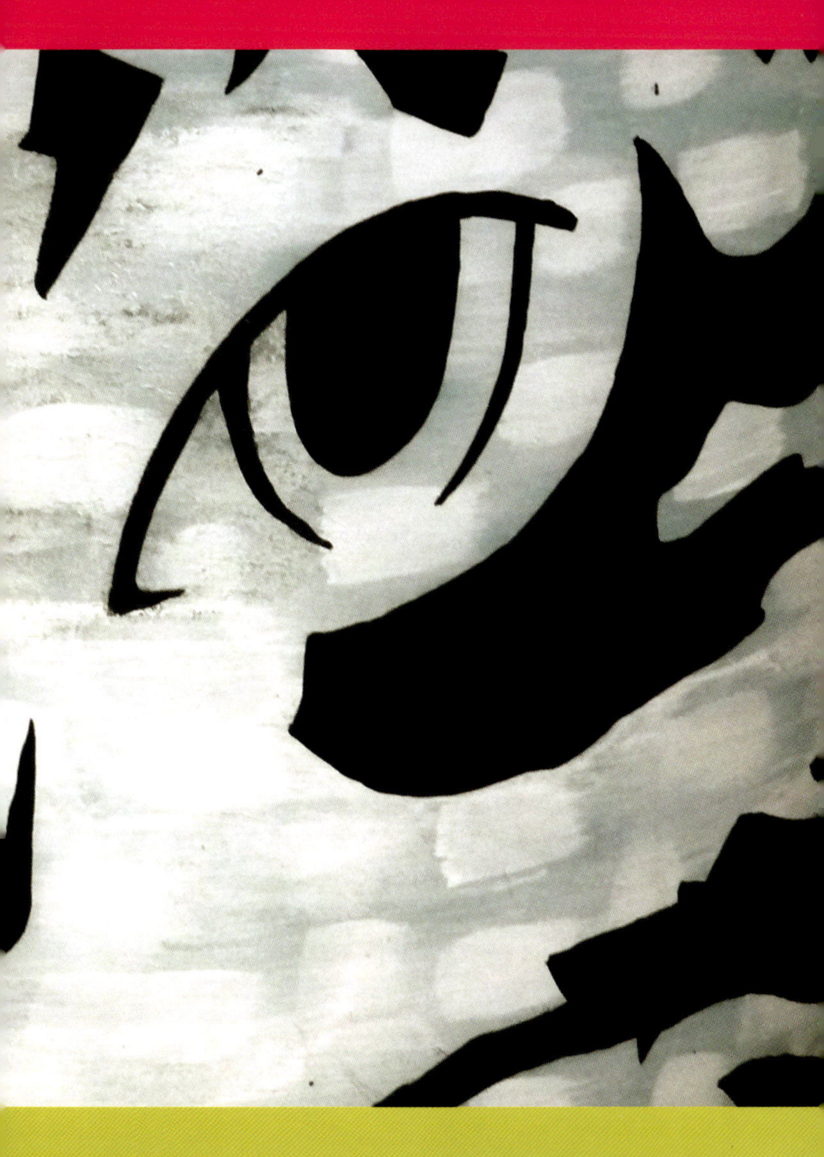

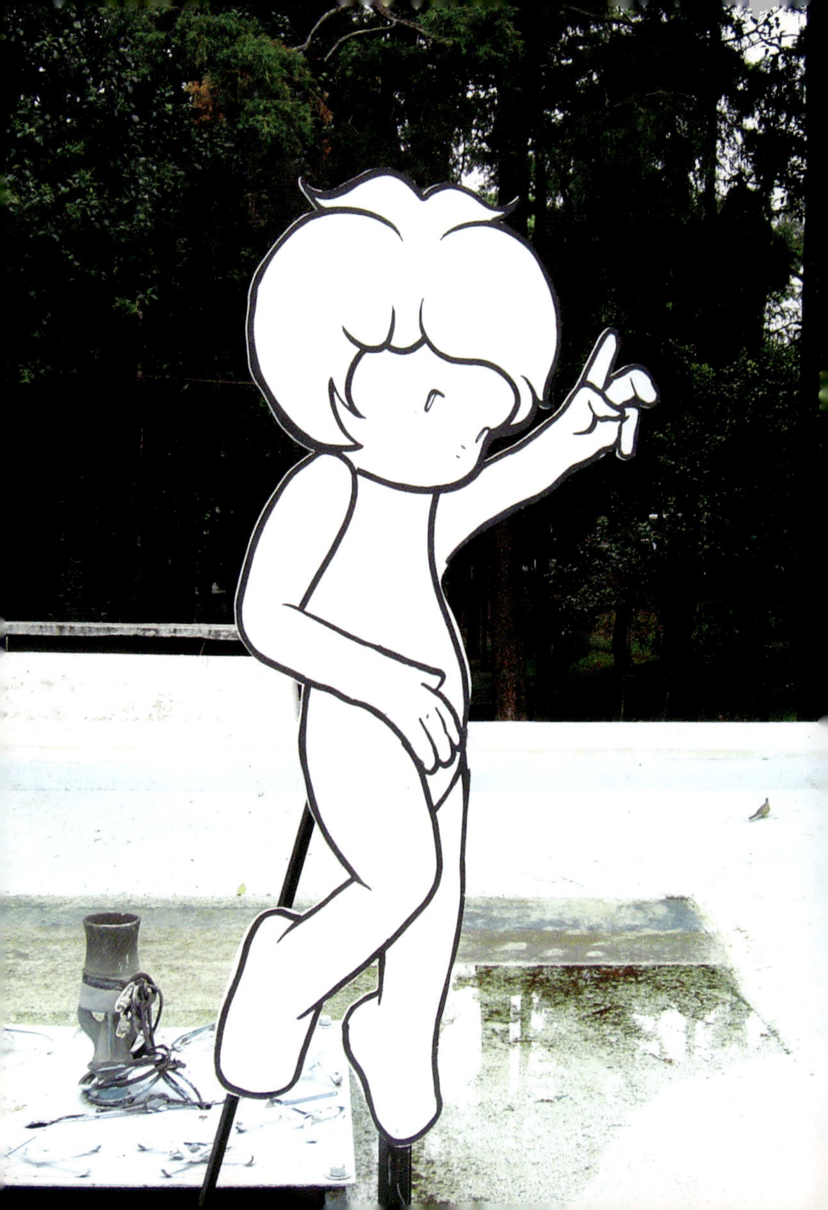

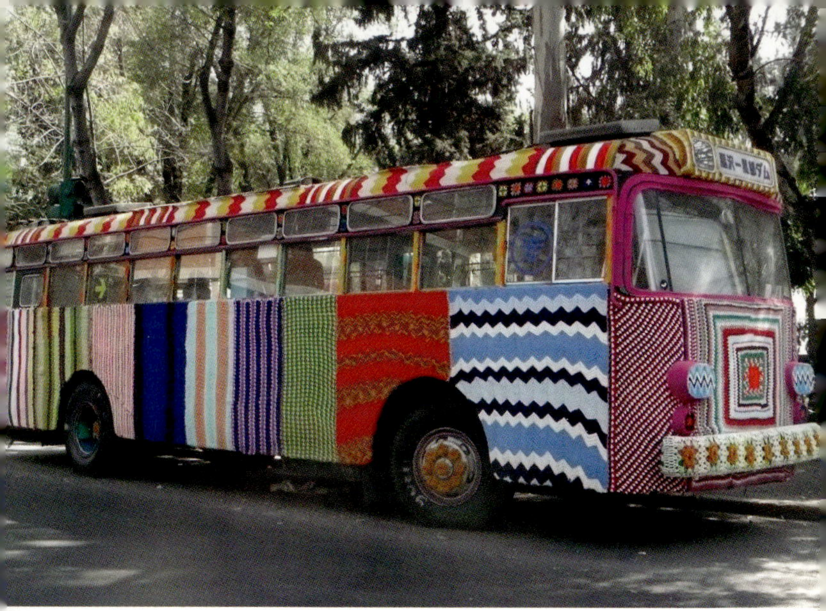

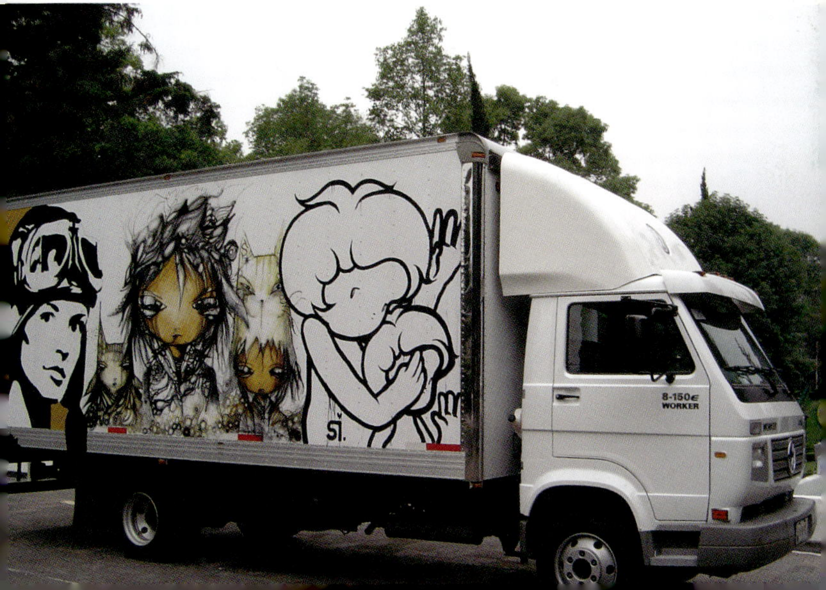

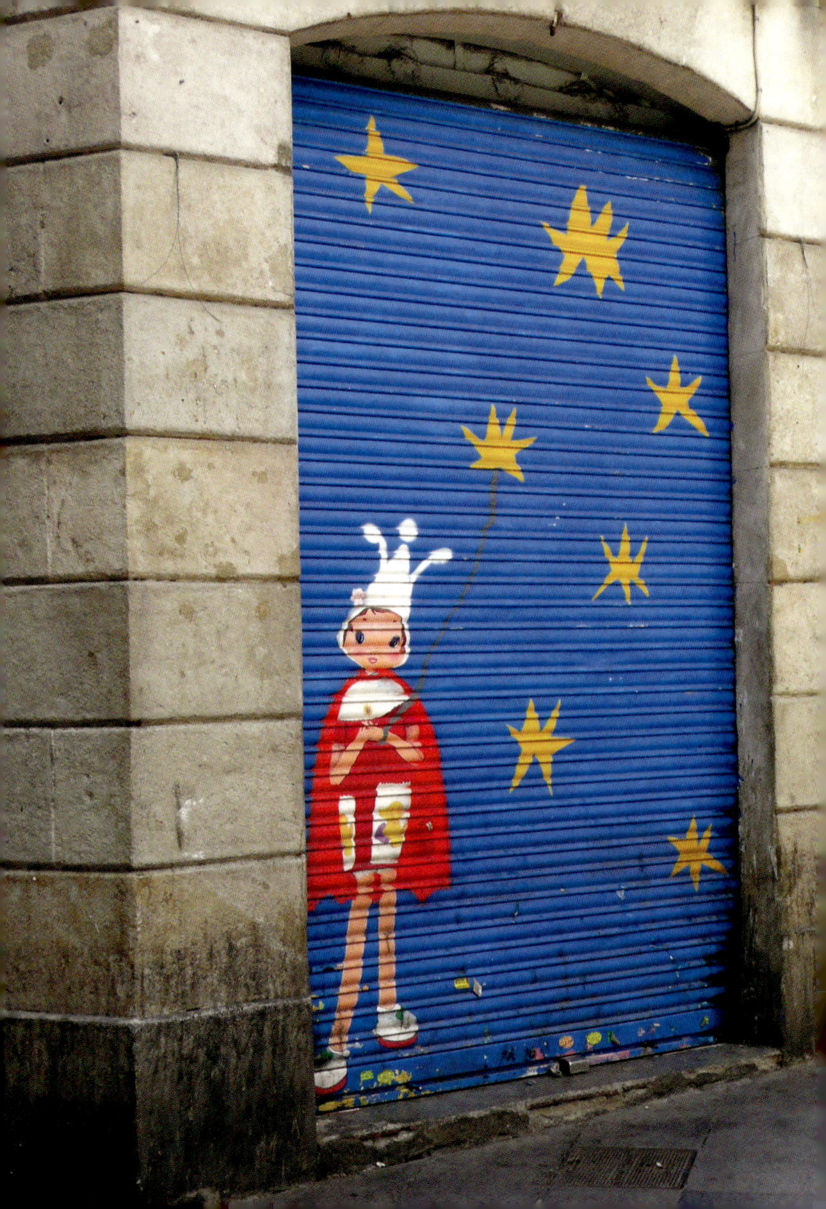

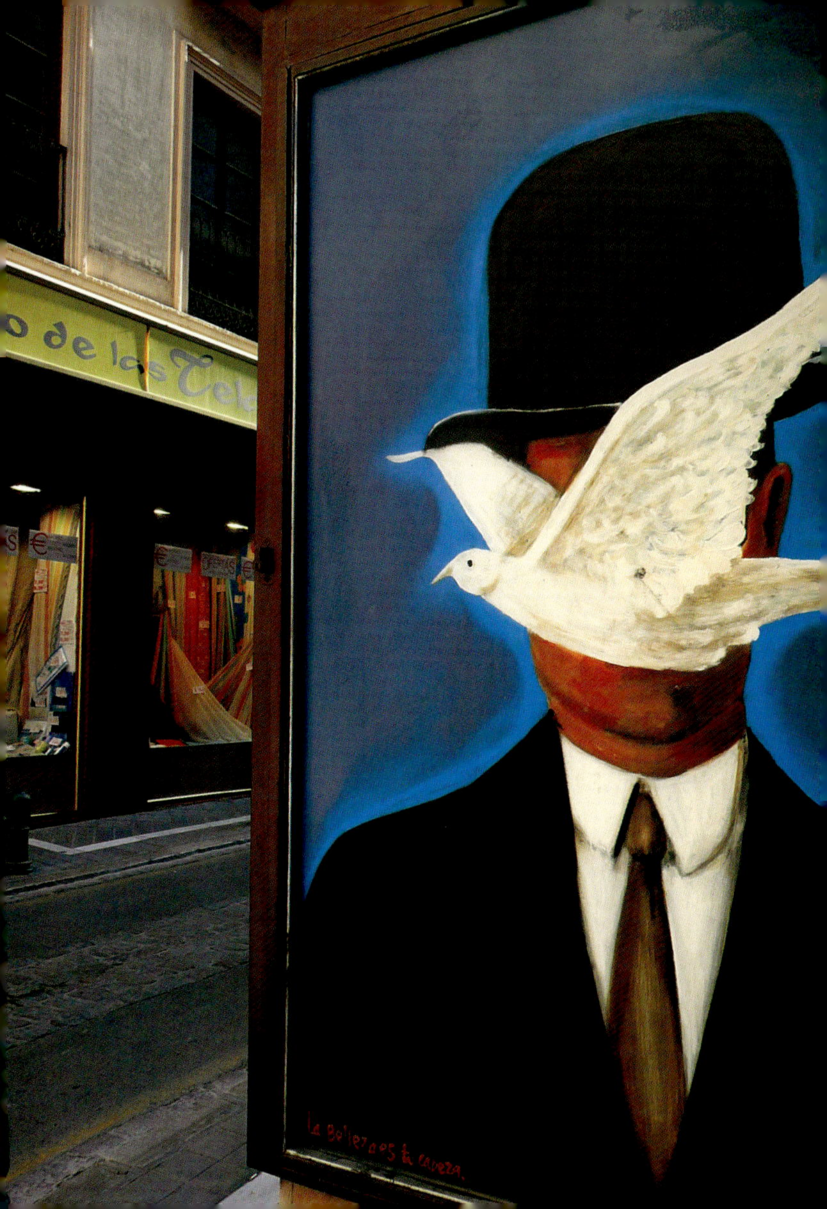
de las
La Belleza es la cabeza.

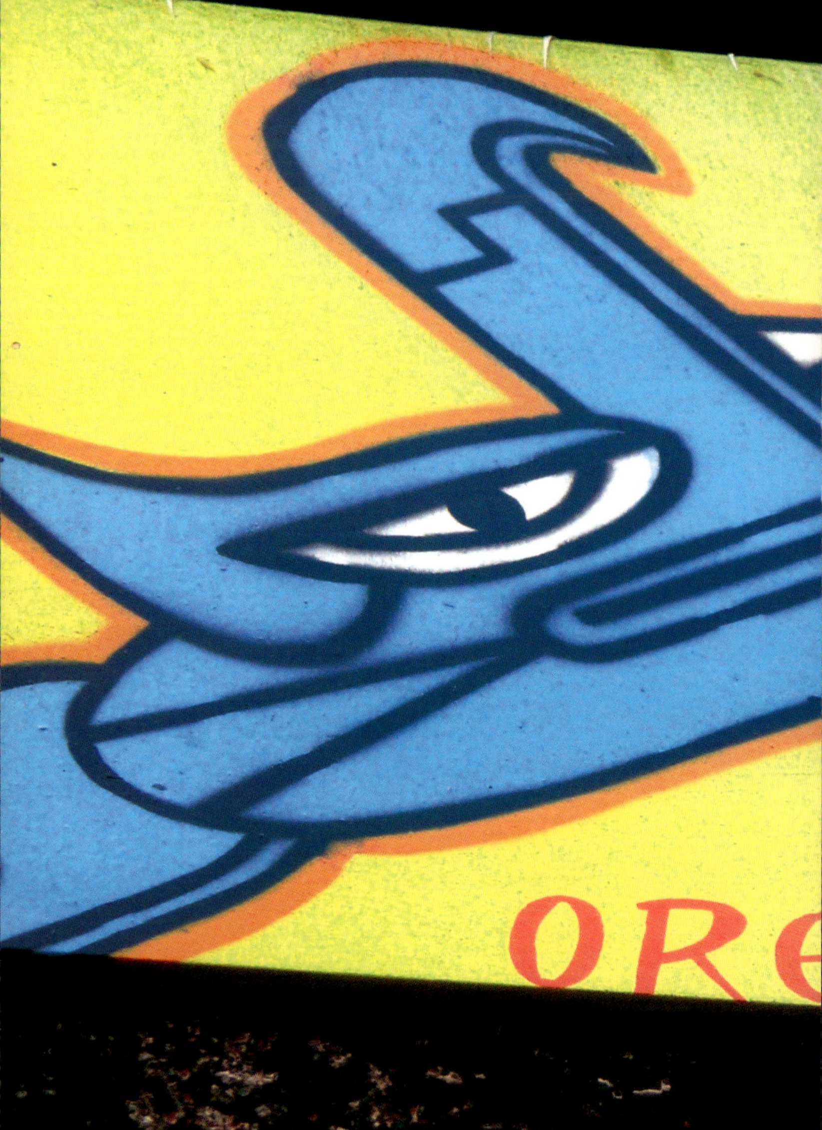

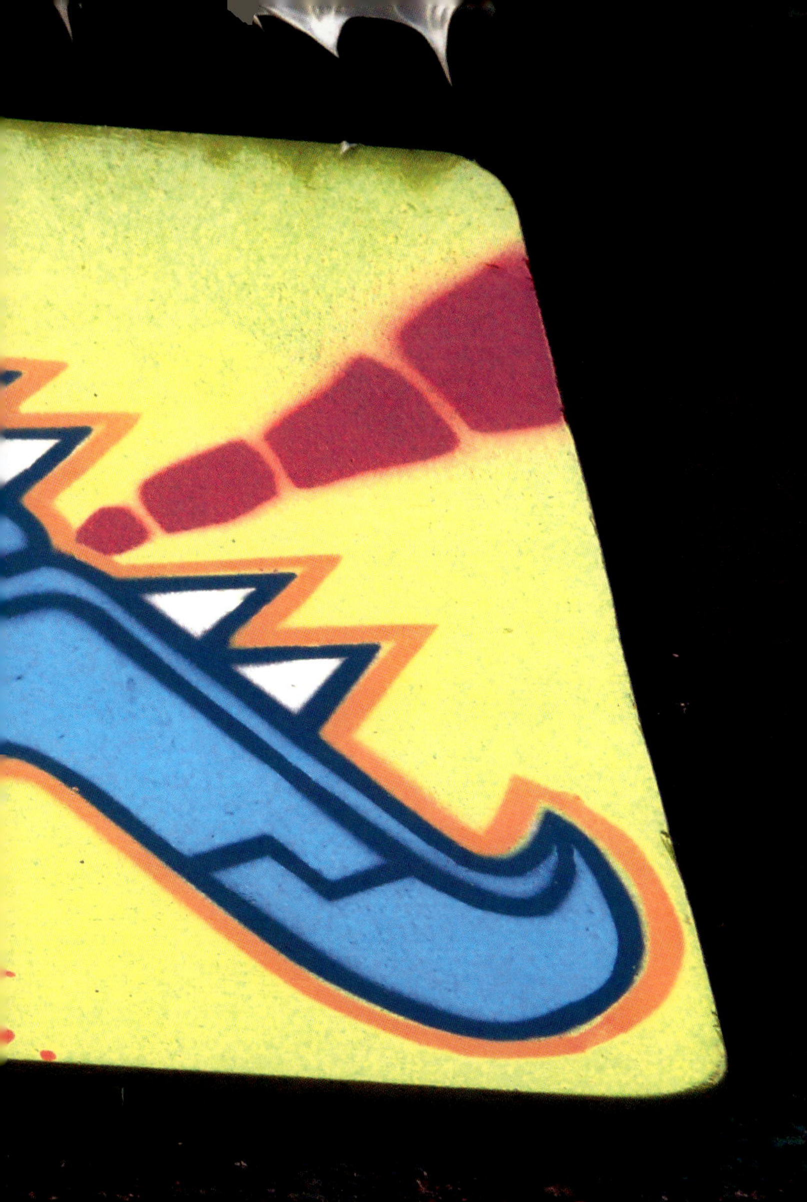

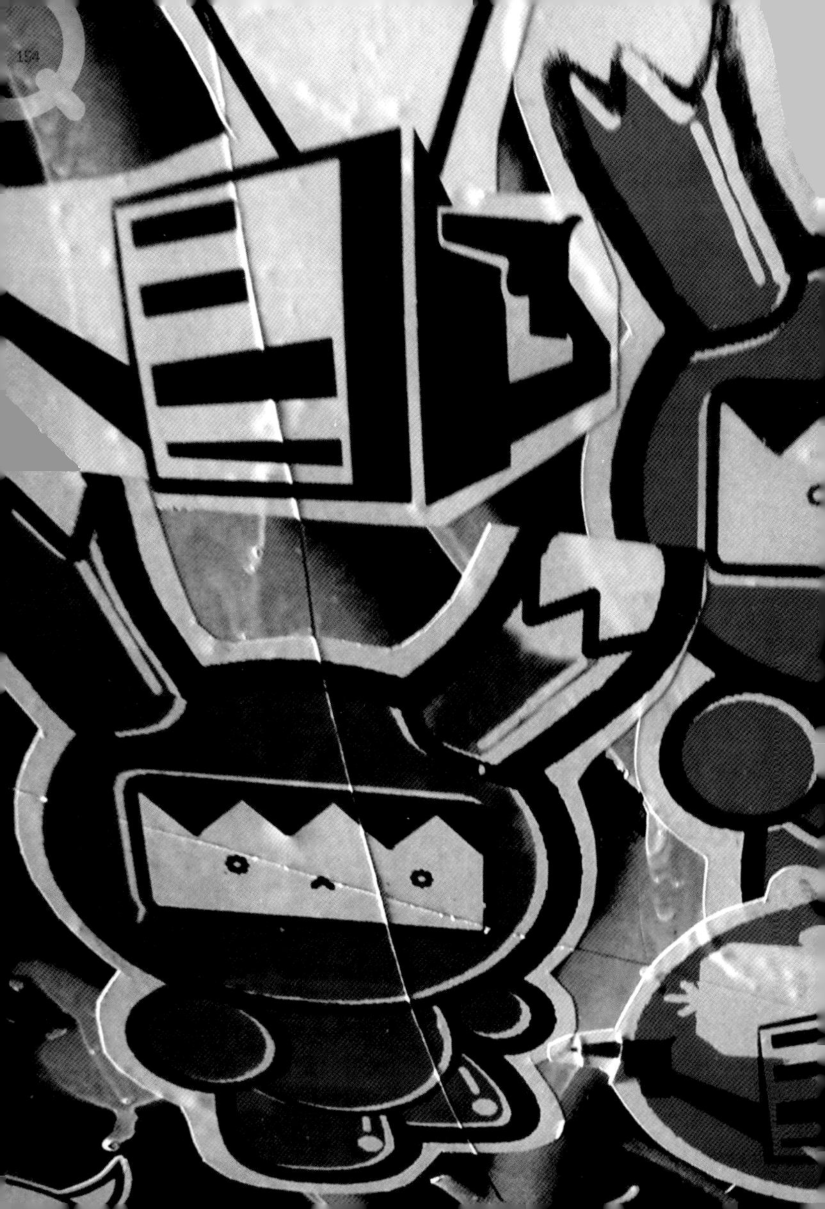

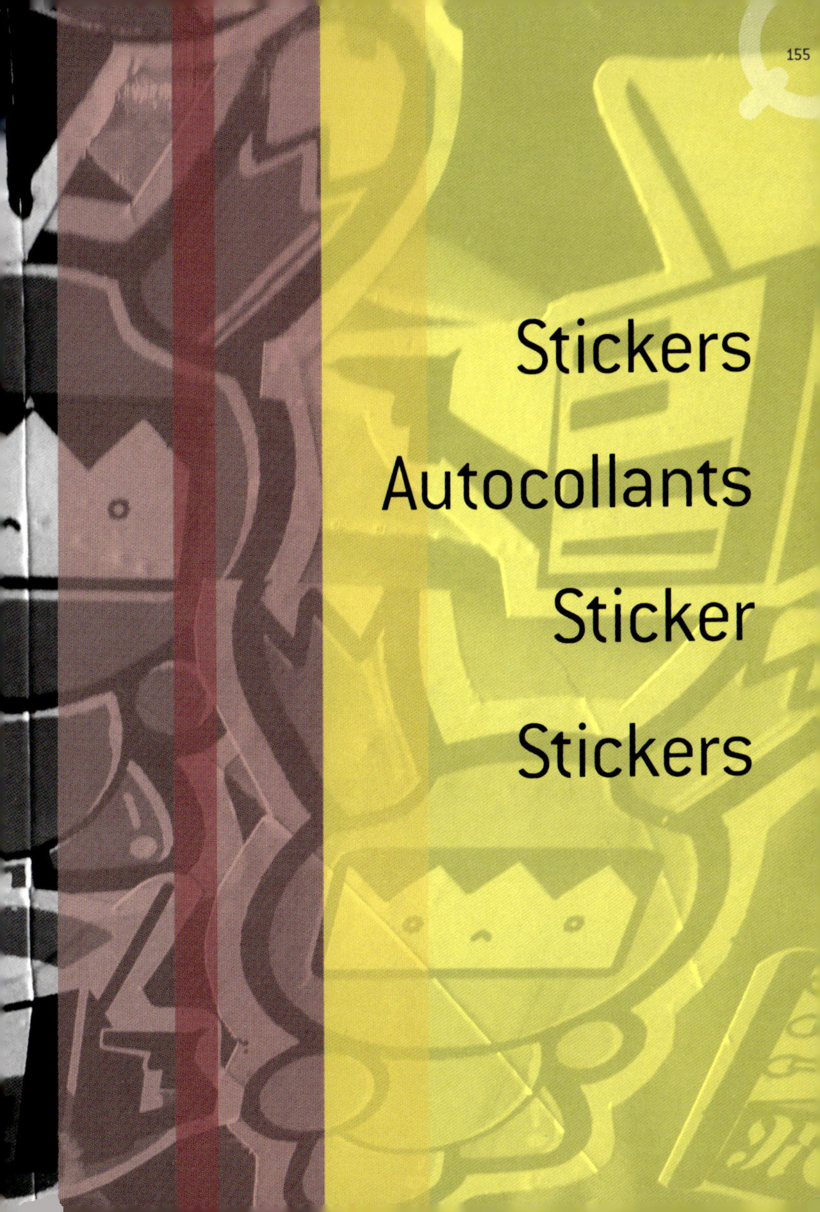

Stickers

Autocollants

Sticker

Stickers

Stickers (sheets of paper or vinyl with an image printed on the front and with a layer of glue on the back) have begun to vie for the throne reserved for graffiti as the eminent street art technique. But what is so great about stickers? They are cheap, quick to manufacture, mechanically reproducible, and, most of all, they are flexible. You no longer need to be able to draw to create street art: being able to manage a simple drawing program is all that is needed.

Les autocollants (feuilles de papier ou vinyle sur la face desquelles a été imprimée une image et disposant au dos d'une couche de colle) ont commencé à usurper le titre de technique par excellence de l'art urbain réservé au graffiti. Leur avantage ? Les autocollants sont bon marché, rapides à fabriquer, reproductibles mécaniquement et, surtout, souples. Il n'est plus nécessaire de savoir dessiner pour faire de l'art urbain : il suffit de maîtriser un simple programme informatique de dessin.

Die Sticker (Papierblätter oder Vinylfolien mit einem Bildaufdruck auf der Vorder- und einer Schicht Klebstoff auf der Rückseite) beginnen allmählich damit, Graffiti als Straßenkunstform par excellence den Rang abzulaufen. Ihre Vorzüge? Sticker sind preisgünstig, schnell herzustellen, mechanisch reproduzierbar und vor allem flexibel, da es für die Schaffung urbaner Kunst nun nicht mehr notwendig ist, zeichnen zu können: es reicht die Beherrschung eines einfachen Computerprogramms.

Stickers (papiertjes of stukjes vinyl waarop aan de voorkant een afbeelding is afgedrukt en aan de achterkant een laag lijm is voorzien) beginnen zich de troon toe te eigenen die gereserveerd was voor de graffiti als techniek bij uitstek van de urban art. De werkingskracht ervan? Stickers zijn goedkoop, snel te maken, machinaal reproduceerbaar en met name flexibel. Het is namelijk voor het maken van straatkunst niet meer nodig om te kunnen tekenen: de beheersing van een simpel computertekenprogramma is voldoende.

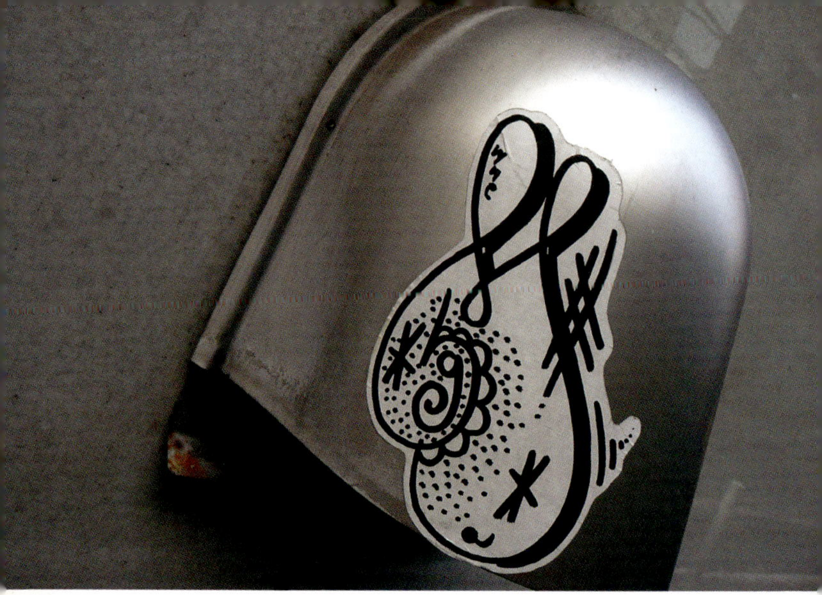

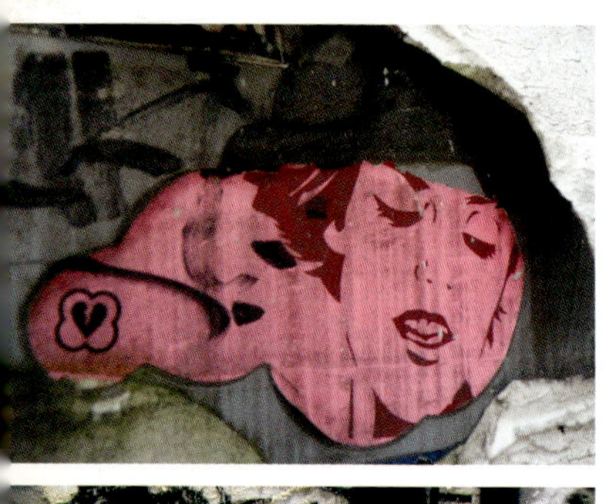

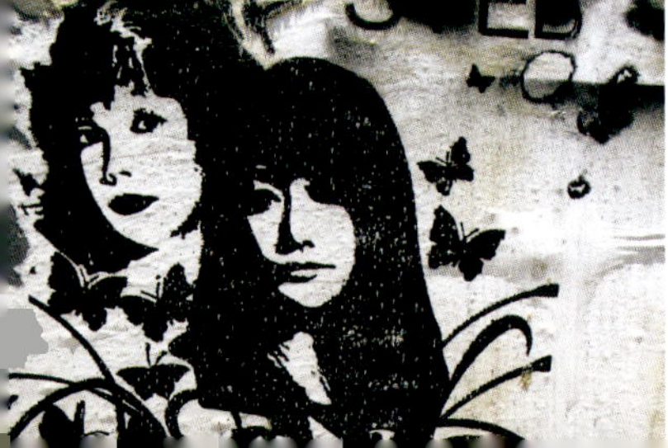

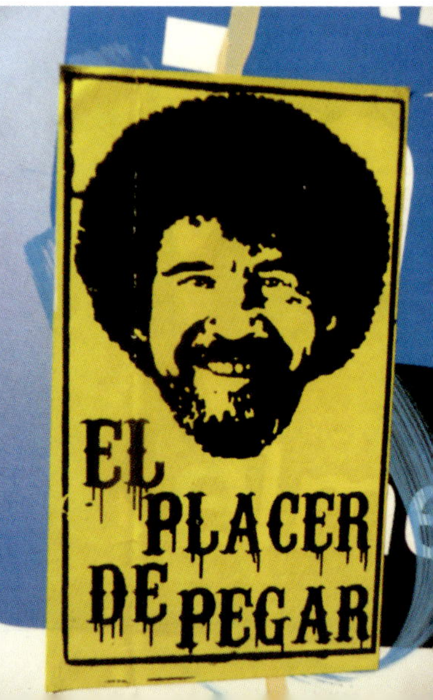
EL PLACER DE PEGAR

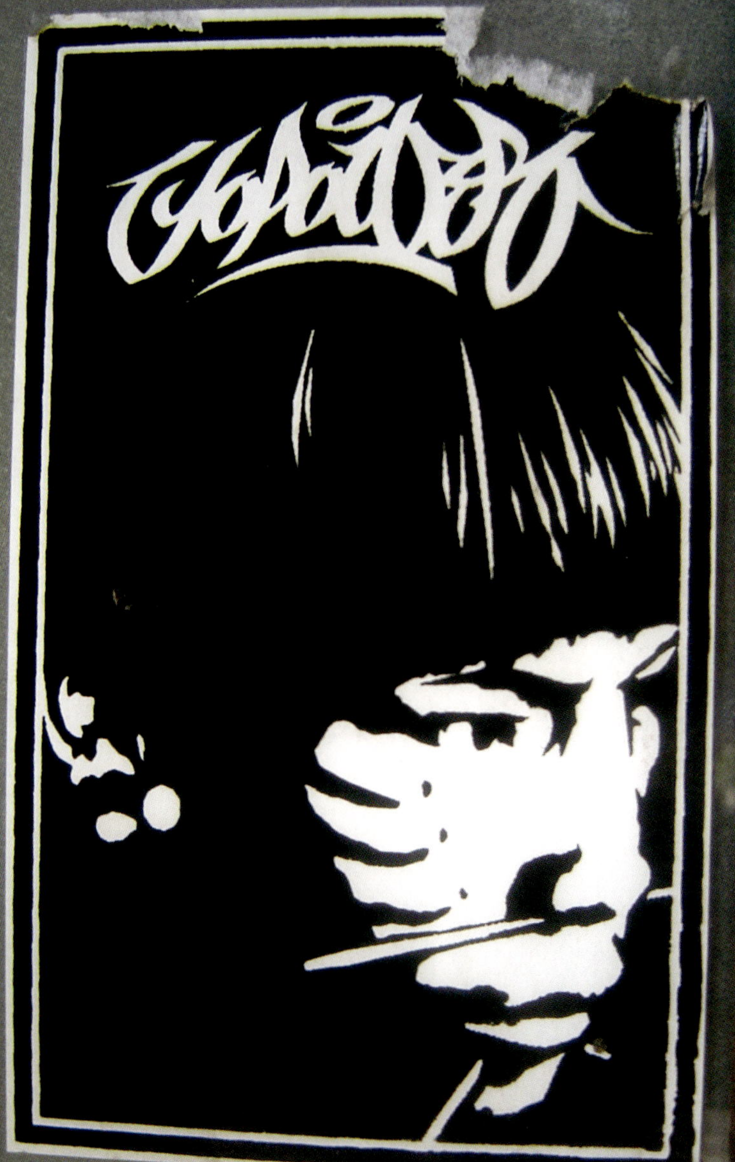

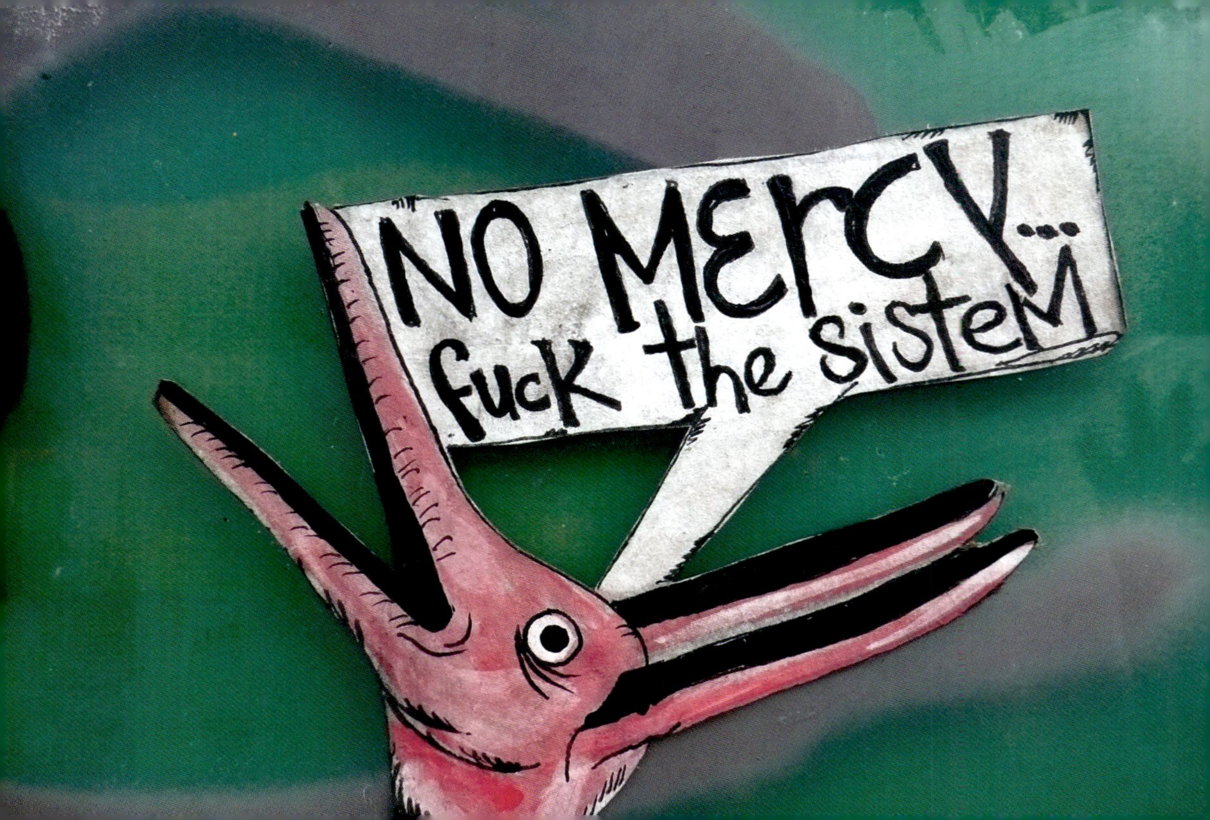
NO MErCY...
fuck the sistem

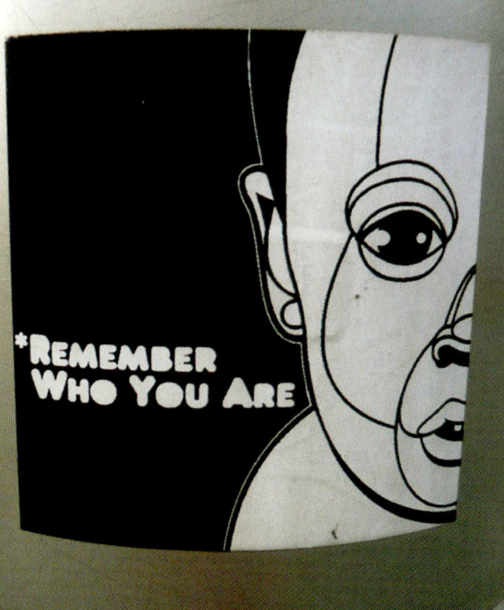
*Remember
Who You Are

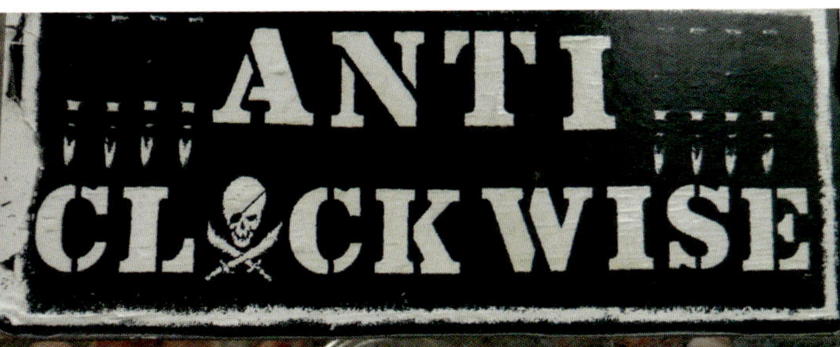
ANTI
CLOCKWISE
ANTI
CLOCKWISE

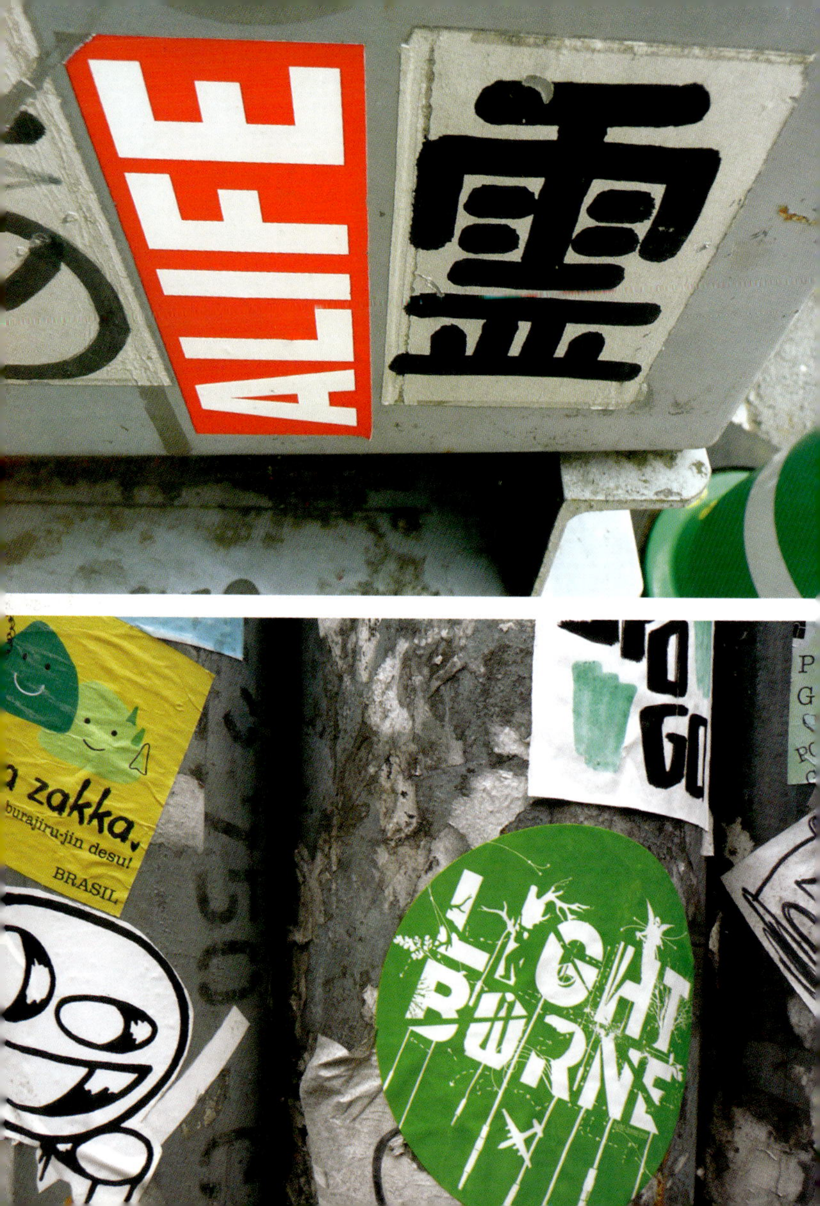
ALIFE
霊
a zakka.
burajiru-jin desu!
BRASIL

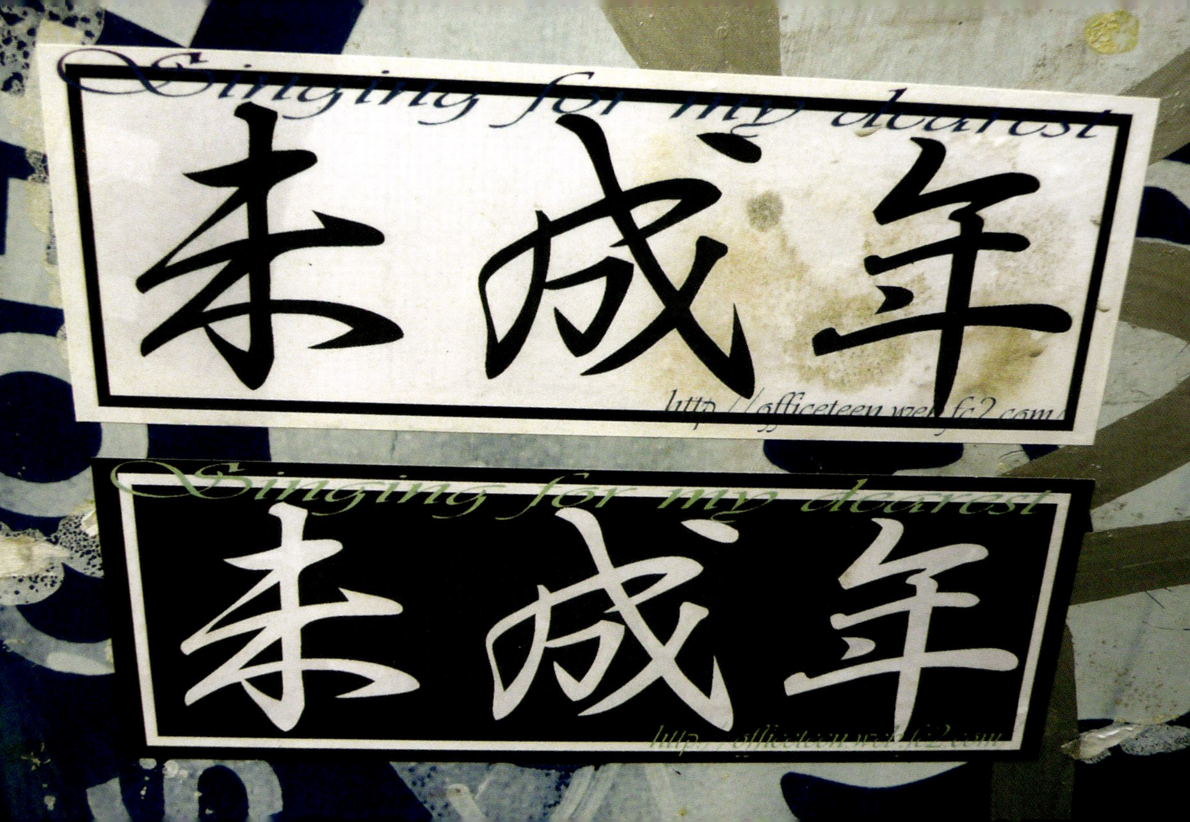
Singing for my dearest
未成年
http://officeteen.web.fc2.com
Singing for my dearest
未成年

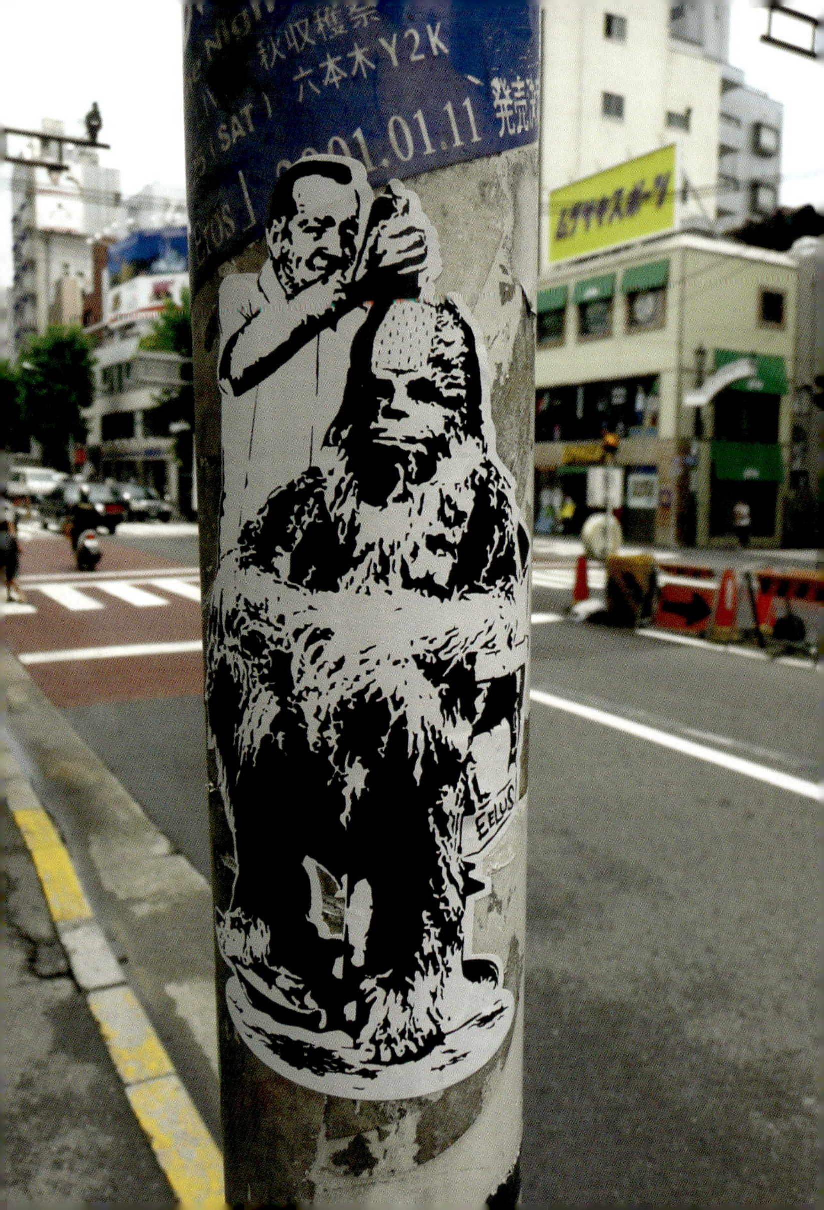

秋収穫祭
(SAT) 六本木 Y2K
EELUS

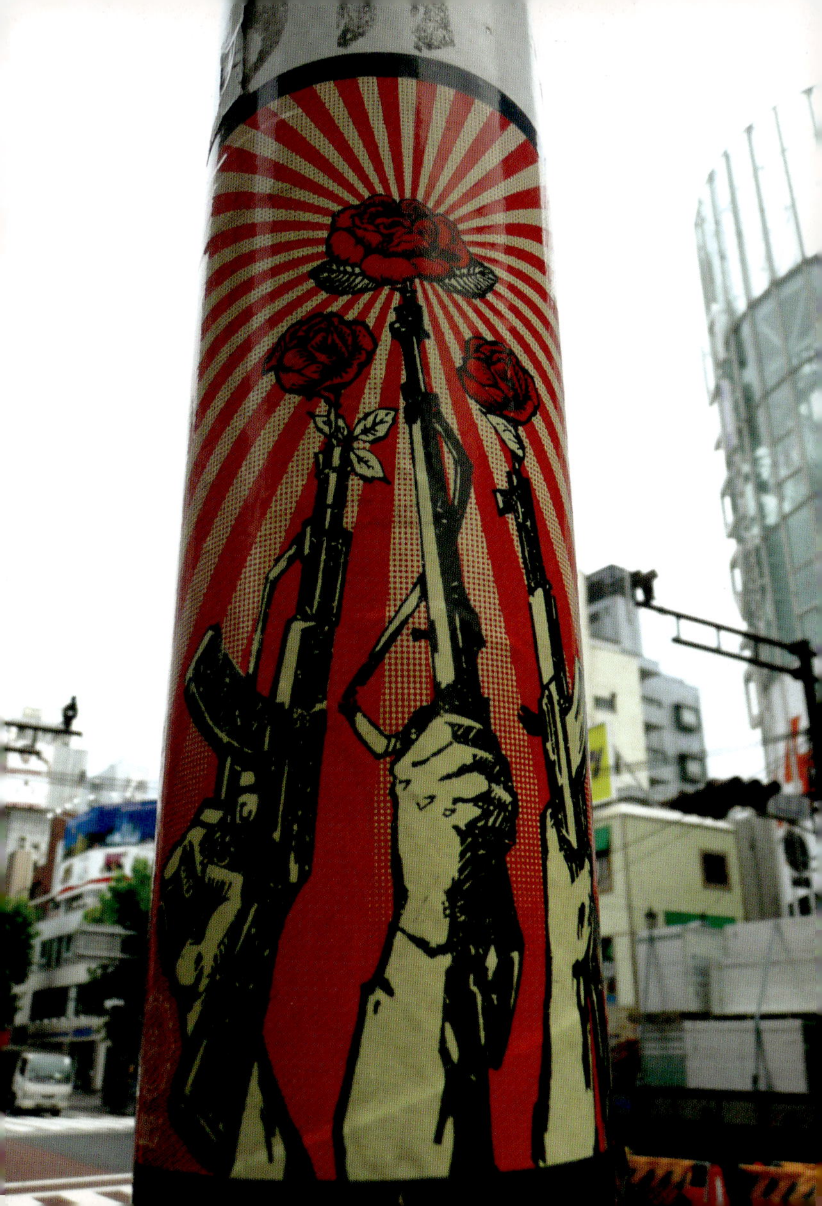

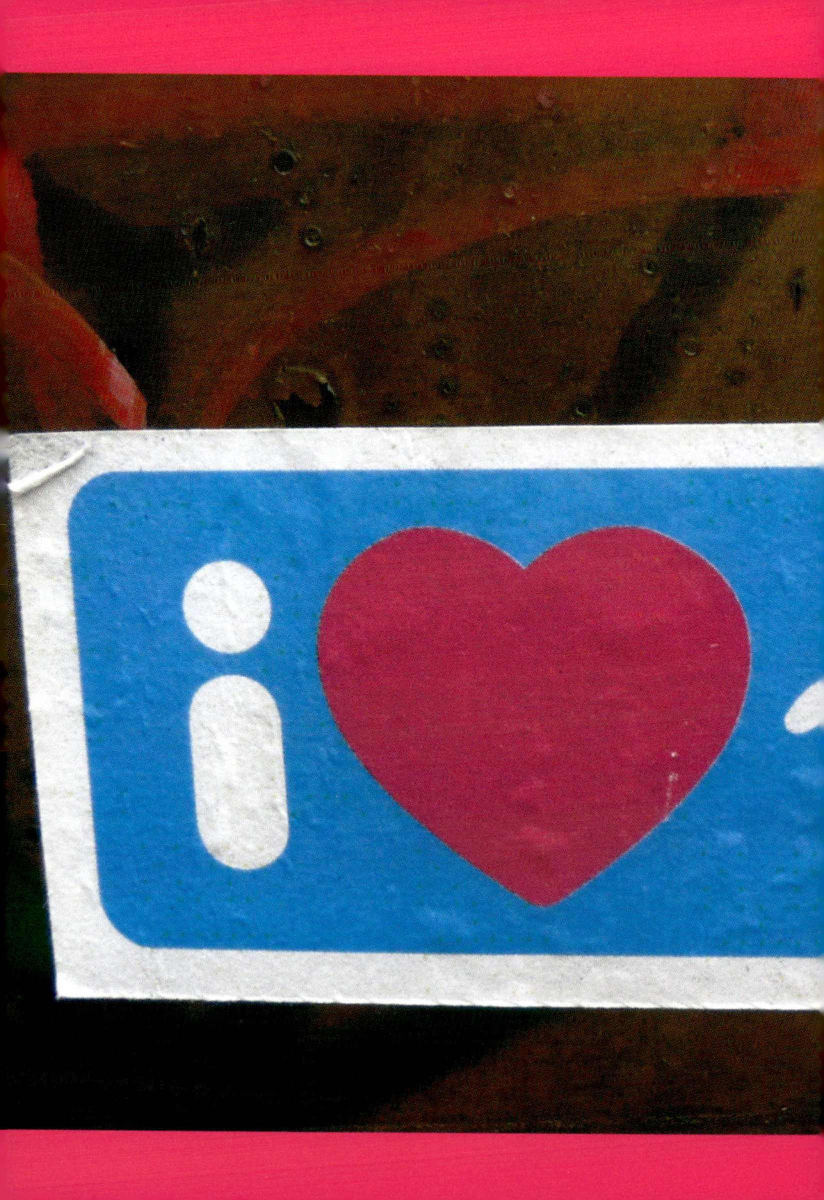
i ♥

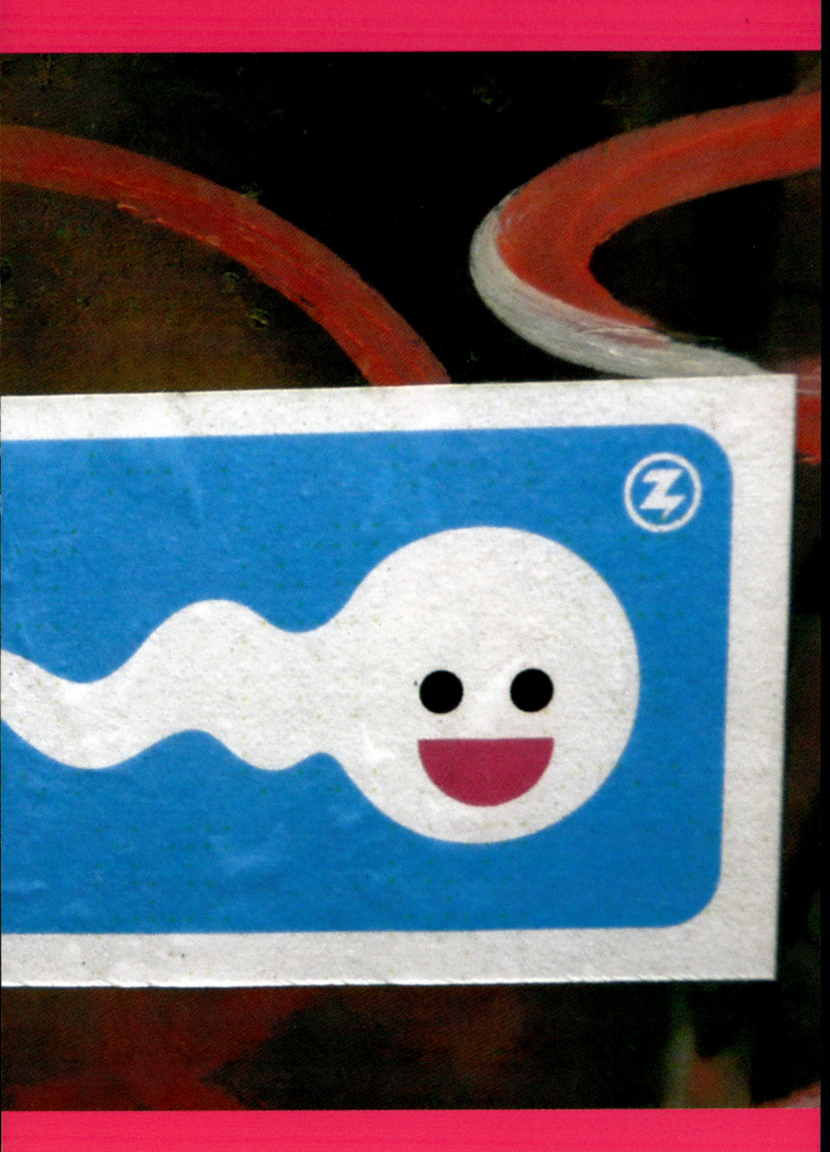

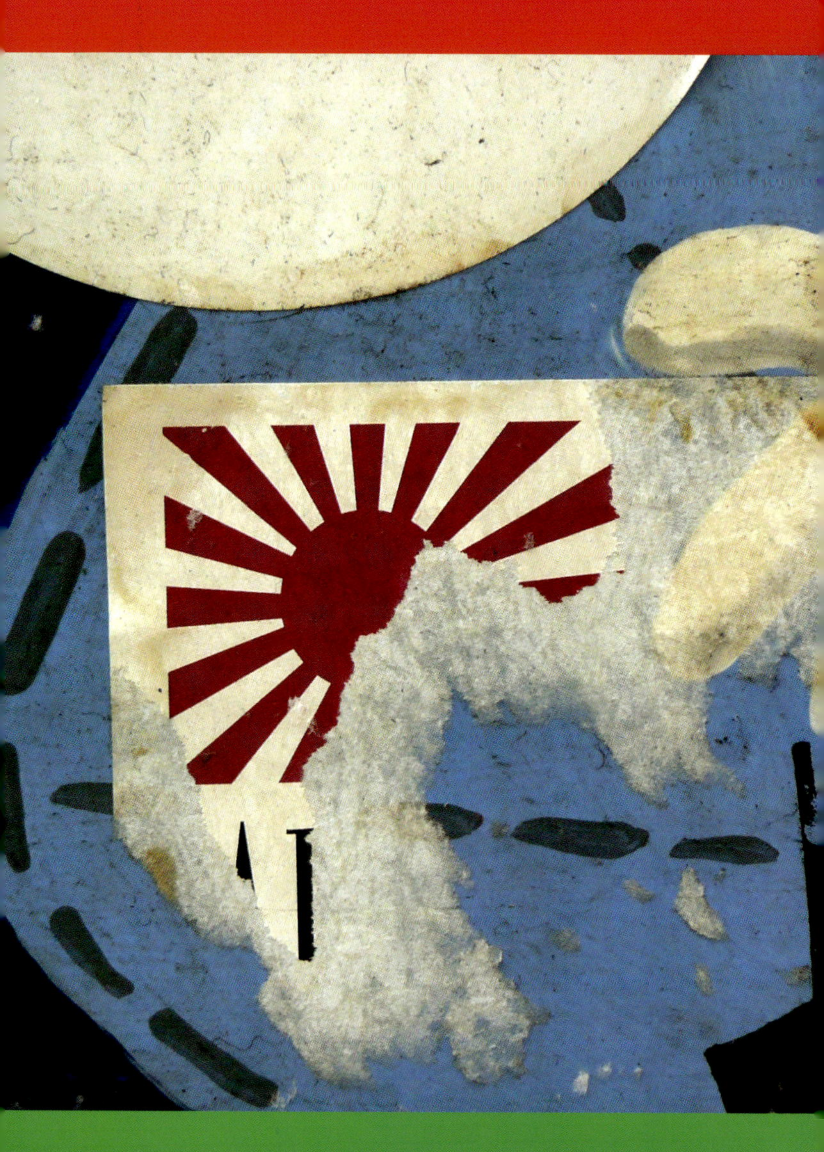

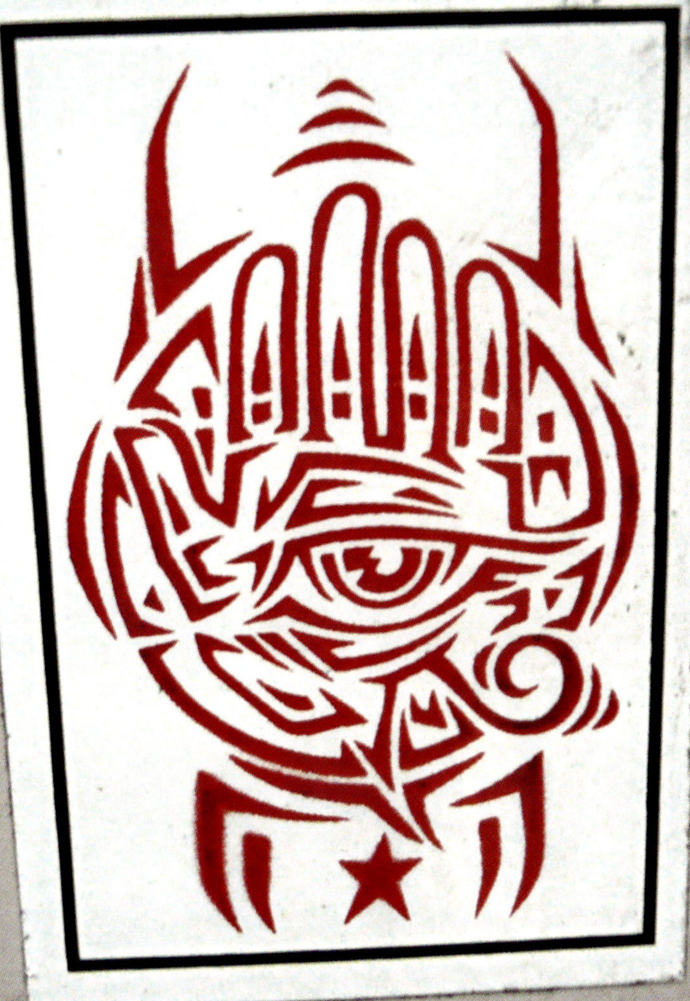

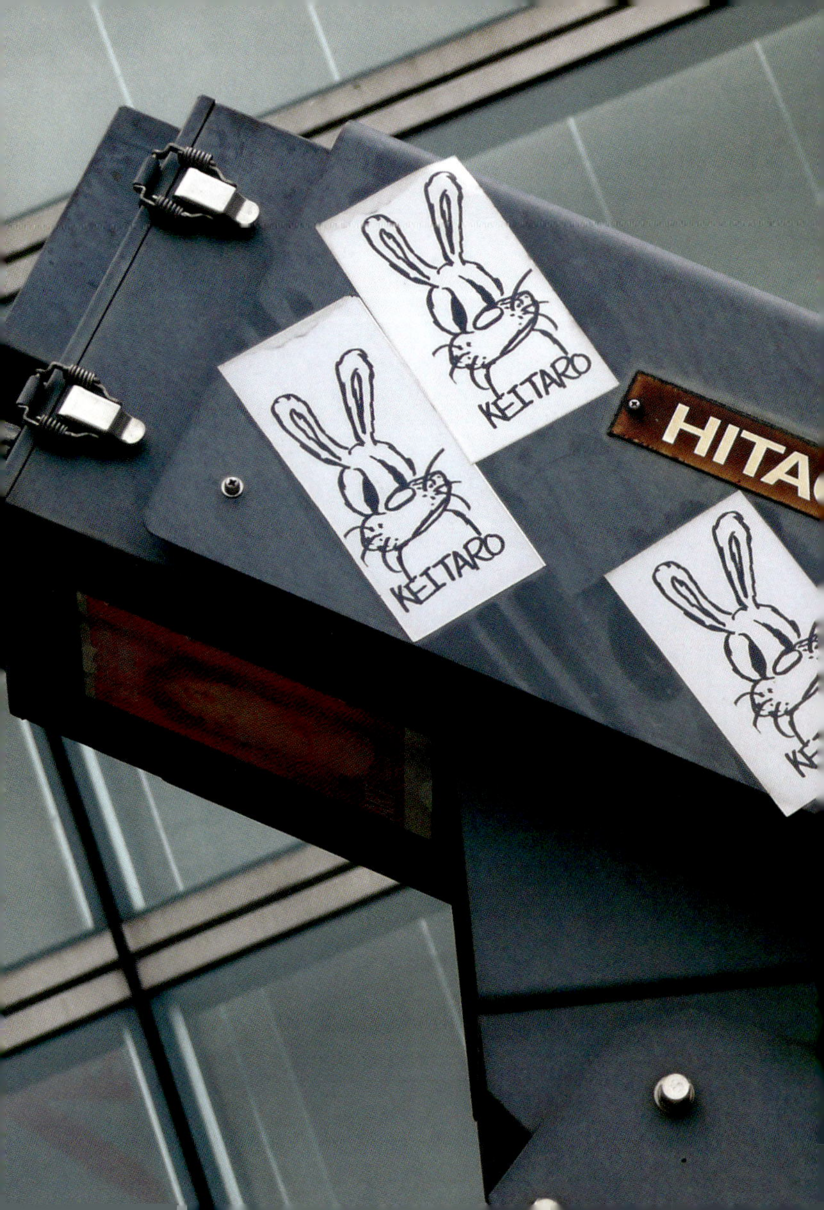
KEITARO
KEITARO

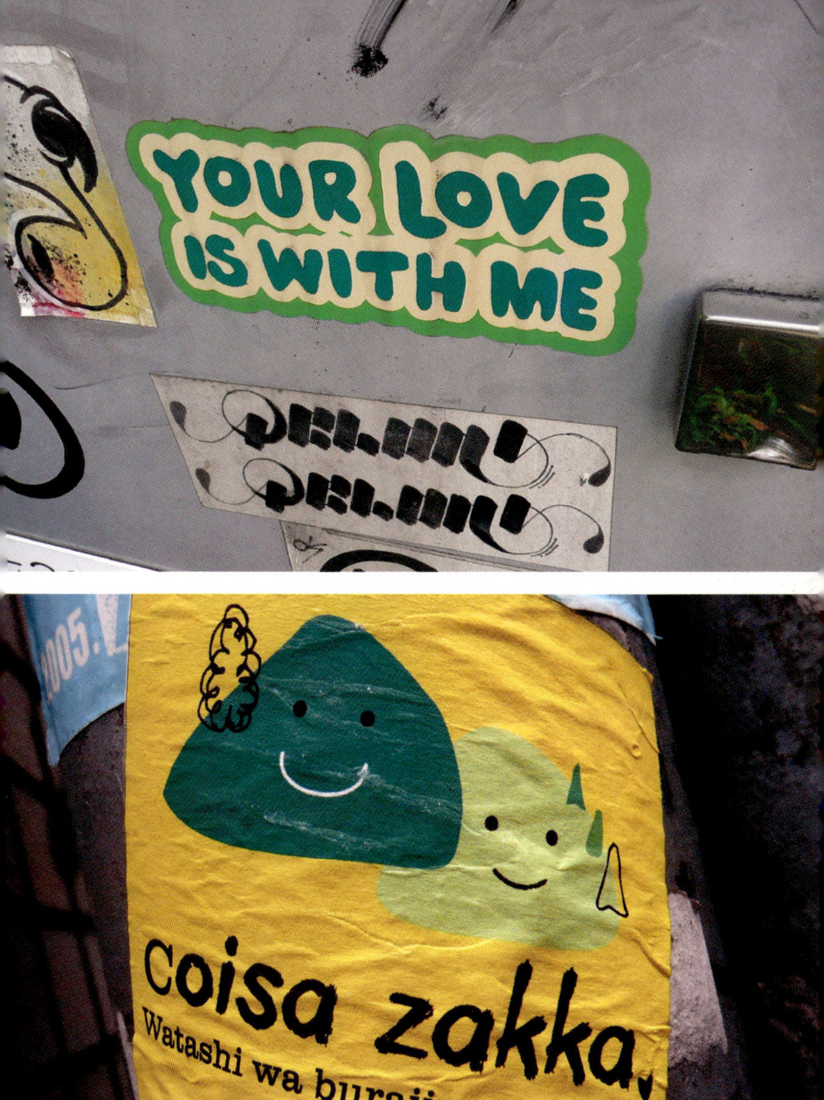
YOUR LOVE IS WITH ME
coisa zakka.
Watashi wa burajiru-jin desu!

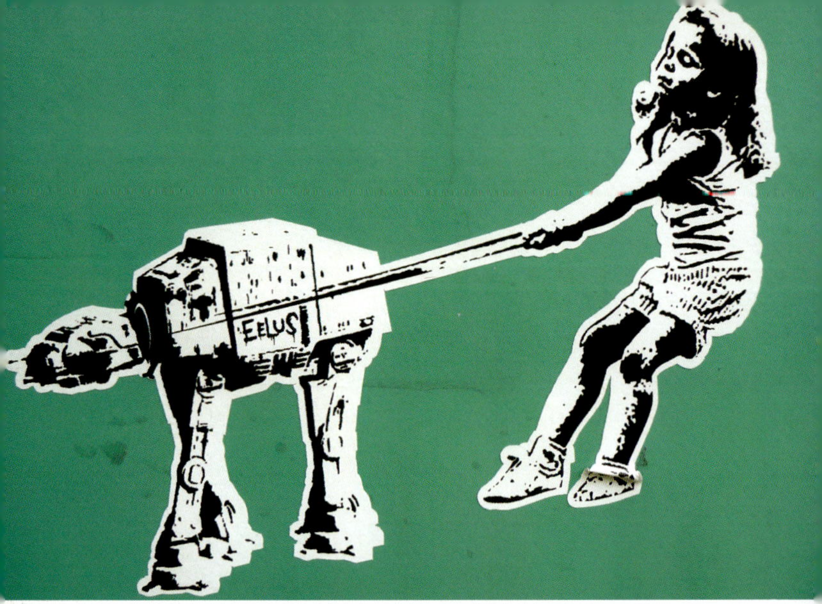

EELUS

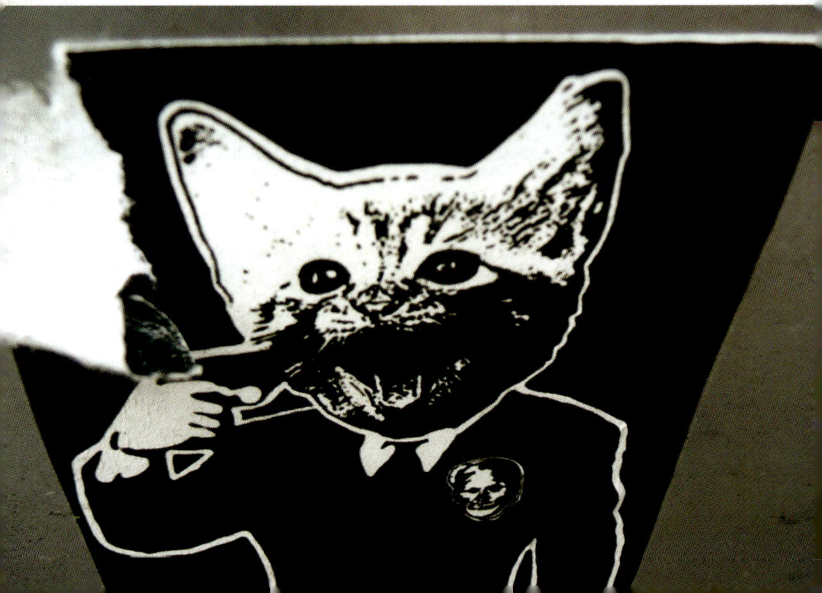

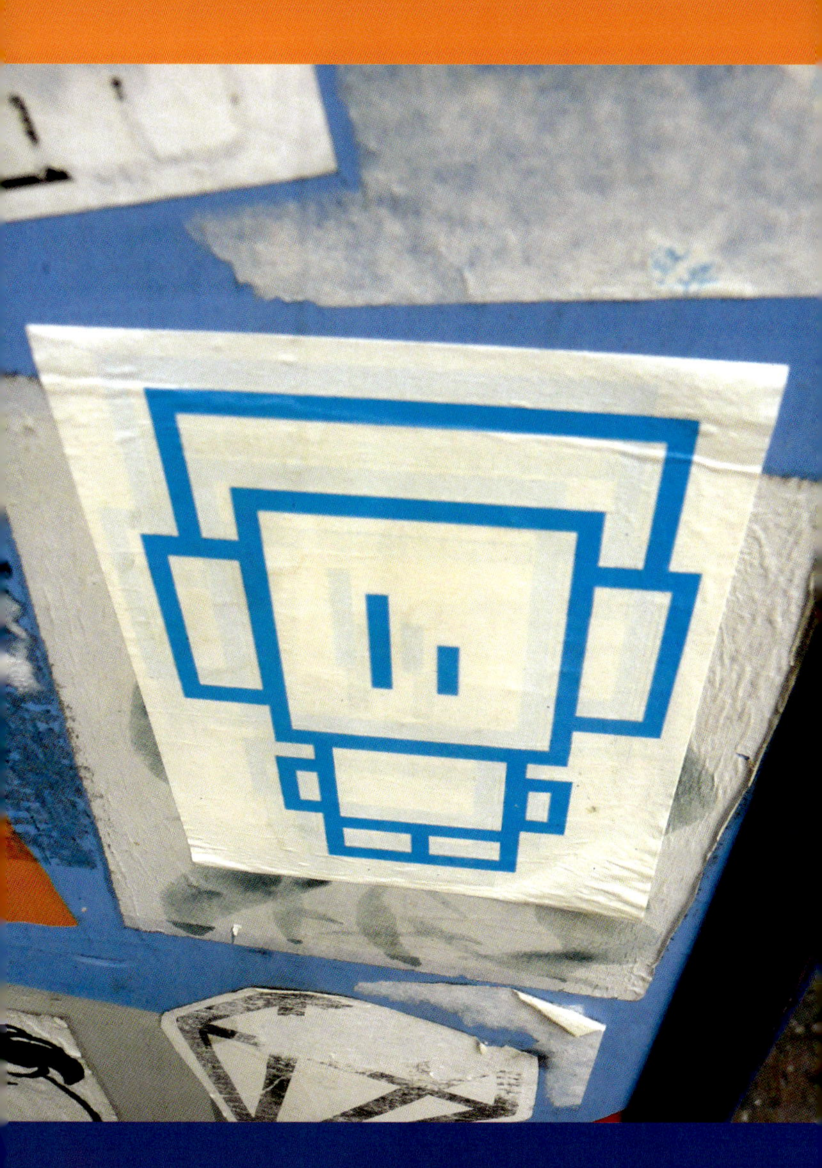

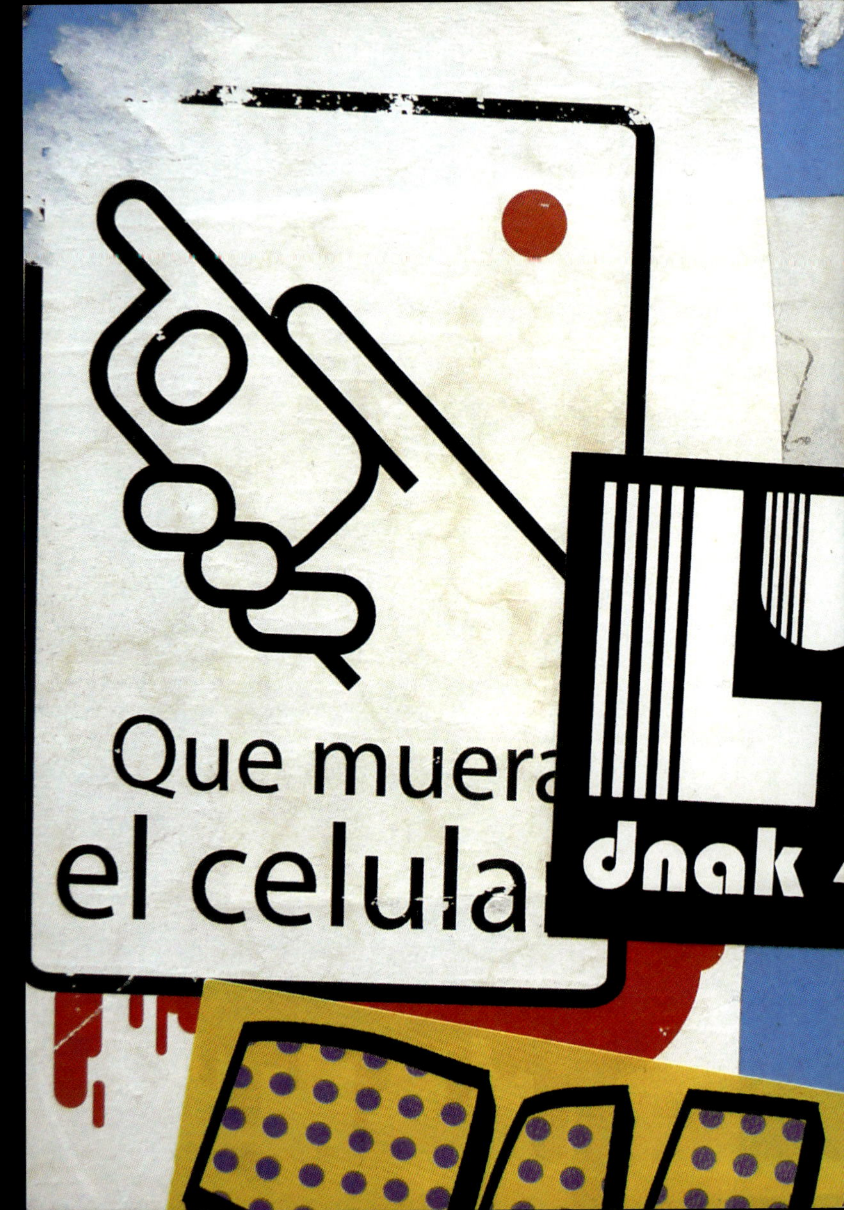
Que muera
el celular
dnak

BREATH
music phenomenon.
新宿リ

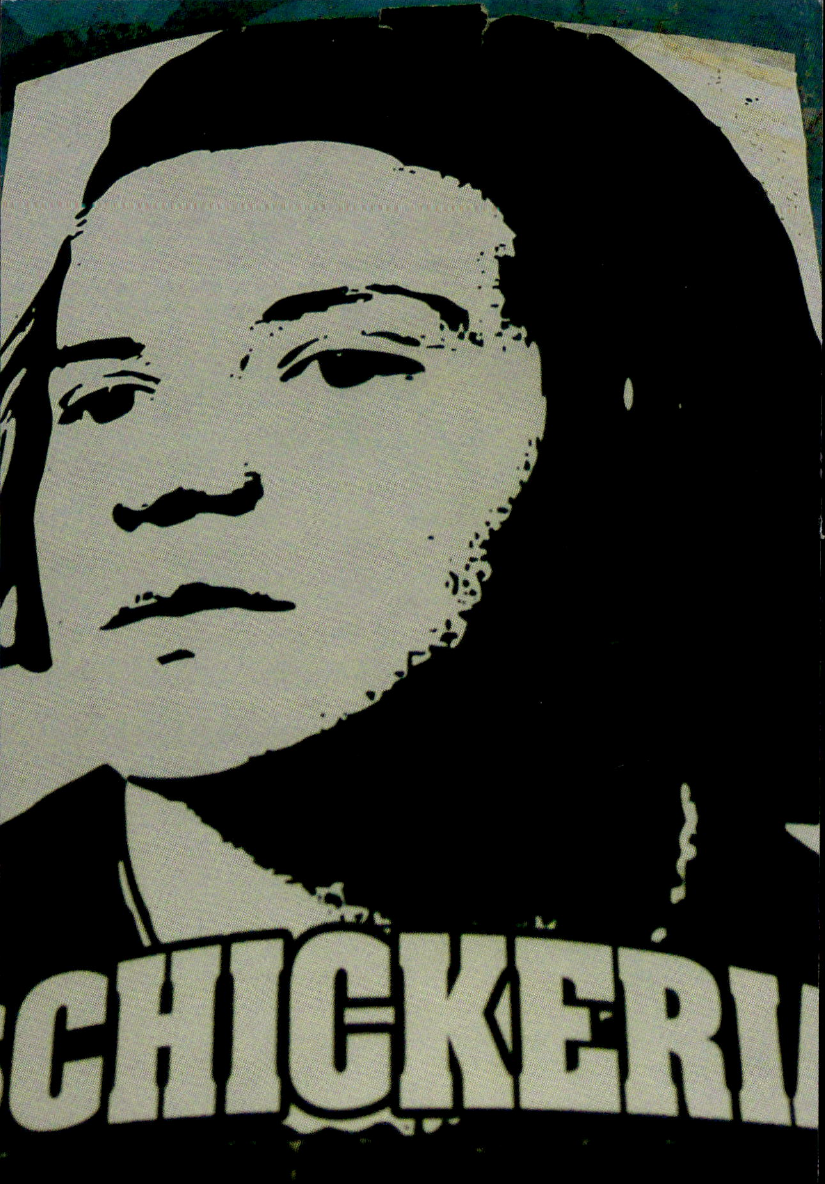
CHICKERI

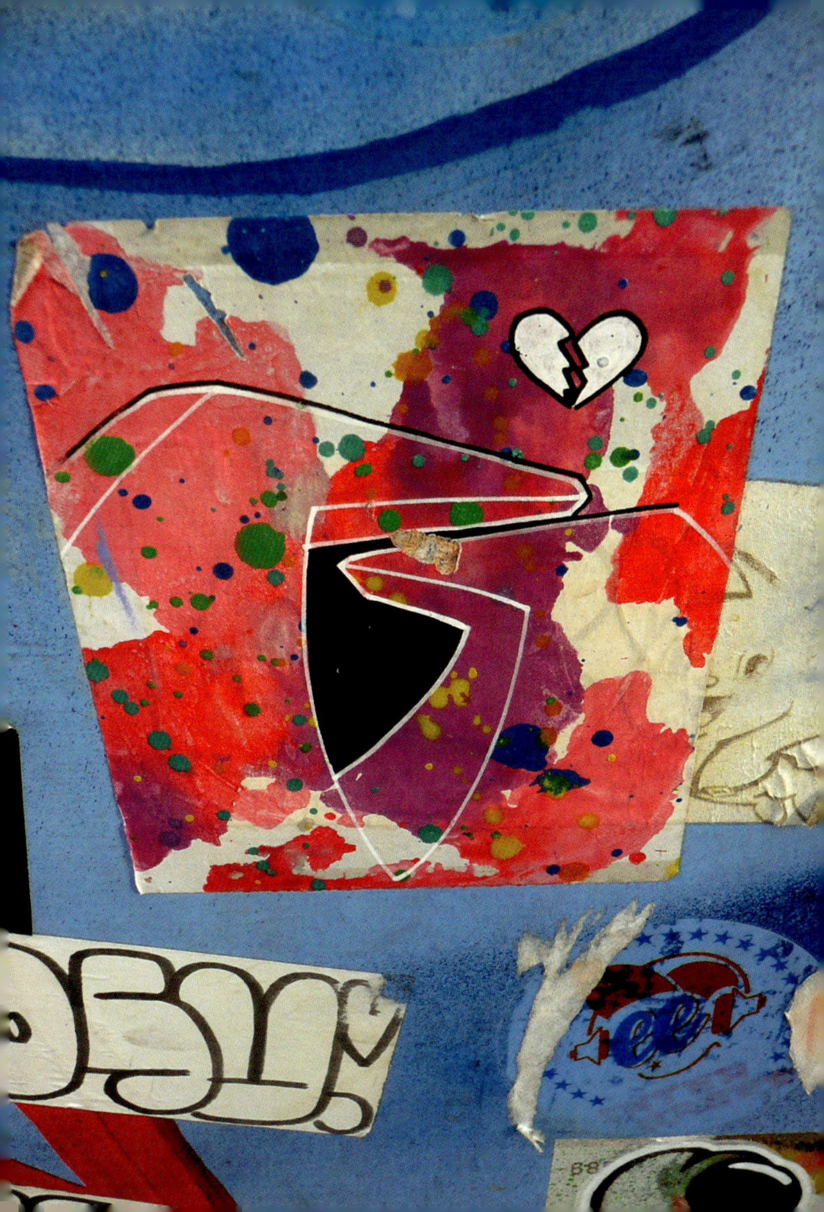

DUB
AINU

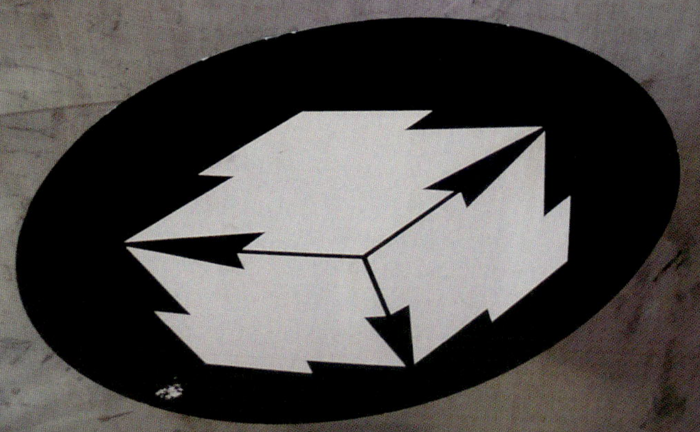

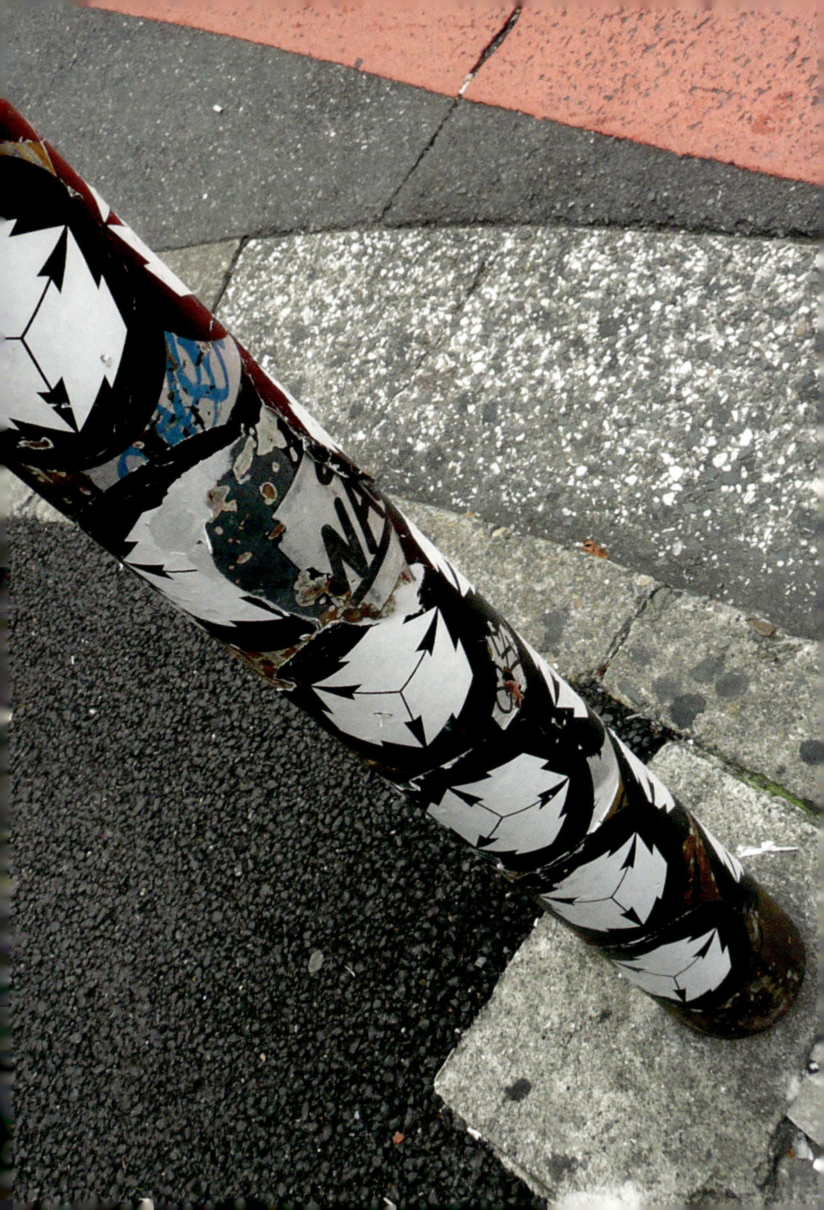

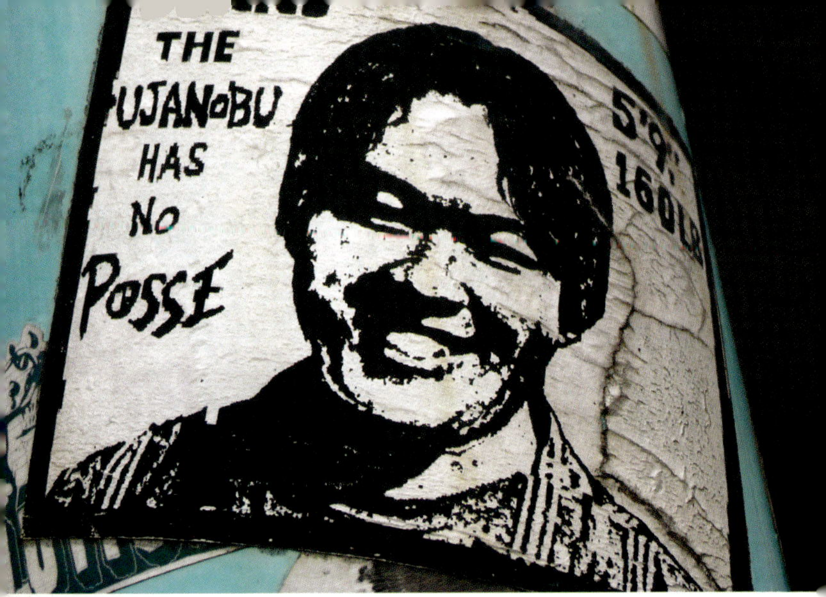

THE
UJANOBU
HAS
NO
POSSE
5'9"
160LB

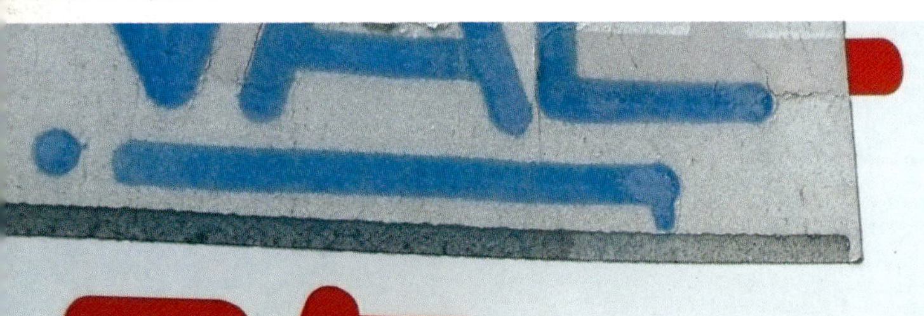

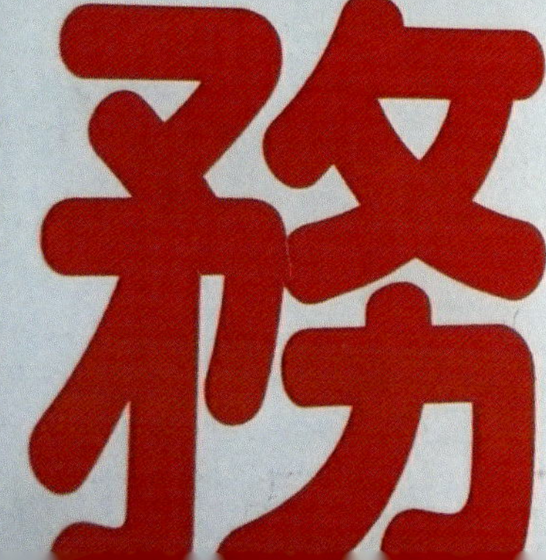

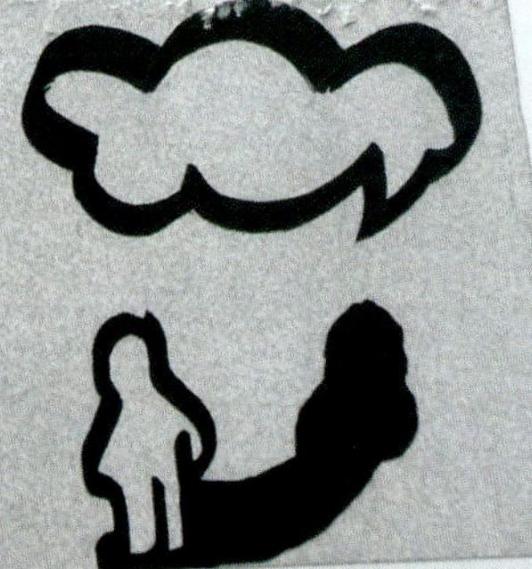

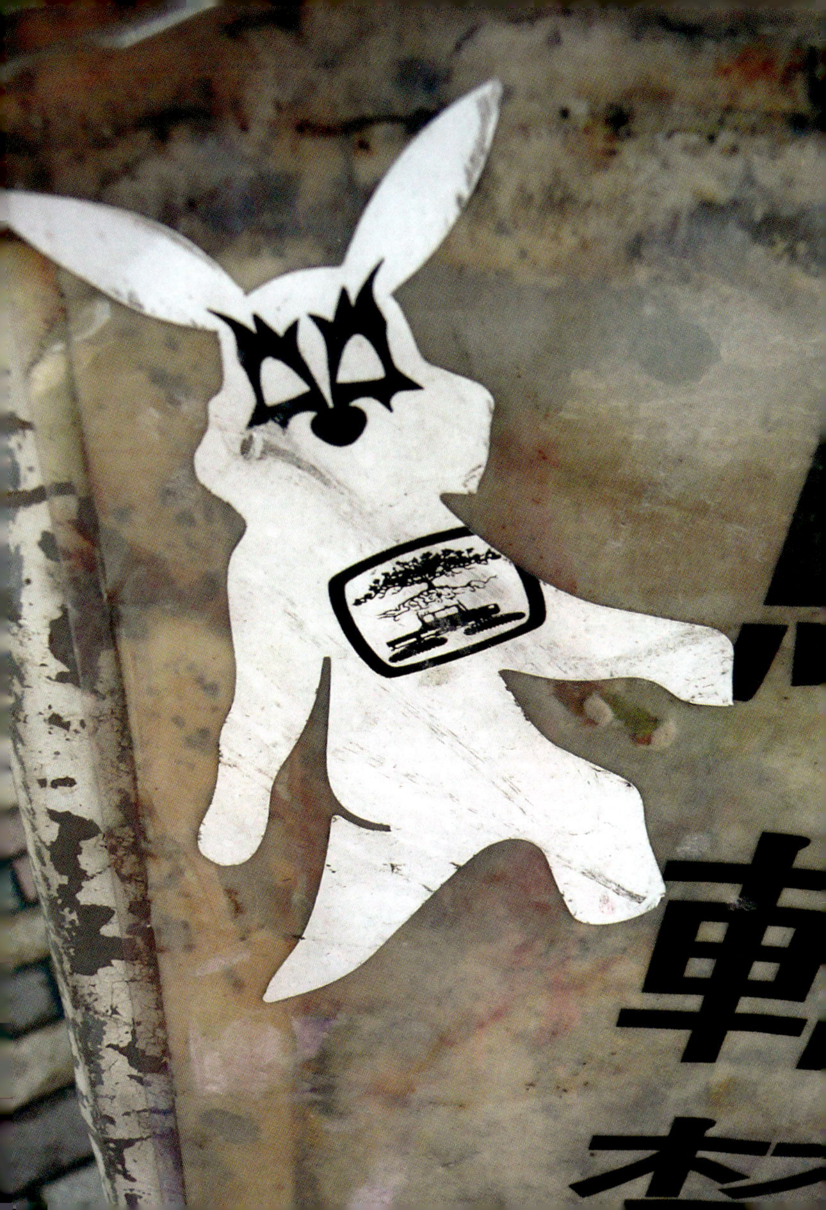

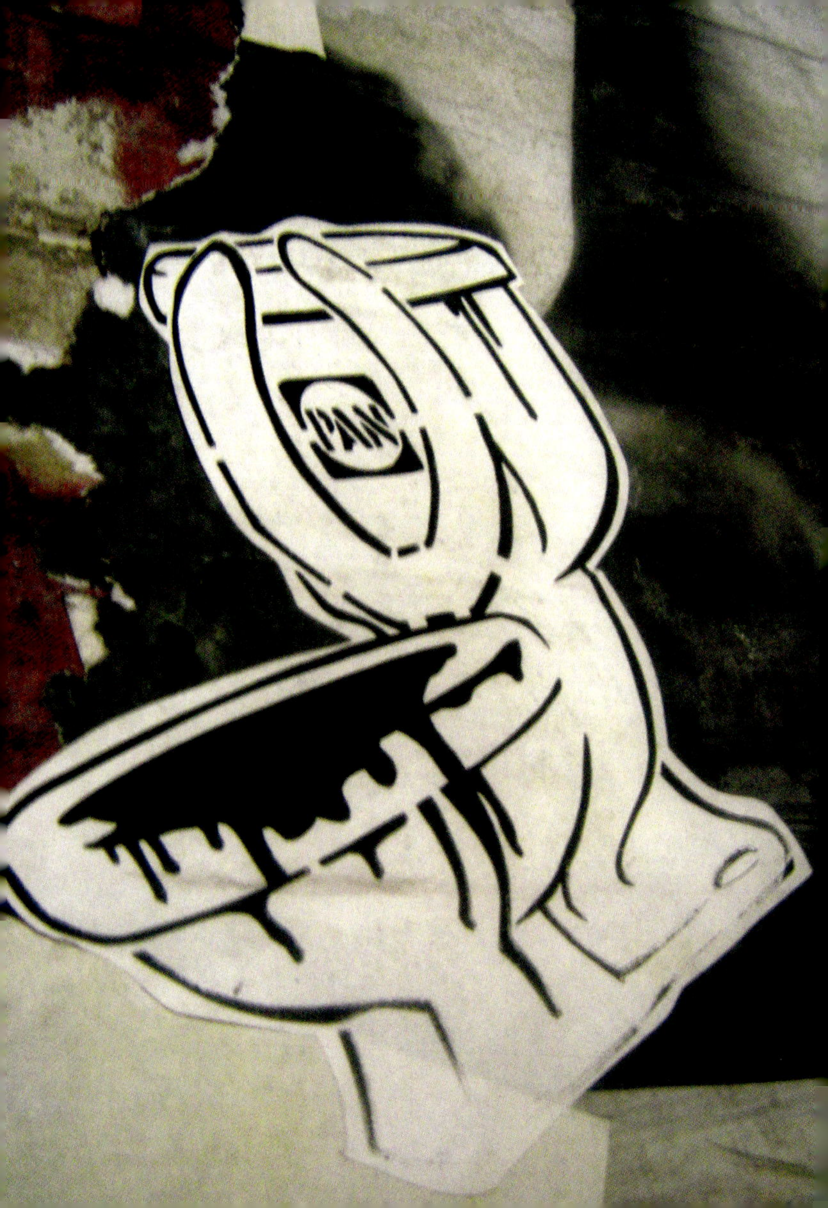
PAN

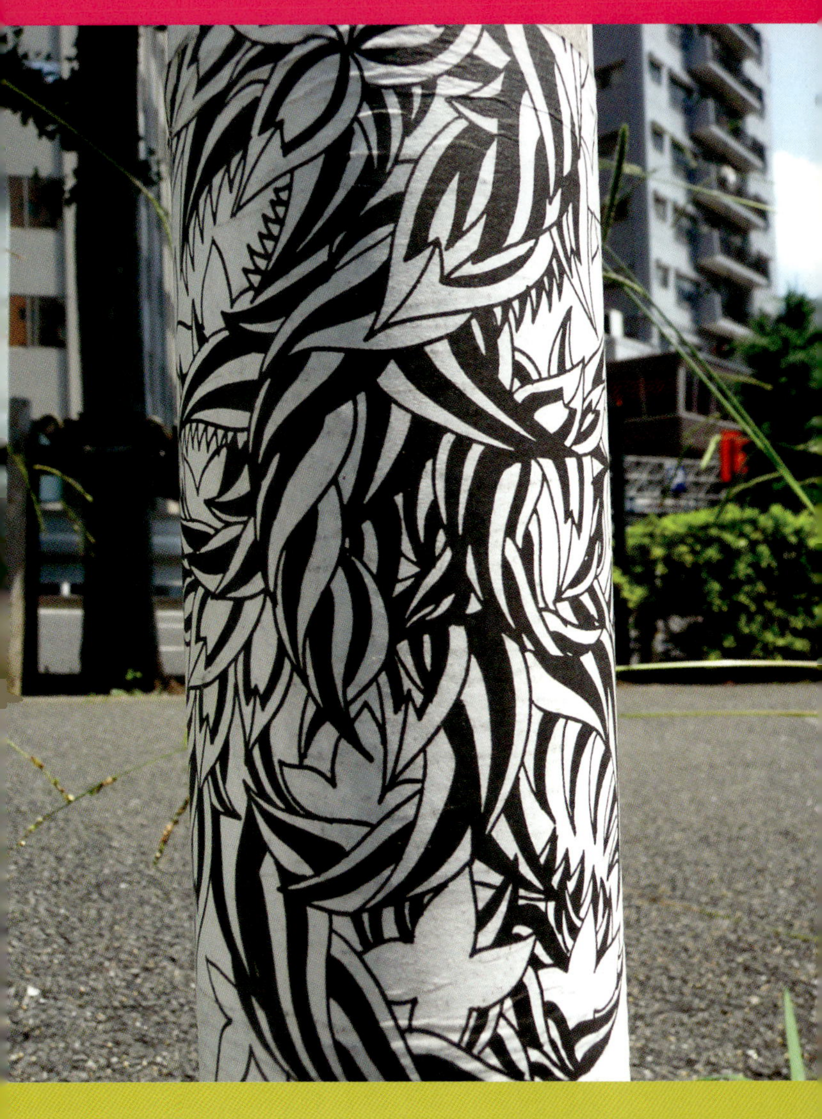

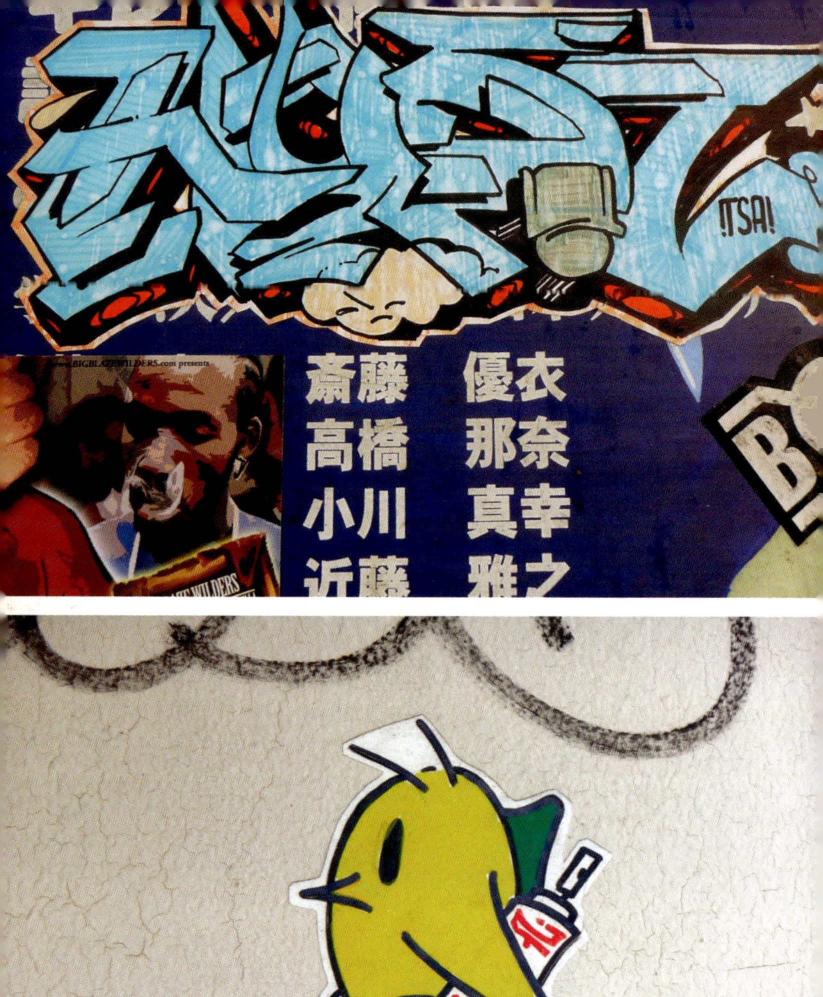
!TSA!
www.BIGBLAZEWILDERS.com presents
斎藤　優衣
高橋　那奈
小川　真幸
近藤　雅之

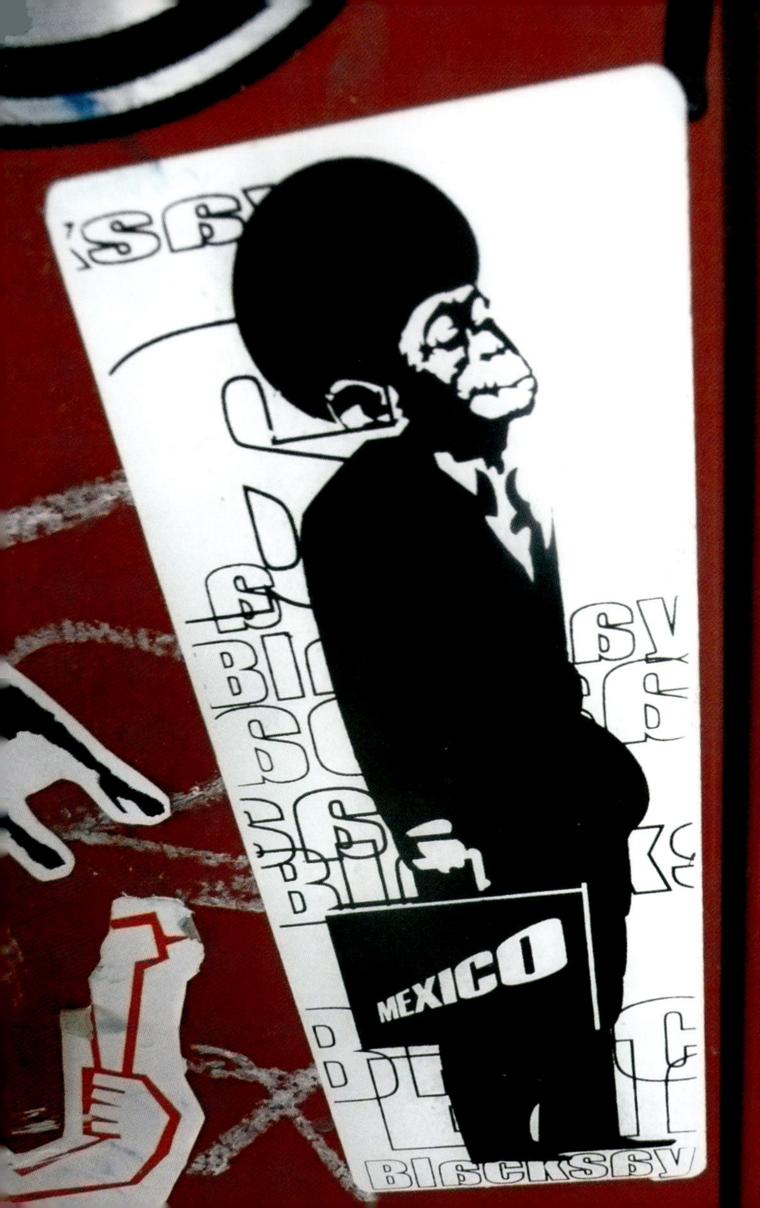
MEXICO

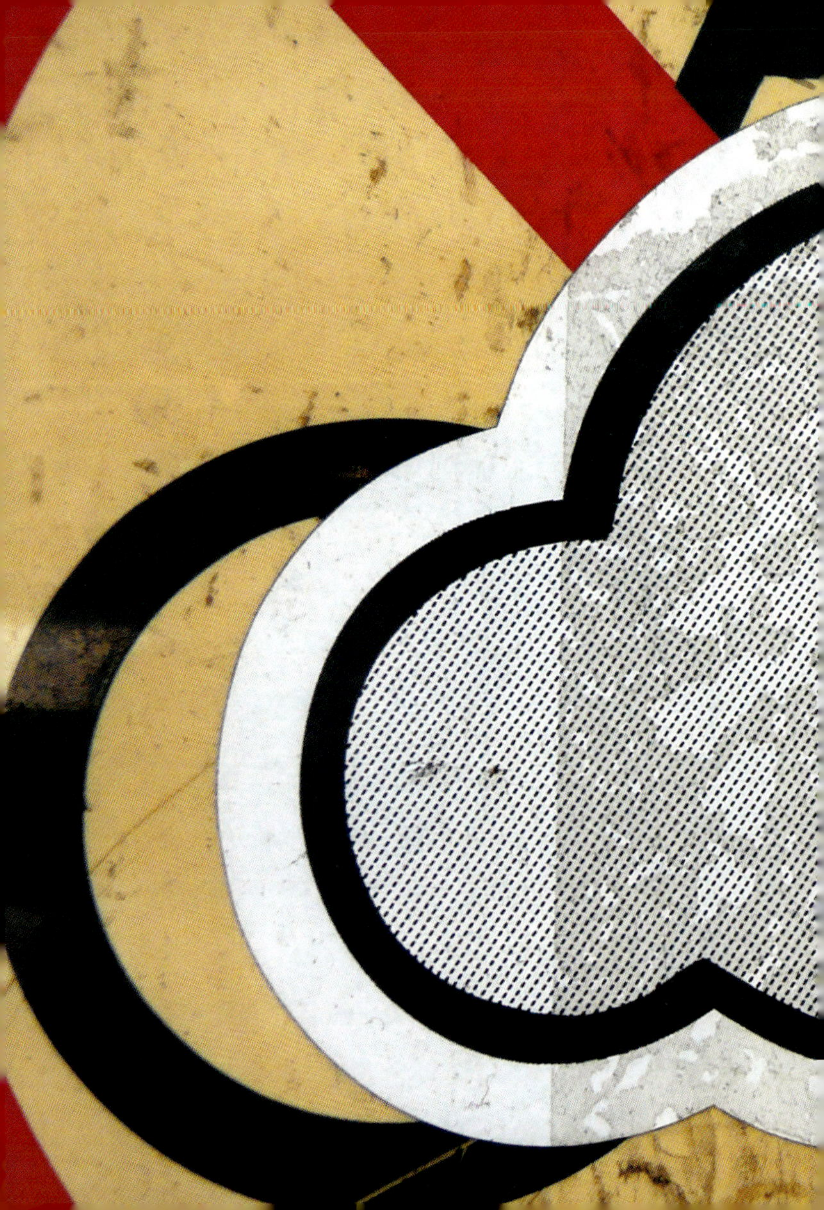

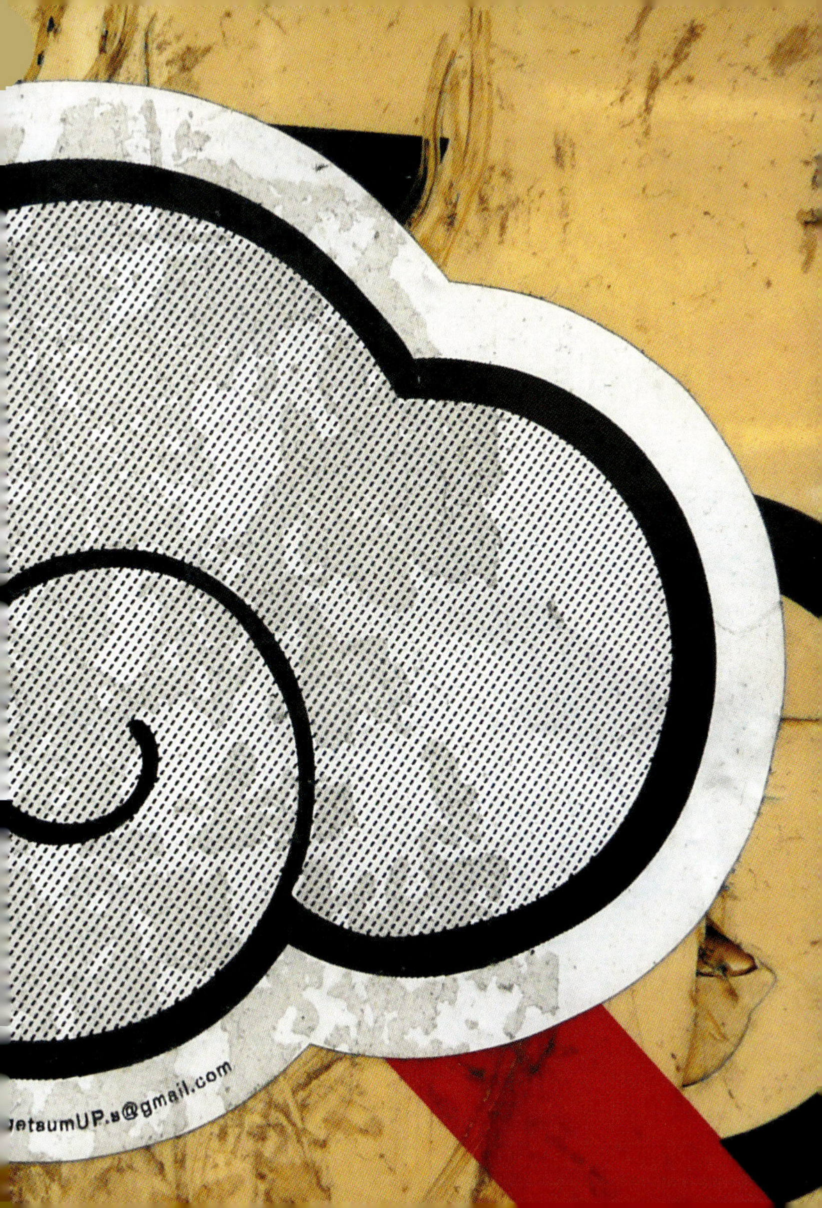
etsumUP.s@gmail.com

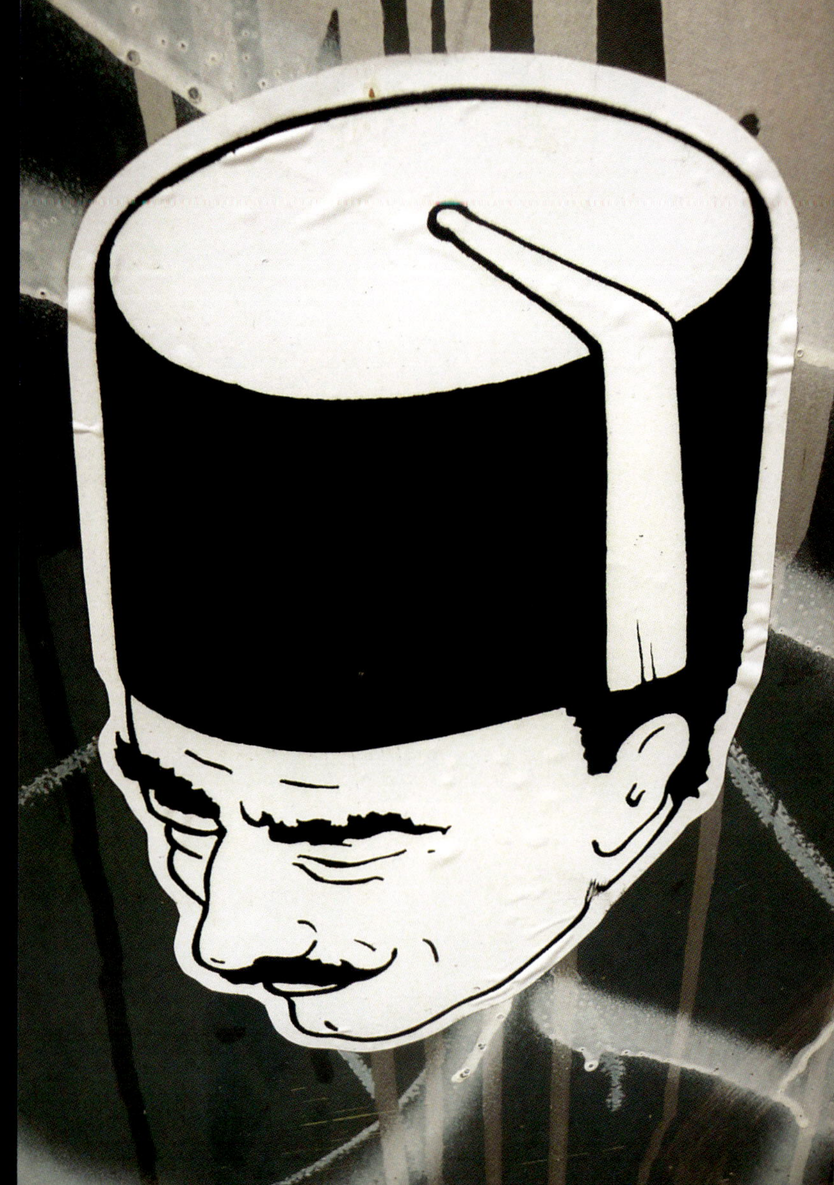

¥TWOS

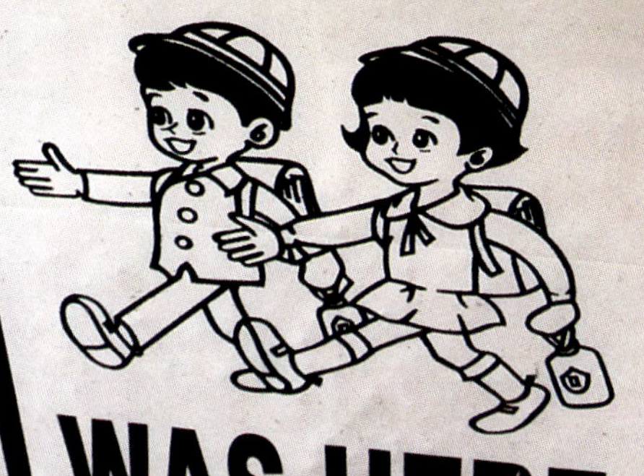

WAS HERE

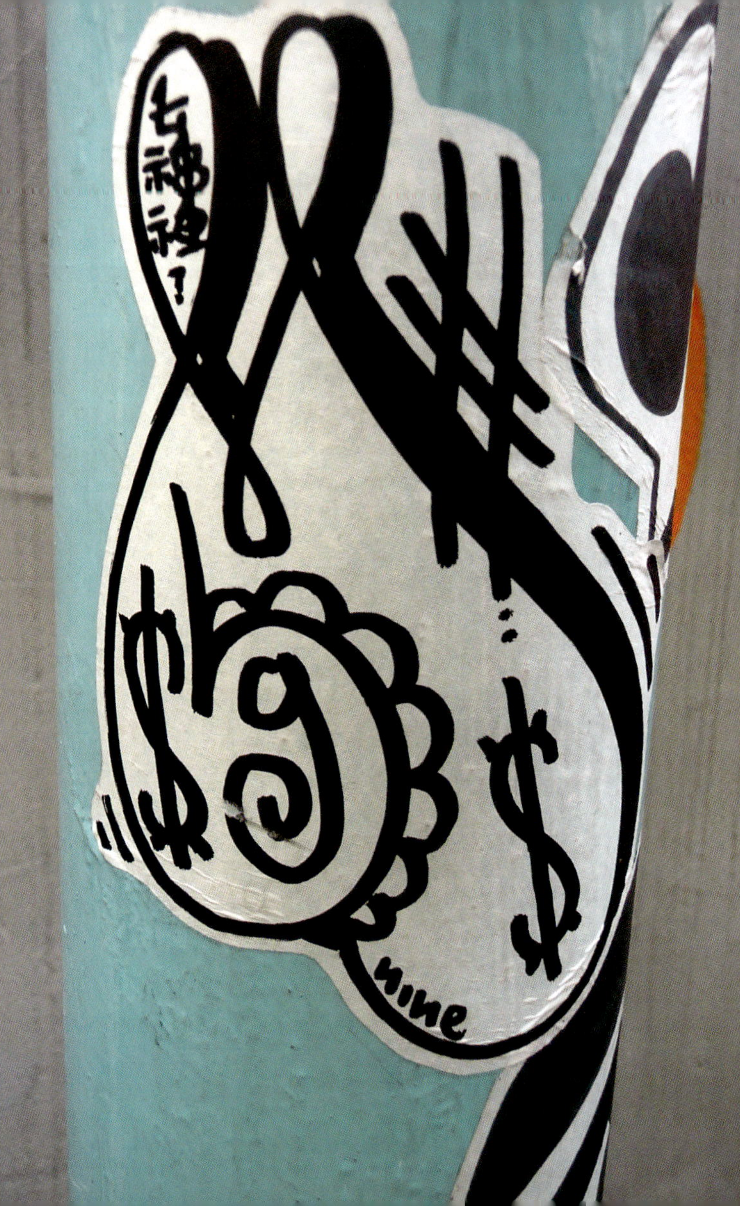
9
nine

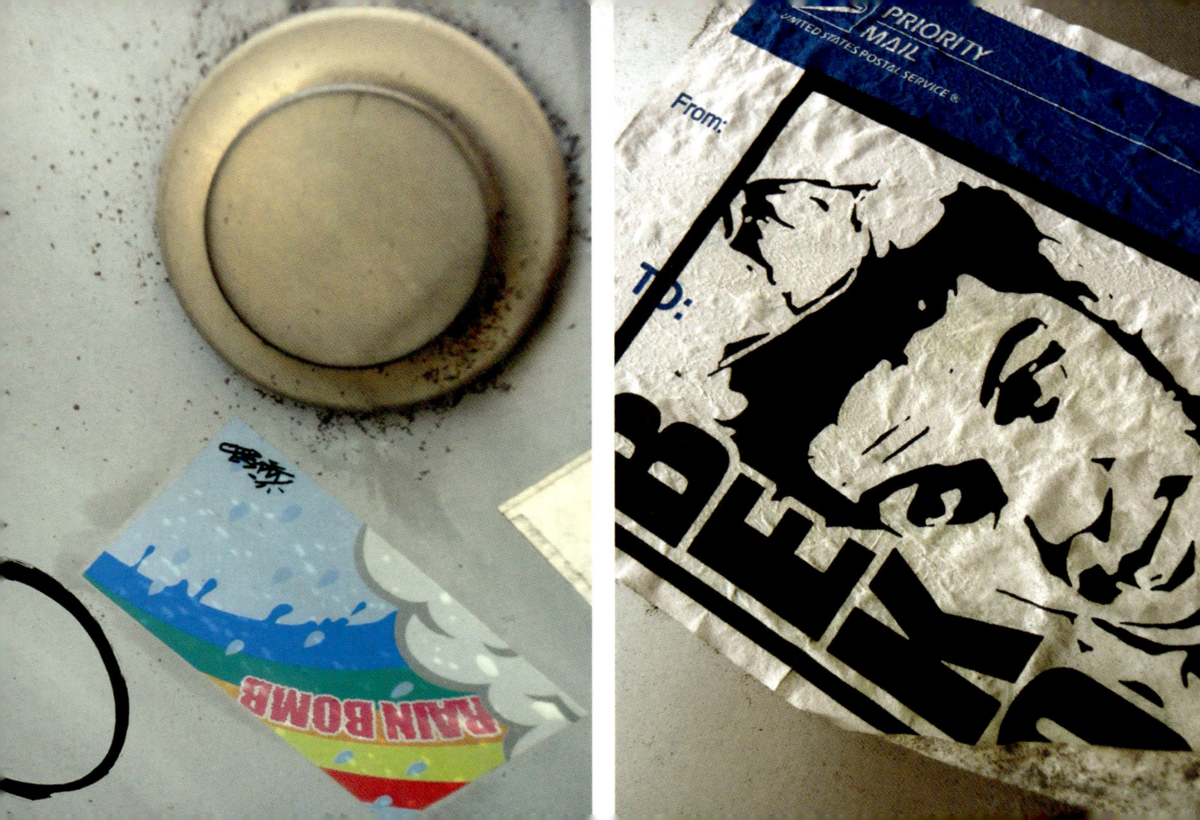
RAIN BOMB
PRIORITY
MAIL
UNITED STATES POSTAL SERVICE ®
From:
TO:

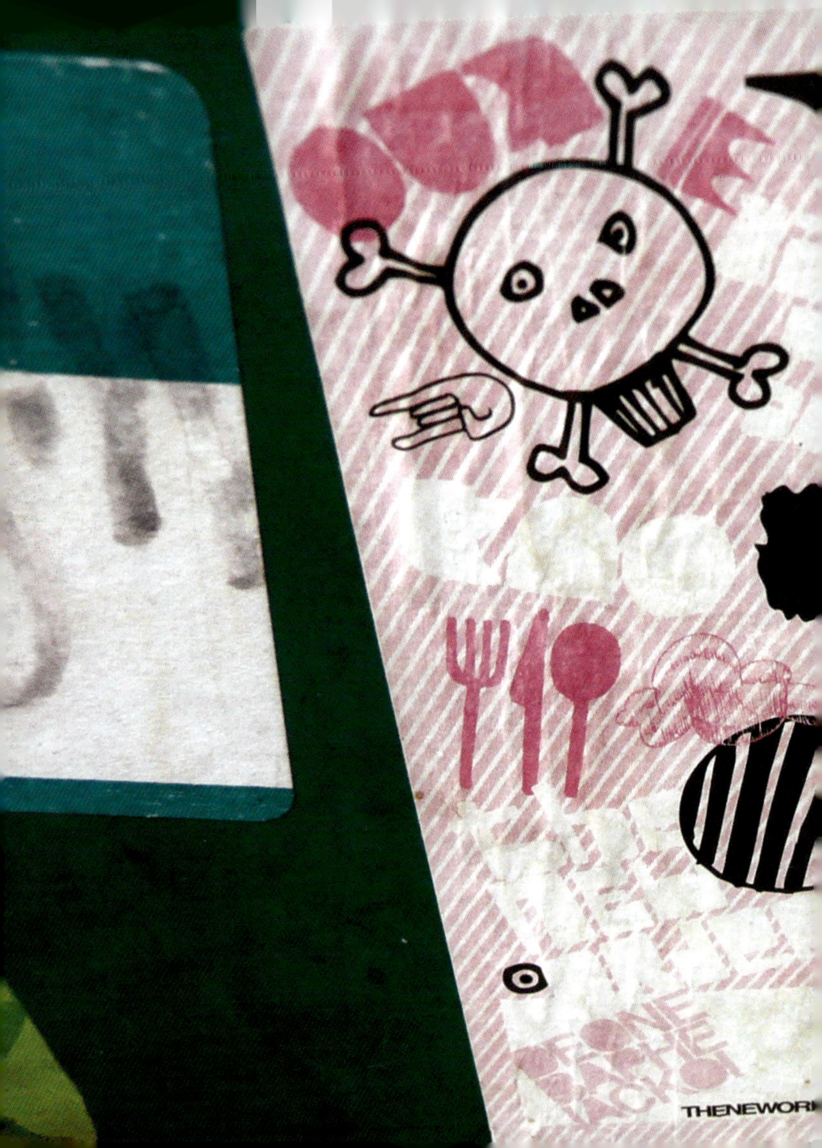
THENEWORK

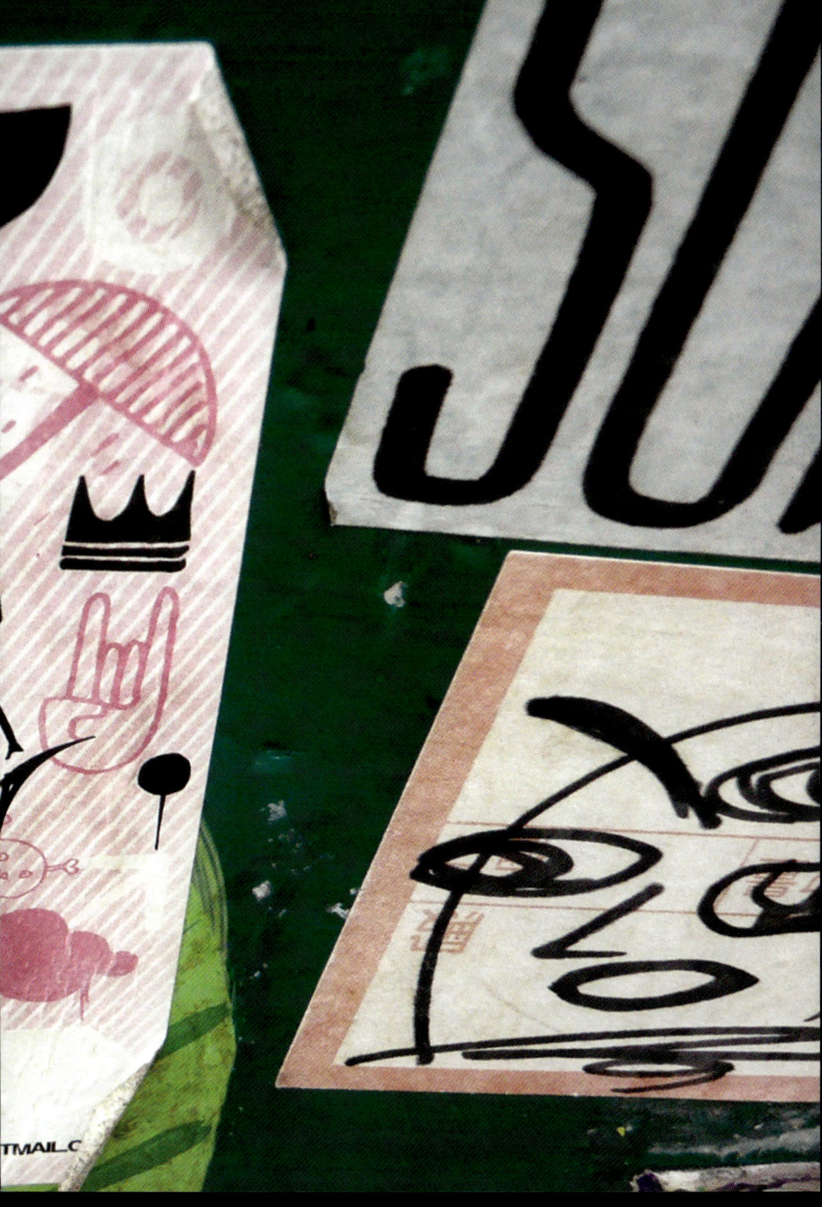
TMAIL.C

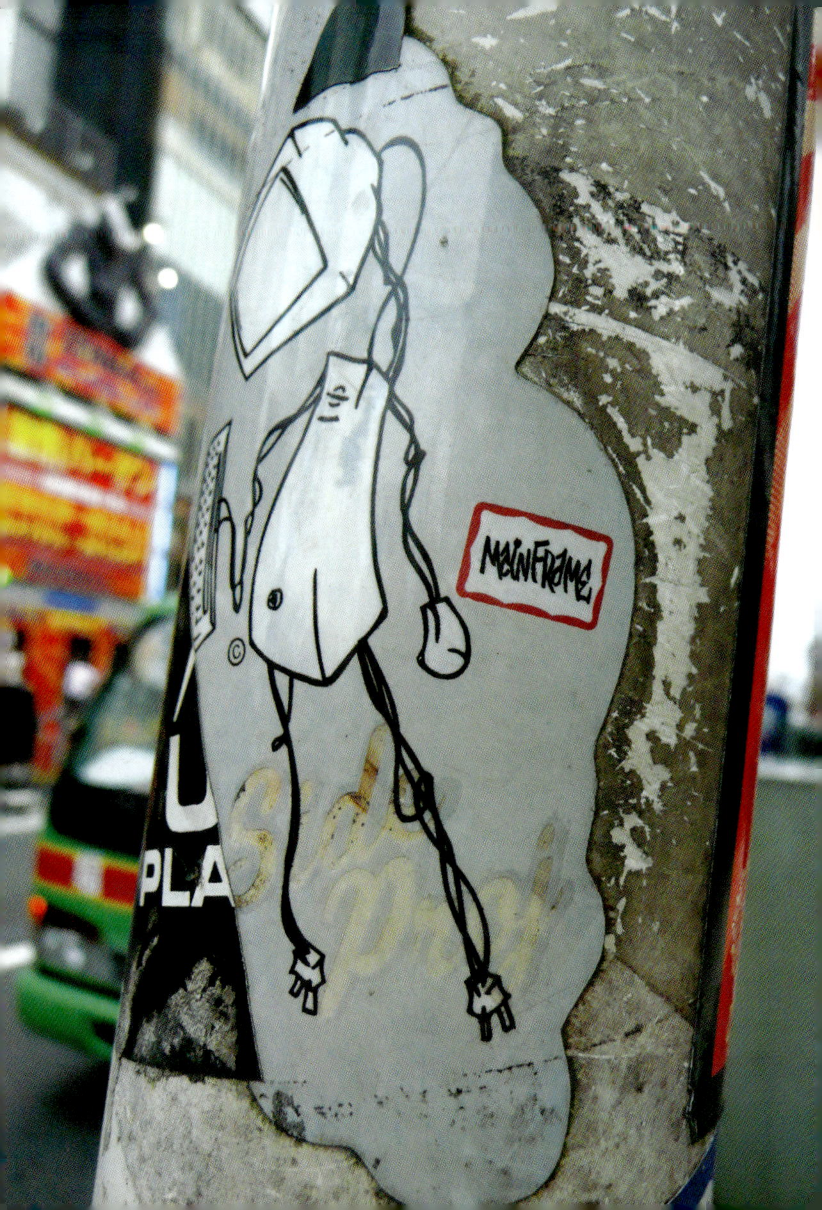
MAINFRAME
©
PLA

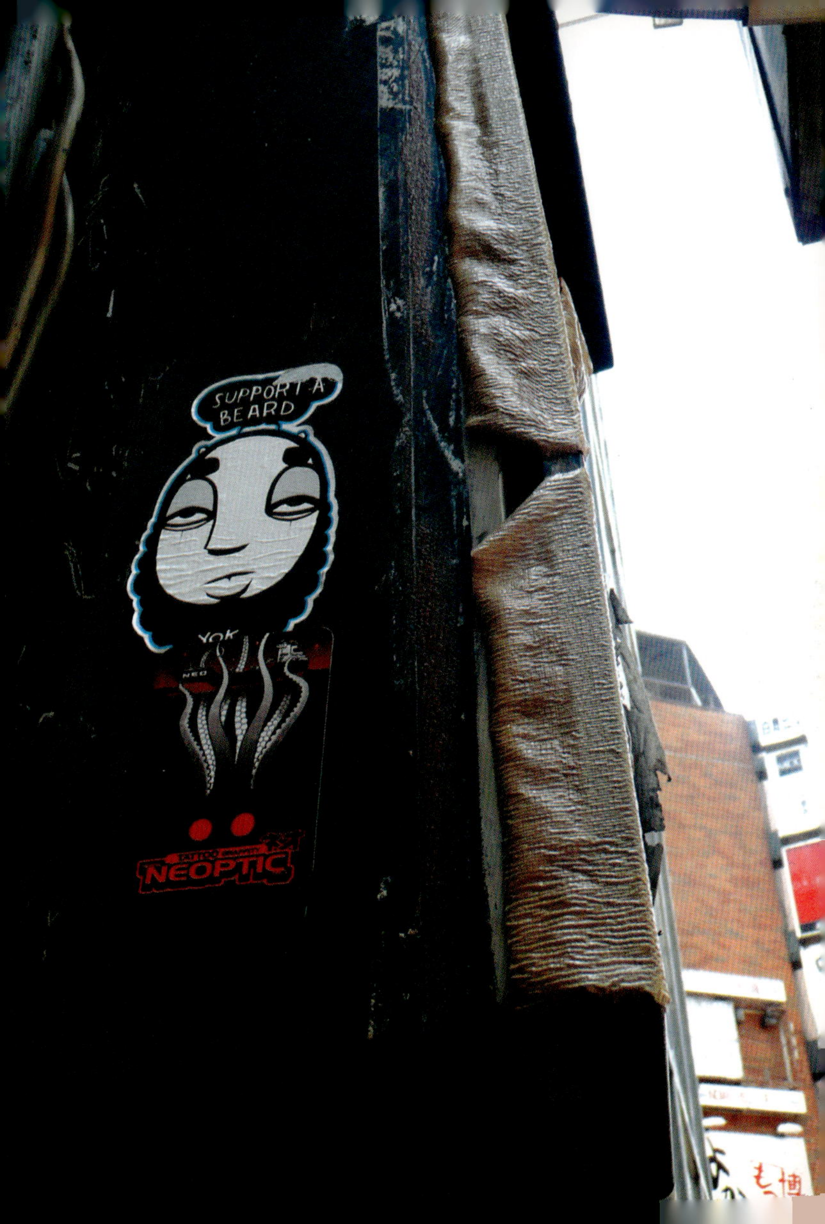
SUPPORT A BEARD
YOK
NEOPTIC

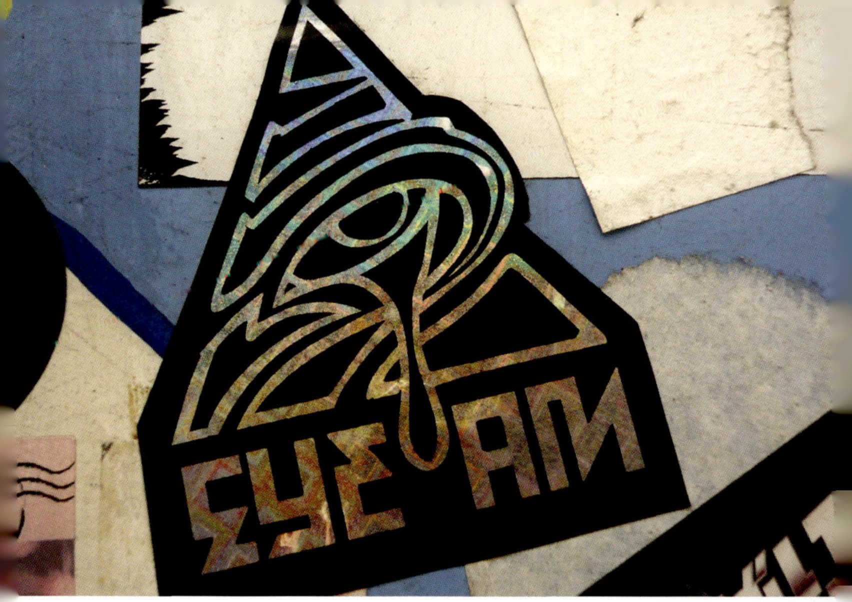

EYE AM
Z5.14.

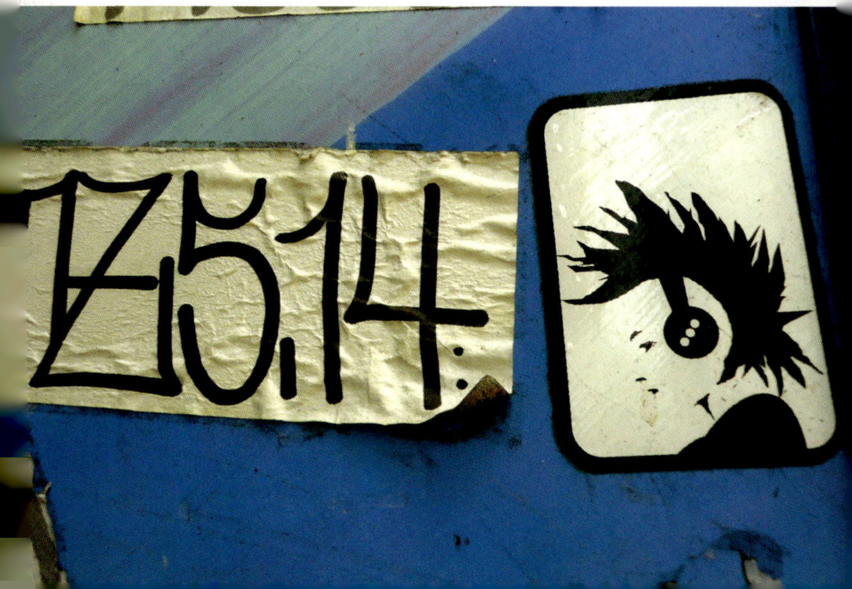

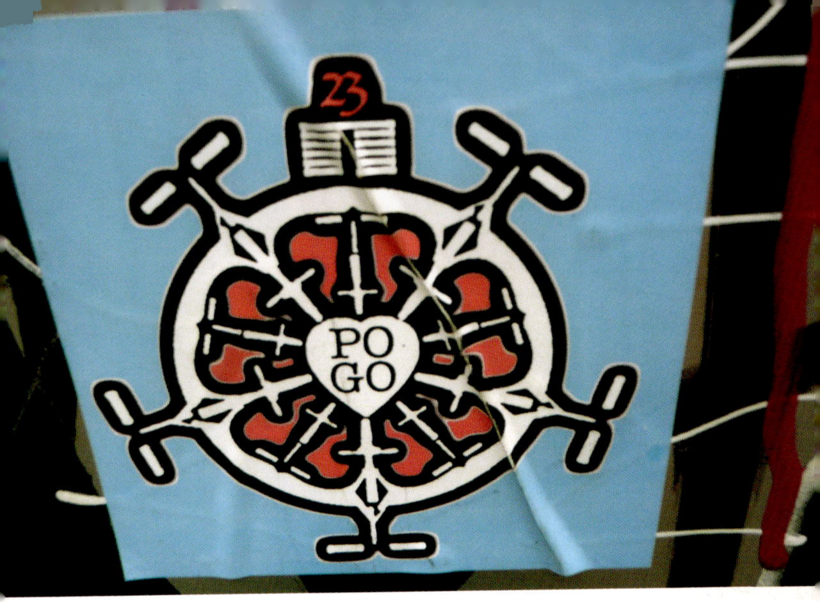

23

PO
GO

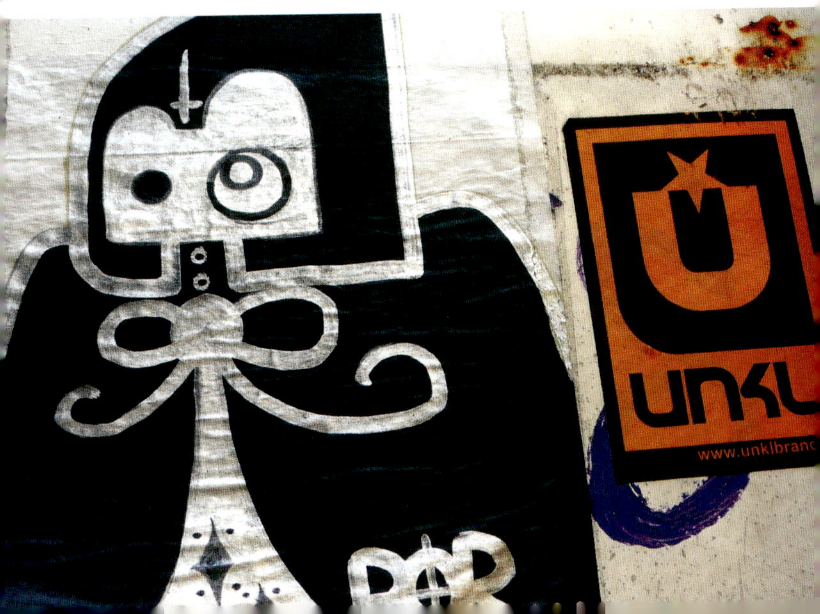

UNKL

www.unklbranc

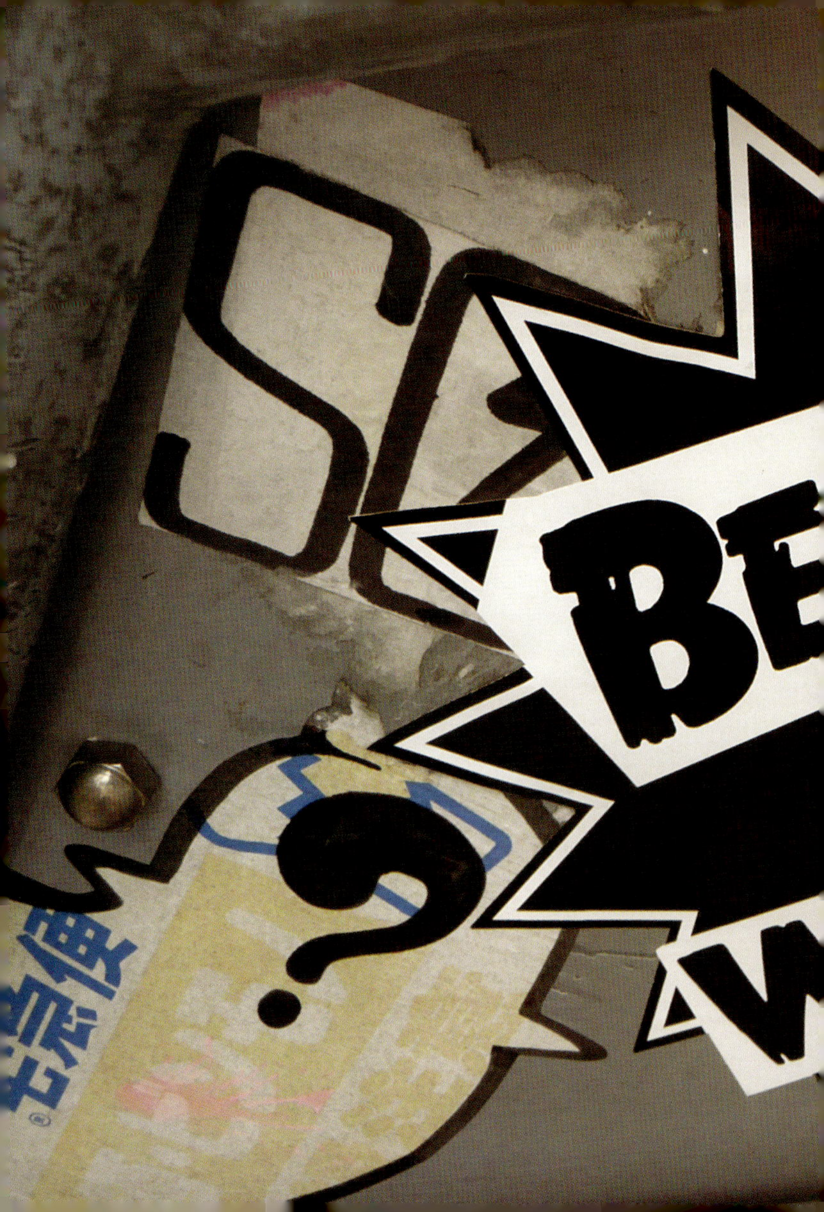

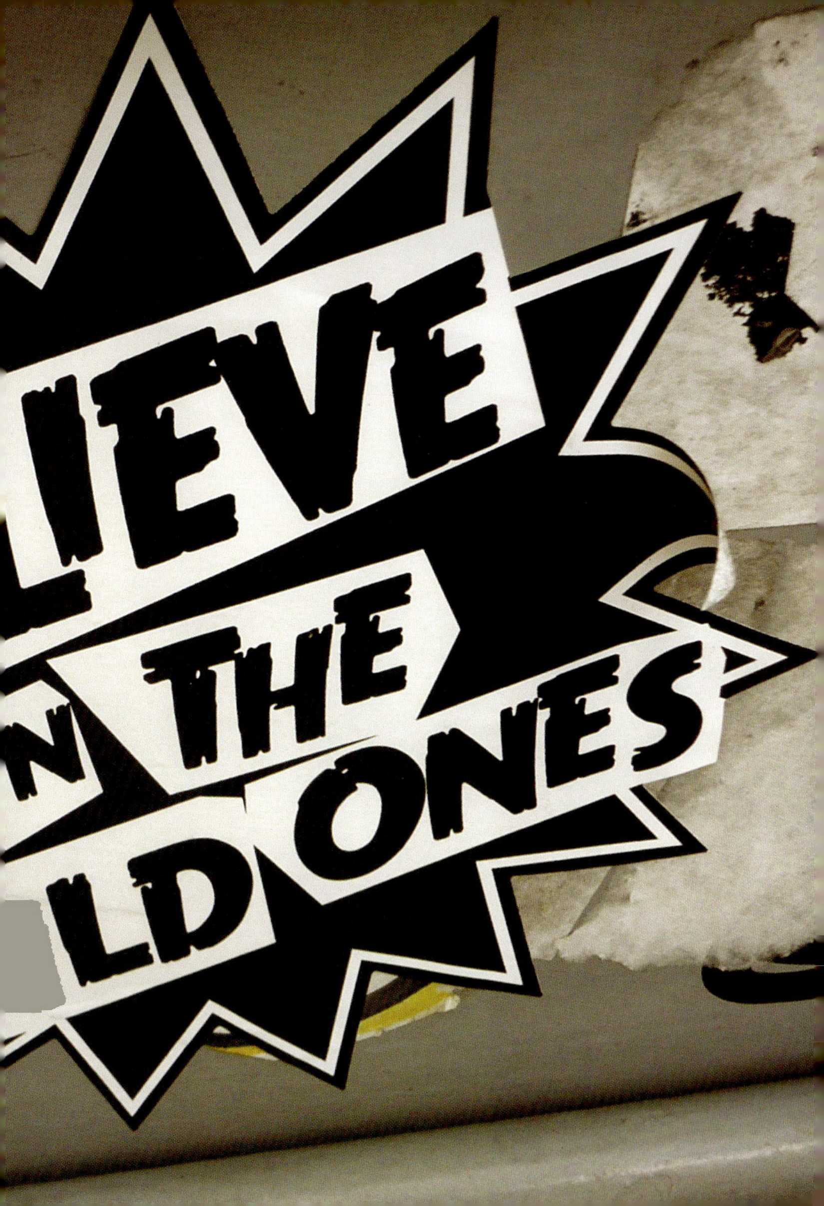
LIEVE
N THE
LD ONES

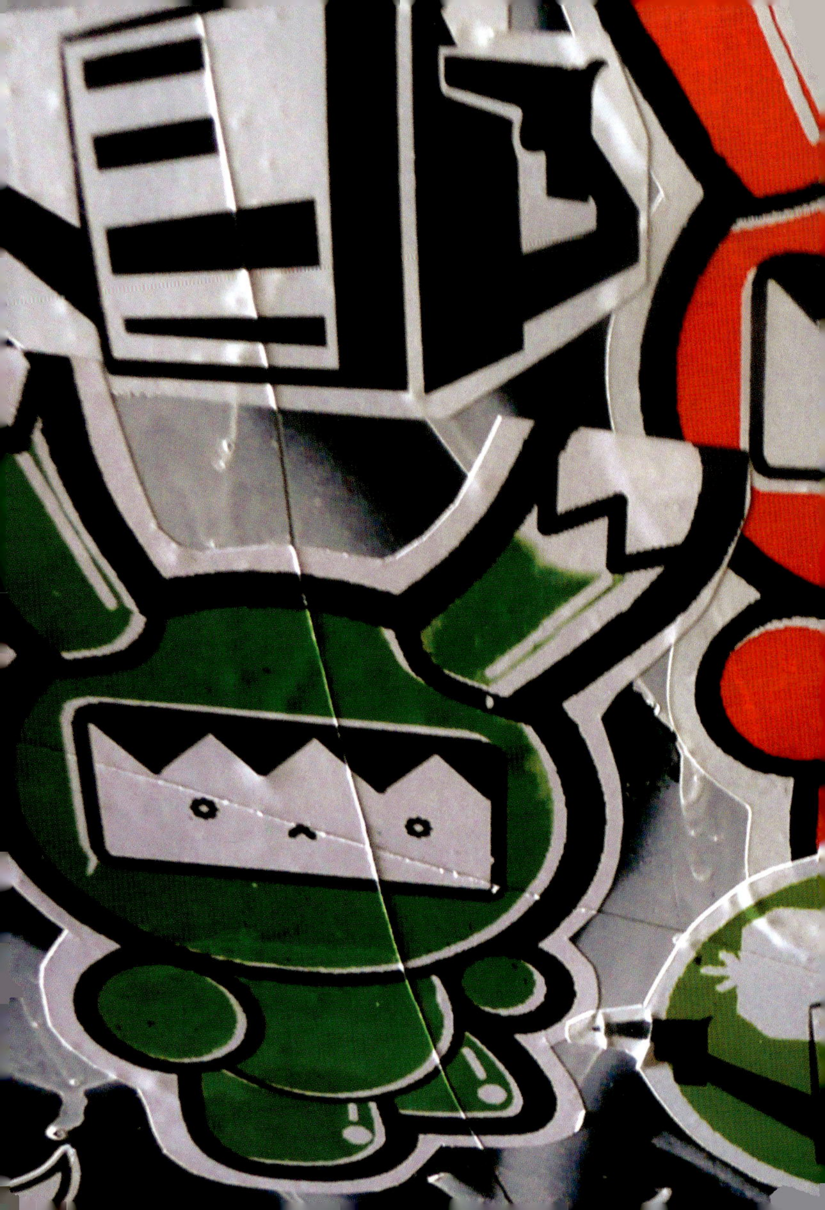

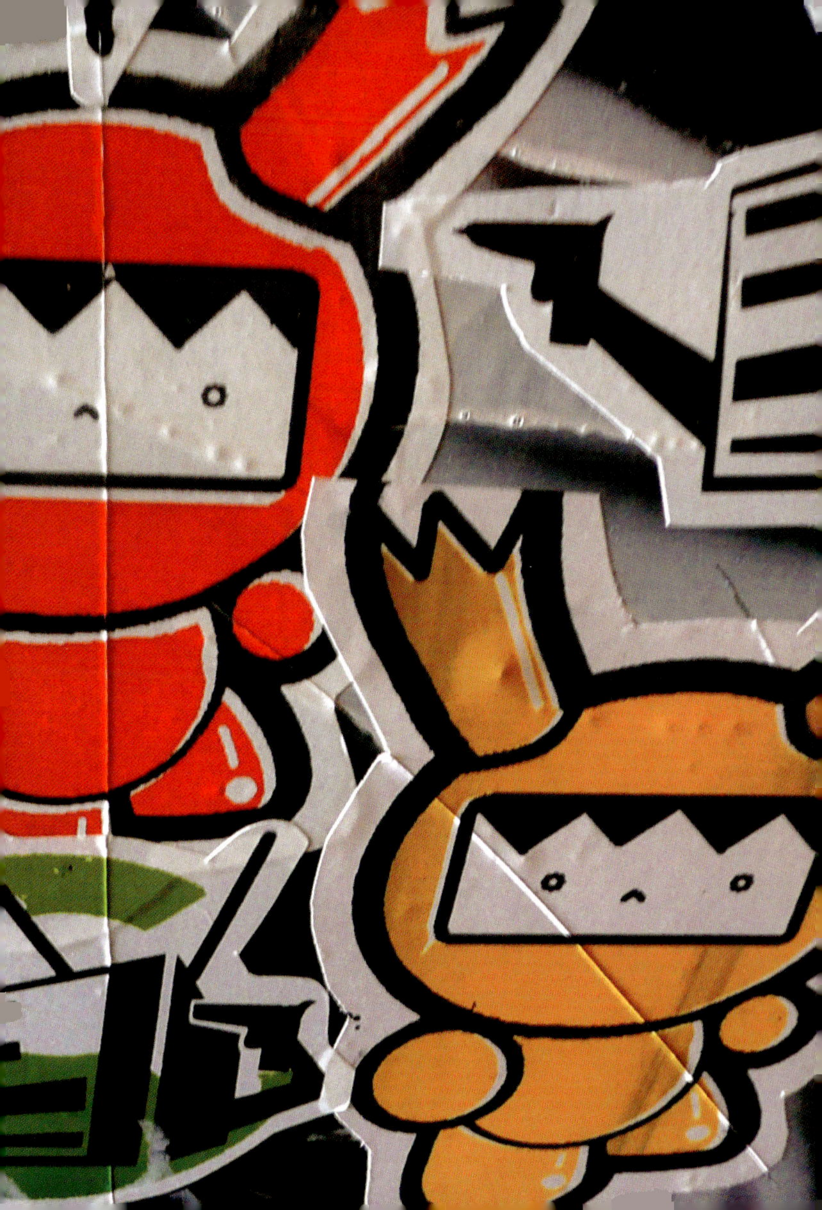

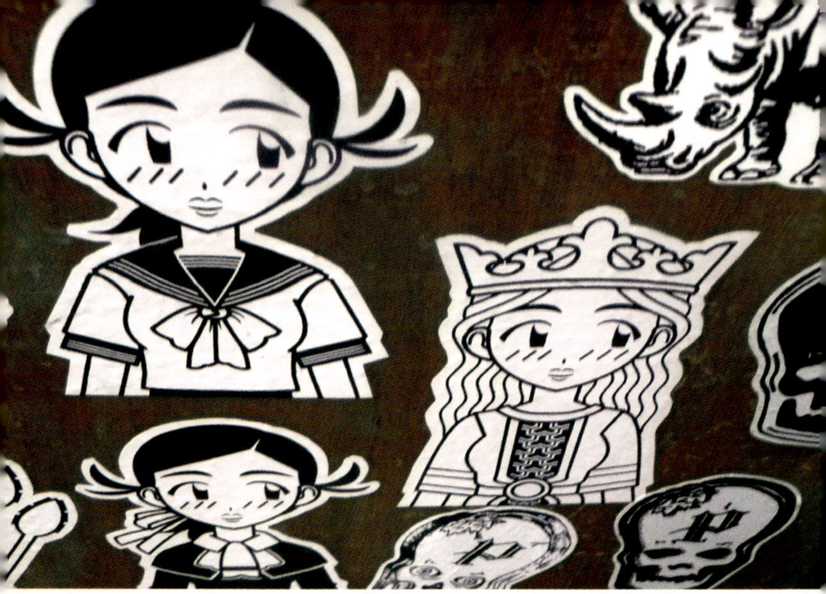

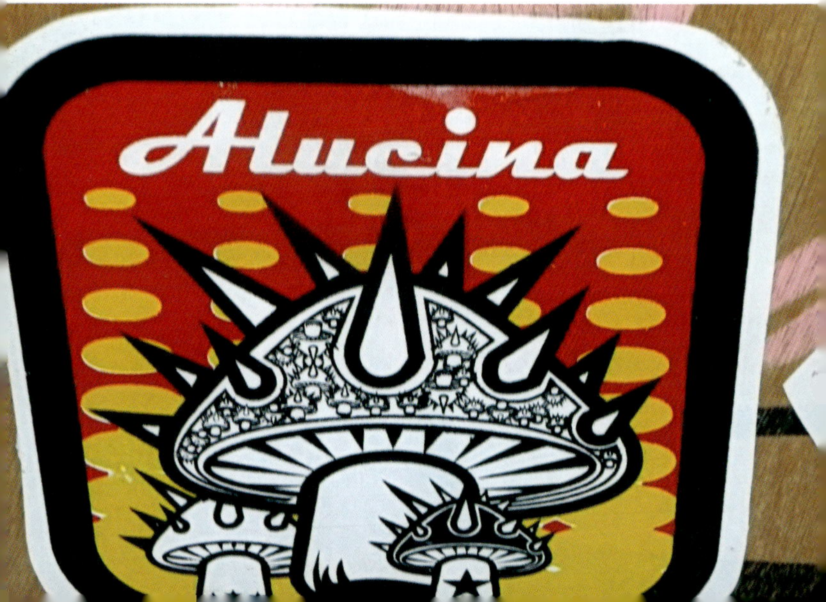

Alucina

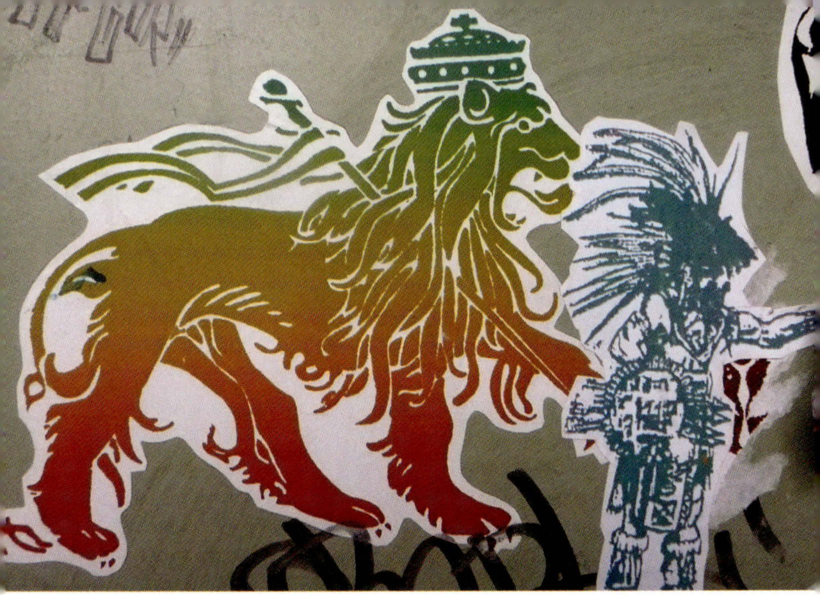

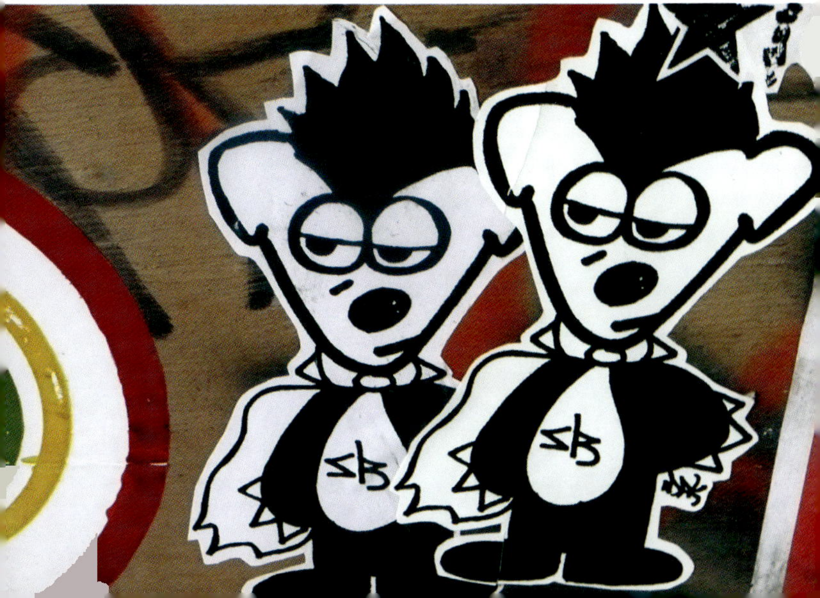

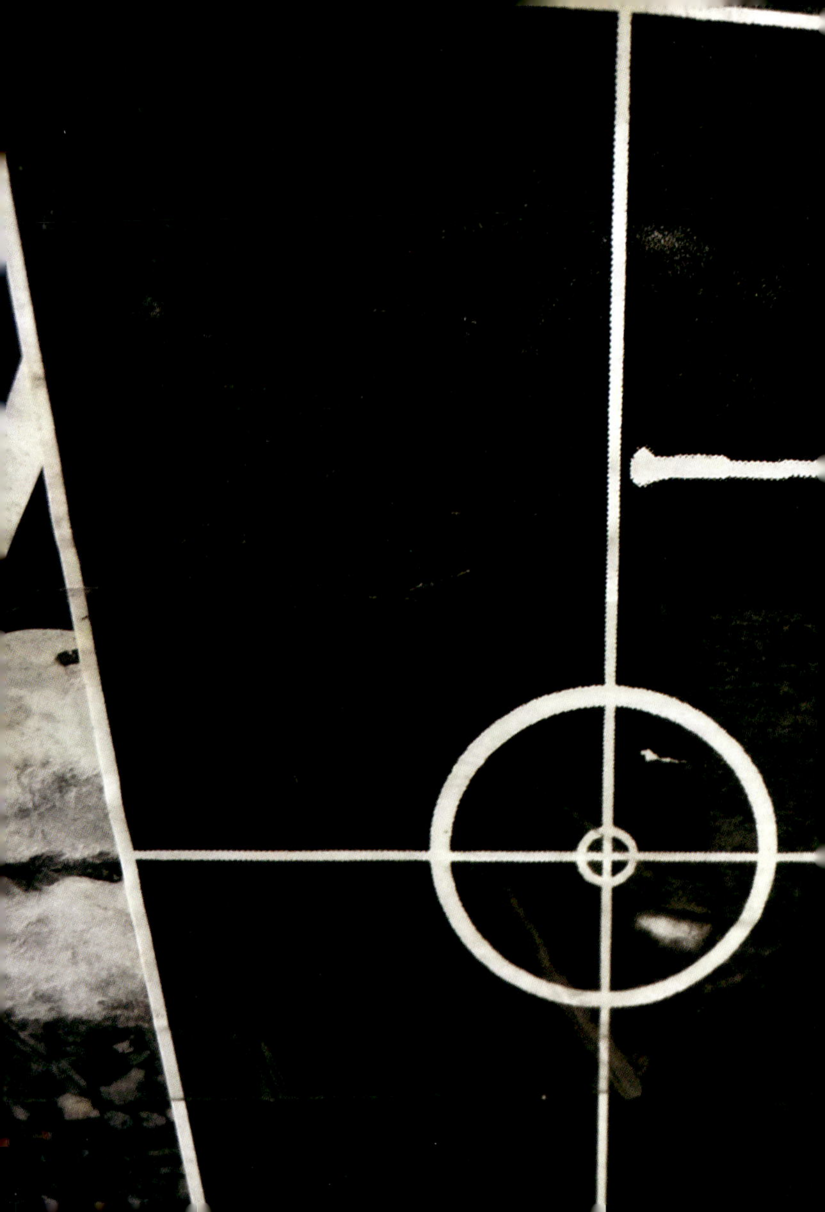

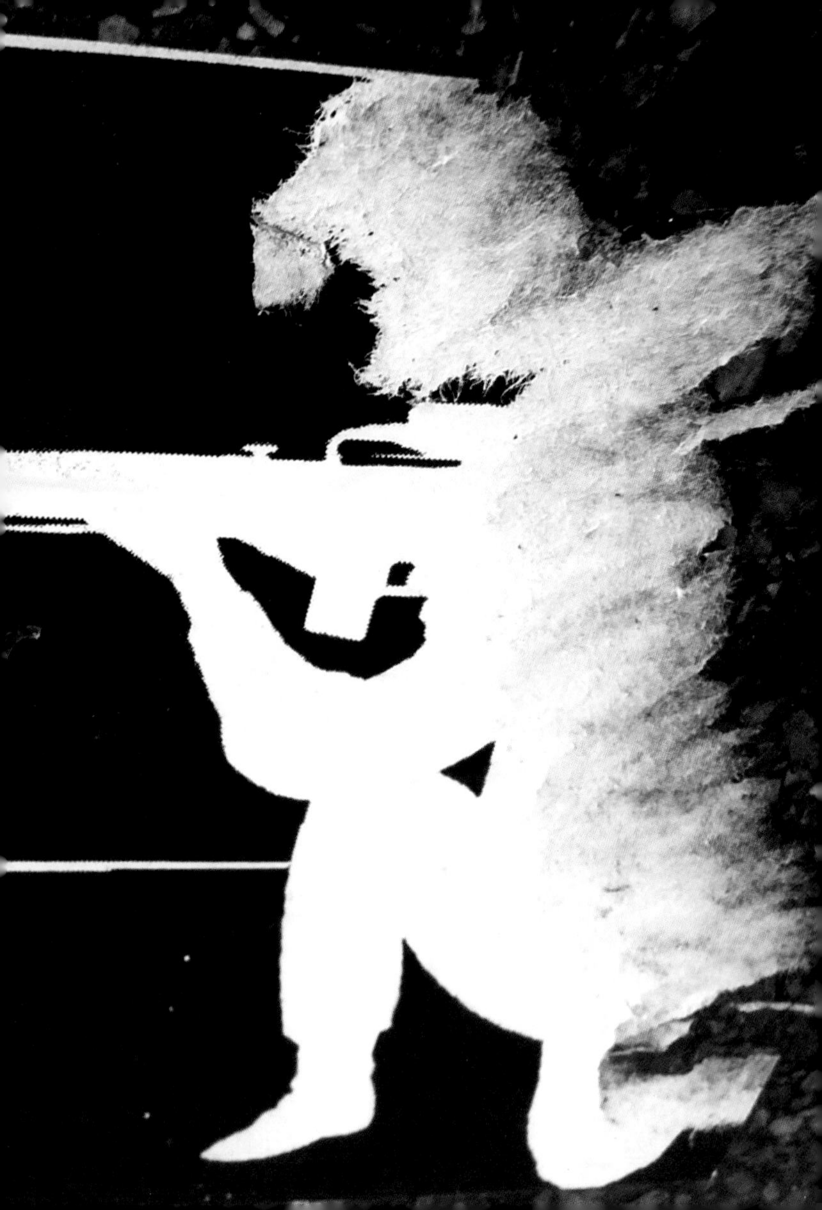

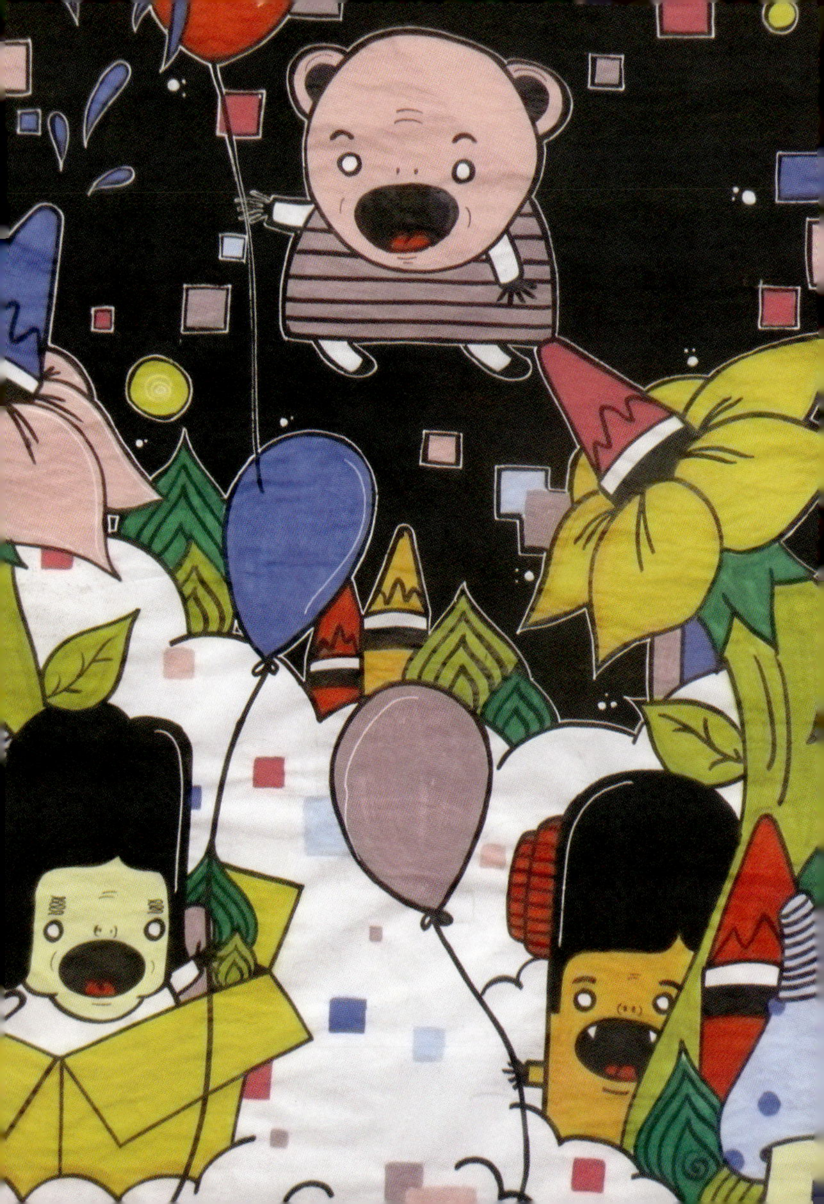

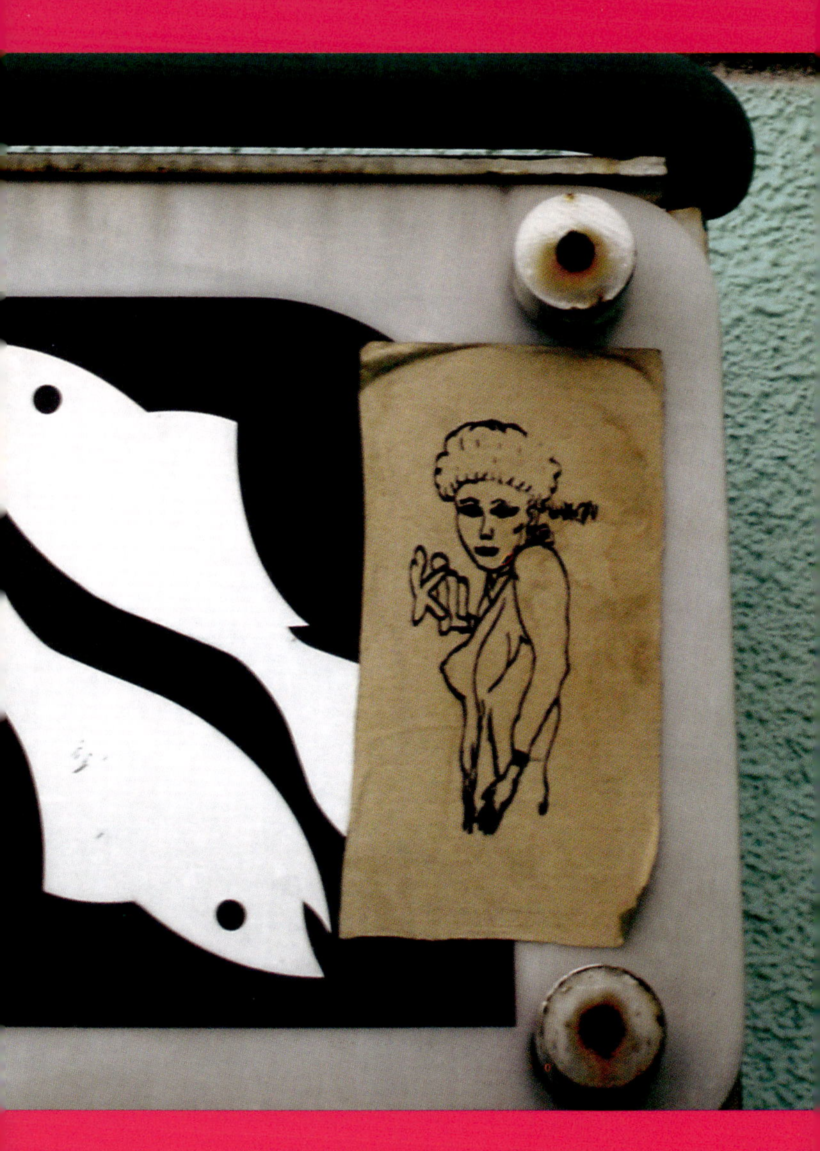

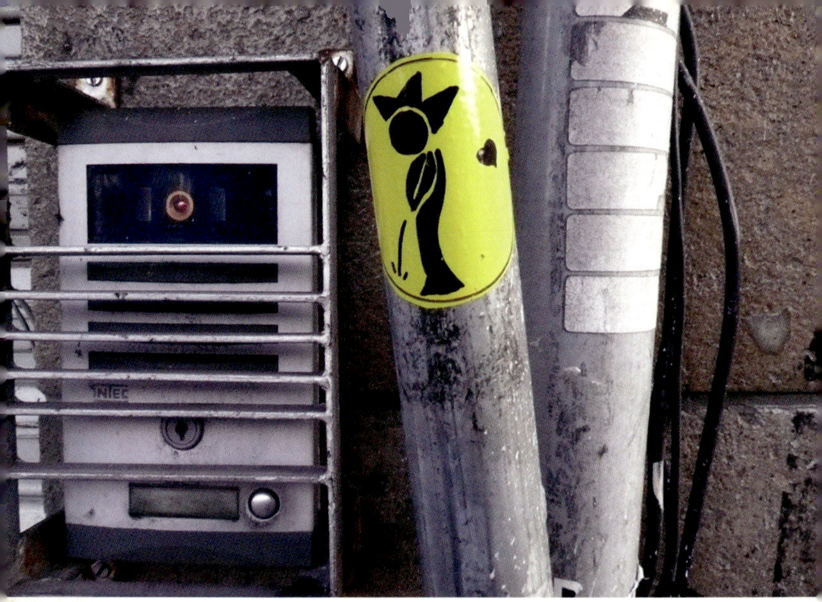

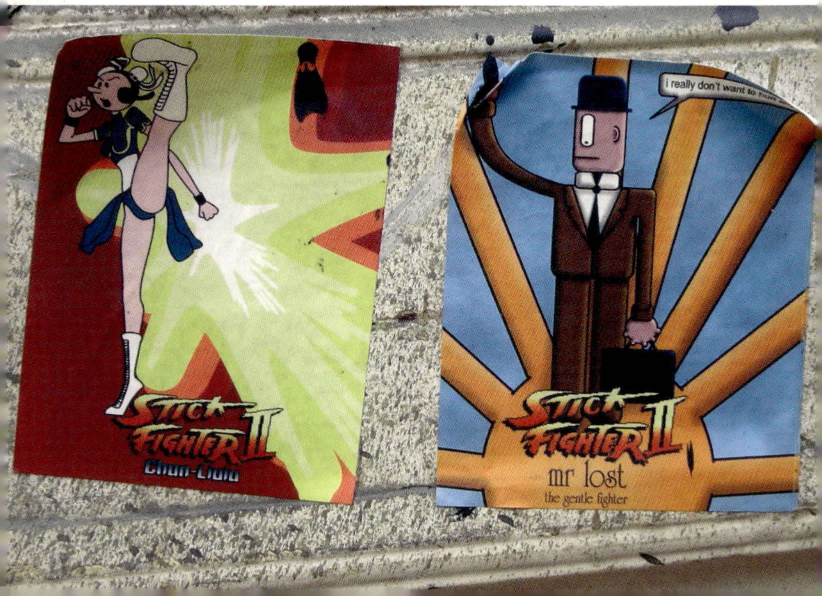

INTEC
Stick Fighter II
Stick Fighter II
mr lost
the gentle fighter

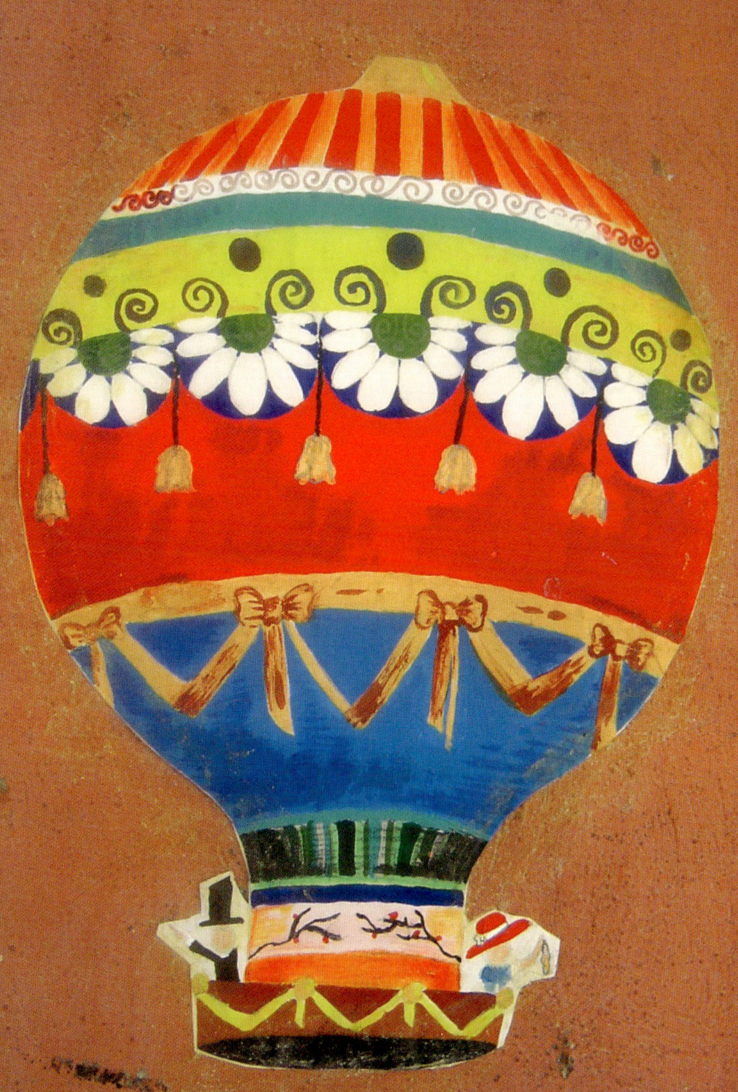

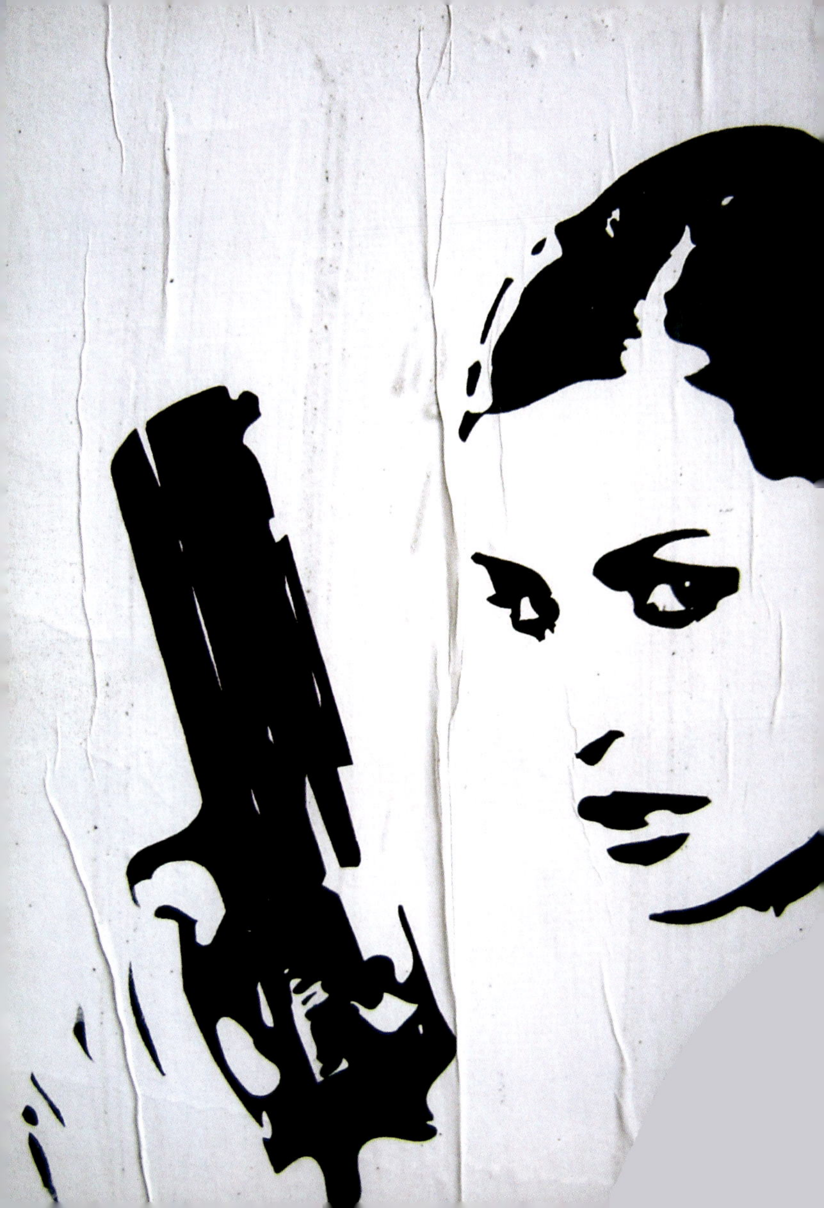

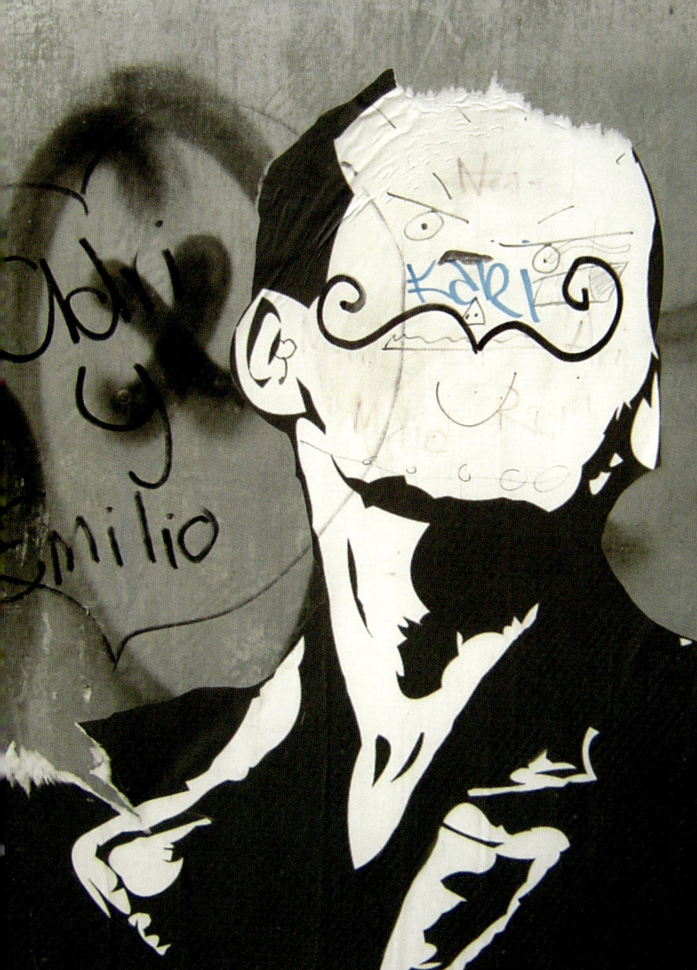
Blume
milio

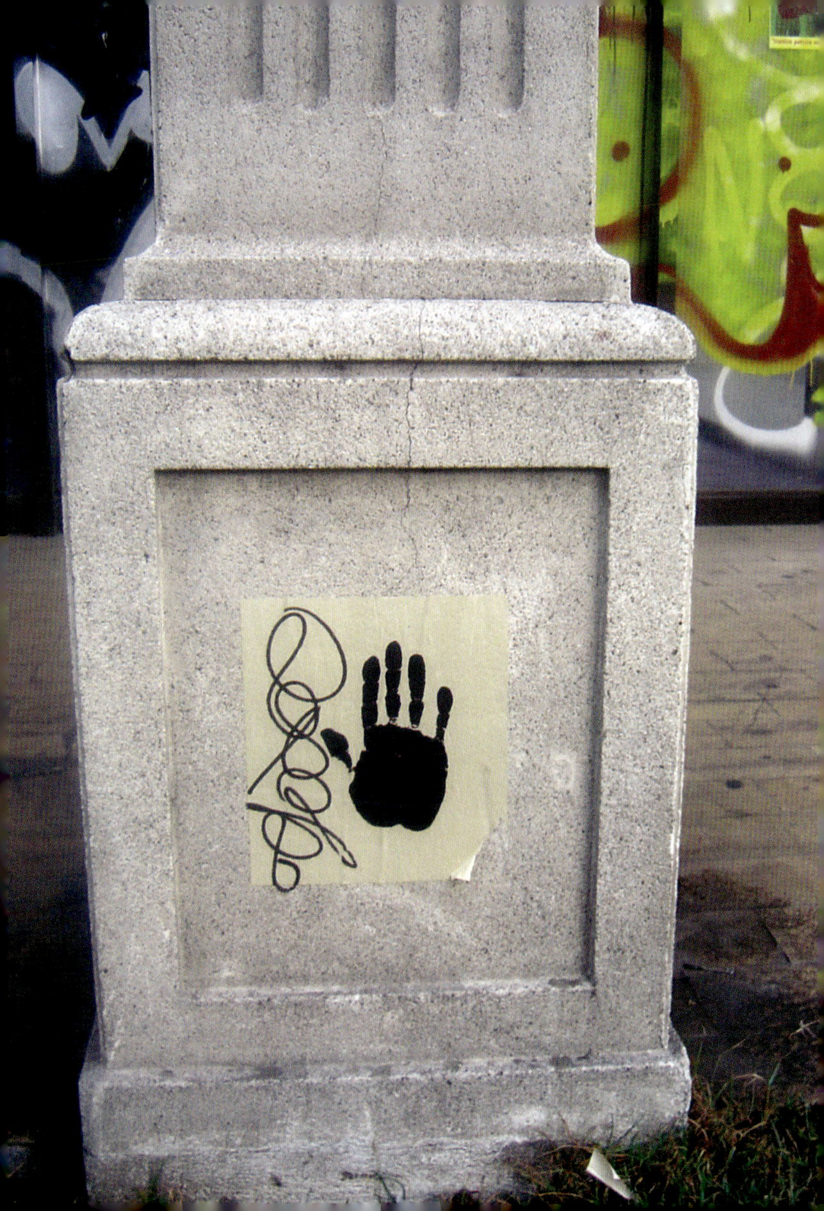

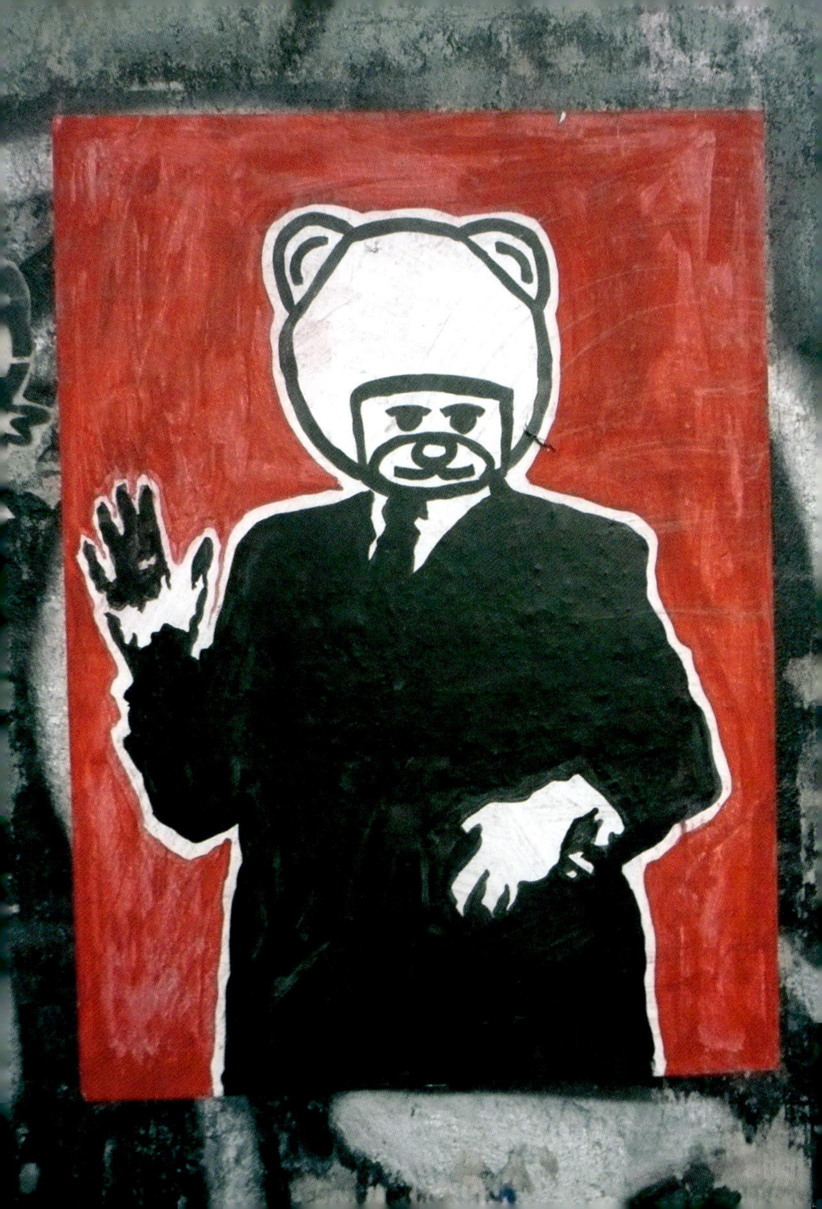

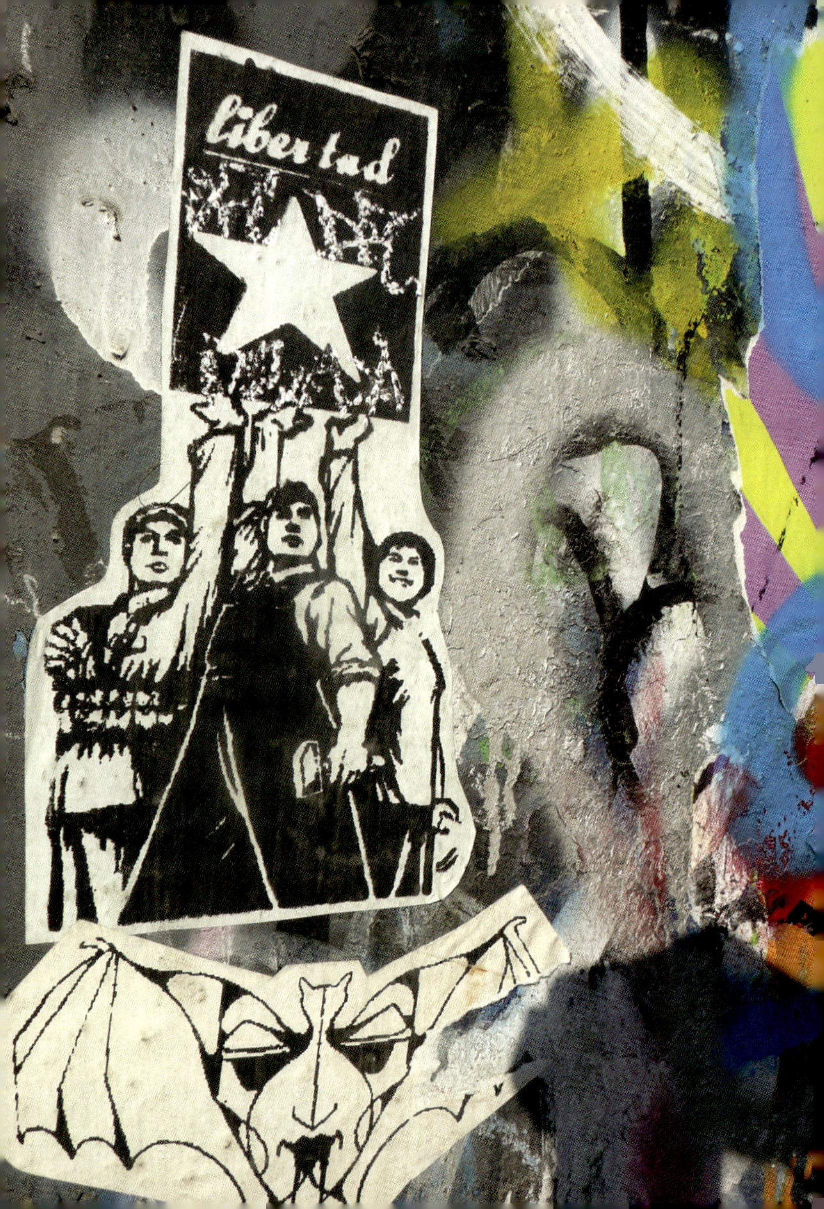
liber tad

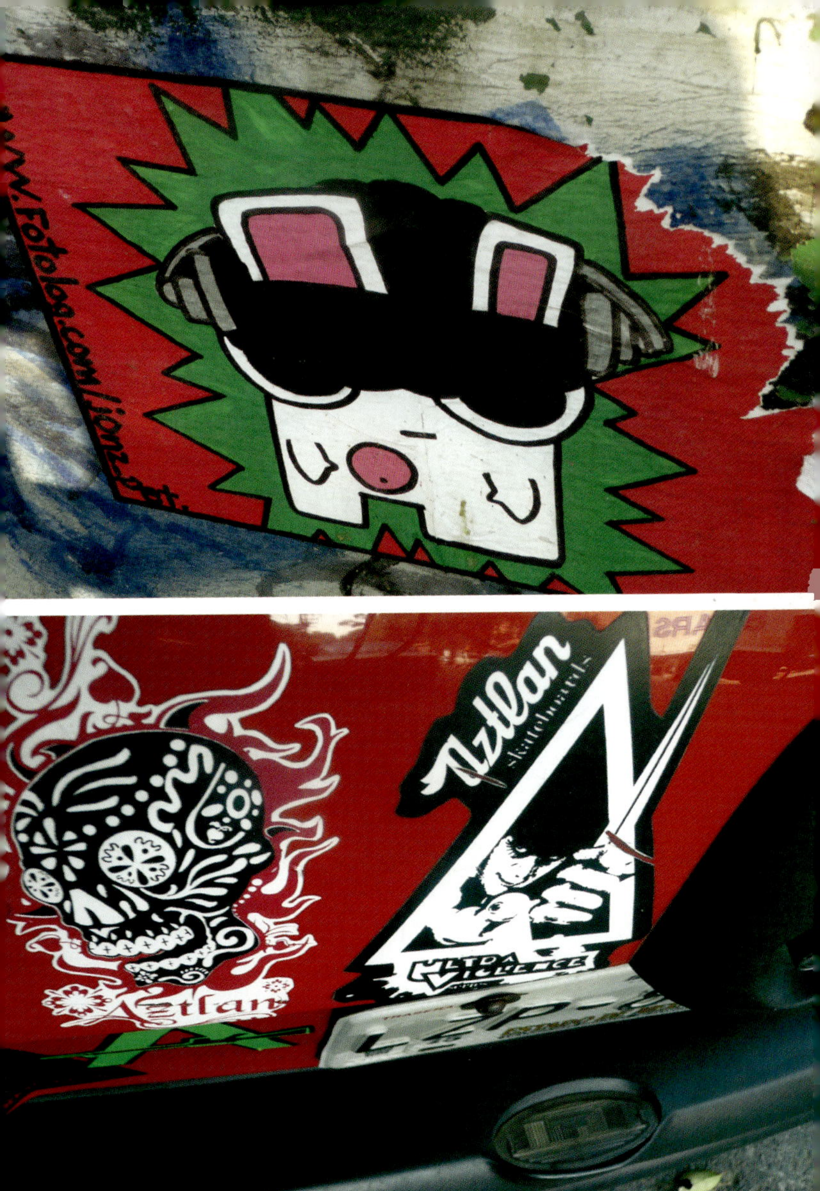
Aztlan
skateboards
Aztlan

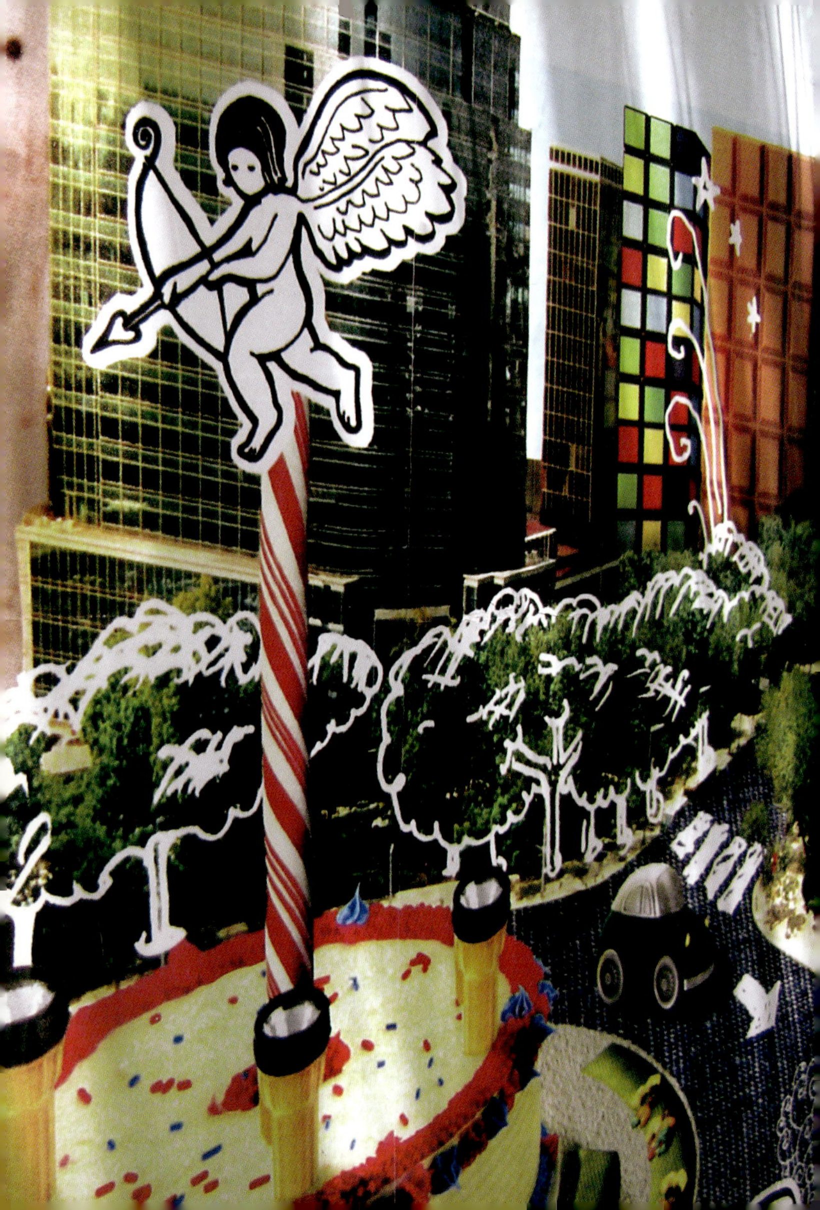

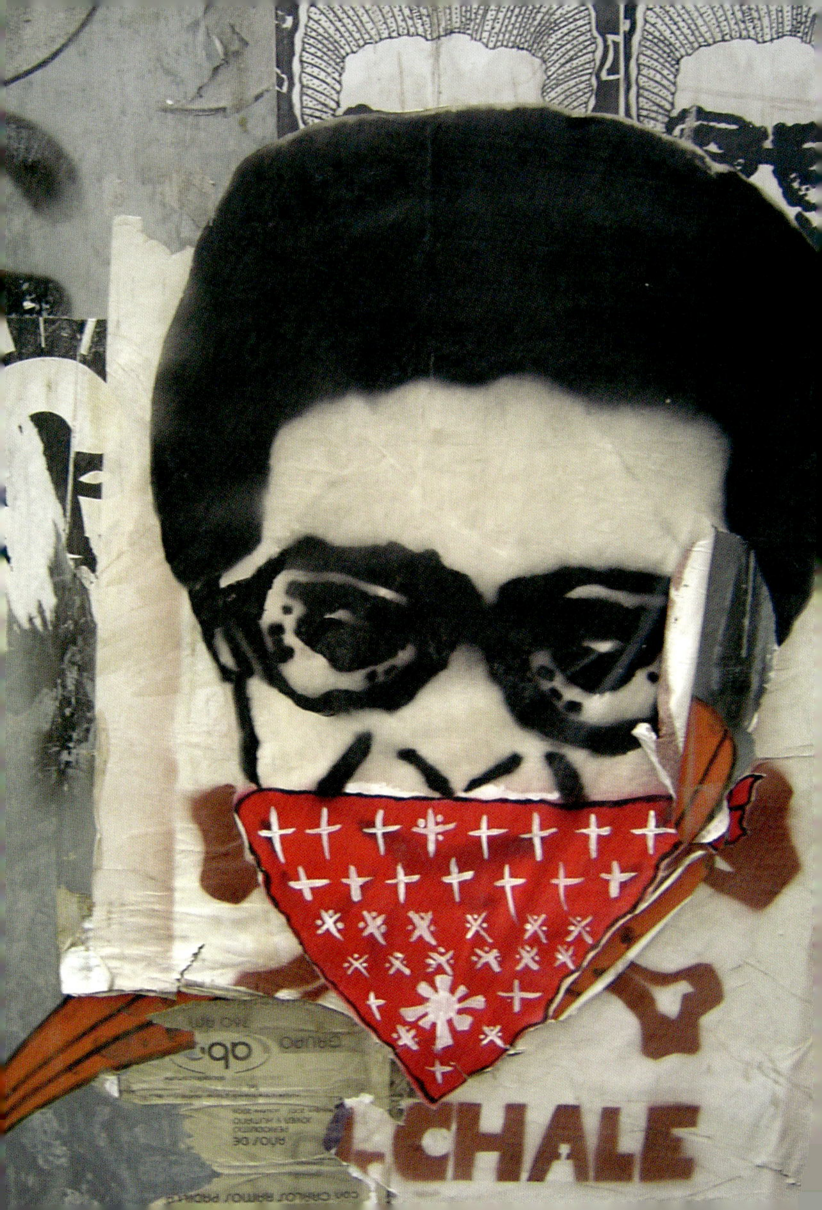
CHALE

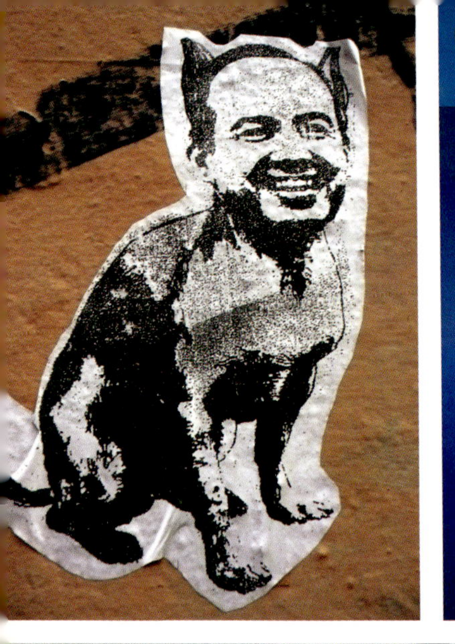

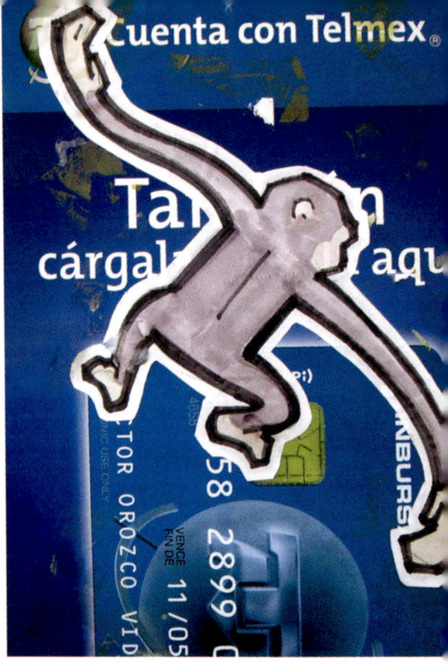
Cuenta con Telmex

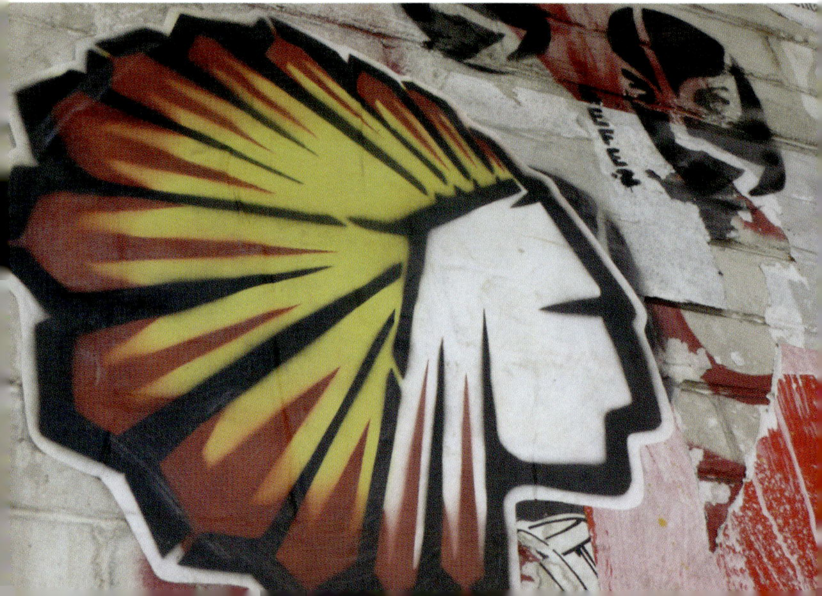

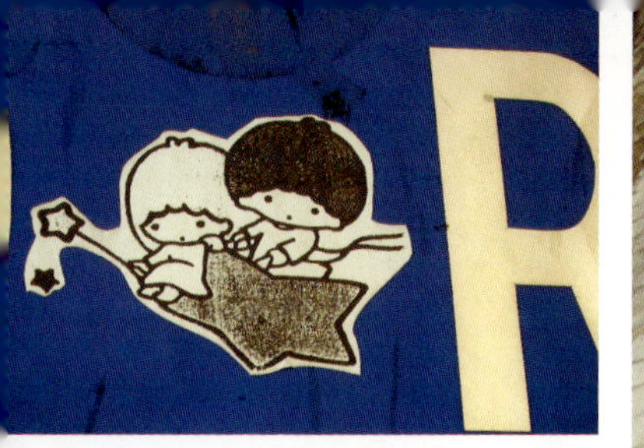

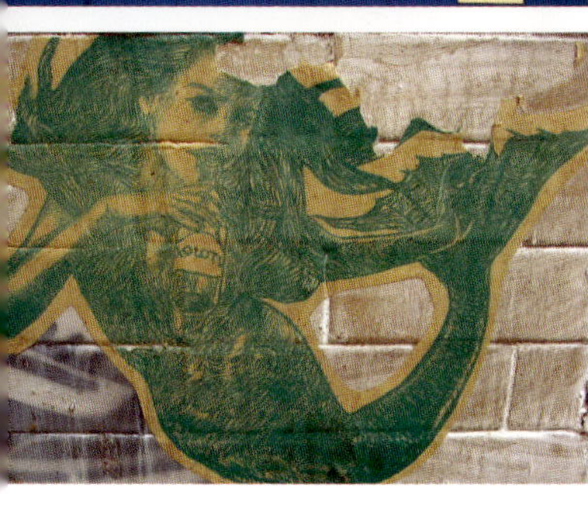

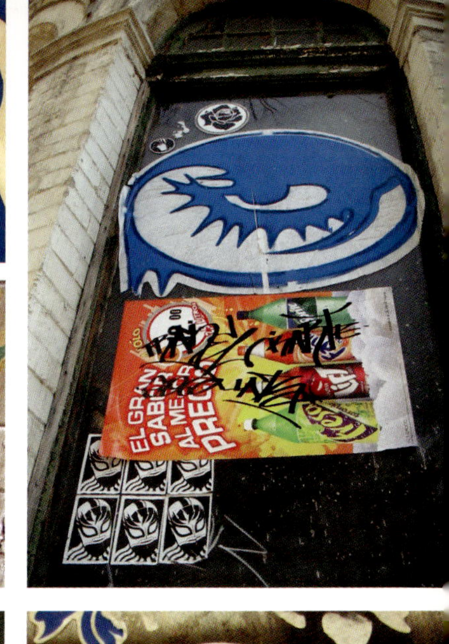

EL GRAN

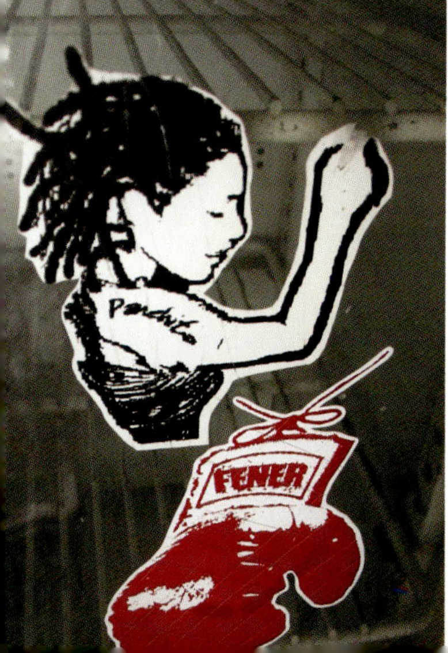

FENER

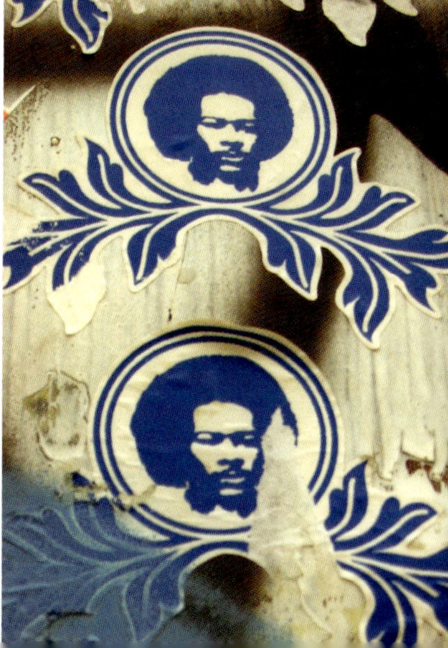

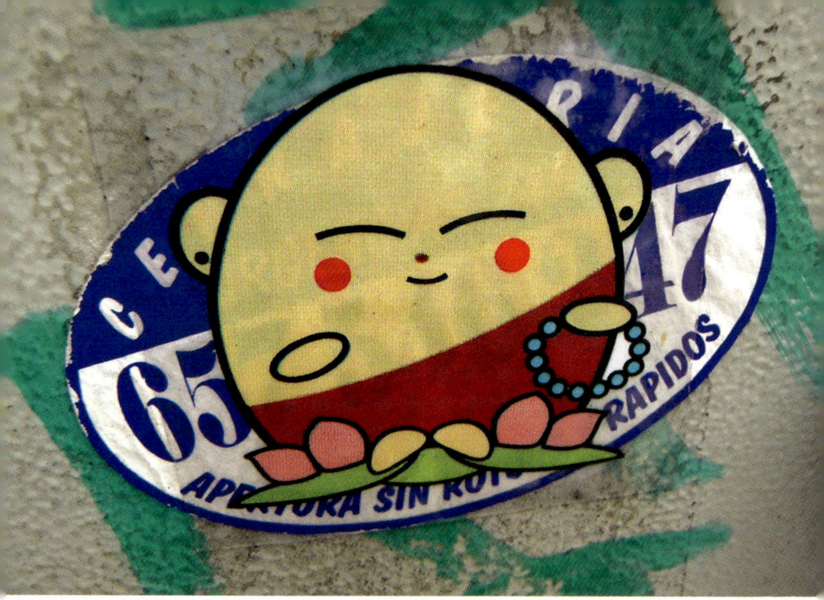

RAPIDOS

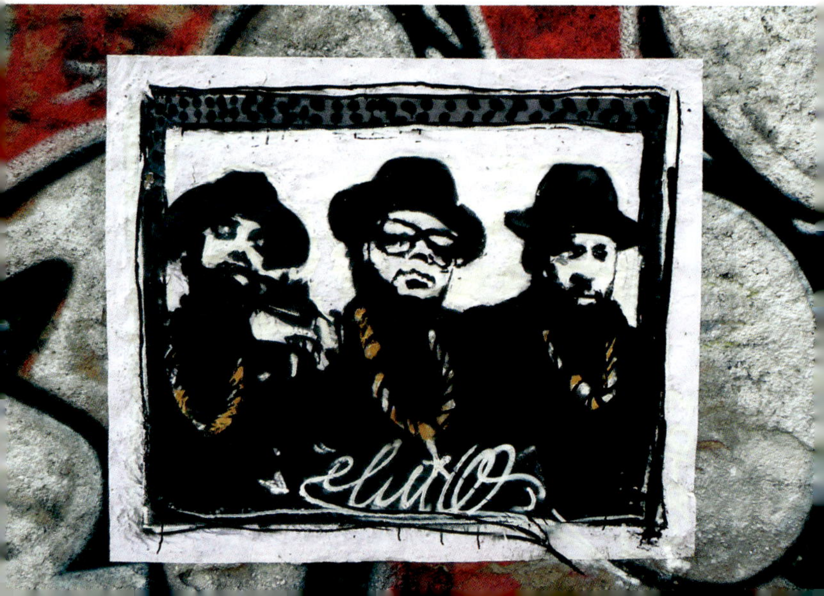

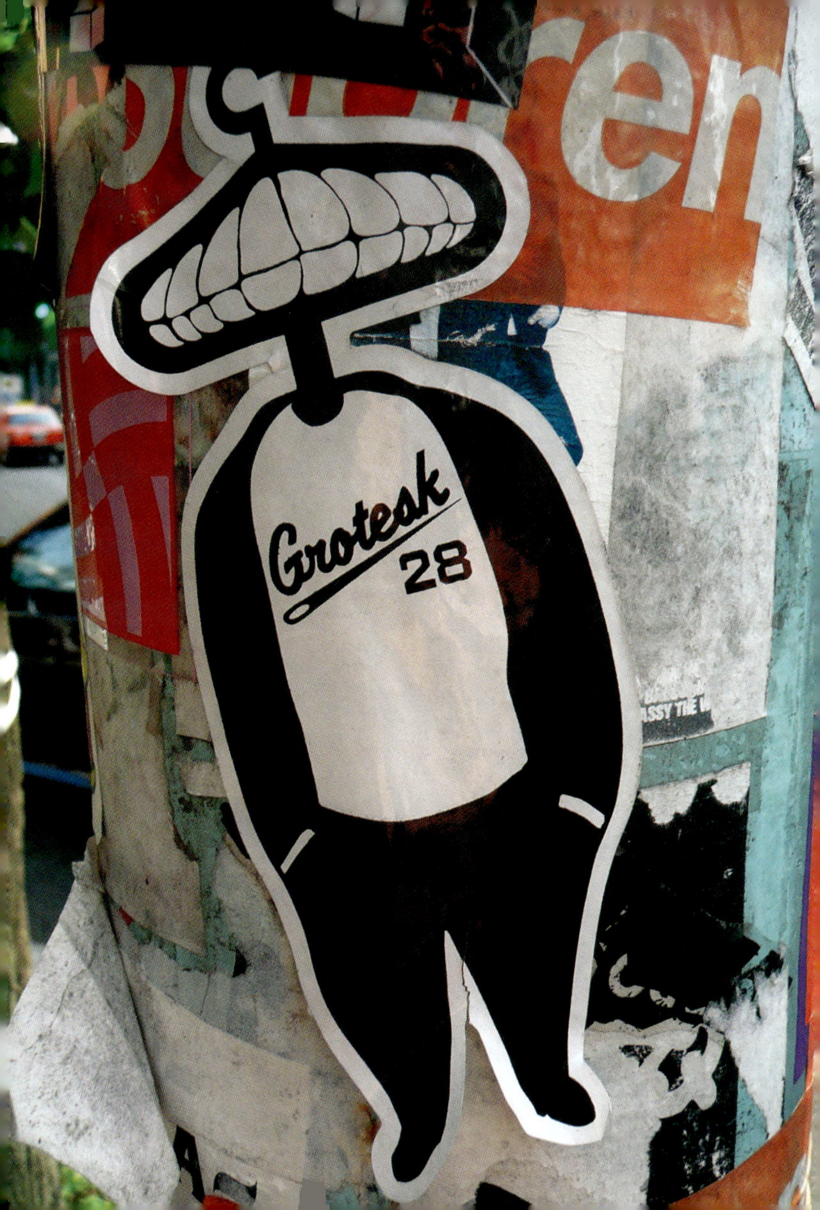
Grotesk
28

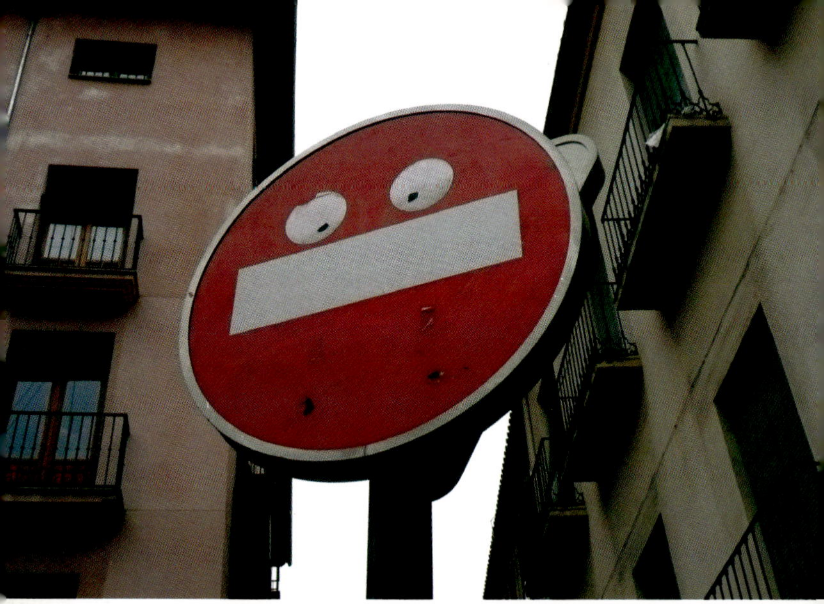

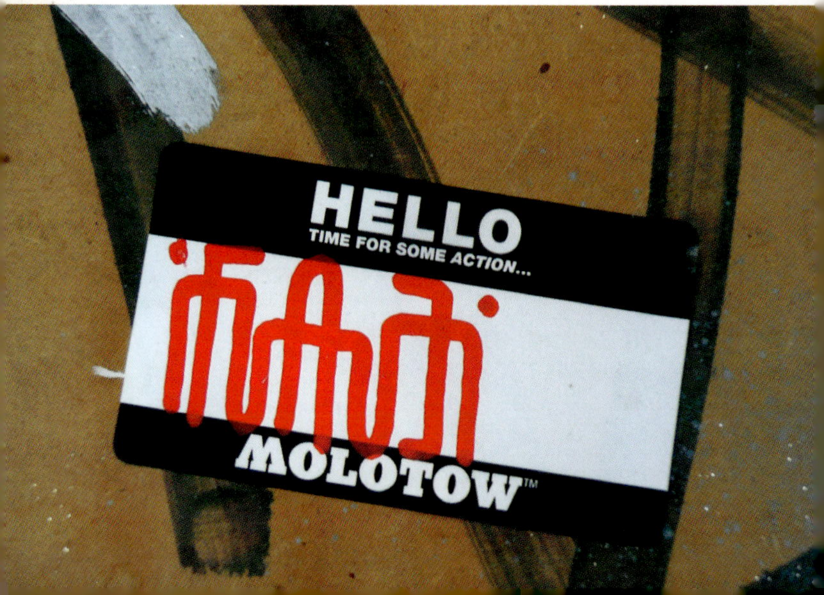

HELLO
TIME FOR SOME ACTION...
MOLOTOW™

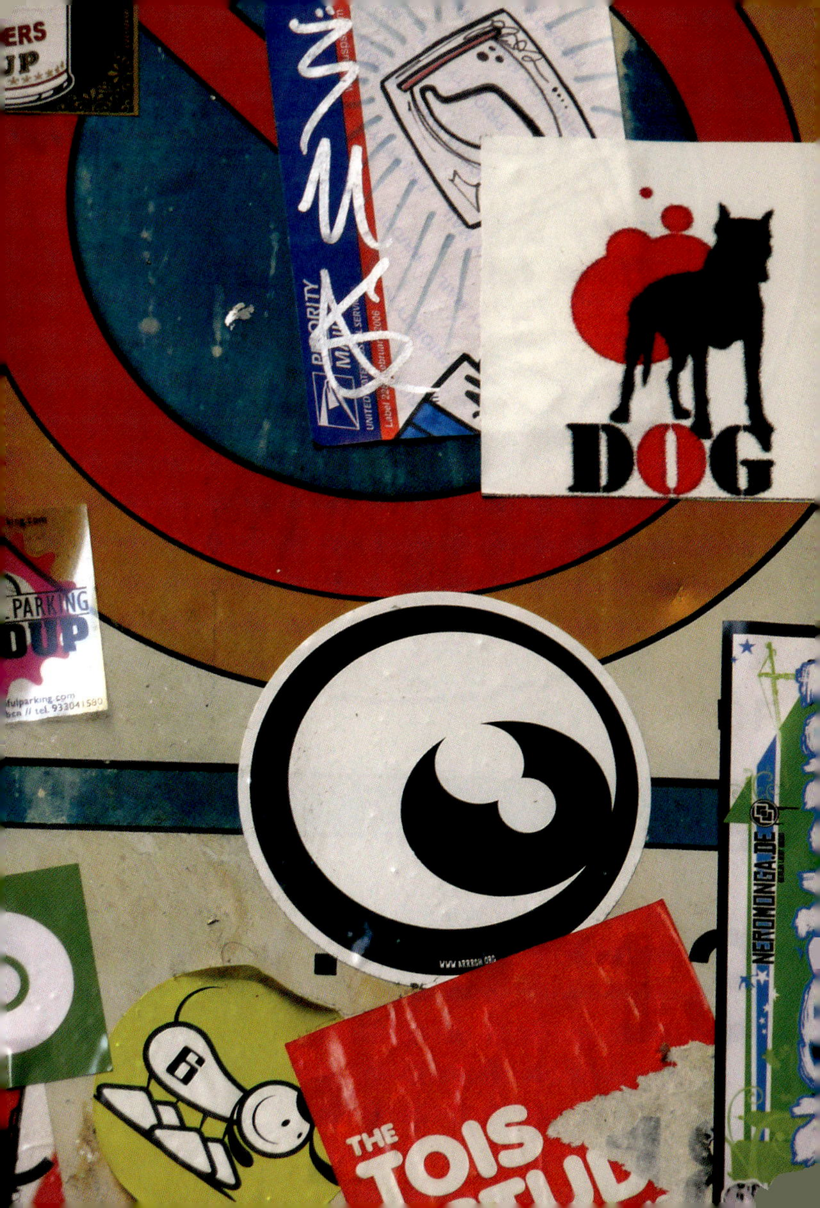

PRIORITY
DOG
PARKING
NEROMONGA.DE
THE
TOIS

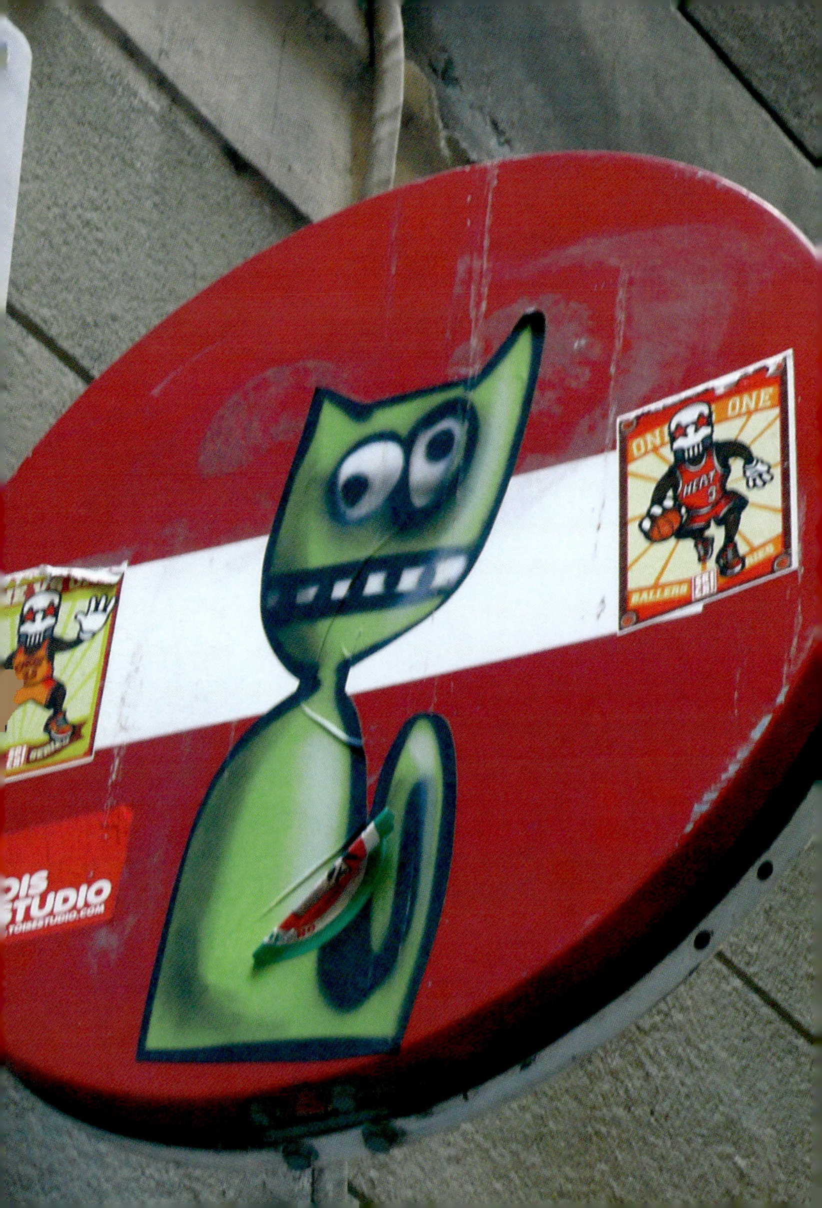
ONE
HEAT

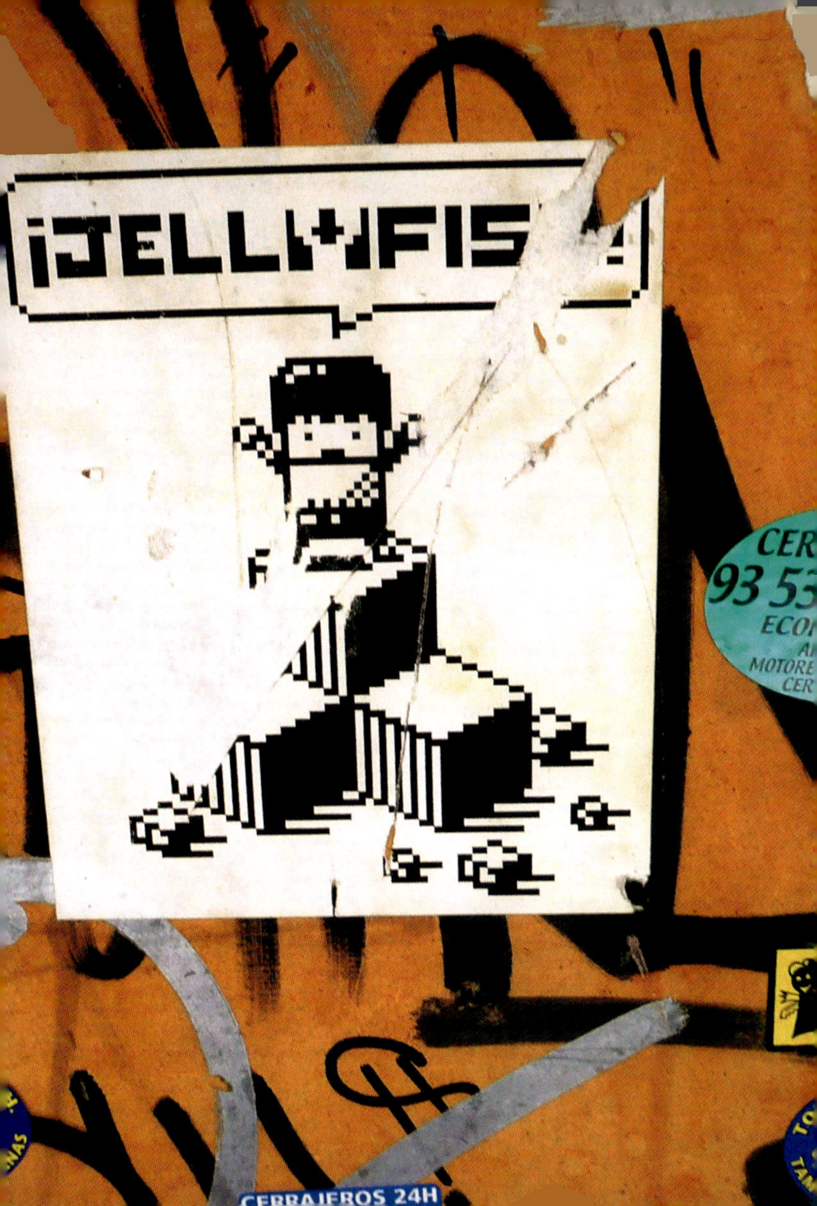
¡JELLYFIS
CERRAJEROS 24H

Be Hope
Shin Shin

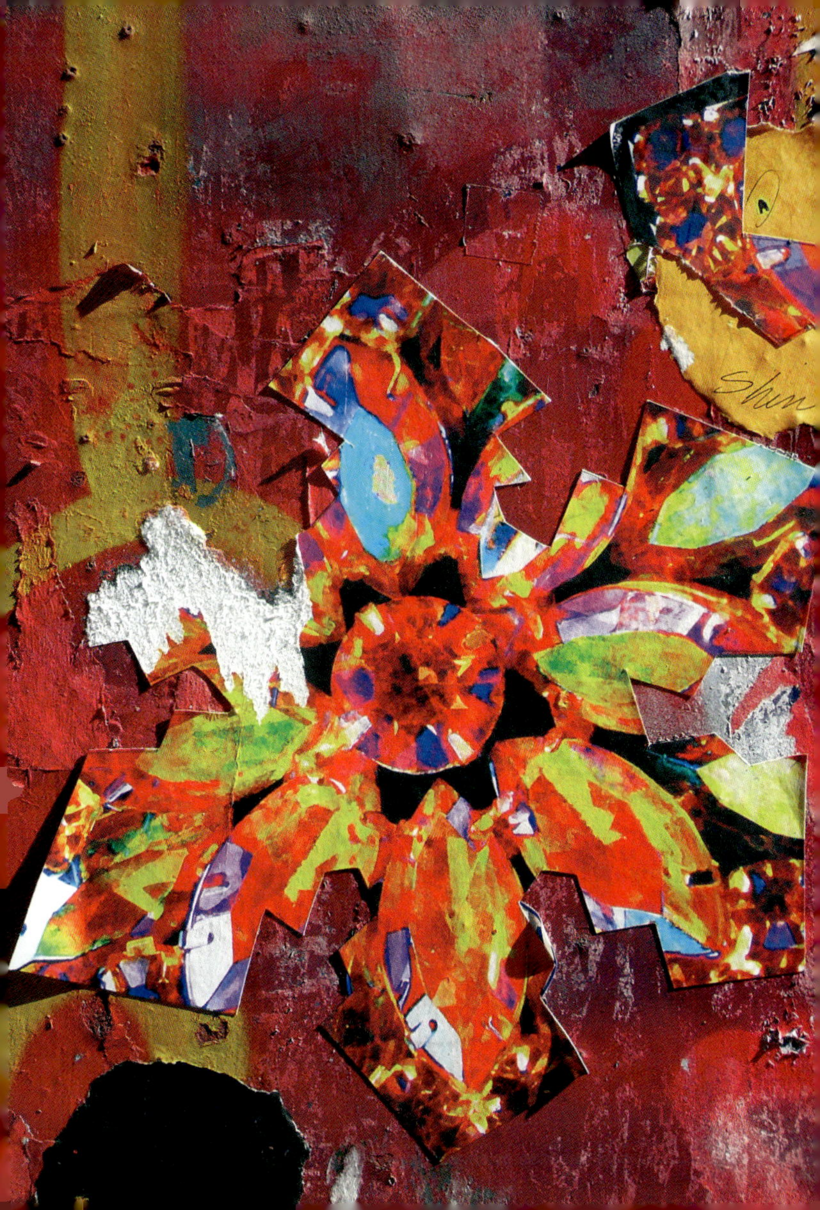
Shun

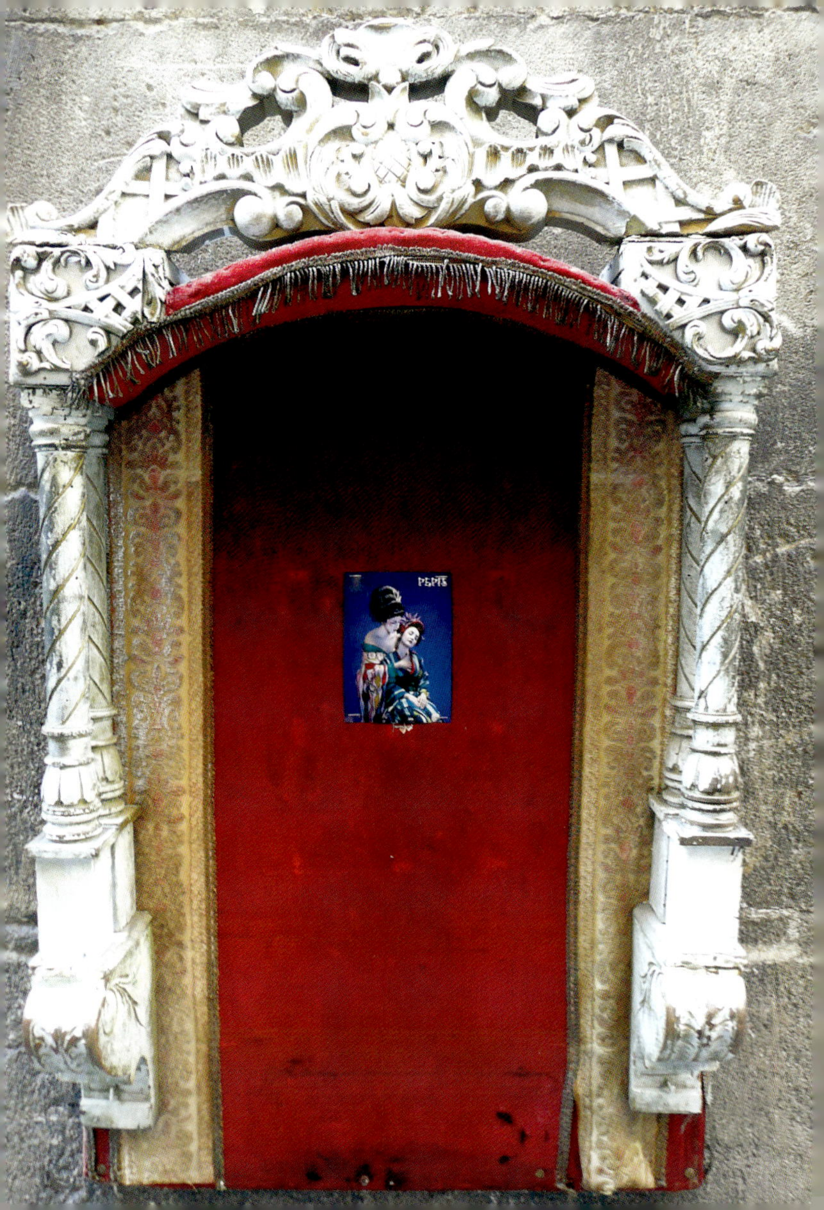

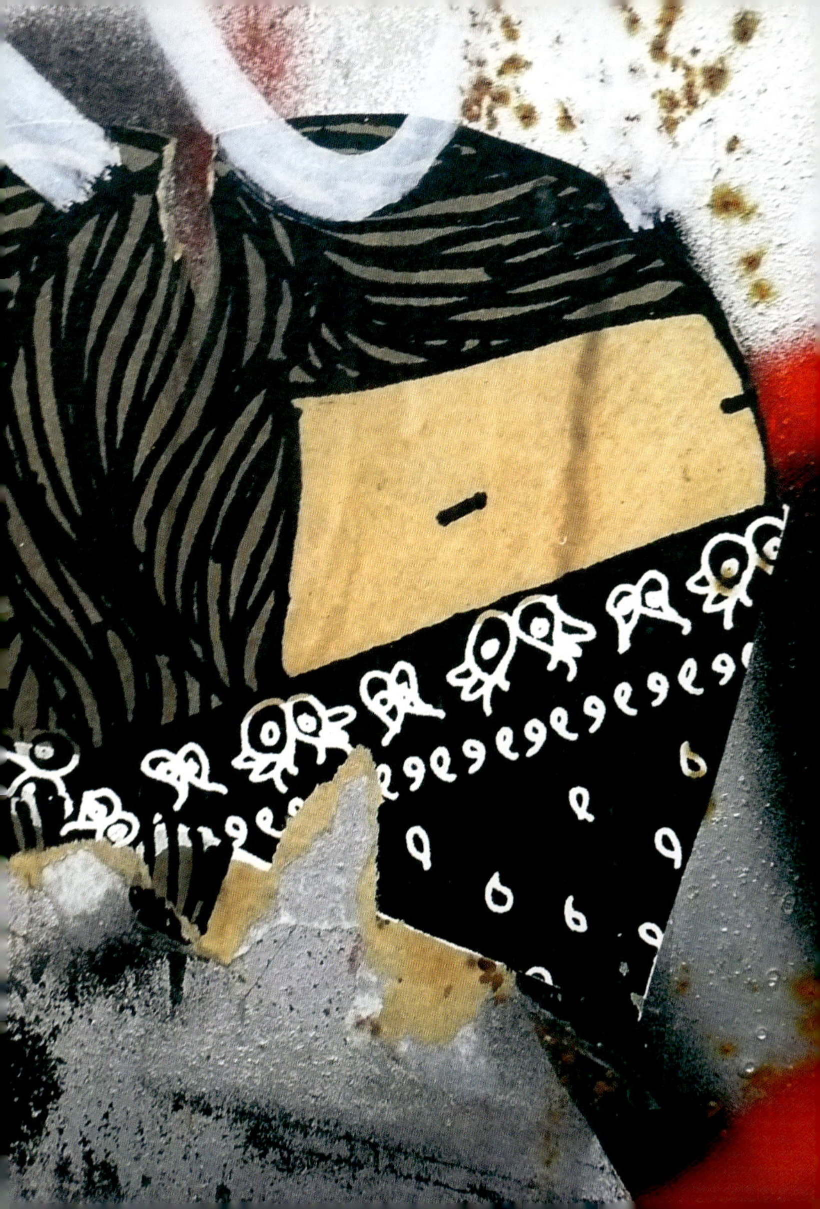

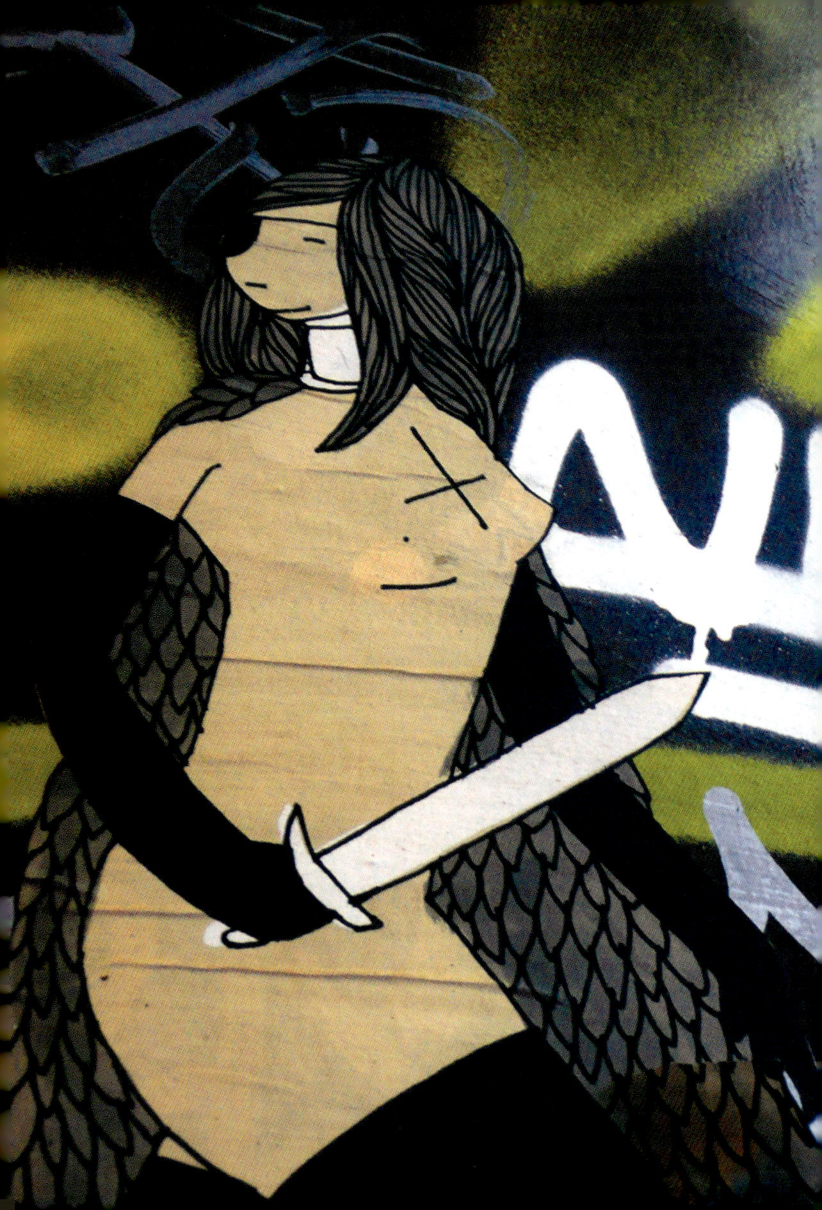

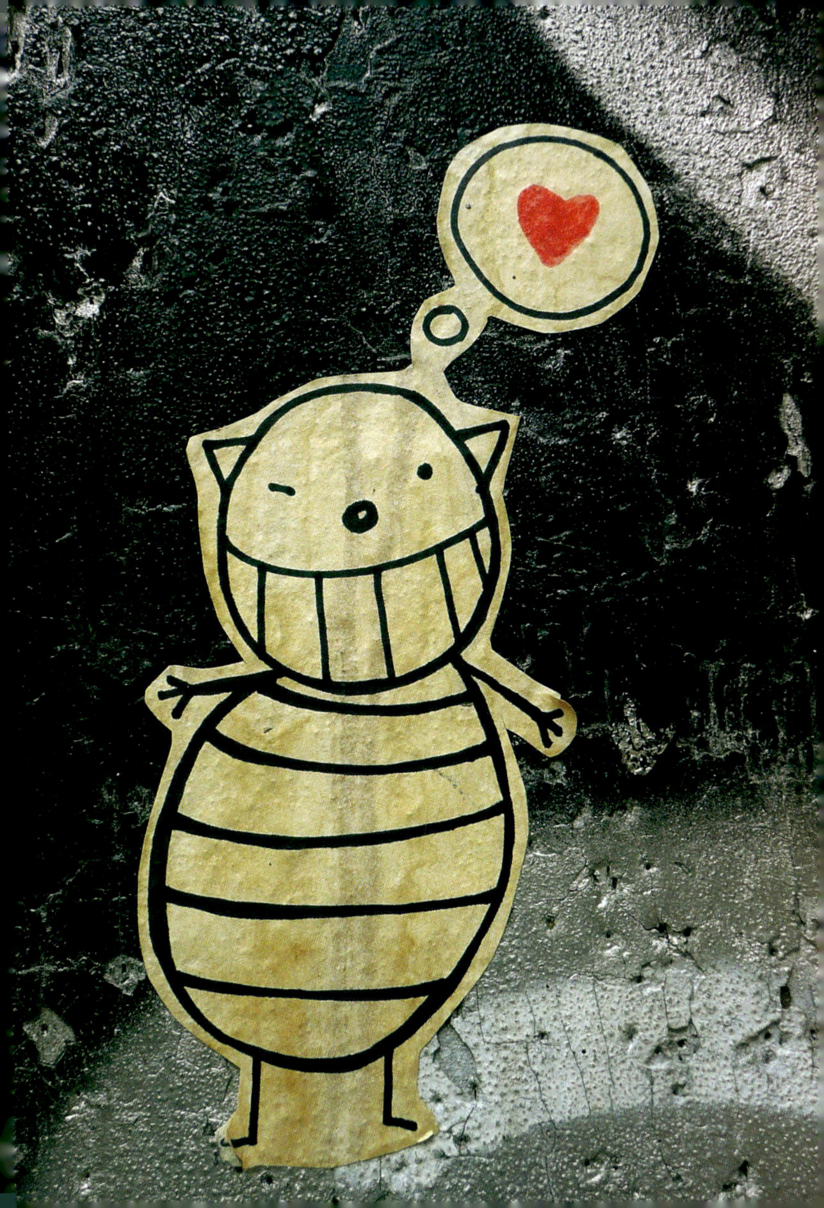

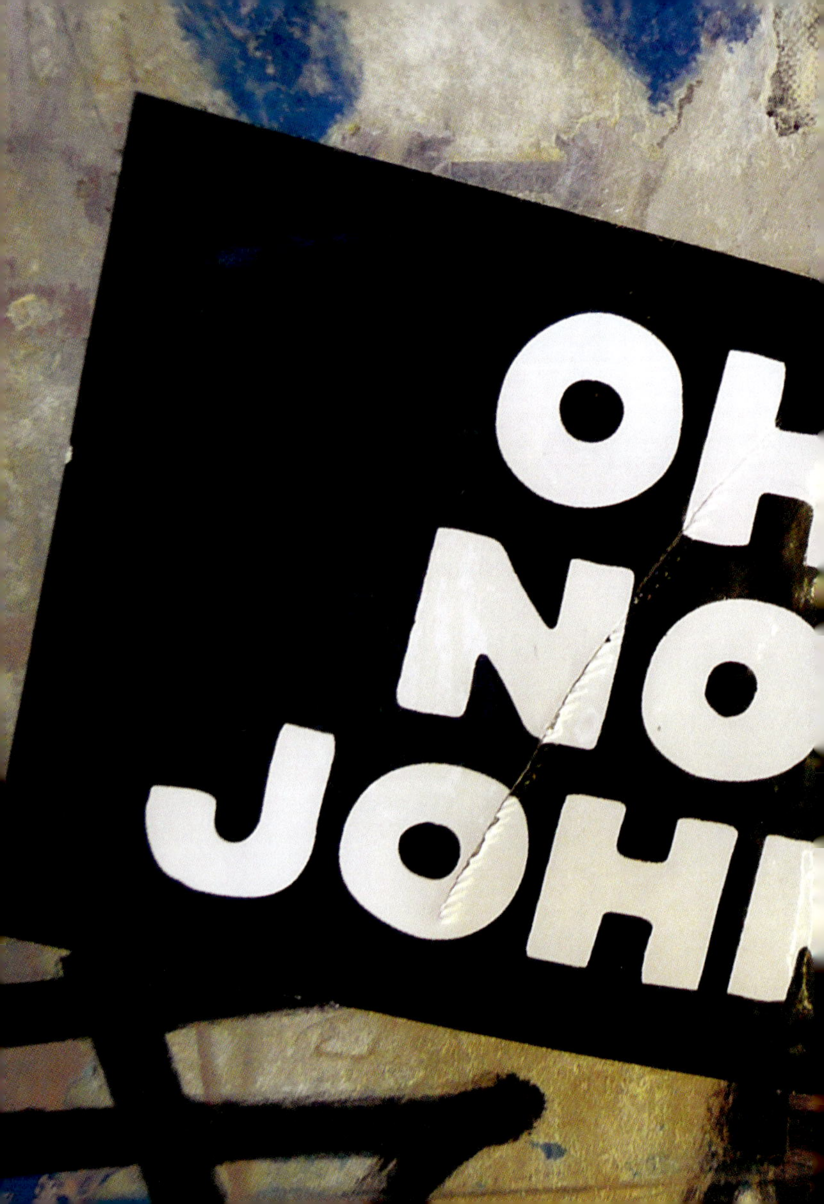
OH
NO
JOH

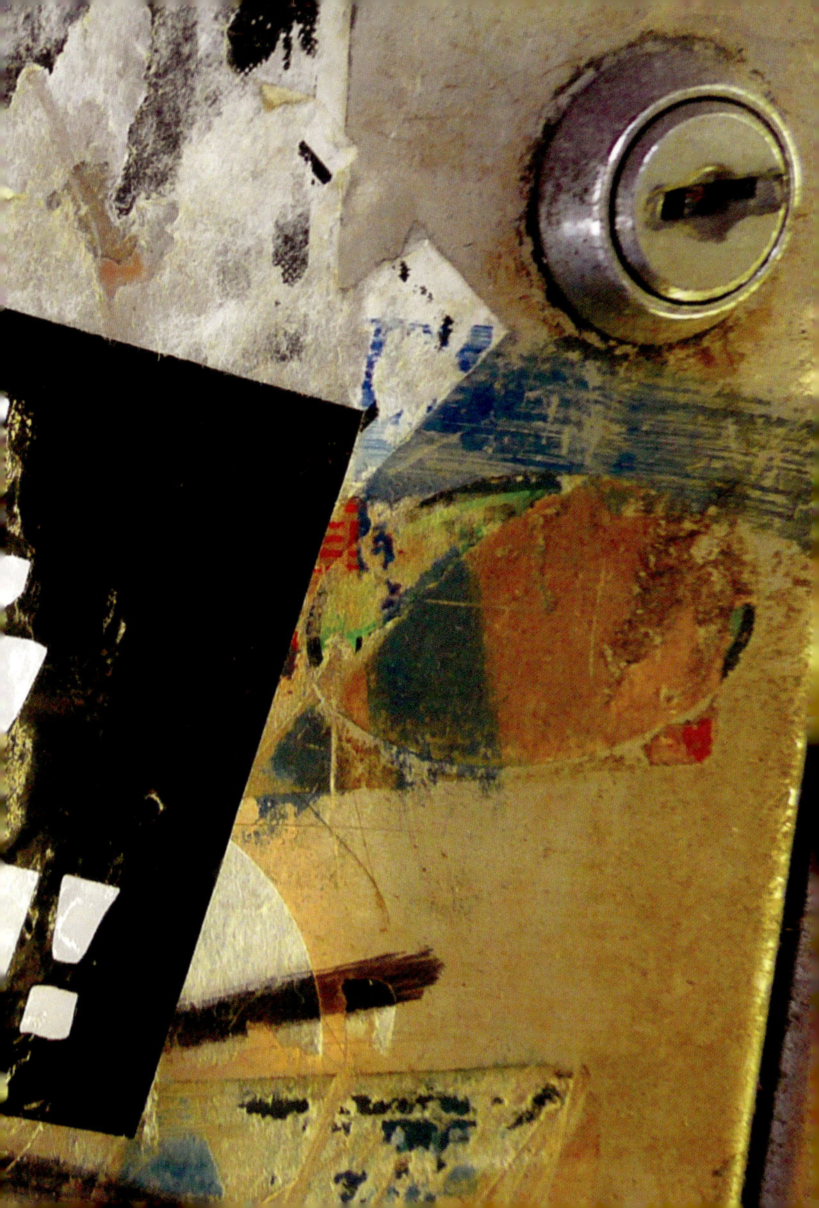

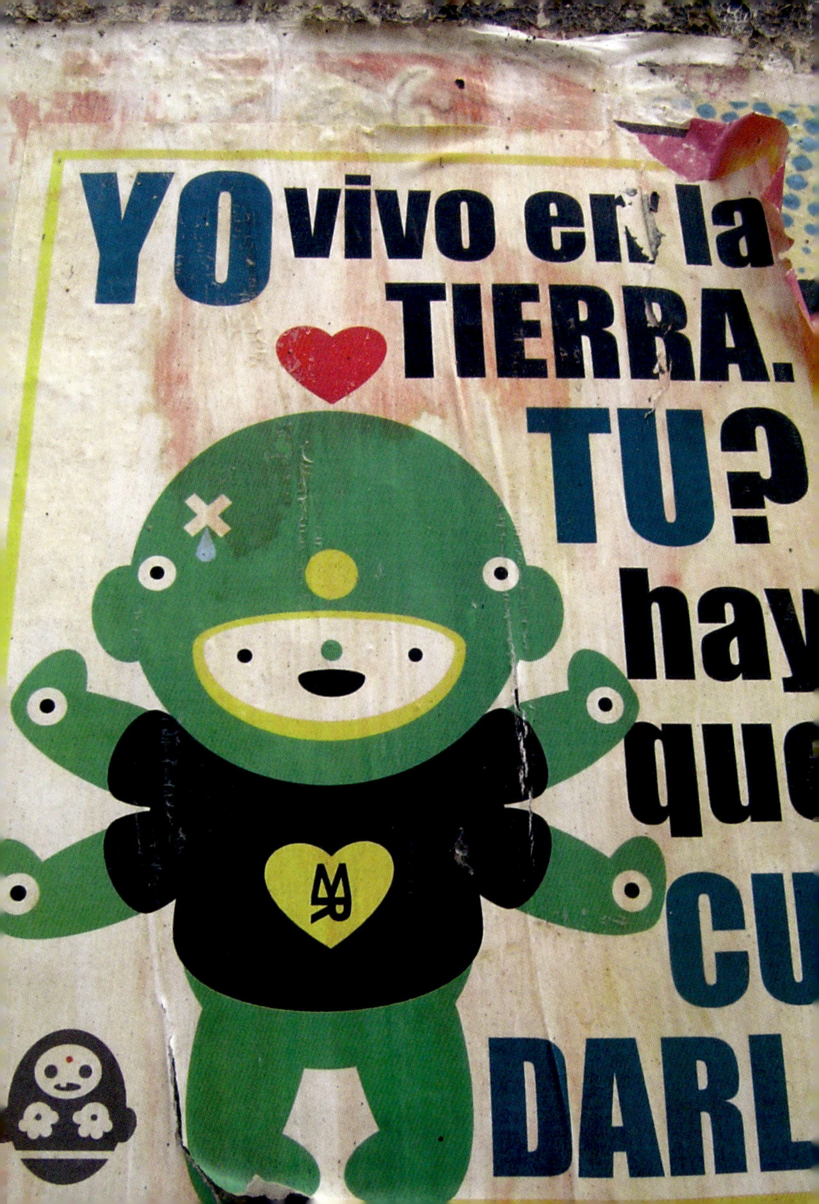
YO vivo en la
TIERRA.
TU?
hay
qu
CU
DARL

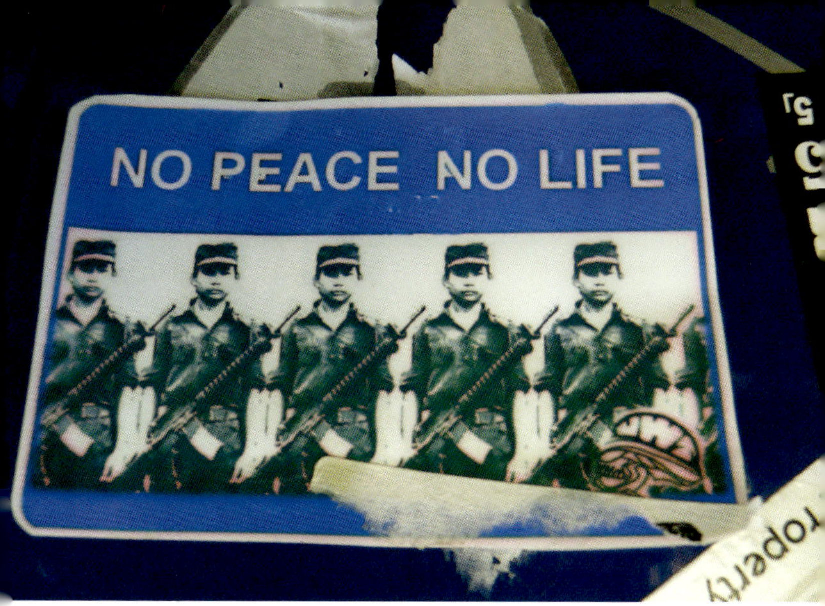

NO PEACE NO LIFE

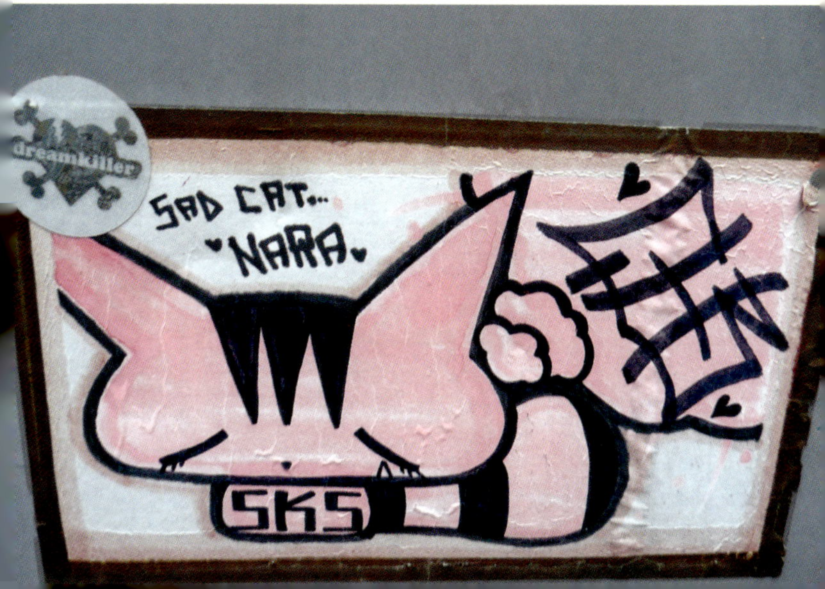

dreamkiller

SAD CAT...
NARA

SKS

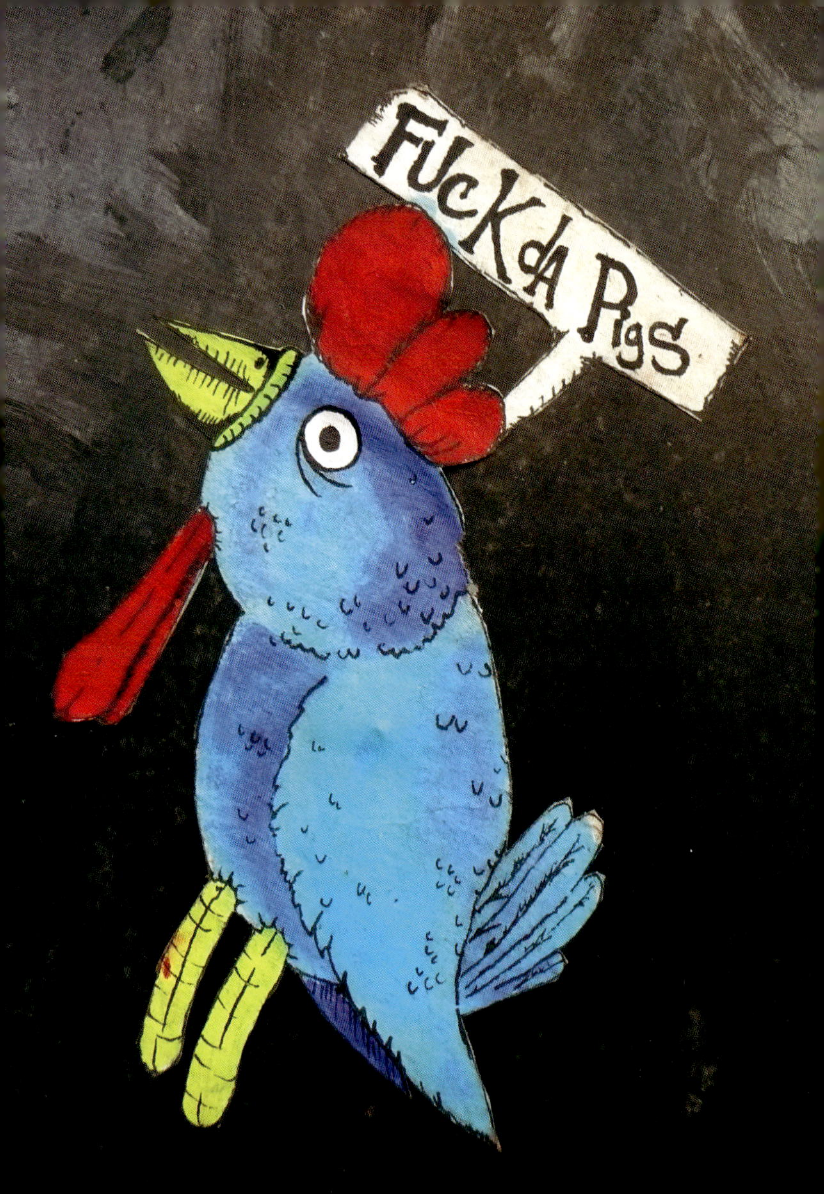
FUcK dA Pigs

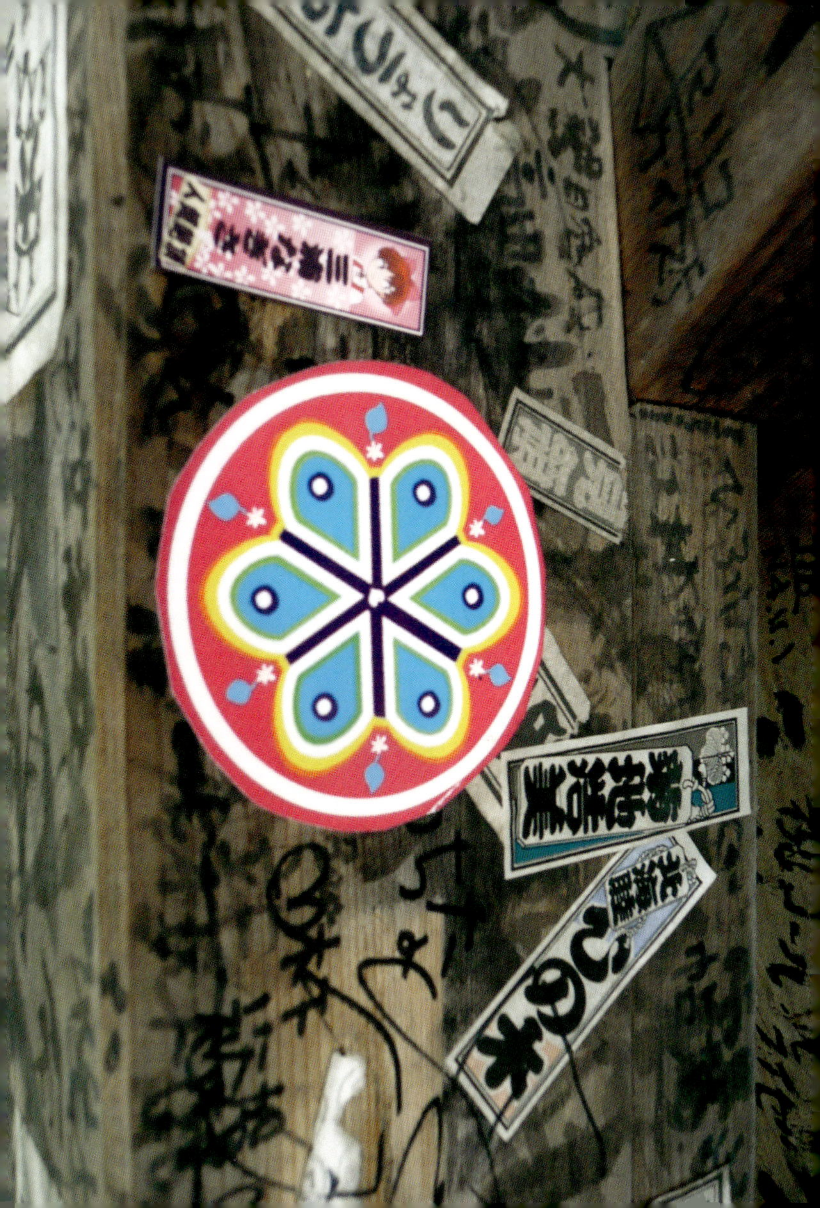

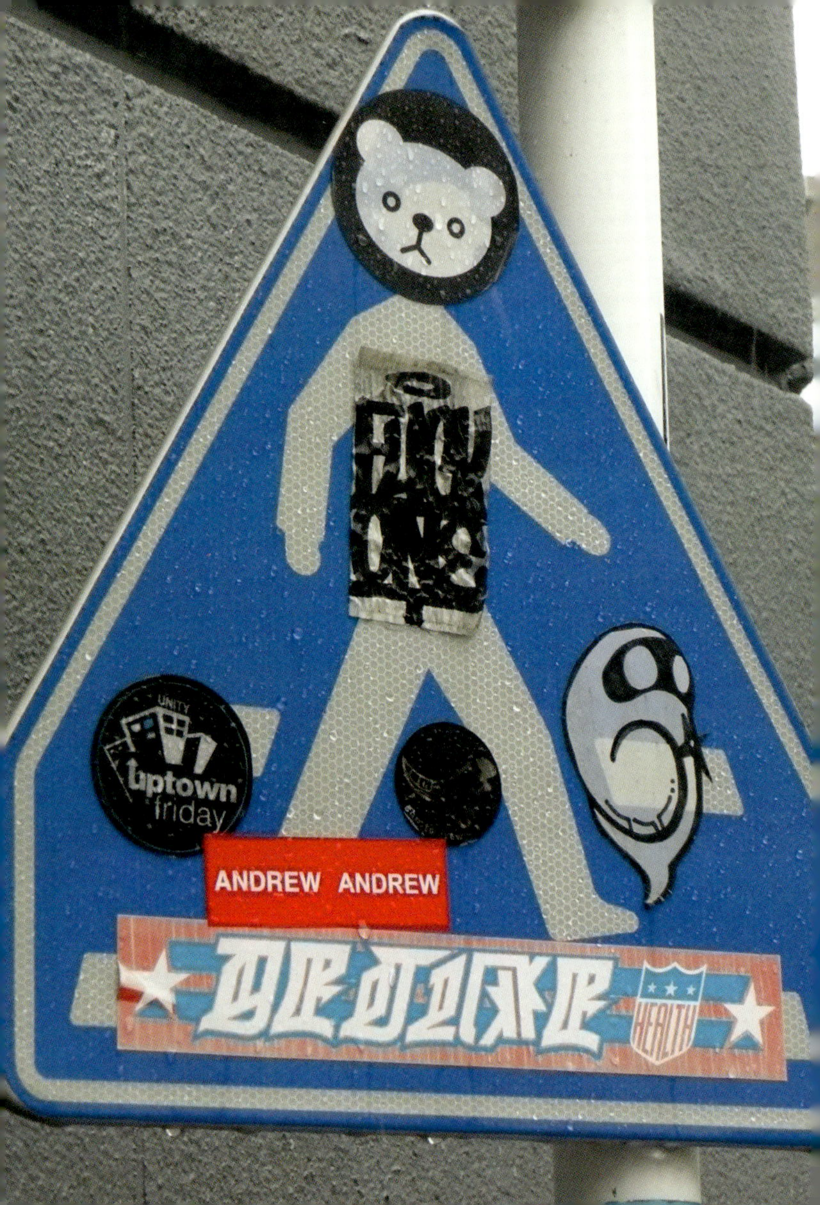
UNITY
uptown
friday
ANDREW ANDREW
HEALTH

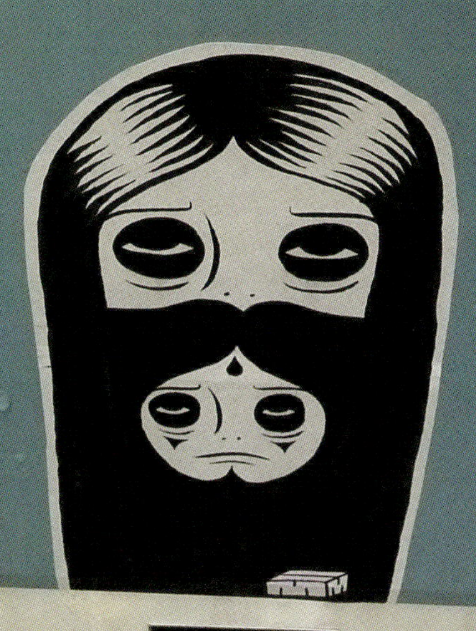
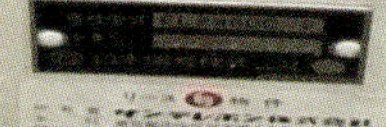

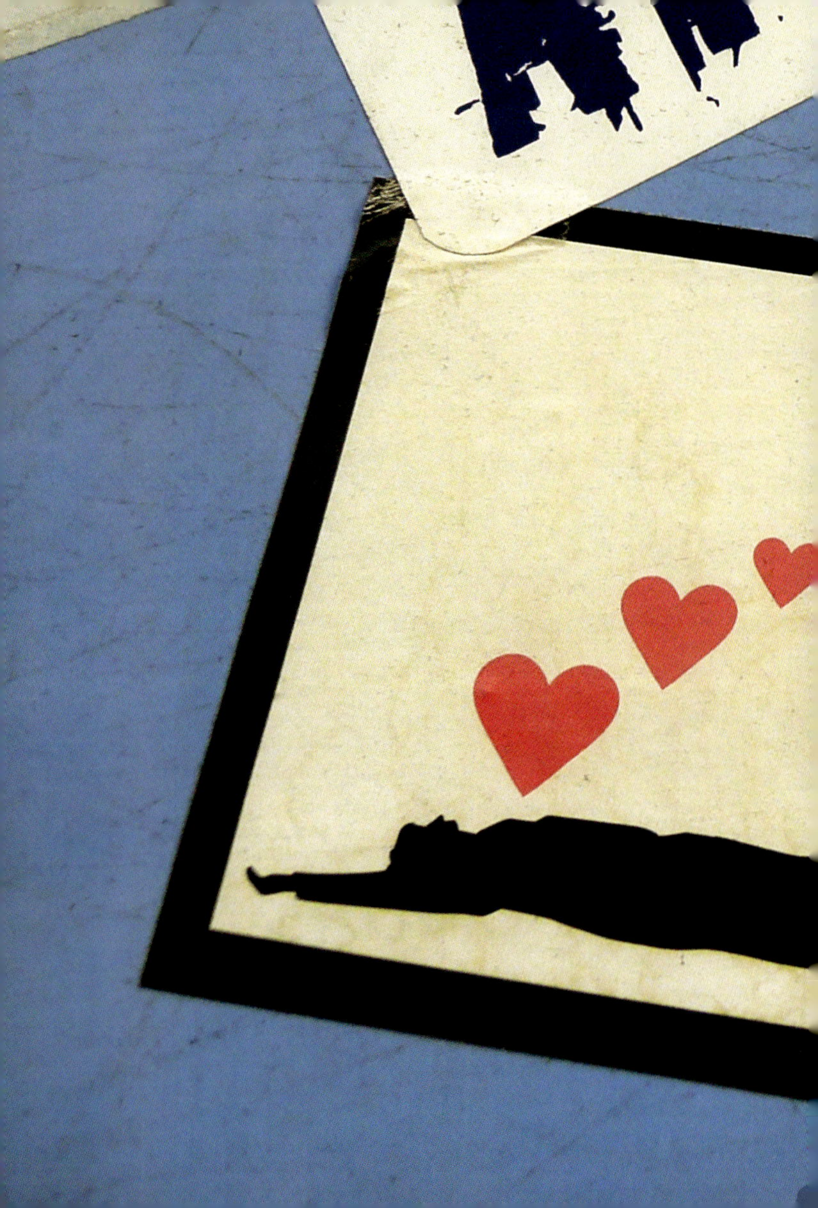

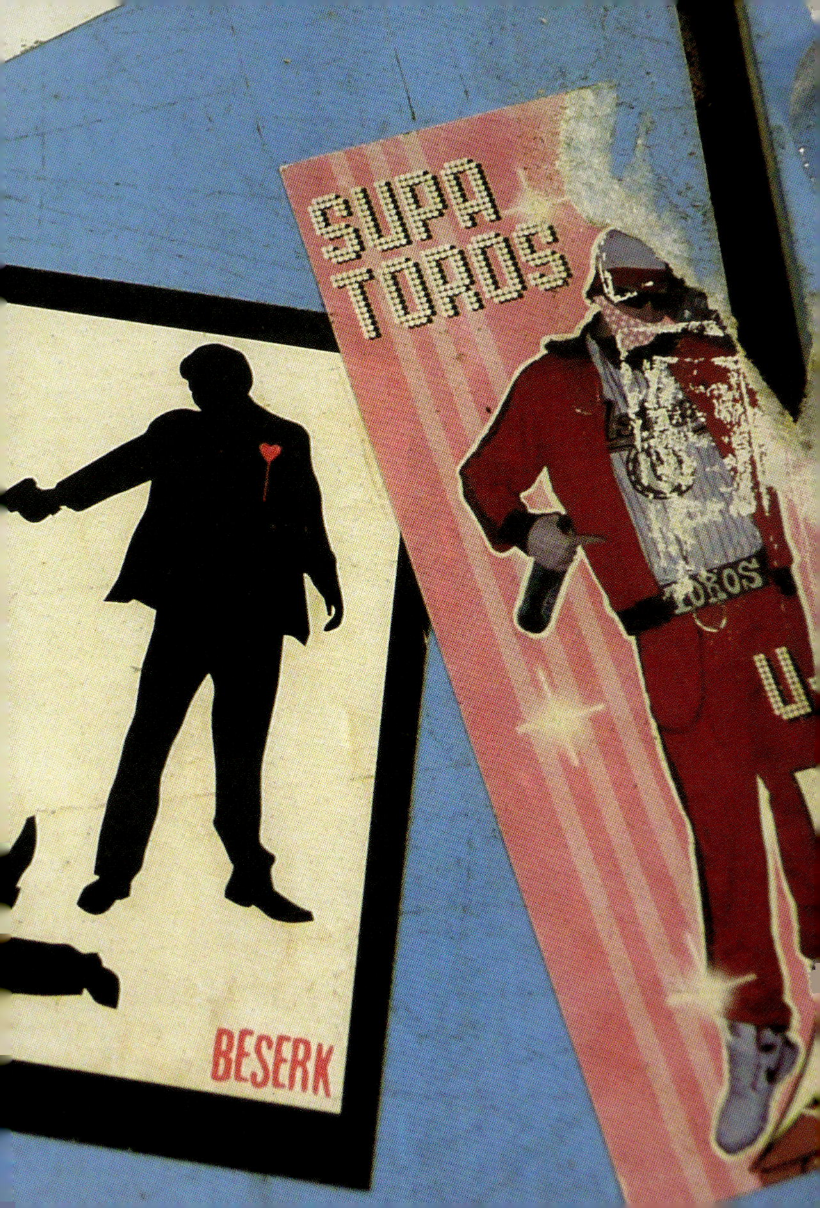
BESERK
SUPA
TOROS
TOROS

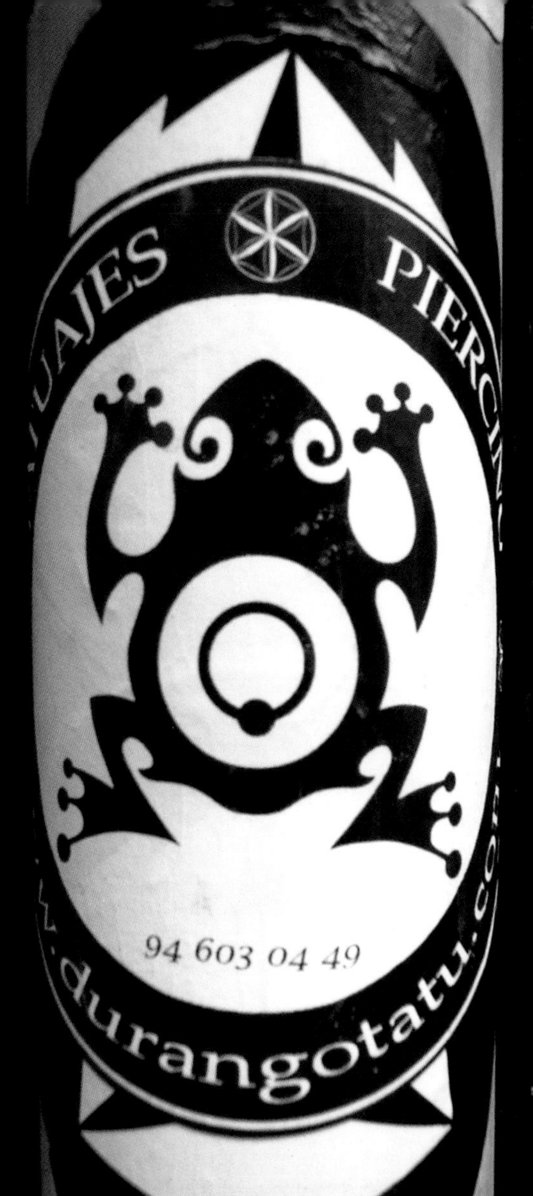
UAJES
PIERC
94 603 04 49
durangotatu.

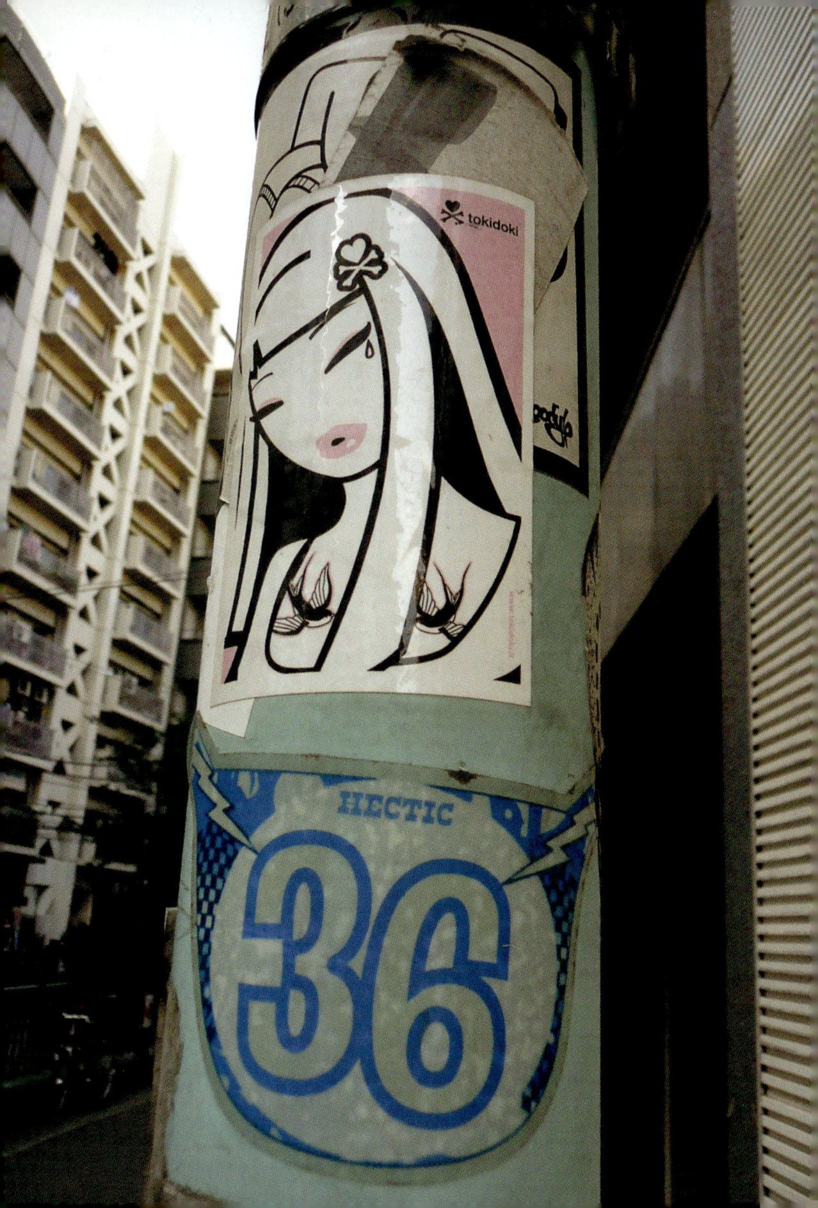

tokidoki
HECTIC
36

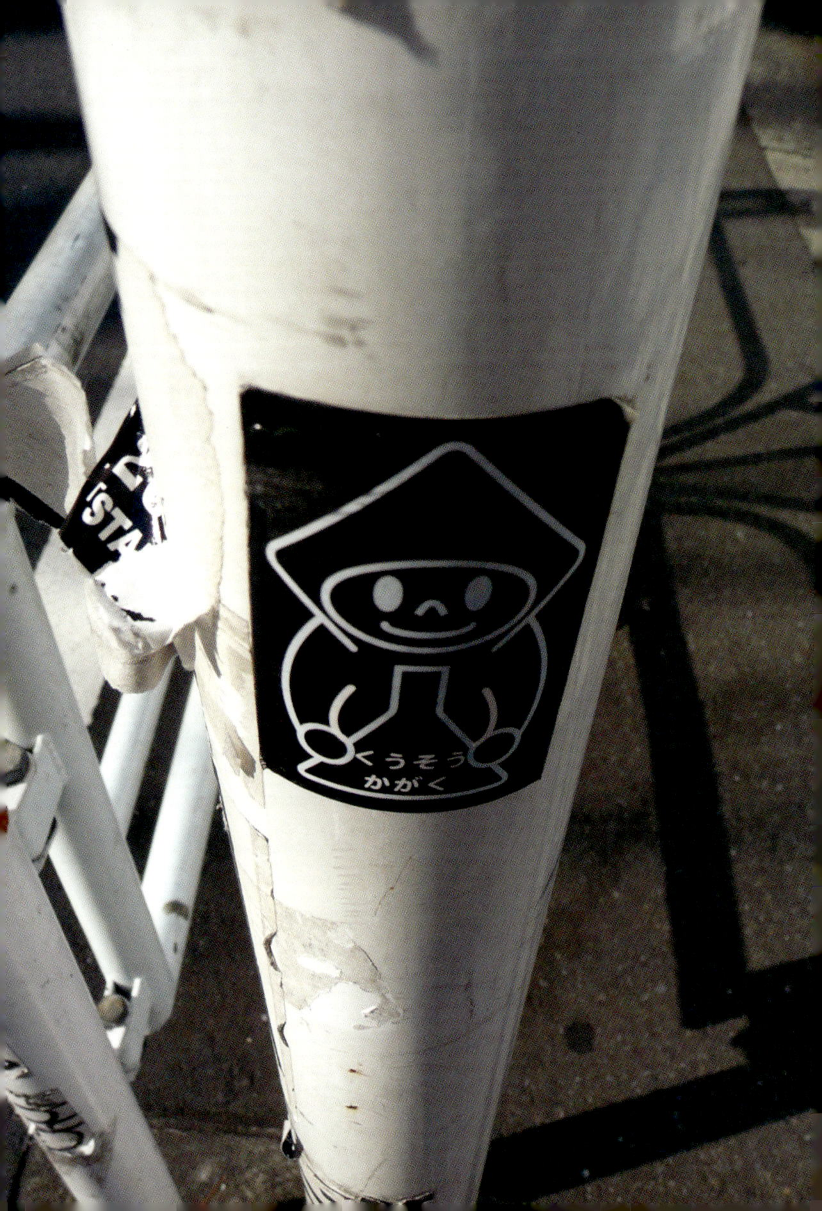
くうそう
かがく

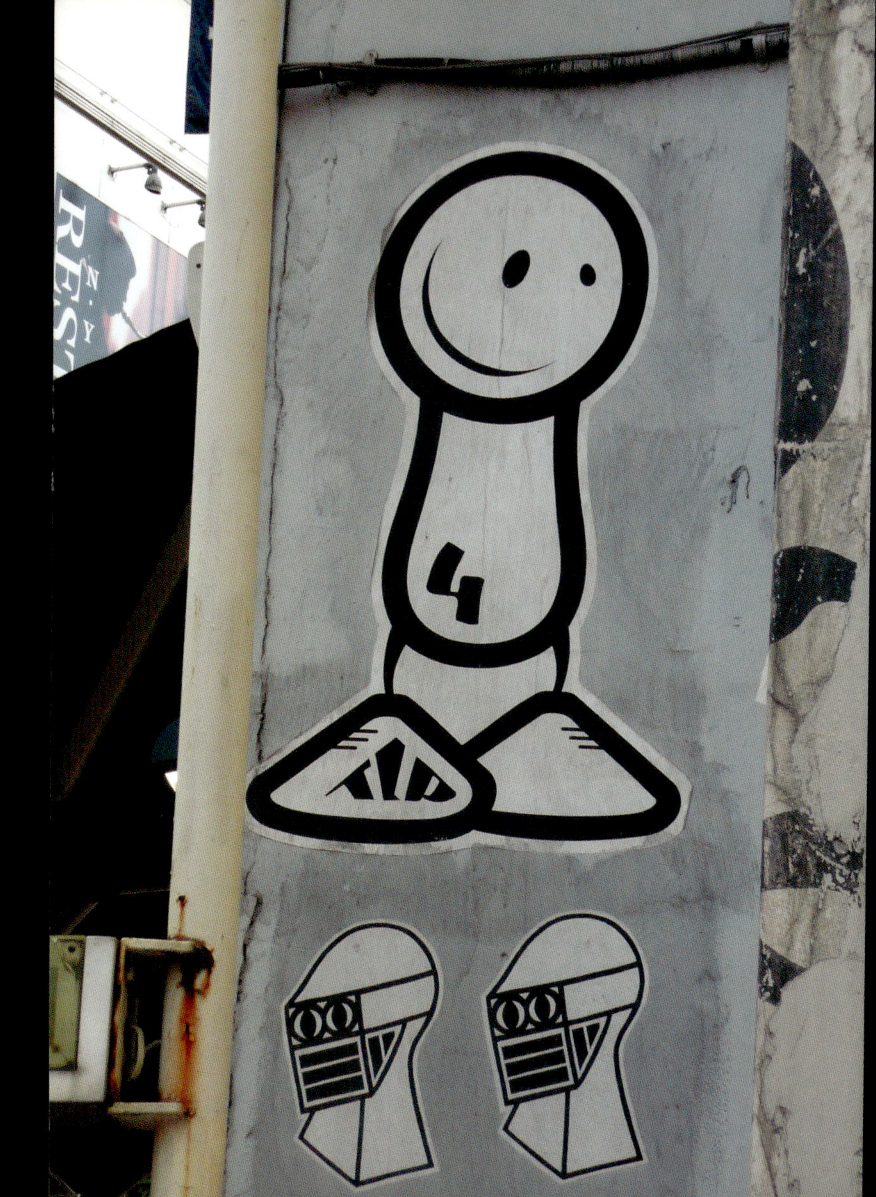
N.Y

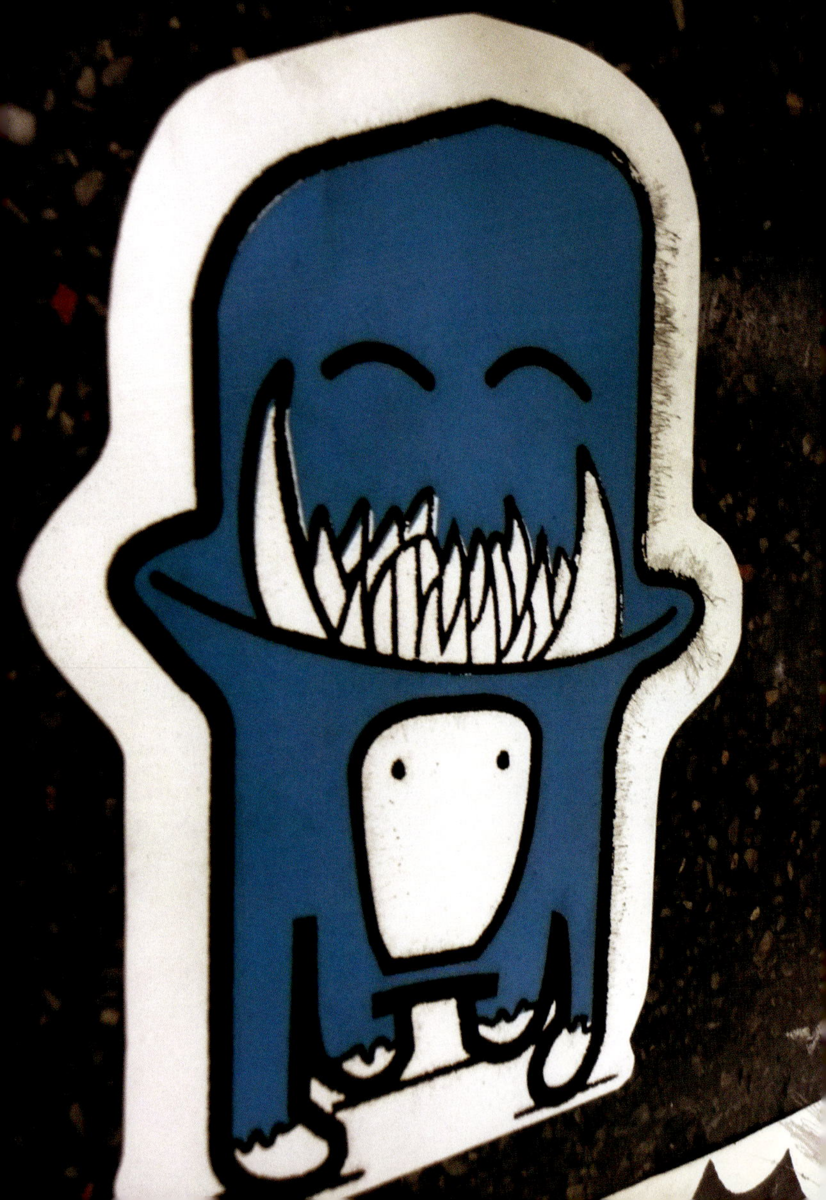

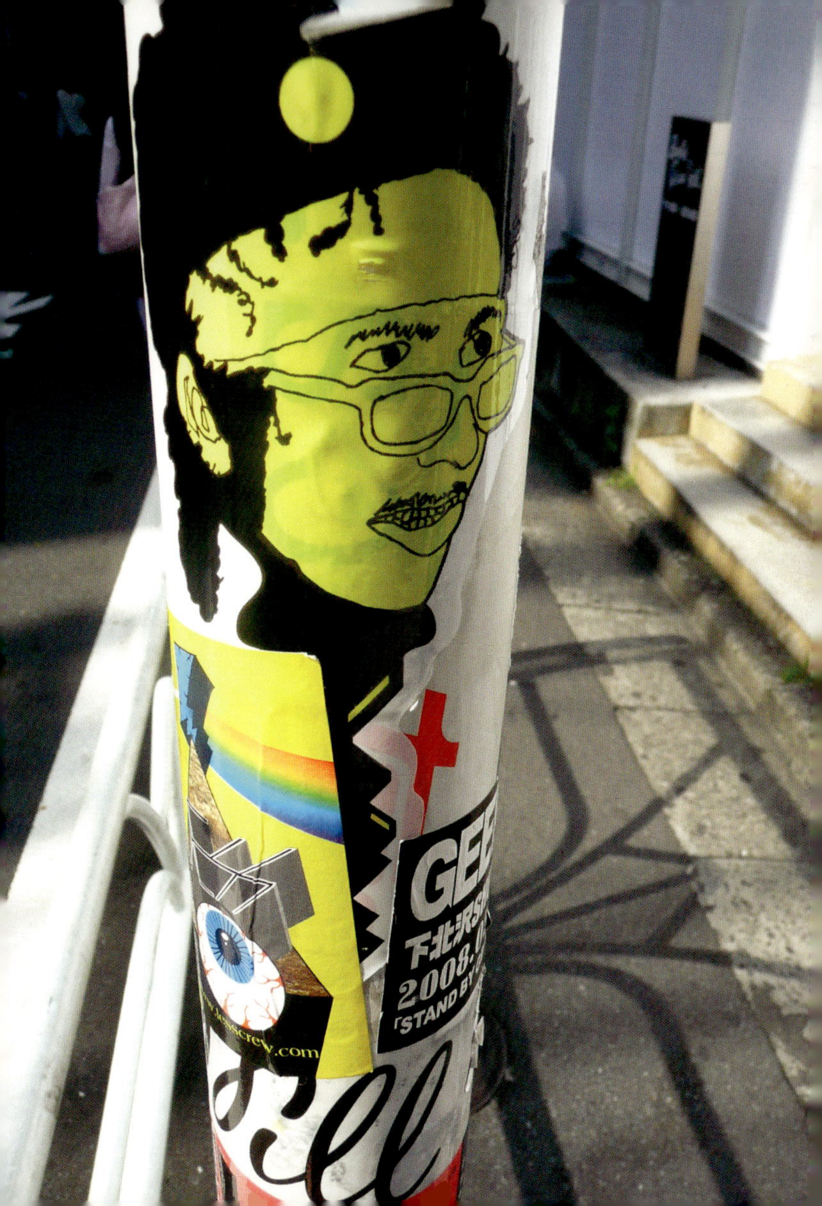
GEE
下北沢S
2008.
「STAND BY
screw.com

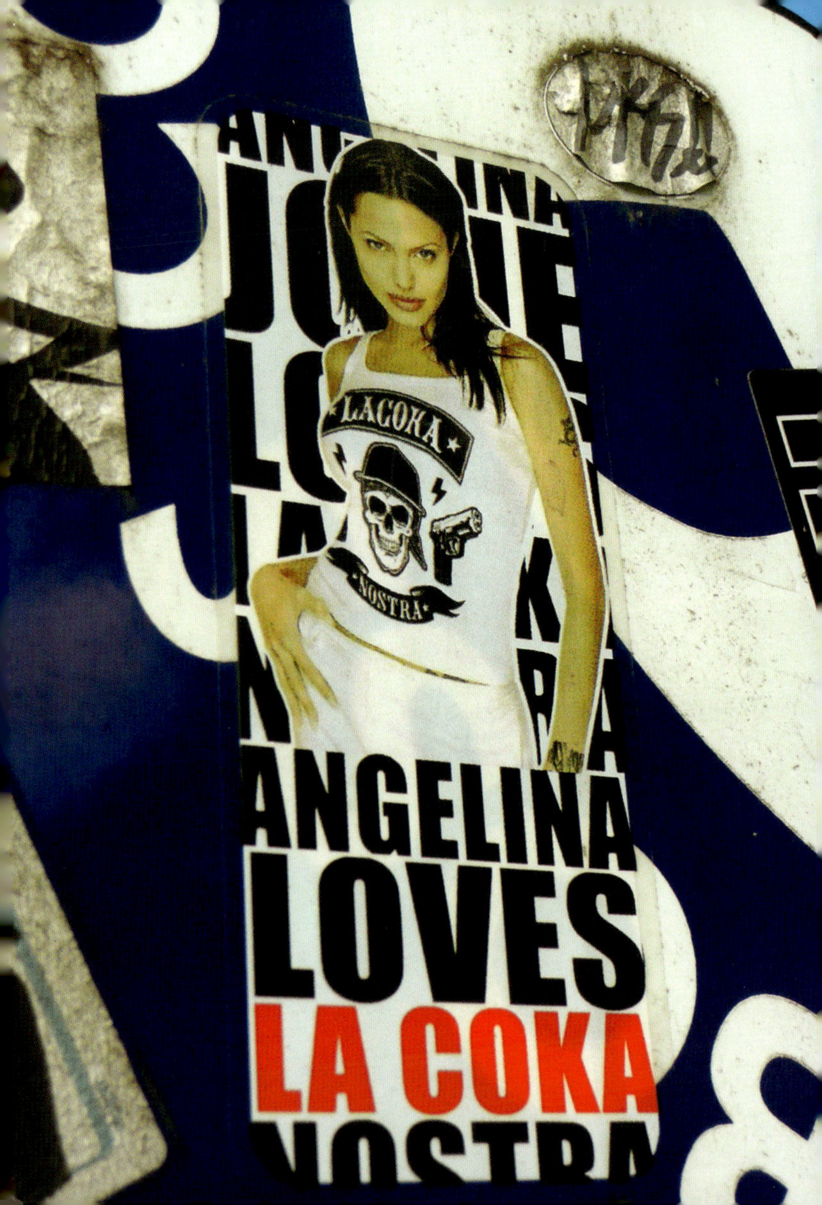
LACOKA
NOSTRA
ANGELINA
LOVES
LA COKA
NOSTRA

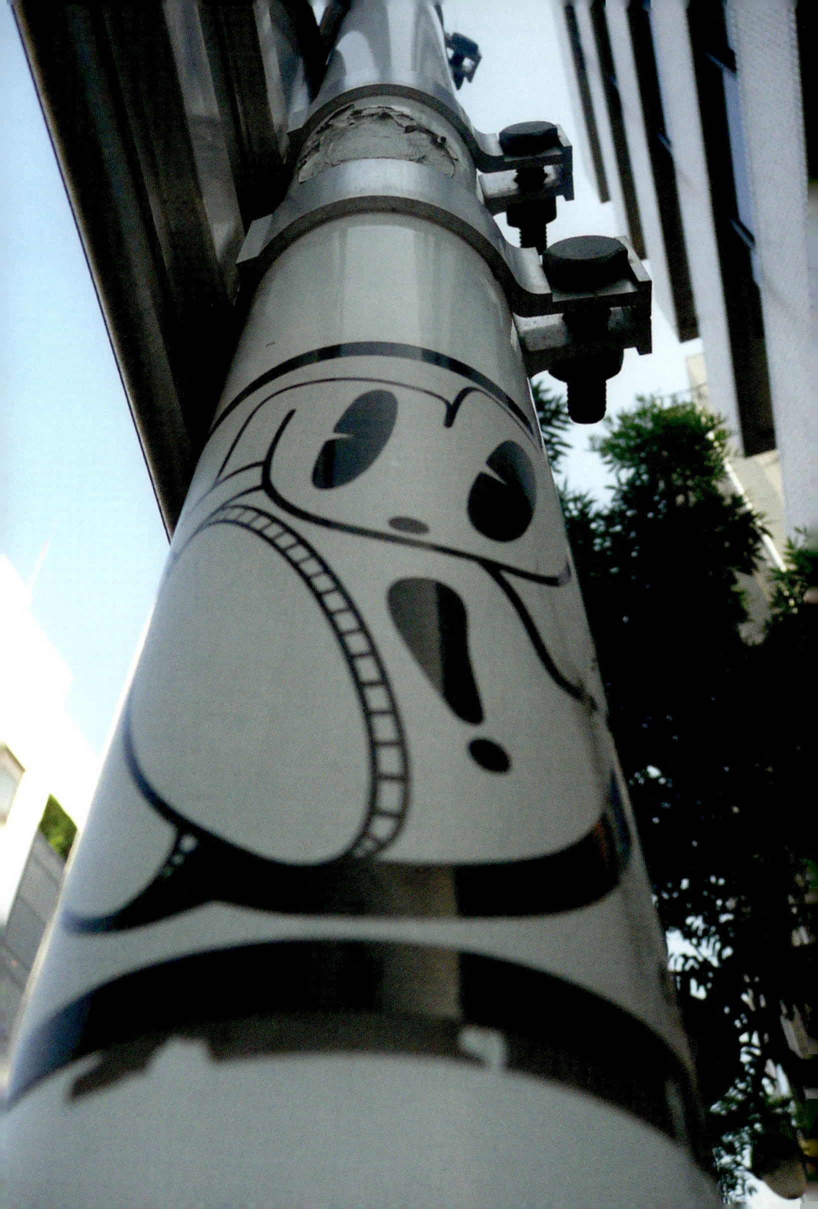

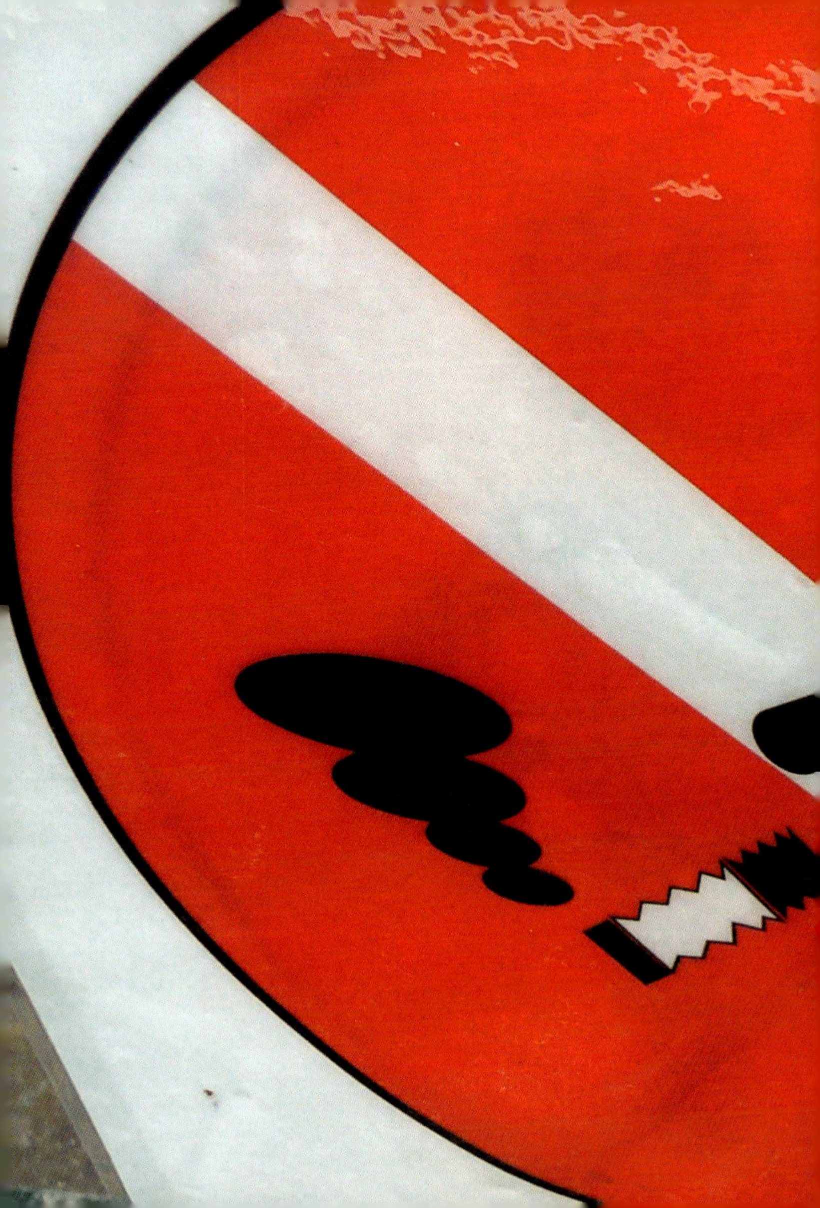

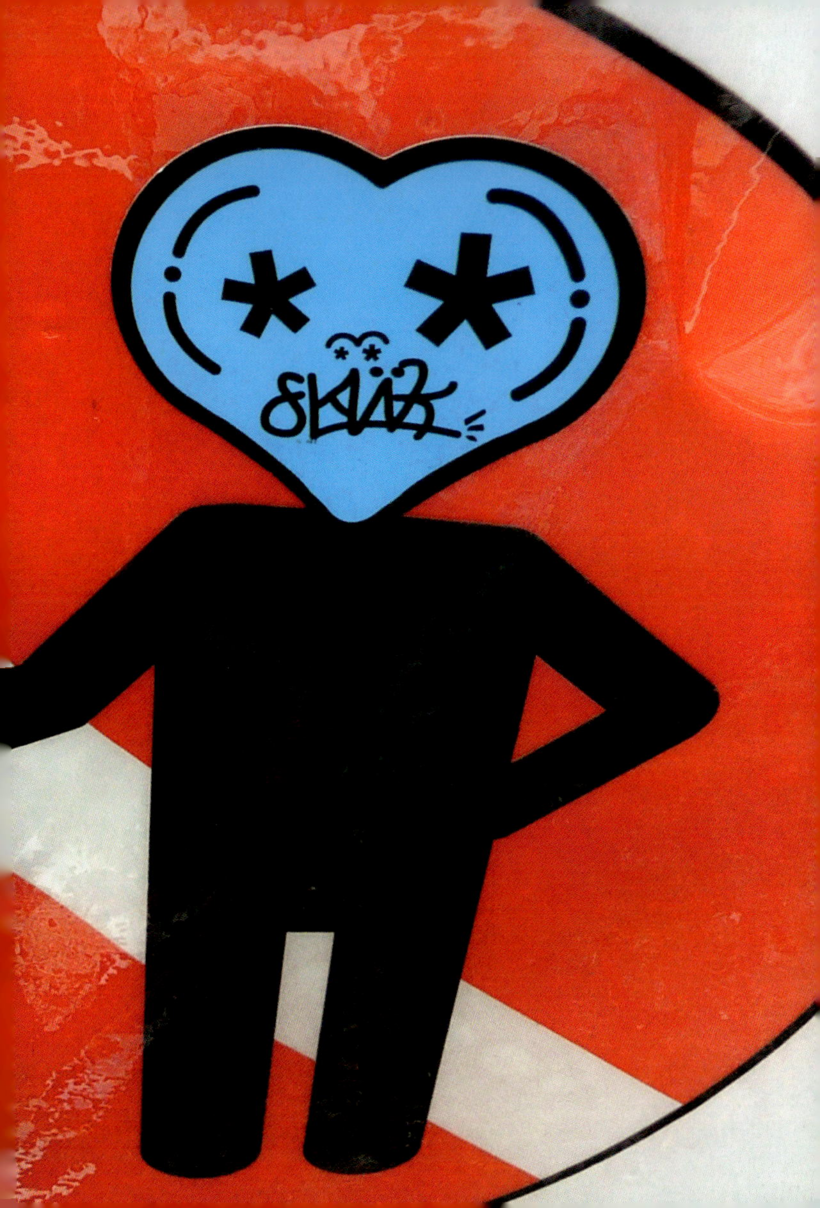

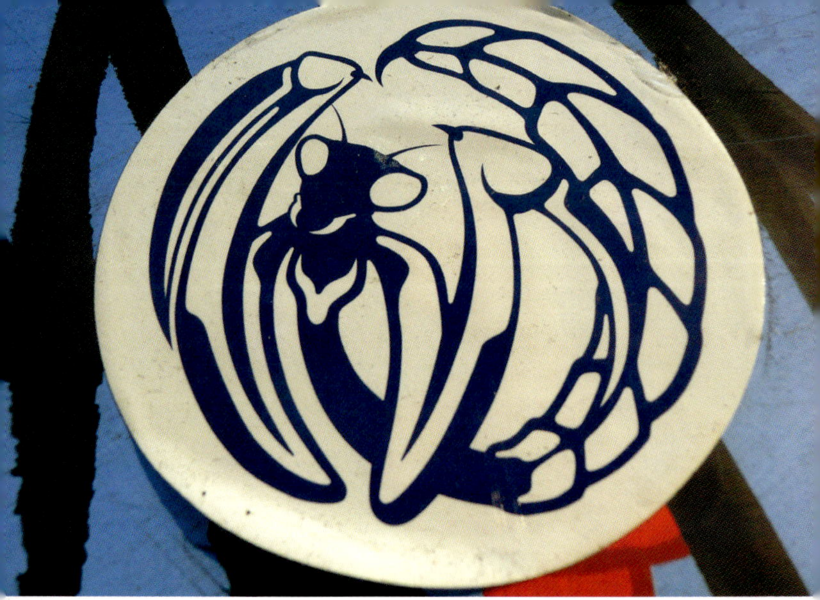

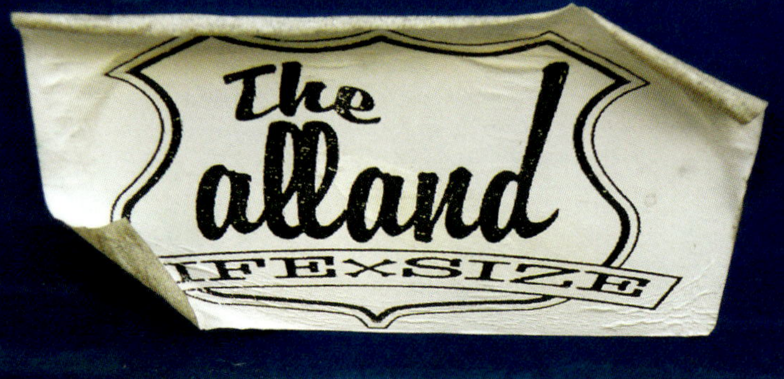
The
alland
IFE×SIZE

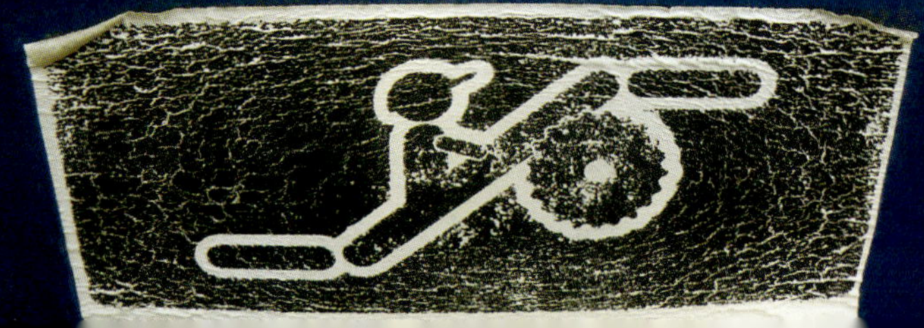

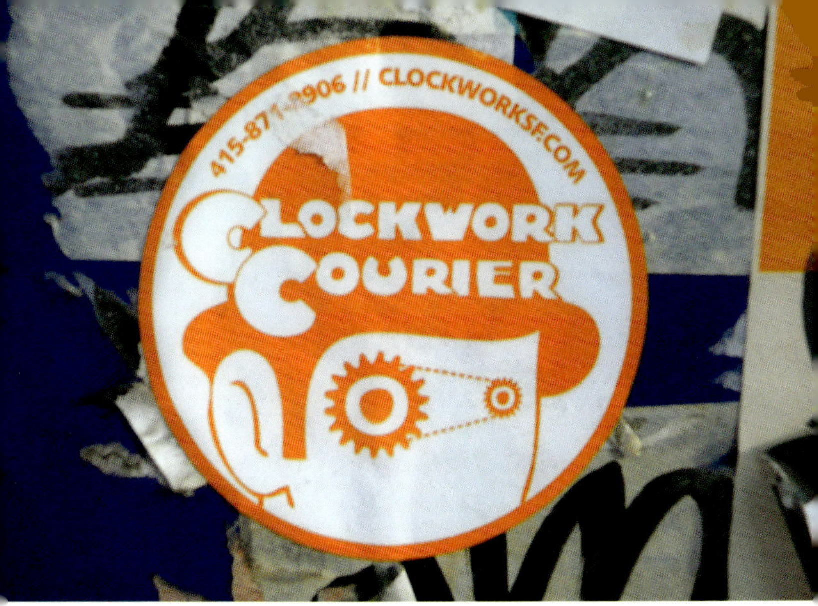

415-871-2906 // CLOCKWORKSF.COM
CLOCKWORK
COURIER

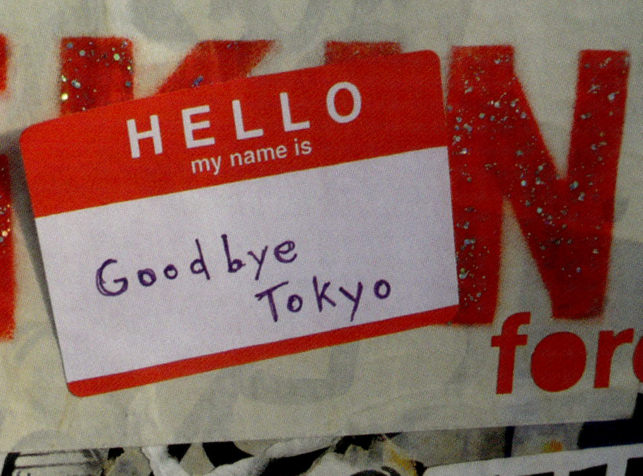
HELLO
my name is
Goodbye
Tokyo
fore

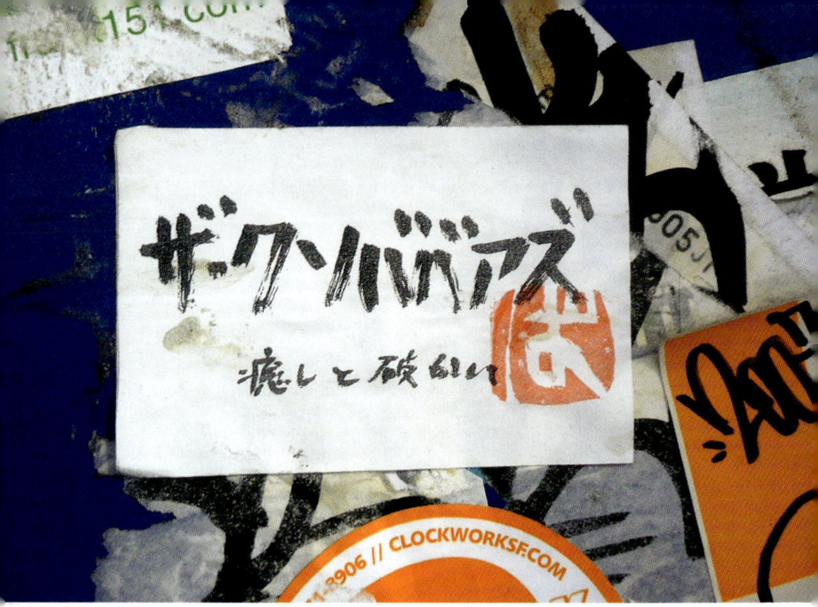

CLOCKWORKSF.COM

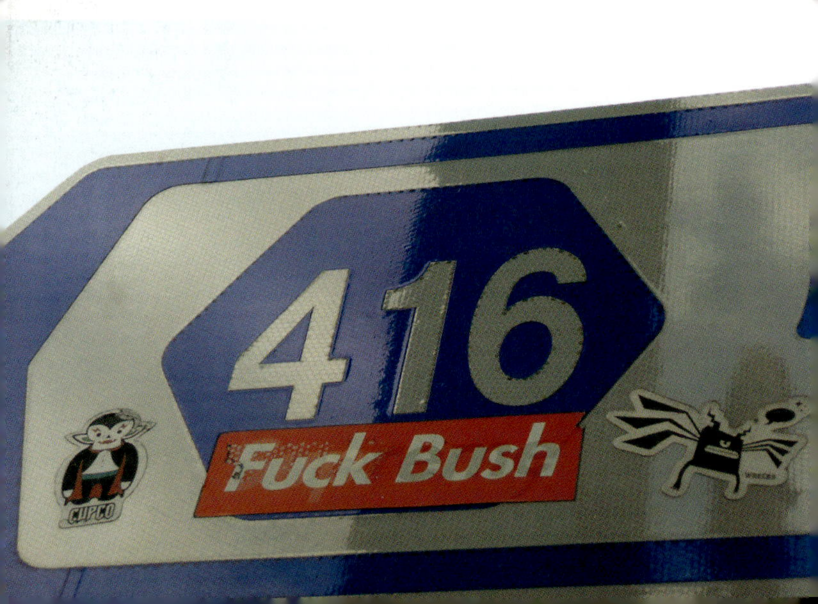

416

Fuck Bush

CUPCO

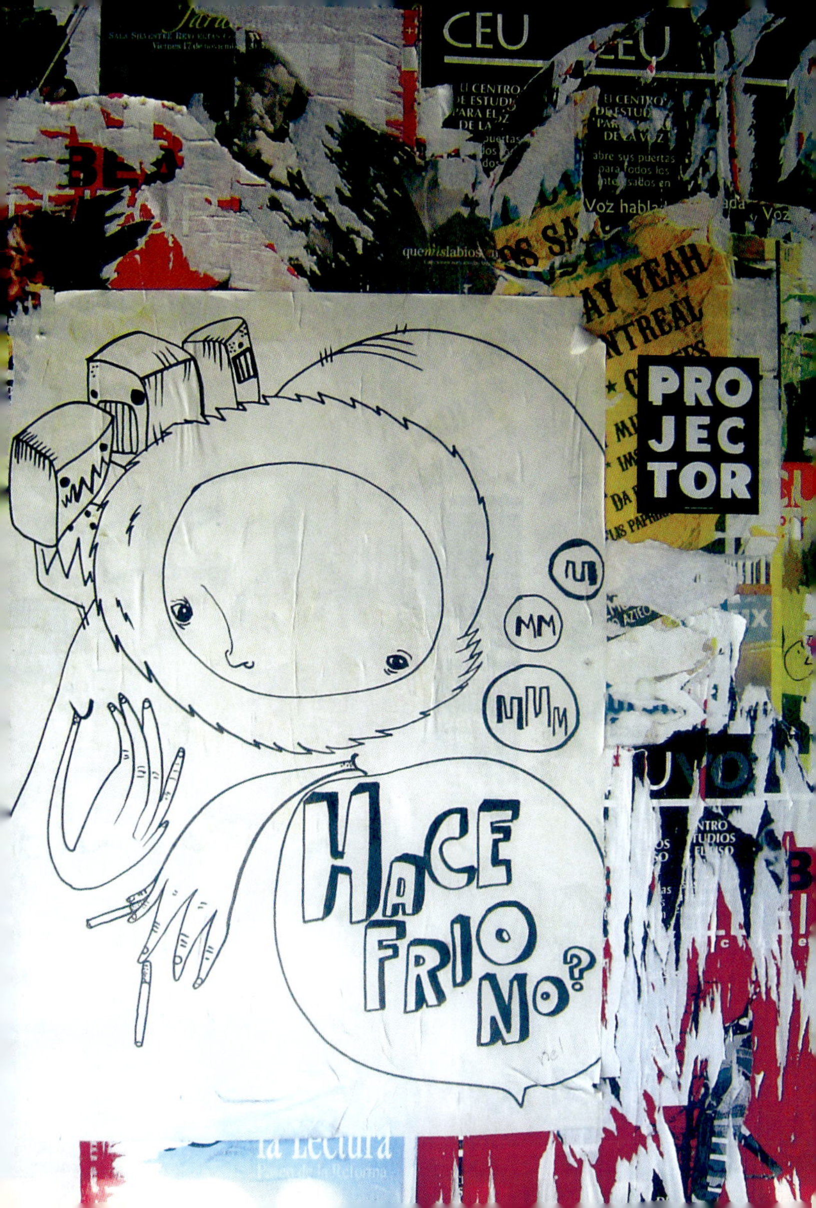
CEU
El CENTRO DE ESTUDIOS PARA EL USO DE LA VOZ
abre sus puertas para todos los interesados en
AY YEAH
PRO JEC TOR
MM
MMM
HACE FRIO NO?
la Lectura
Paseo de la Reforma

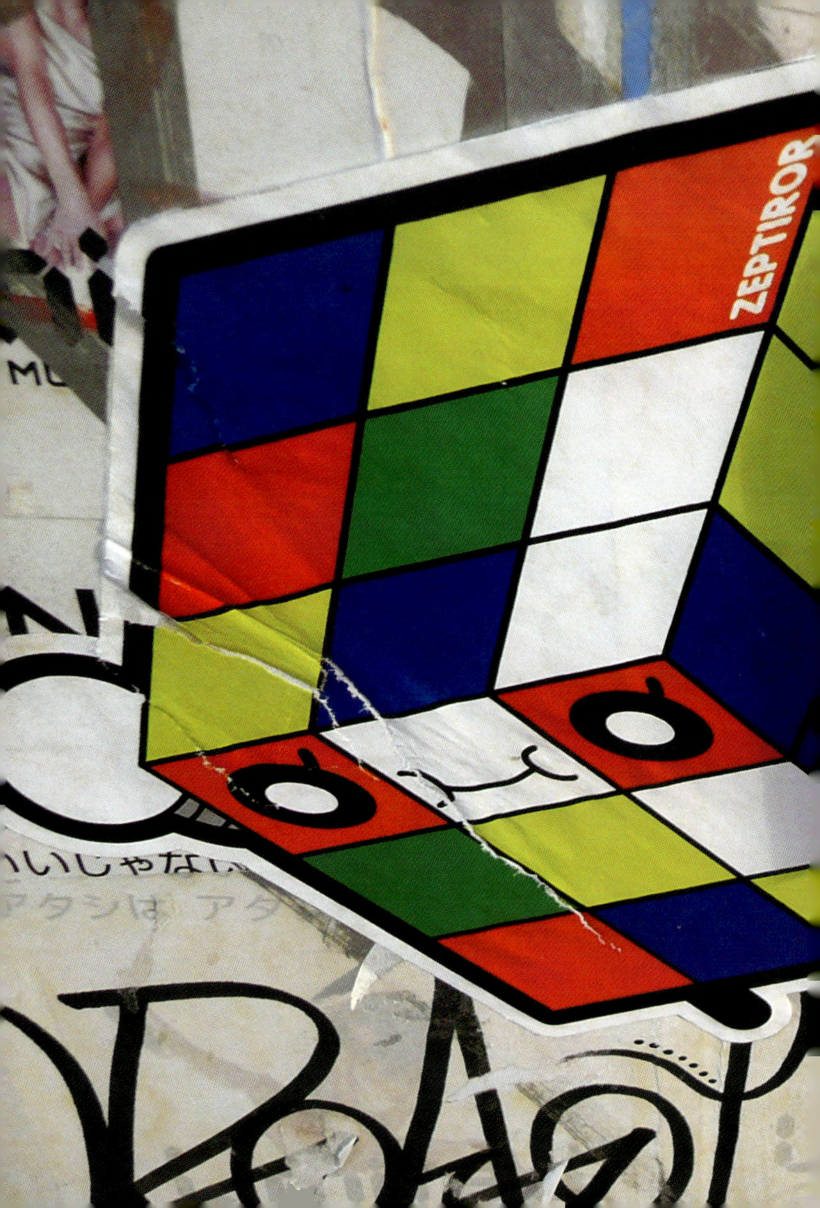
ZEPTIROR

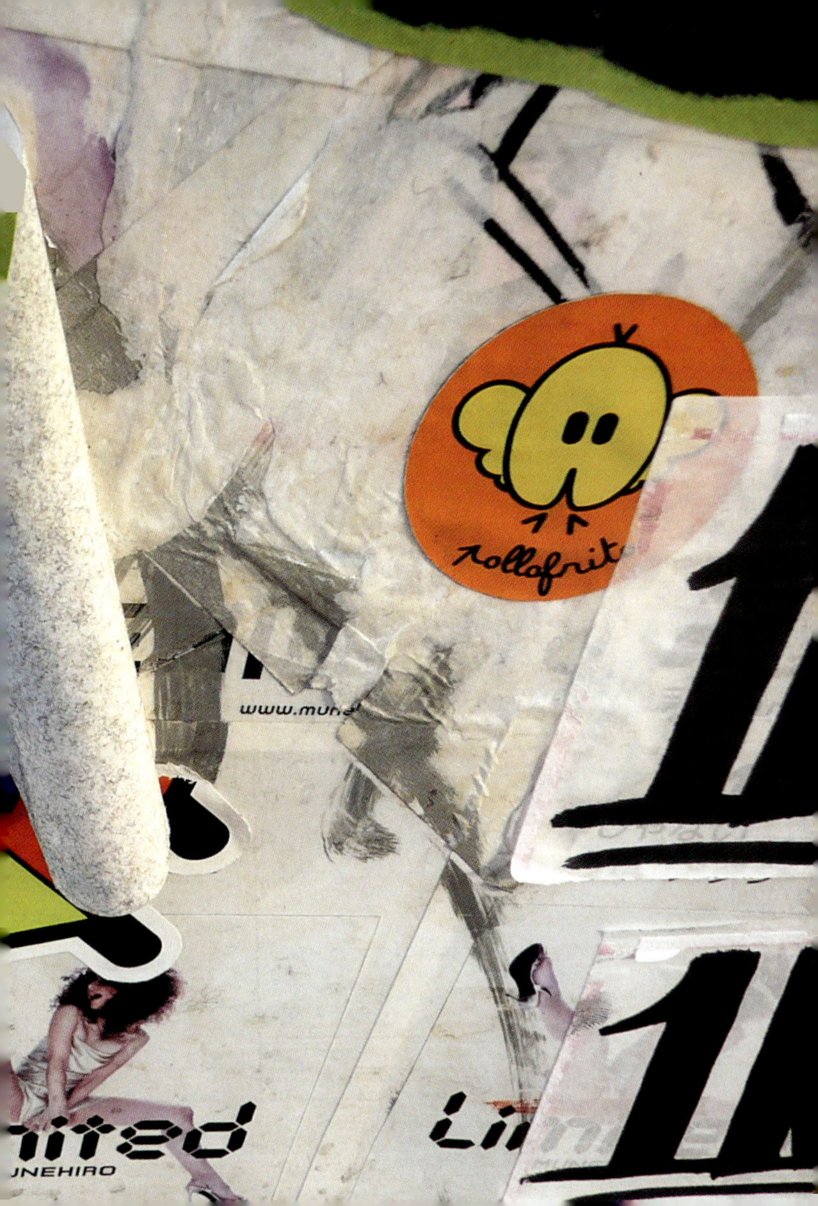
rollofrit
www.mun
ited
UNEHIRO

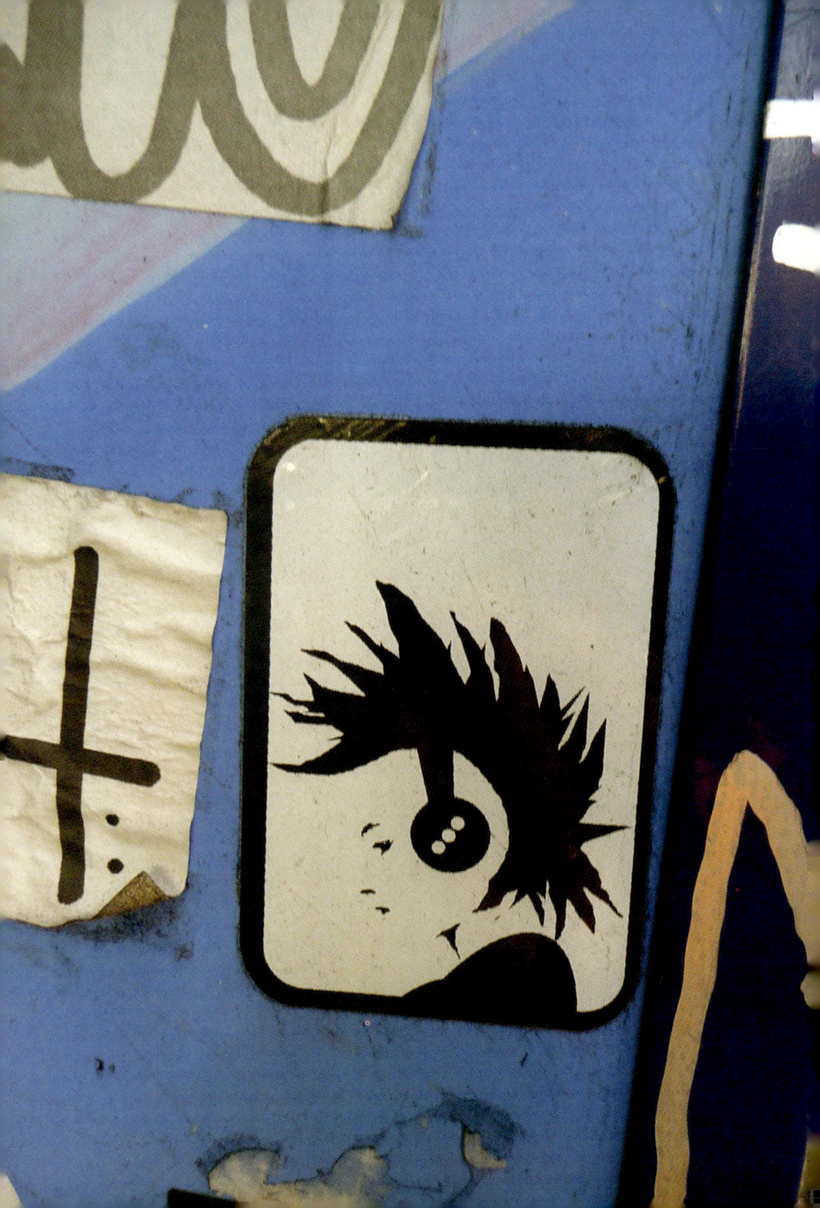

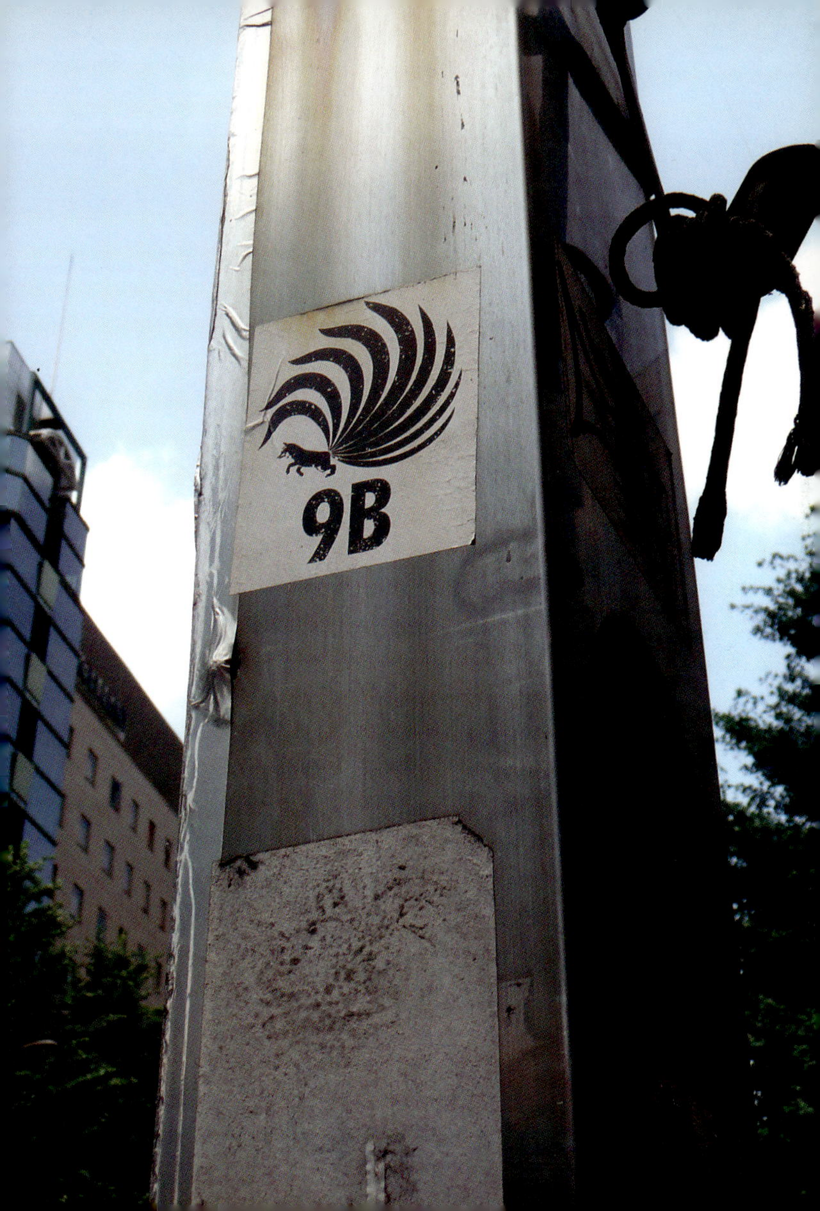
9B

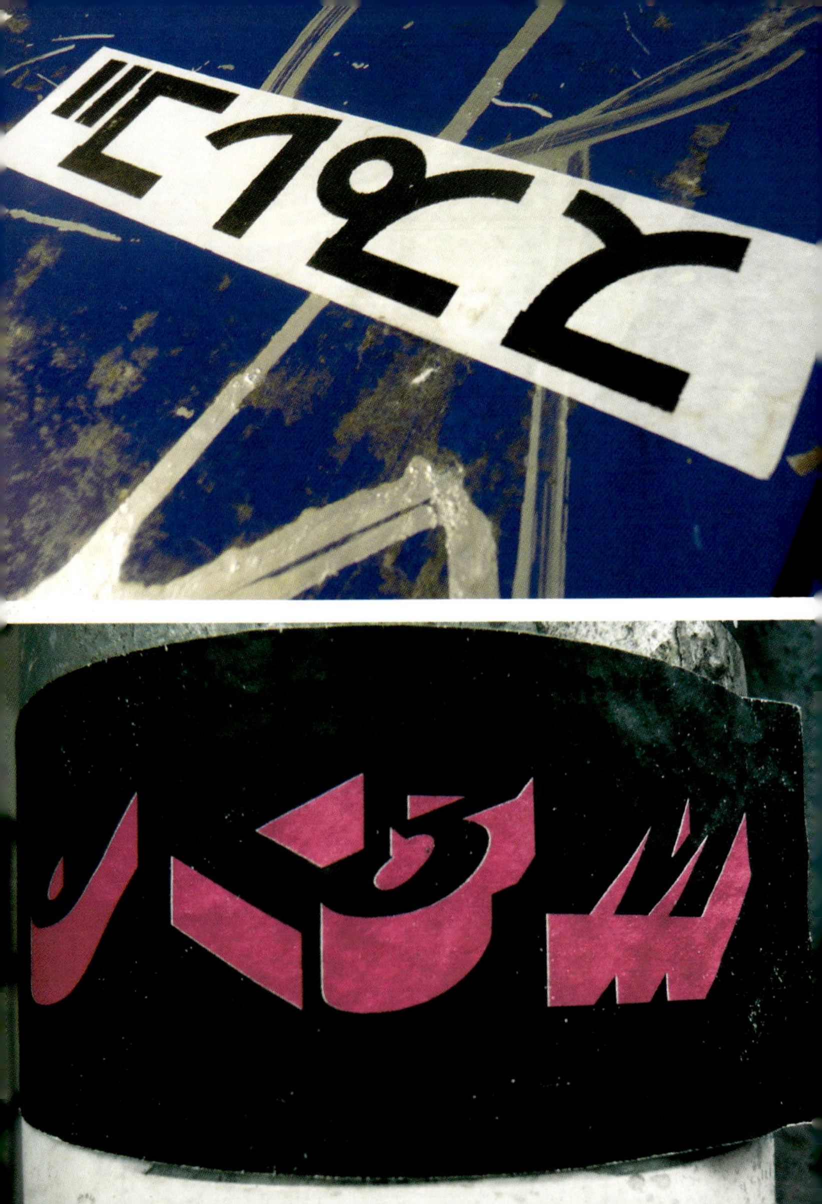

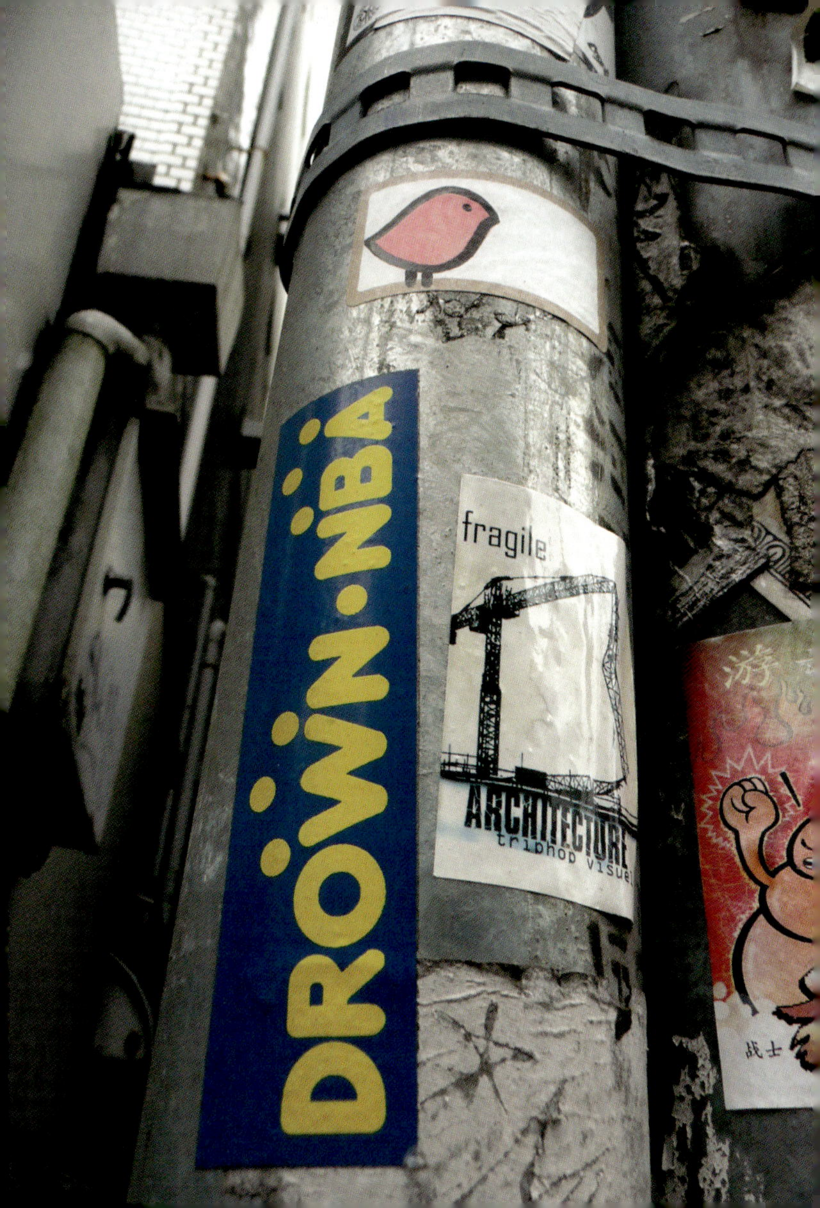
DRÖWN·NBÄ
fragile
ARCHITECTURE
triphop visuel
游
战士

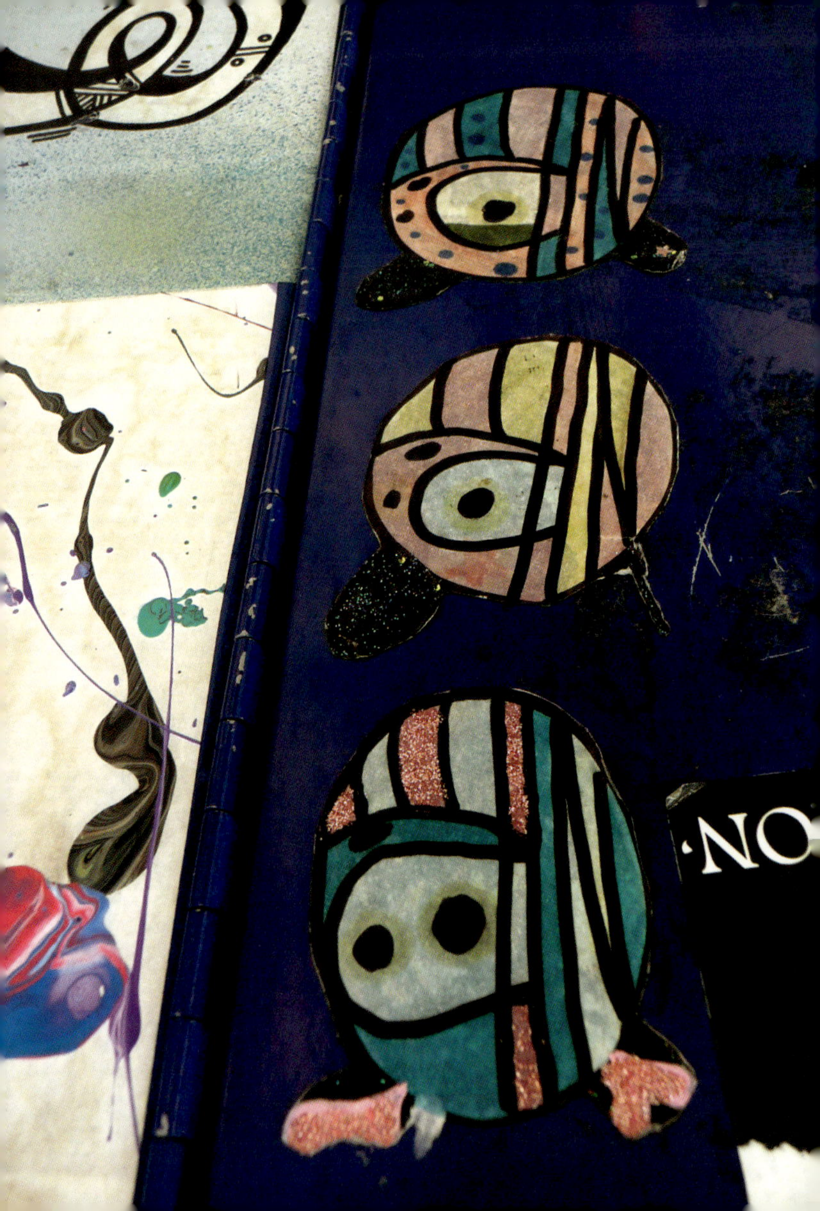

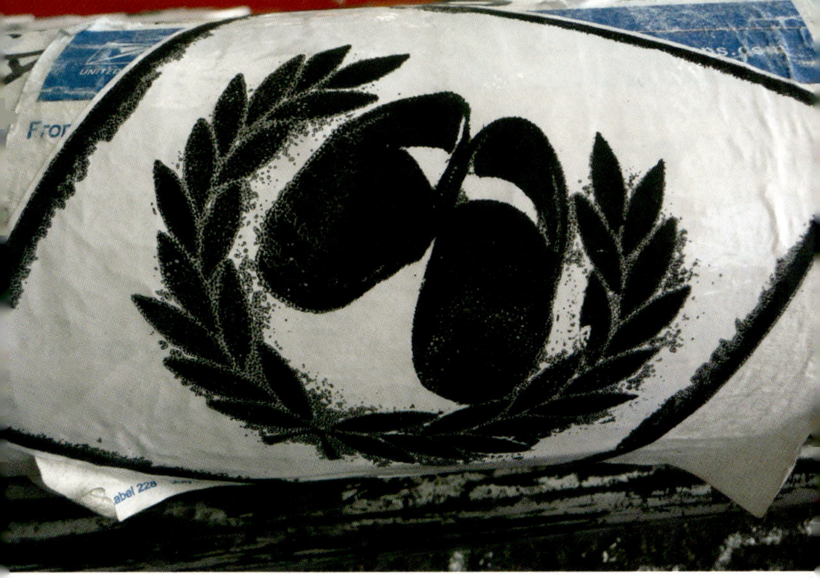

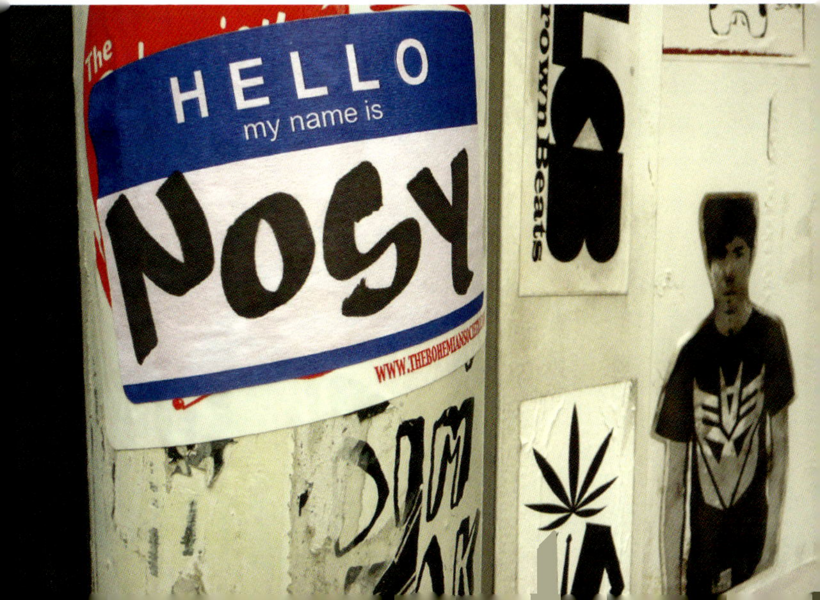

HELLO
my name is
NOSY

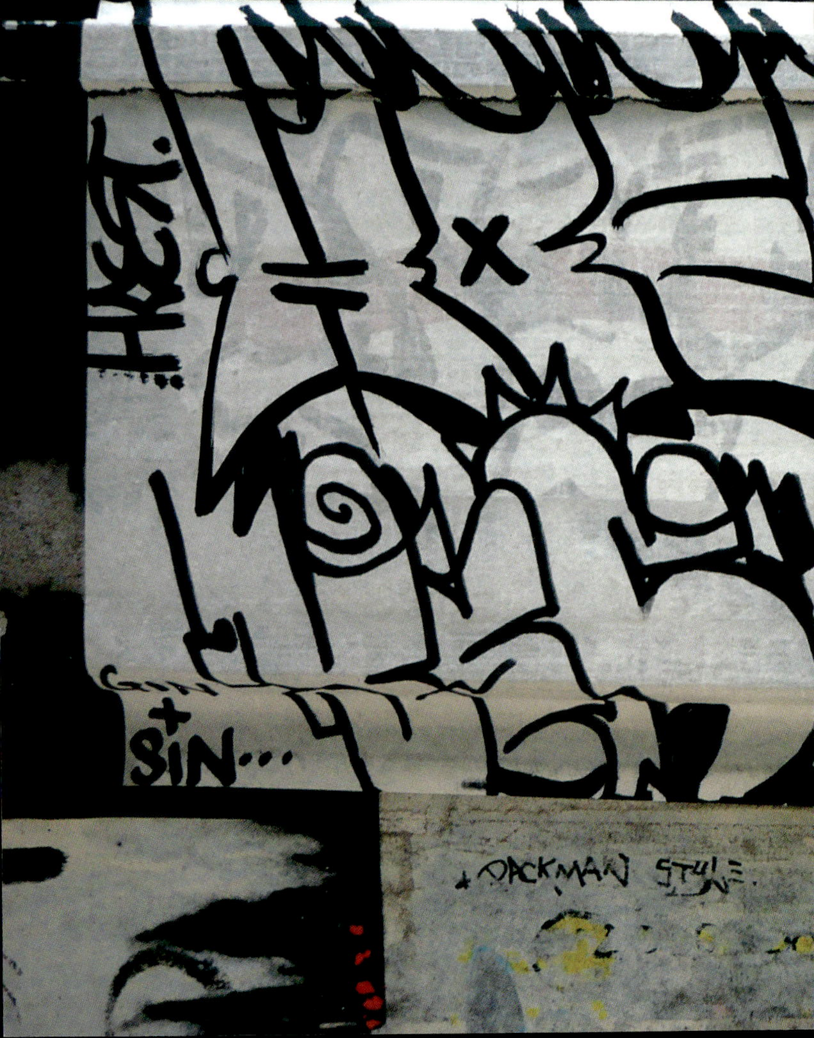
+ SIN...

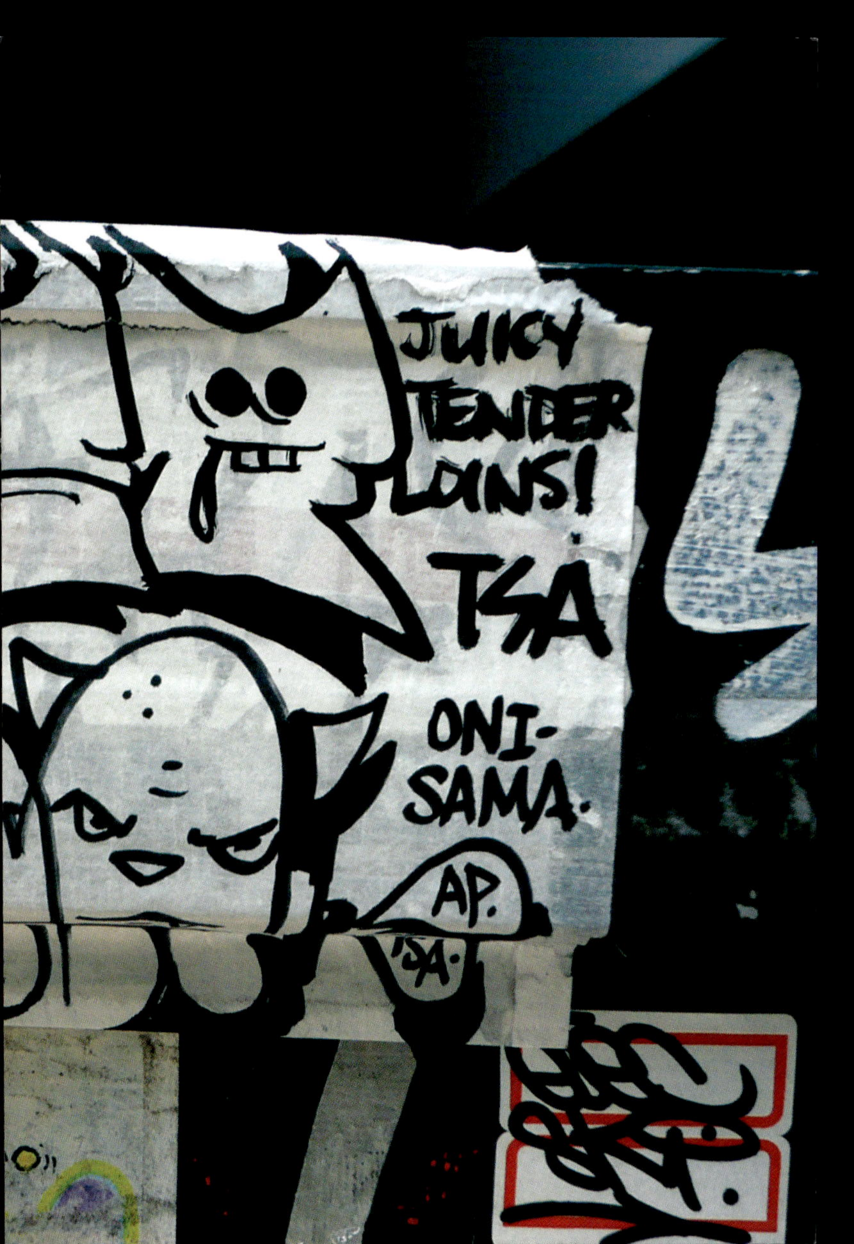

JUICY
TENDER
LOINS!
TSA
ONI-
SAMA.
AP.
TSA.

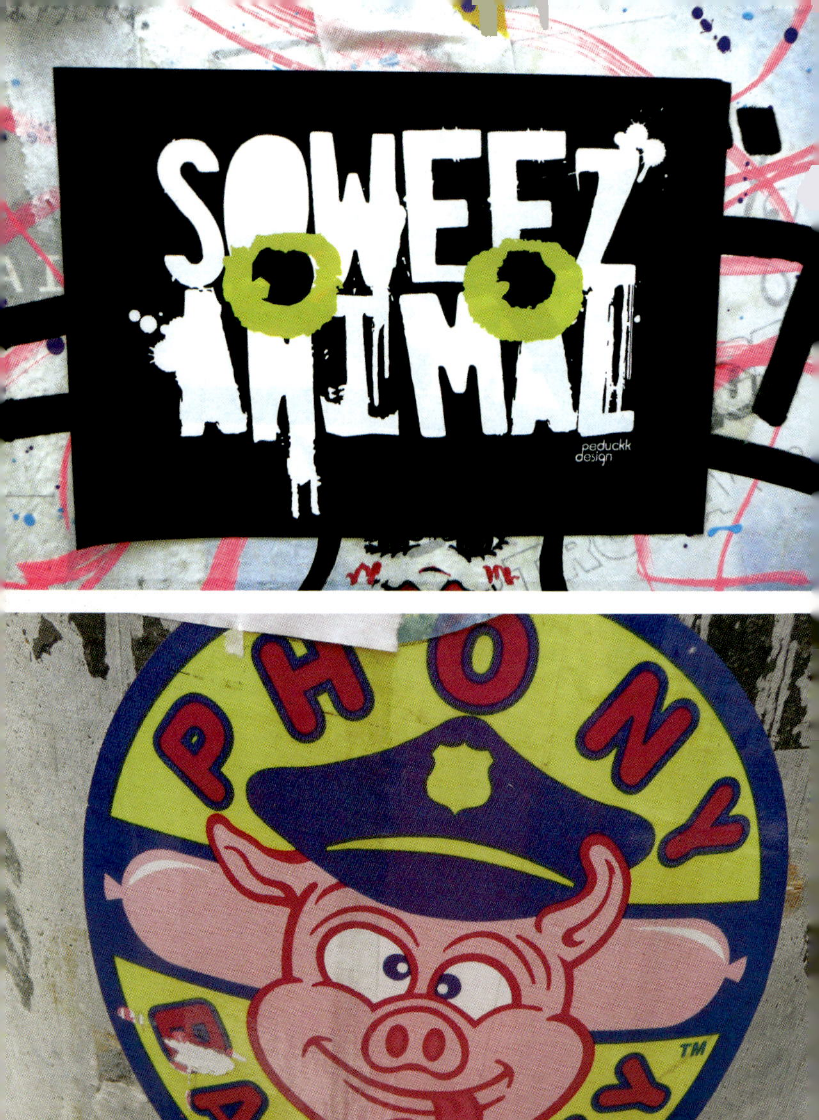
peduckk design
PHONY
TM

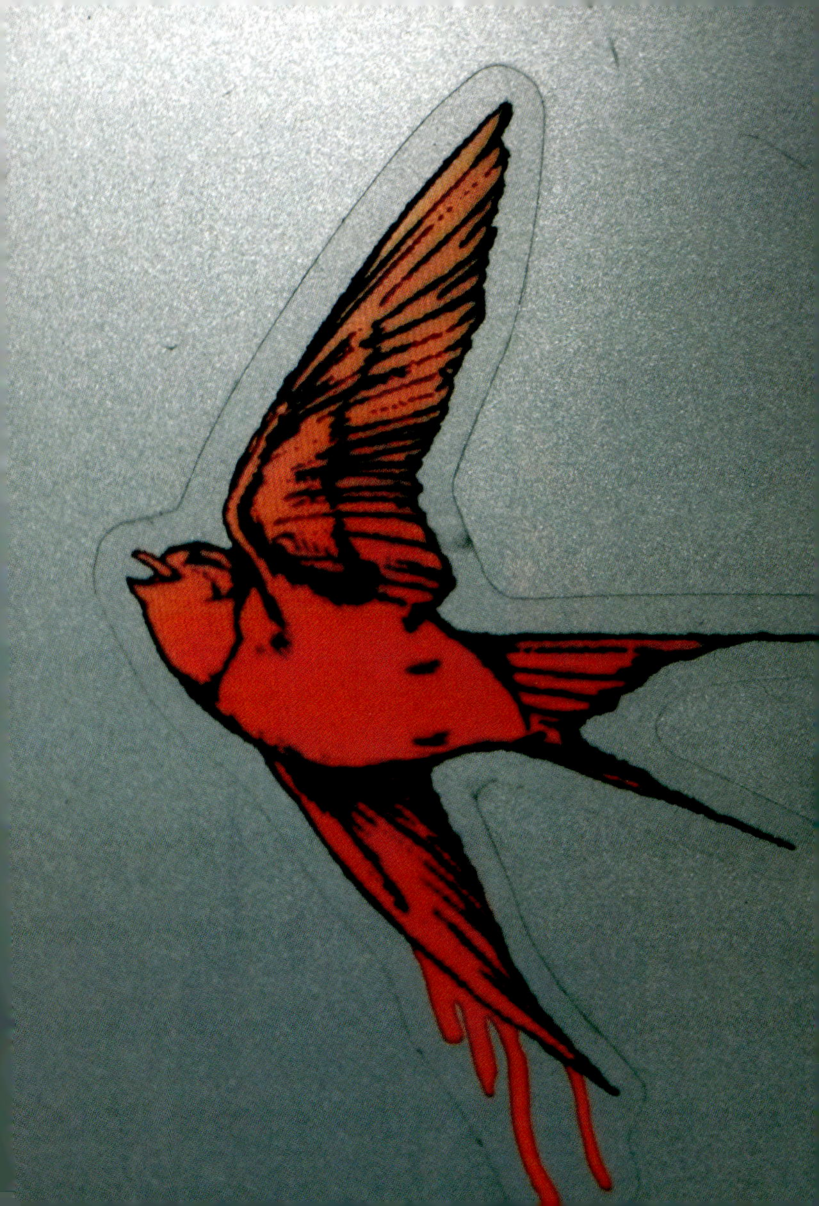

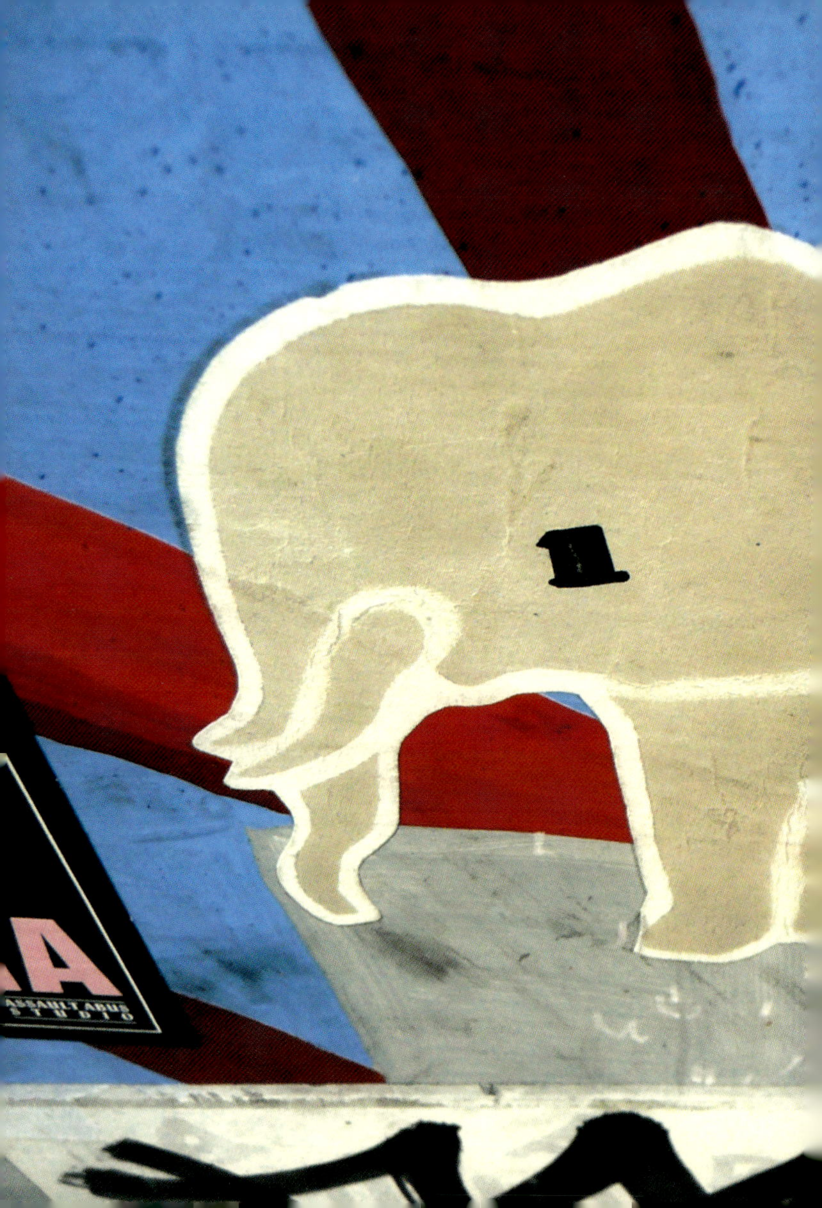
ASSAULT ABUS
STUDIO

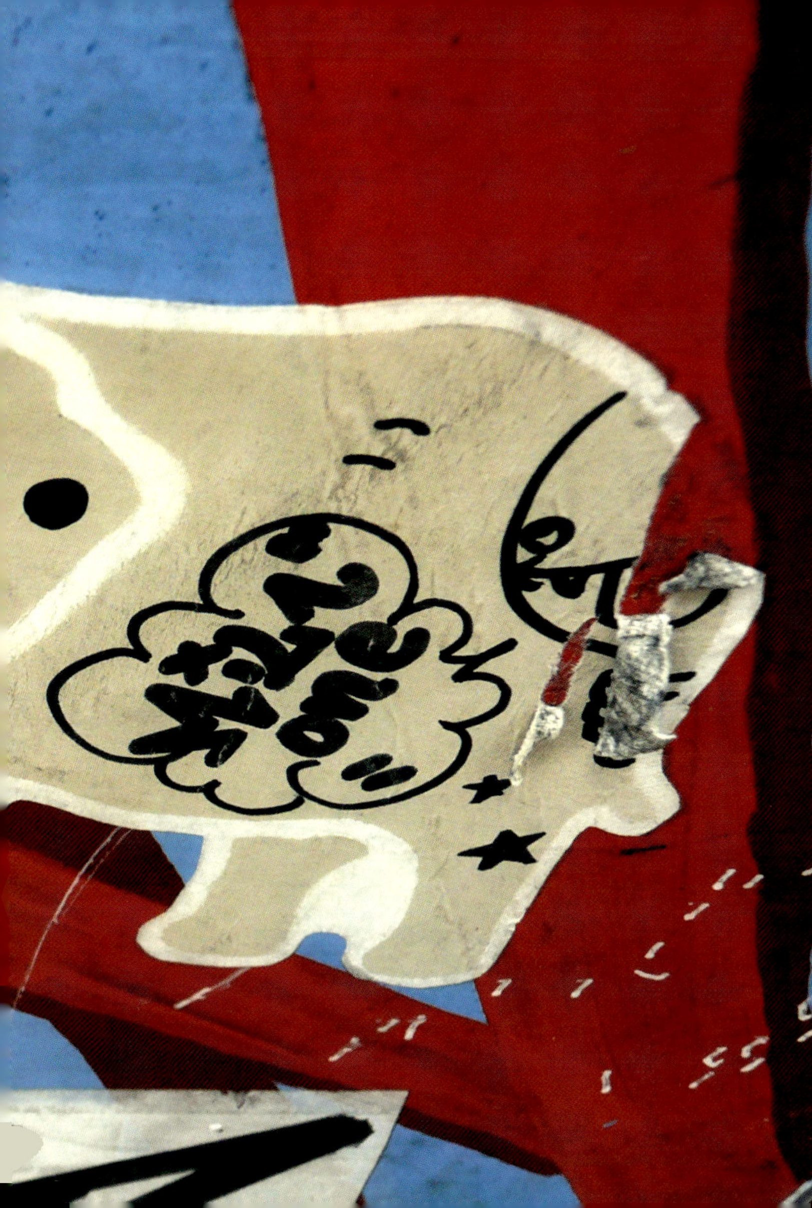

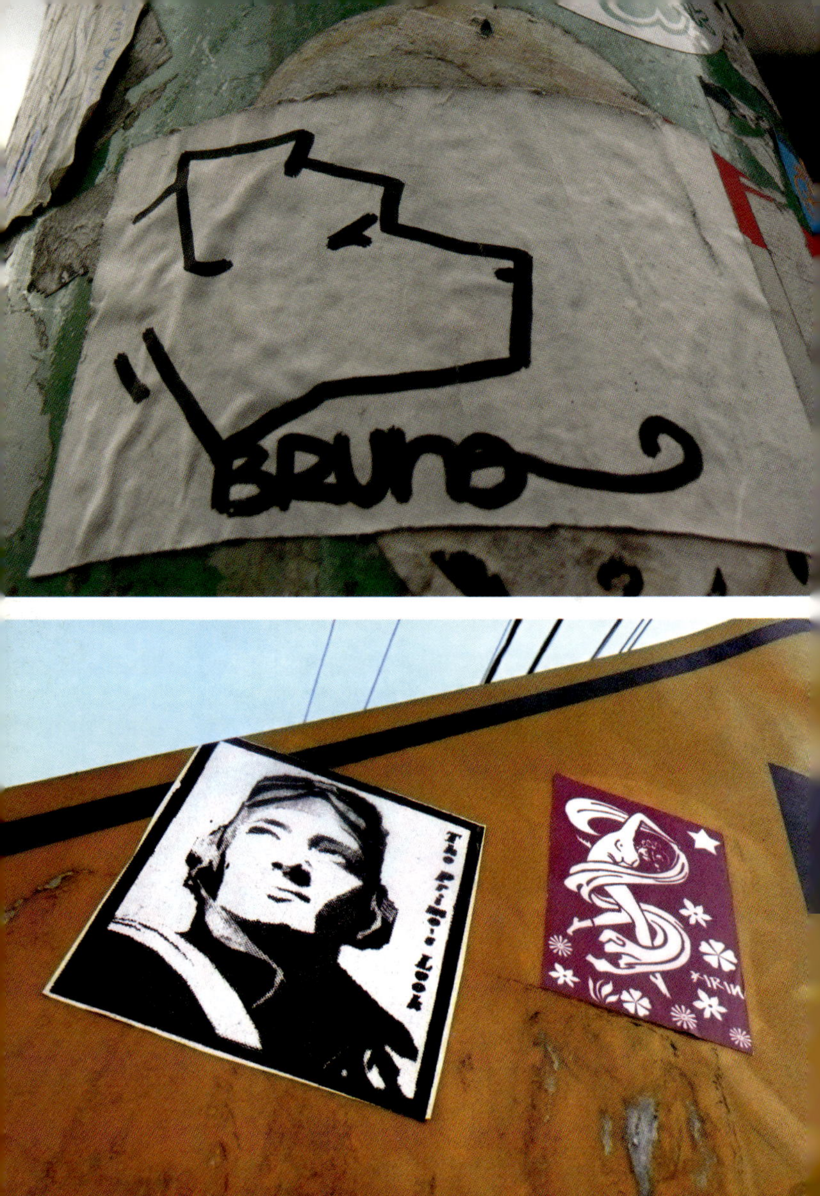
BRUNO

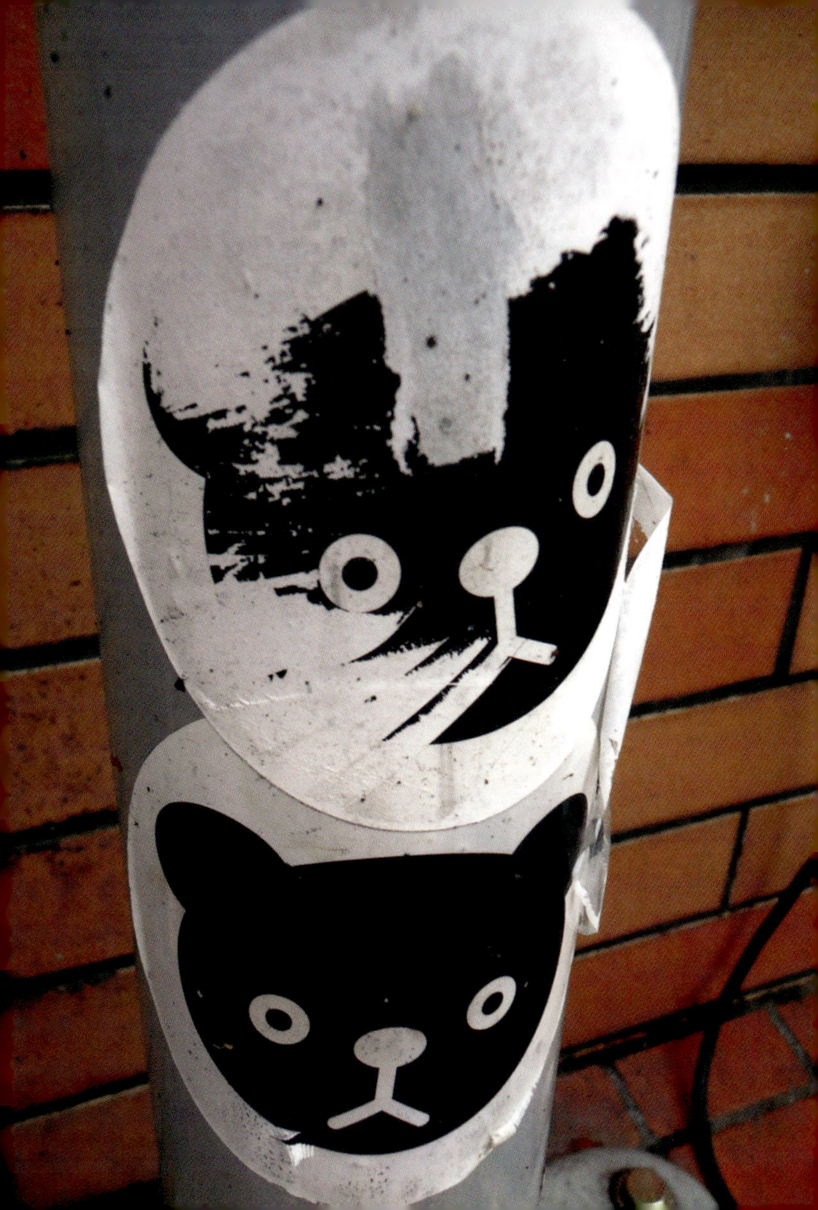

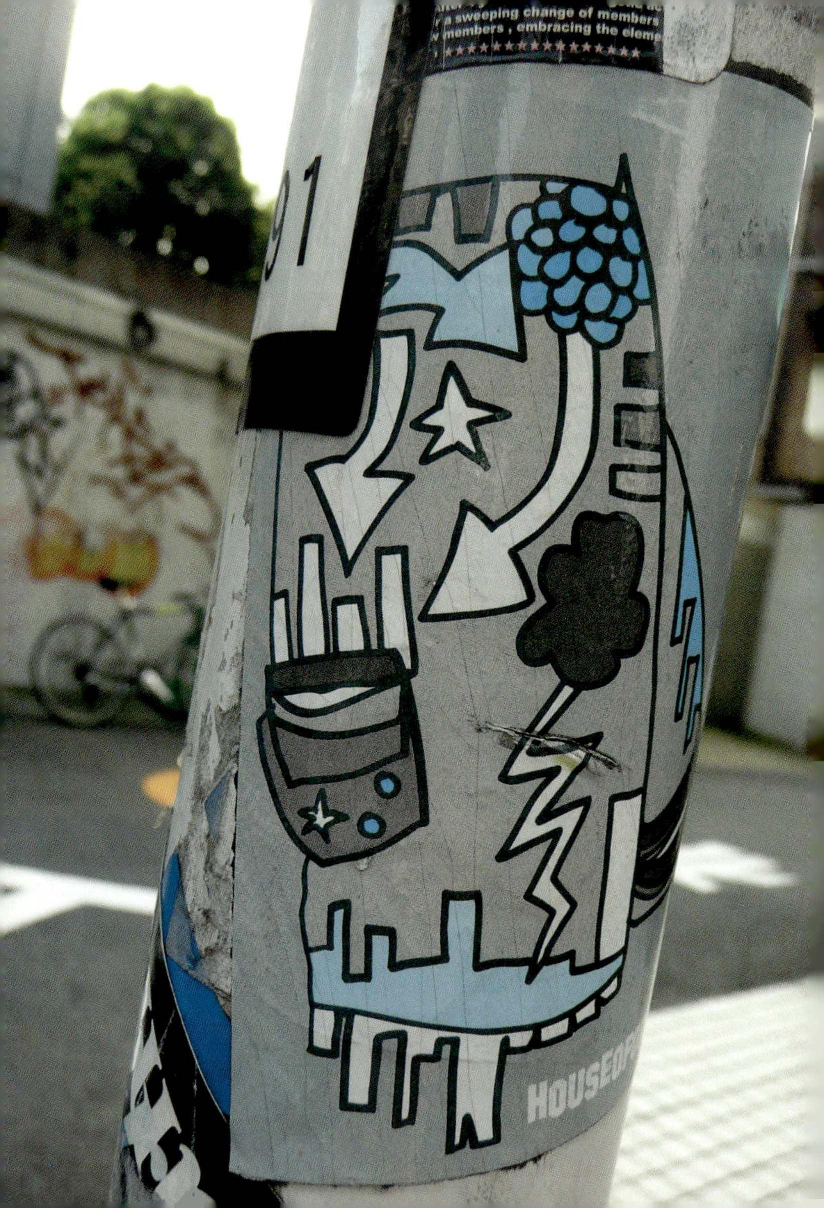
a sweeping change of members
members , embracing the eleme
91
HOUSEOF

ww.shinobispirit.com
Memento
REMEMBER THAT YOU ARE MORTAL
CARPE DIEM

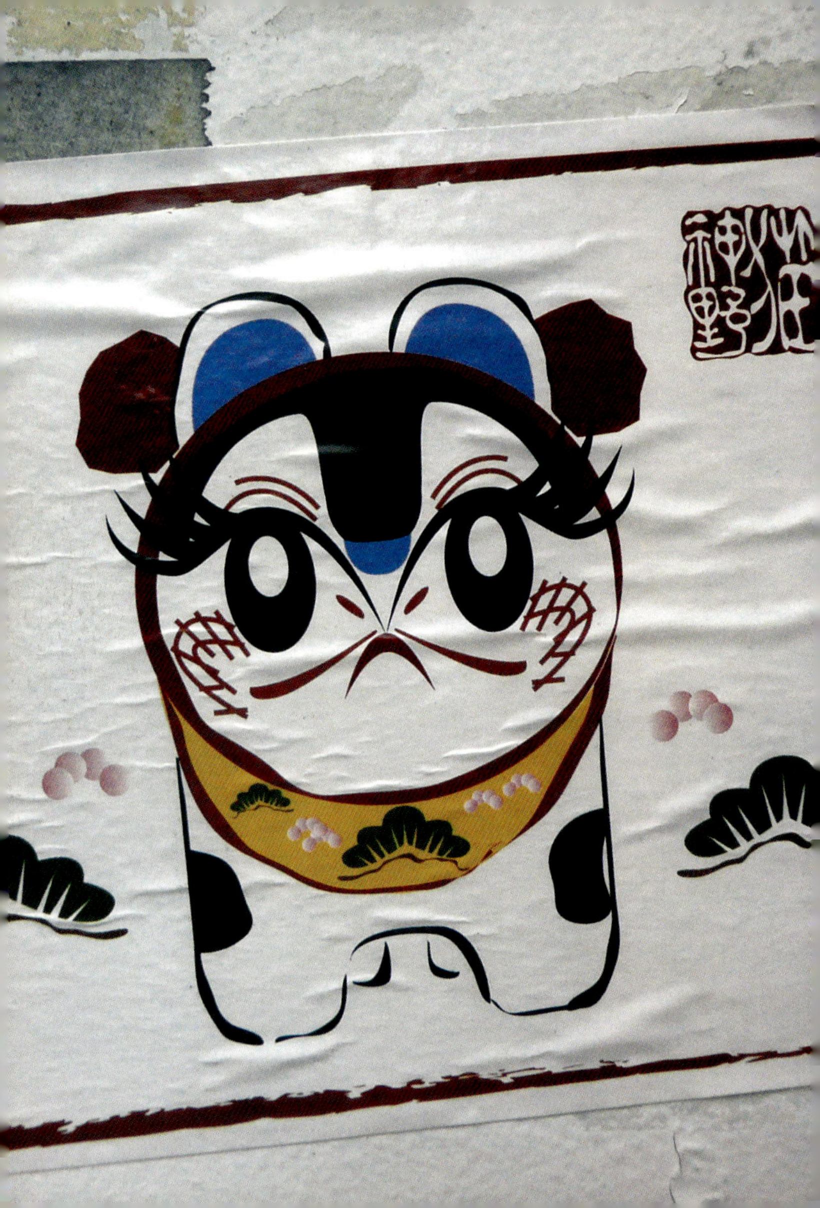

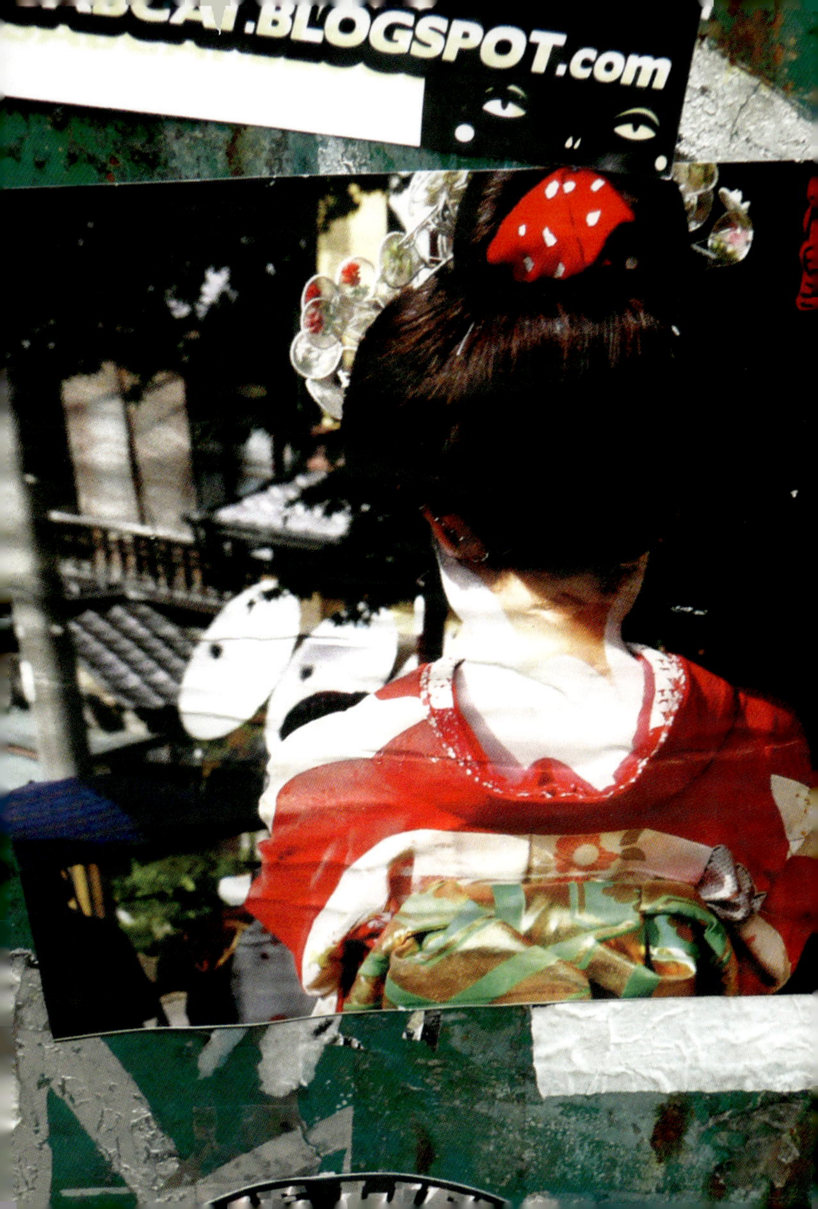
.BLOGSPOT.com

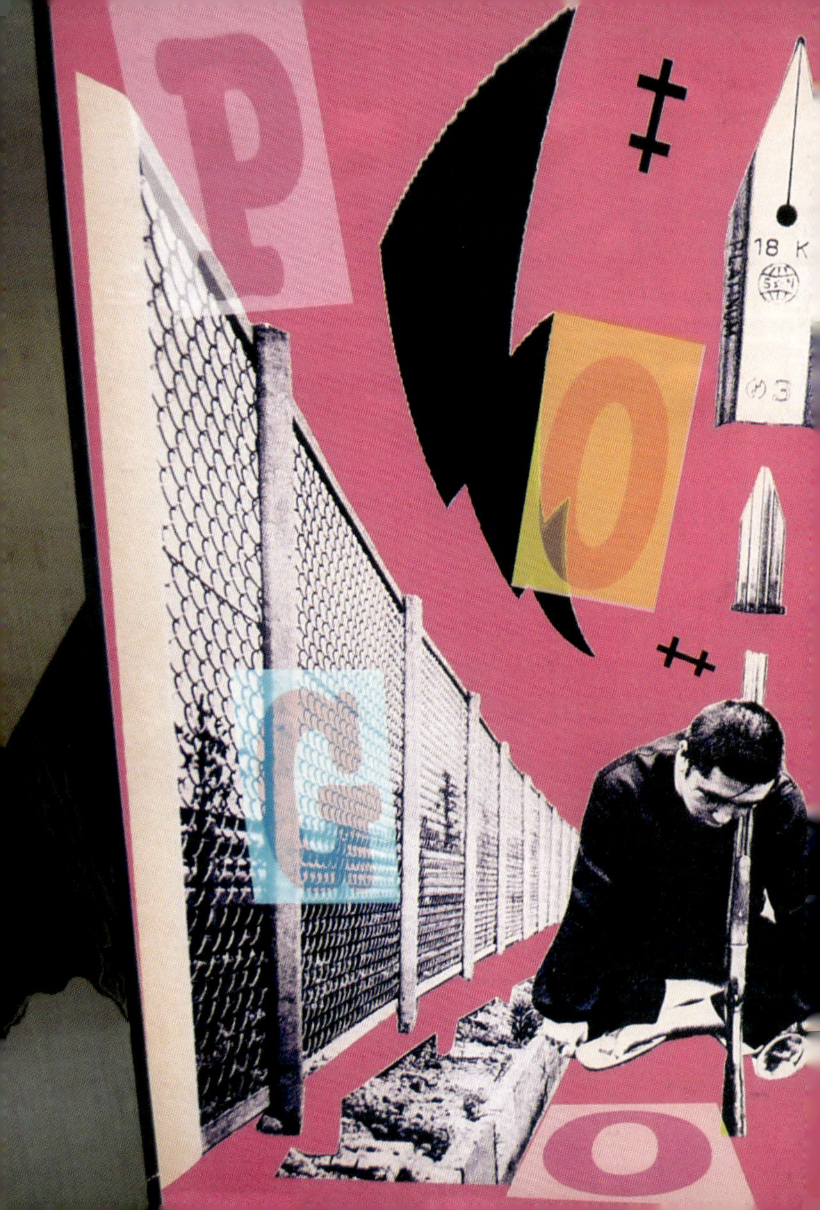
18 K

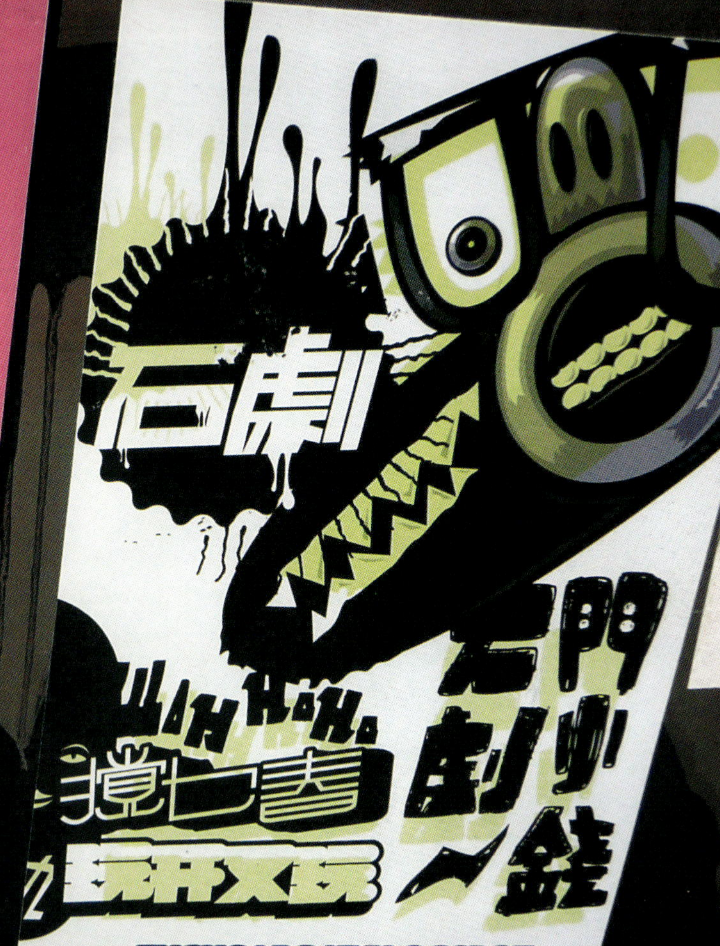
www.FUCKSABCAT.BLOGSPOT.com

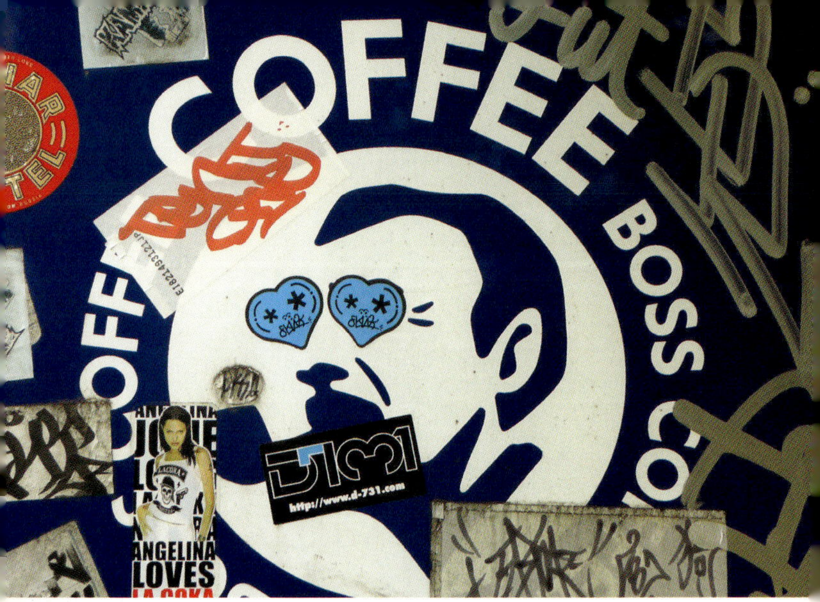

COFFEE
BOSS
ANGELINA
LOVES
LA COKA
http://www.d-731.com 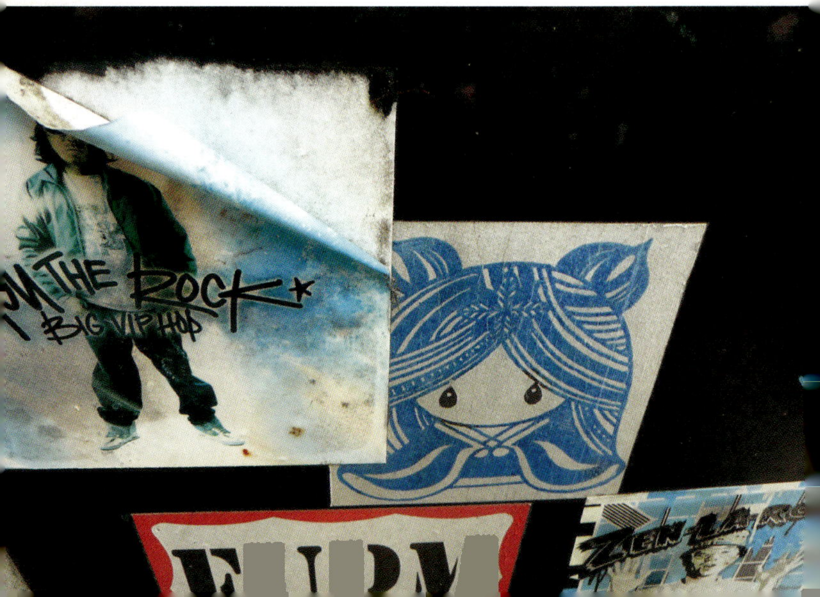
ON THE ROCK
BIG VIP HOP

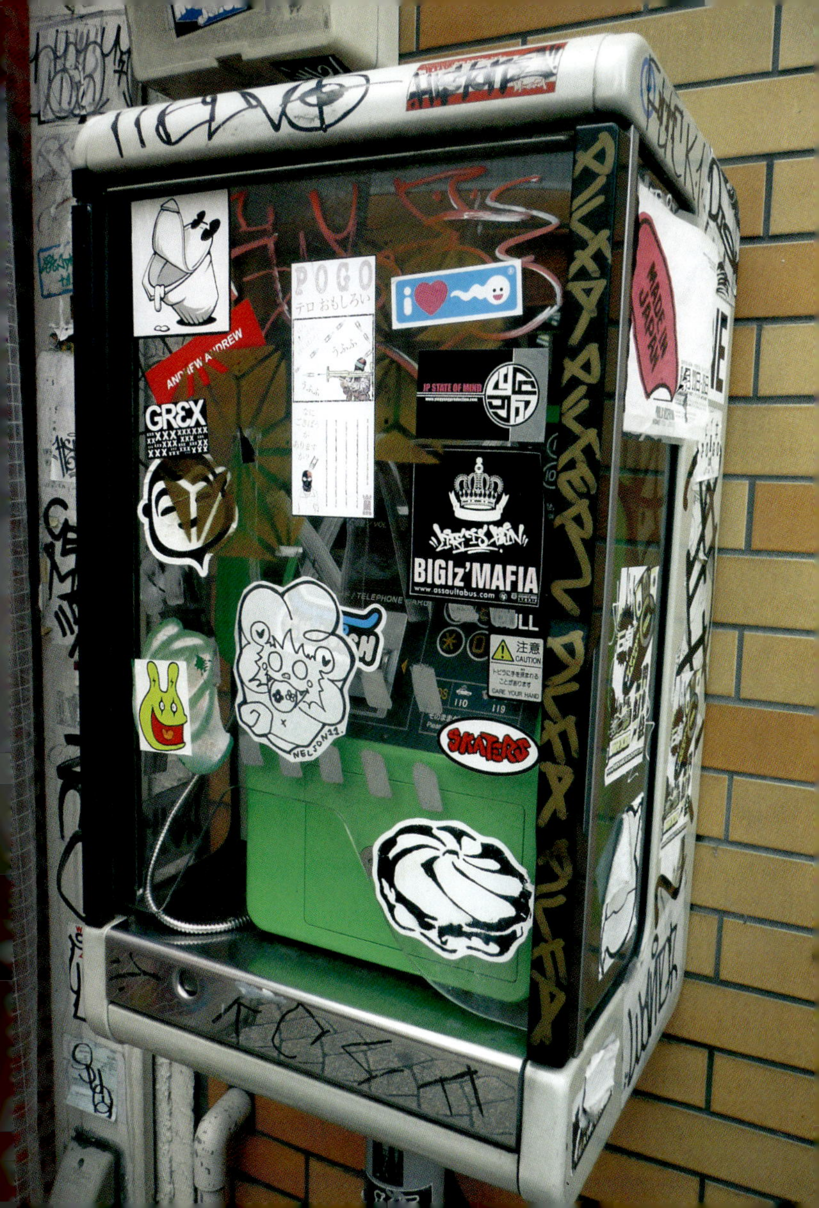
POGO
テロ おもしろい
ANDREW ANDREW
GREX
JP STATE OF MIND
BIGIz'MAFIA
www.assaultabus.com
注意
CAUTION
CARE YOUR HAND
MADE IN JAPAN
SKATERS
110
119

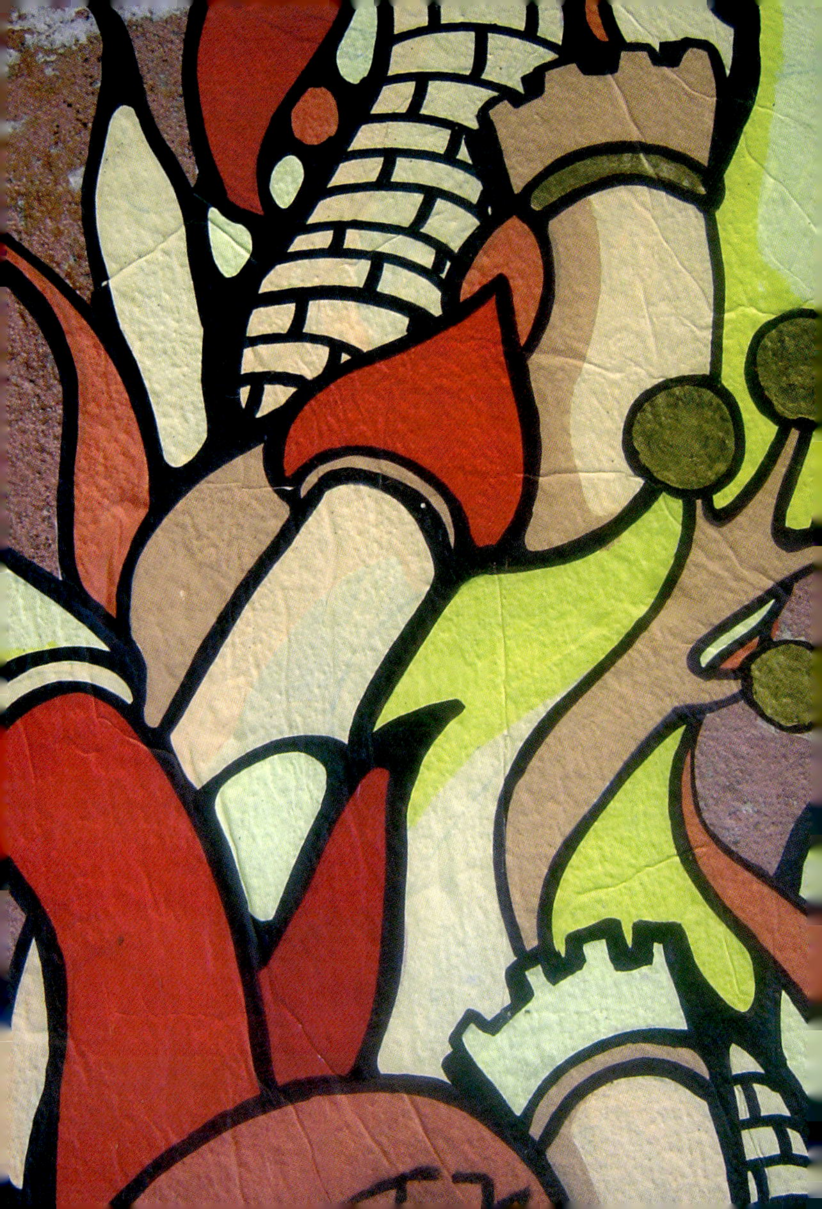

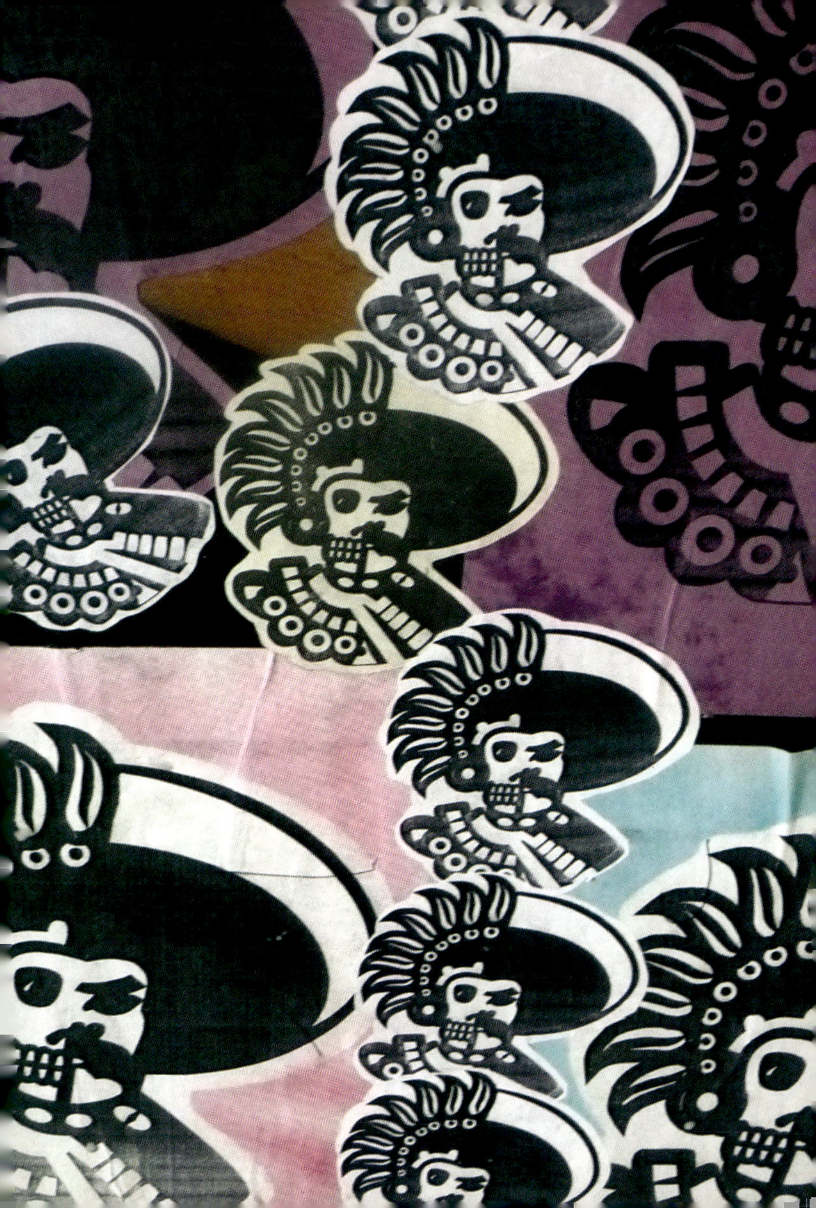

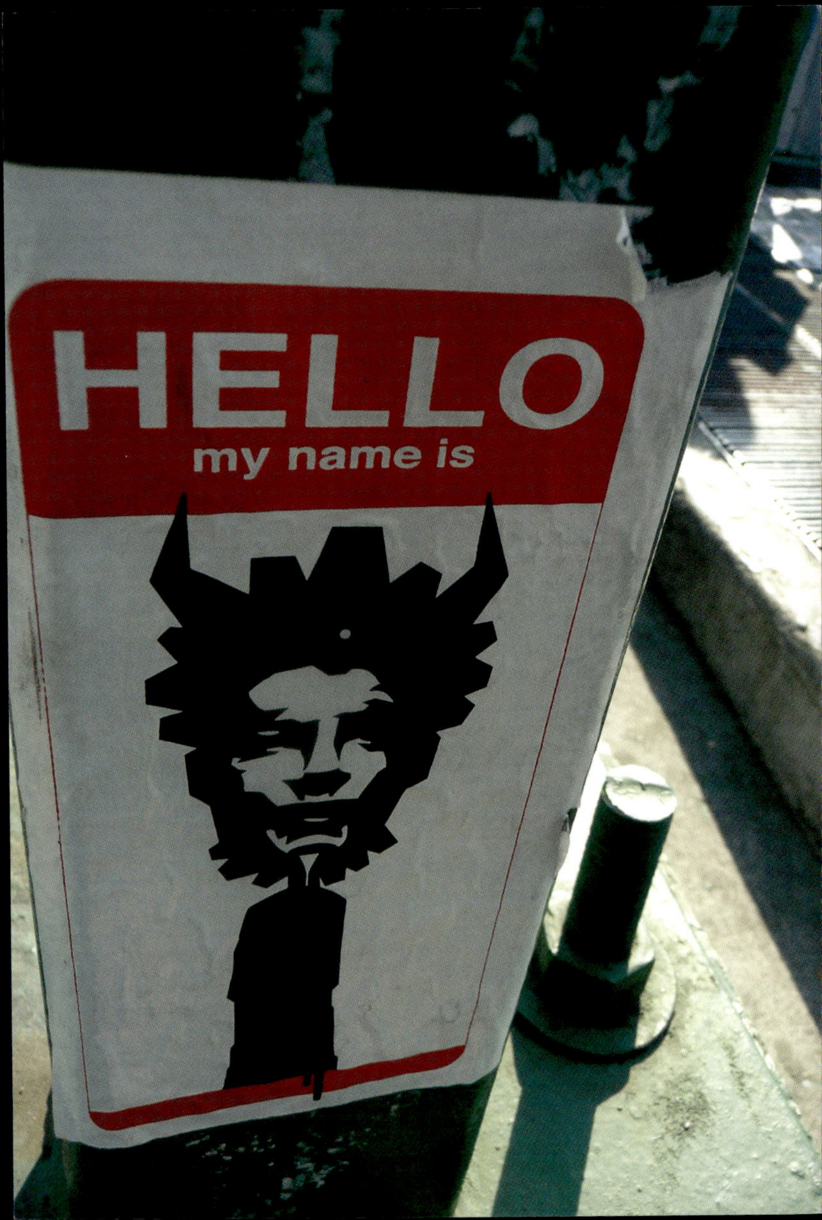
HELLO
my name is

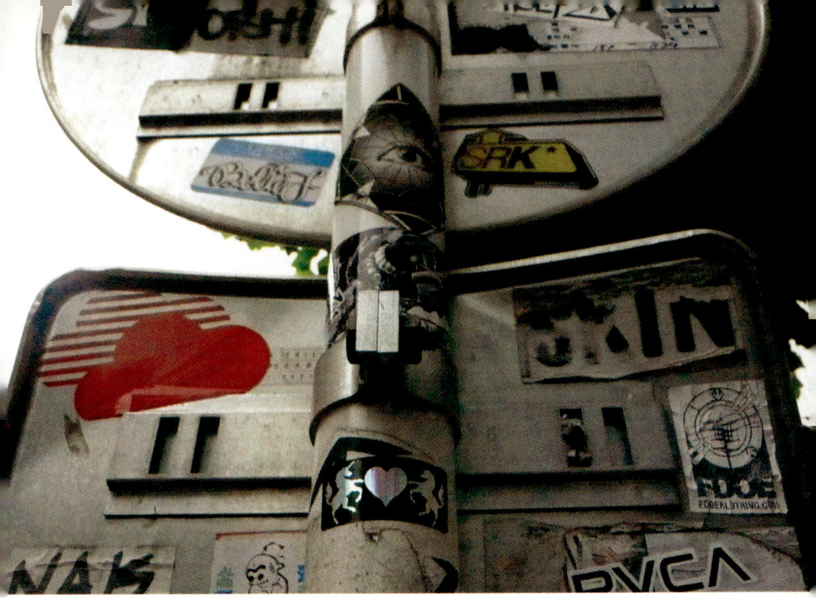

RVCA
THE KICK ABOUT SOUND OF 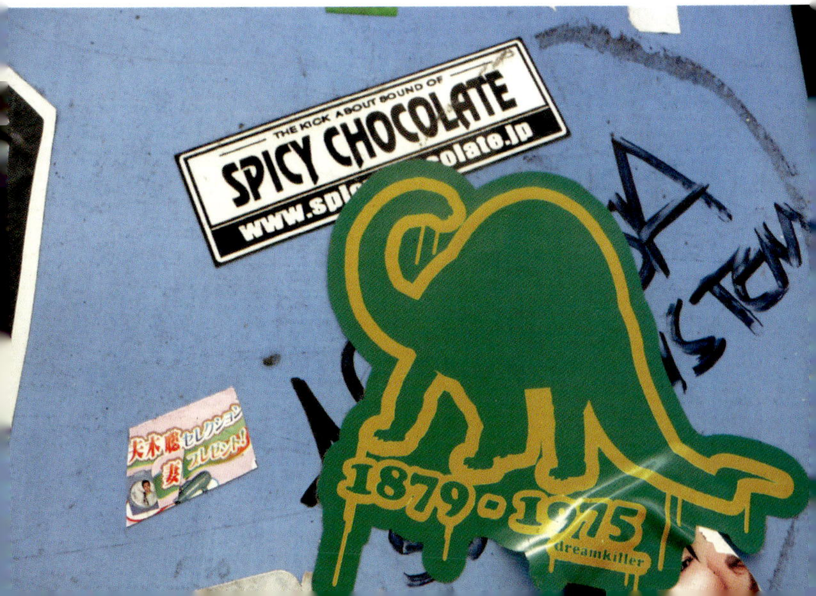
SPICY CHOCOLATE
1879-1975
dreamkiller

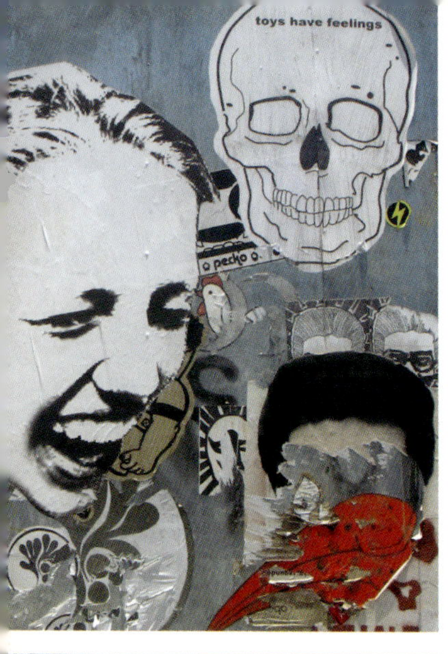
toys have feelings
pecko

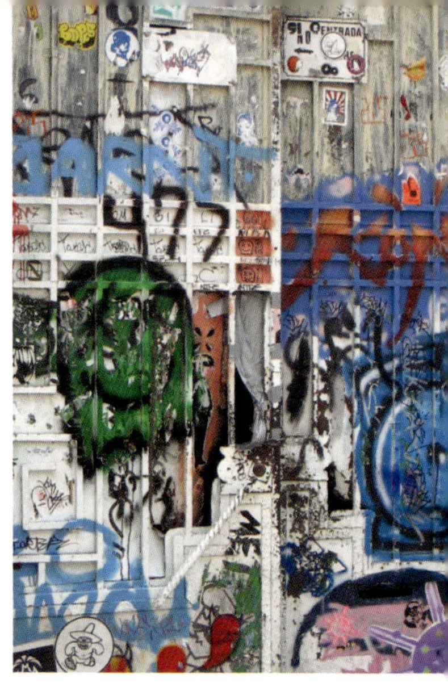

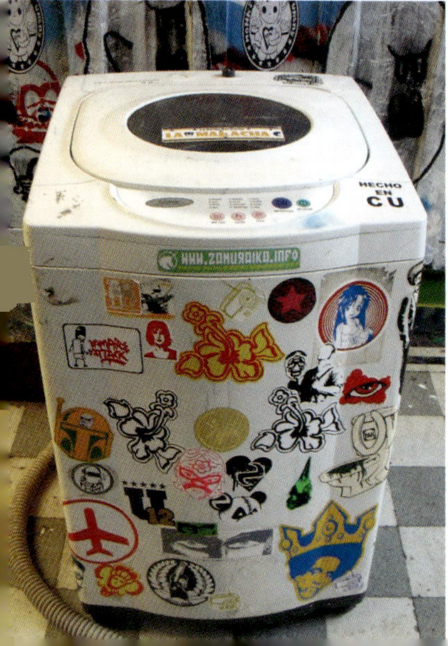
HECHO
EN
CU

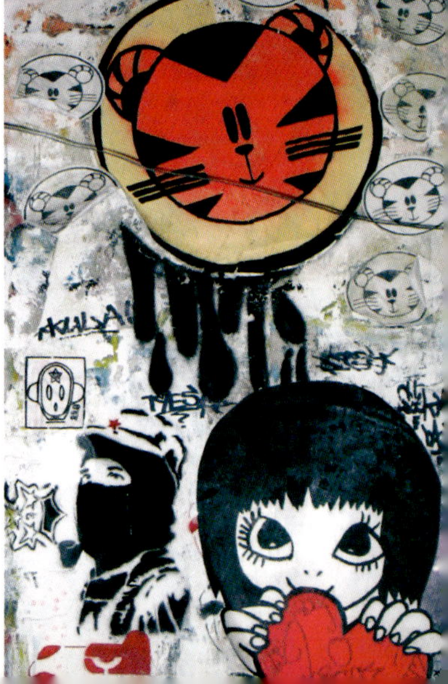

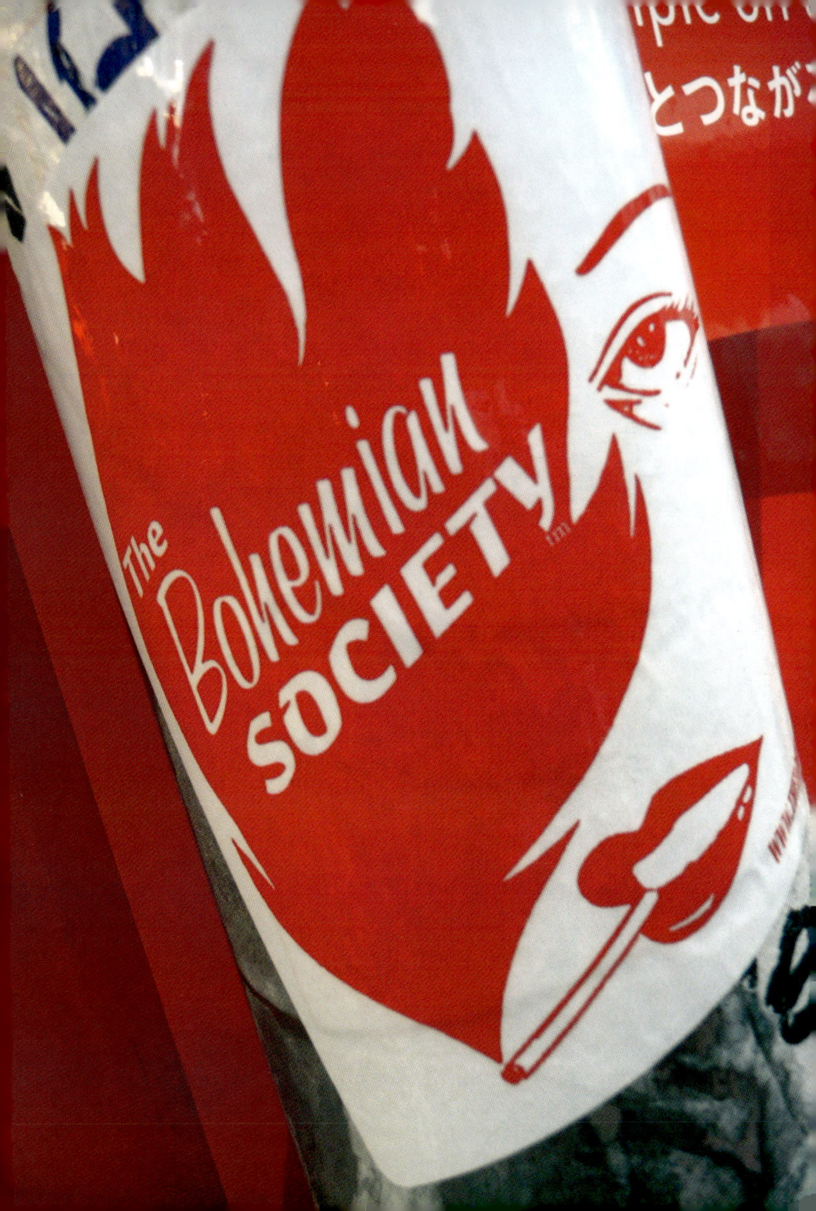

The Bohemian SOCIETY

とつなが

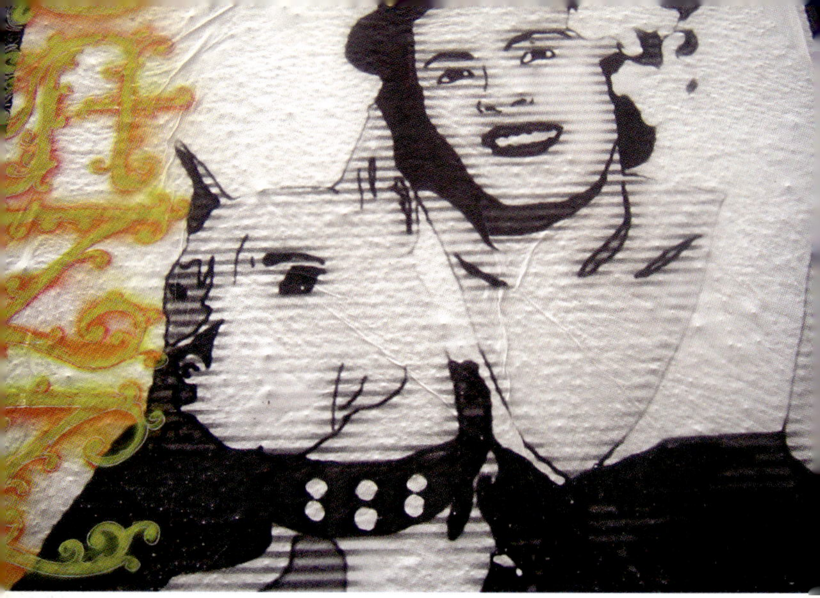

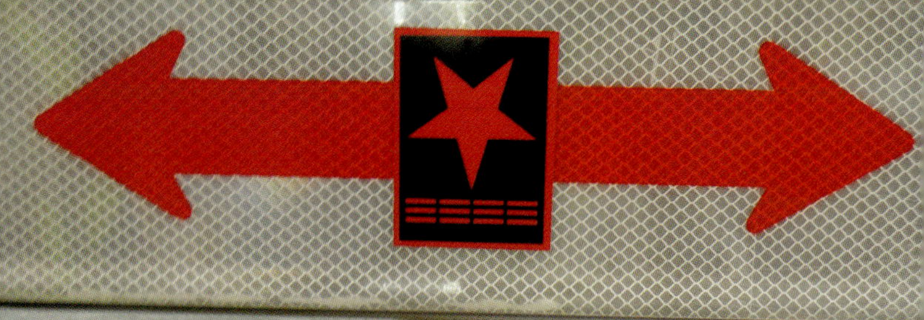

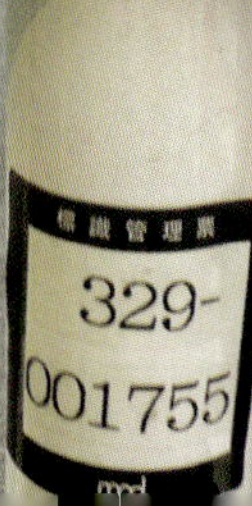
329-
001755

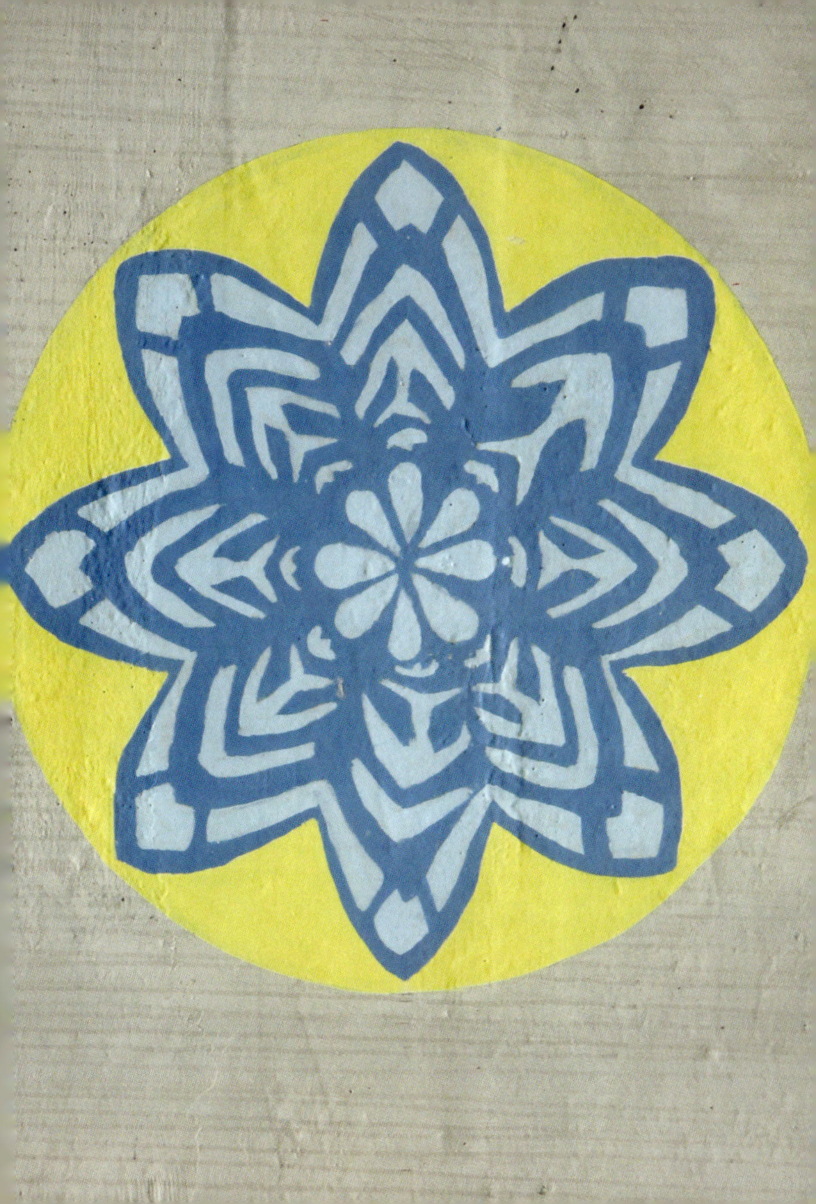

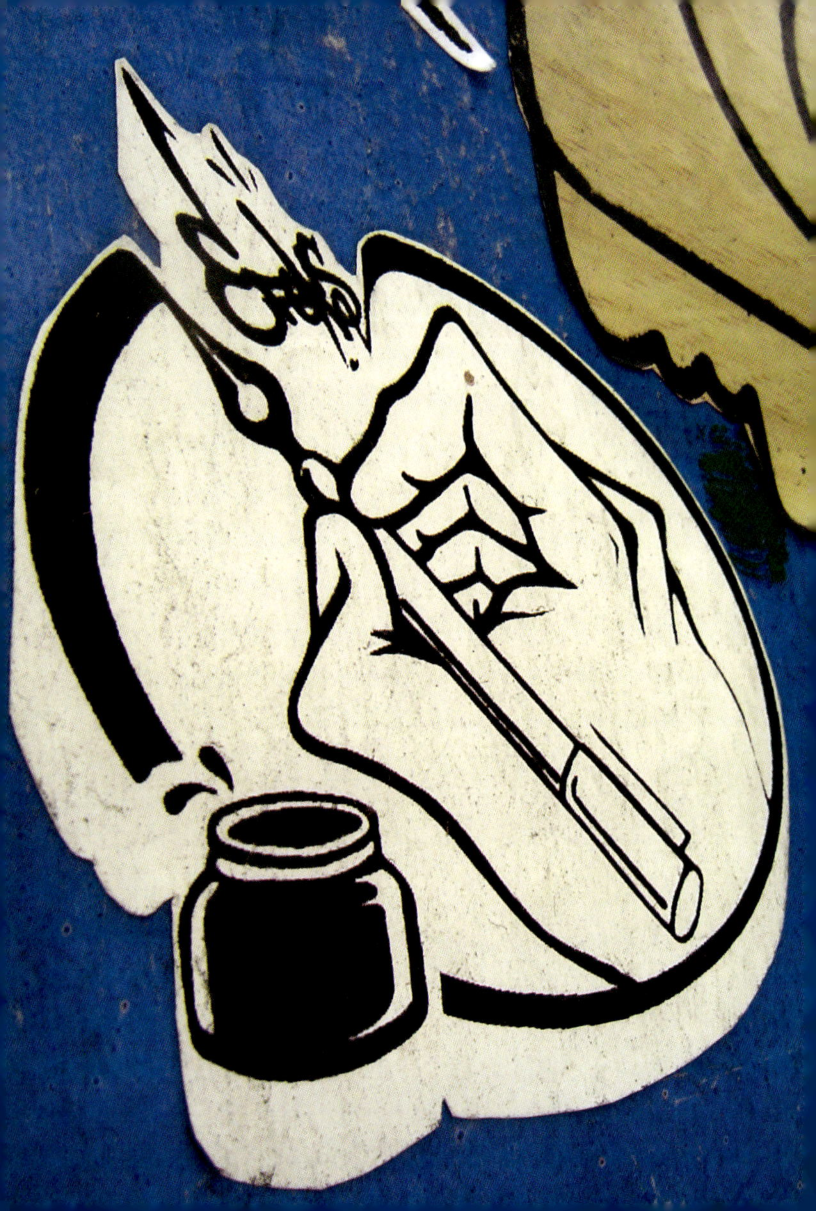

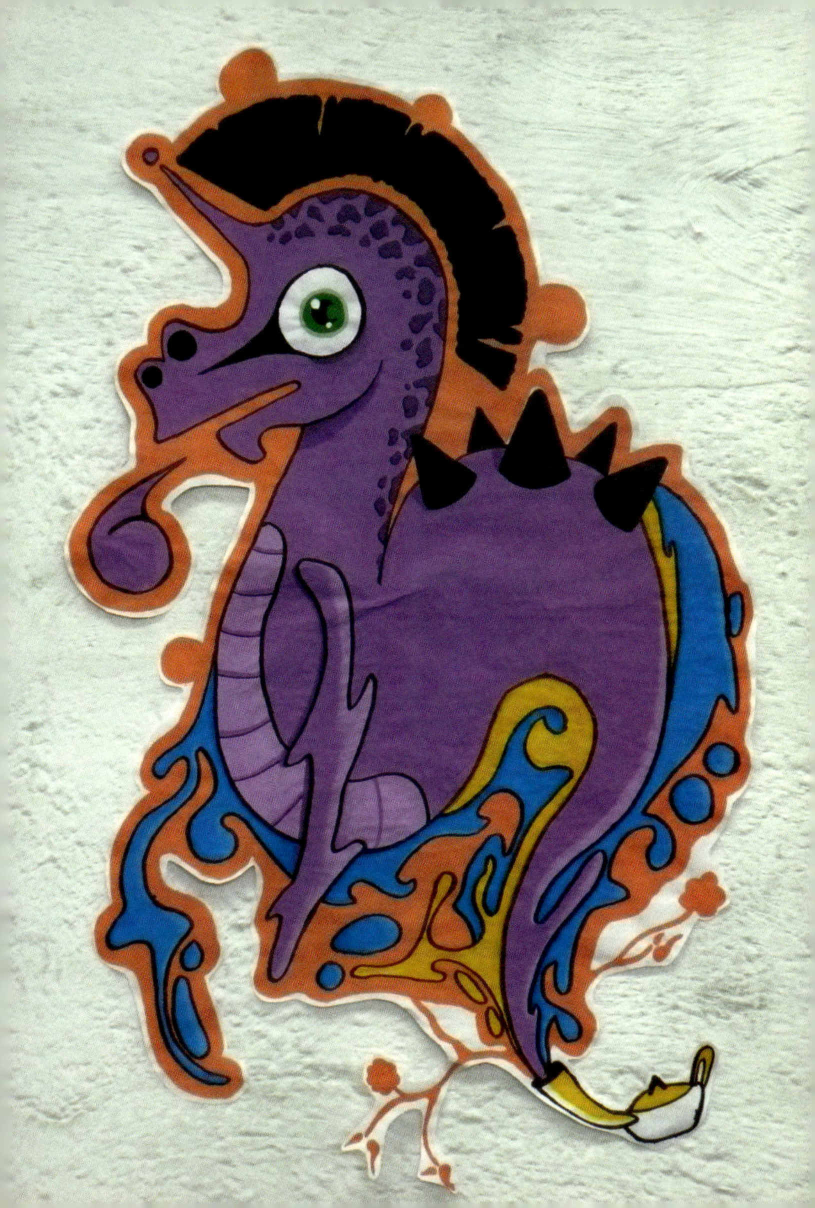

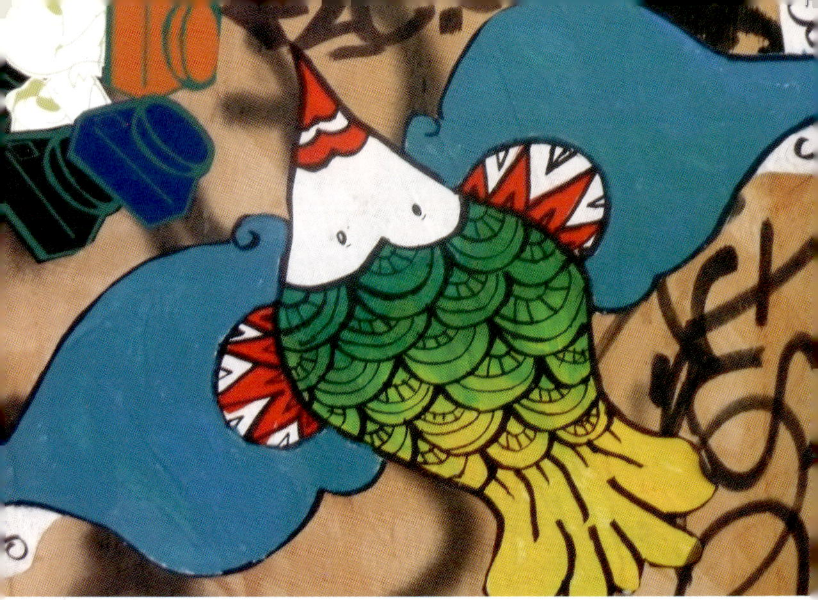

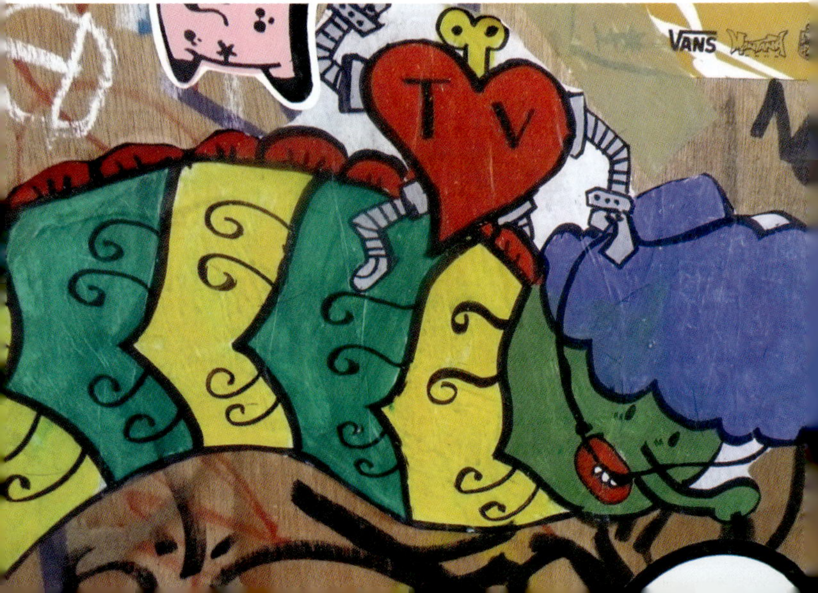

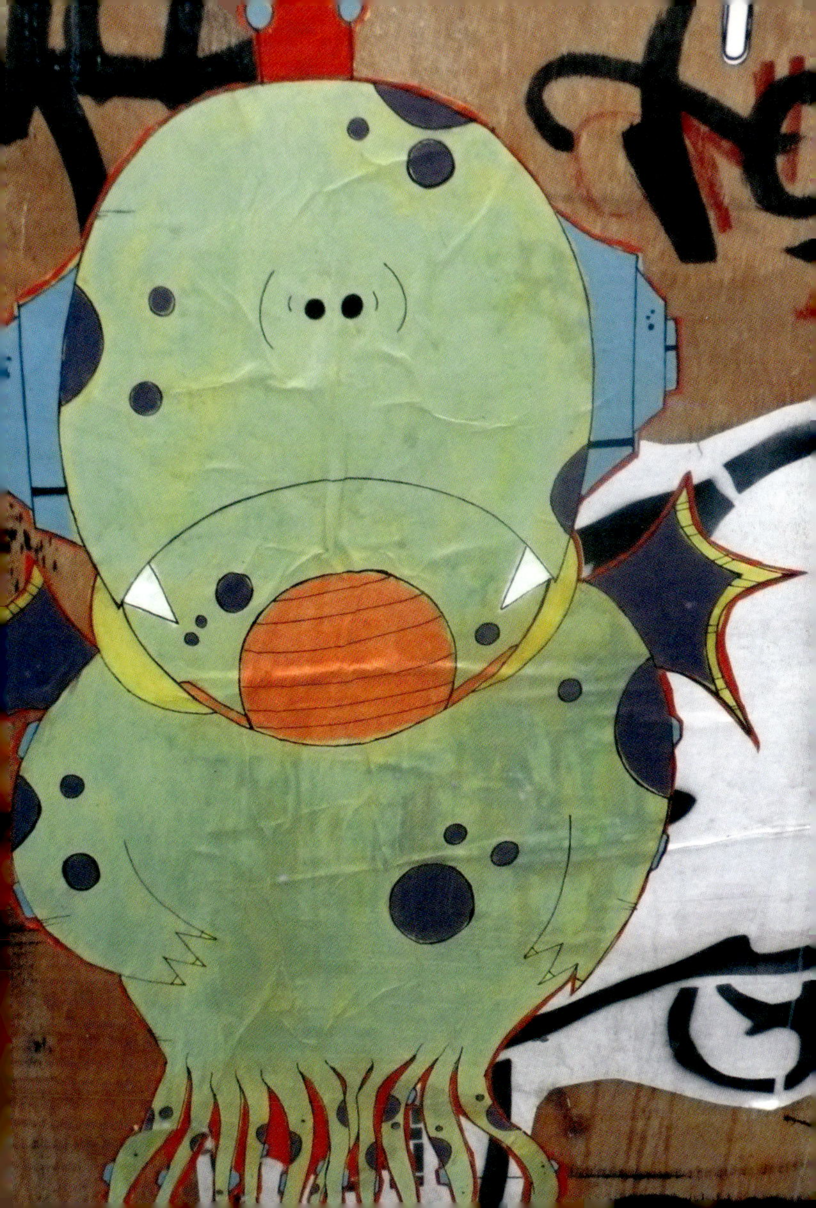

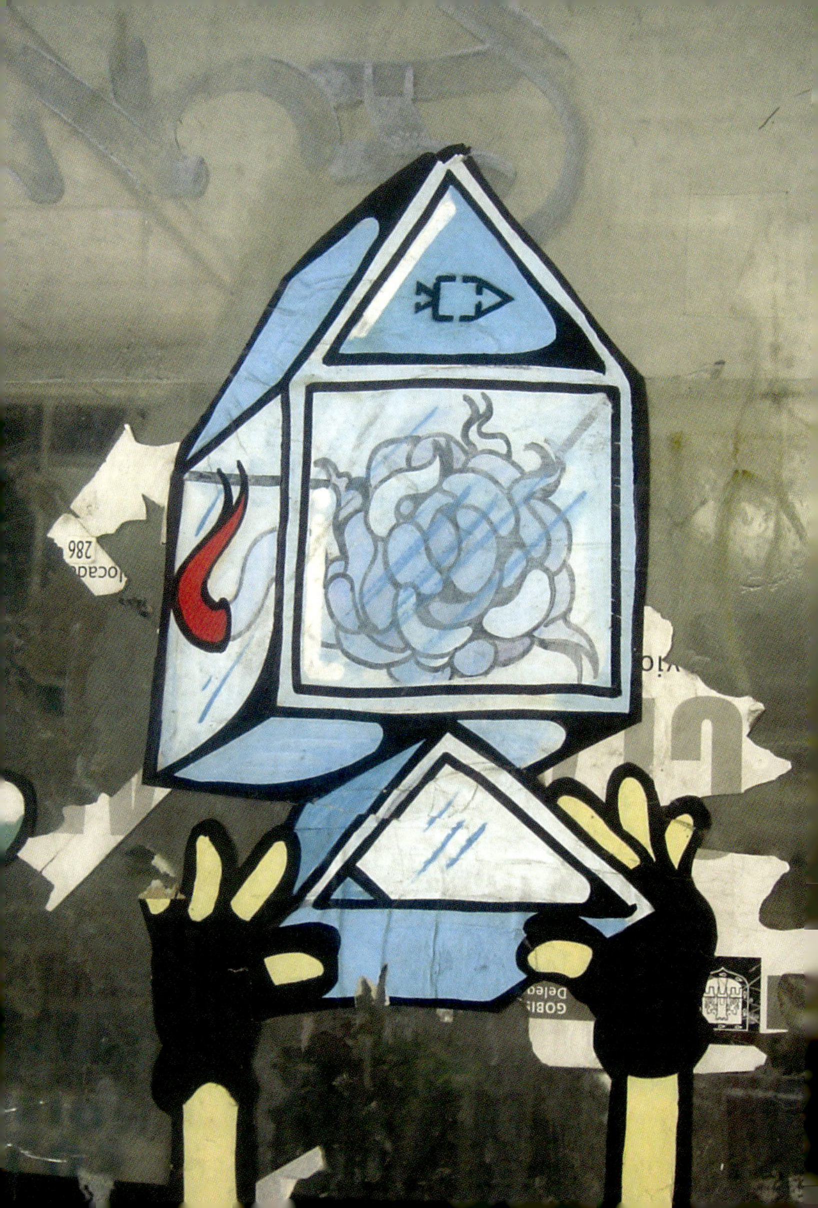

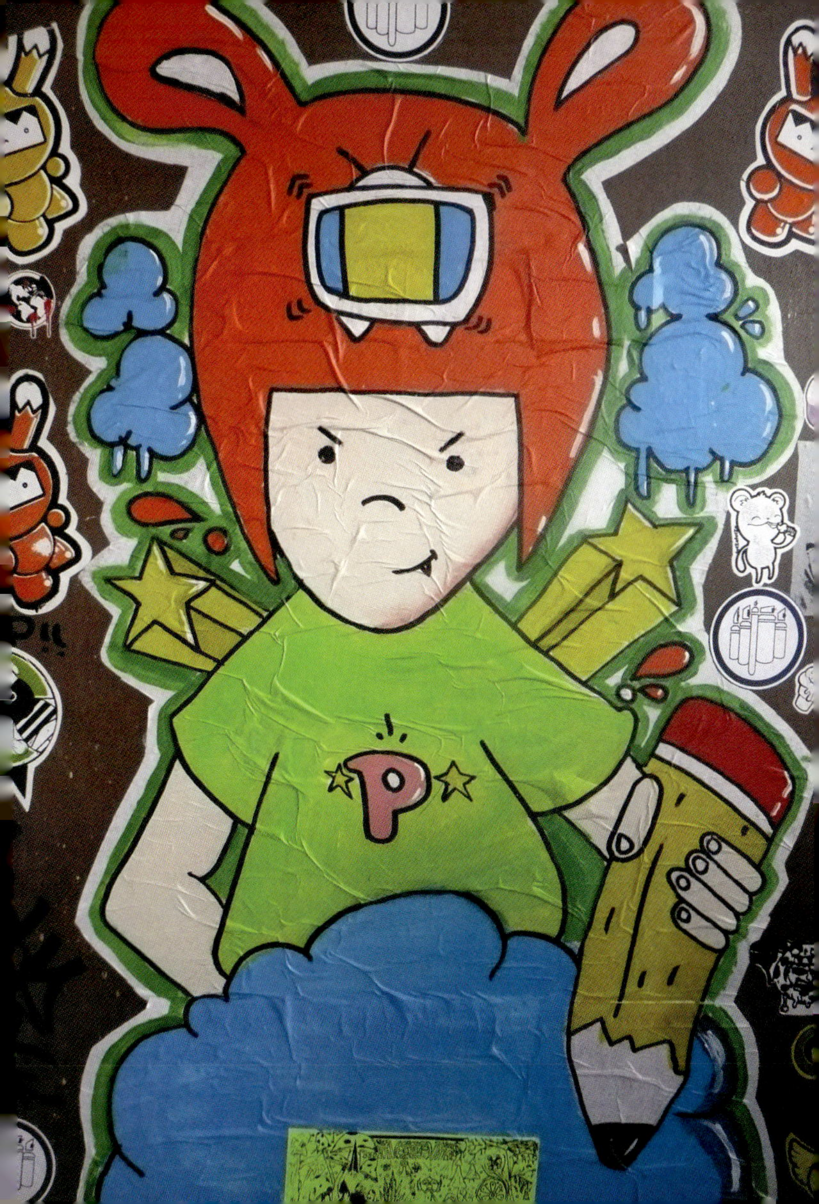

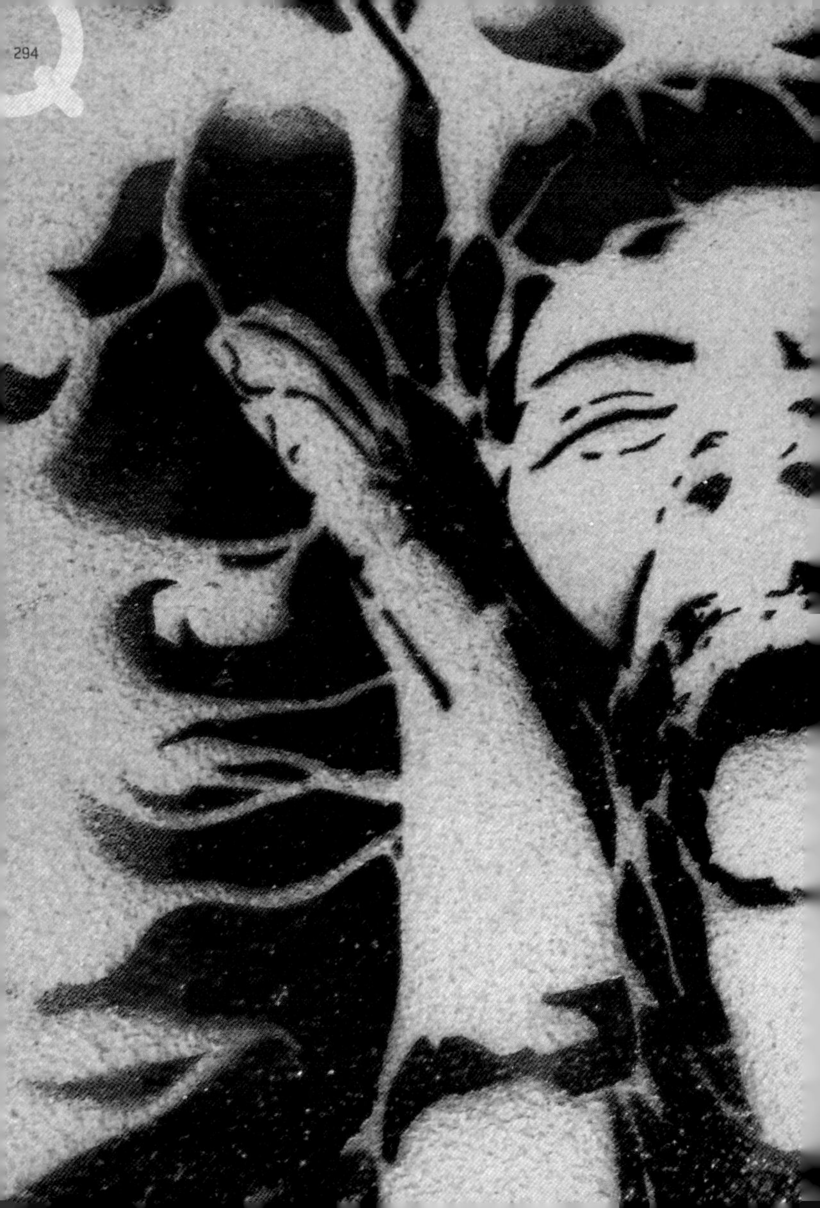

Templates and posters

Pochoirs et affiches

Schablonen und Plakate

Sjablonen en posters

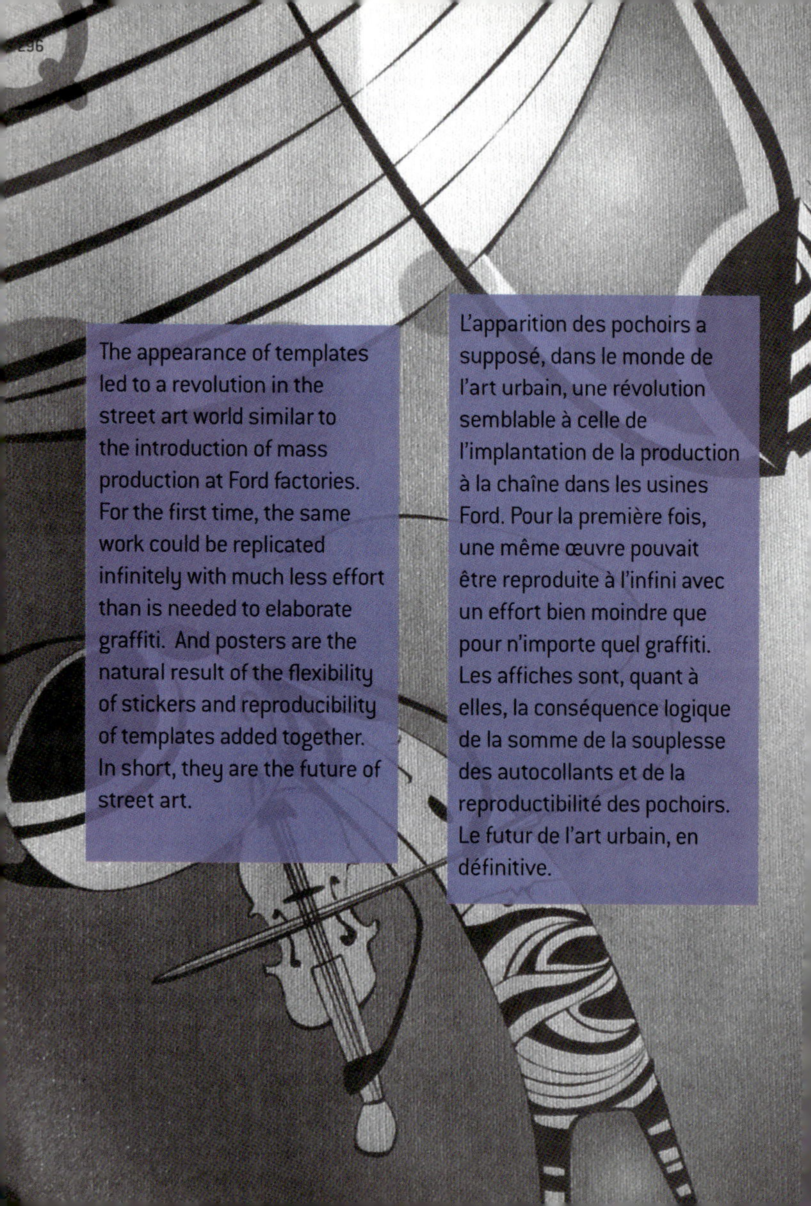

The appearance of templates led to a revolution in the street art world similar to the introduction of mass production at Ford factories. For the first time, the same work could be replicated infinitely with much less effort than is needed to elaborate graffiti. And posters are the natural result of the flexibility of stickers and reproducibility of templates added together. In short, they are the future of street art.

L'apparition des pochoirs a supposé, dans le monde de l'art urbain, une révolution semblable à celle de l'implantation de la production à la chaîne dans les usines Ford. Pour la première fois, une même œuvre pouvait être reproduite à l'infini avec un effort bien moindre que pour n'importe quel graffiti. Les affiches sont, quant à elles, la conséquence logique de la somme de la souplesse des autocollants et de la reproductibilité des pochoirs. Le futur de l'art urbain, en définitive.

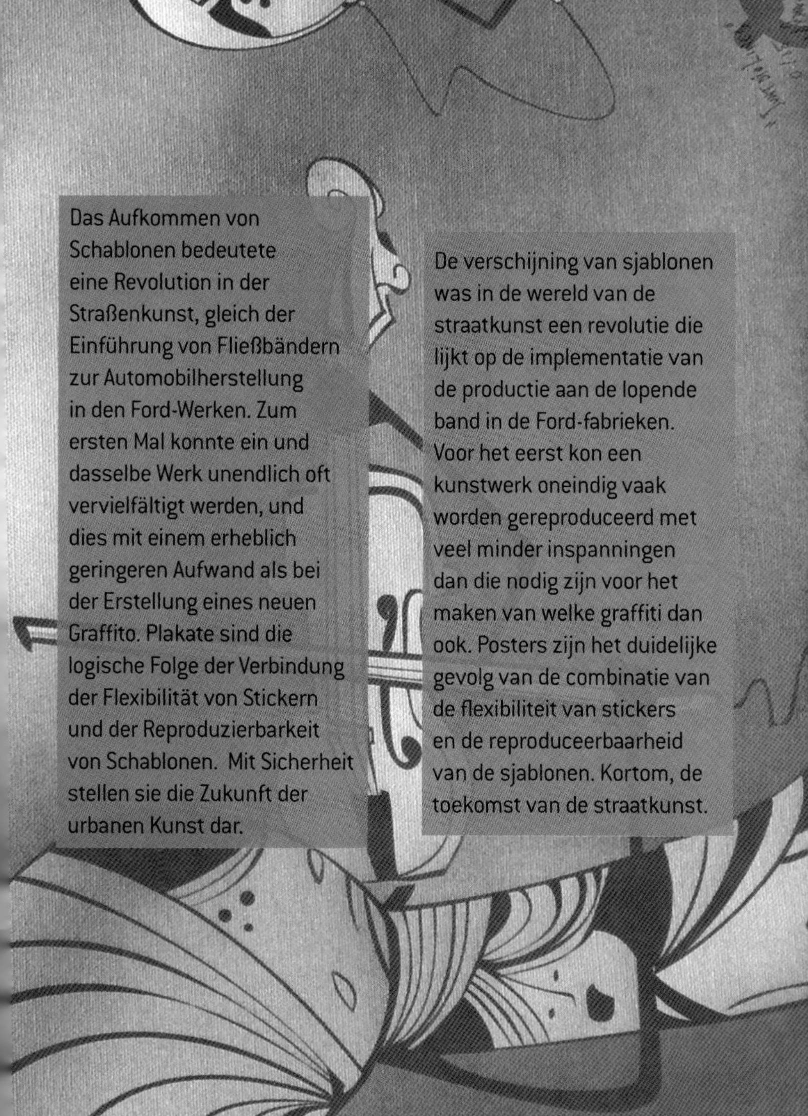

Das Aufkommen von Schablonen bedeutete eine Revolution in der Straßenkunst, gleich der Einführung von Fließbändern zur Automobilherstellung in den Ford-Werken. Zum ersten Mal konnte ein und dasselbe Werk unendlich oft vervielfältigt werden, und dies mit einem erheblich geringeren Aufwand als bei der Erstellung eines neuen Graffito. Plakate sind die logische Folge der Verbindung der Flexibilität von Stickern und der Reproduzierbarkeit von Schablonen. Mit Sicherheit stellen sie die Zukunft der urbanen Kunst dar.

De verschijning van sjablonen was in de wereld van de straatkunst een revolutie die lijkt op de implementatie van de productie aan de lopende band in de Ford-fabrieken. Voor het eerst kon een kunstwerk oneindig vaak worden gereproduceerd met veel minder inspanningen dan die nodig zijn voor het maken van welke graffiti dan ook. Posters zijn het duidelijke gevolg van de combinatie van de flexibiliteit van stickers en de reproduceerbaarheid van de sjablonen. Kortom, de toekomst van de straatkunst.

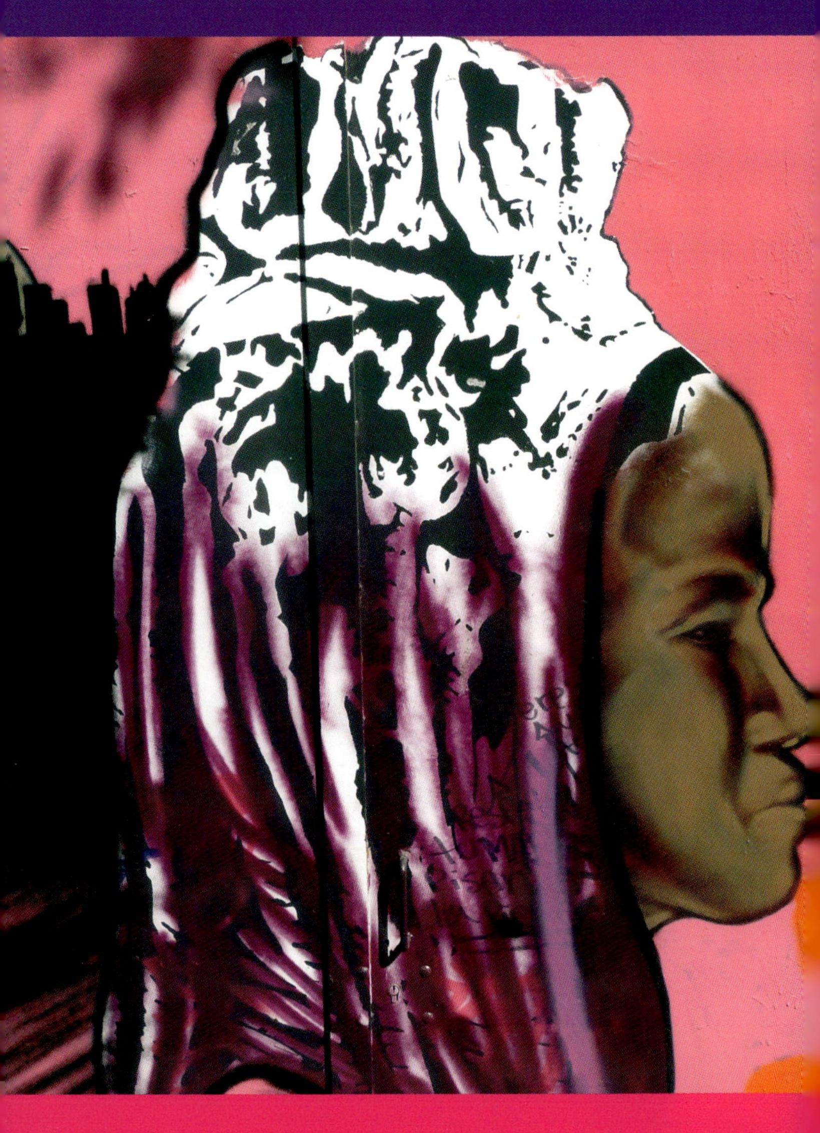

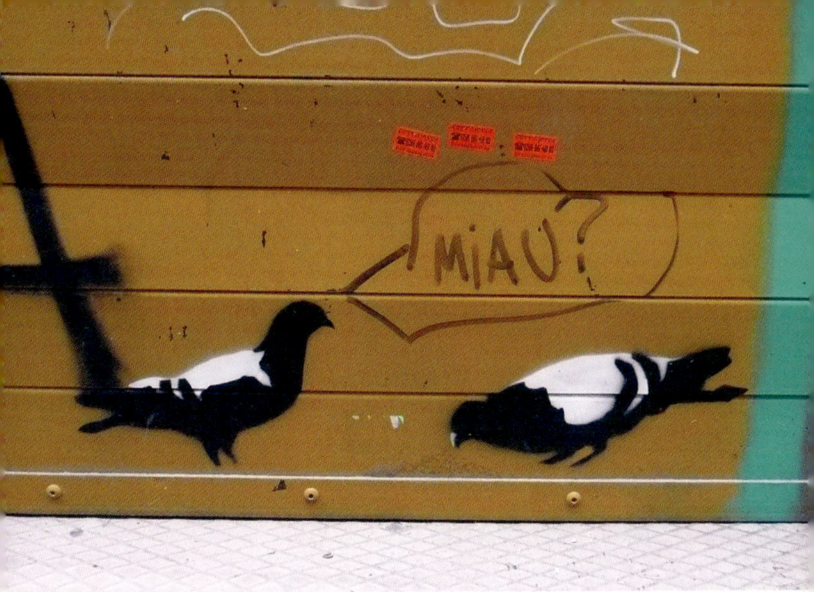

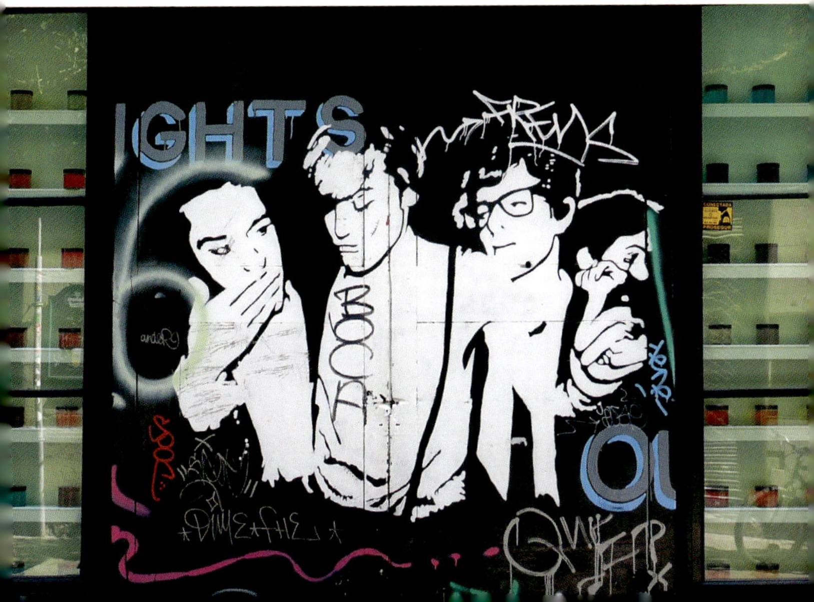

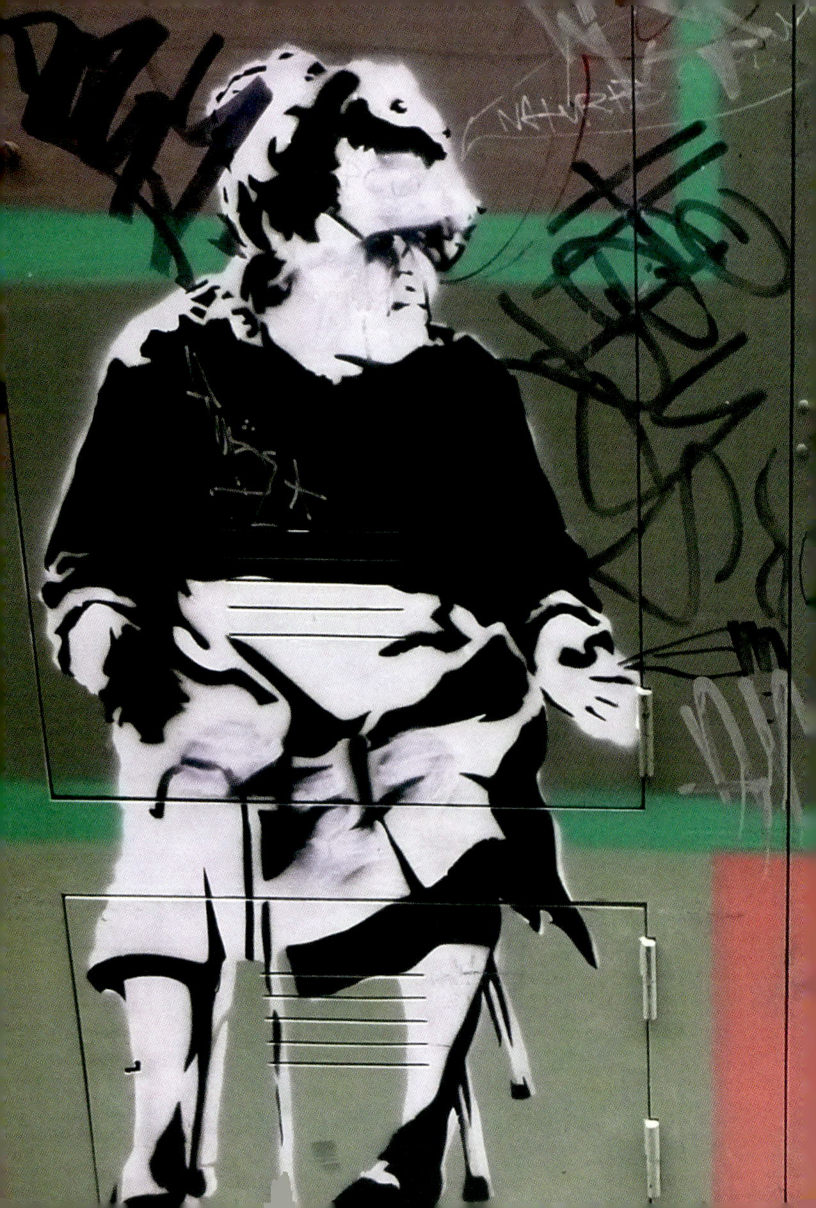

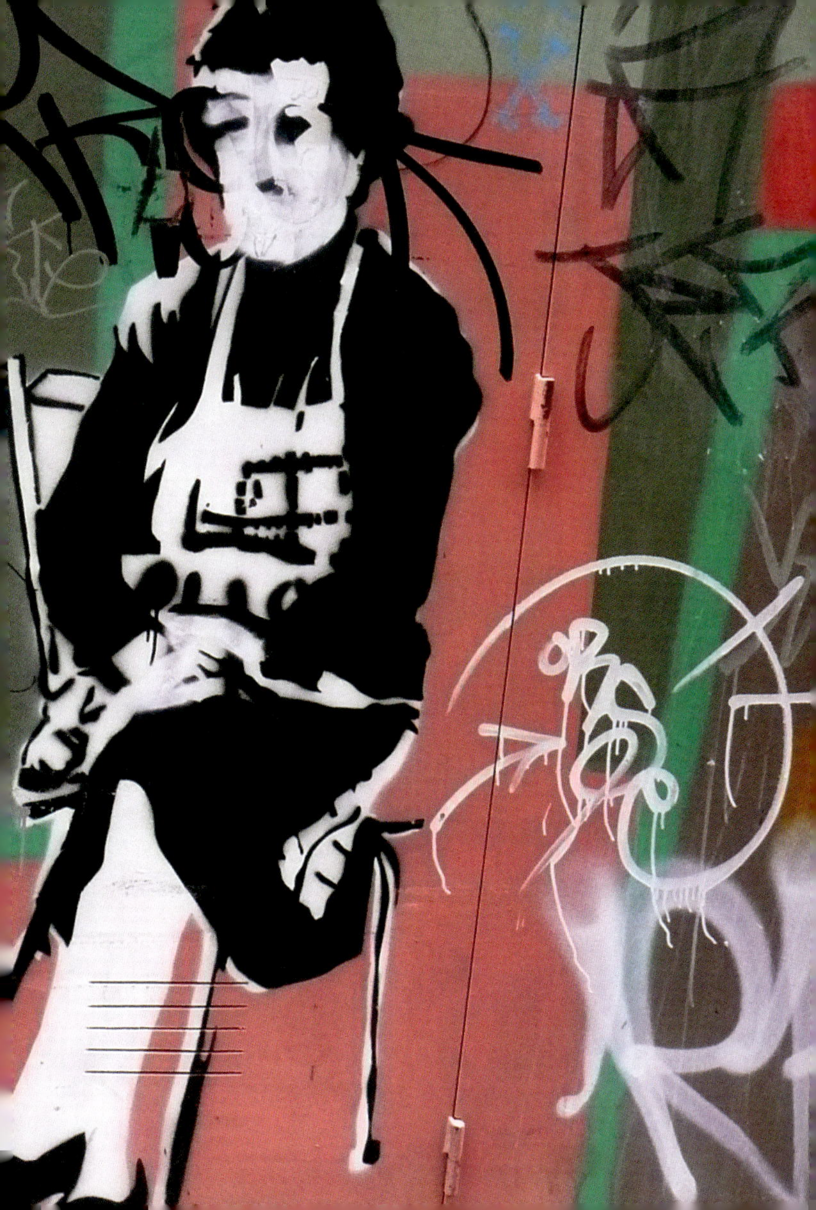

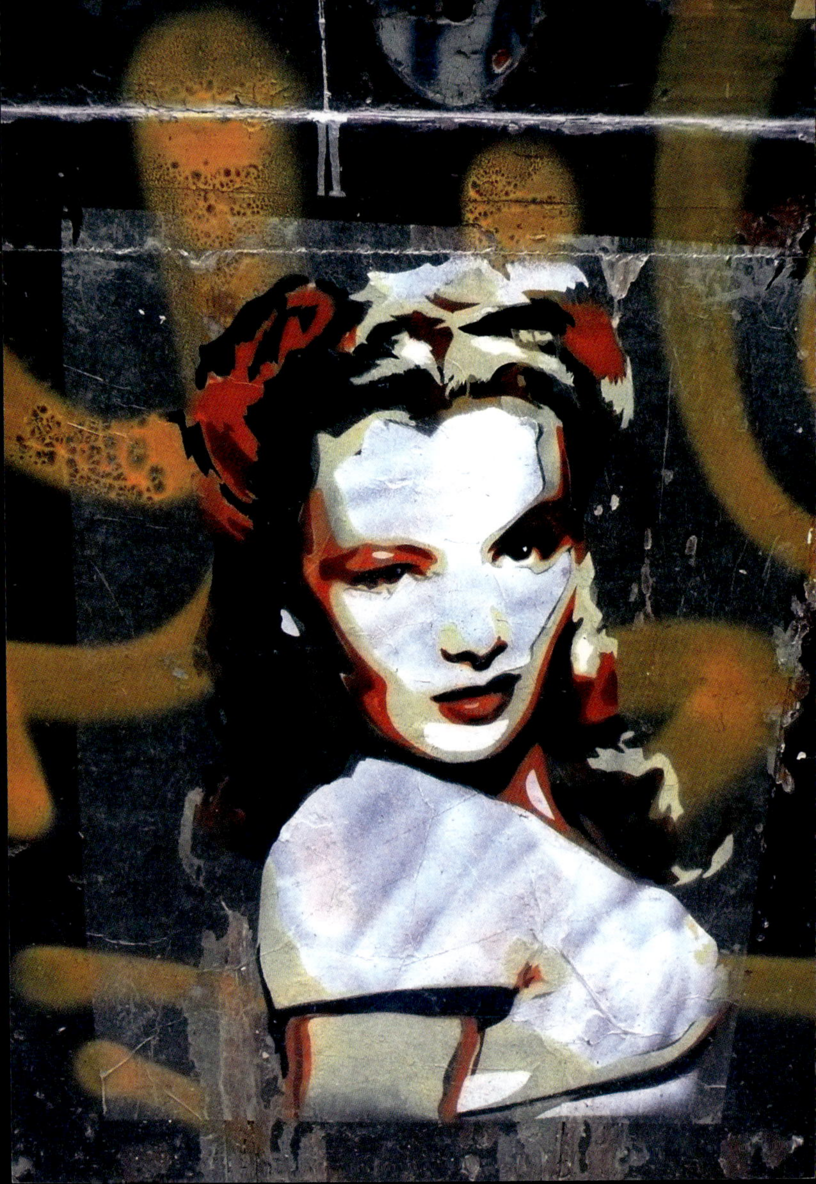

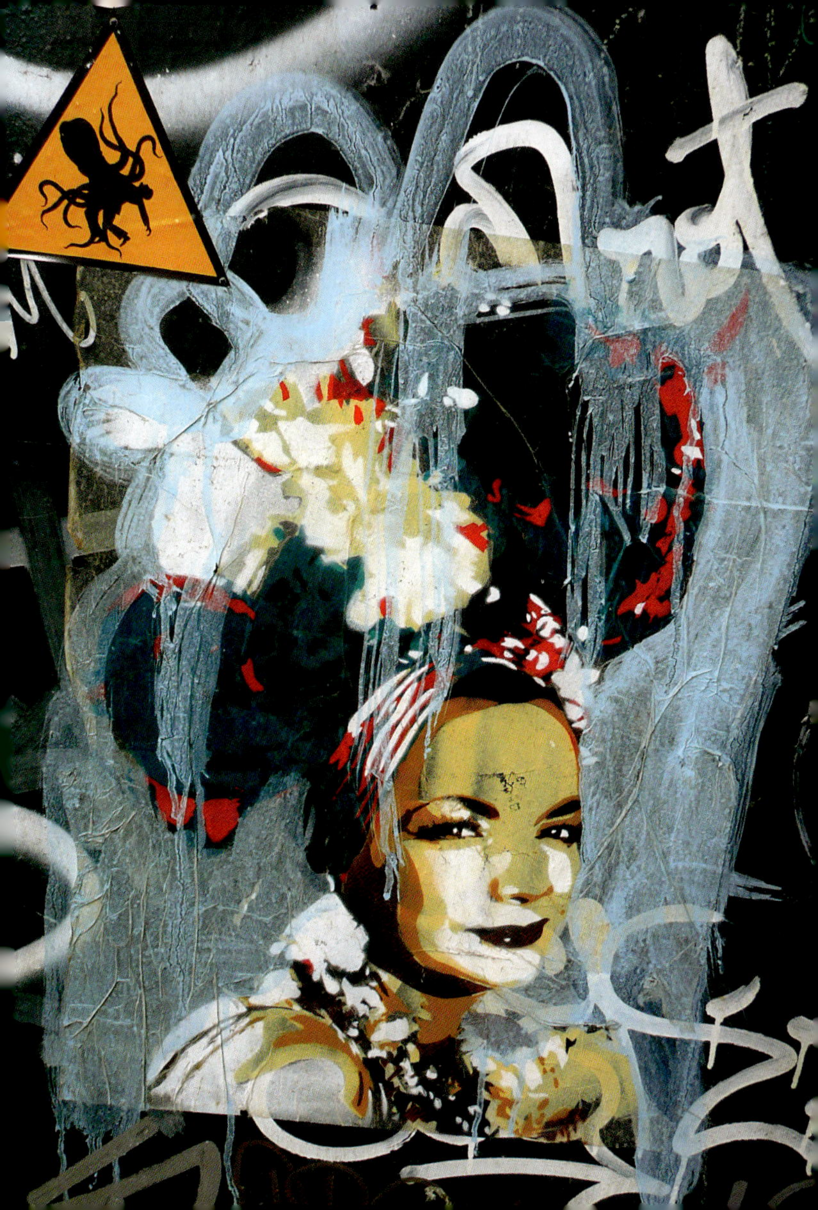

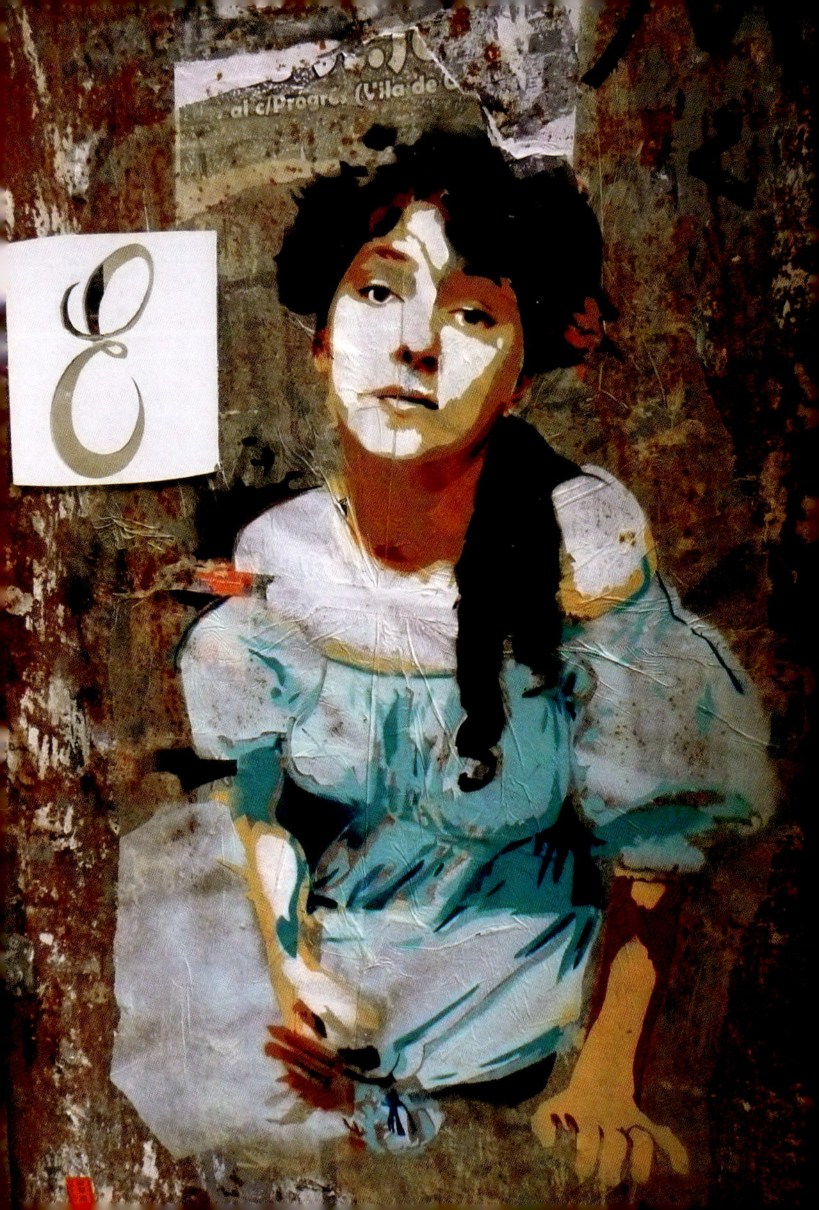
(Vila de
E

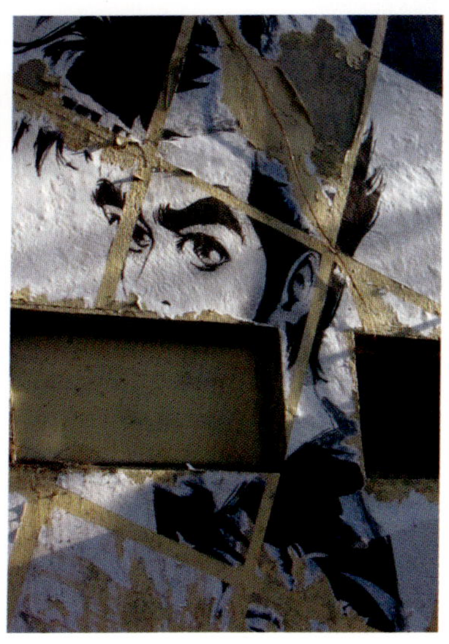

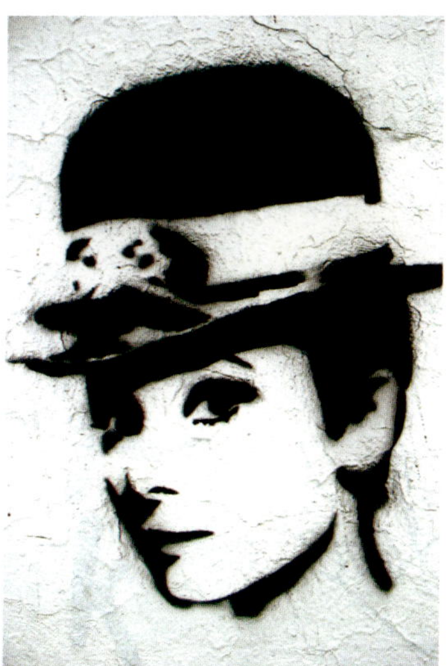

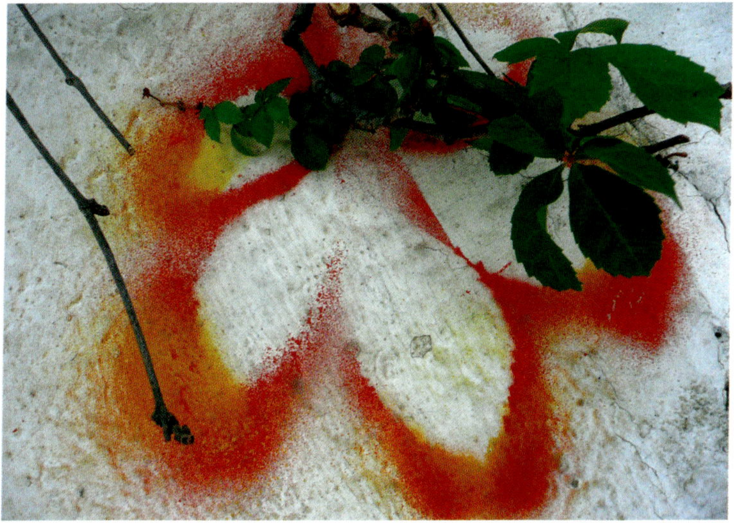

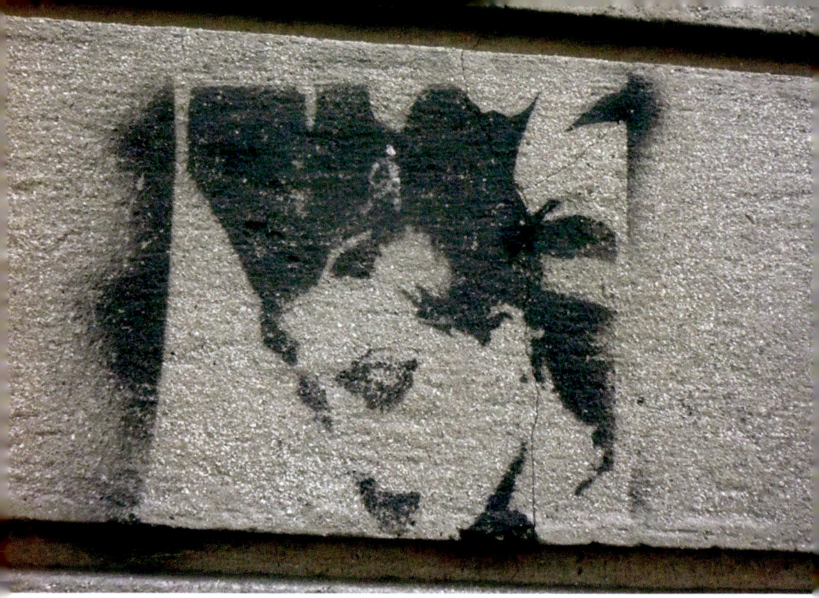

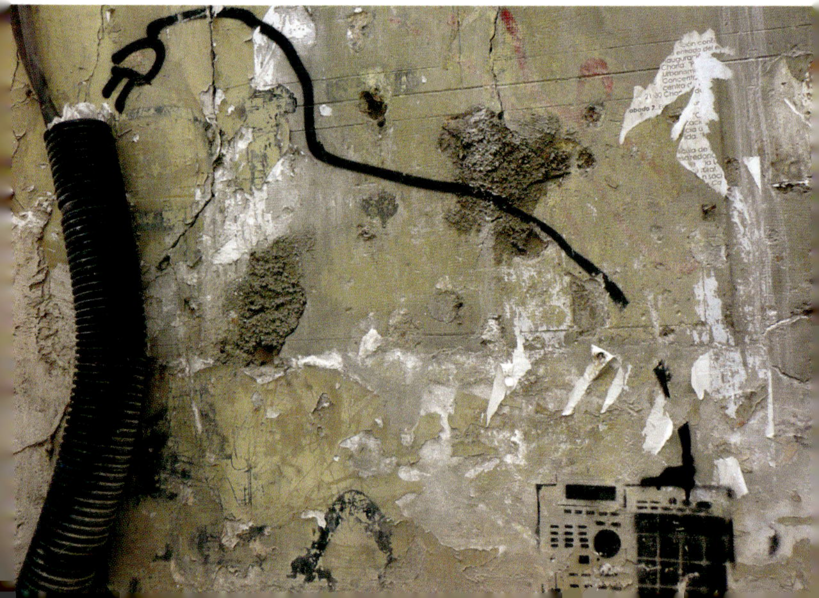

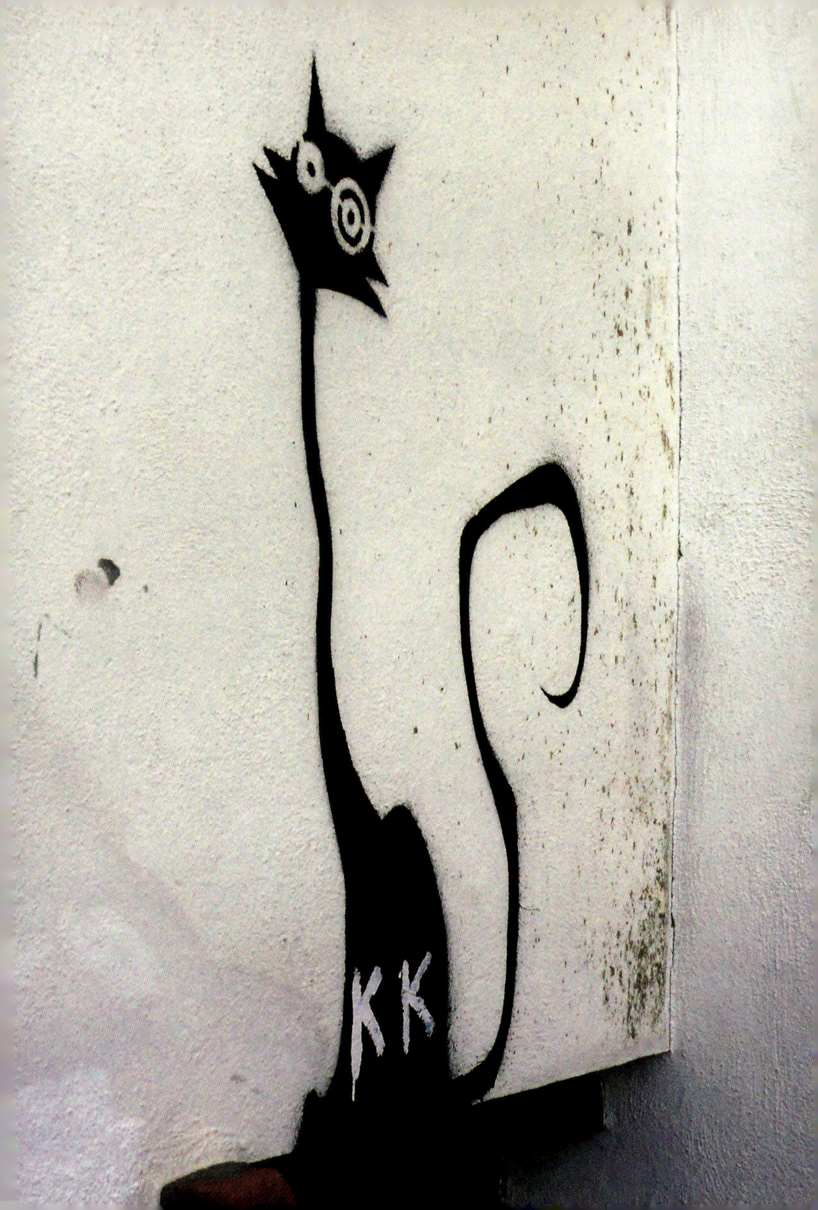
KK

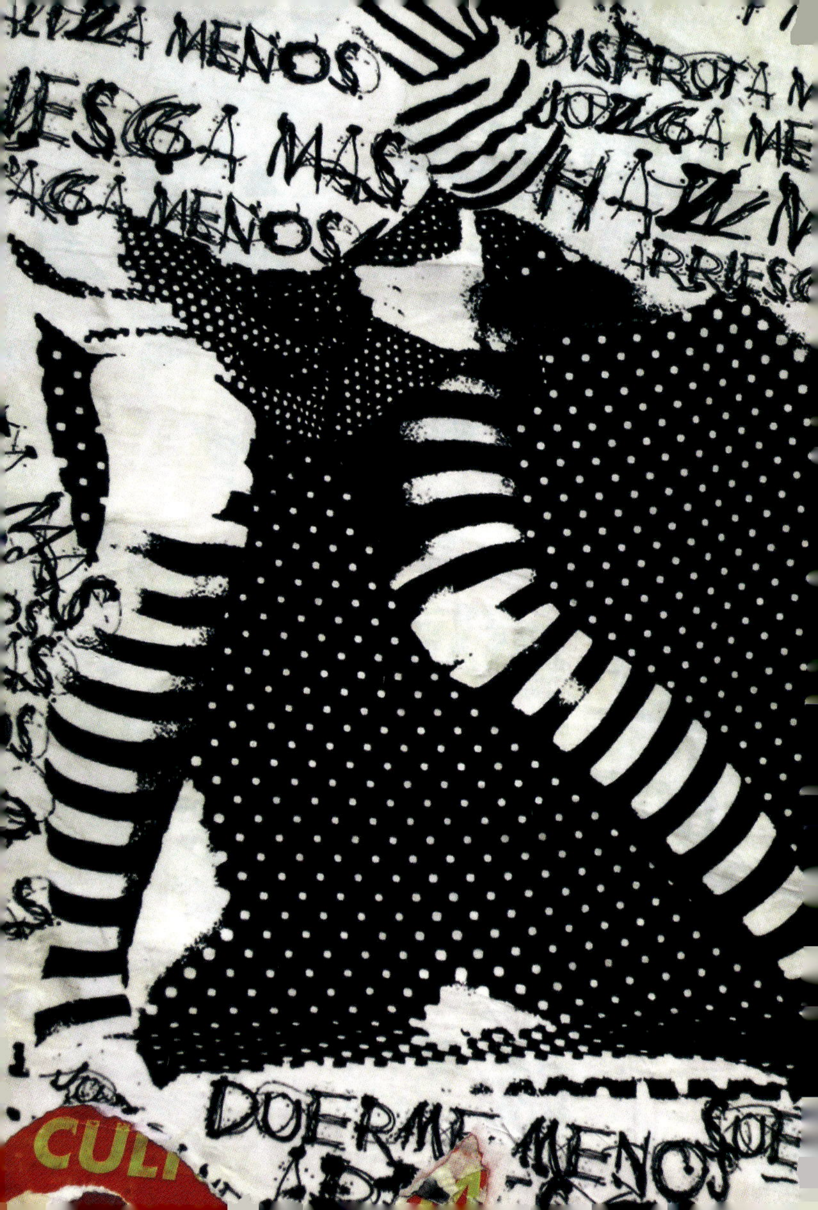
MENOS
DISFRUTA
JUZGA
MÁS
MENOS
DUERME MENOS

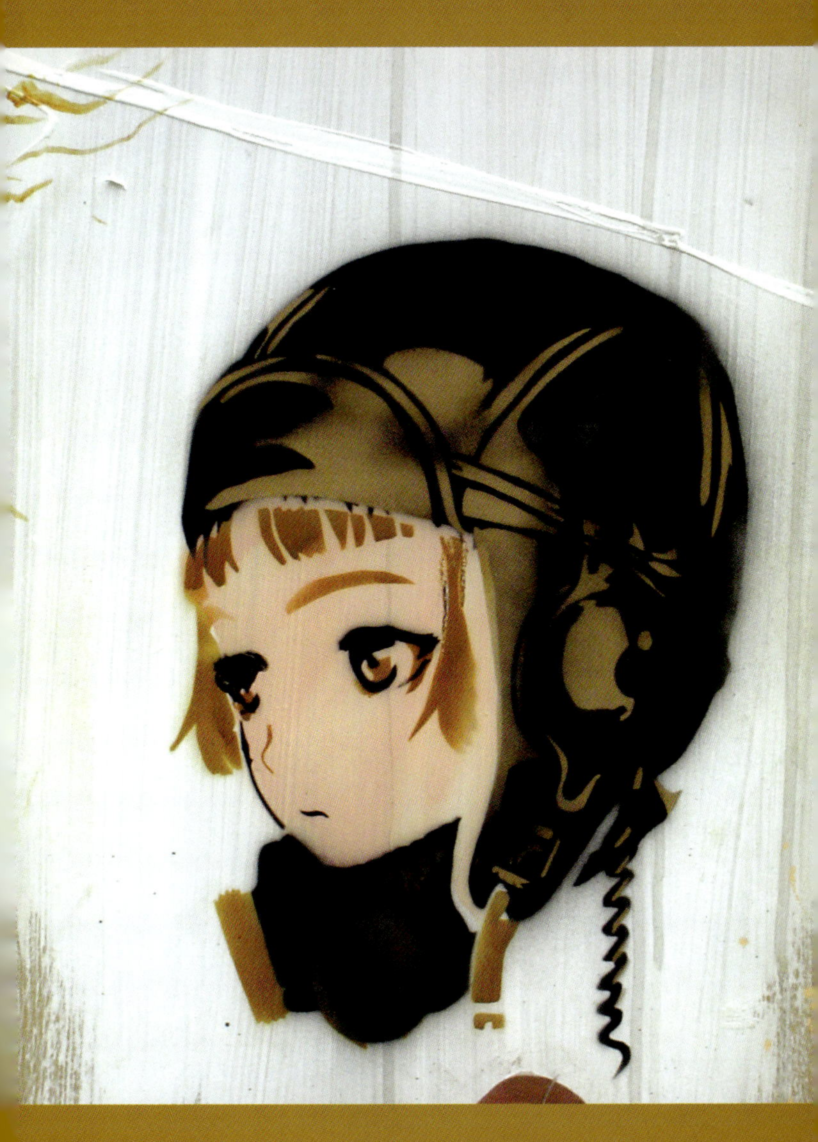

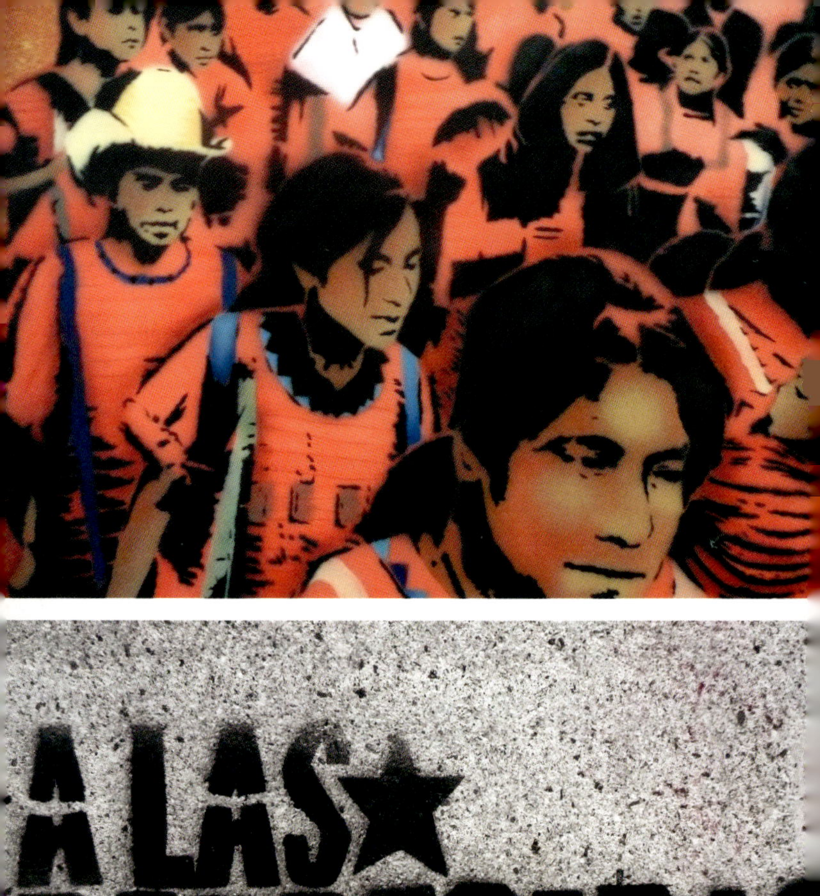
A LAS
BARRICADAS

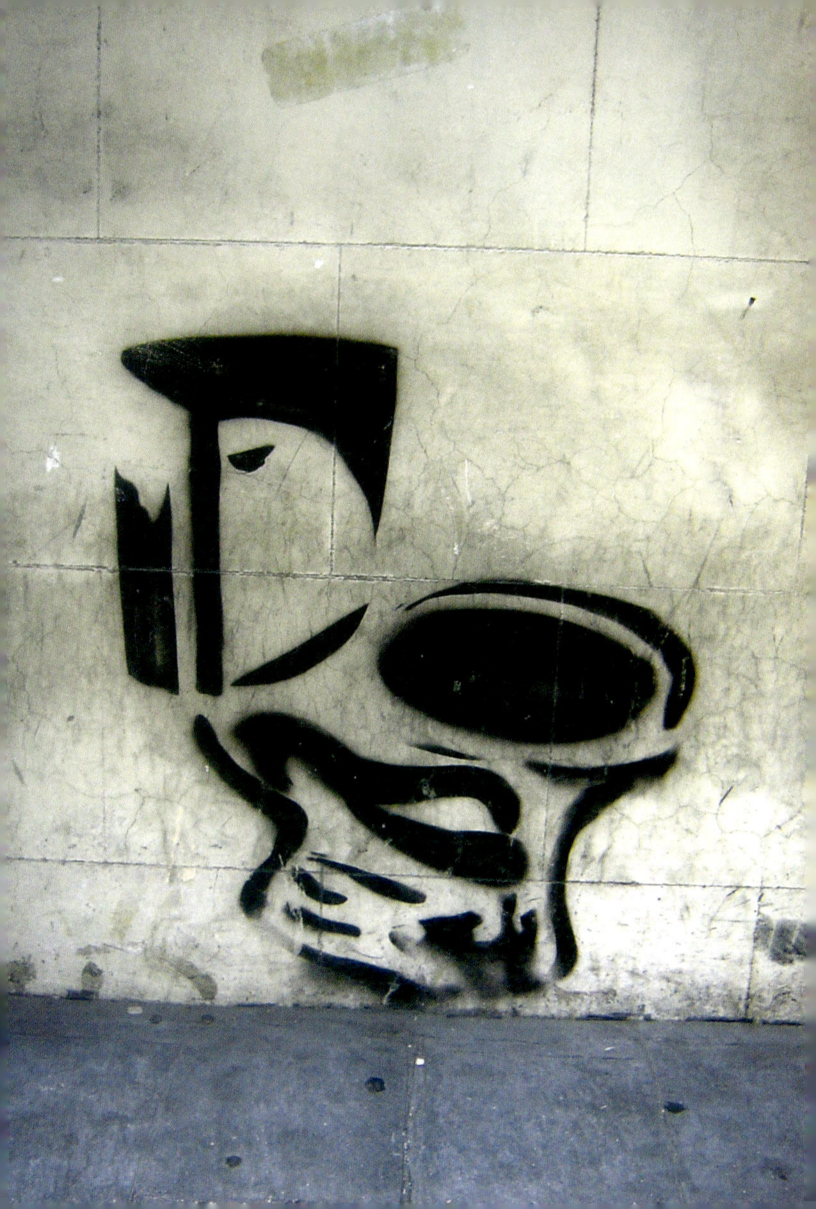

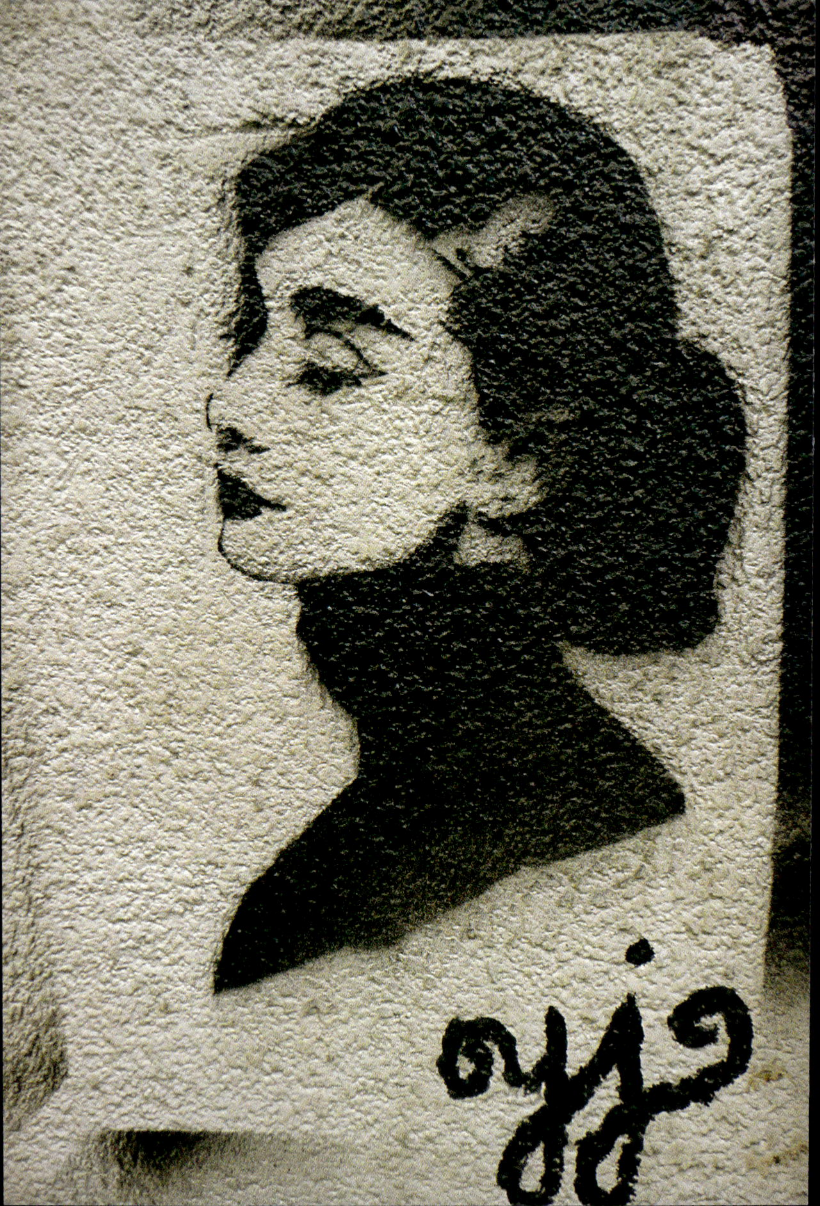

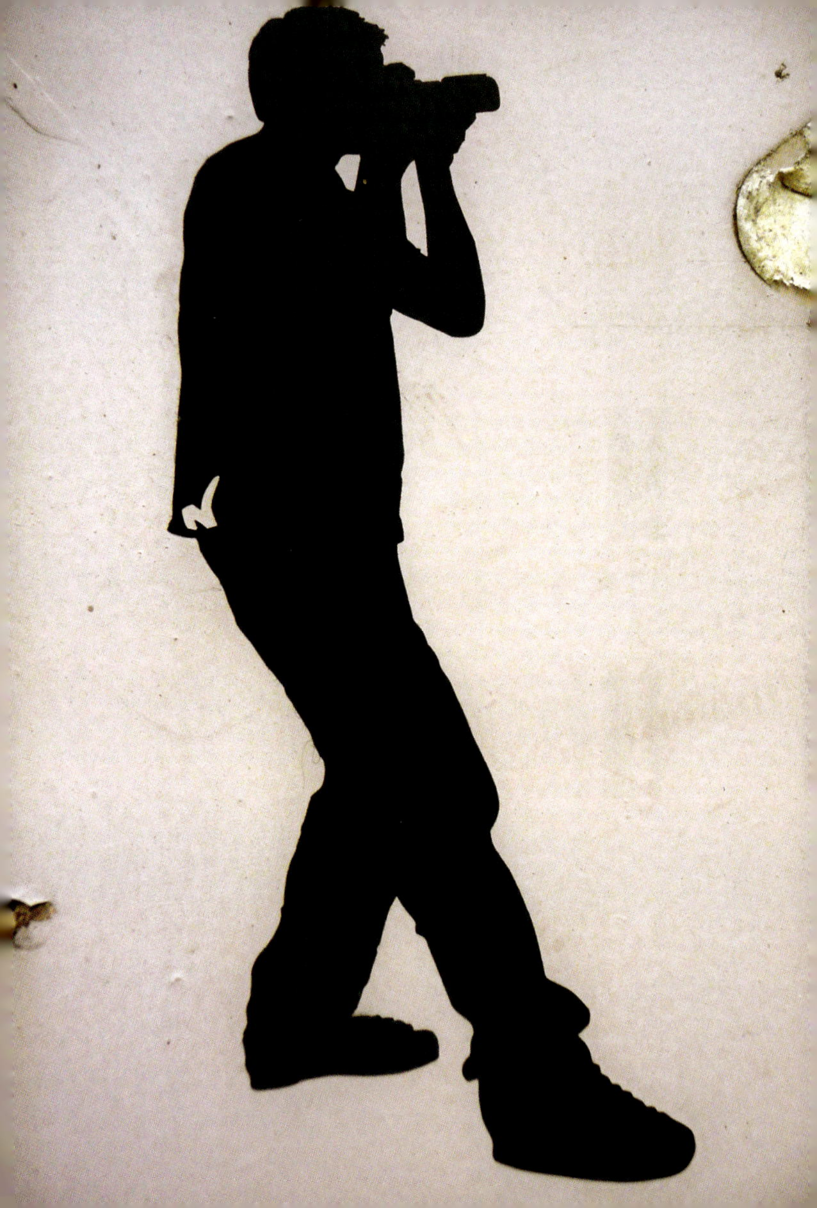

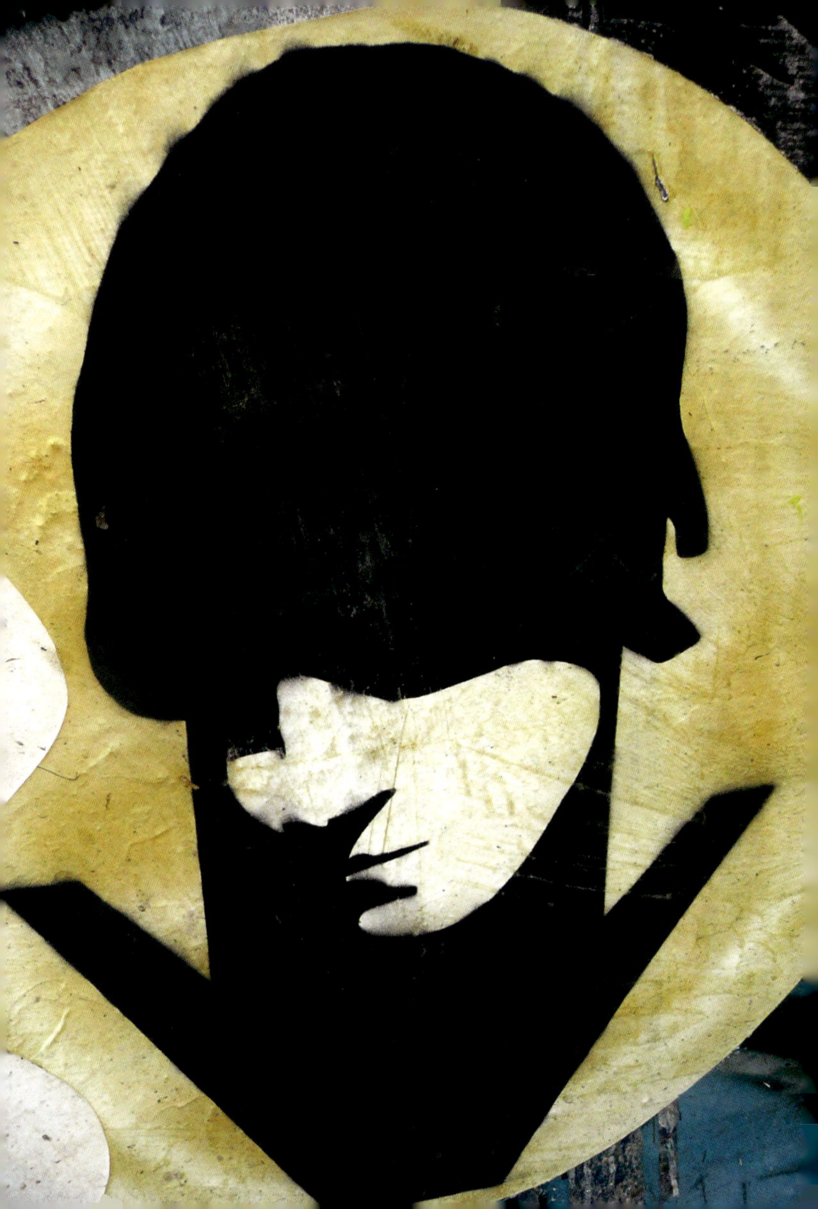

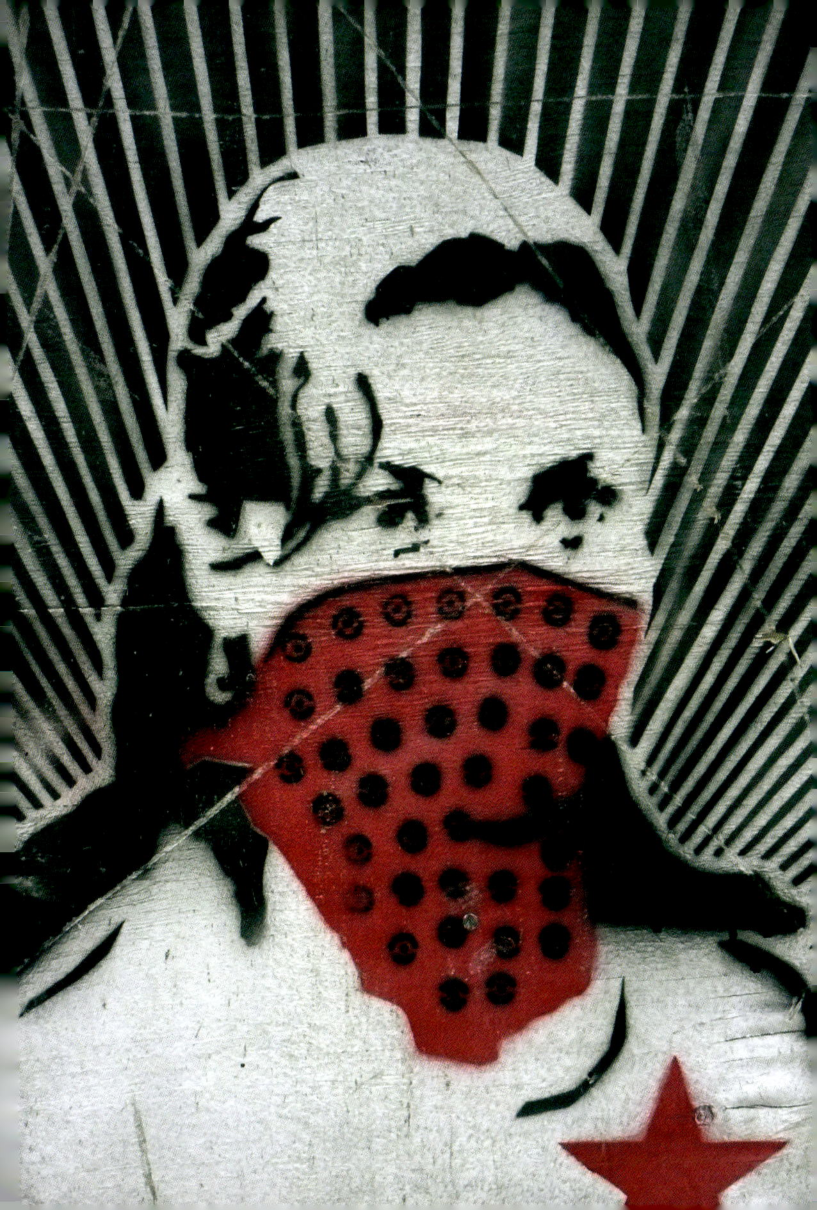

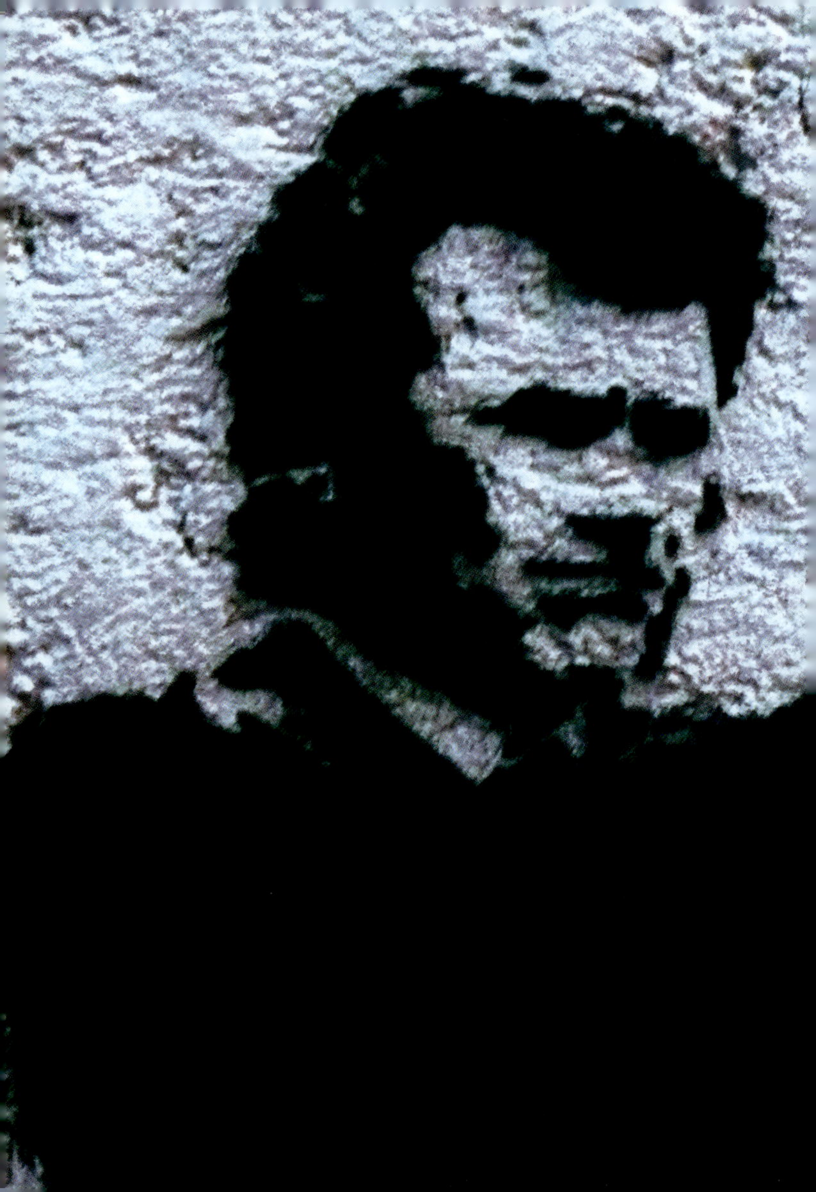

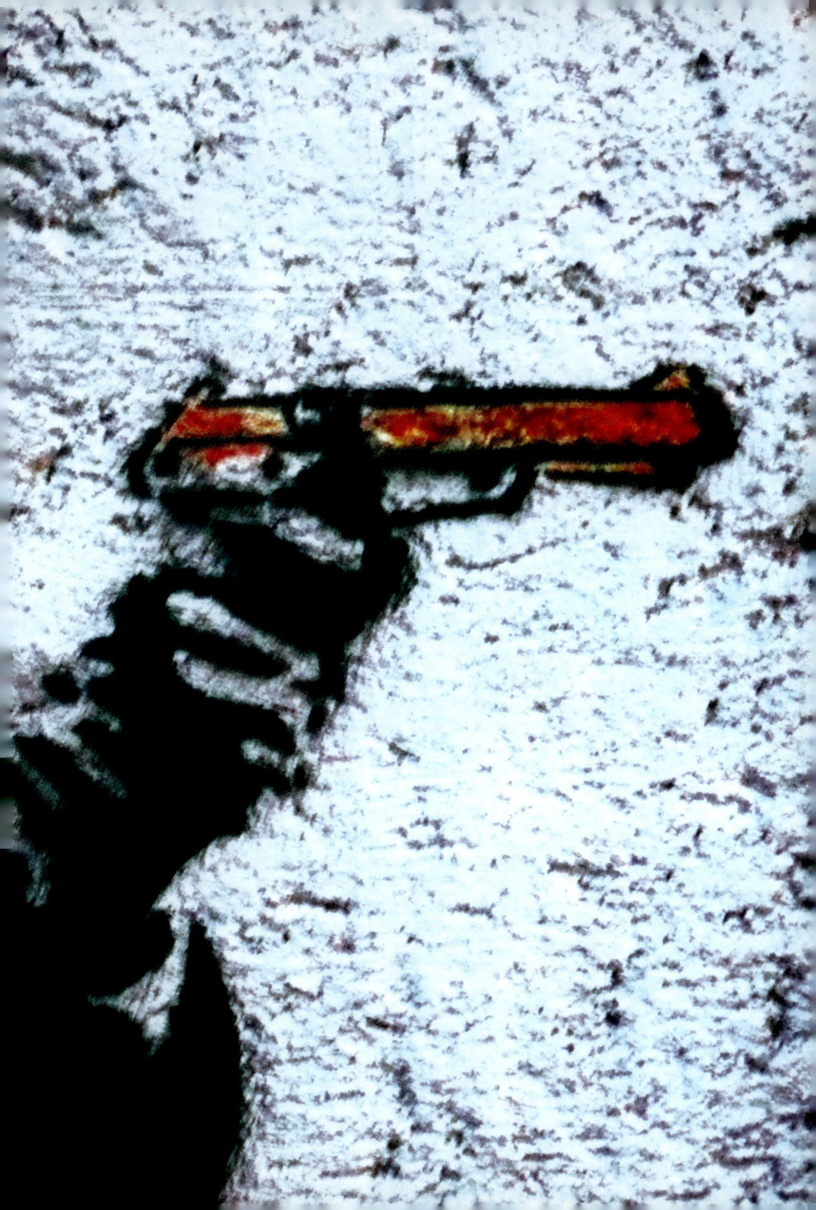

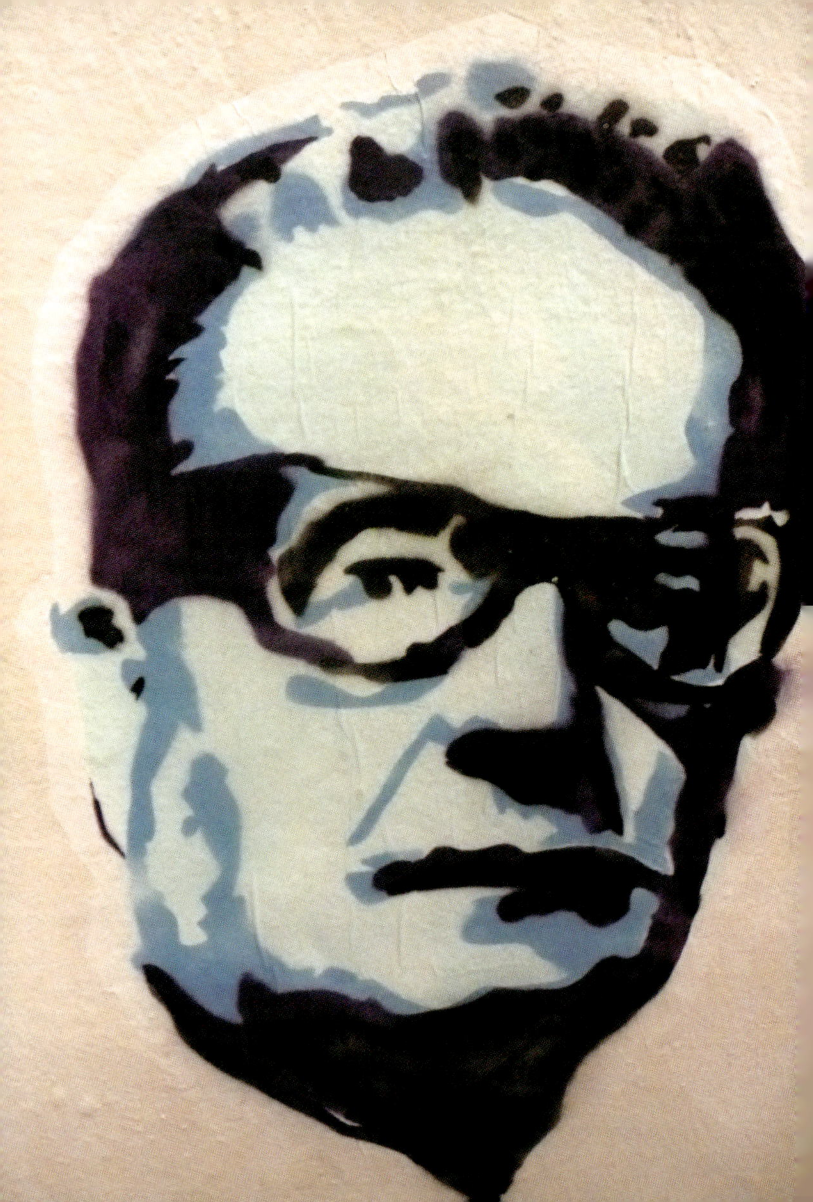

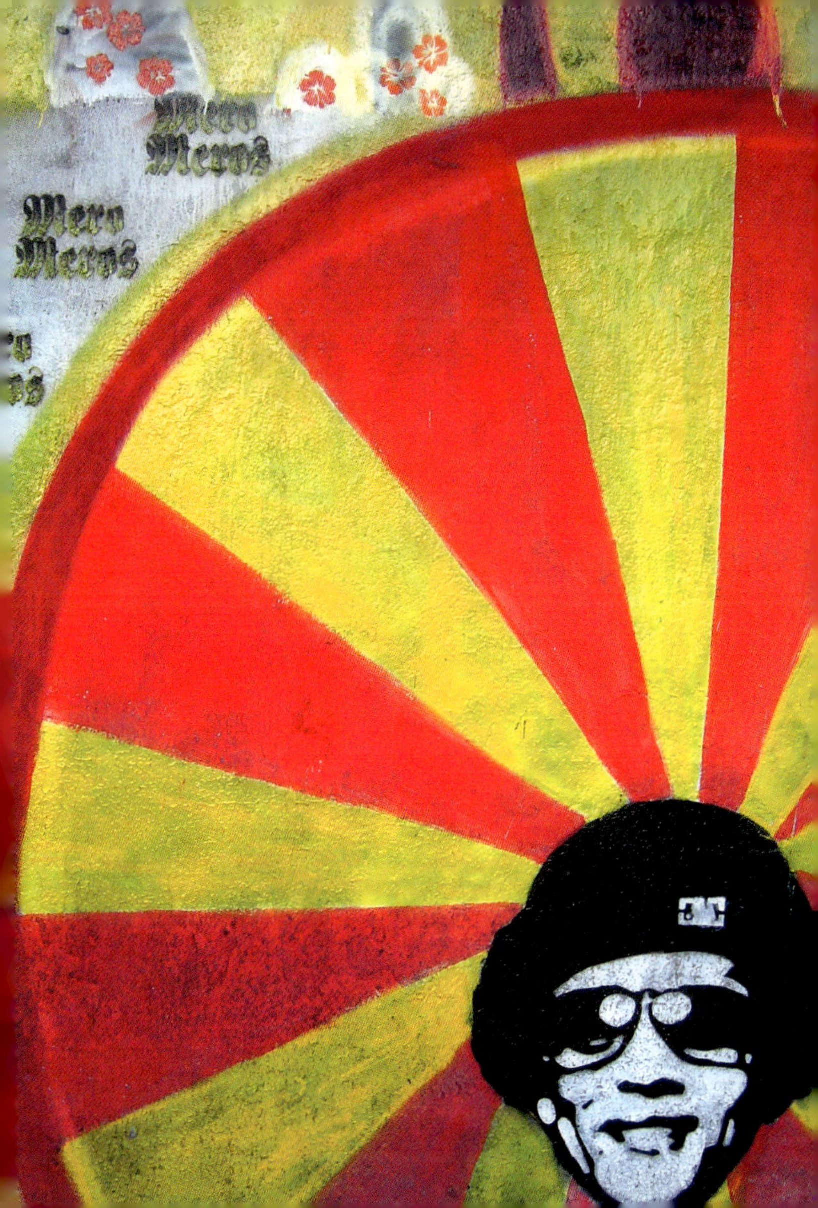
Mero Meros
Mero Meros

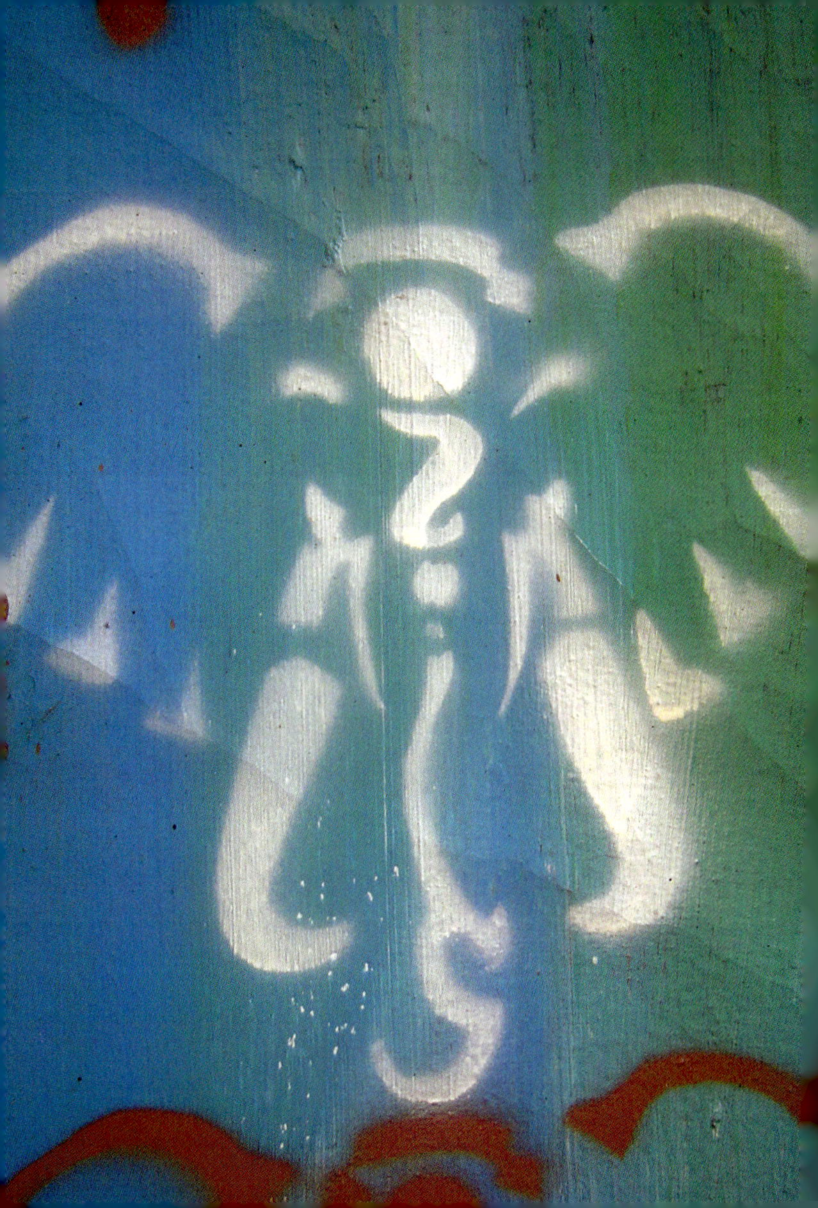

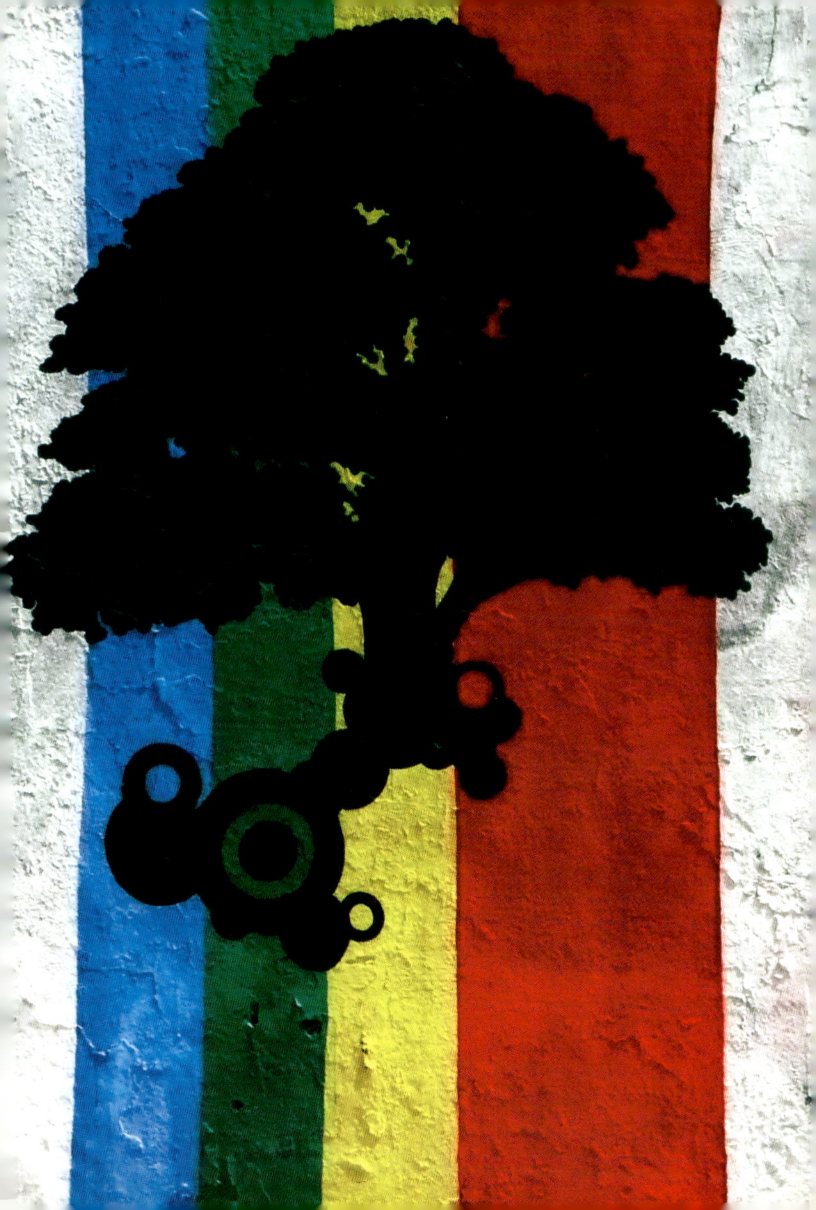

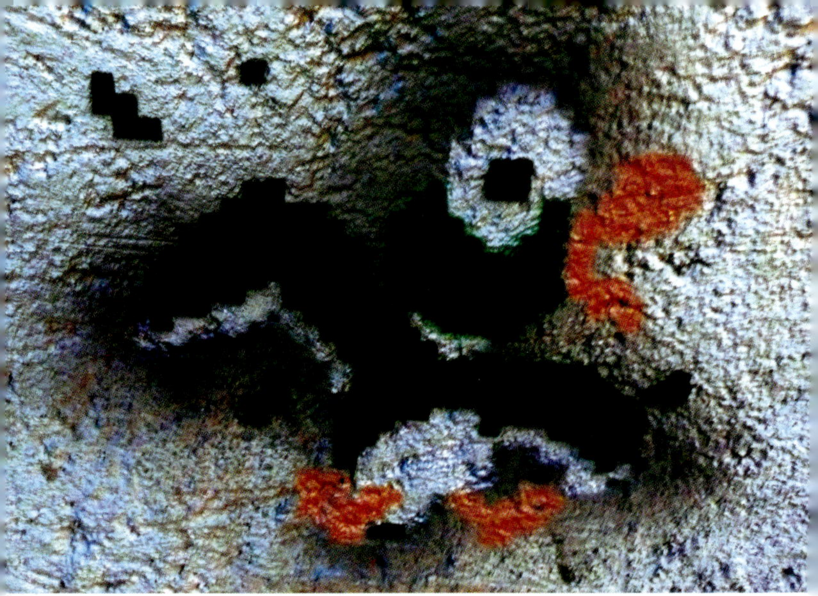

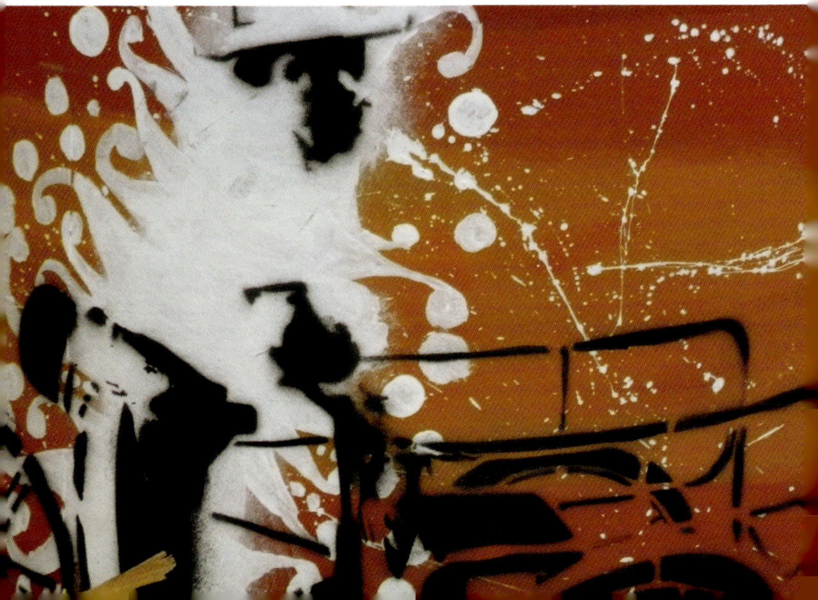

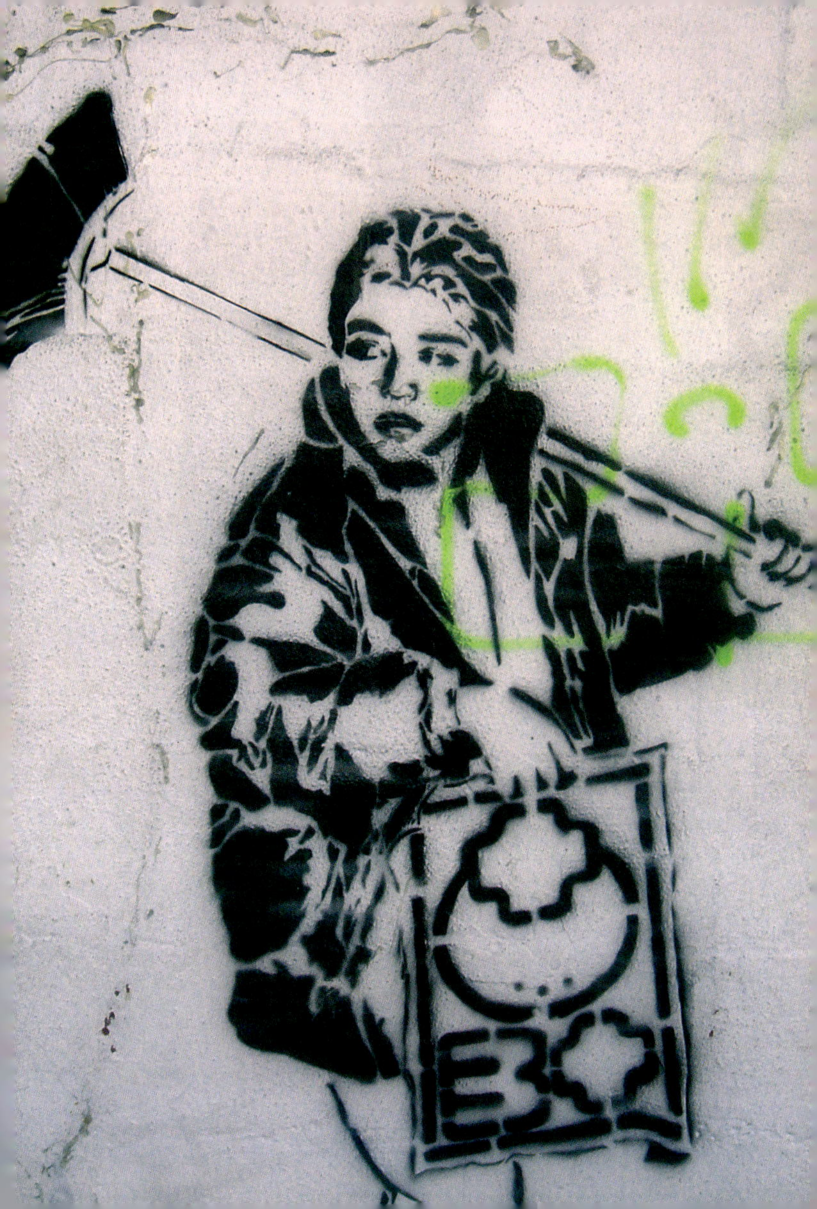

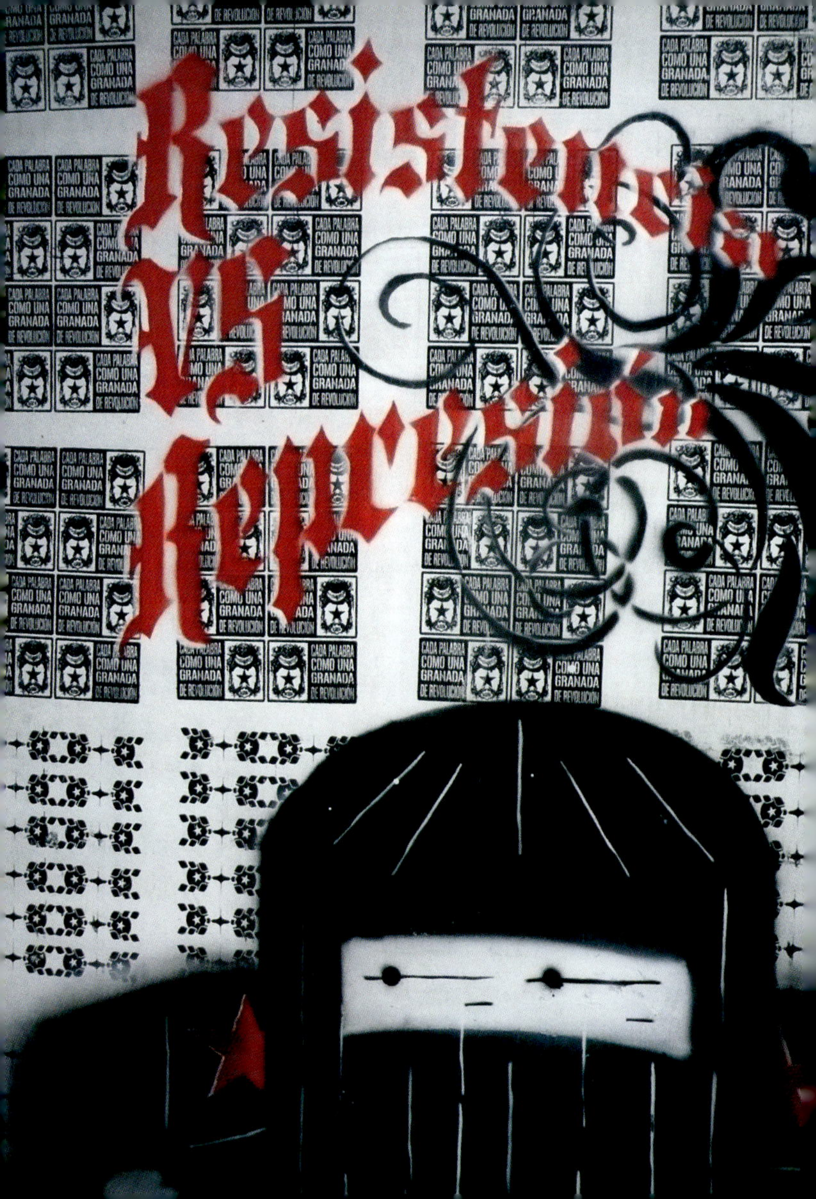
CADA PALABRA COMO UNA GRANADA DE REVOLUCIÓN

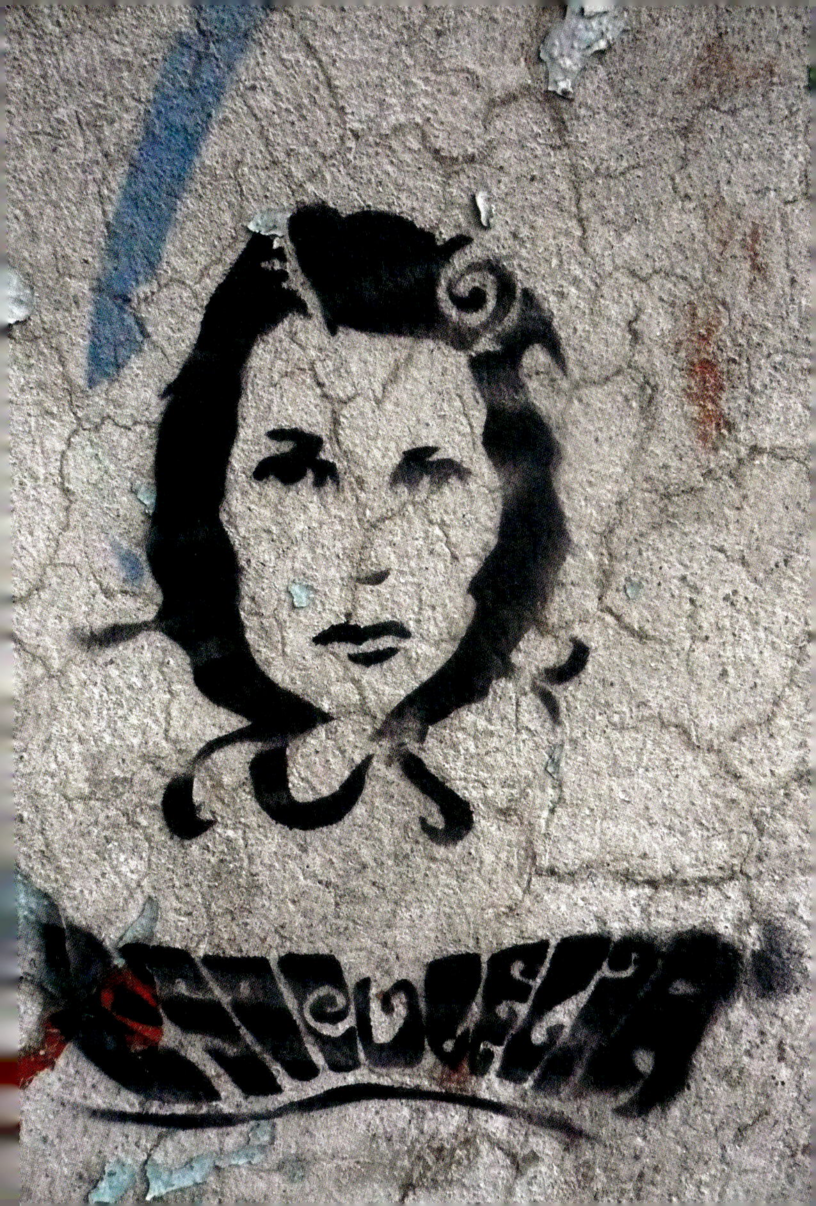

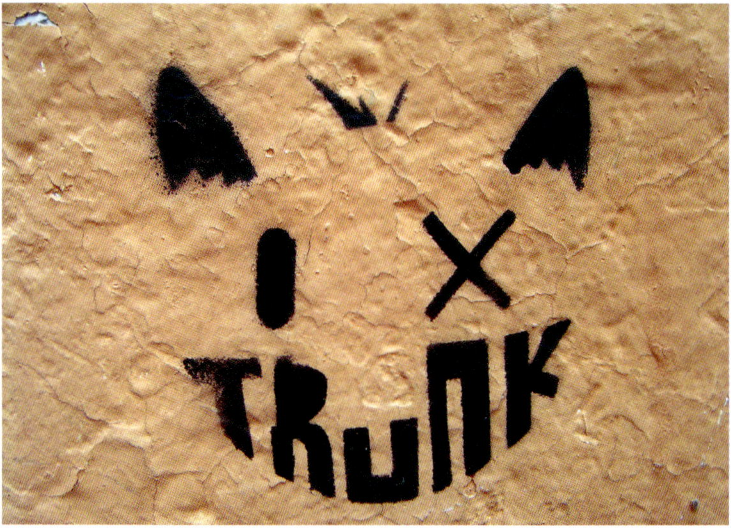

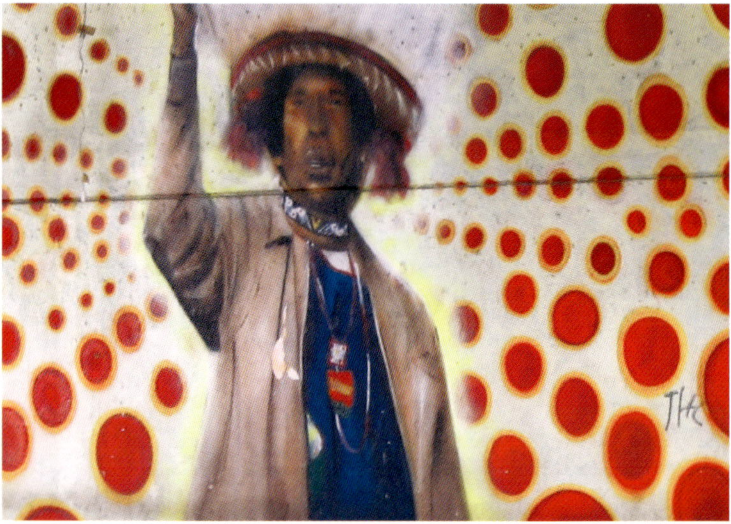

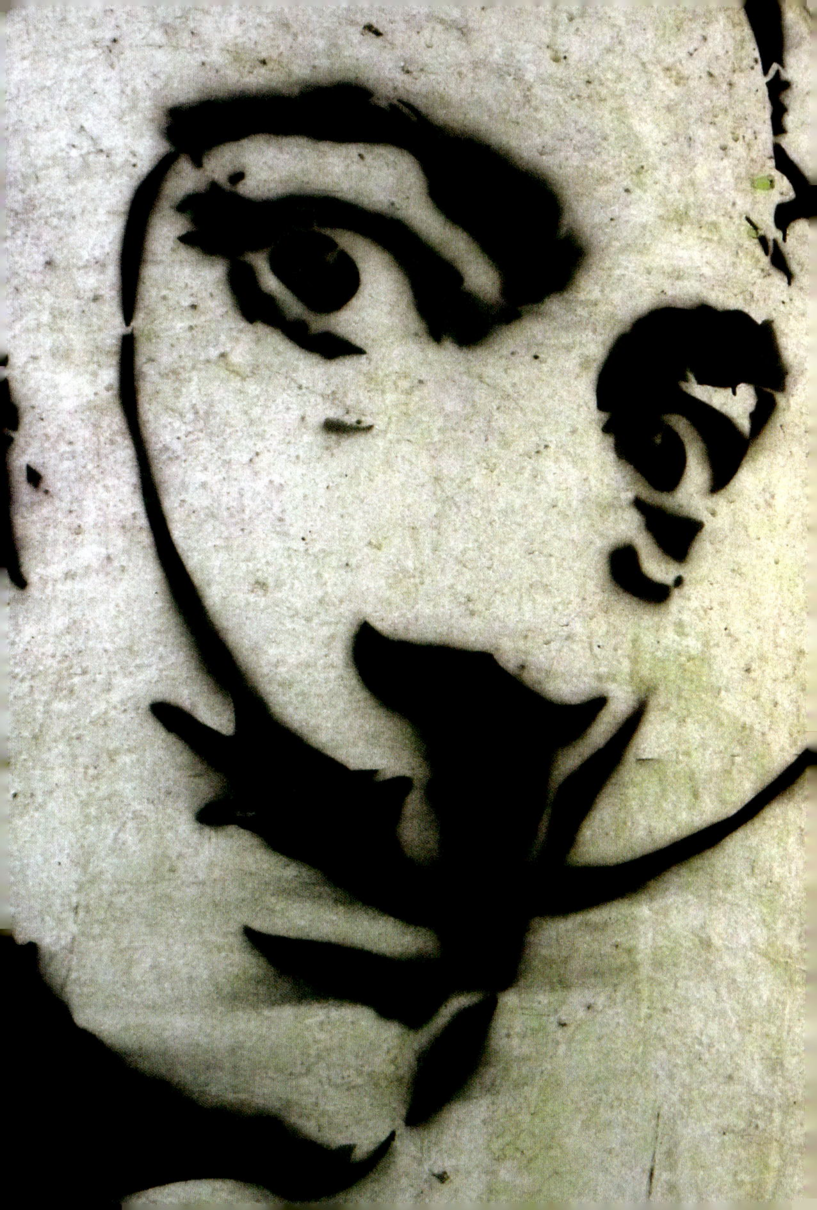

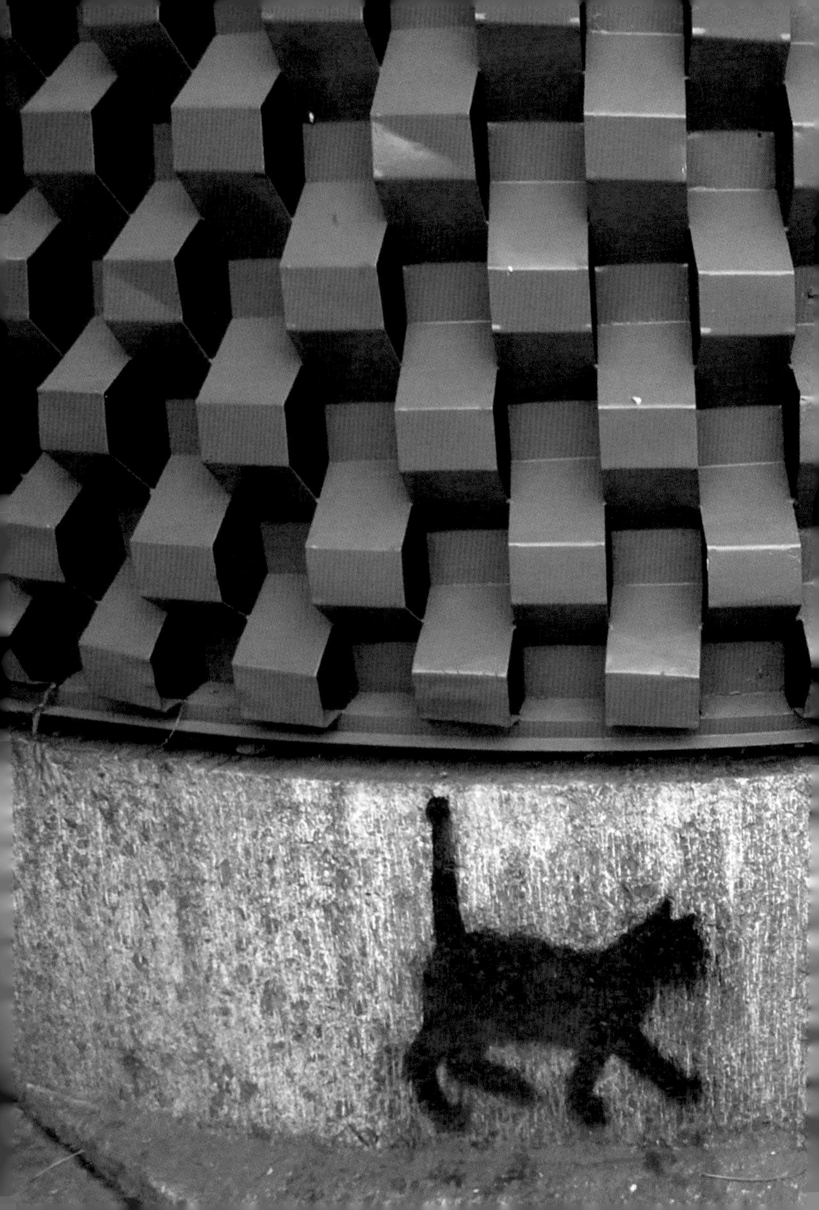

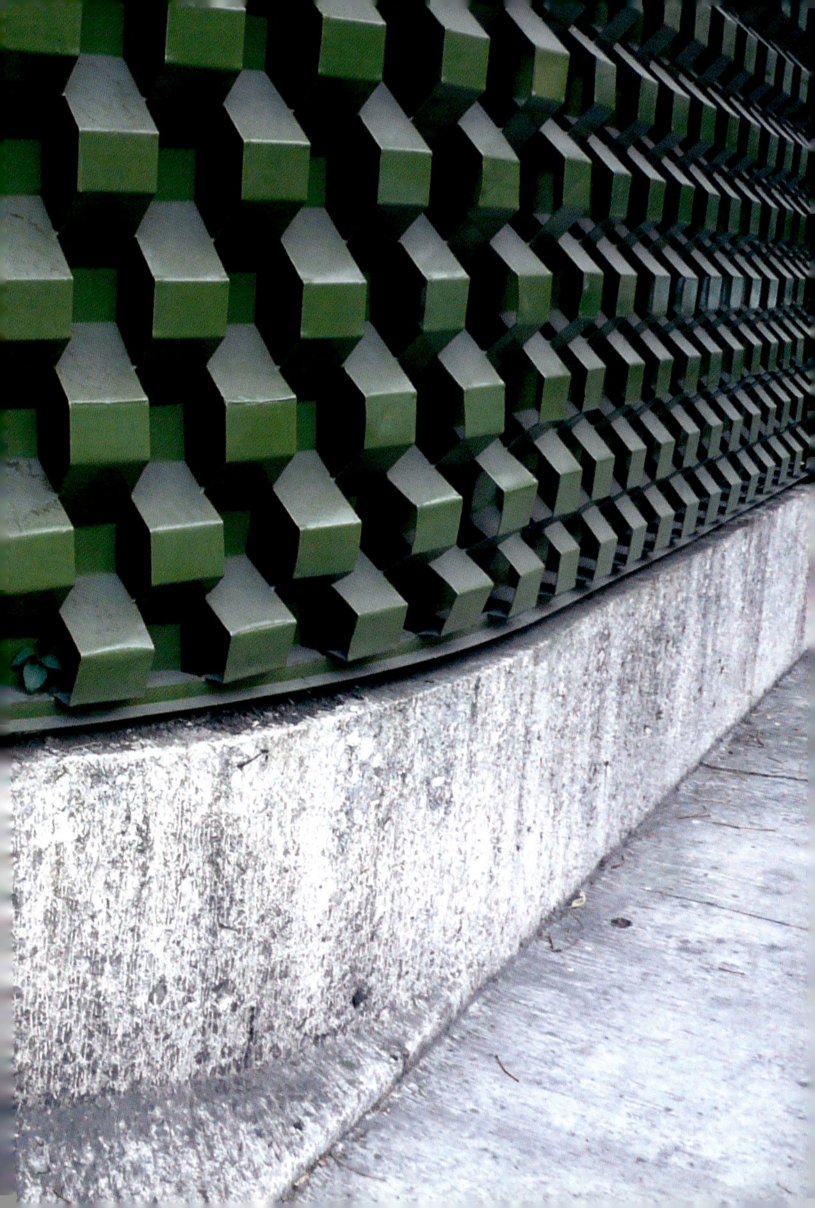

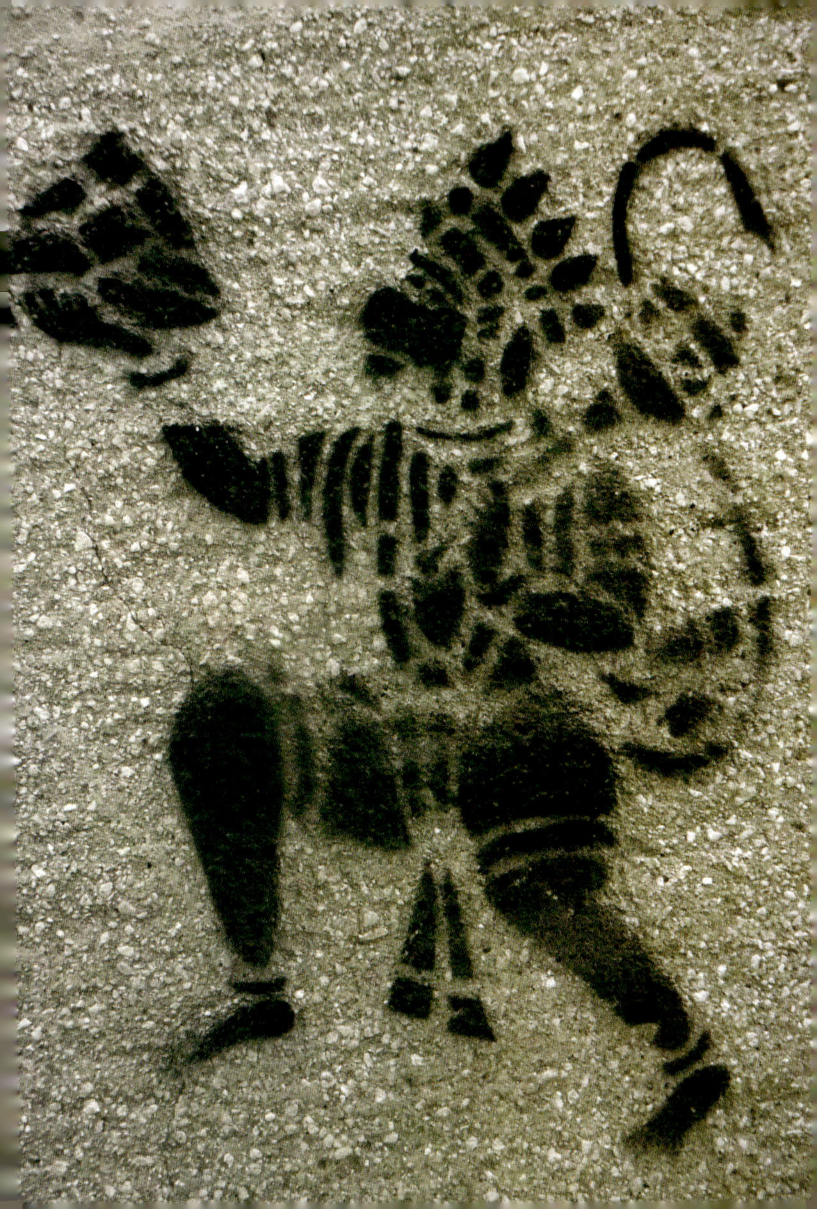

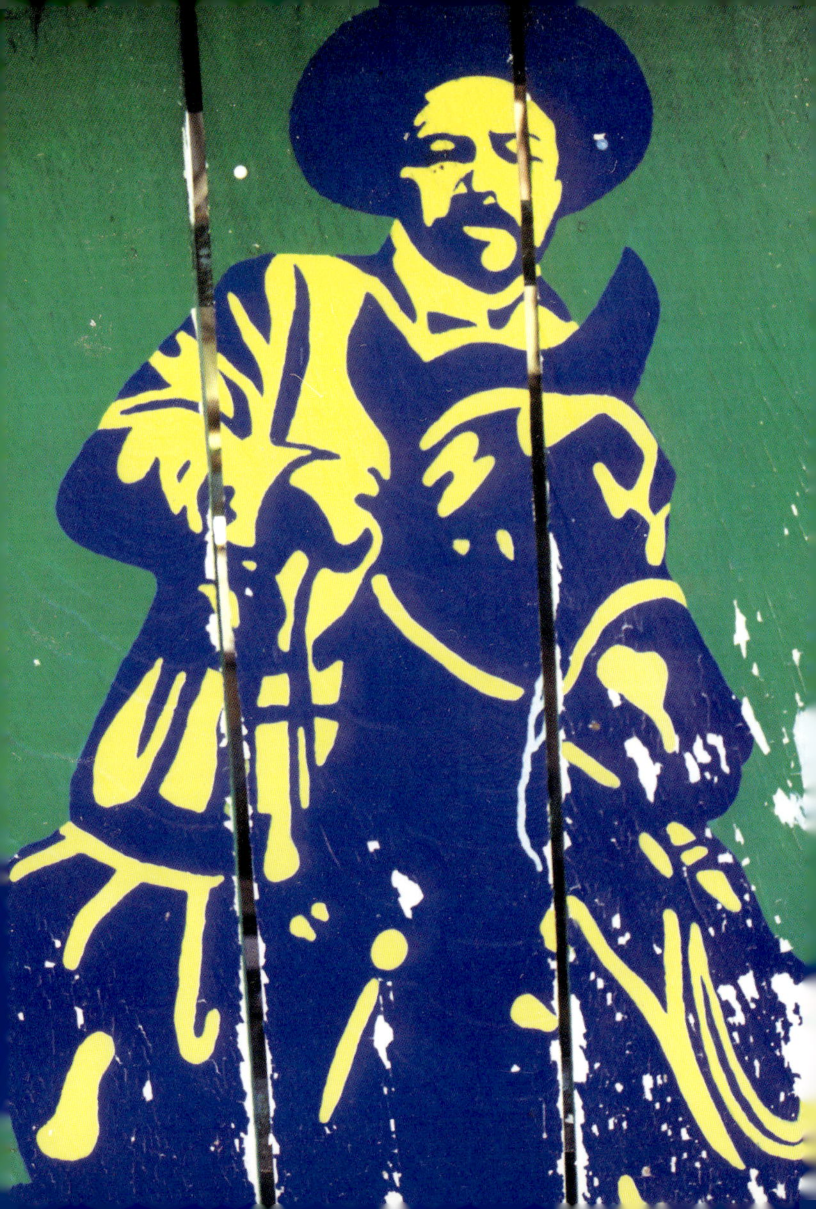

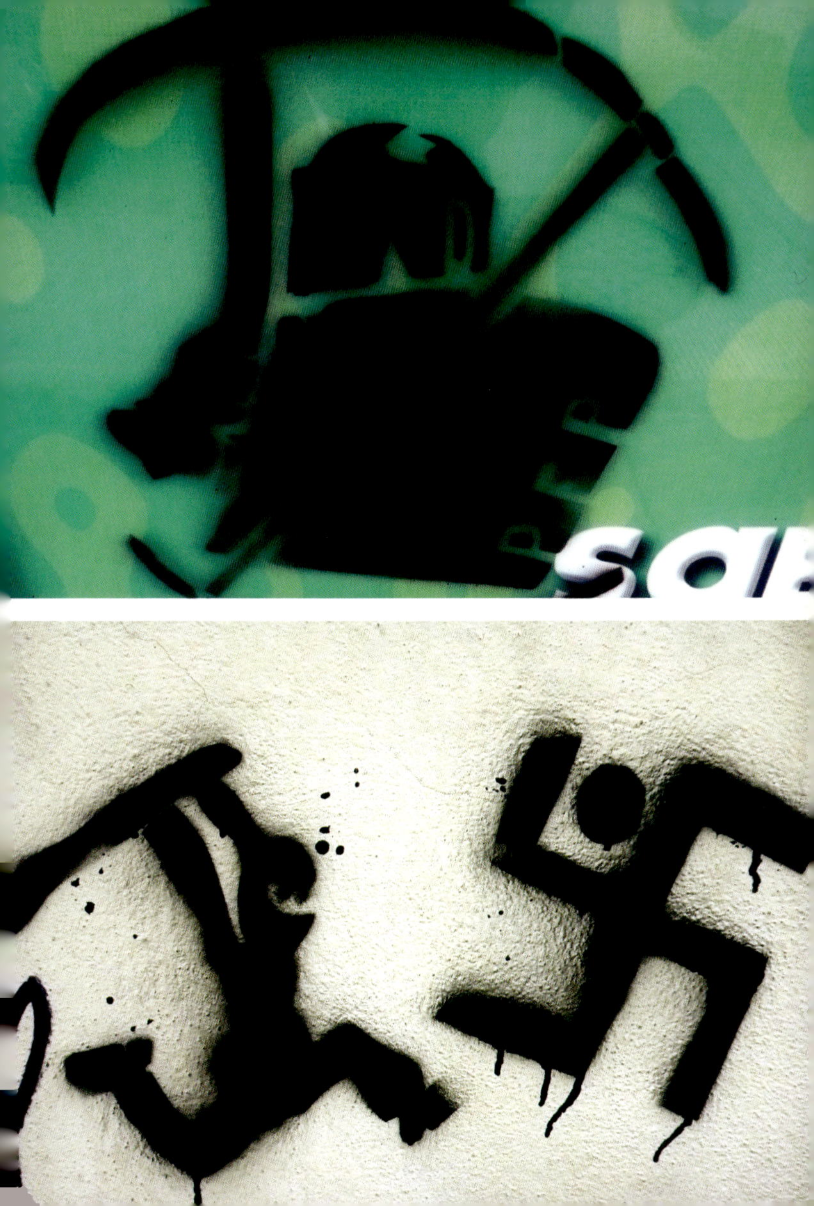

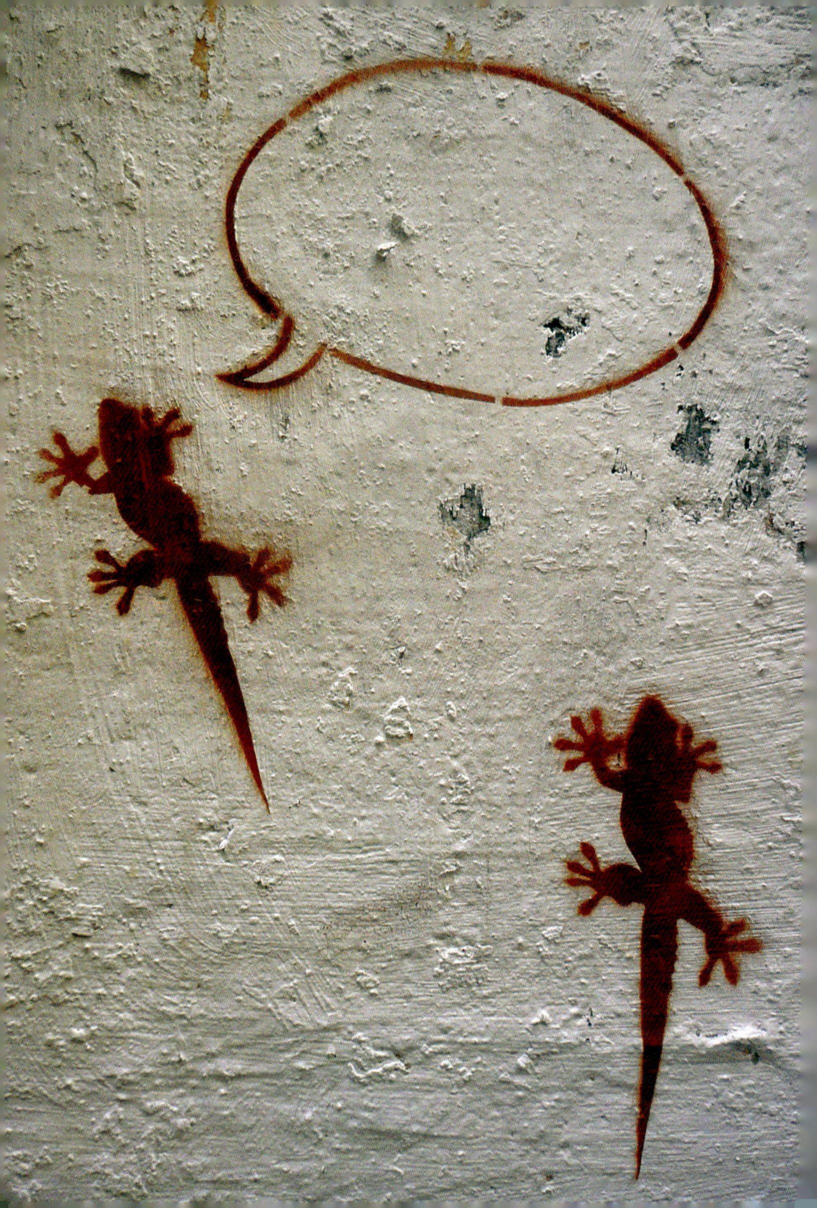

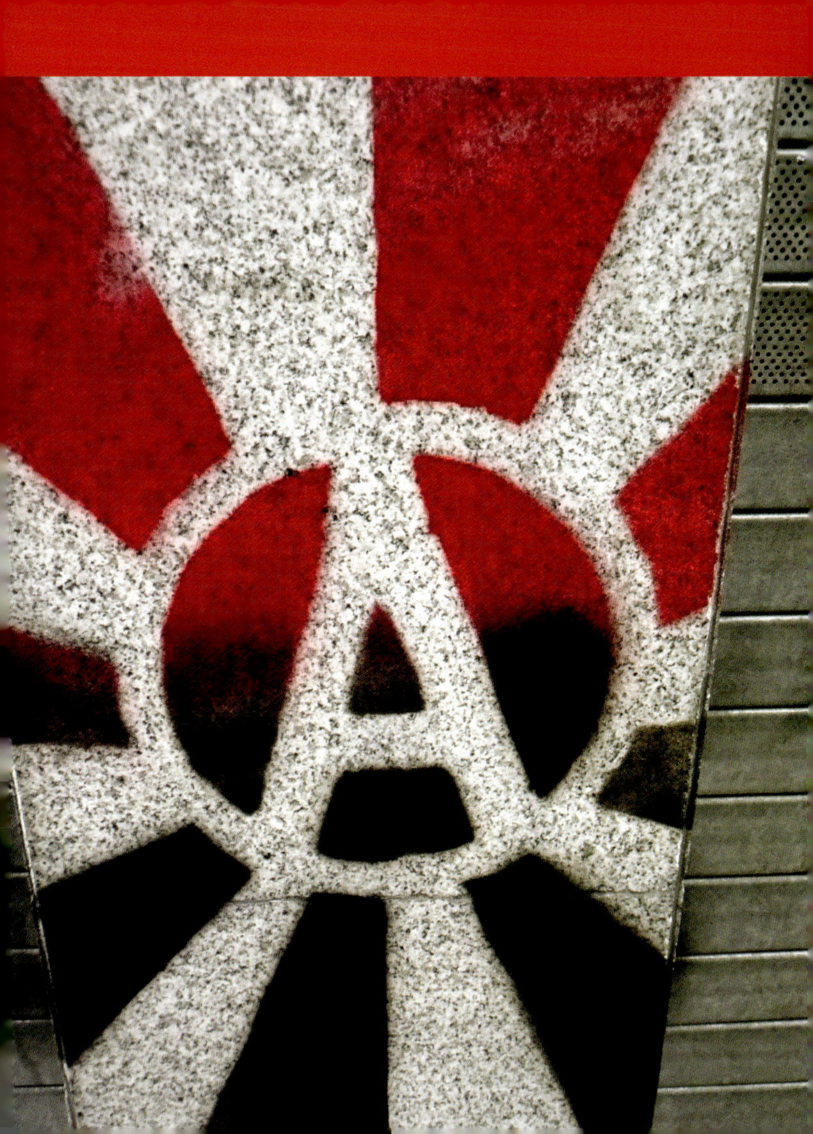

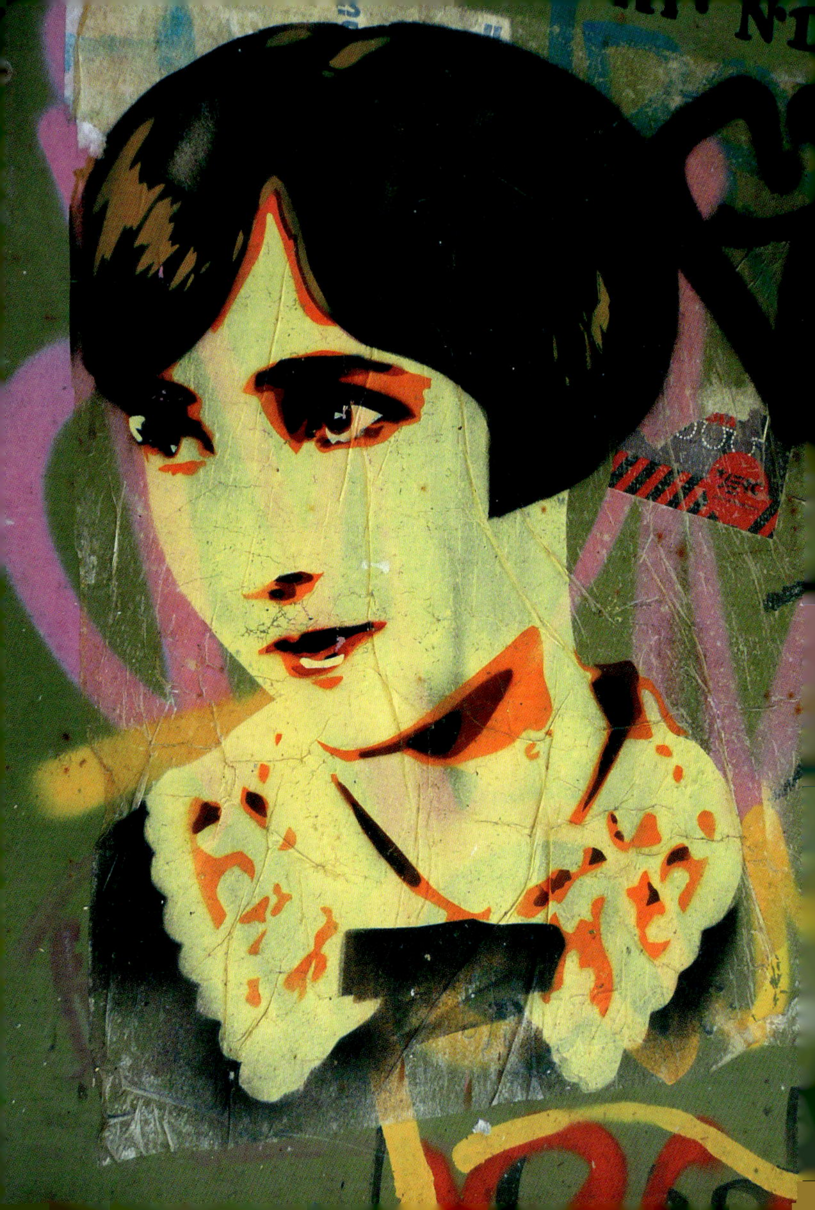

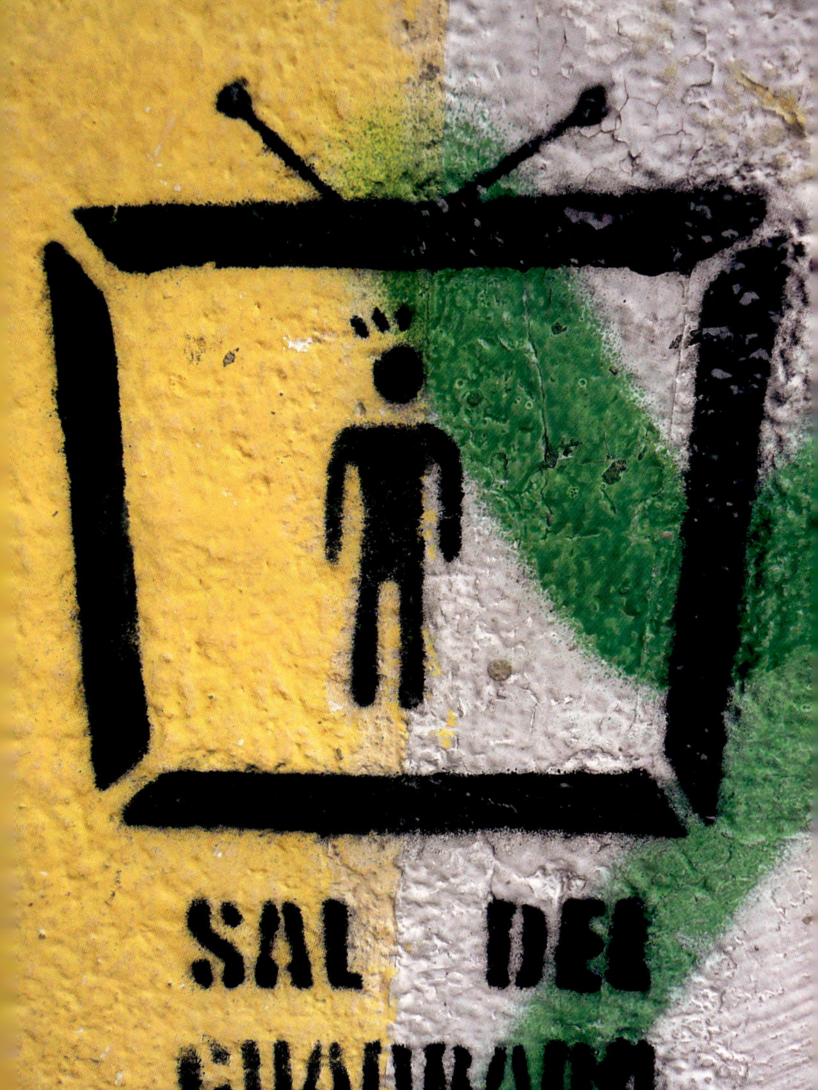
SAL DEL
CUADRADO

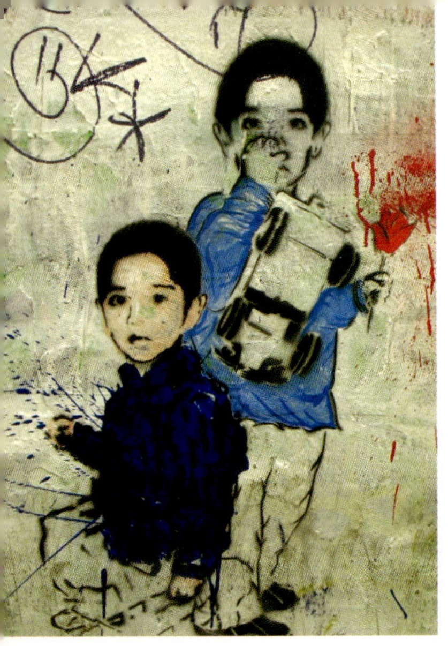

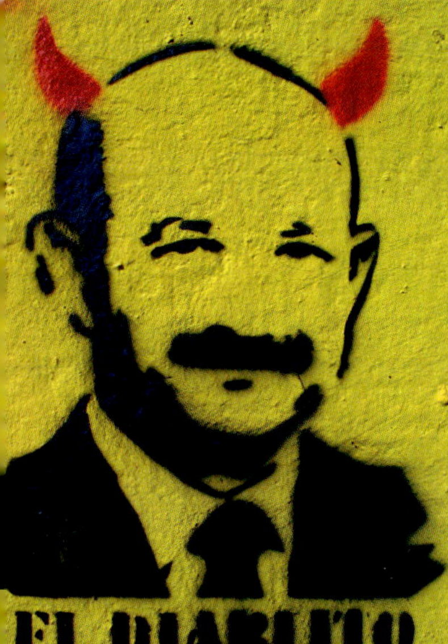
EL DIABLITO

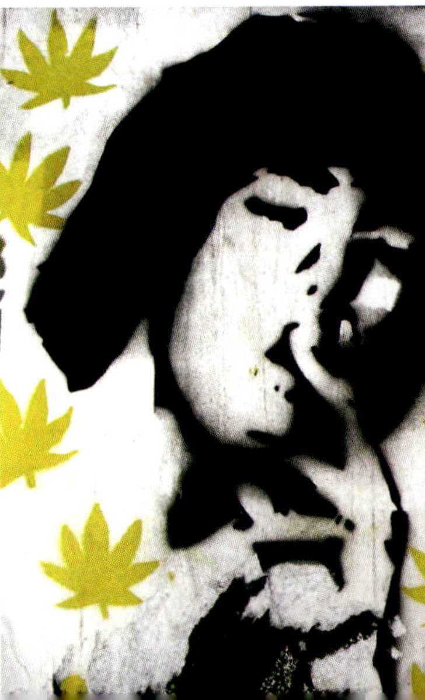

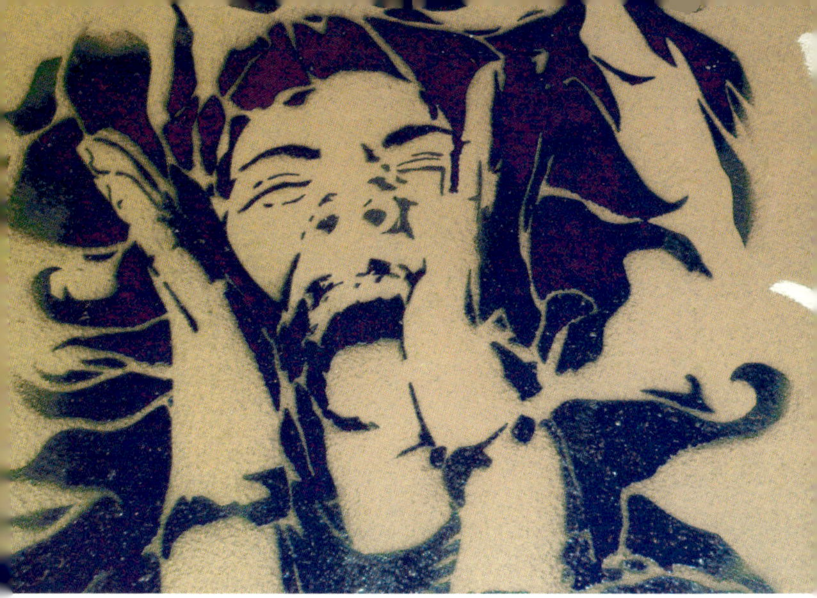

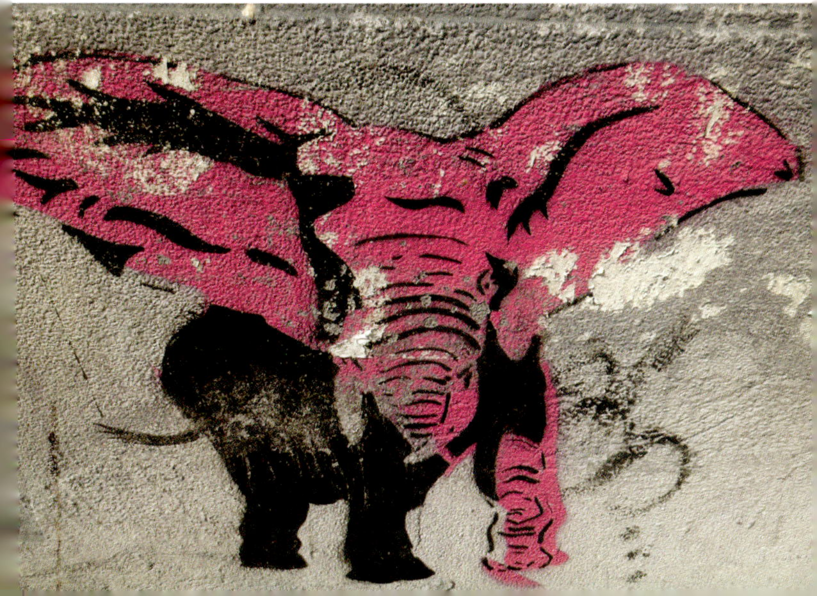

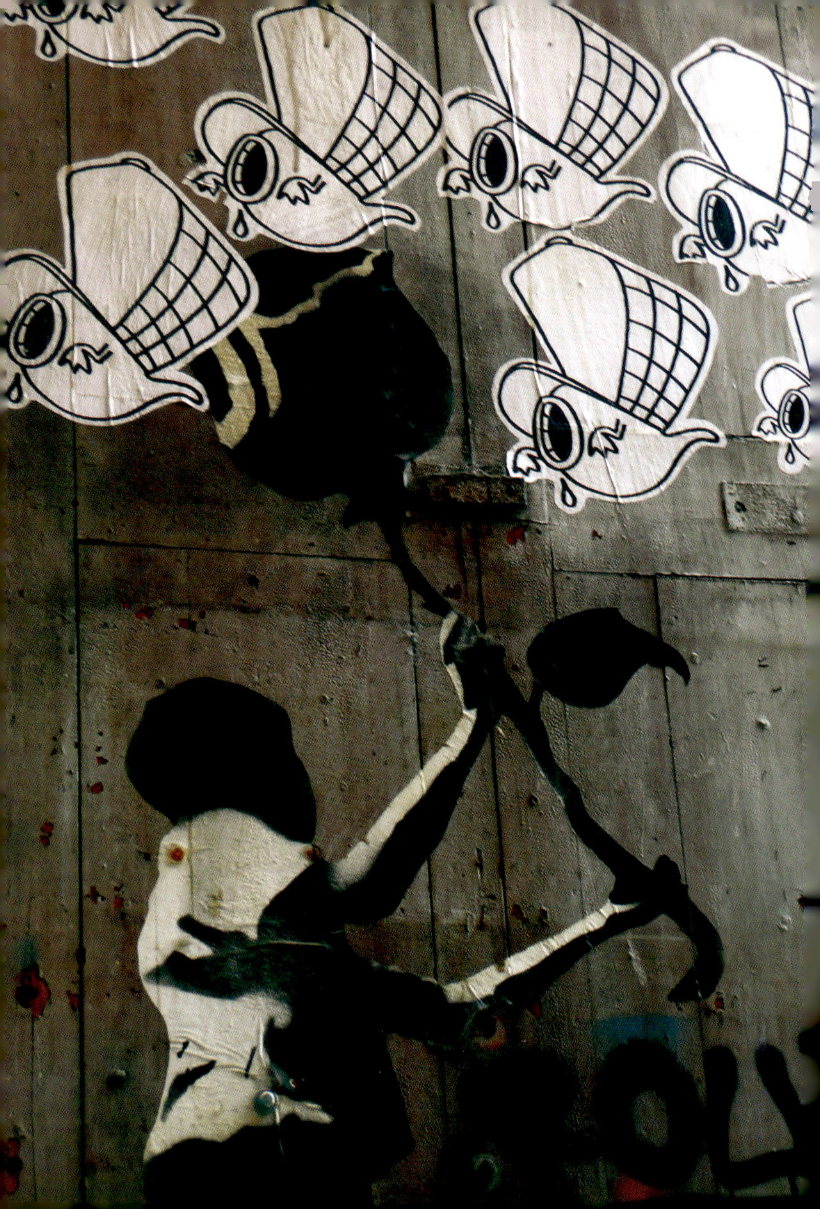

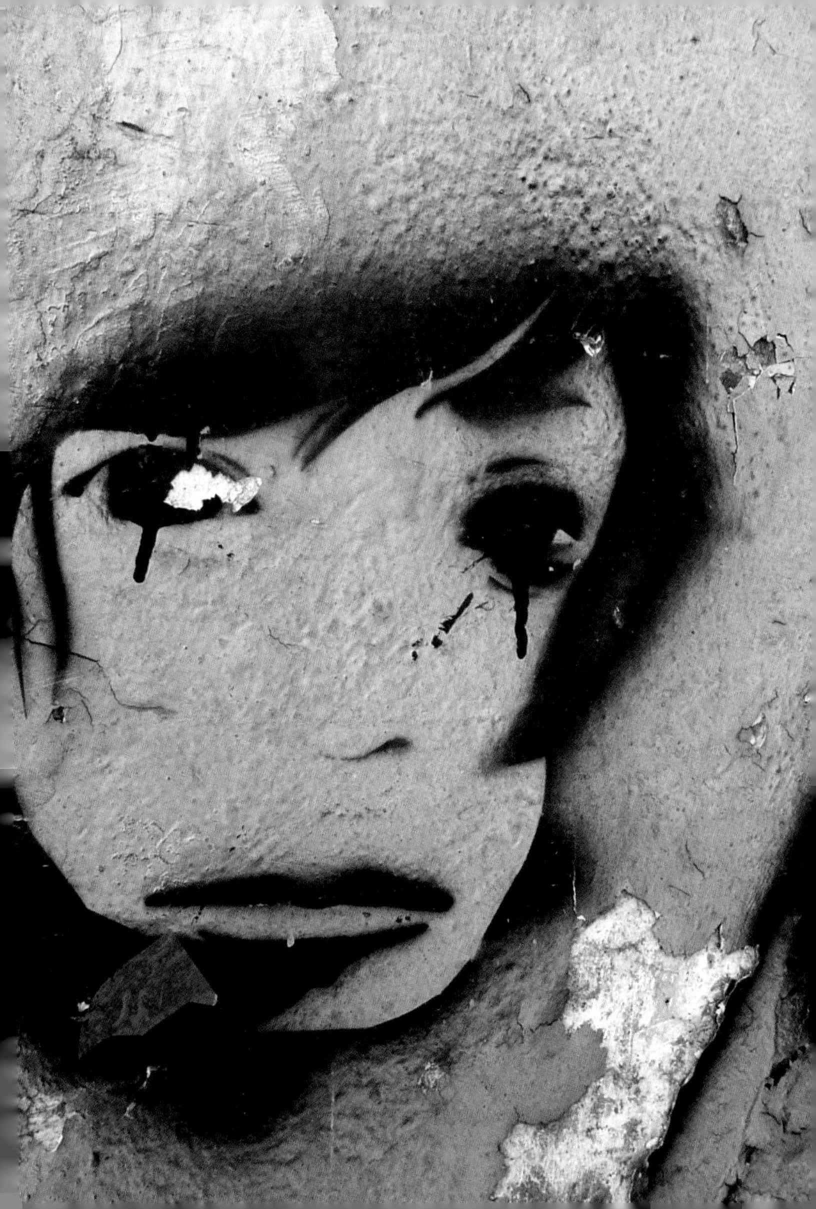

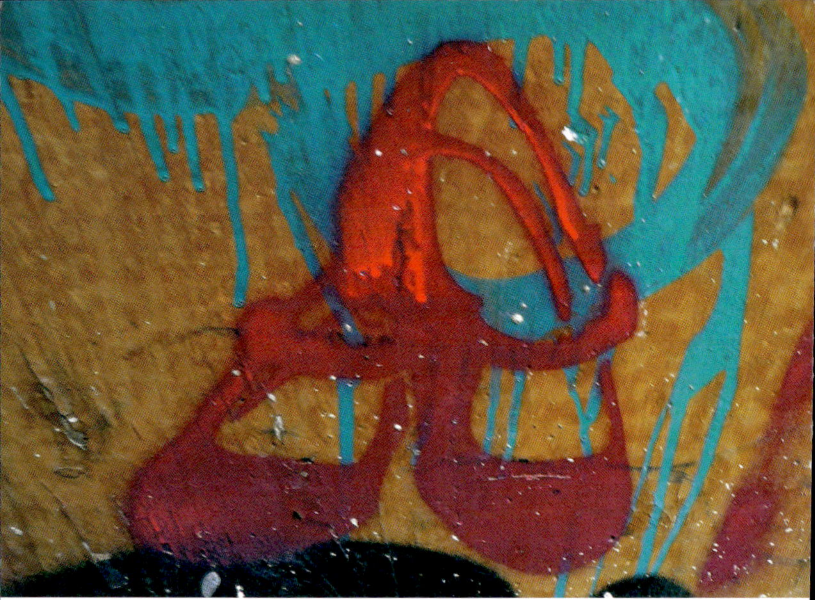

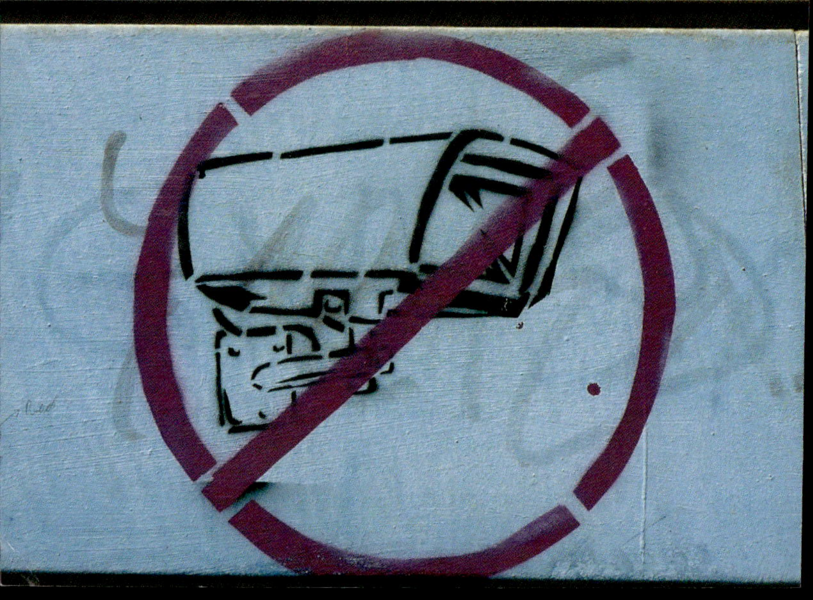

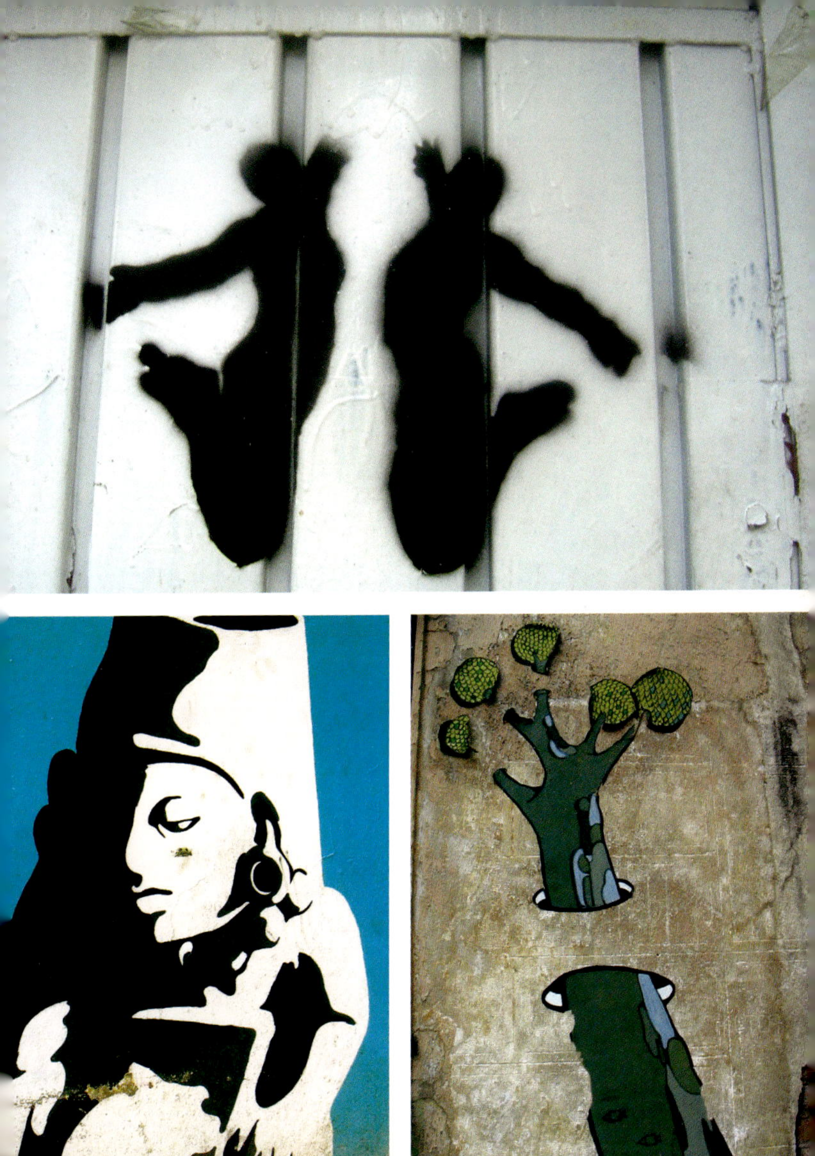

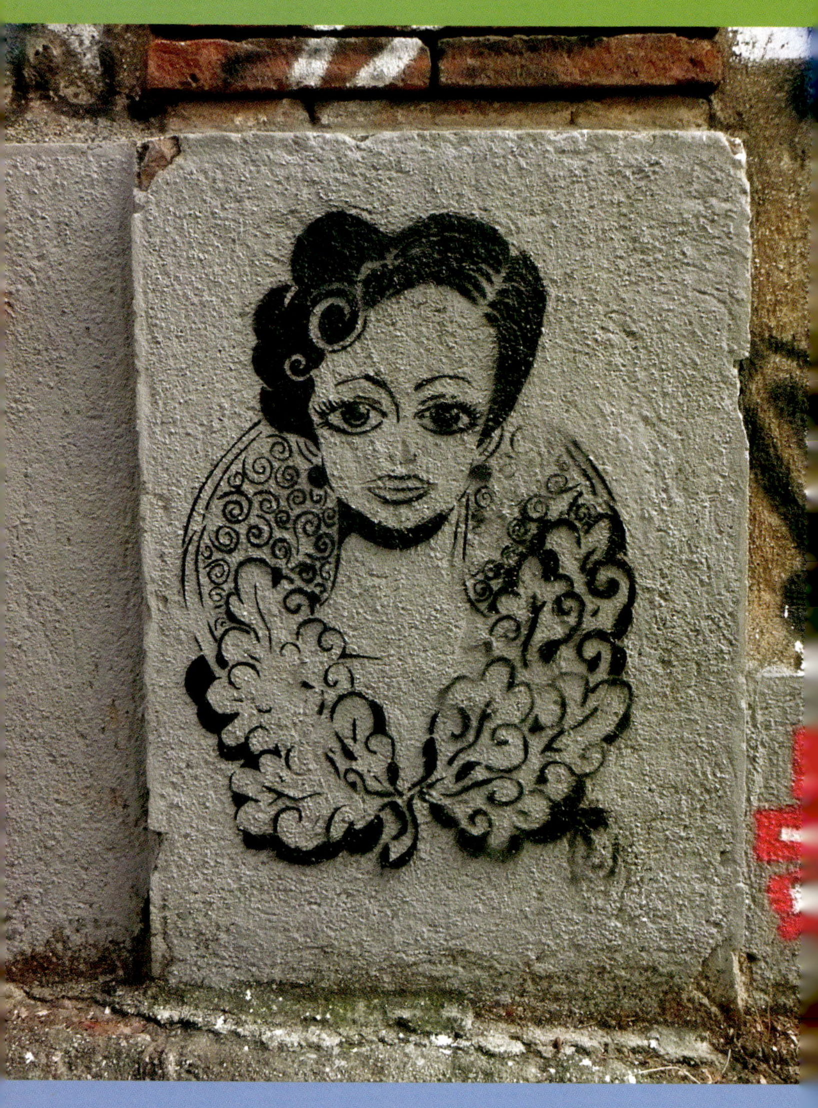

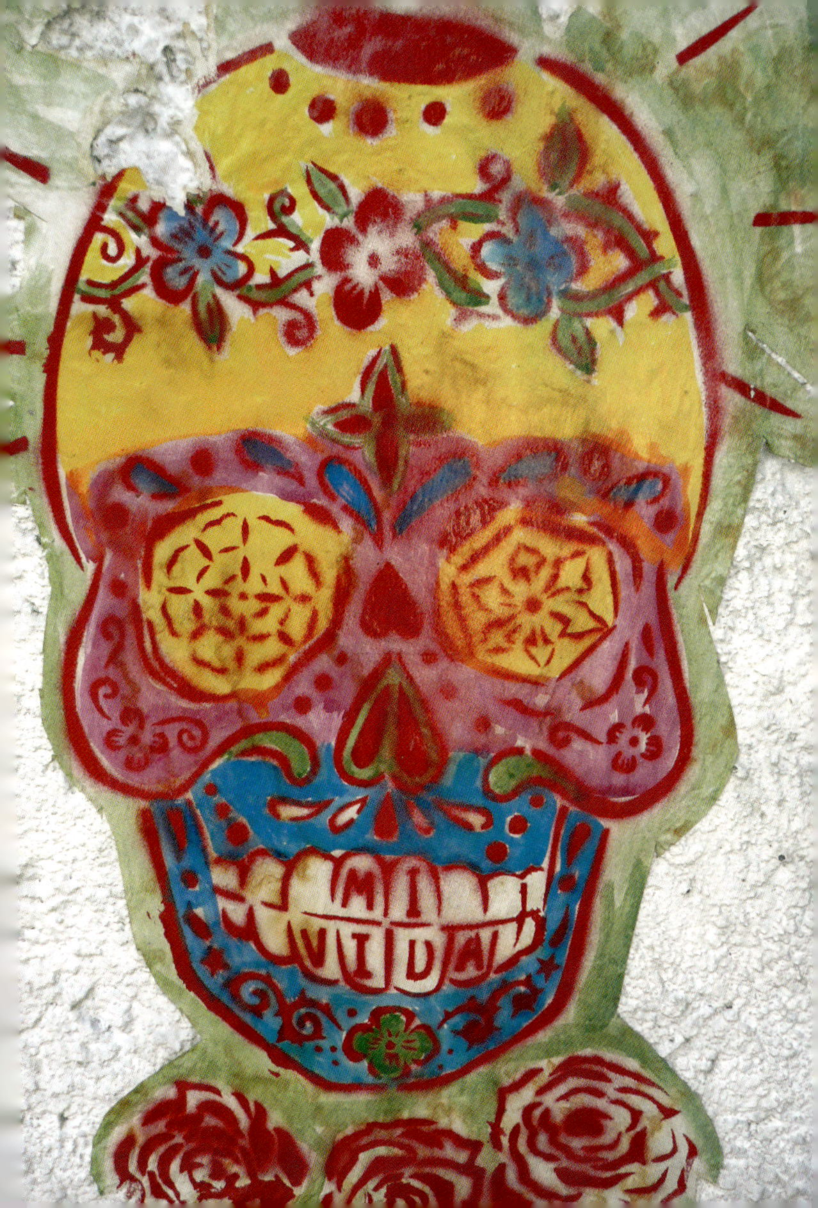
MI
VIDA

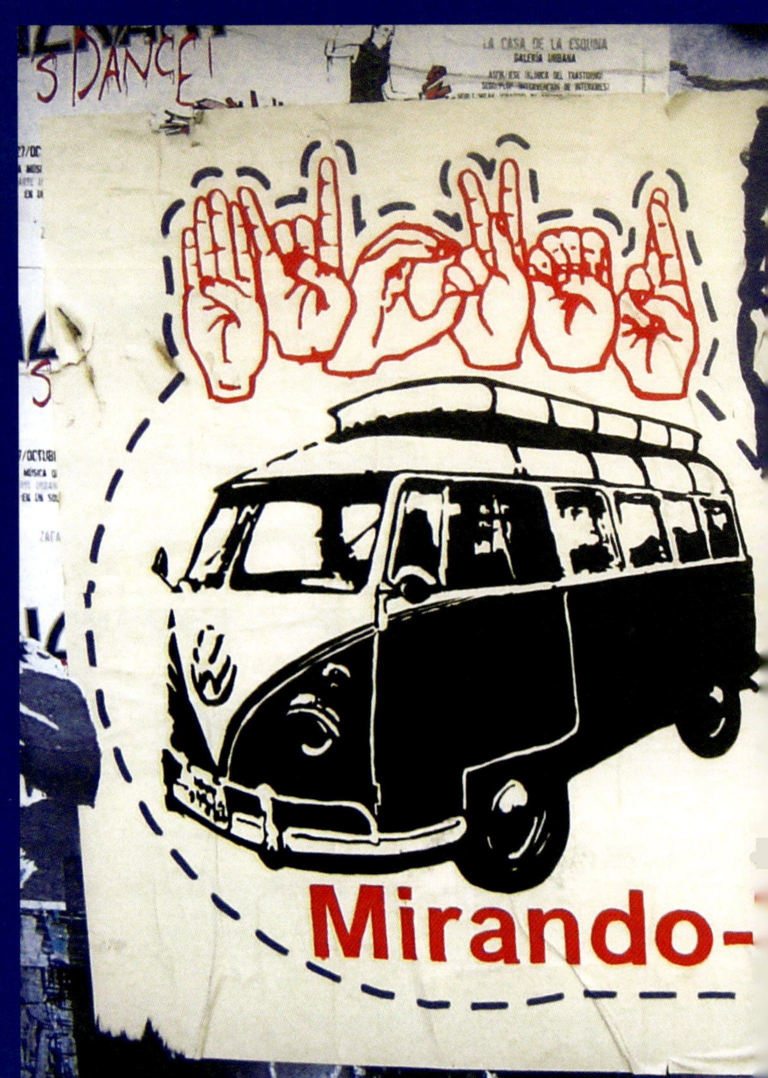
S DANCE!
LA CASA DE LA ESQUINA
GALERÍA URBANA
Mirando-

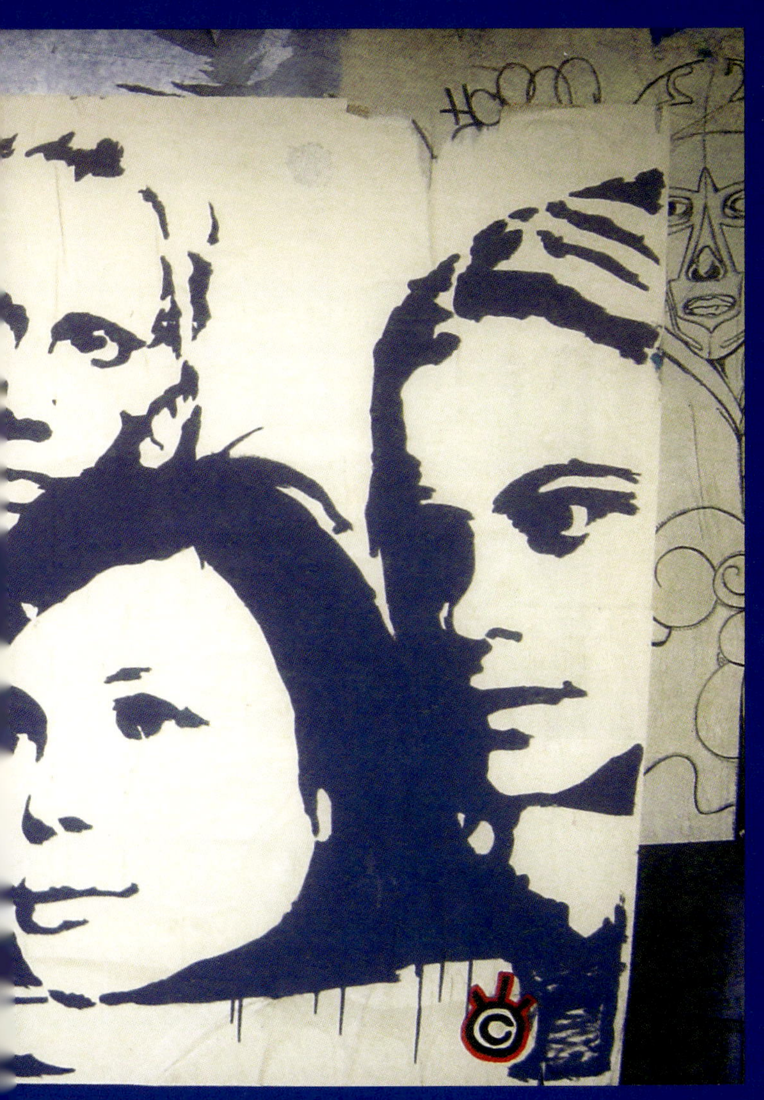

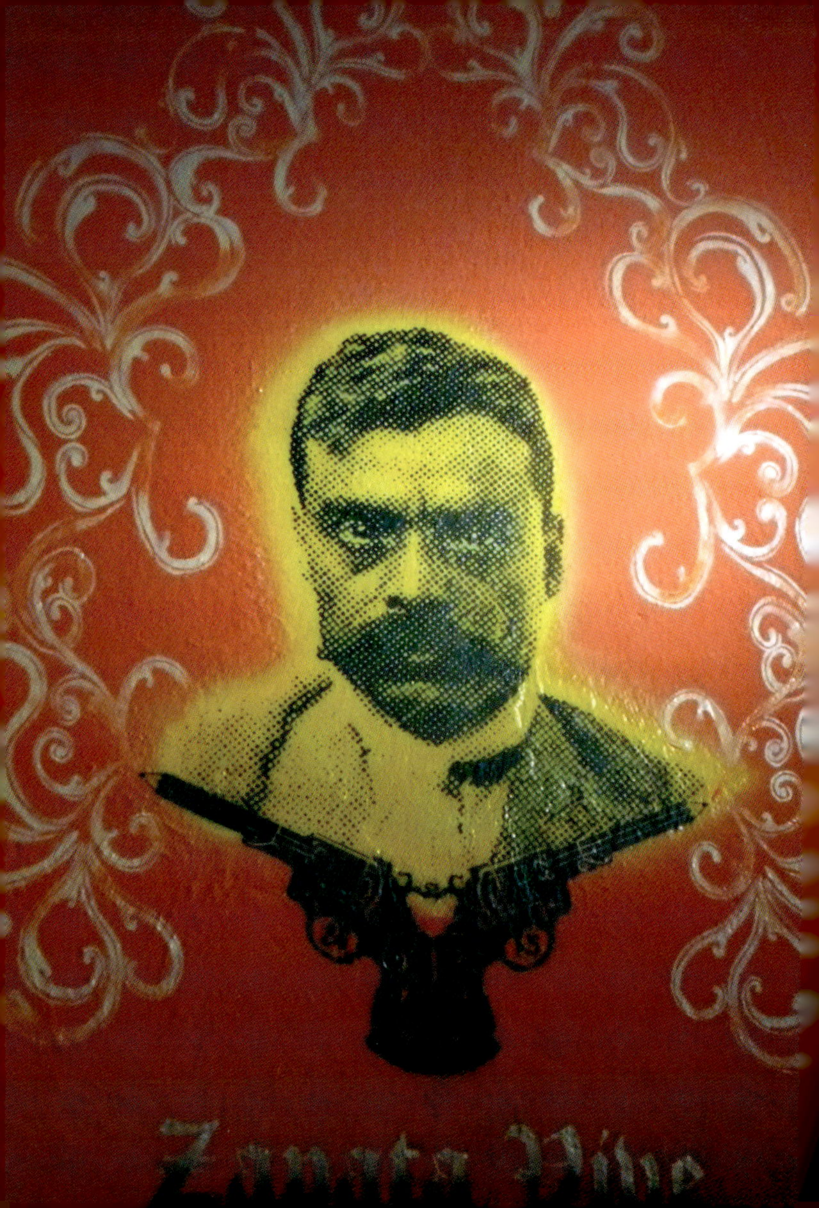
Zapata Vive

¡QUÉ BONITO ES
LO BONITO,
ÁSTIMA QUE SEA
PECADO!

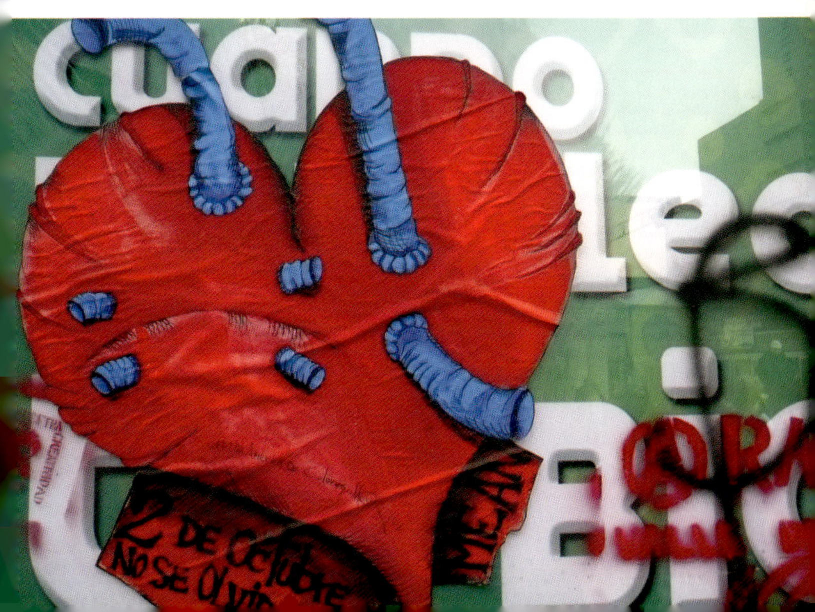

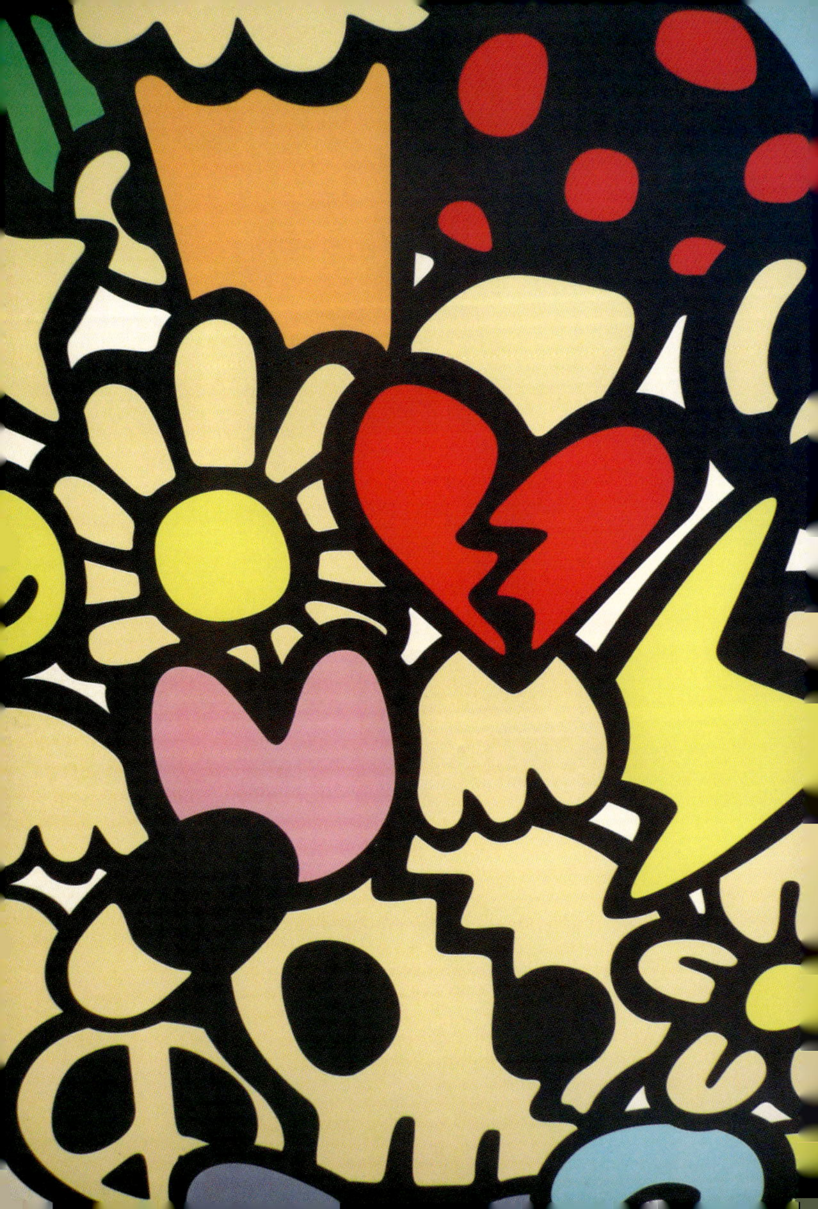

C

YOA

CHOOSE

YOUROWN

ADVENTURE

CYOACYOACYOA

HEARTSREVOLUTION

LIVEEACHMOMENT

LIKEITSYOURLAST

ALWAYSINTHEPRESENT

NEVERINTHEPAST

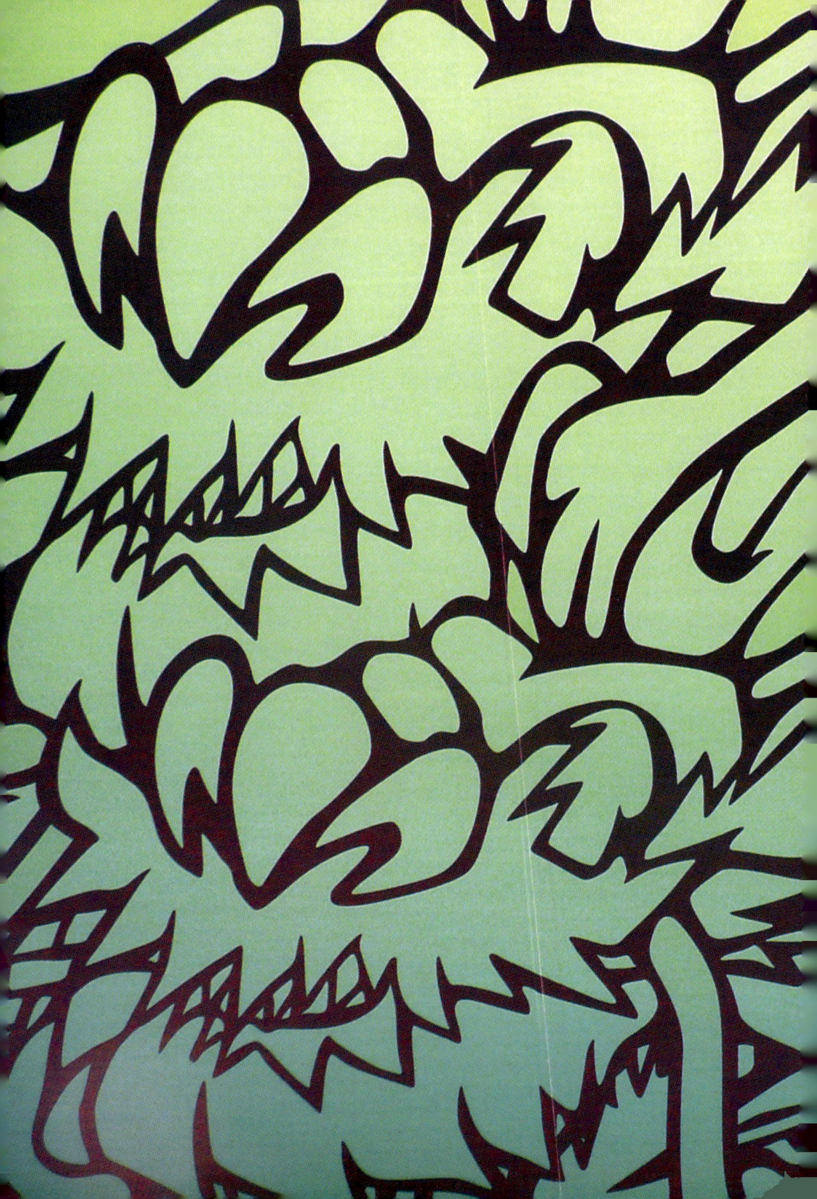

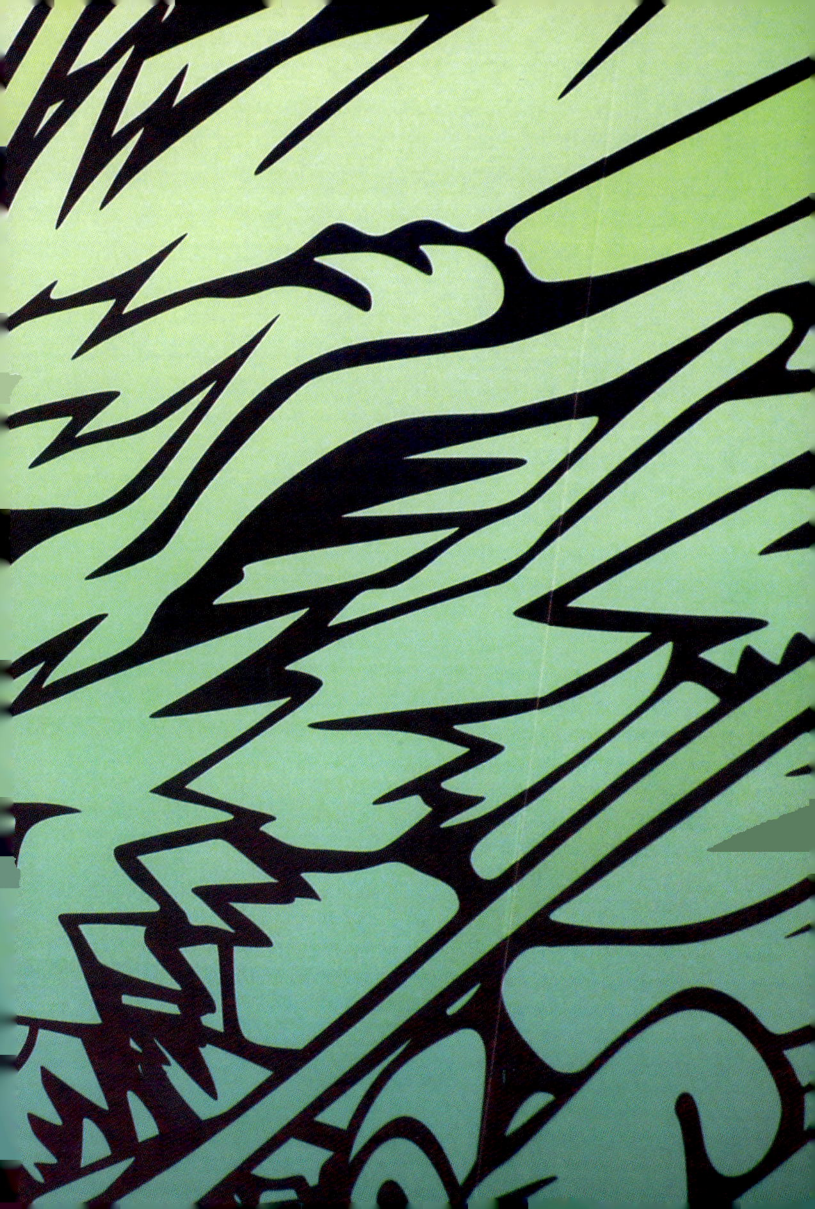

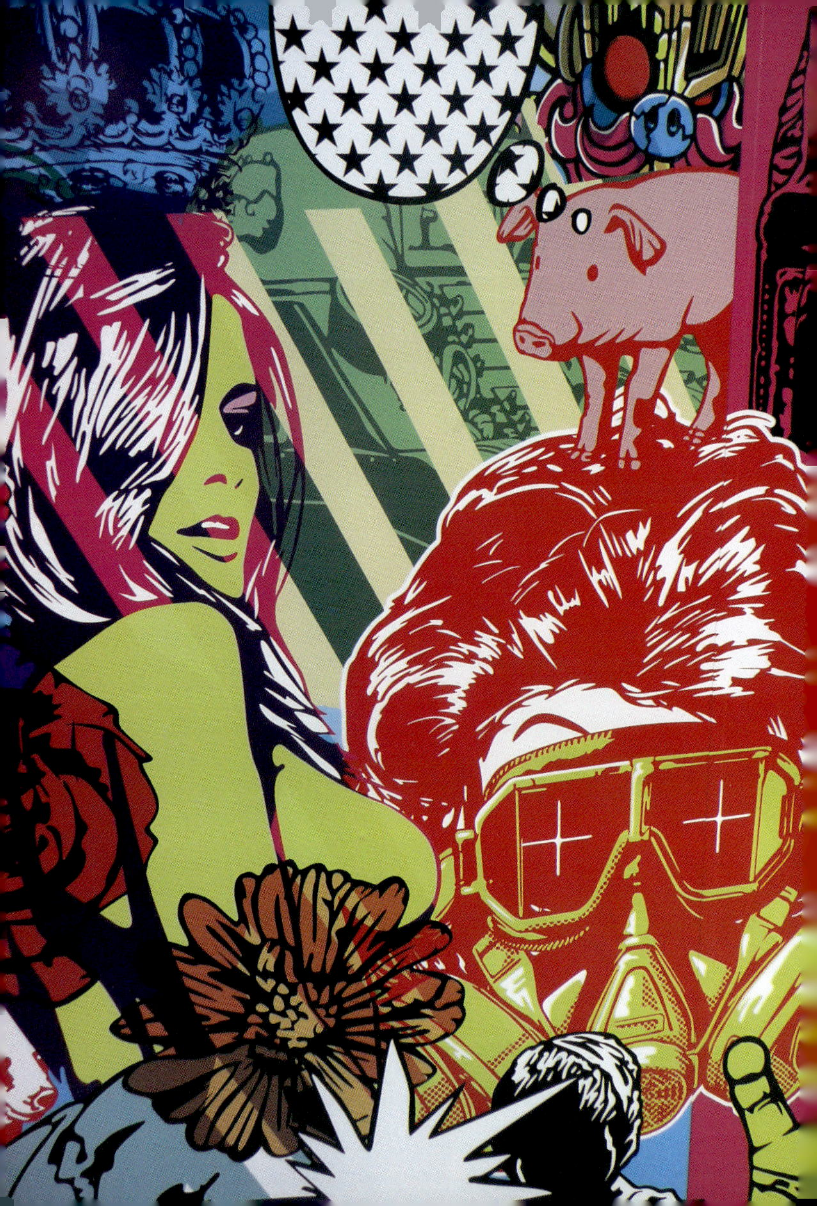

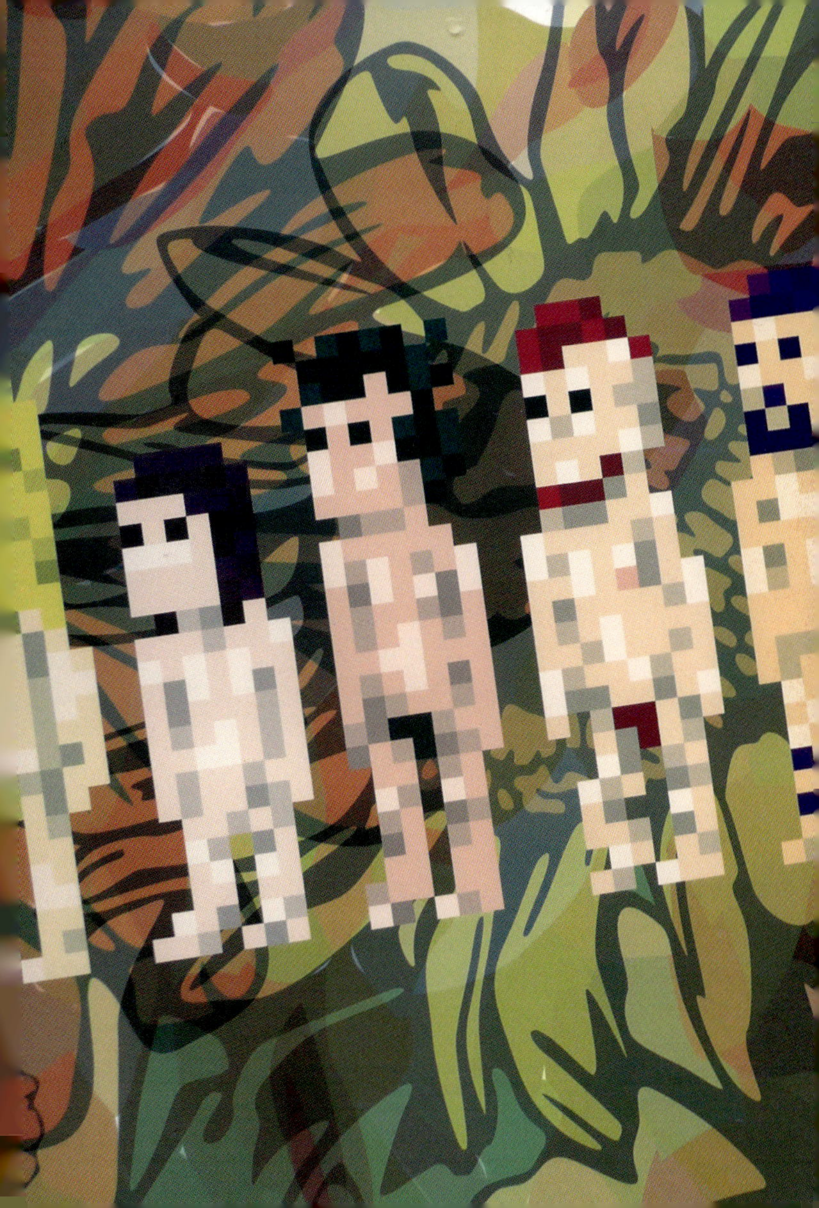

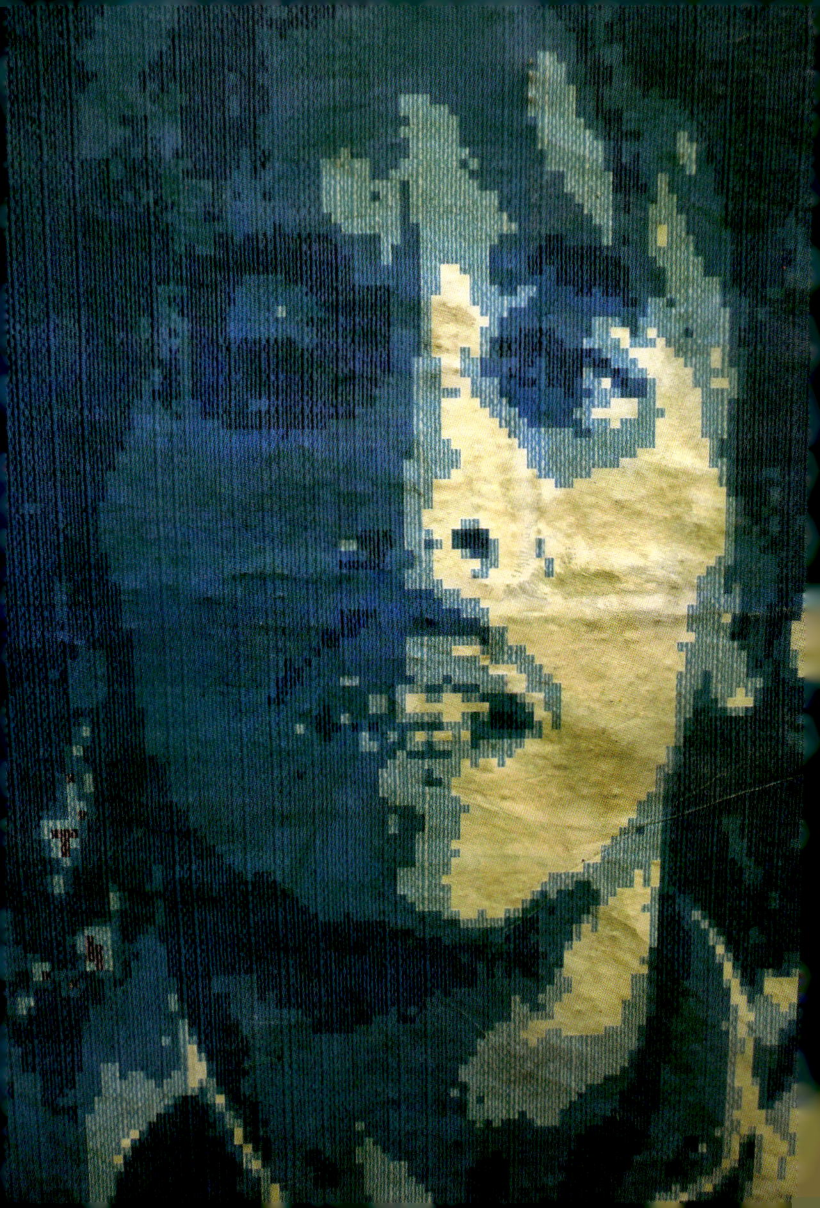

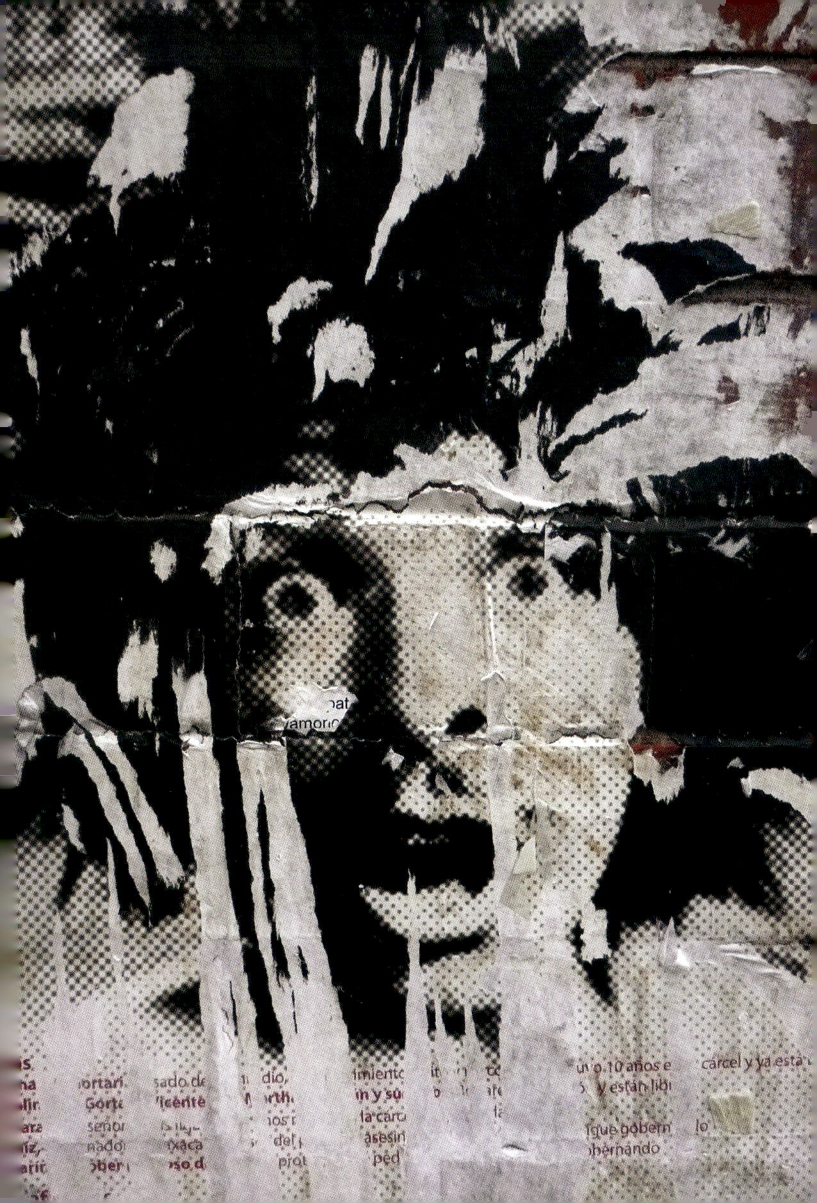

10 años e
carcel y ya está
y están lib
sigue gobern
gobernando

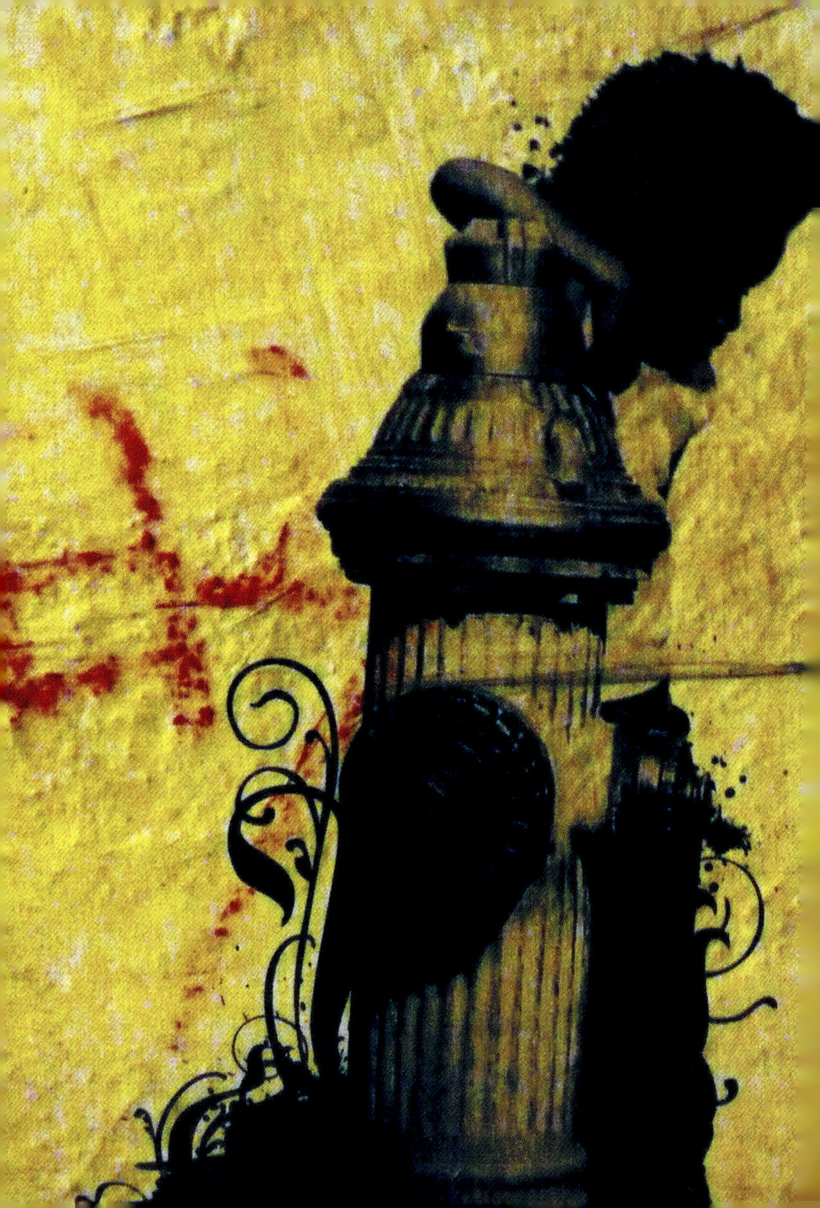

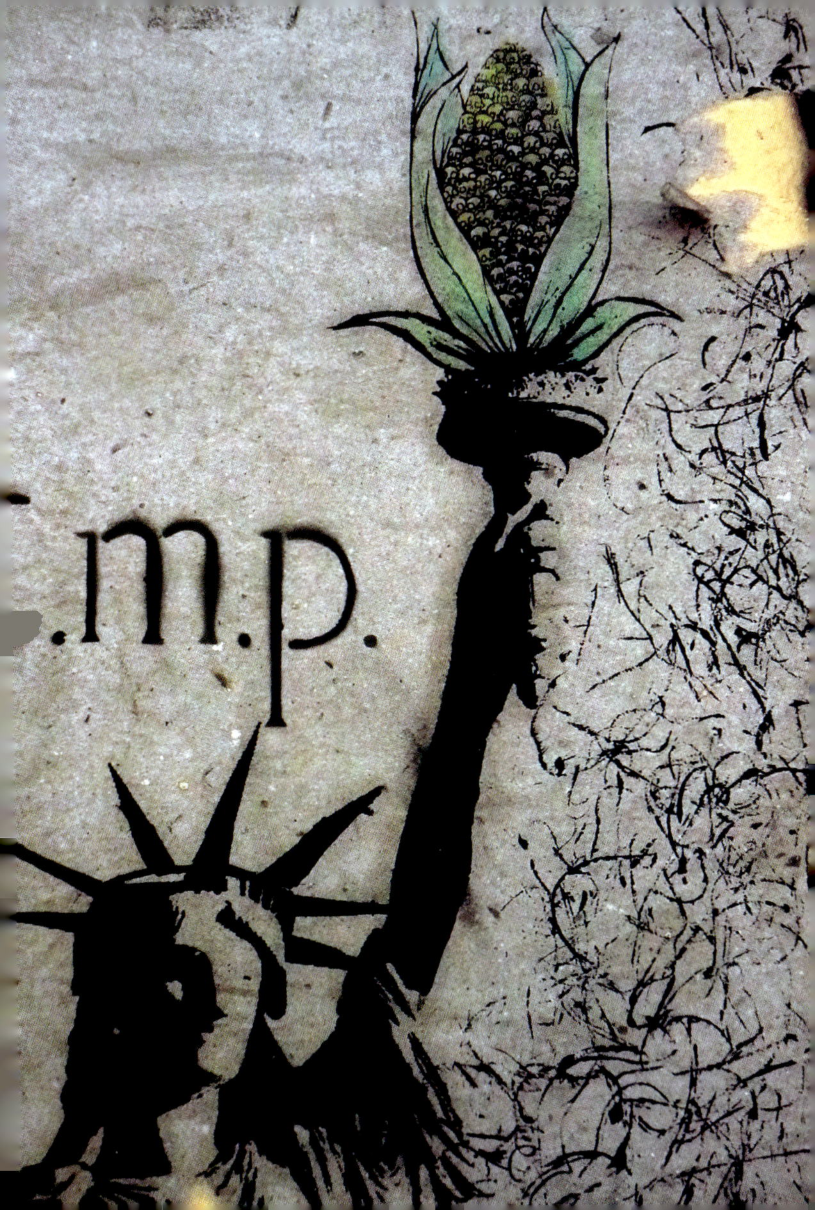

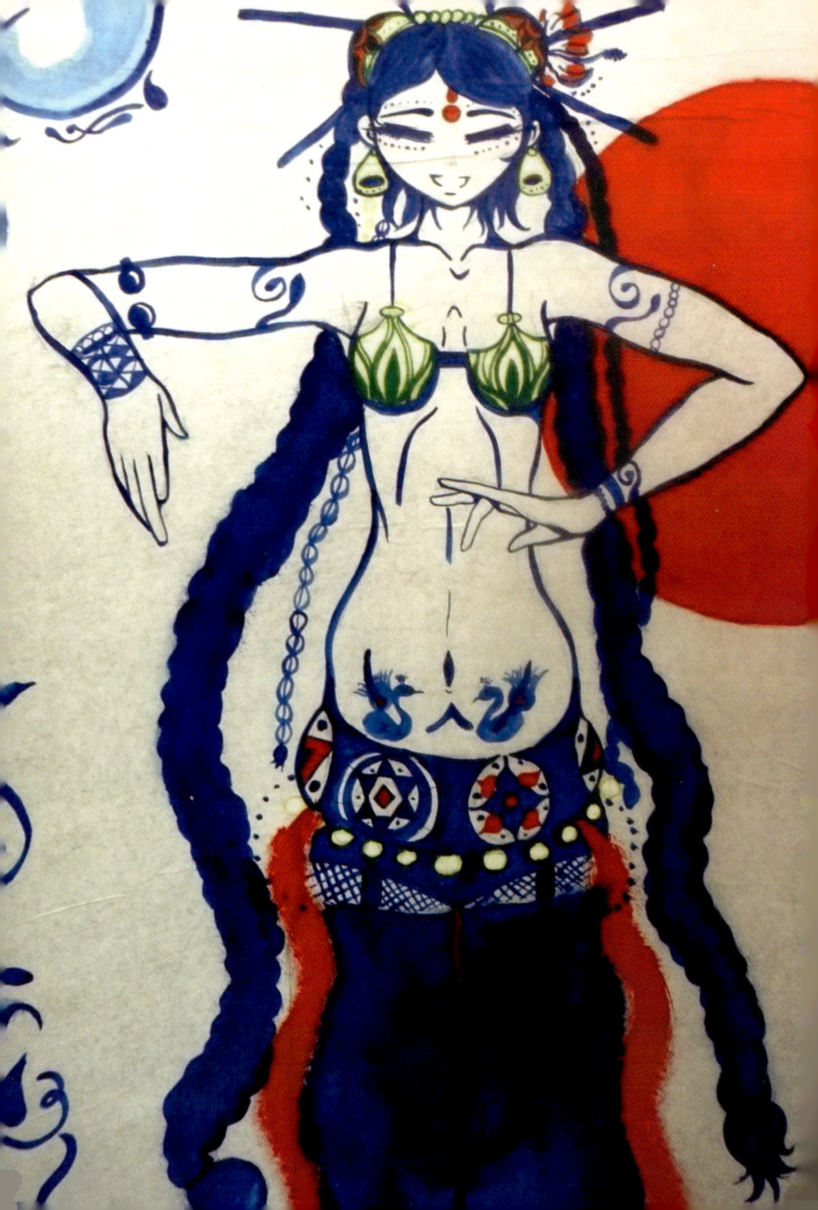

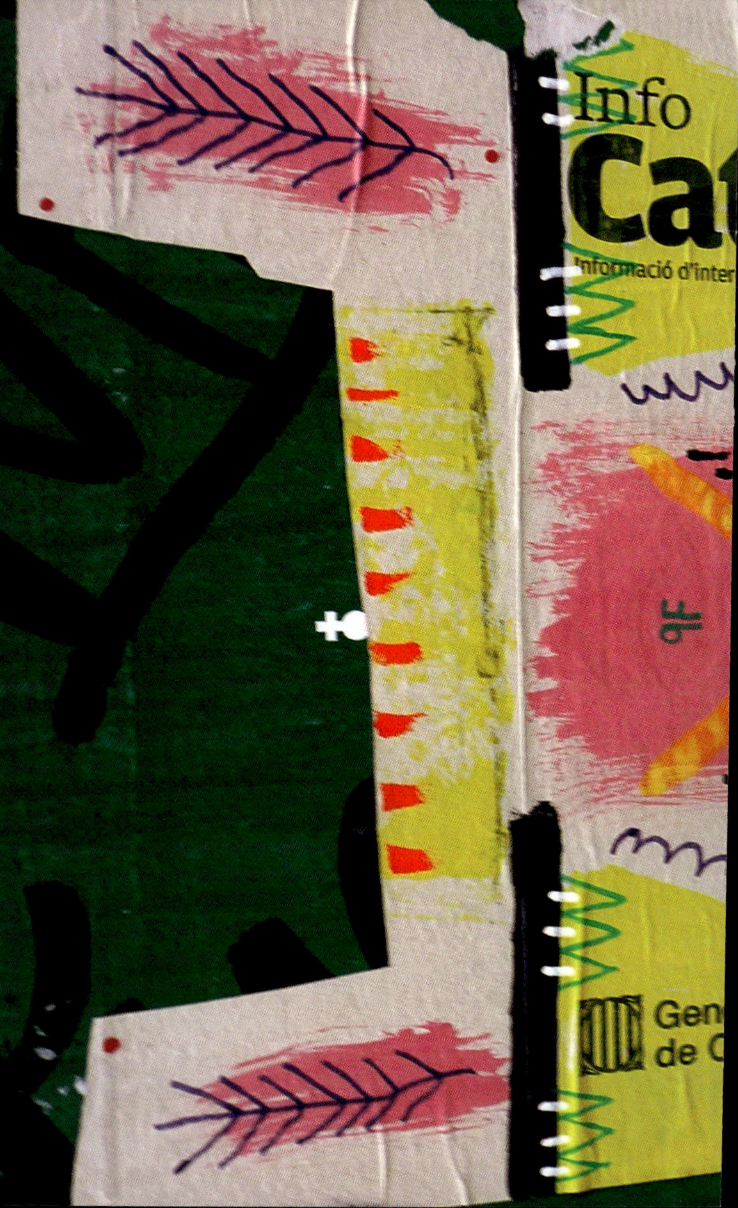
Info

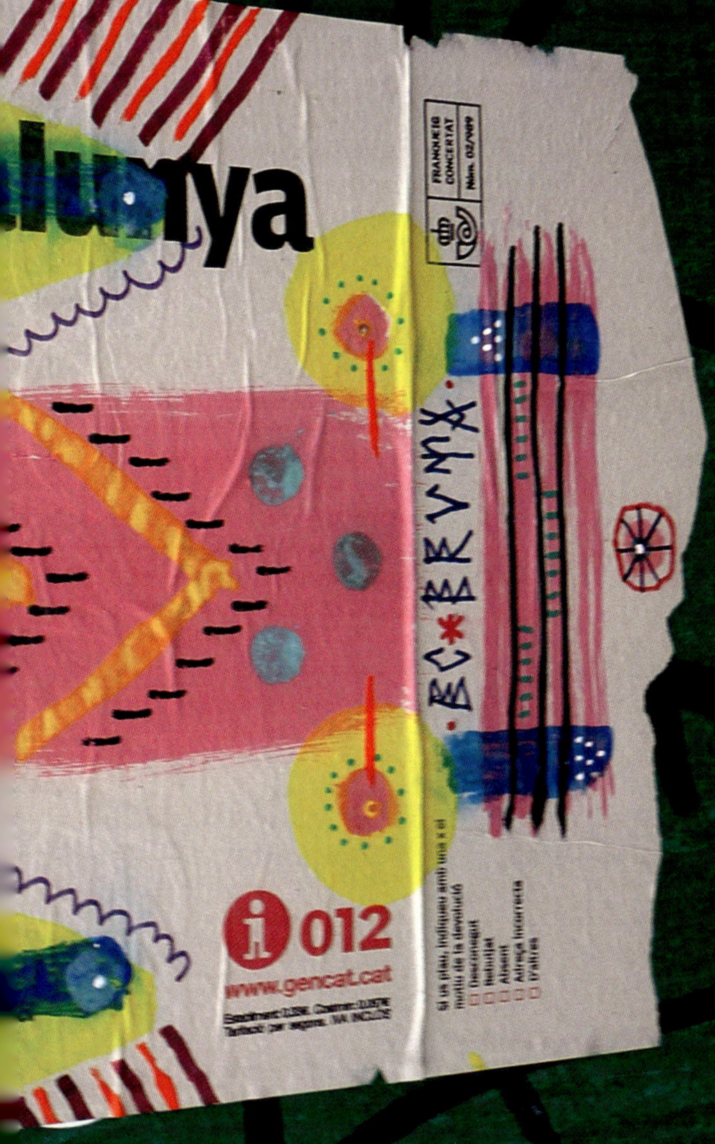

lunya
012
www.gencat.cat
FRANQUEIG CONCERTAT
Núm. 02/989
Si us plau, indiqueu amb una x el motiu de la devolució
Desconegut
Rebutjat
Absent
Adreça incorrecta
D'altres

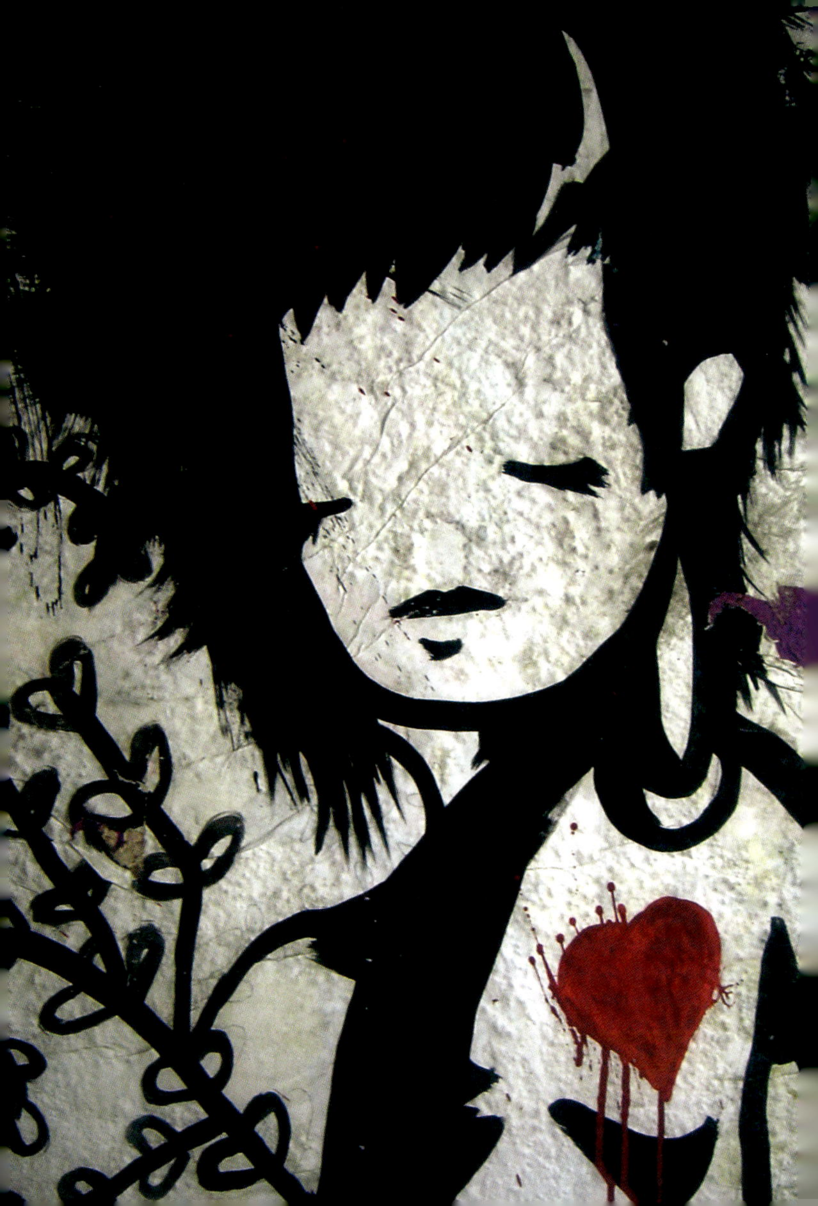

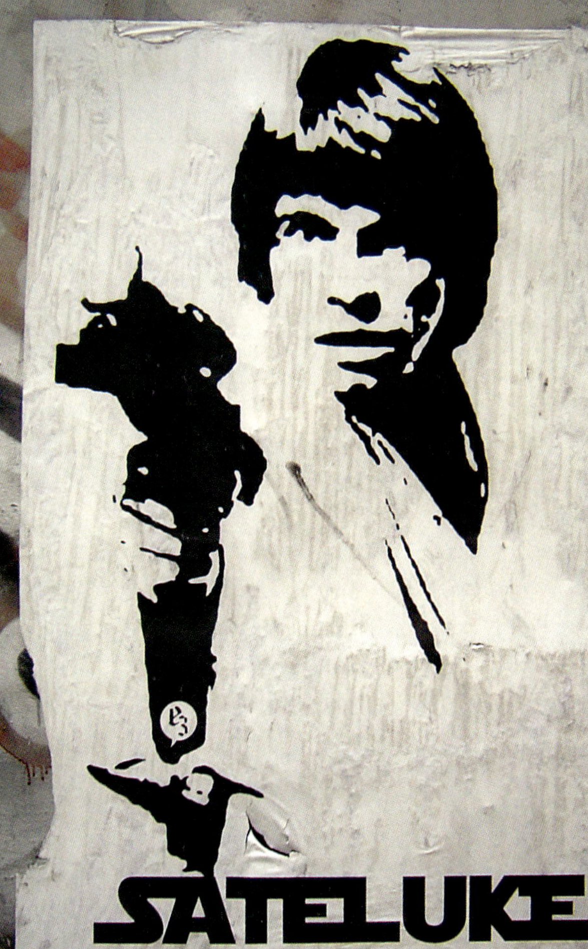
SATELUKE

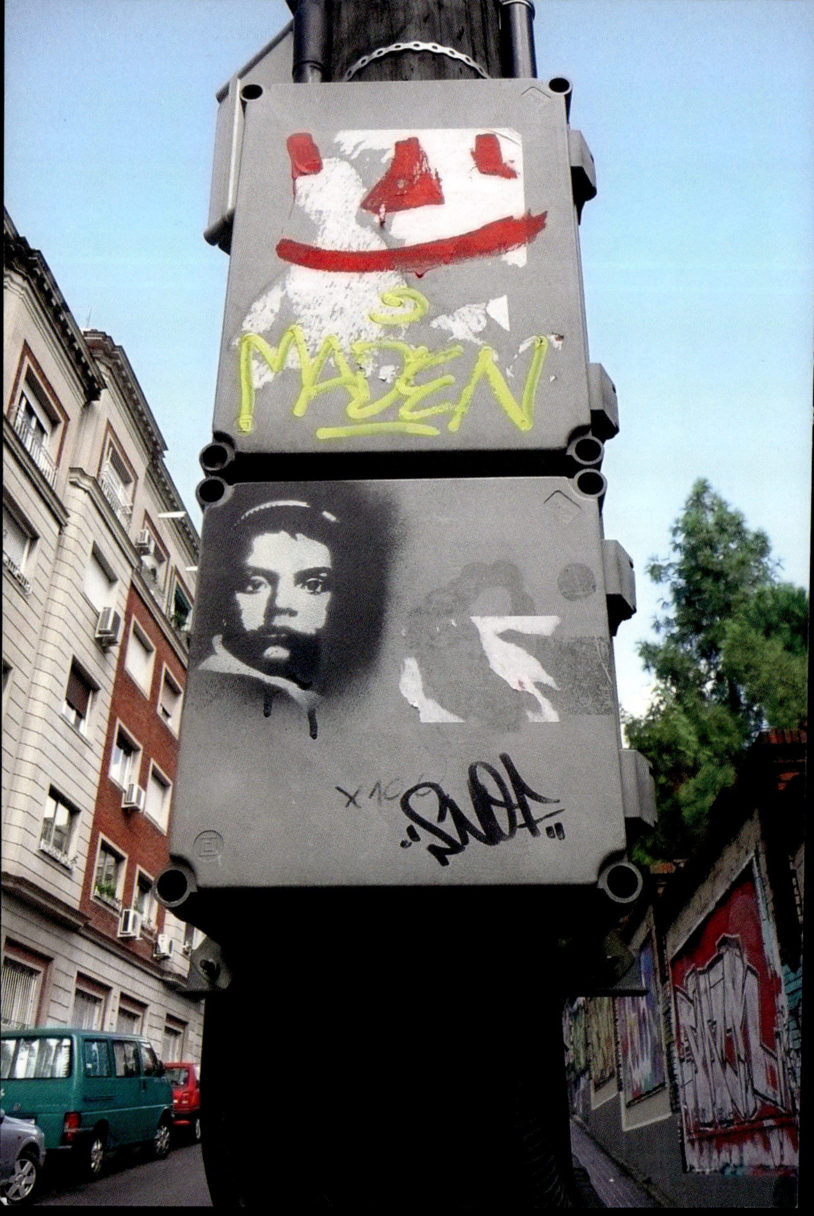
MADEN

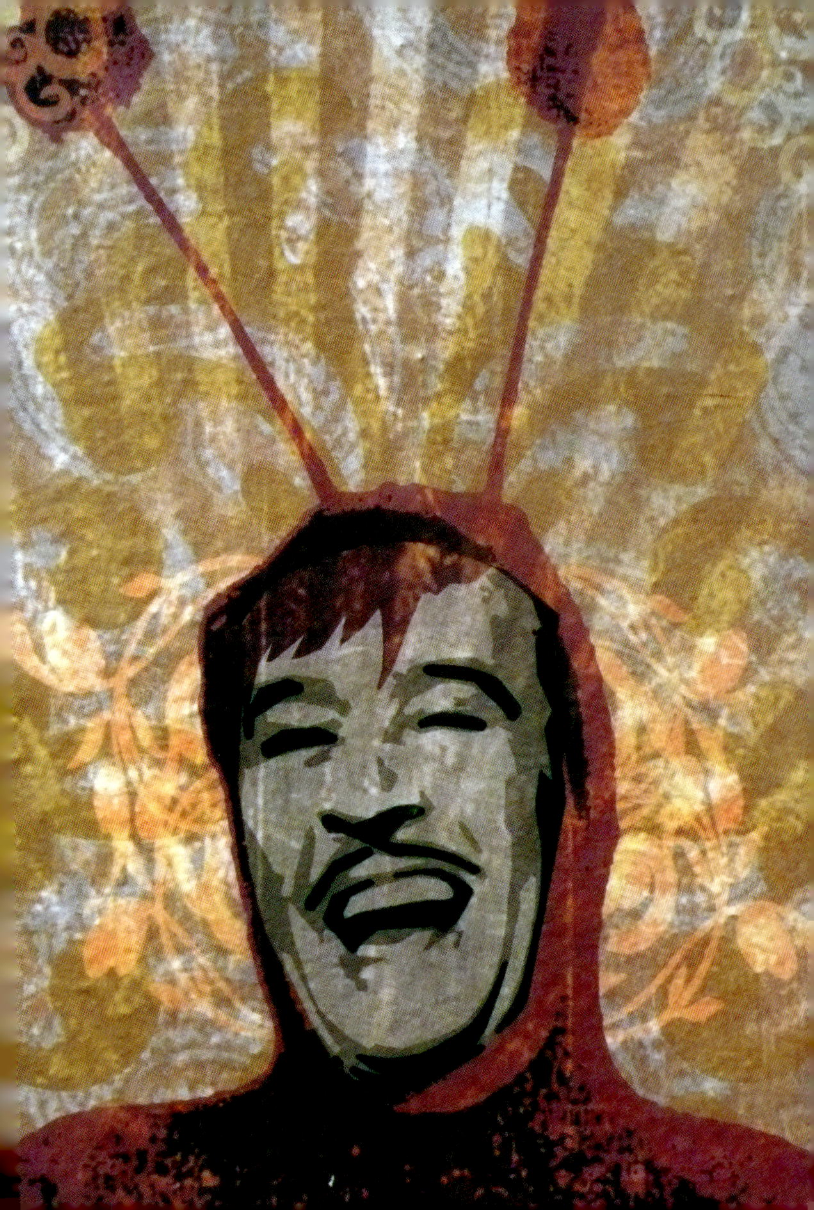

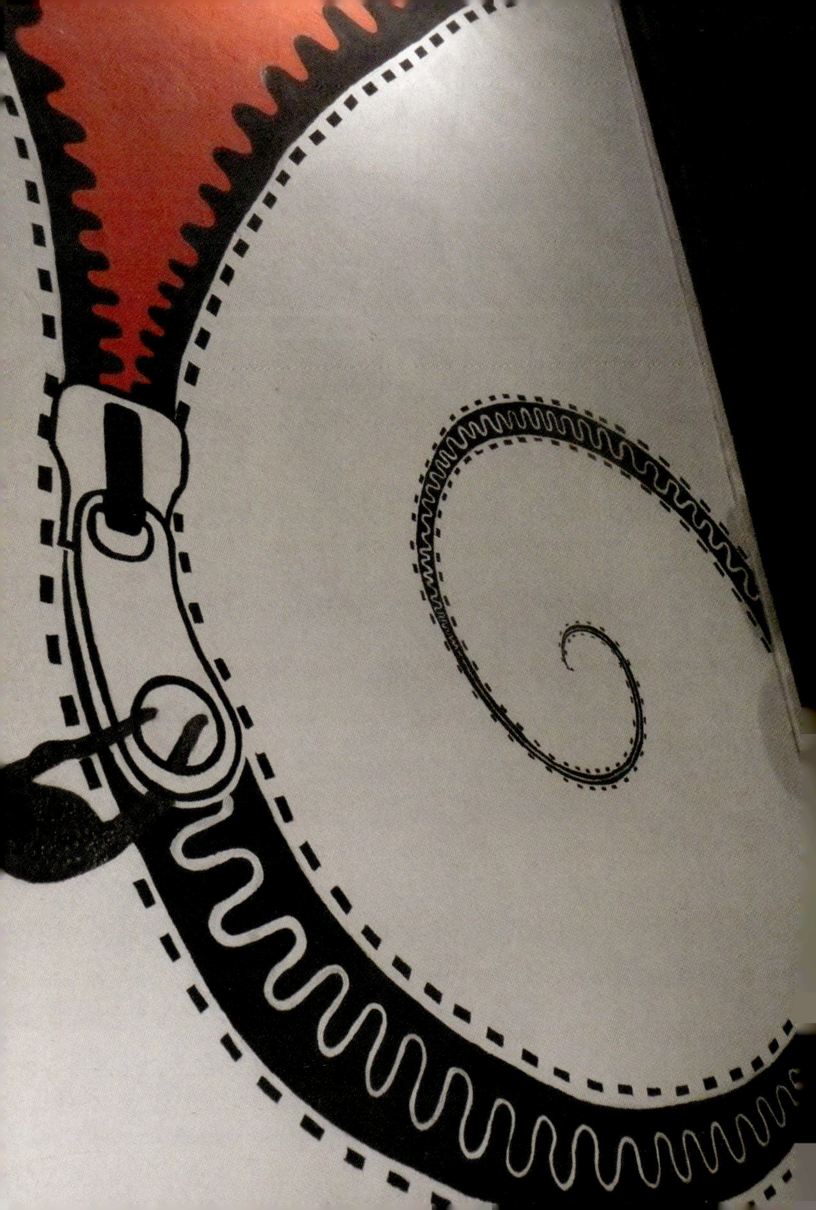

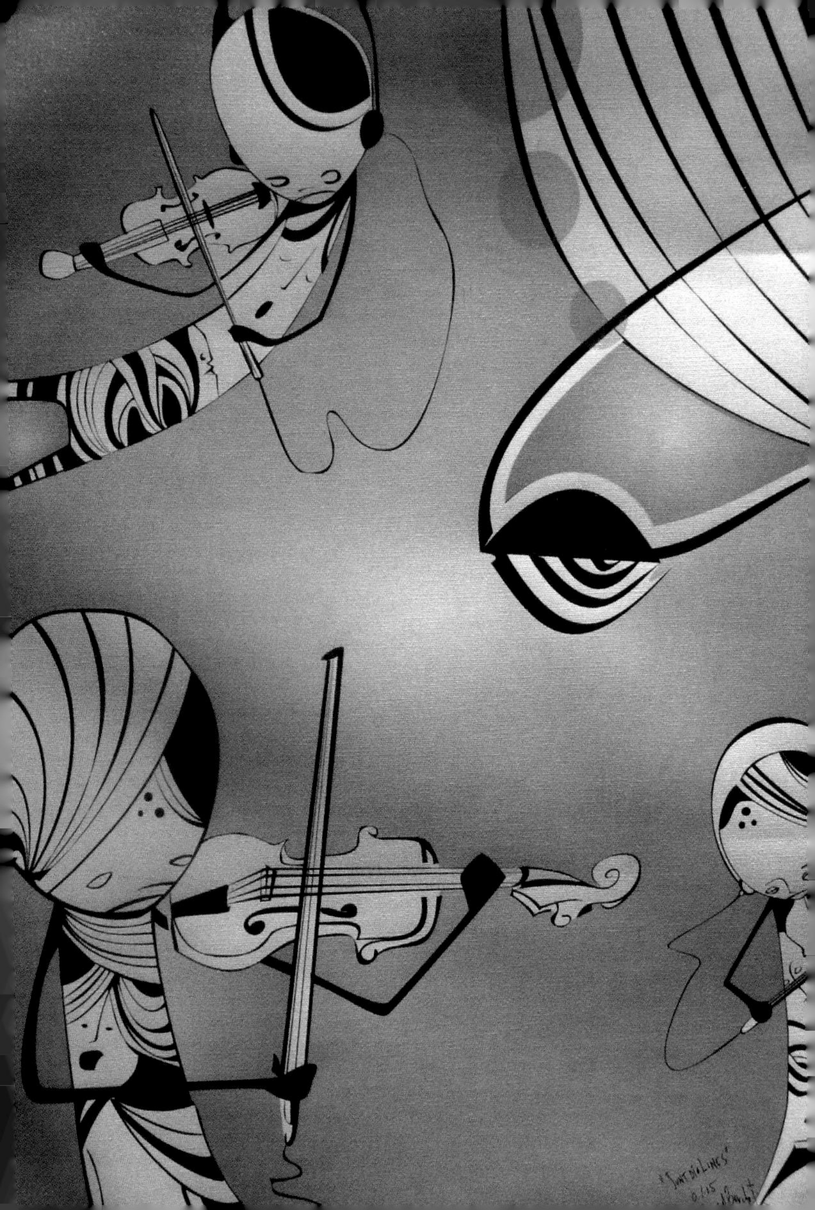

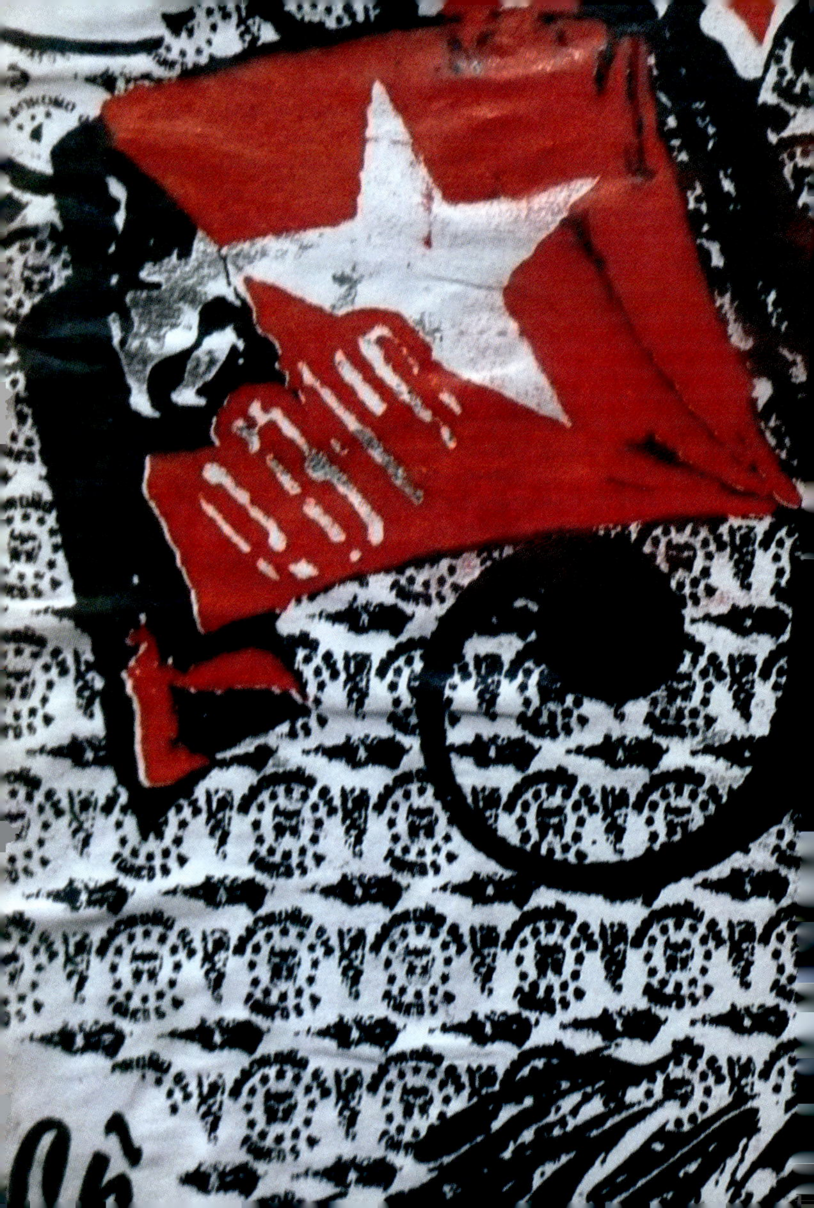

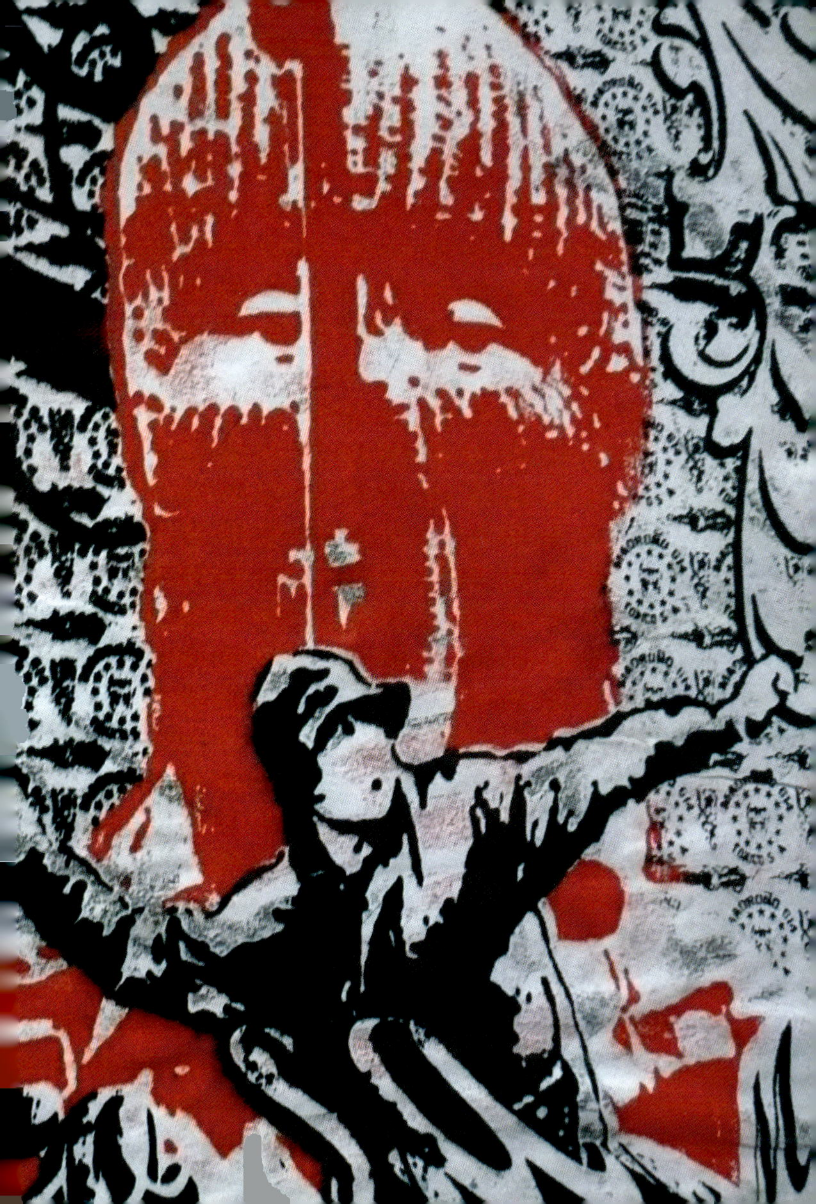

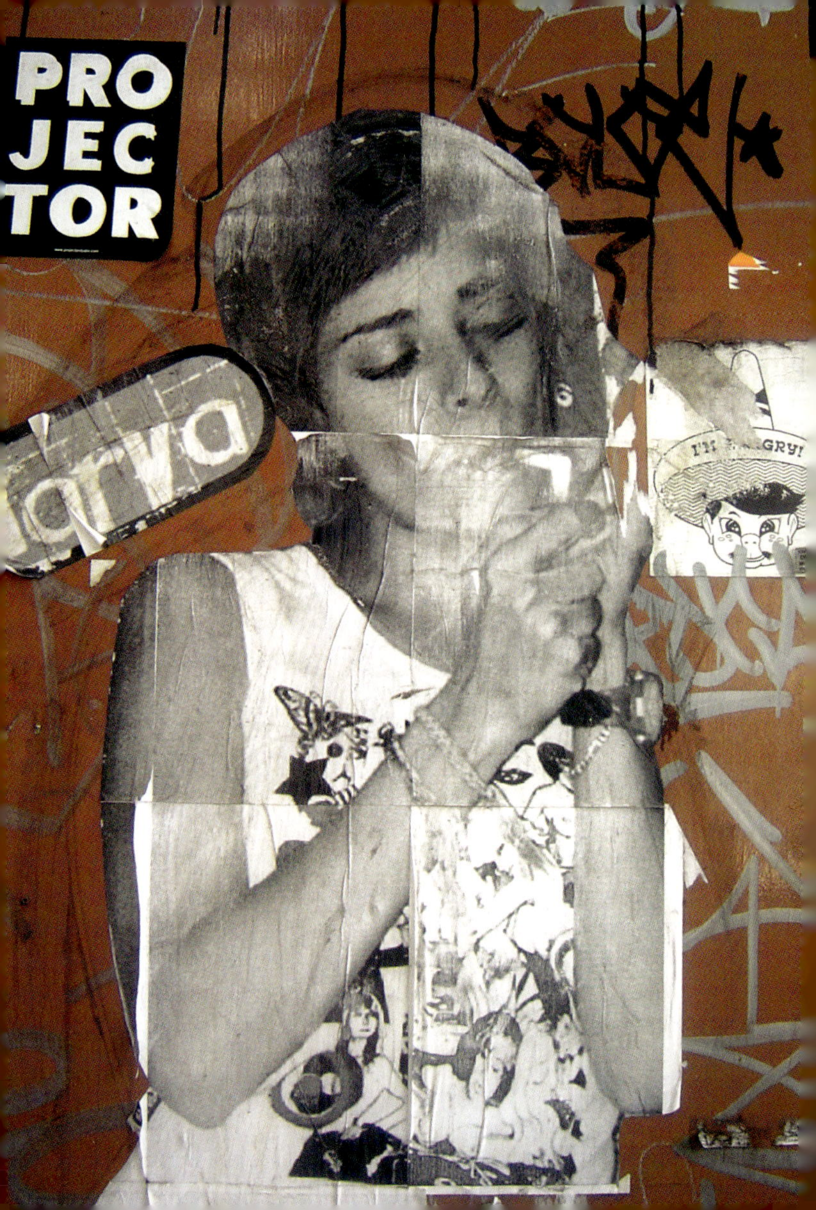
PRO
JEC
TOR
arva

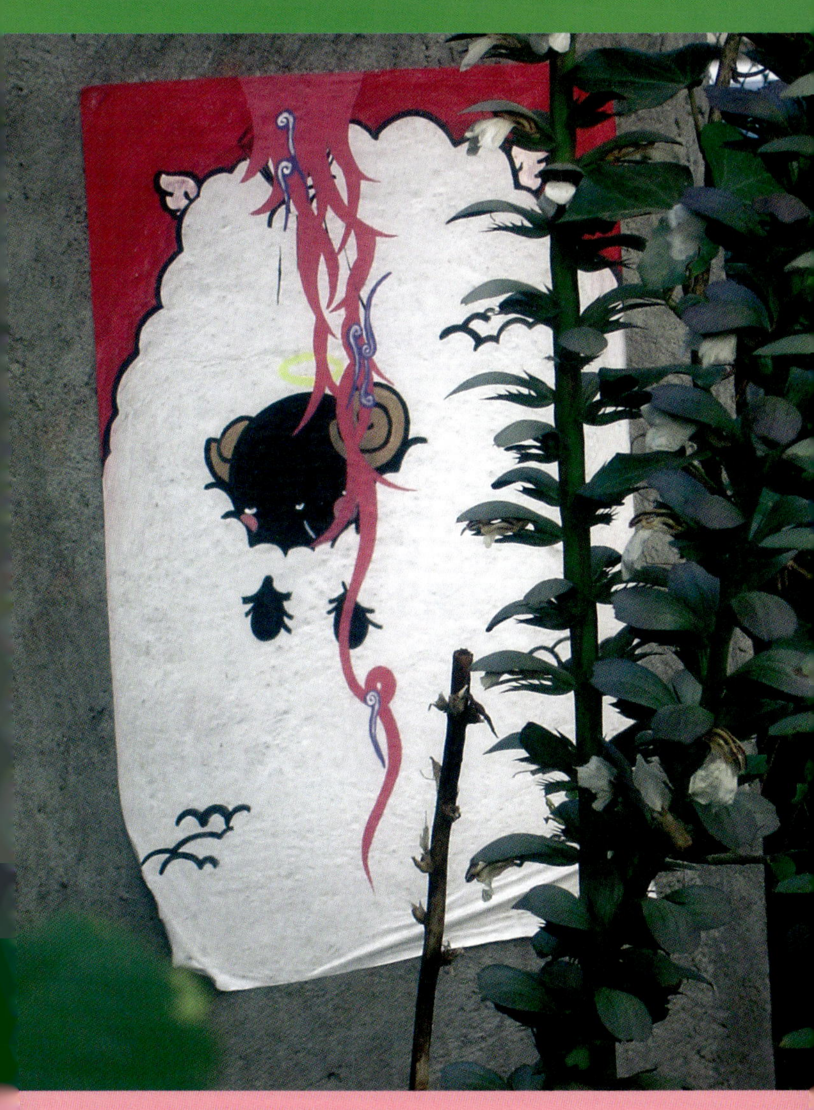

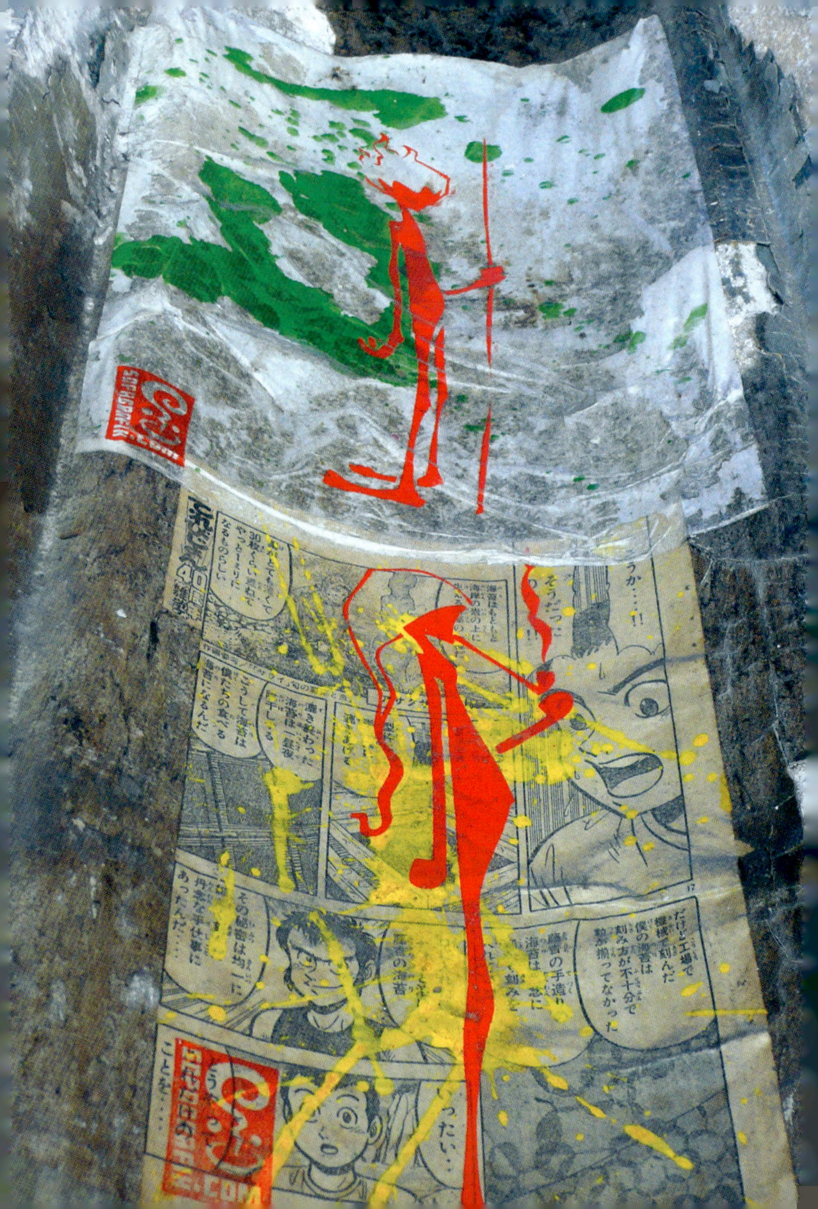

そうか…!!
だけど工場で機械で刻んだ僕の海苔は刻み方が不十分で粒が揃ってなかった
こうして海苔は僕たちの食べる海苔になるんだ
その秘密は均一に丹念な手仕事にあったんだ……

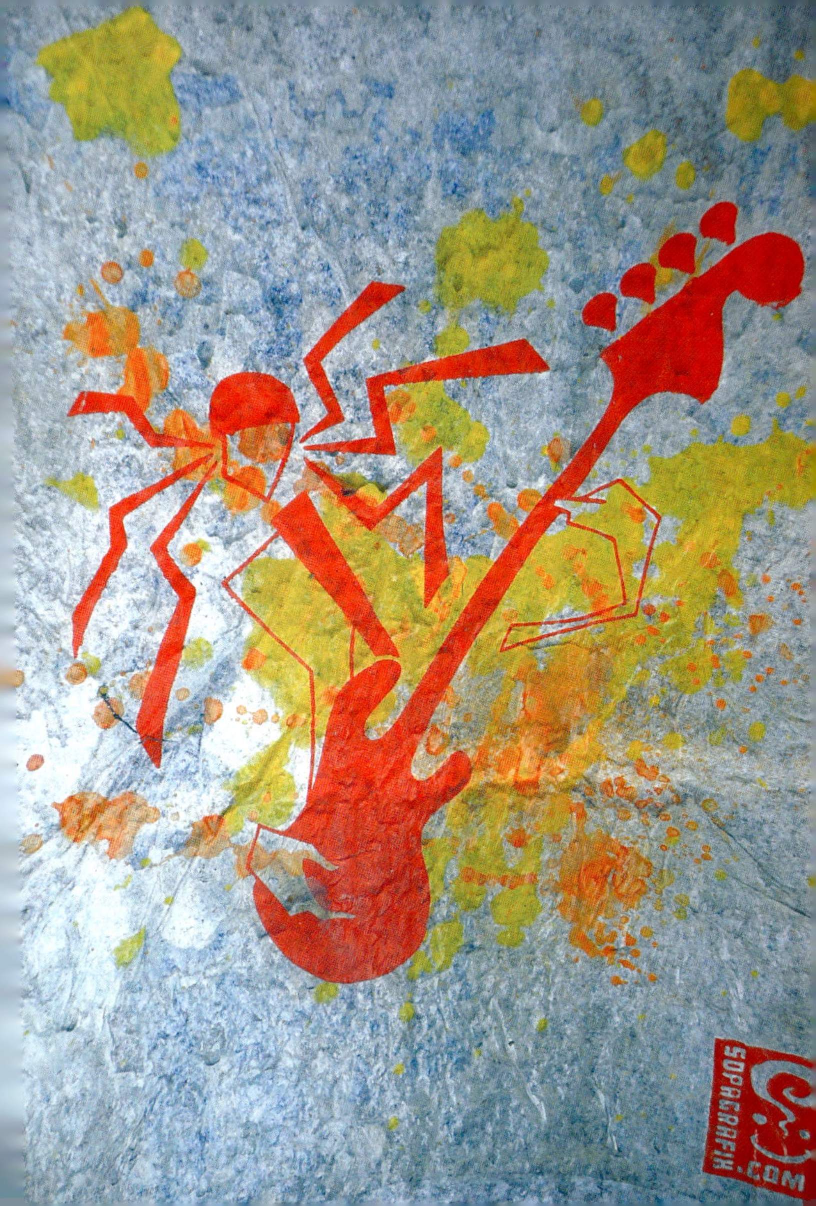
SOPAGRAFIK
.COM

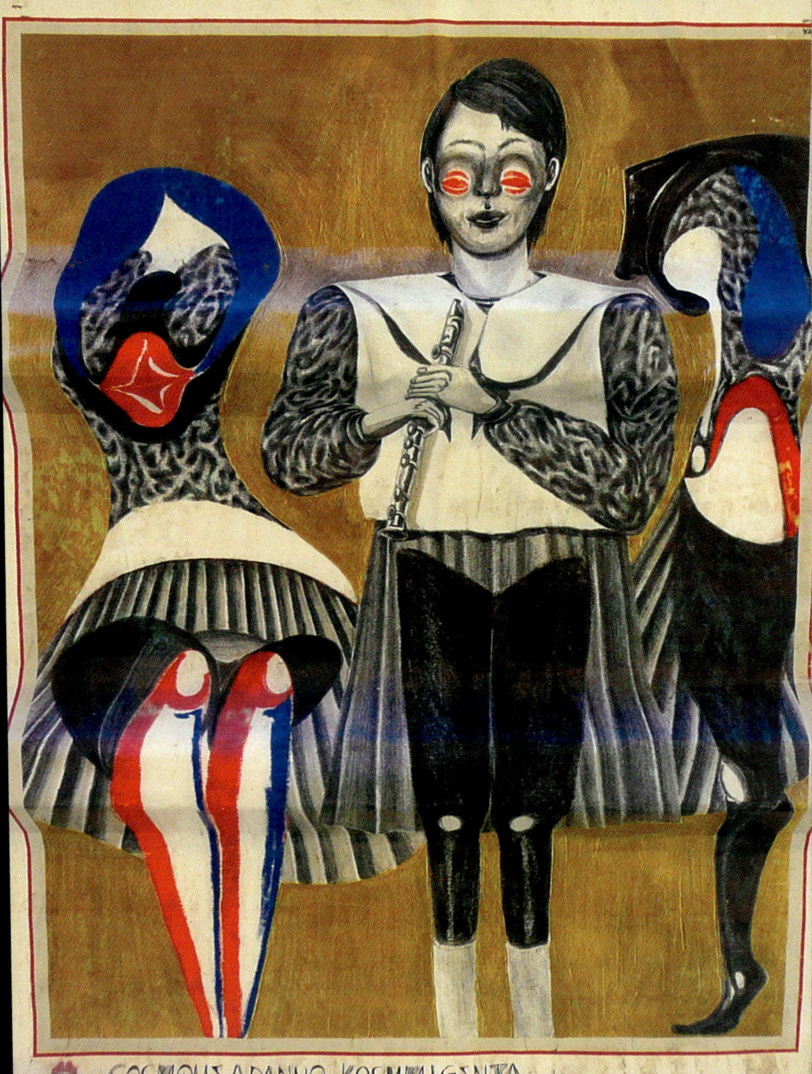
COSMOHΣAΔANNO KOSUMIGΣNTA

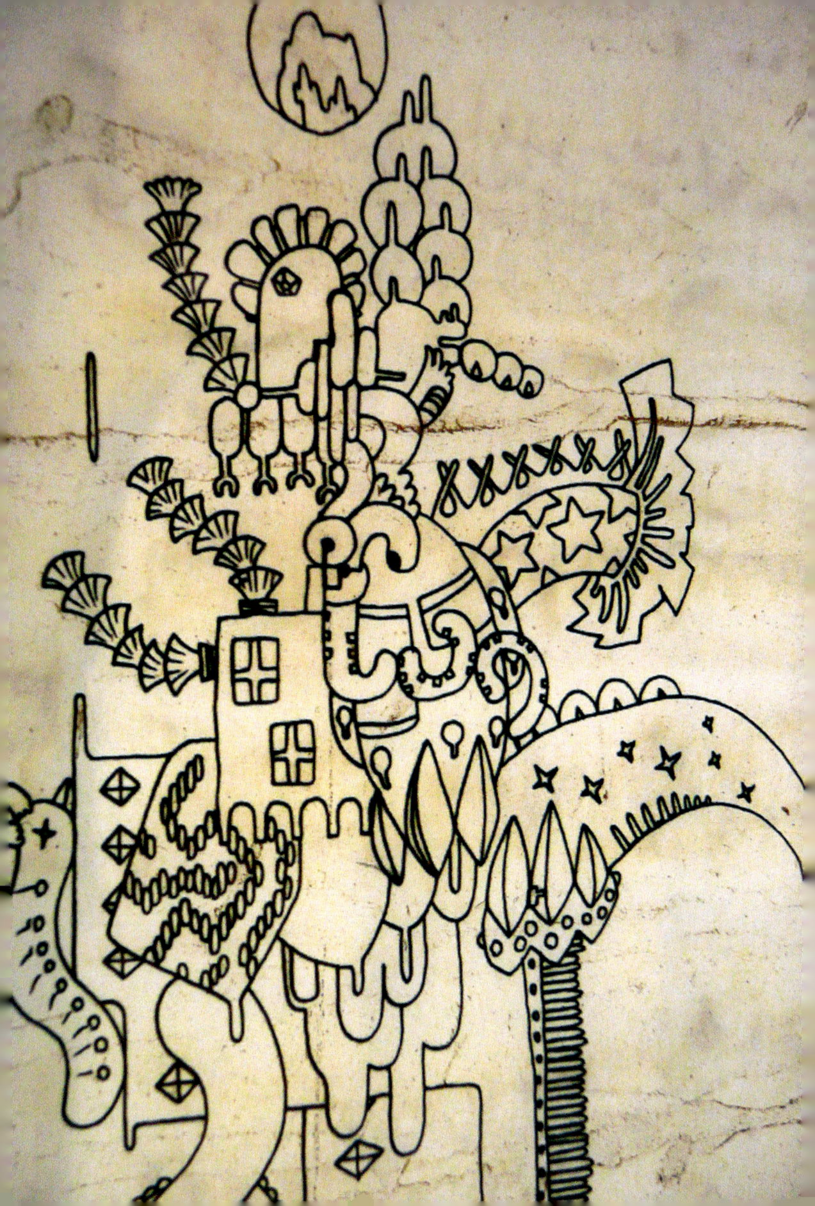

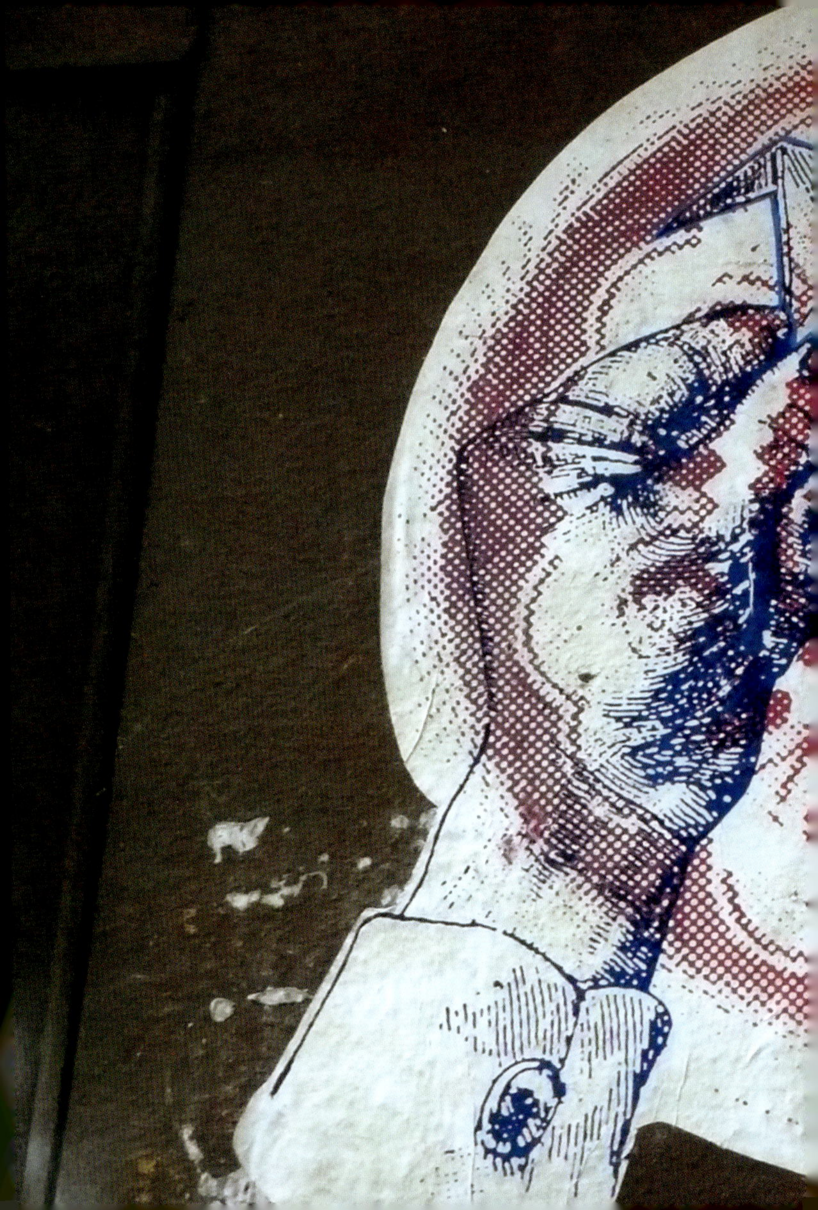

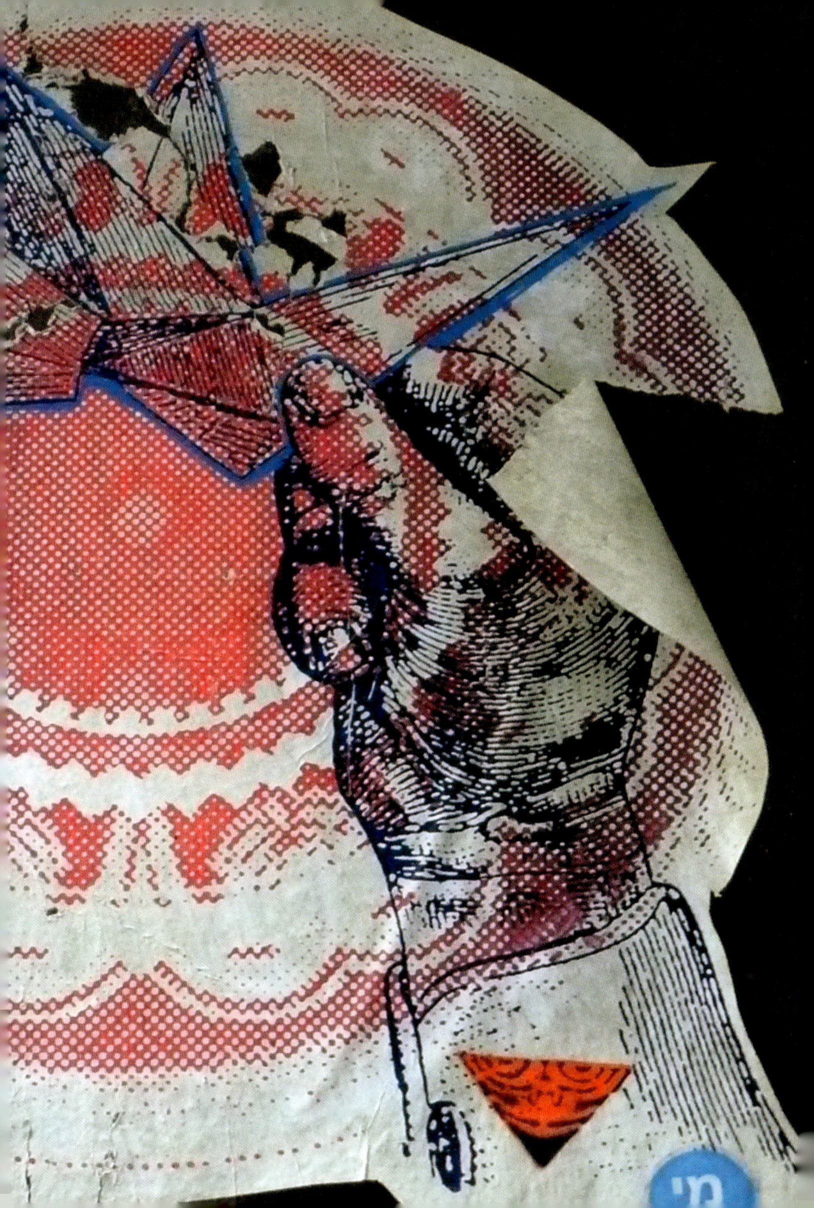

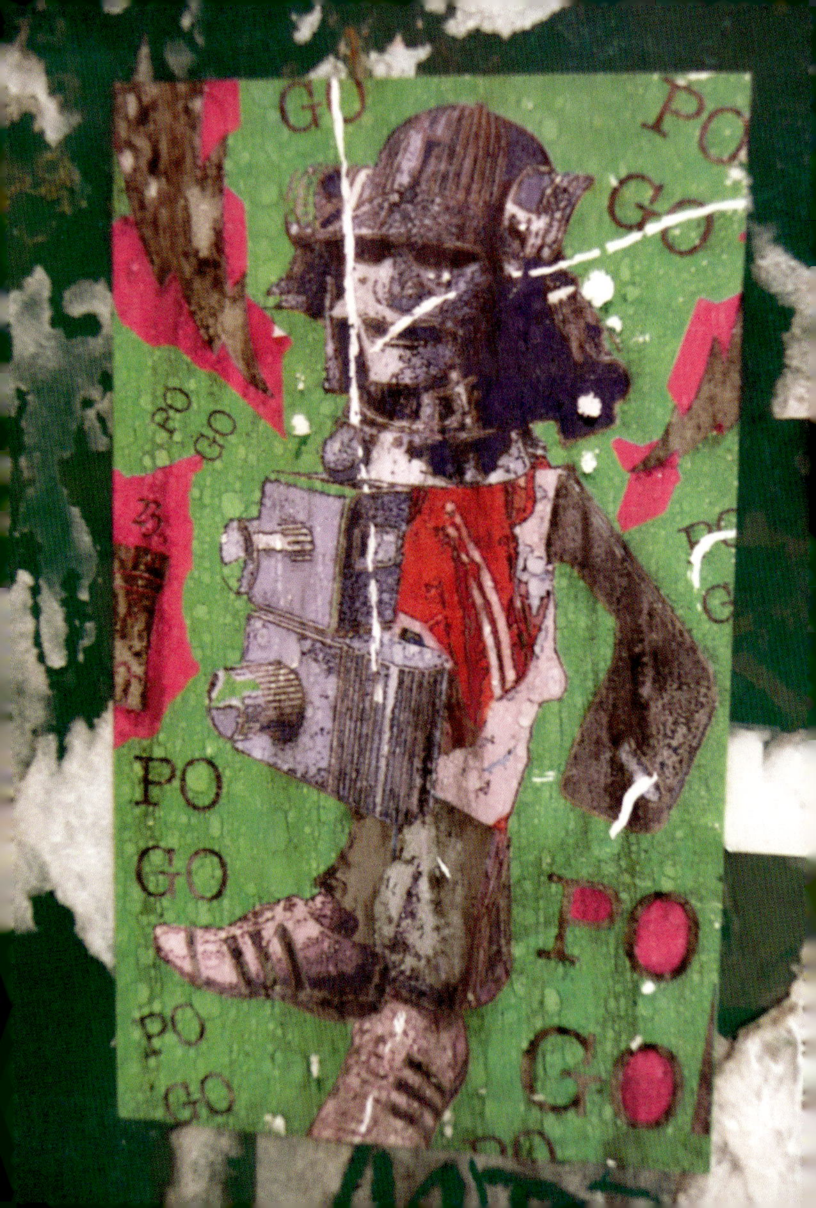

GO
PO
GO
PO
GO
PO
GO
PO
GO
PO
GO
PO
GO

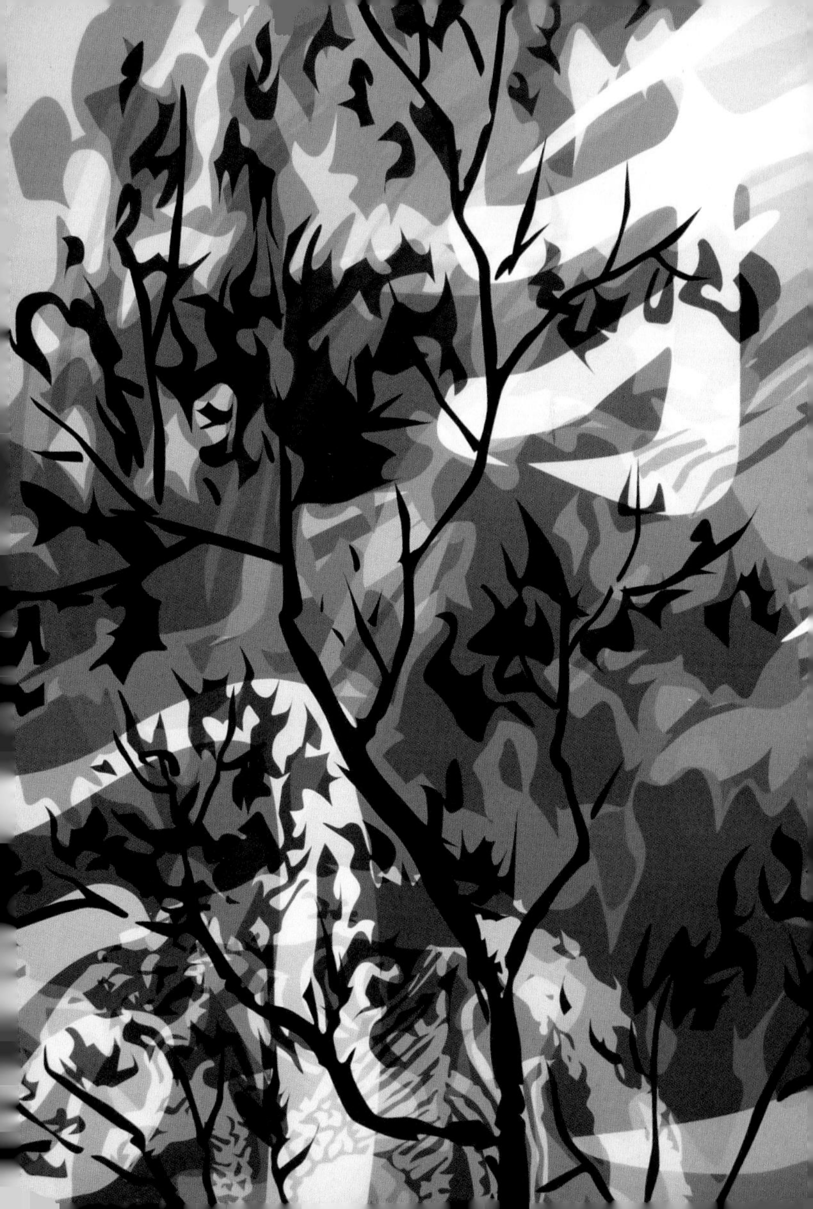

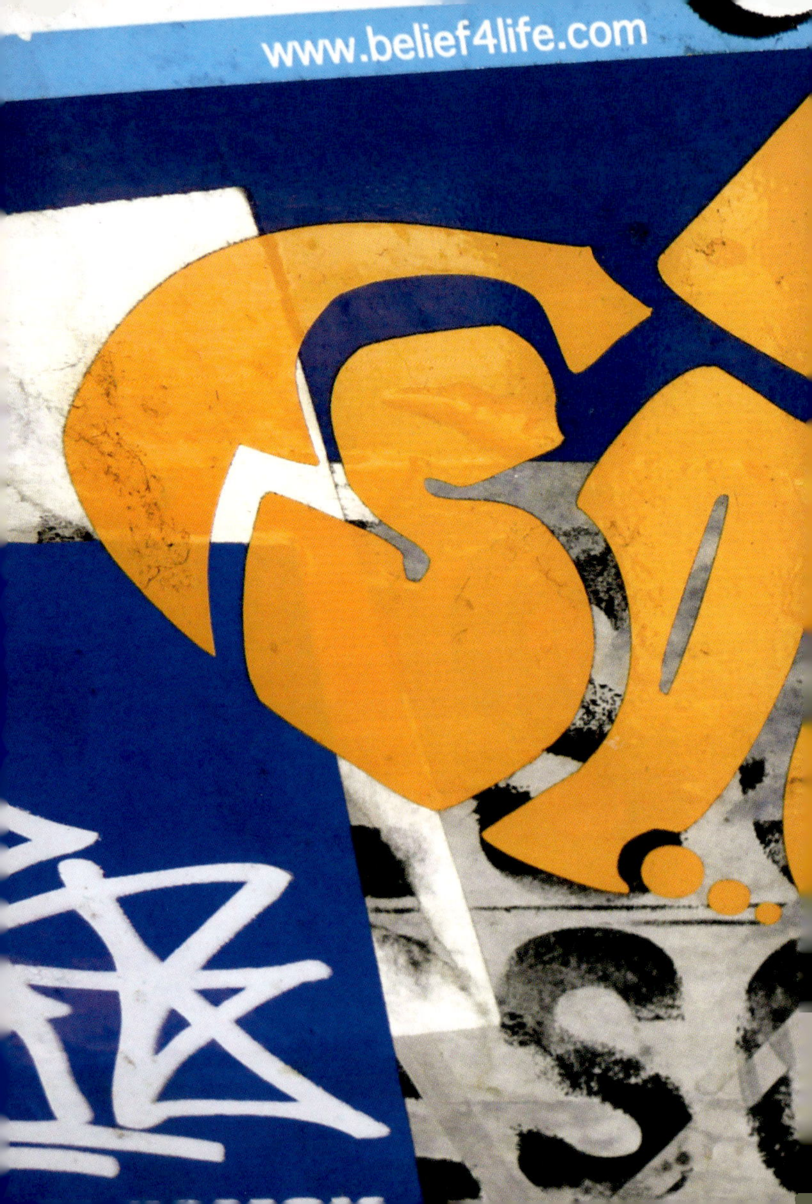
www.belief4life.com

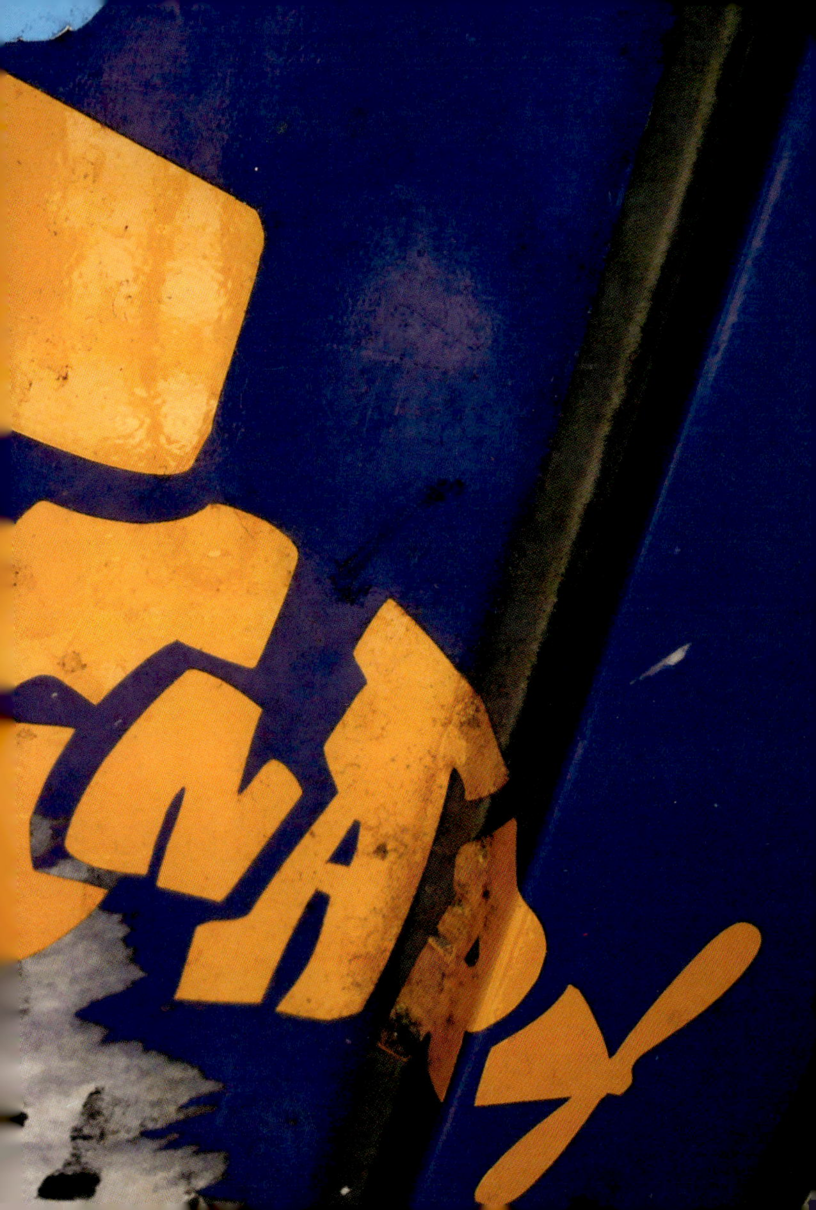

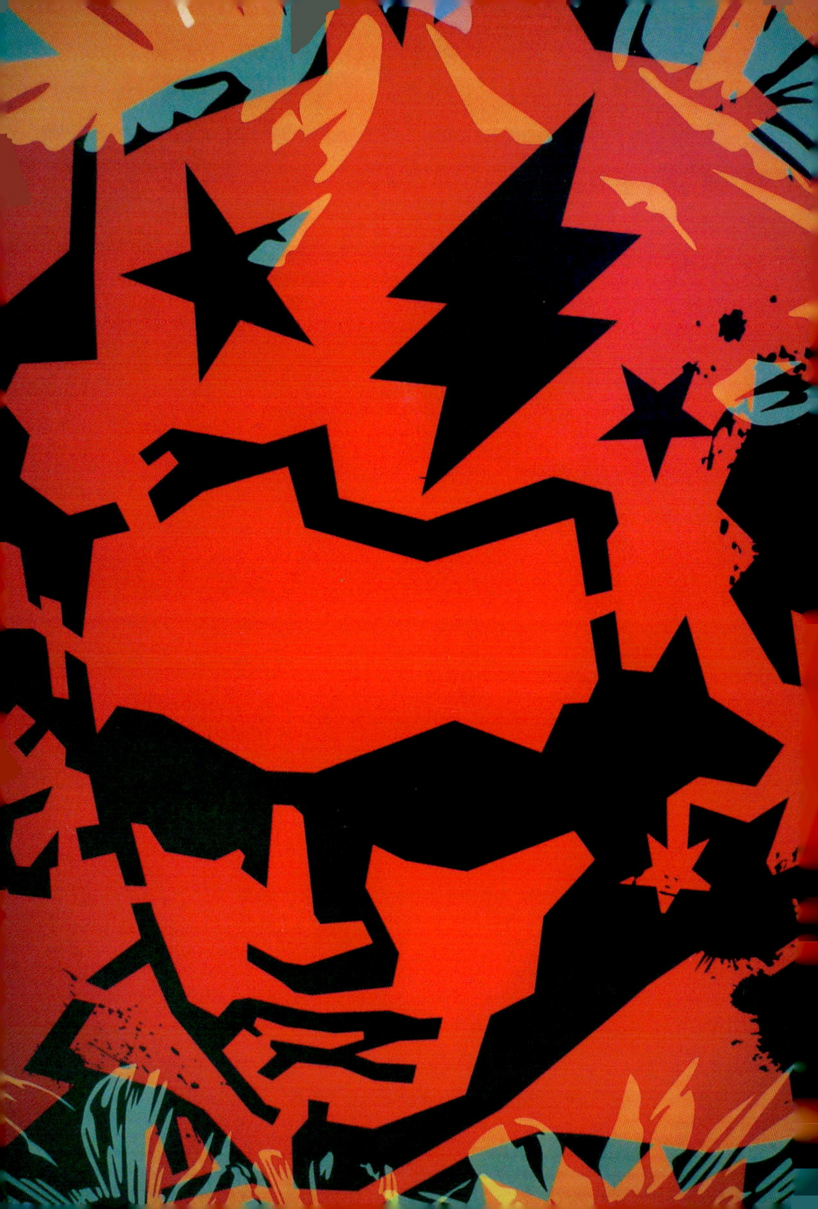

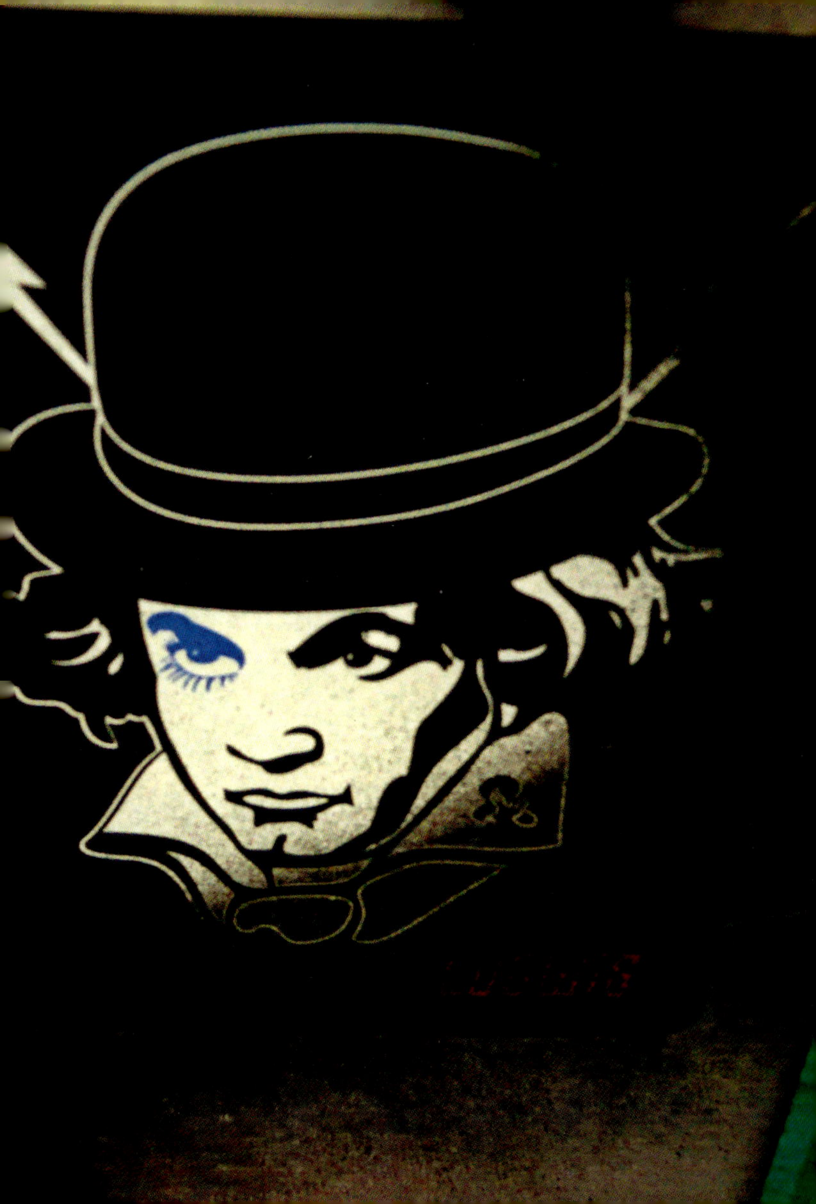

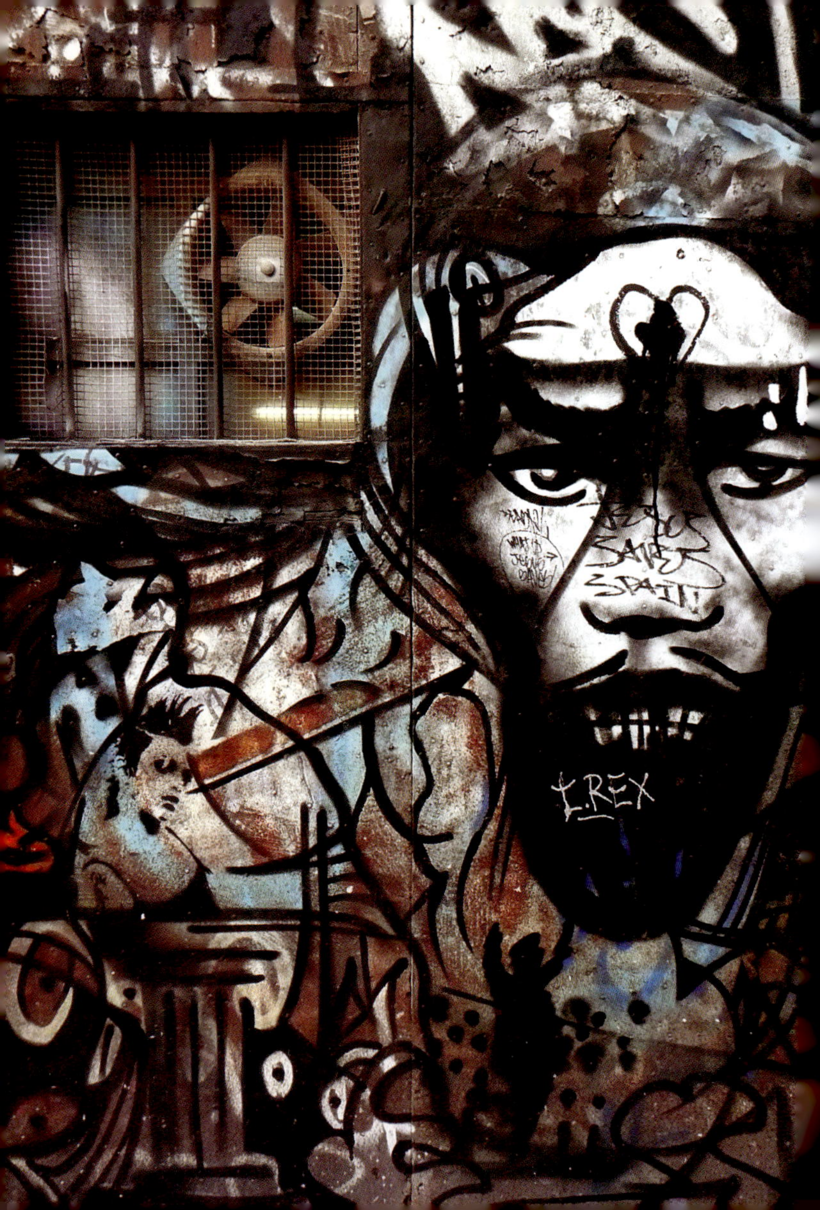
T.REX

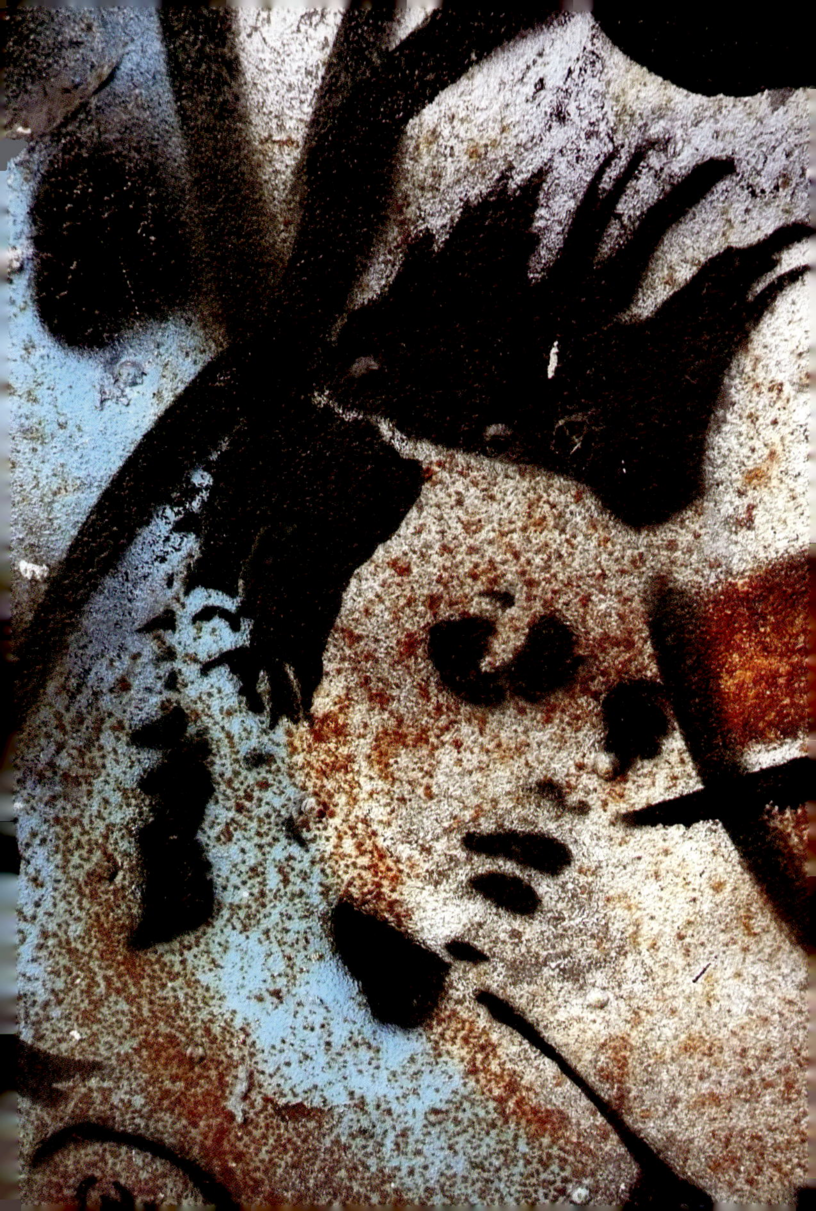

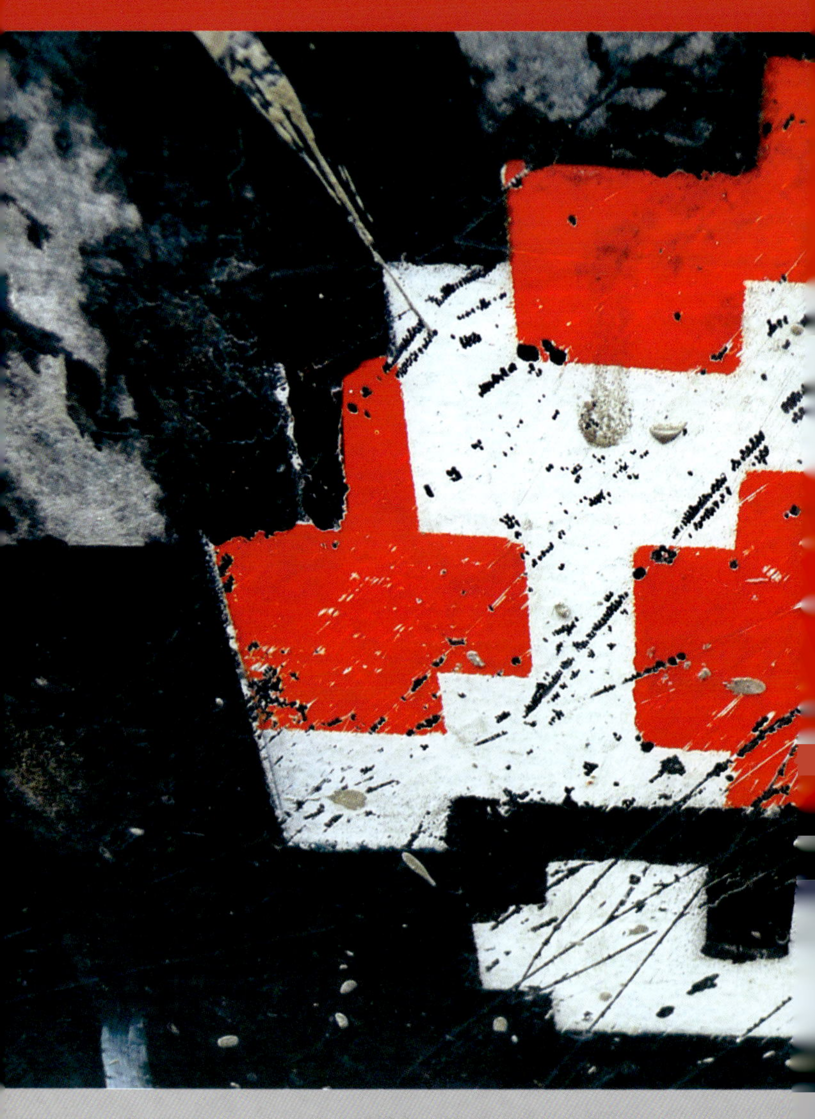

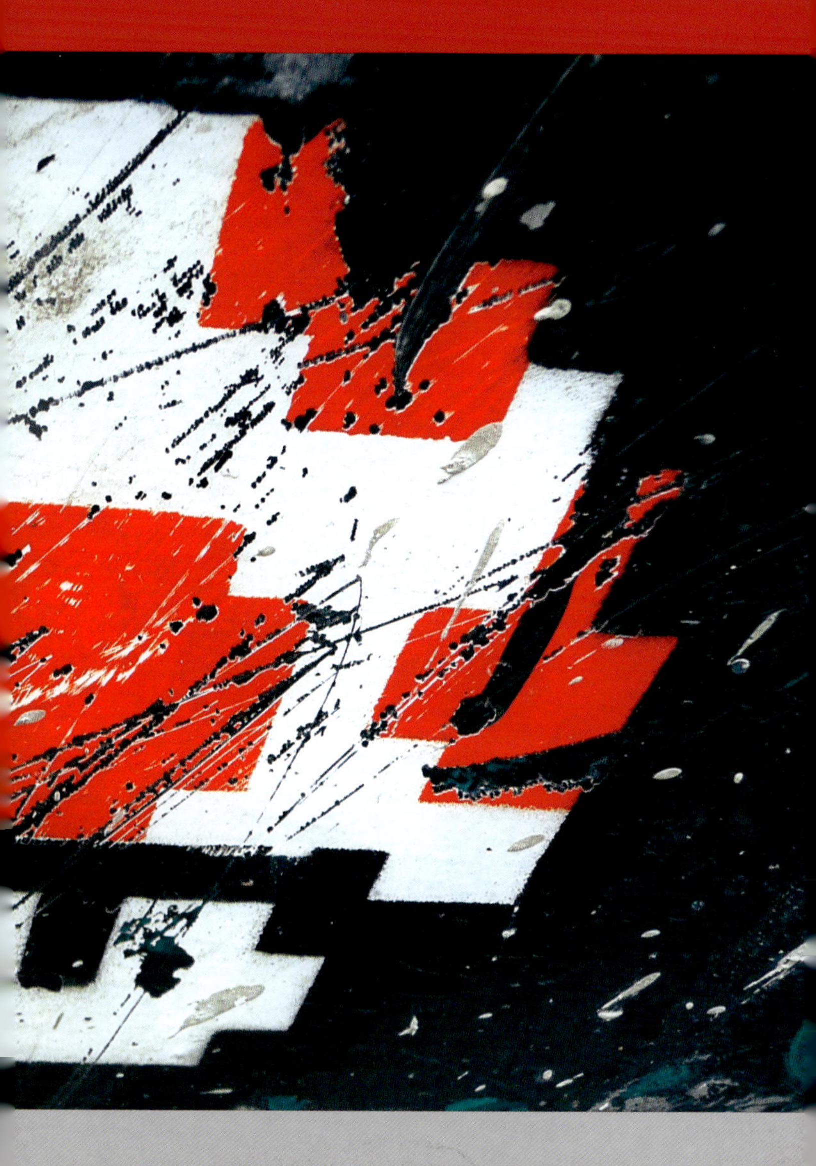

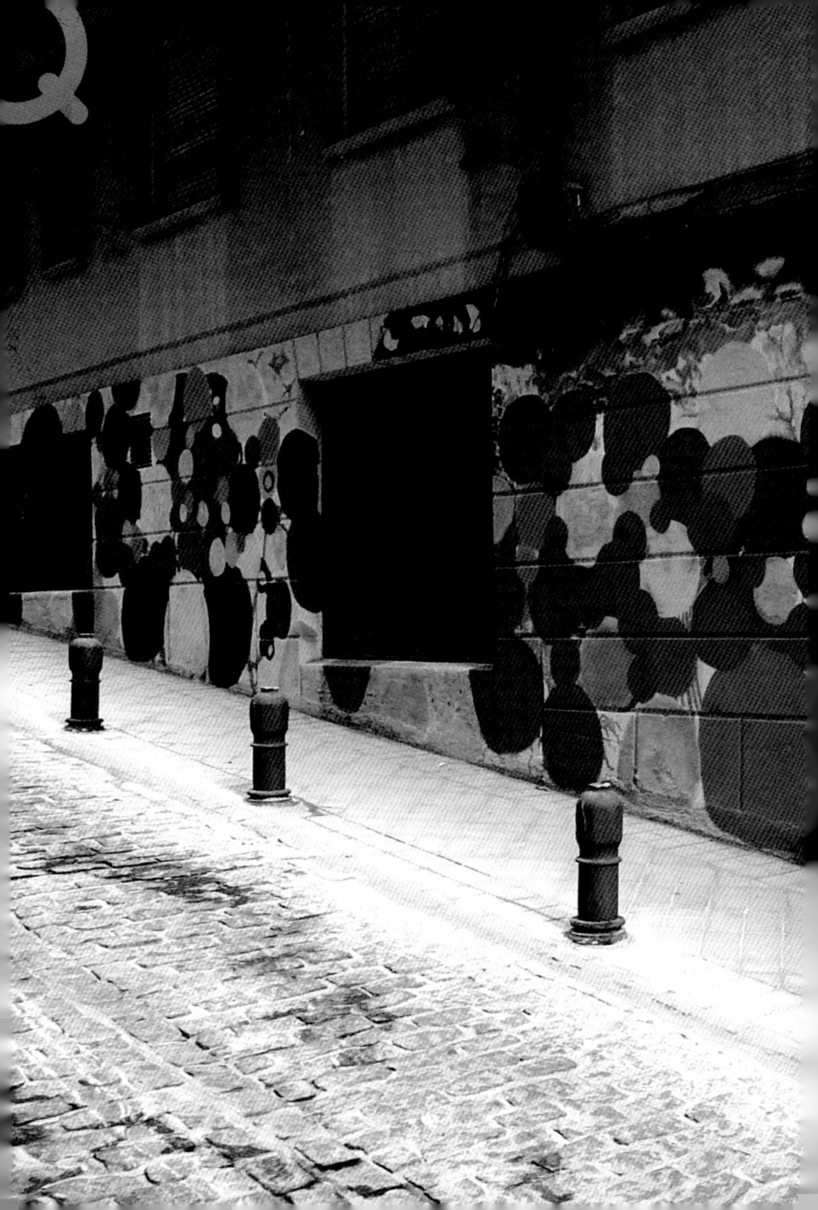

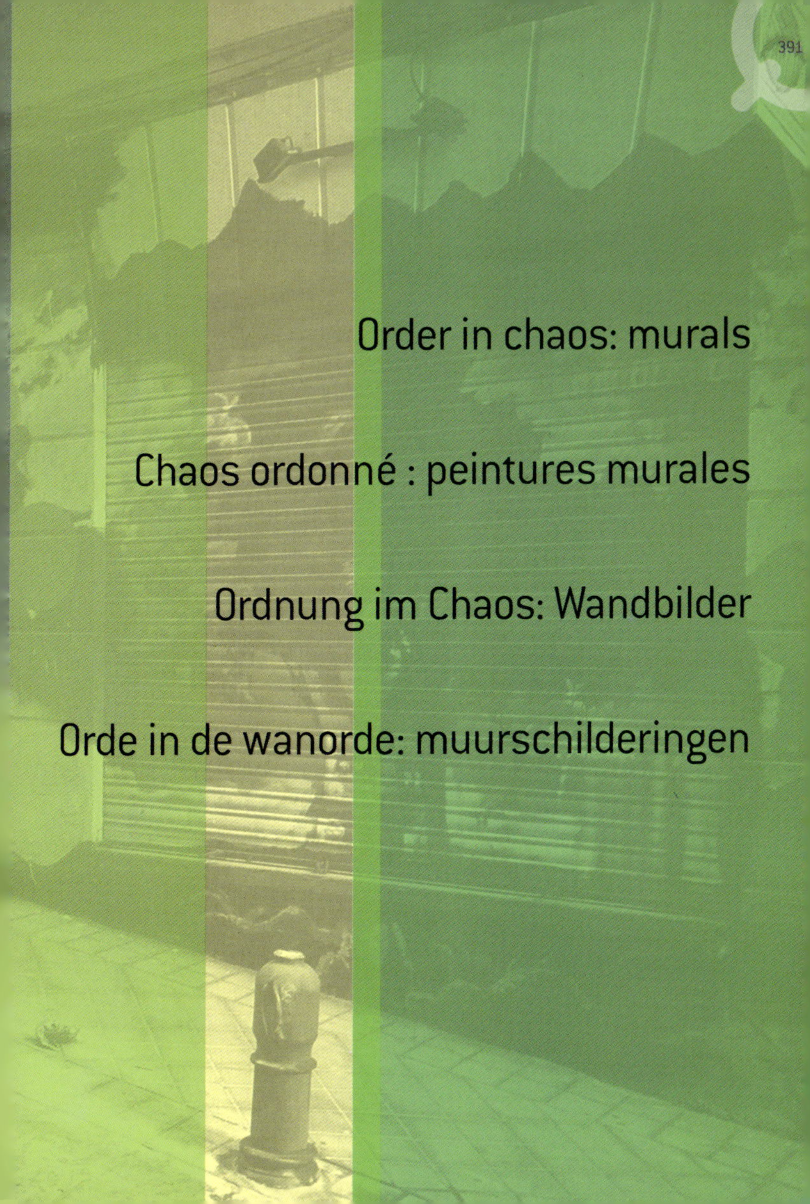

Order in chaos: murals

Chaos ordonné : peintures murales

Ordnung im Chaos: Wandbilder

Orde in de wanorde: muurschilderingen

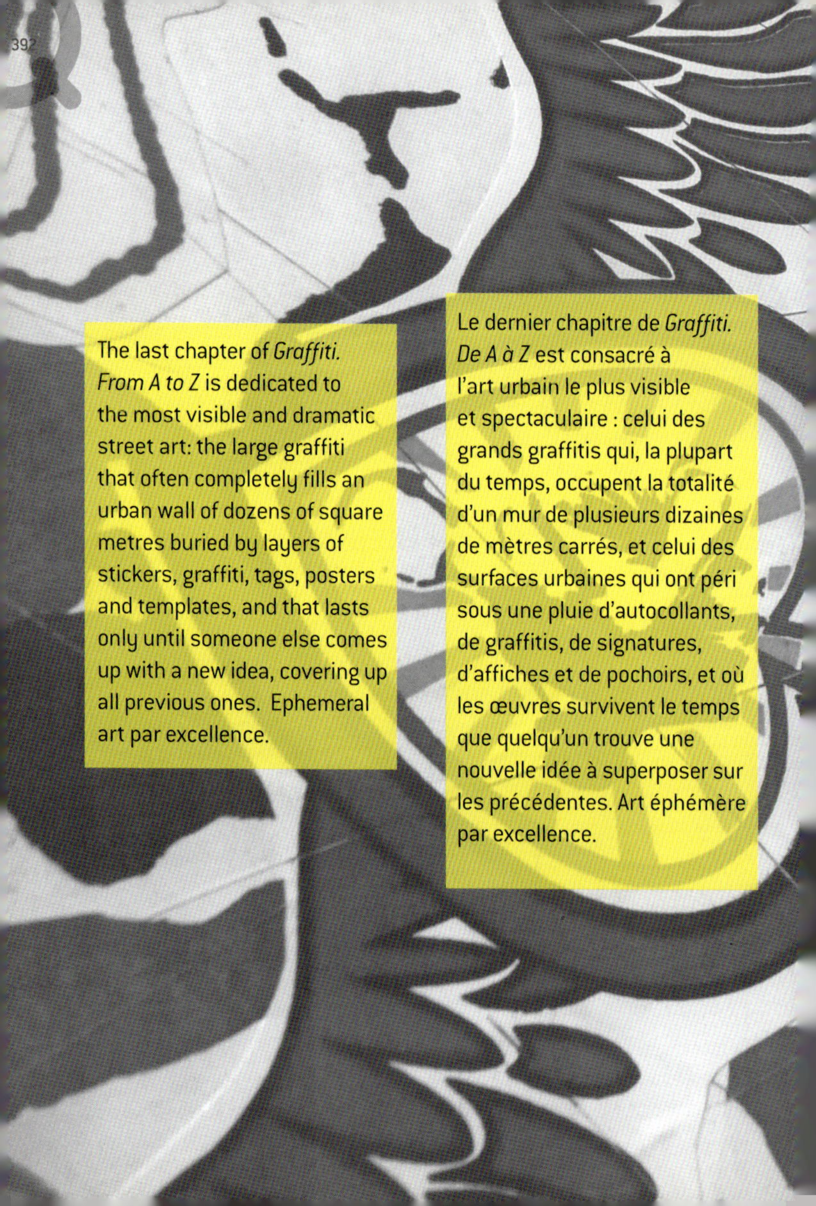

The last chapter of *Graffiti. From A to Z* is dedicated to the most visible and dramatic street art: the large graffiti that often completely fills an urban wall of dozens of square metres buried by layers of stickers, graffiti, tags, posters and templates, and that lasts only until someone else comes up with a new idea, covering up all previous ones. Ephemeral art par excellence.

Le dernier chapitre de *Graffiti. De A à Z* est consacré à l'art urbain le plus visible et spectaculaire : celui des grands graffitis qui, la plupart du temps, occupent la totalité d'un mur de plusieurs dizaines de mètres carrés, et celui des surfaces urbaines qui ont péri sous une pluie d'autocollants, de graffitis, de signatures, d'affiches et de pochoirs, et où les œuvres survivent le temps que quelqu'un trouve une nouvelle idée à superposer sur les précédentes. Art éphémère par excellence.

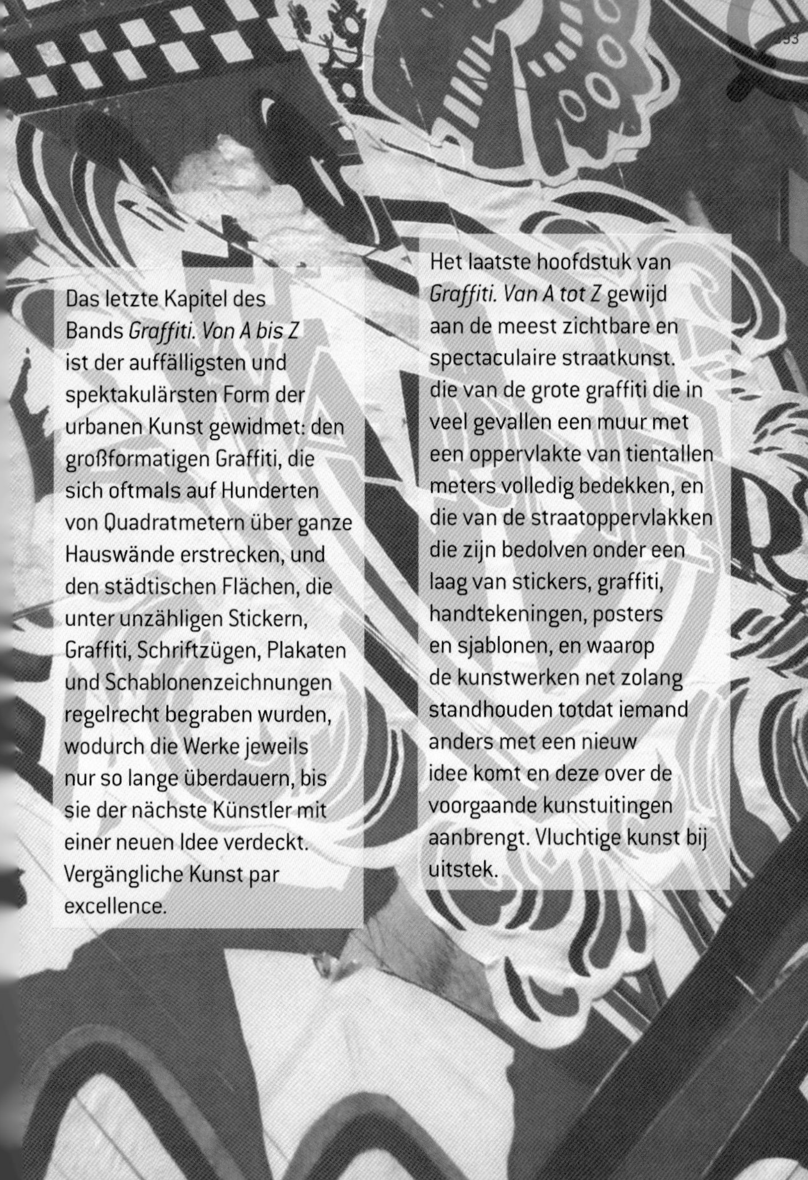

Das letzte Kapitel des Bands *Graffiti. Von A bis Z* ist der auffälligsten und spektakulärsten Form der urbanen Kunst gewidmet: den großformatigen Graffiti, die sich oftmals auf Hunderten von Quadratmetern über ganze Hauswände erstrecken, und den städtischen Flächen, die unter unzähligen Stickern, Graffiti, Schriftzügen, Plakaten und Schablonenzeichnungen regelrecht begraben wurden, wodurch die Werke jeweils nur so lange überdauern, bis sie der nächste Künstler mit einer neuen Idee verdeckt. Vergängliche Kunst par excellence.

Het laatste hoofdstuk van *Graffiti. Van A tot Z* gewijd aan de meest zichtbare en spectaculaire straatkunst. die van de grote graffiti die in veel gevallen een muur met een oppervlakte van tientallen meters volledig bedekken, en die van de straatoppervlakken die zijn bedolven onder een laag van stickers, graffiti, handtekeningen, posters en sjablonen, en waarop de kunstwerken net zolang standhouden totdat iemand anders met een nieuw idee komt en deze over de voorgaande kunstuitingen aanbrengt. Vluchtige kunst bij uitstek.

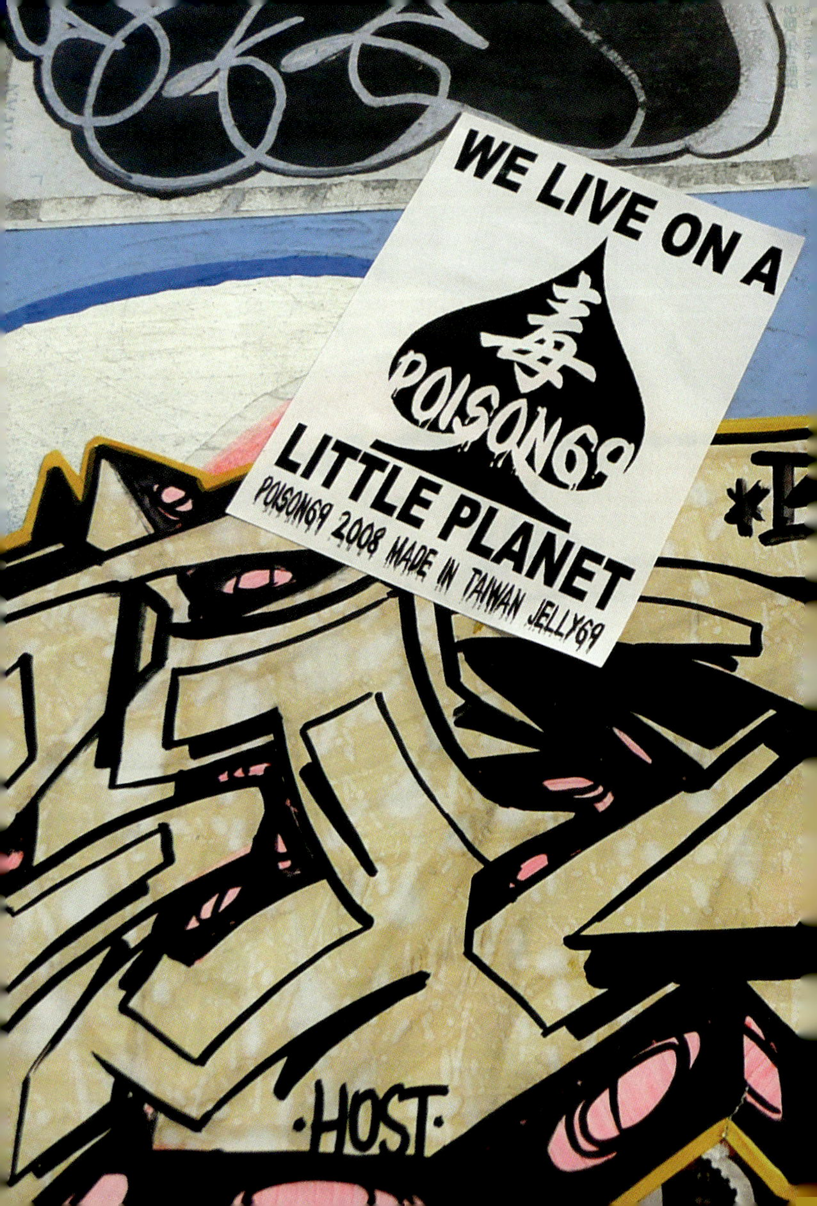
WE LIVE ON A
毒
POISON69
LITTLE PLANET
POISON69 2008 MADE IN TAIWAN JELLY69
HOST

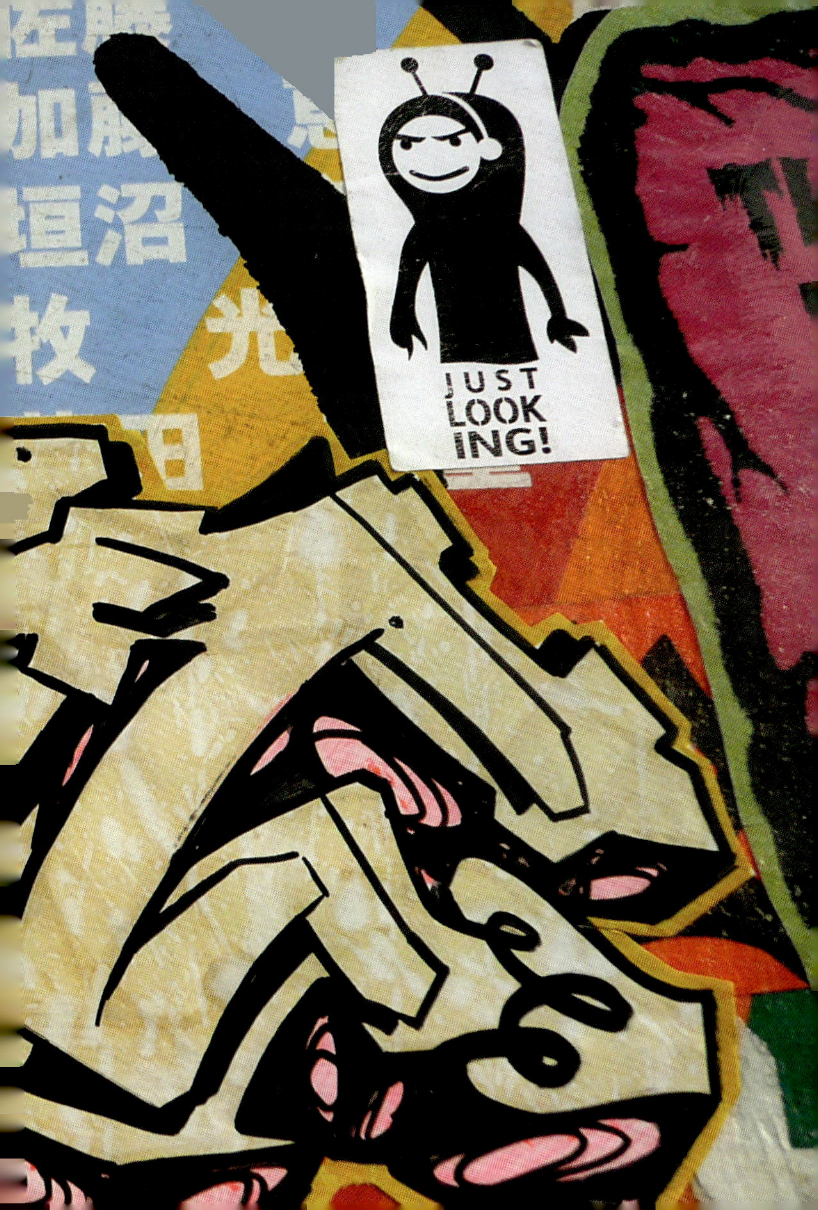
JUST
LOOK
ING!

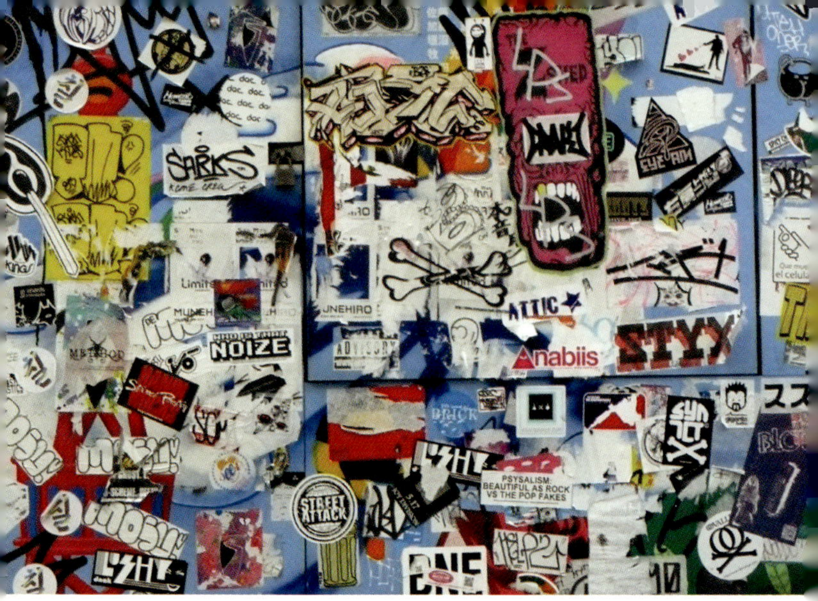

SARKS
NOIZE
ATTIC
STYX
nabiis
PSYSALISM:
BEAUTIFUL AS ROCK
VS THE POP FAKES
STREET ATTACK
e.p.a.
Expresion
Popular
Artistica

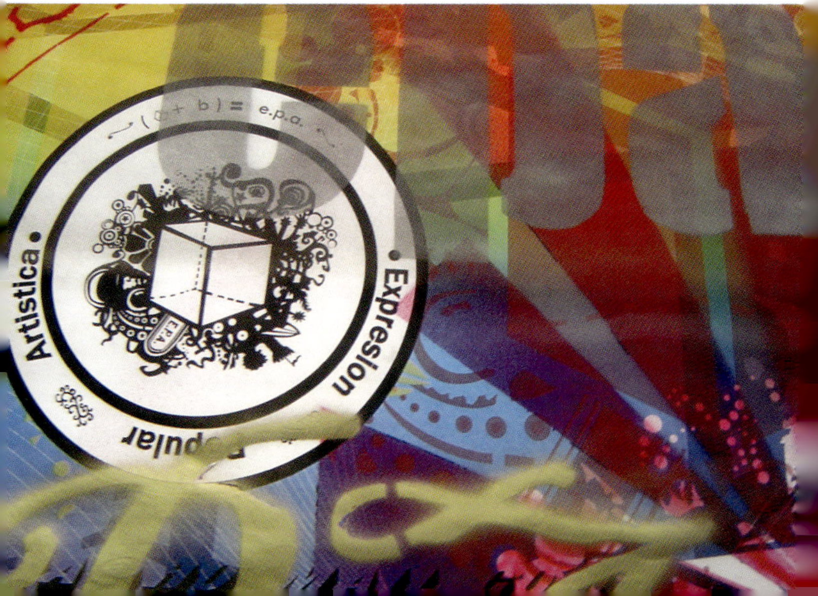

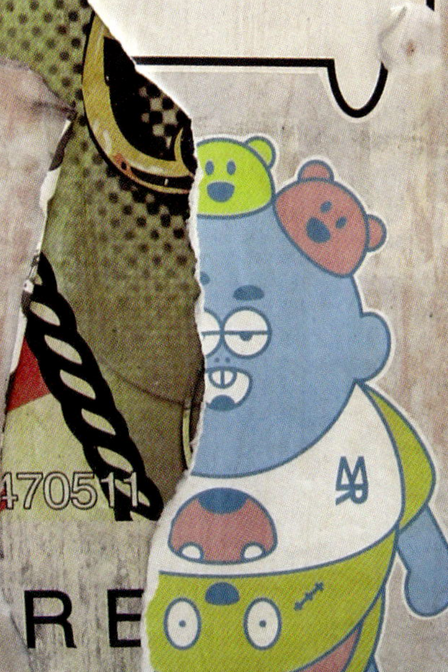
del
GUA
n la
mar
SALVA
TU
PLANETA
TU
PUEDES
470511
RE

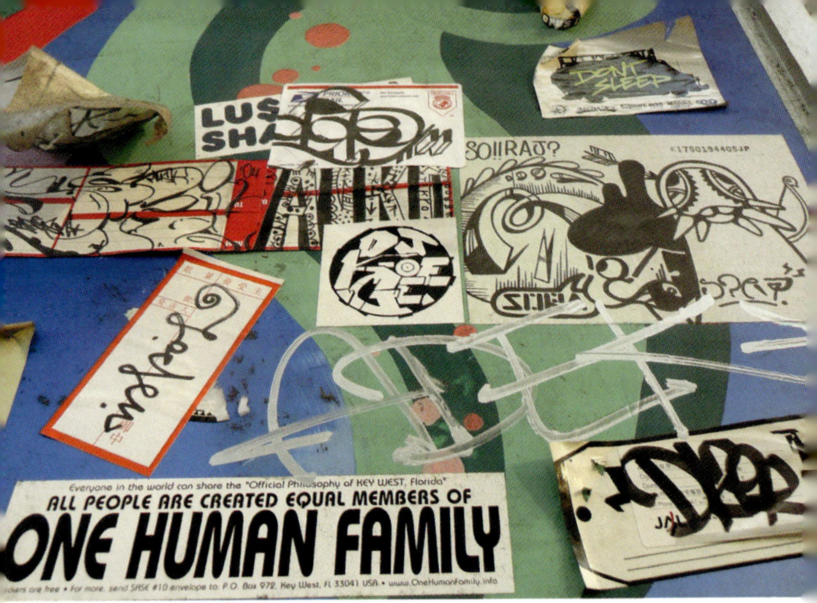

Everyone in the world can share the "Official Philosophy of KEY WEST, Florida"
ALL PEOPLE ARE CREATED EQUAL MEMBERS OF
ONE HUMAN FAMILY
RANE
Pro DJ Mixers
MR CASUAL !

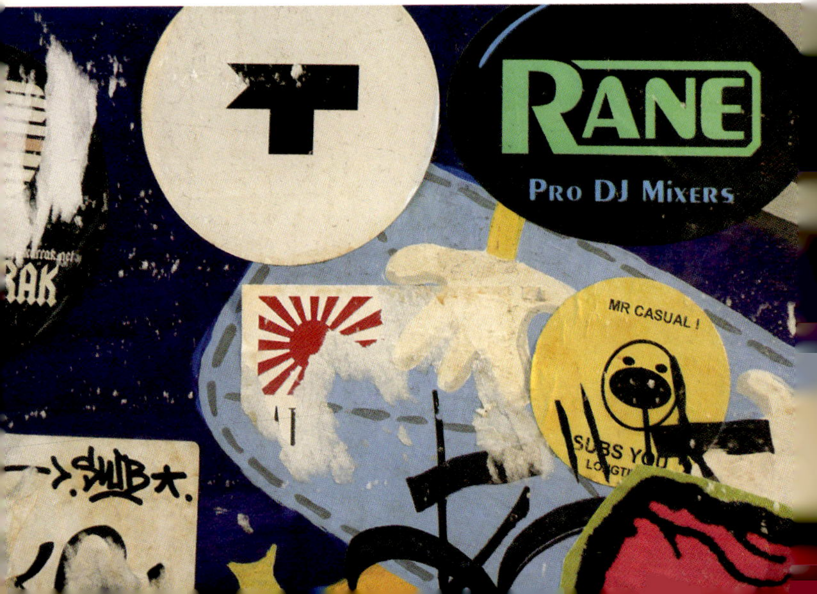

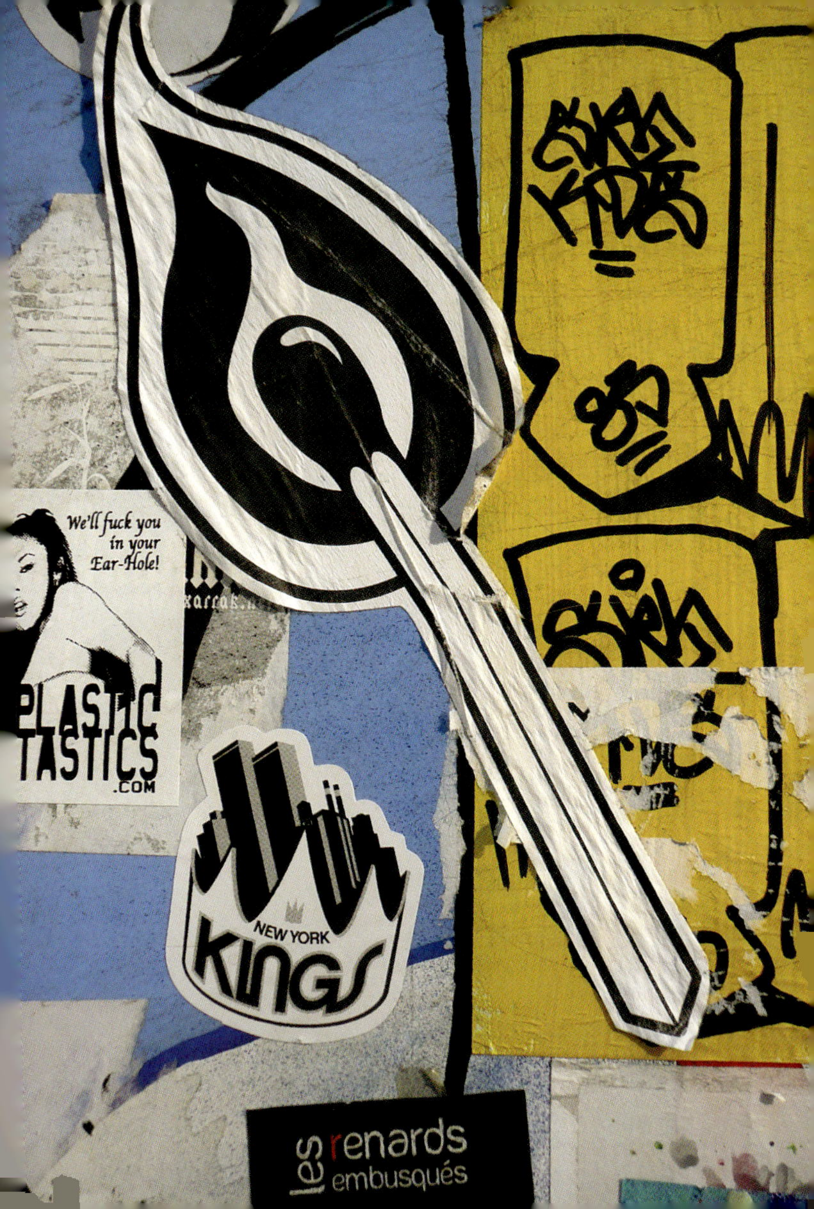
We'll fuck you in your Ear-Hole!
PLASTIC TASTICS .COM
NEW YORK KINGS
les renards embusqués

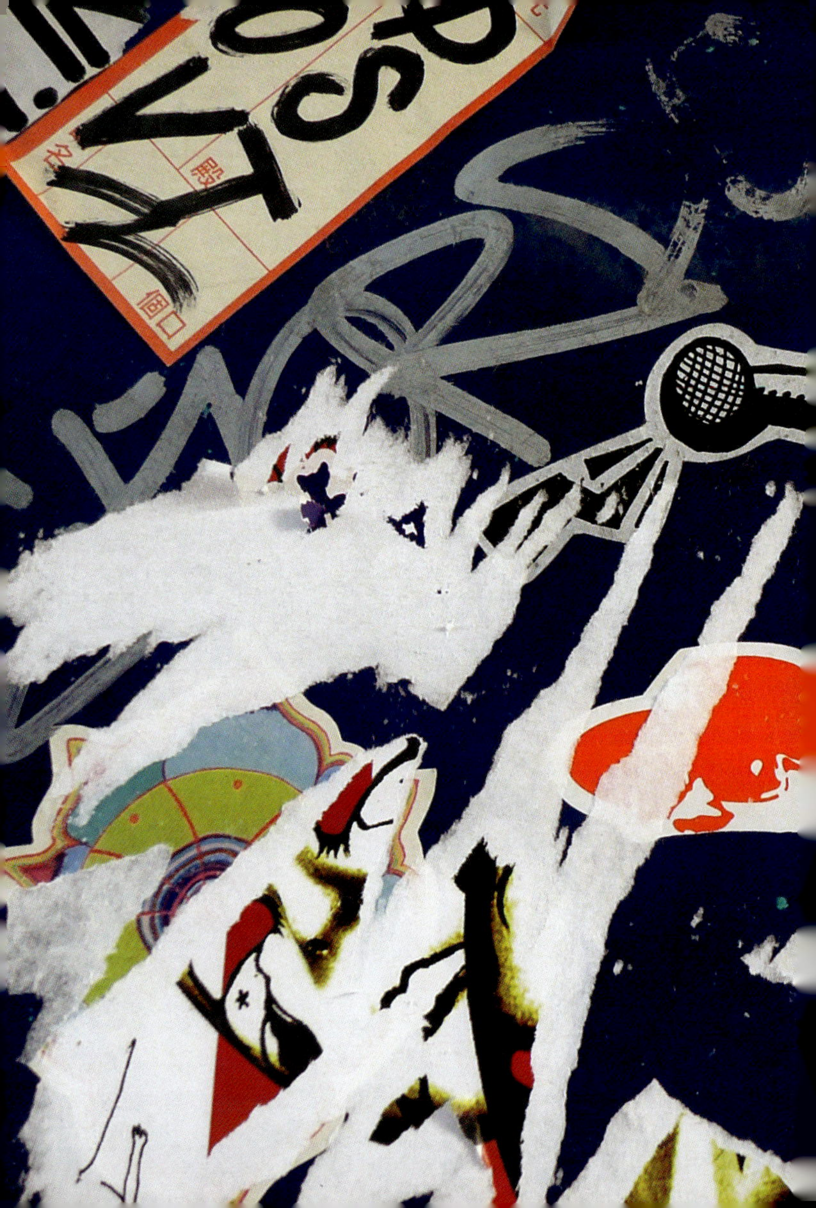

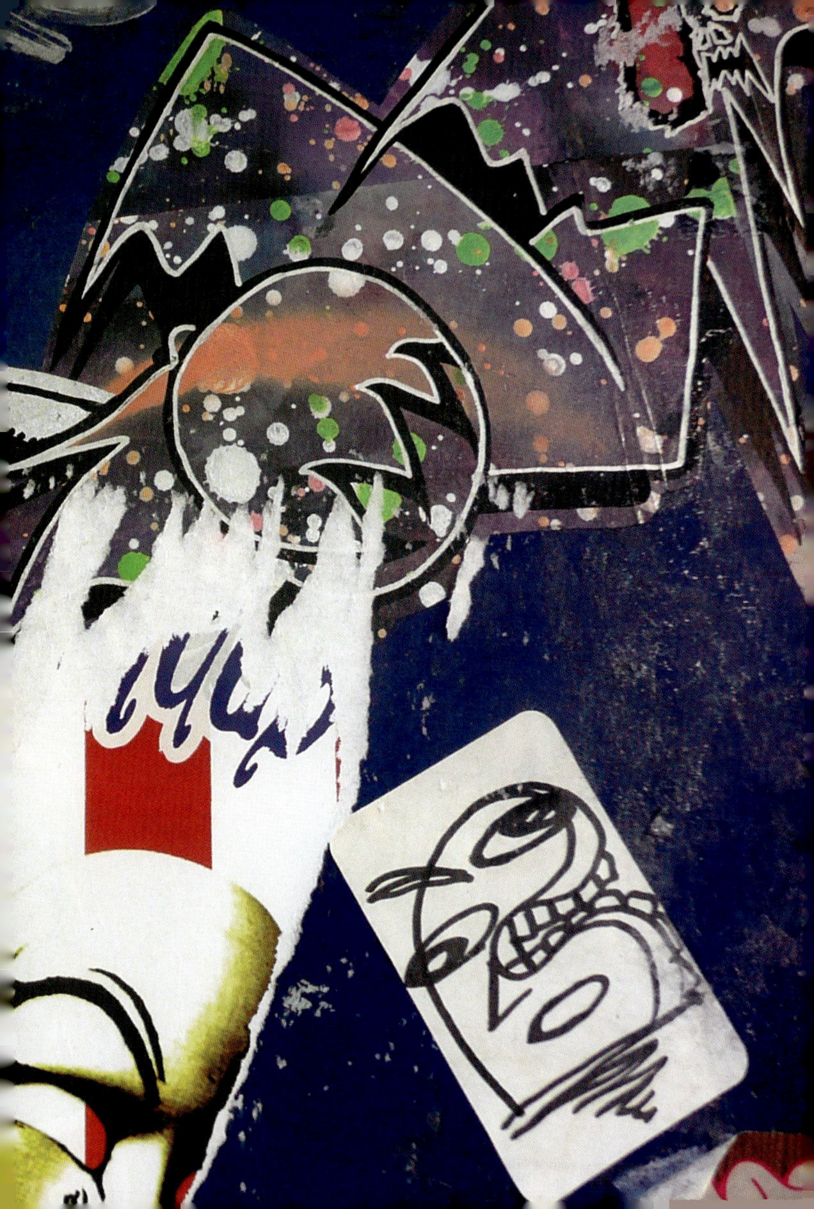

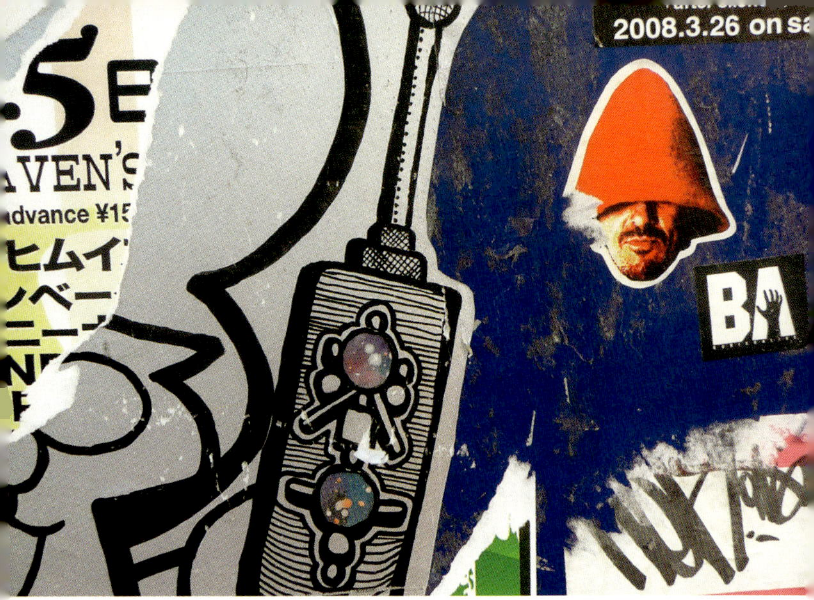

2008.3.26 on sa
advance ¥15
LU$HY SHARK
ONE HUMAN FAMILY
ALL PEOPLE ARE CREATED EQUAL MEMBERS OF
OCTOPUS INK
LU$HY SHARK

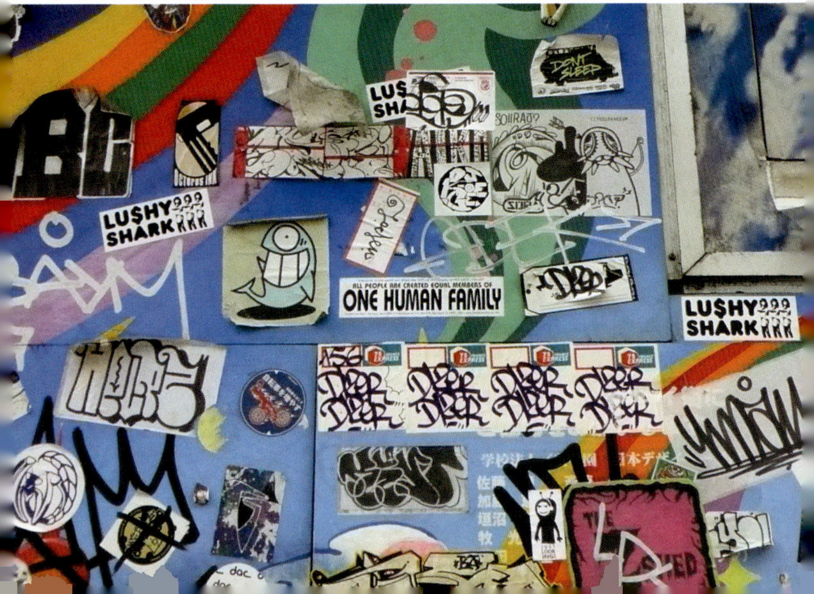

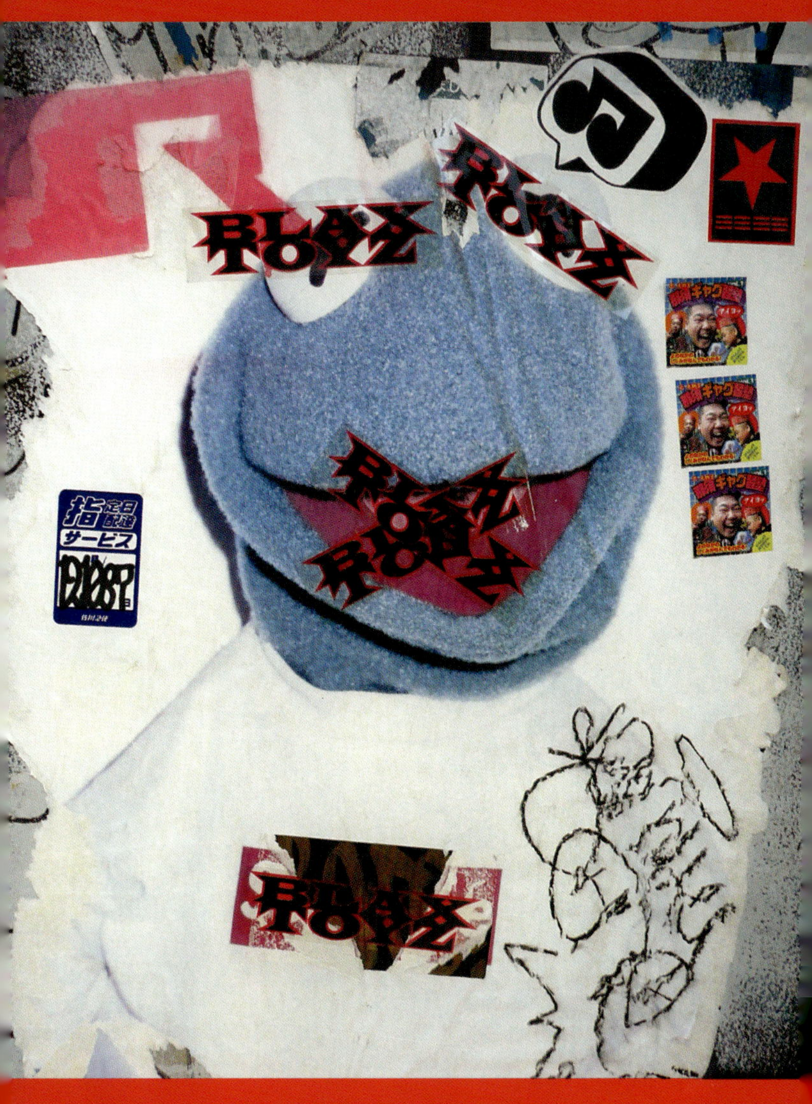

BLAZ TOYZ
指
サービス

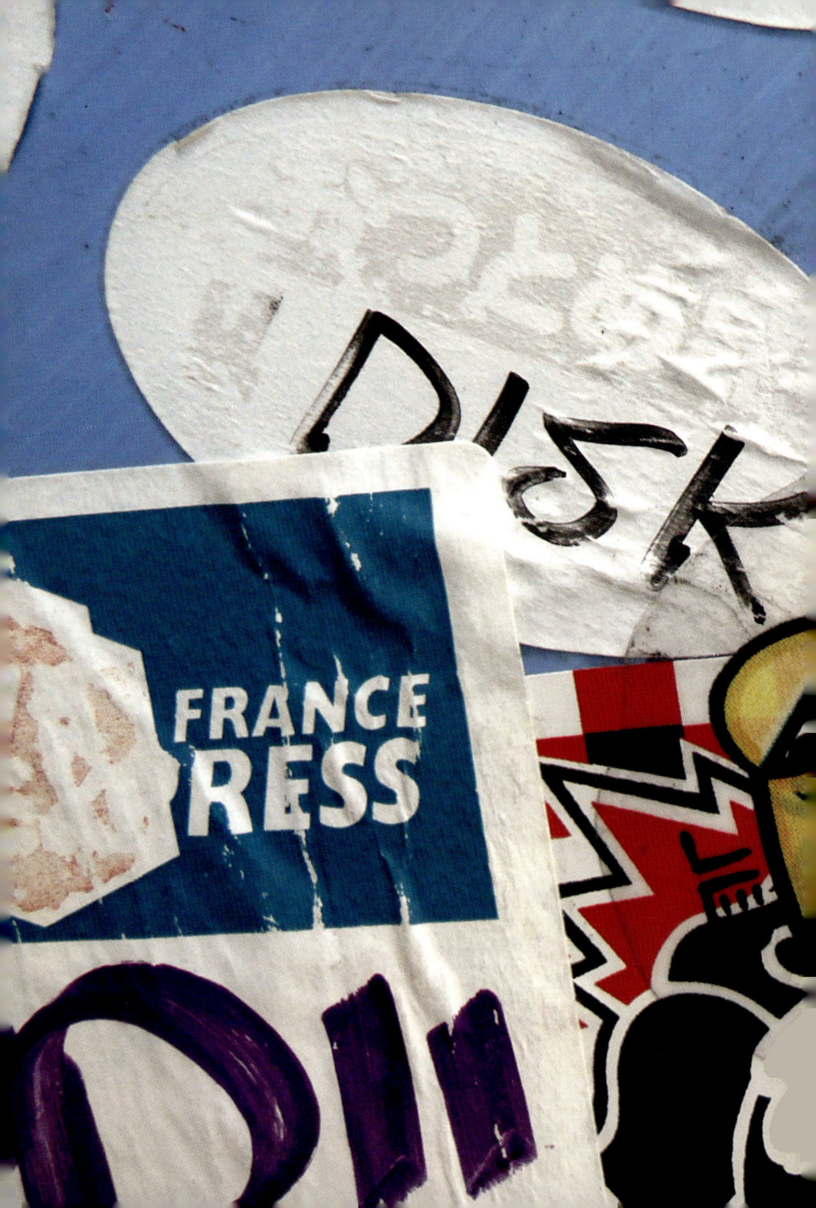
FRANCE
RESS

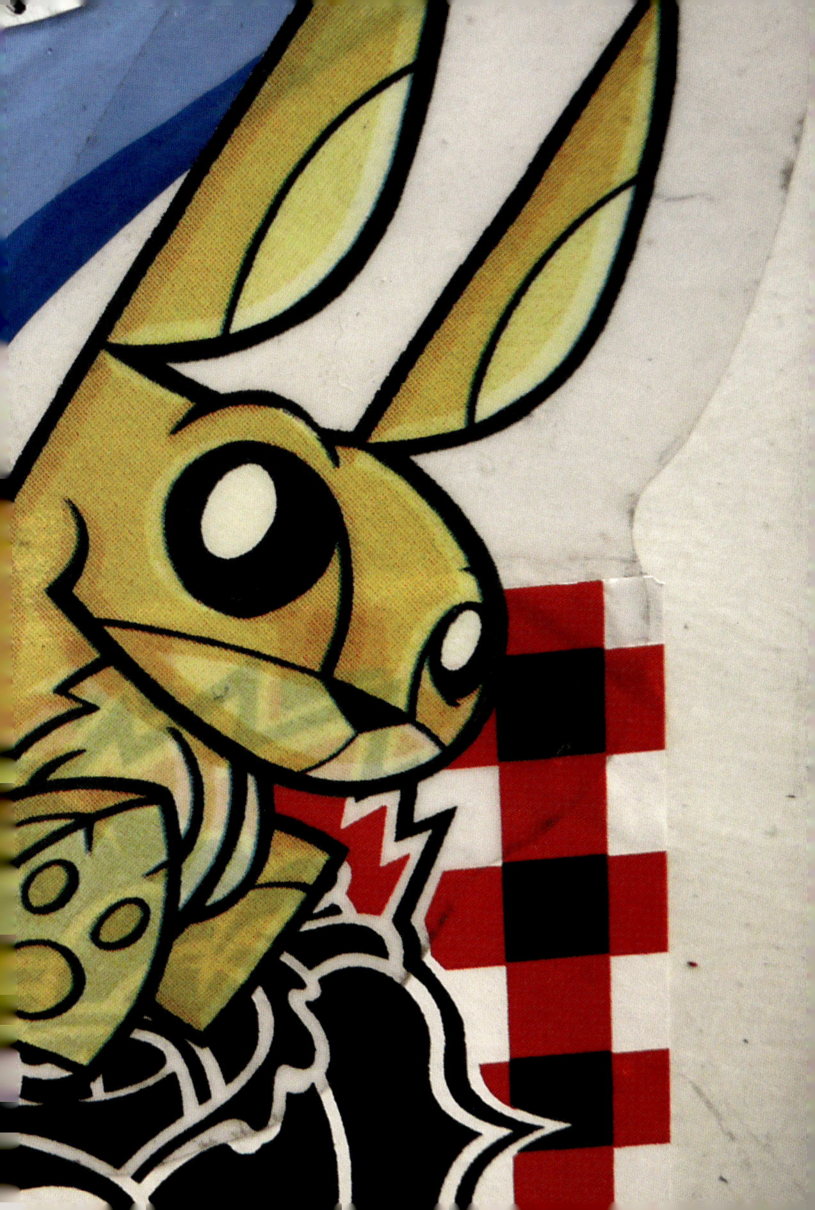

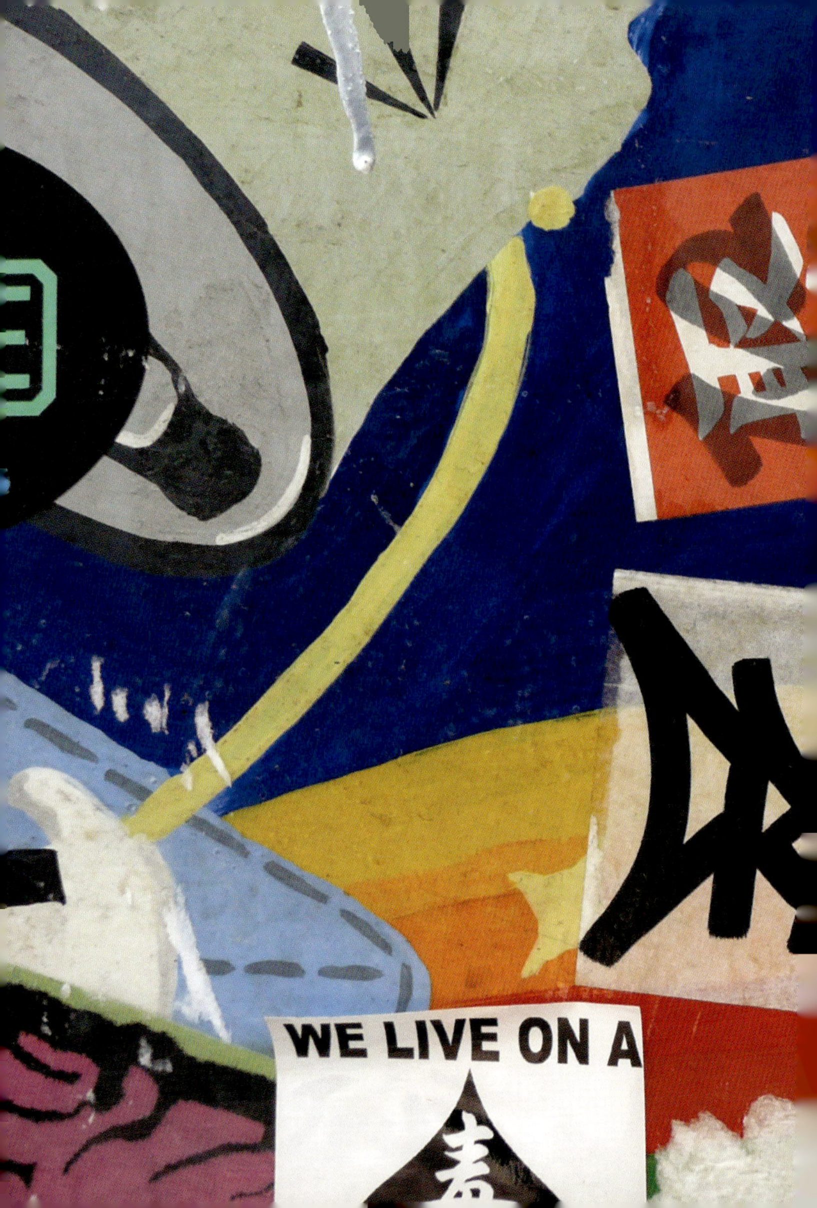
WE LIVE ON A

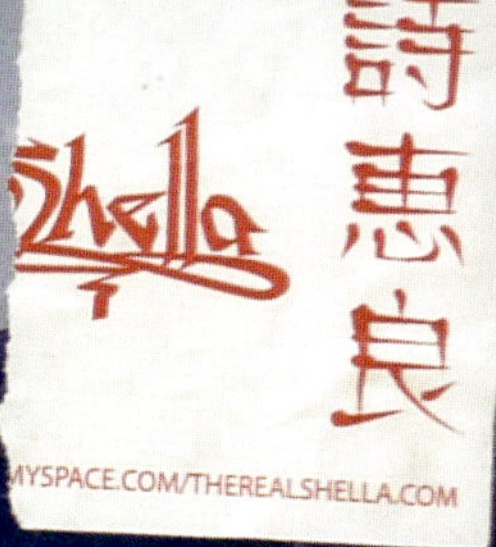
詩恵良
Shella
MYSPACE.COM/THEREALSHELLA.COM

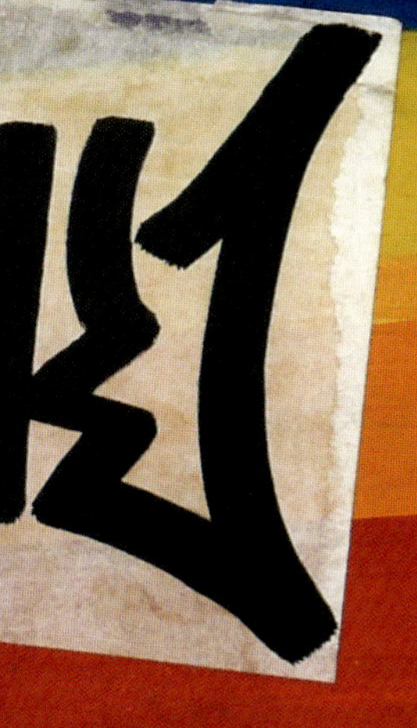

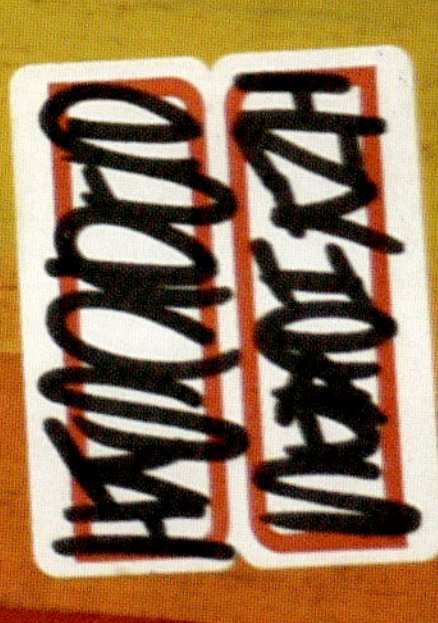

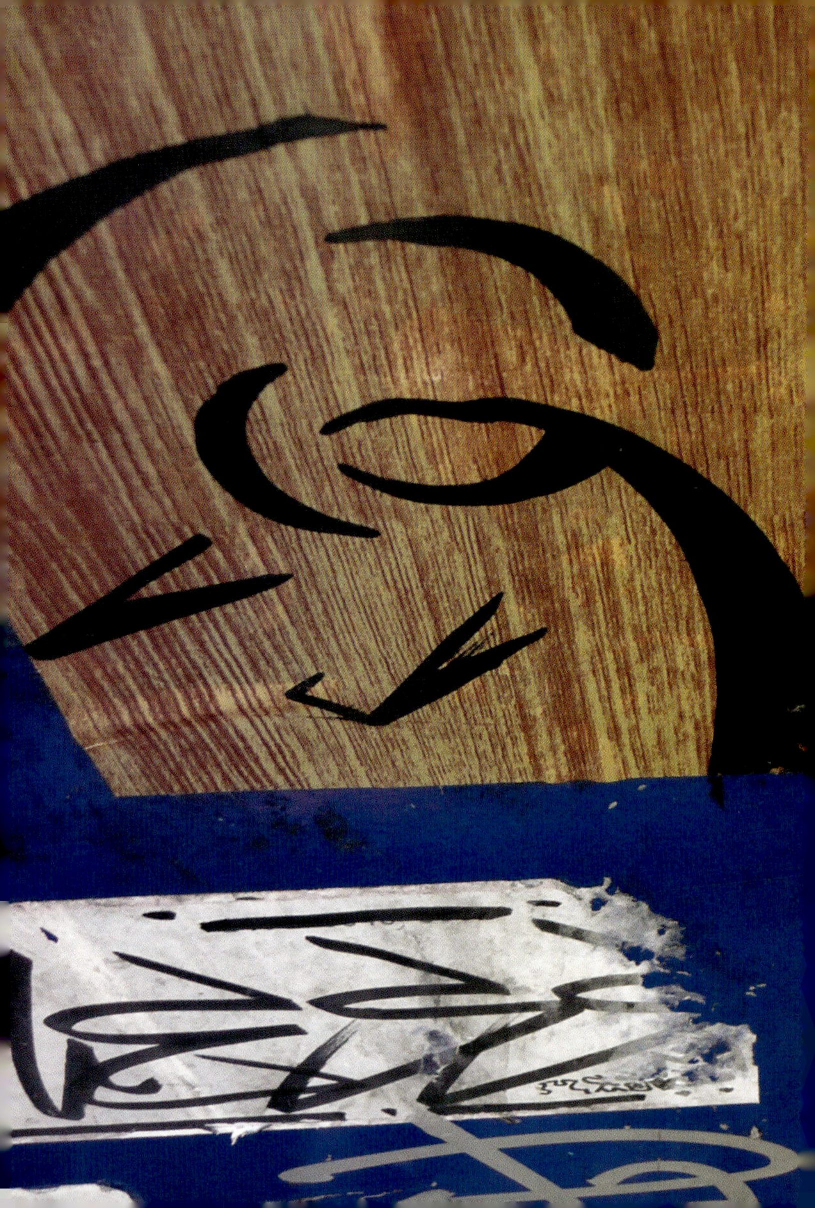

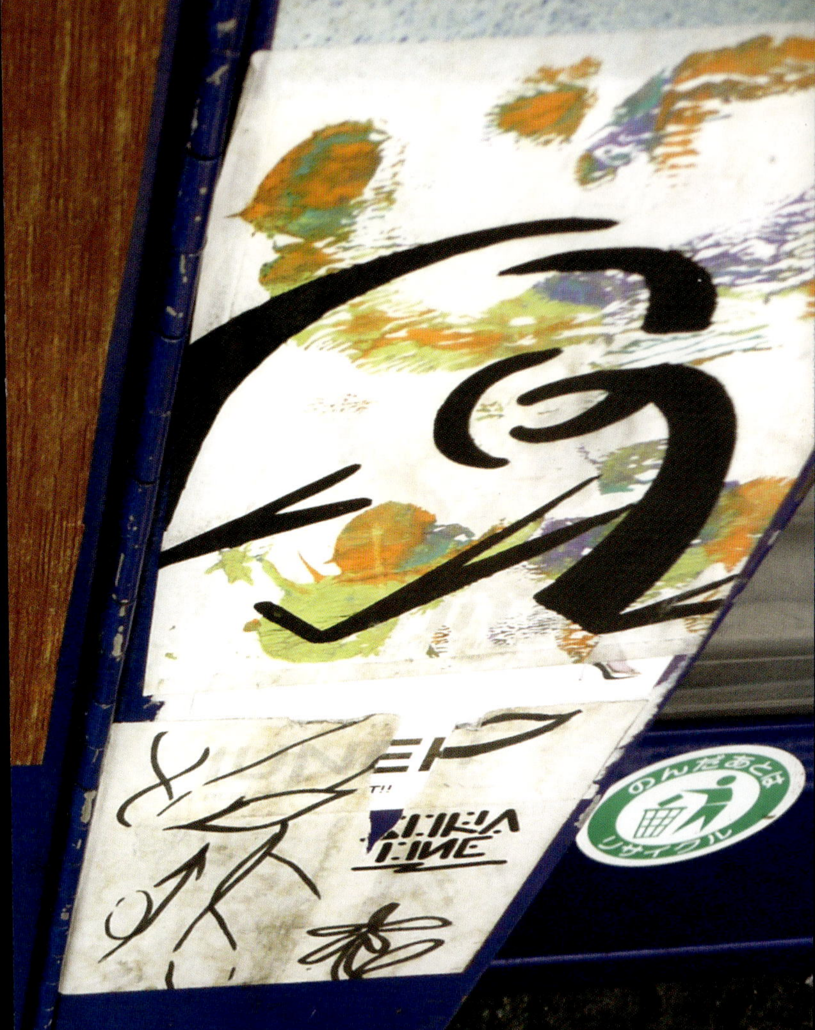
のんだあとは
リサイクル

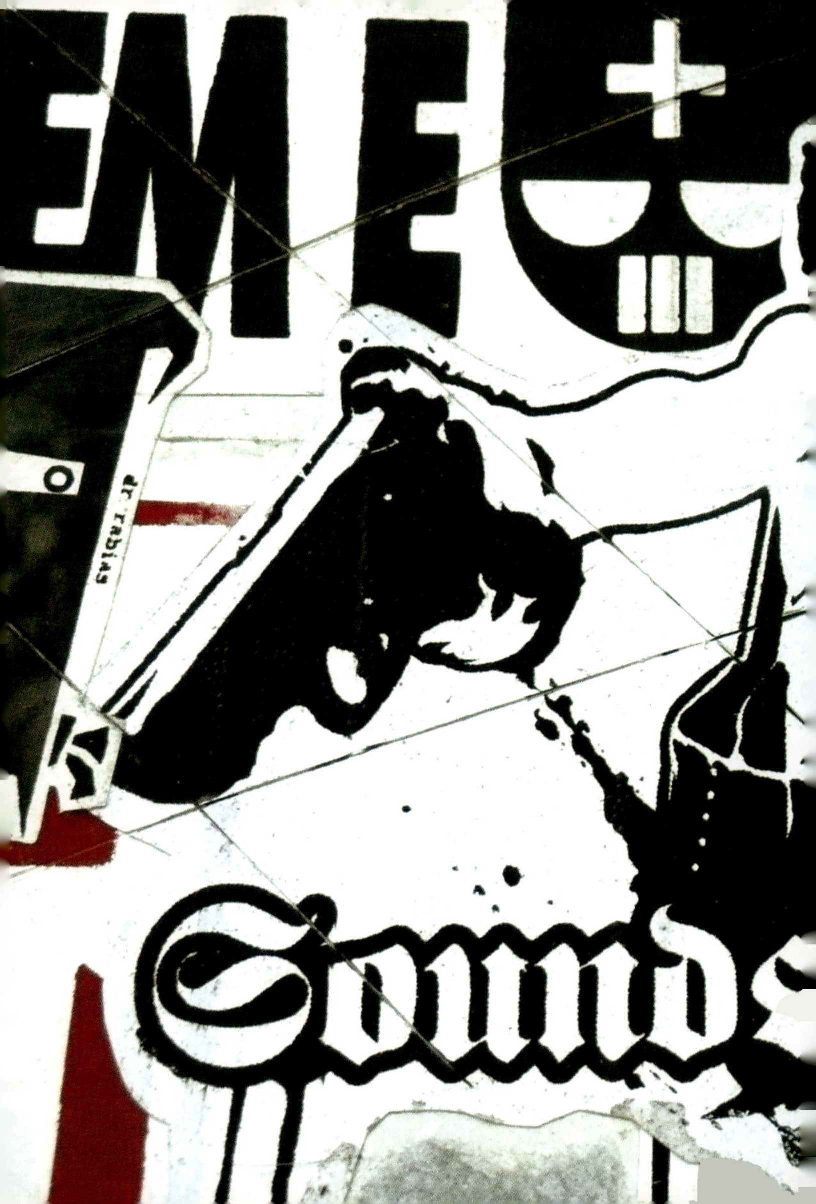
EME
dr rabias

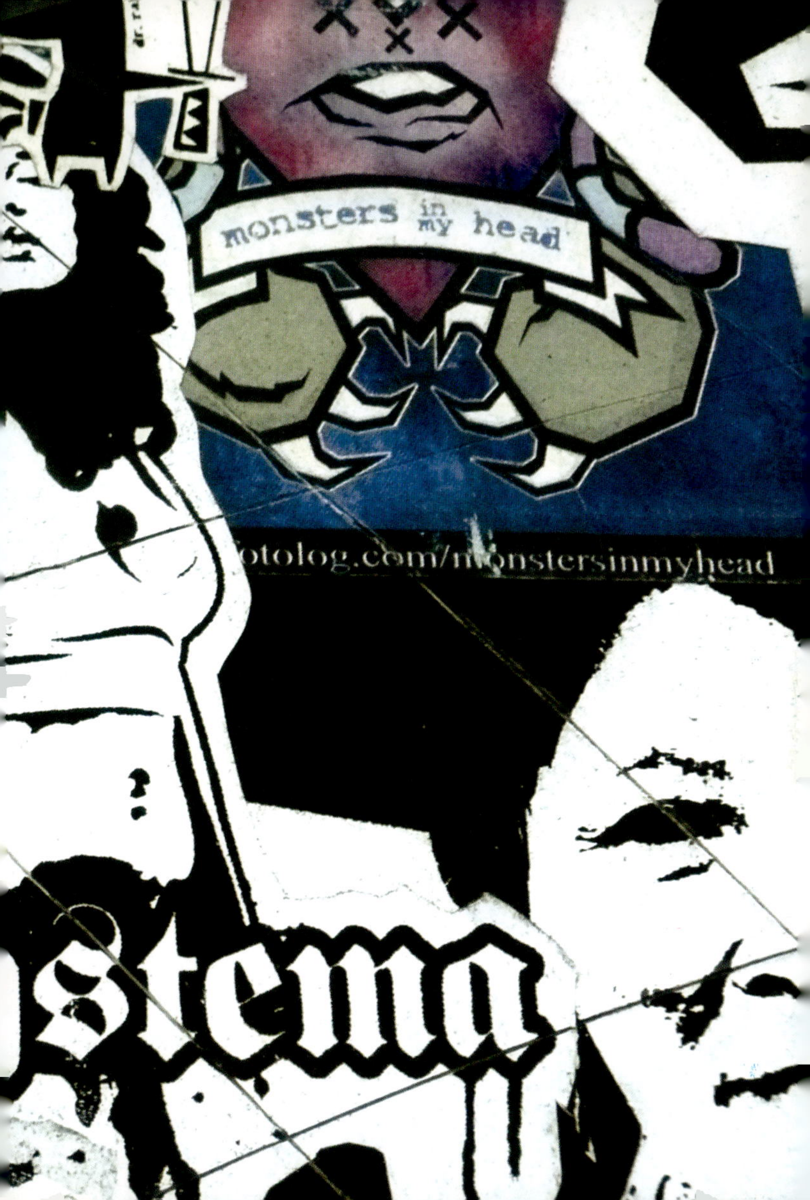
monsters in my head
otolog.com/monstersinmyhead
stema

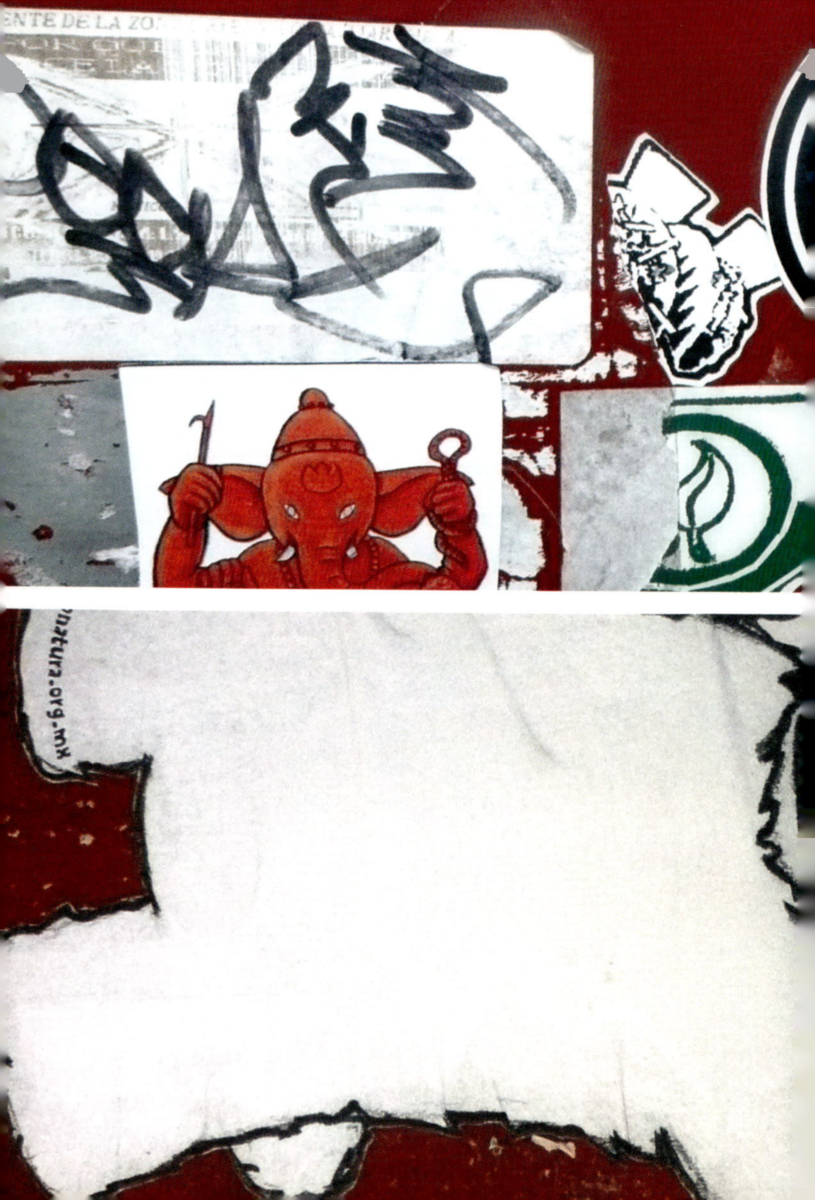
natura.org.mx

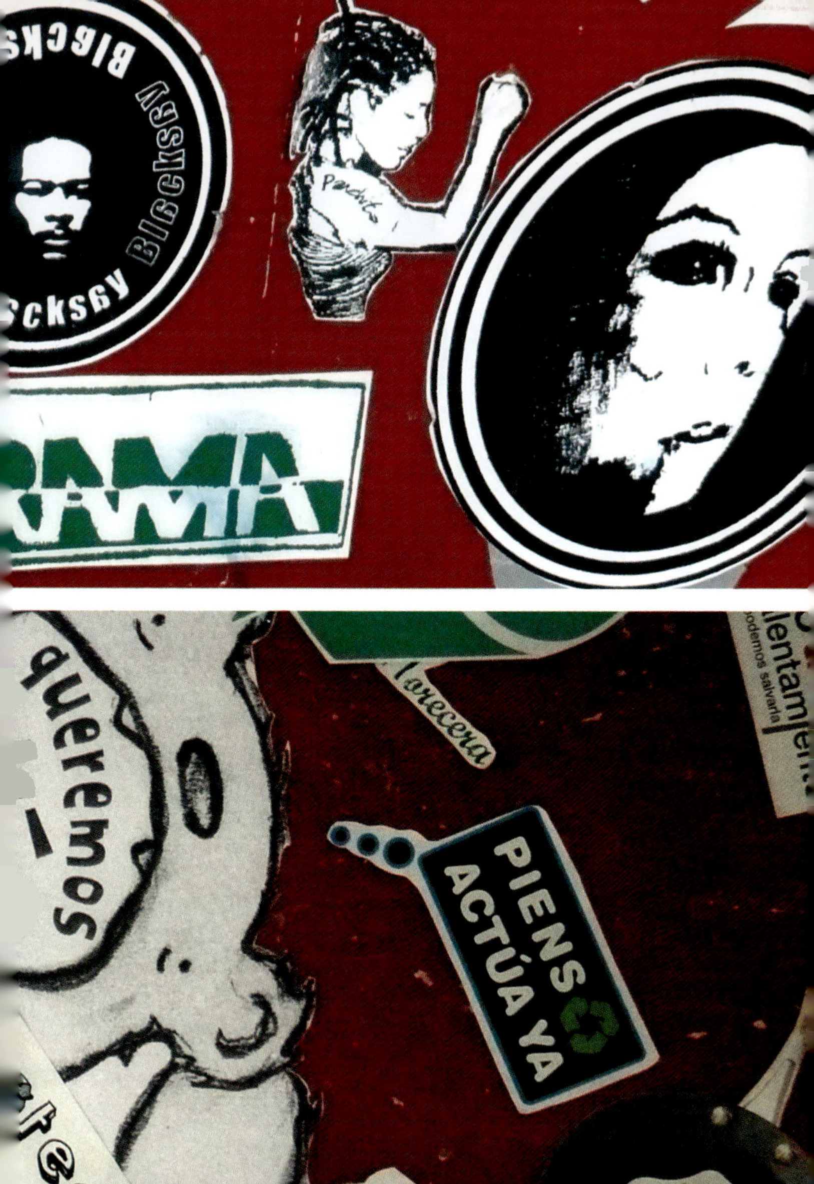

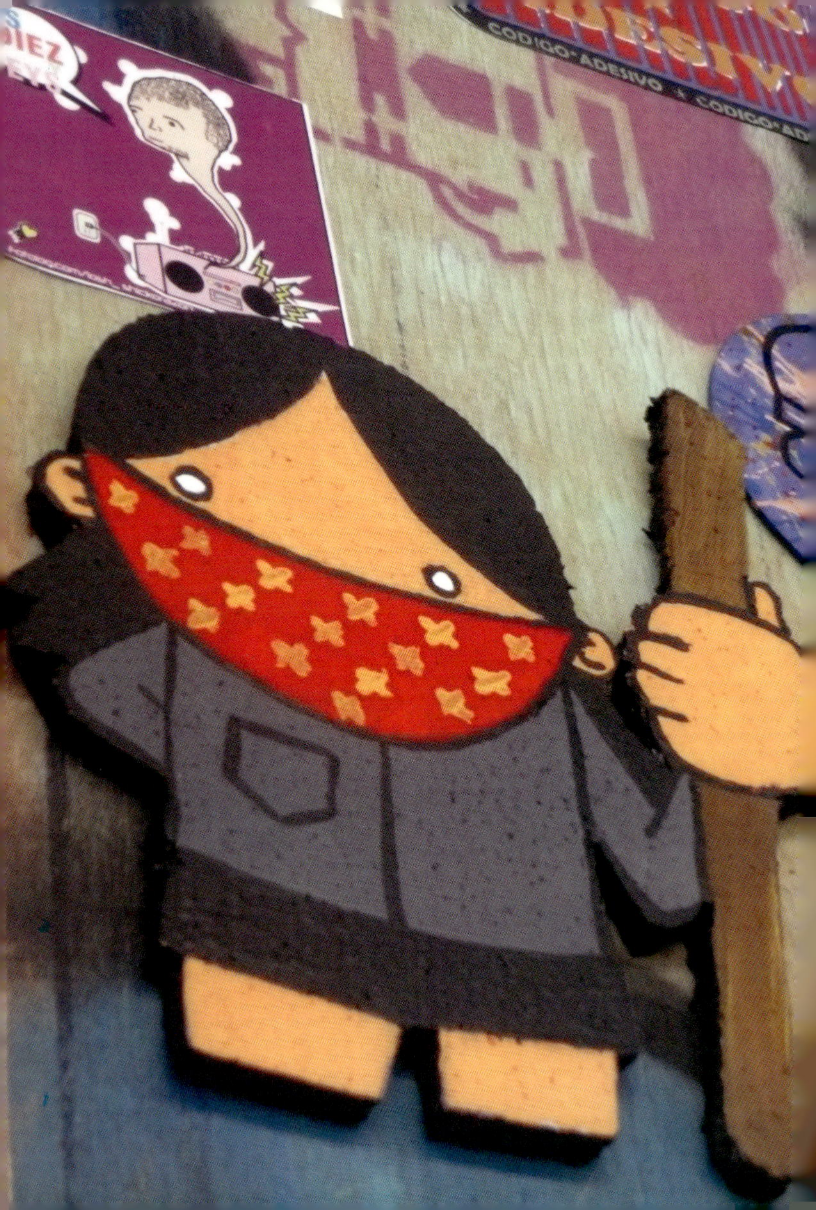
DIEZ
CODIGO ADESIVO
CODIGO ADESIVO

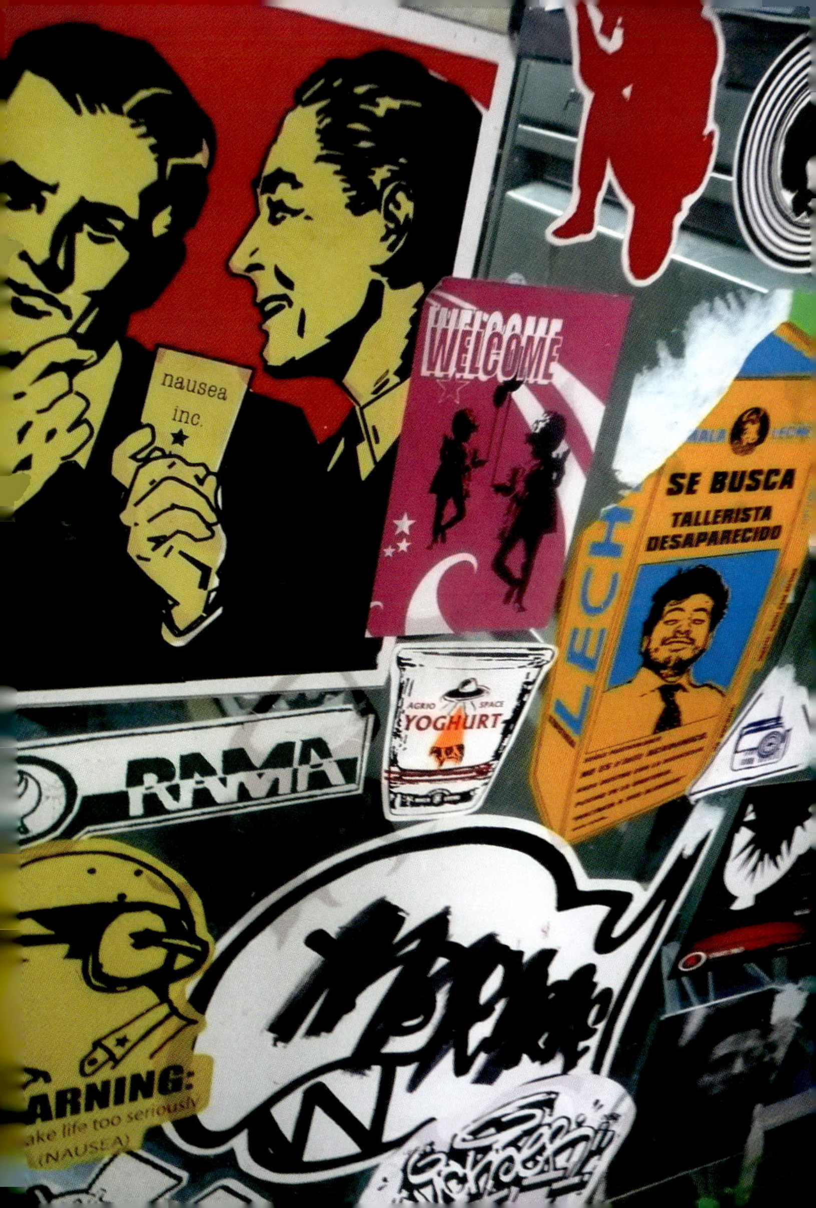
nausea
inc.
WELCOME
SE BUSCA
TALLERISTA
DESAPARECIDO
LECH
AGRIO
SPACE
YOGHURT
RAMA
ARNING:
ake life too seriously
(NAUSEA)

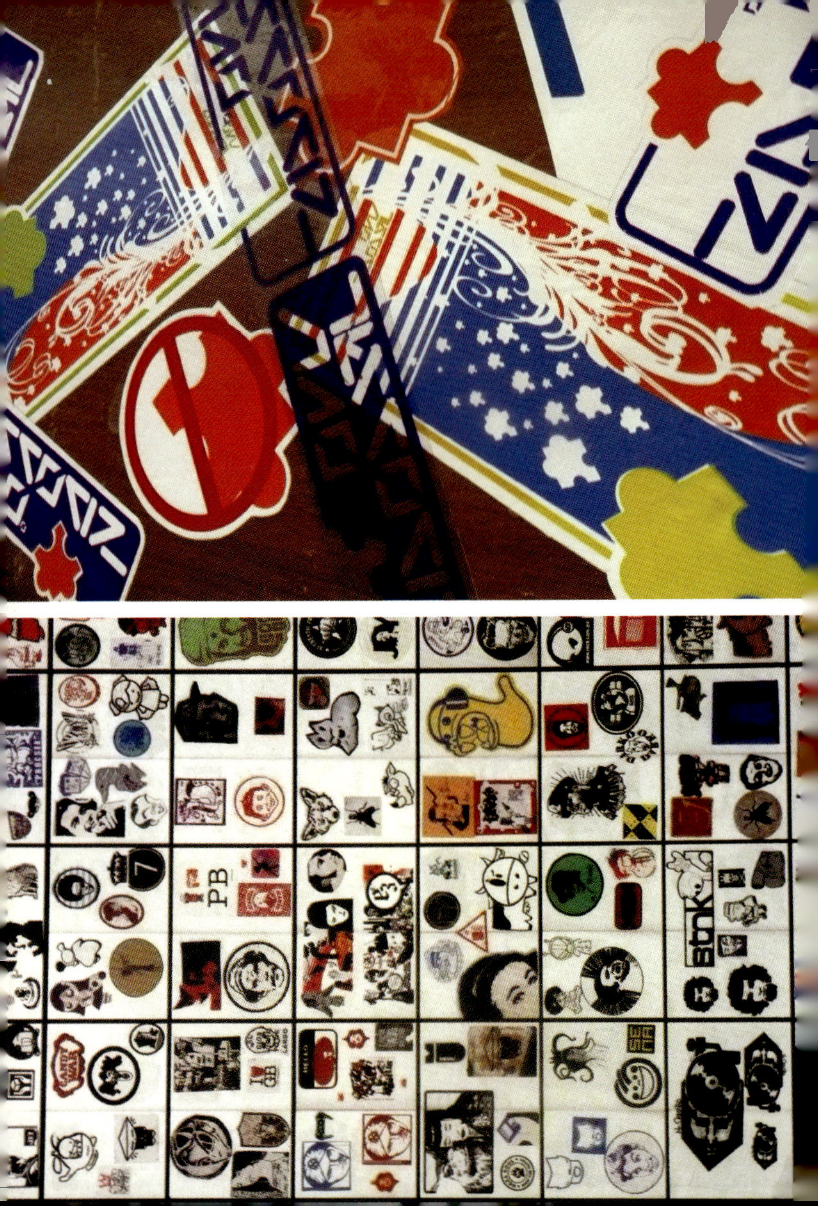

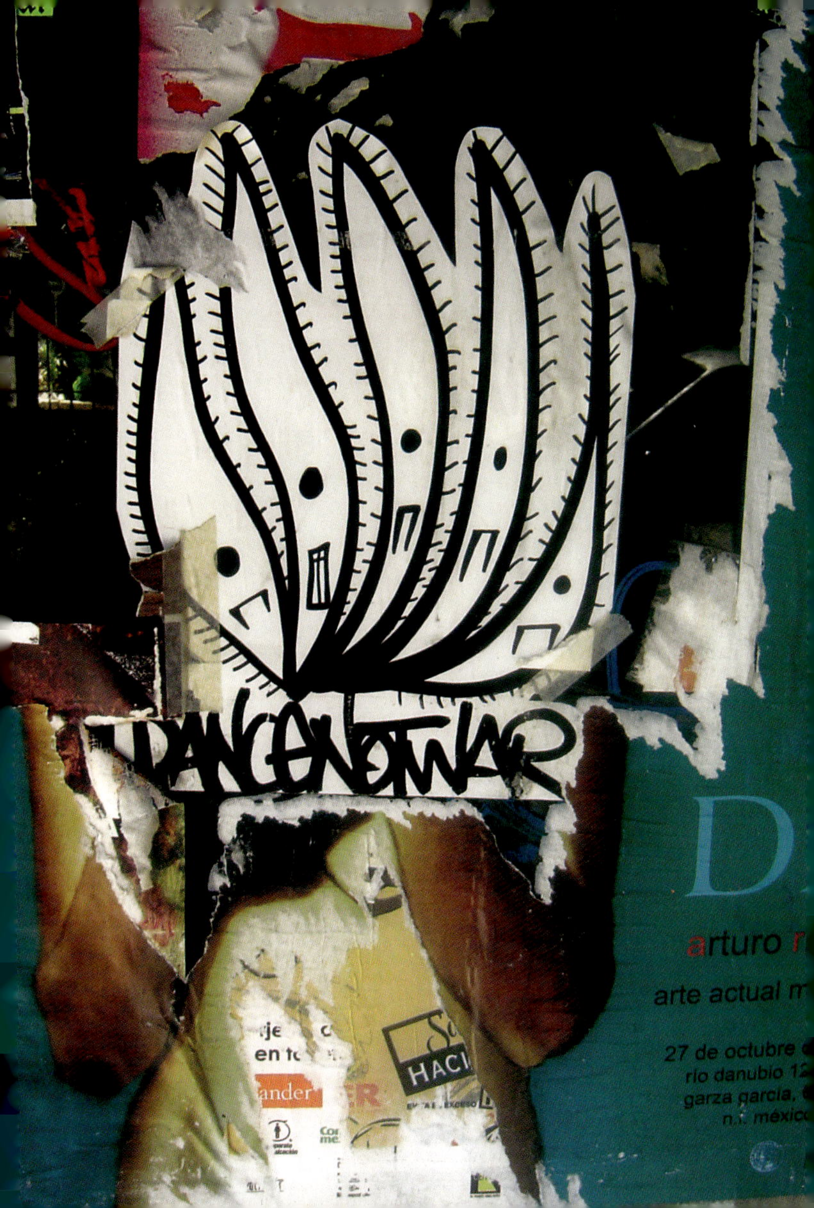
DANCENOTWAR
arturo
arte actual
27 de octubre
río danubio
garza garcía,
n.l. méxico

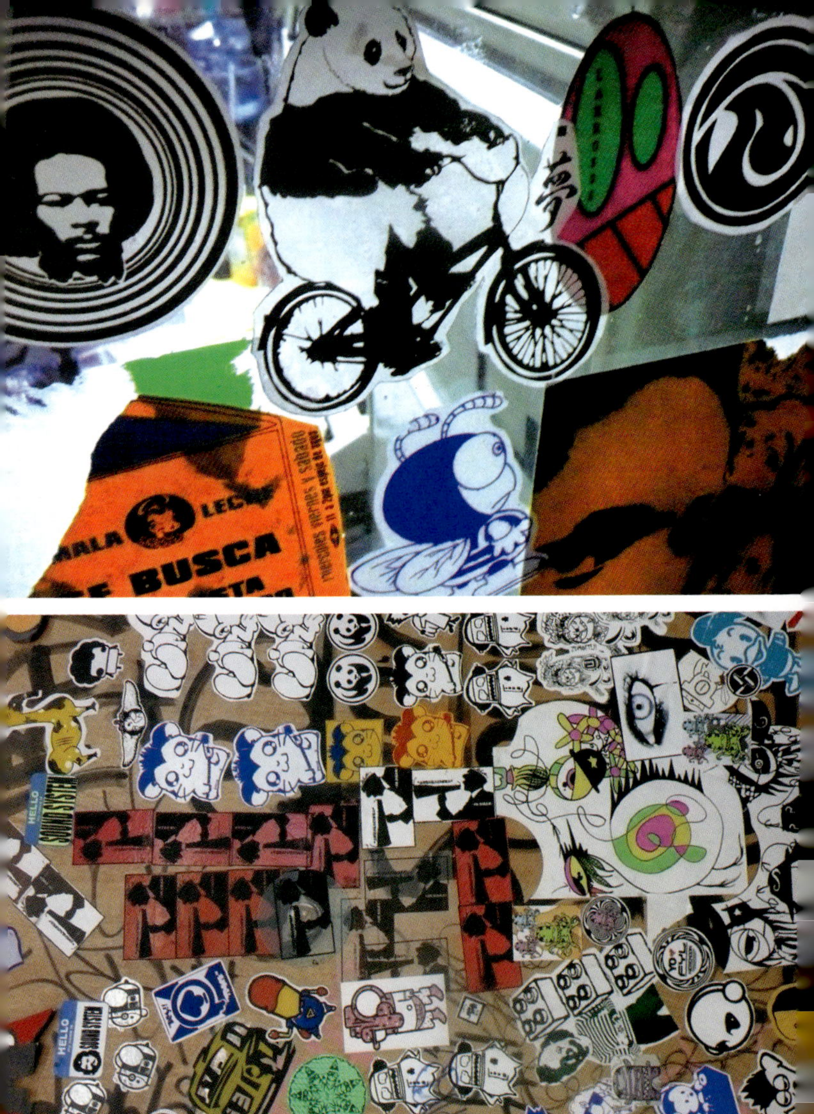
BUSCA
HELLO
SOUND SYSTEM
HELLO
SOUND SYSTEM

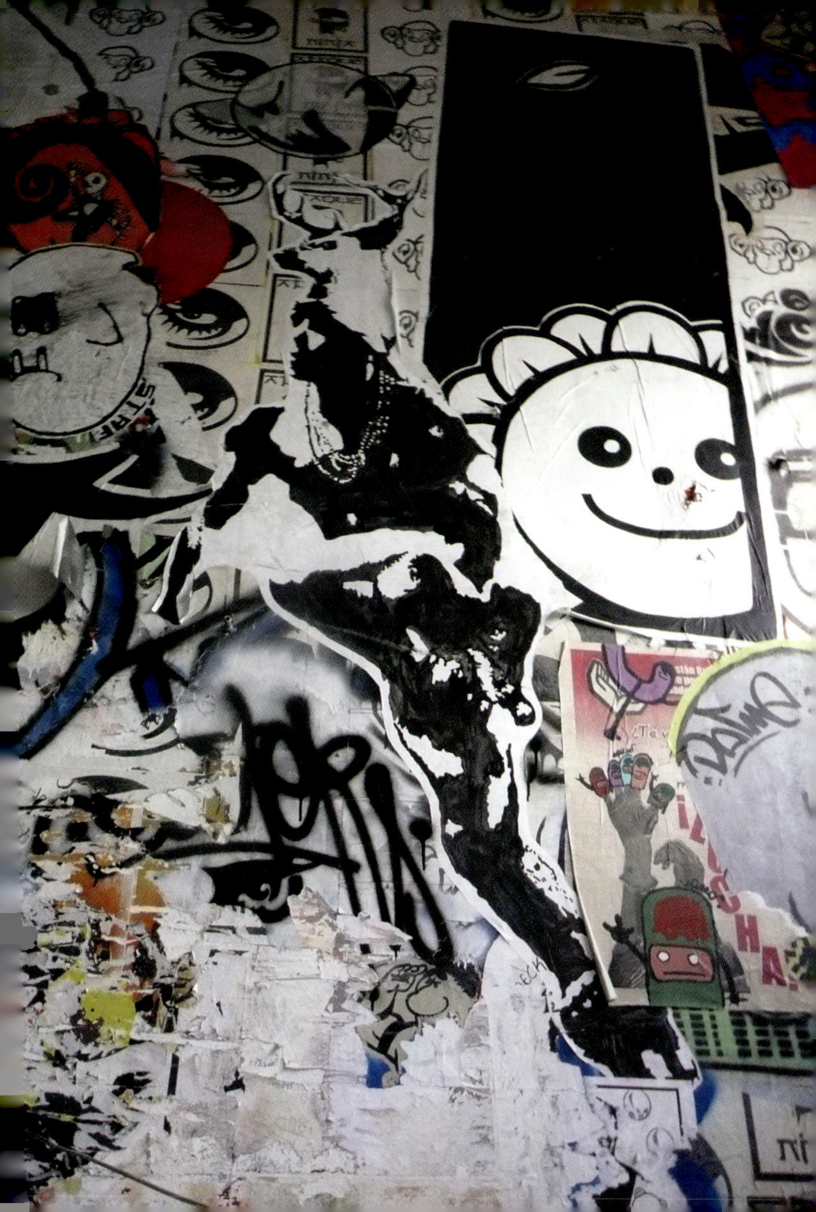

¡LUCHA!

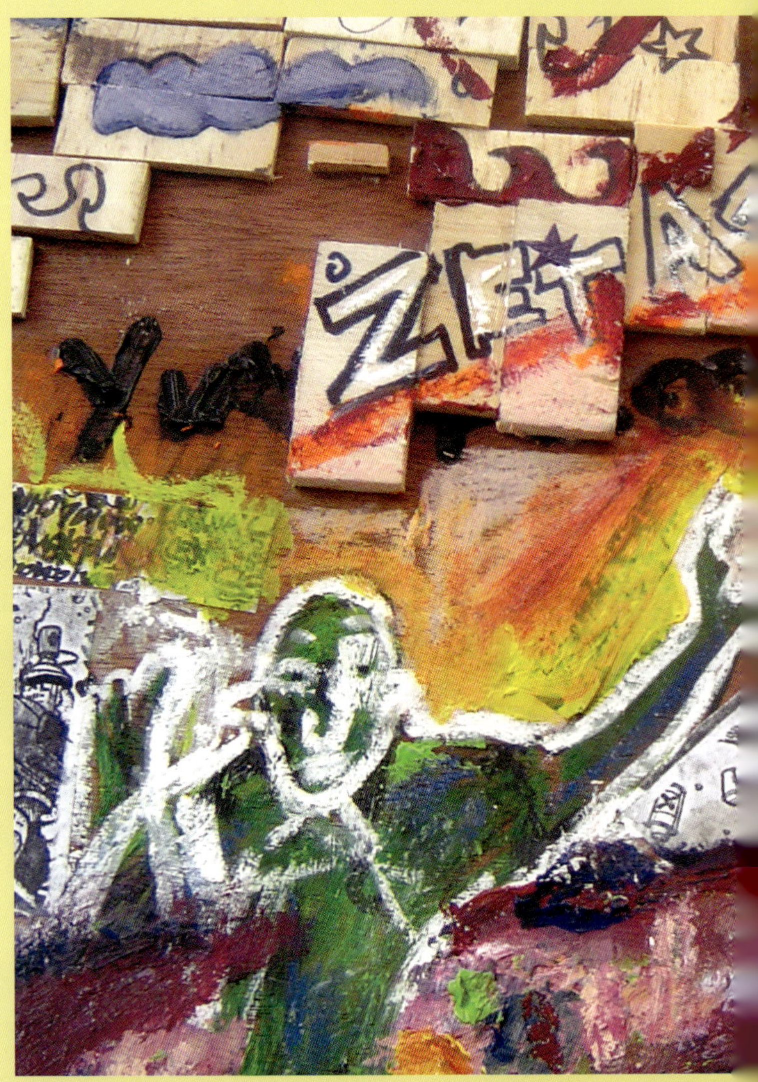

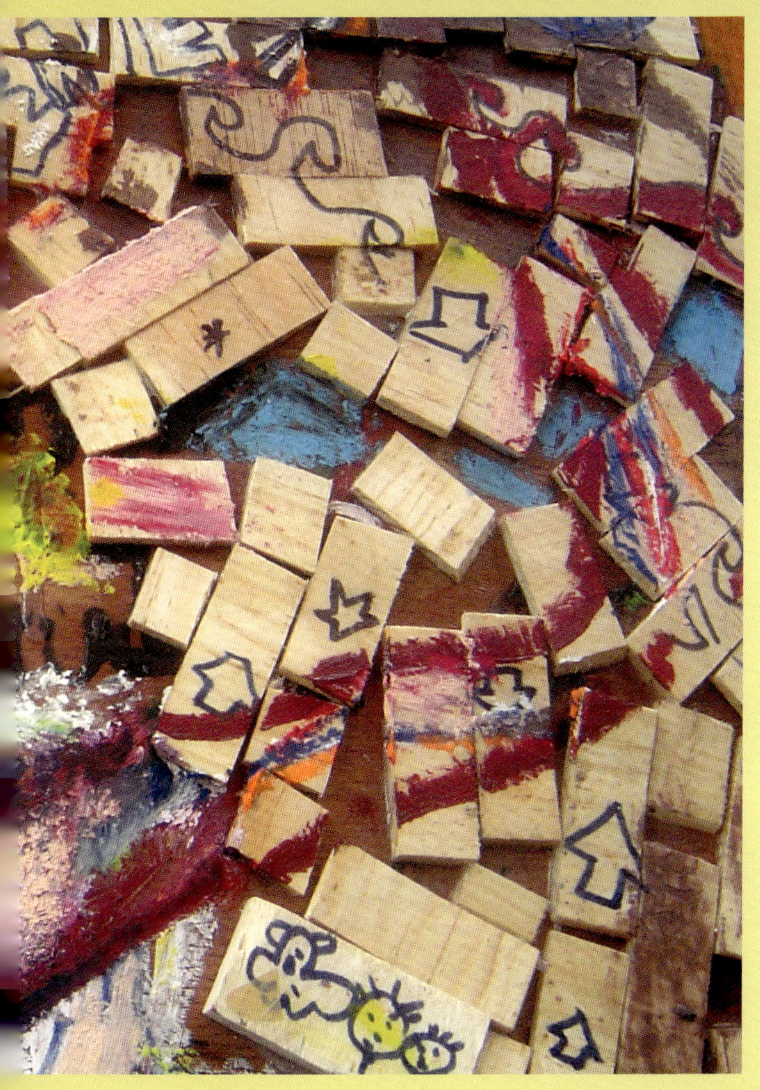

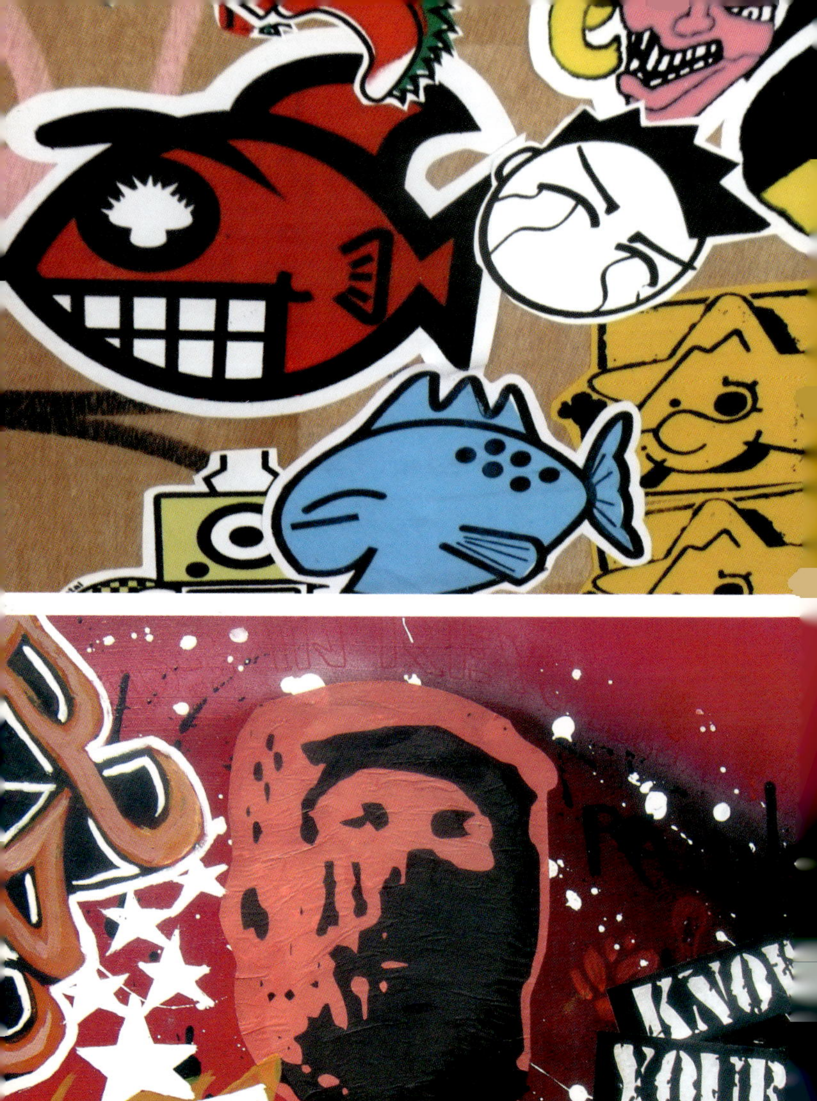
YOUR

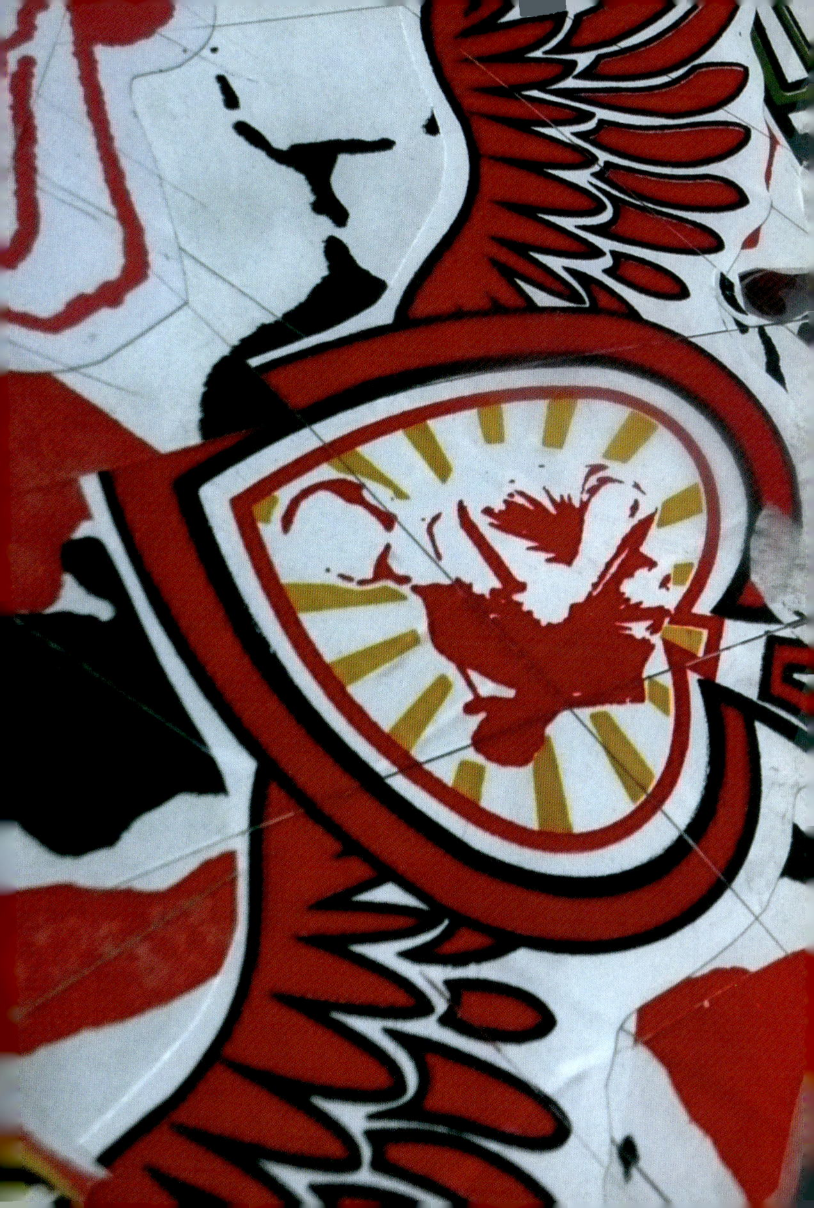

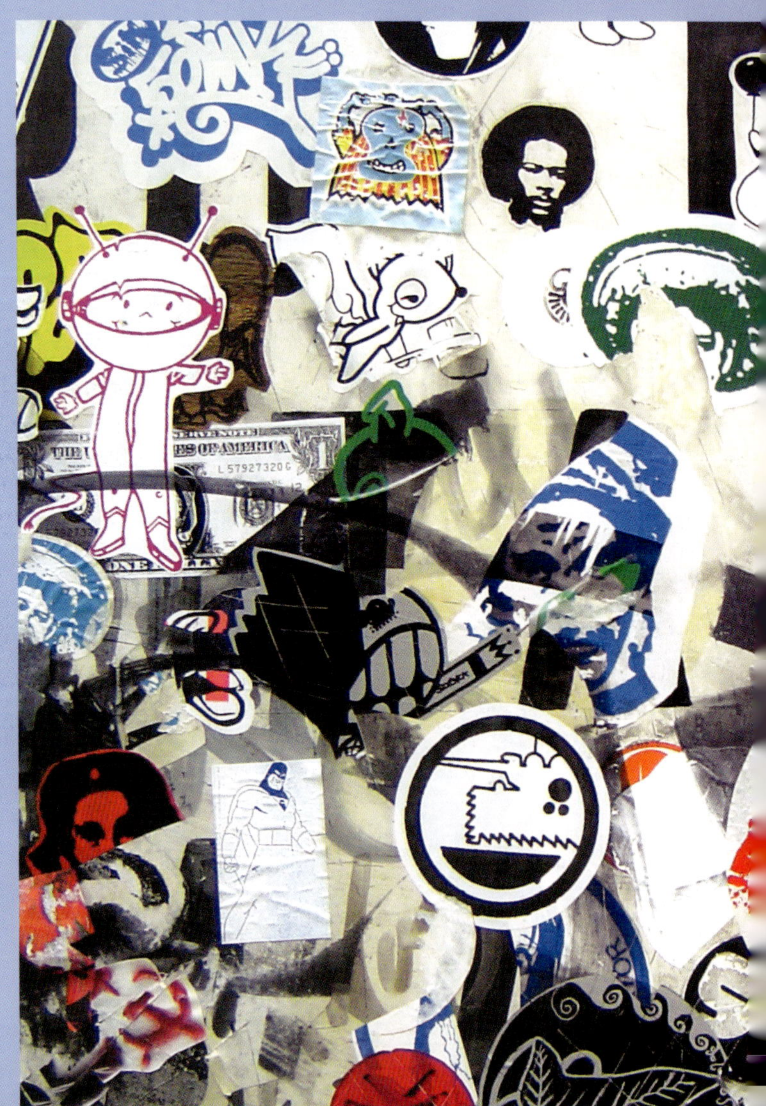

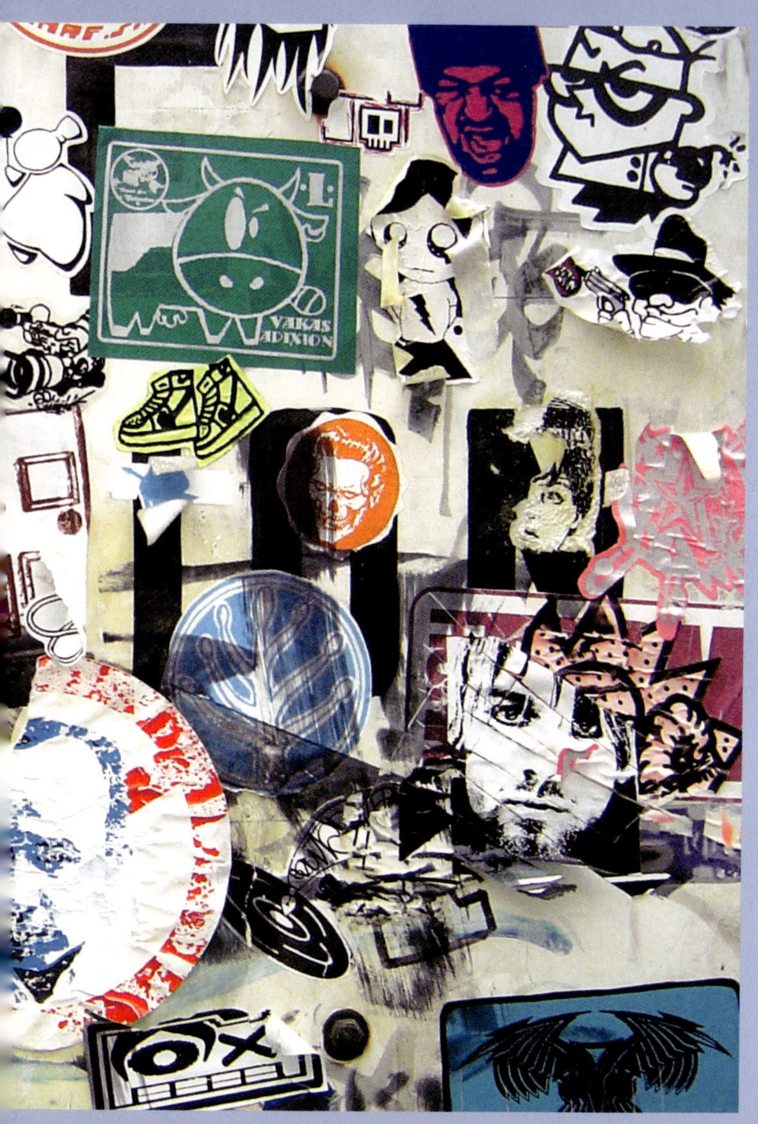
VAKAS
ADIXION

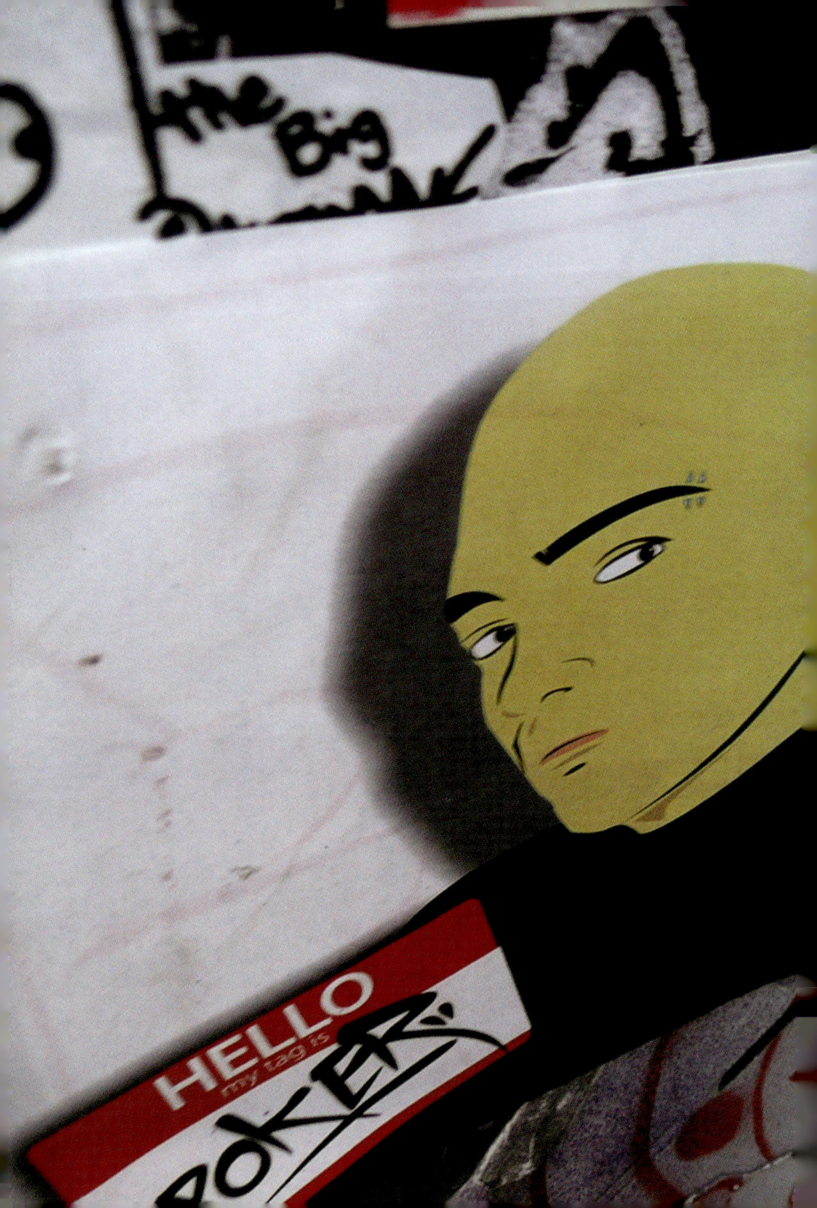
the Big
HELLO
my tag is

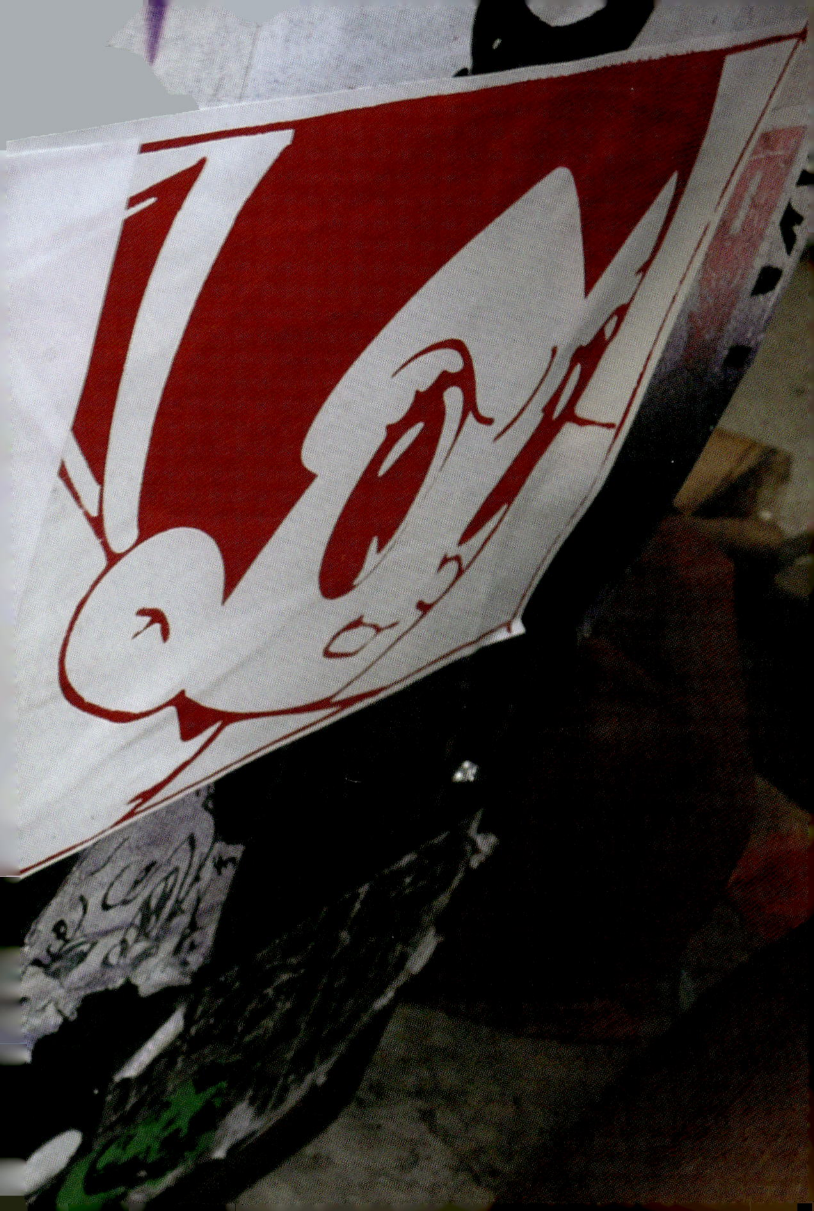

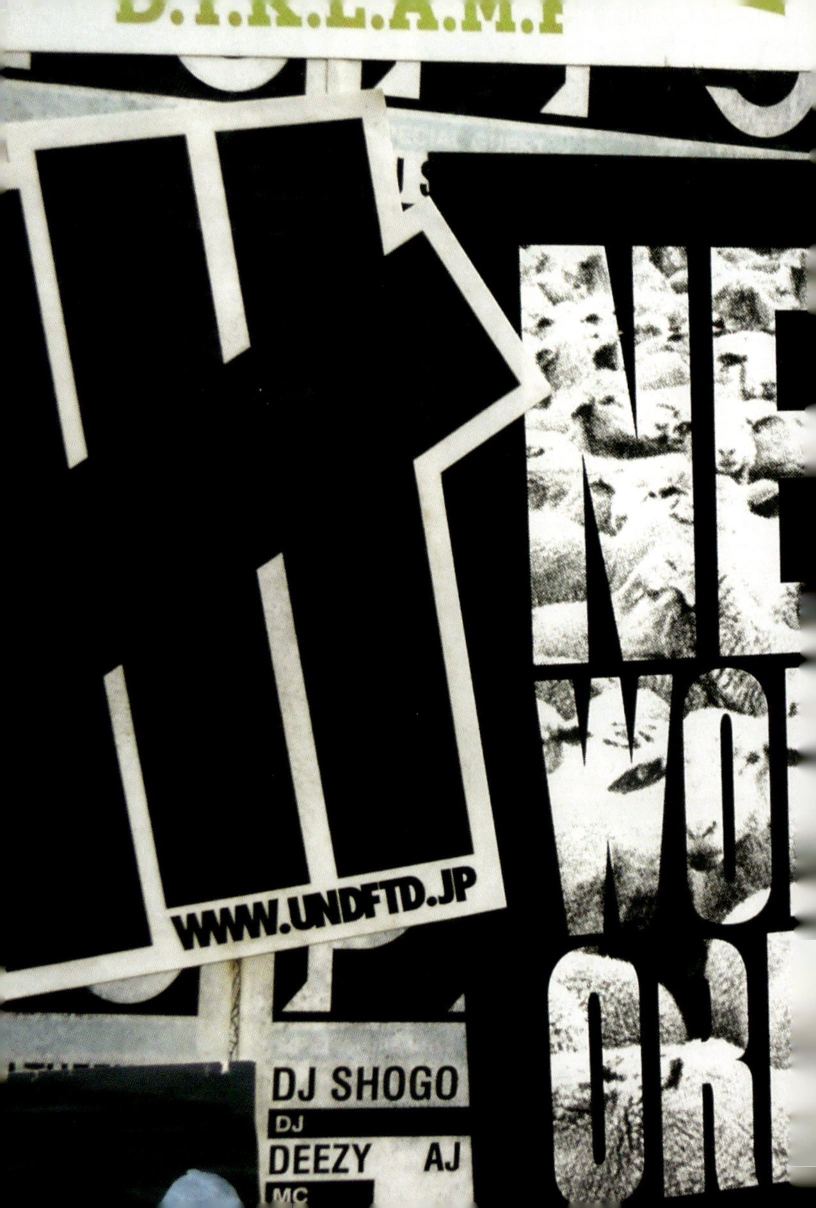
D.I.R.L.A.M.I
WWW.UNDFTD.JP
DJ SHOGO
DJ
DEEZY AJ
MC

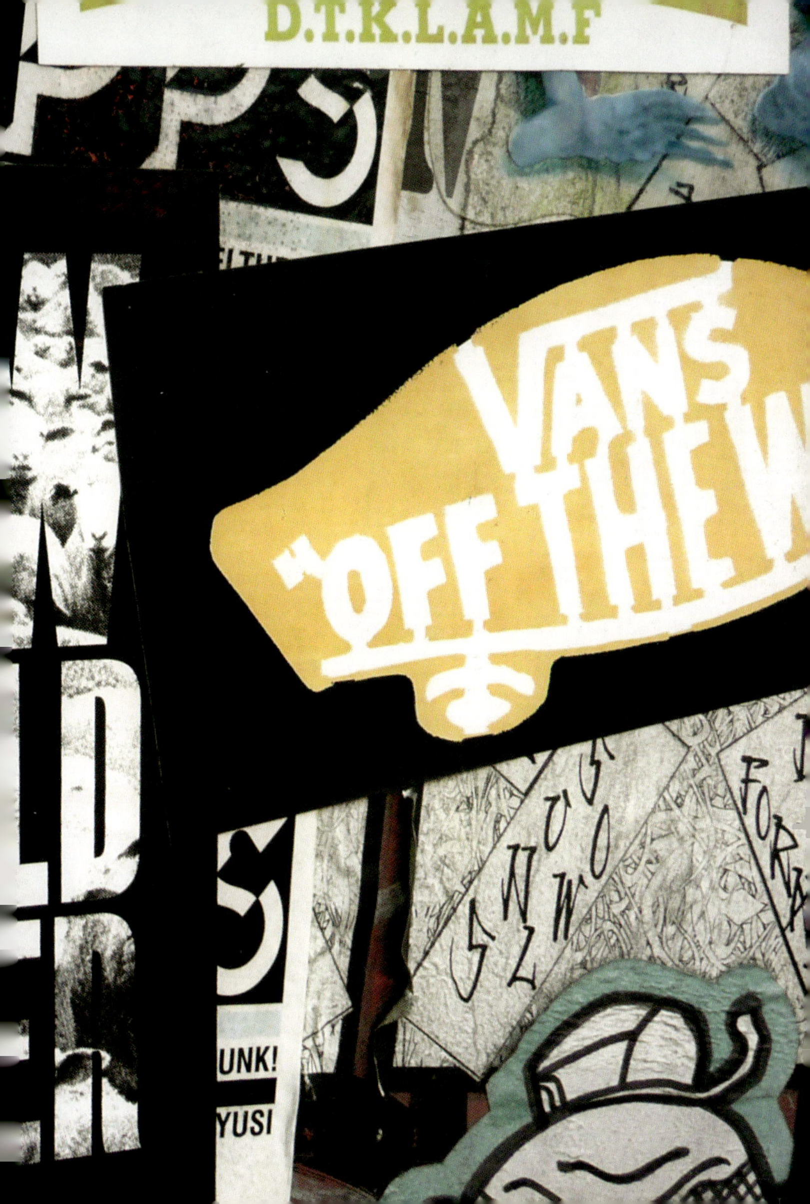
D.T.K.L.A.M.F
VANS
"OFF THE
UNK!
YUSI

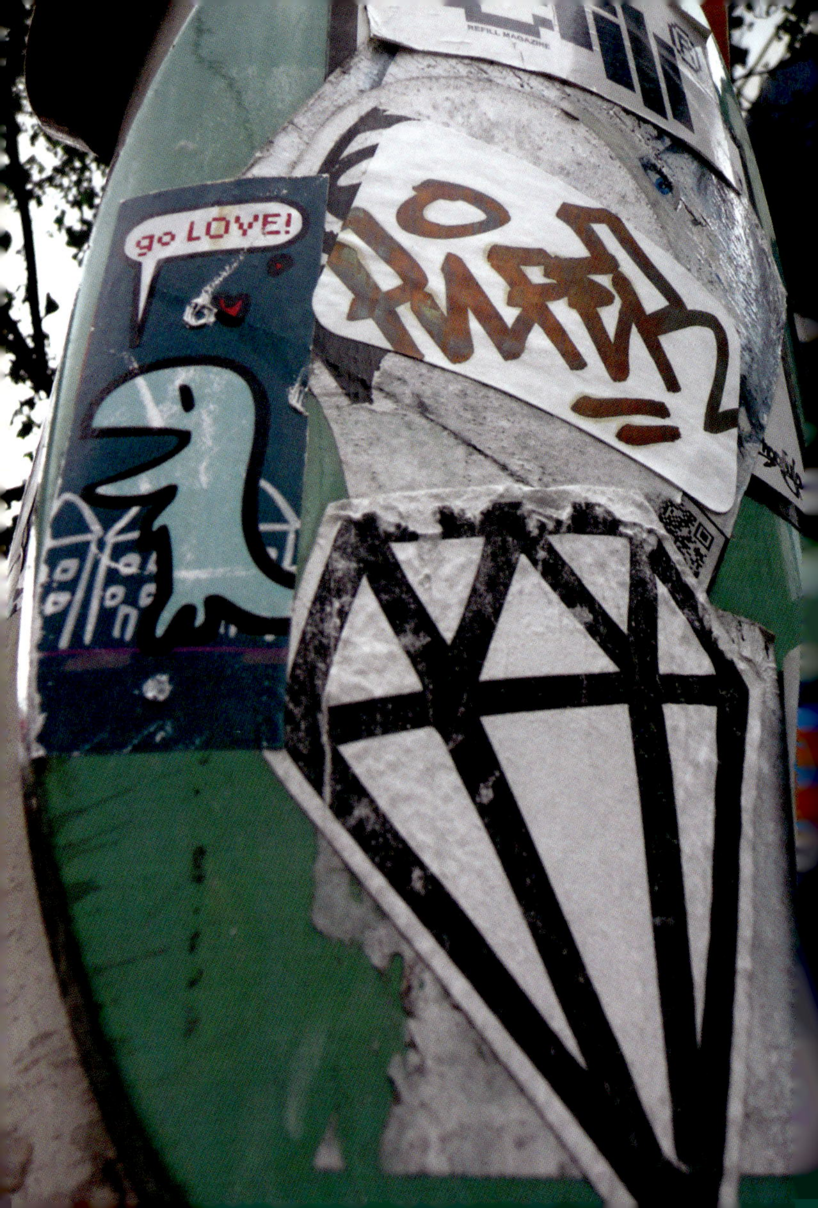
REFILL MAGAZINE
go LOVE!

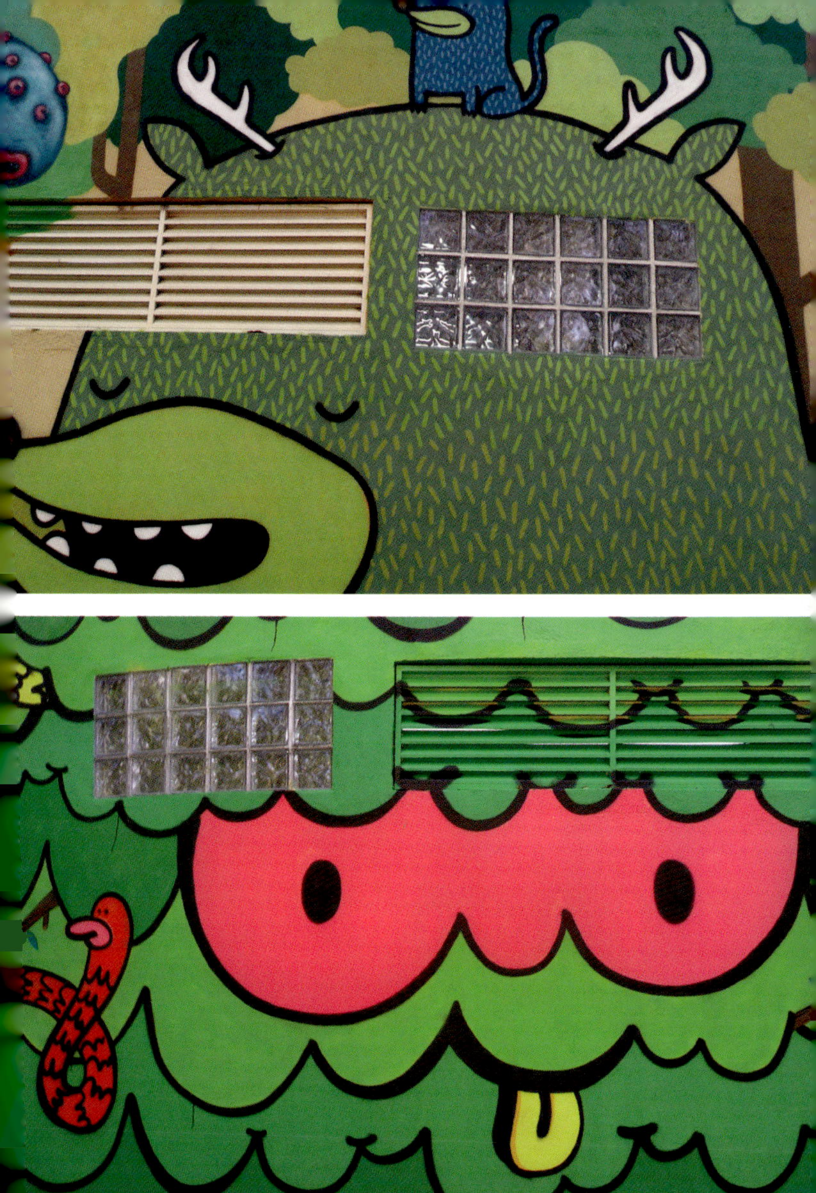

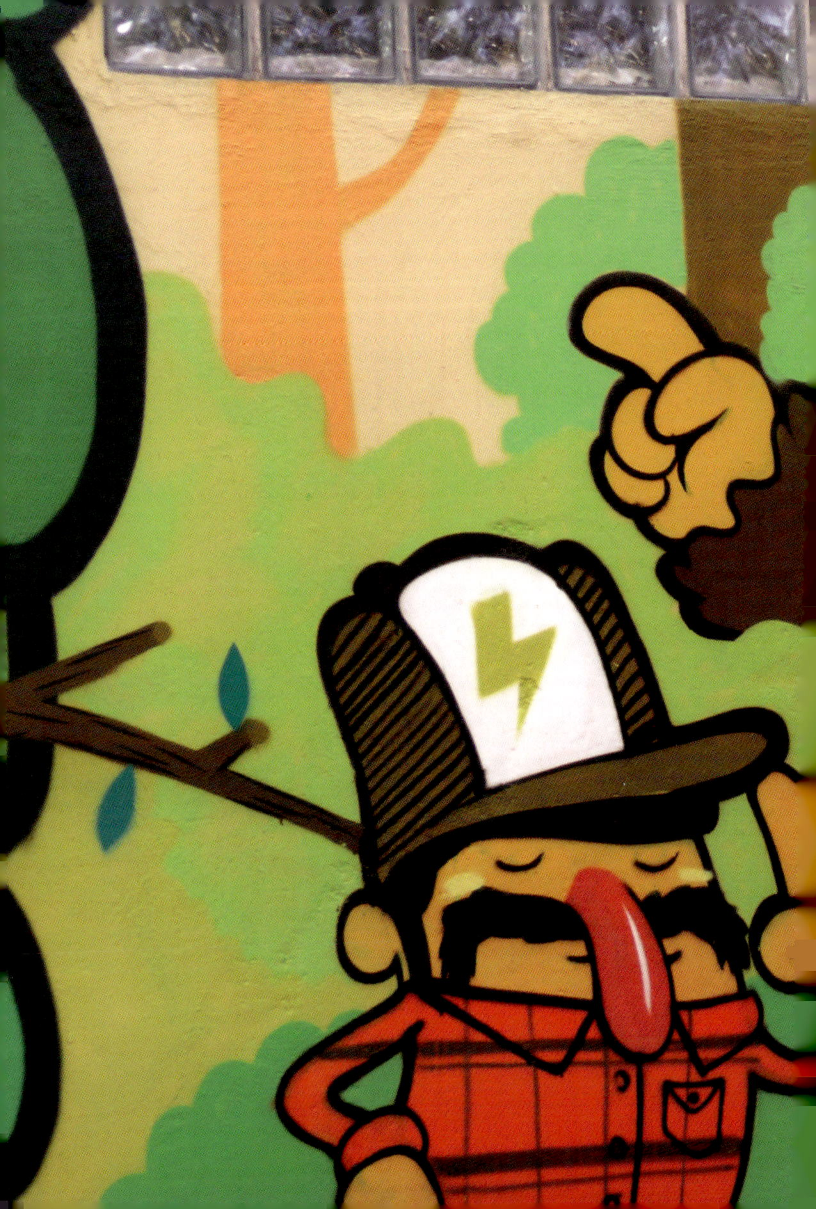

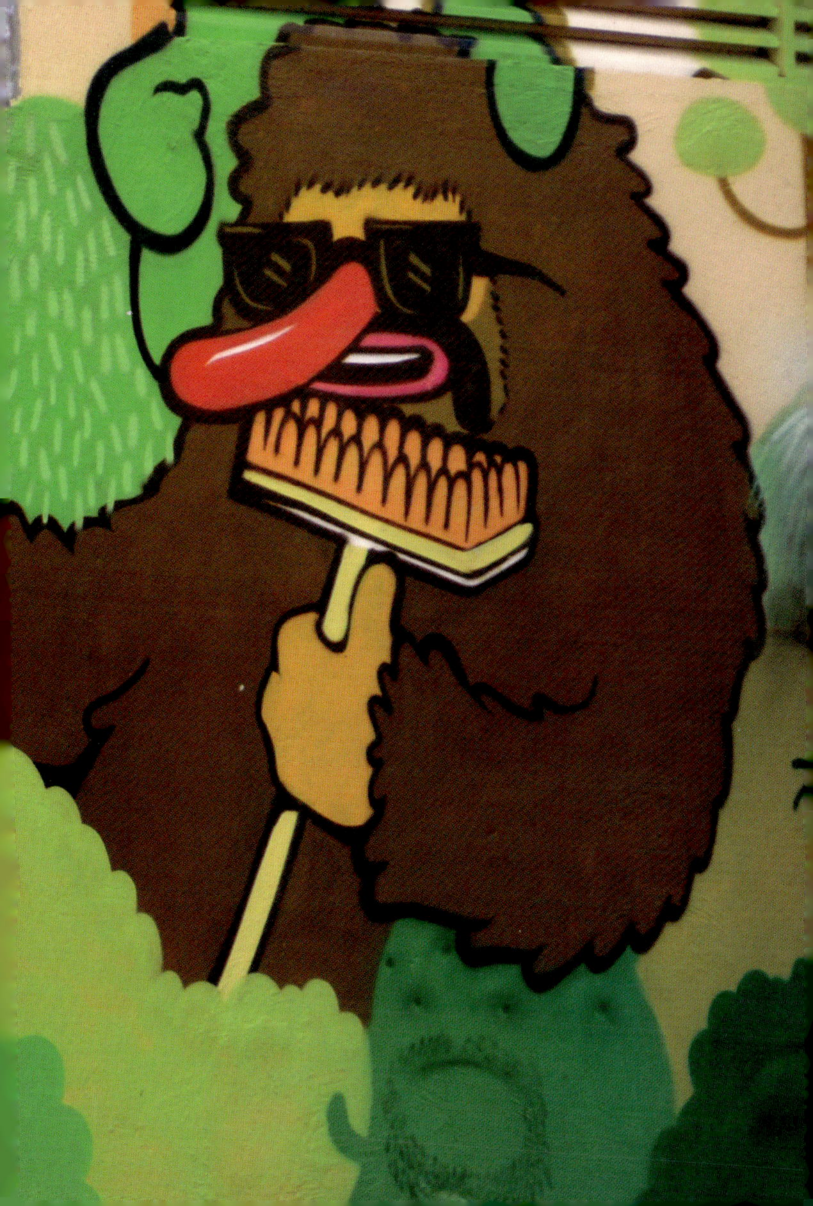

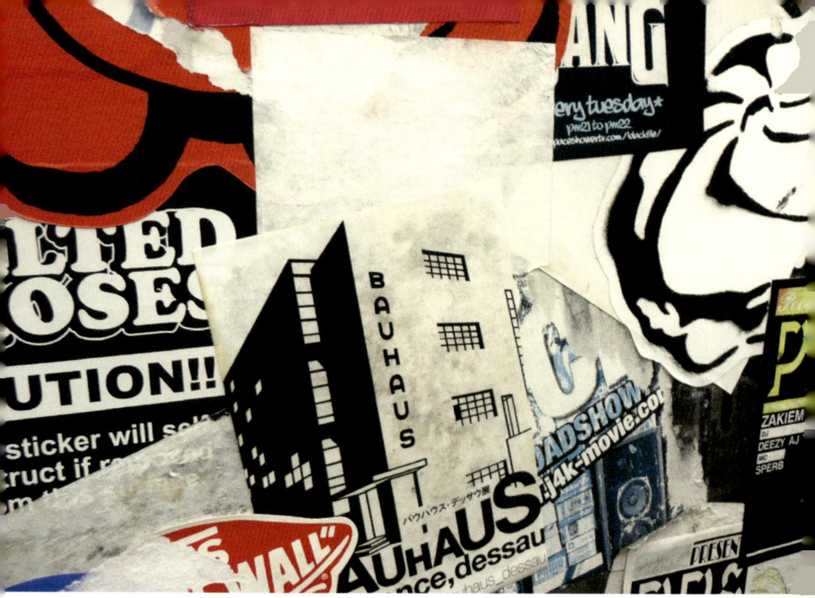

ANG
ery tuesday*
pm21 to pm22
LTED
OSES
UTION!!
sticker will se
truct if re
BAUHAUS
バウハウス・デッサウ展
AUHAUS
nce,dessau
OADSHOW
j4k-movie.co
ZAKIEM
DJ
DEEZY AJ
MC
SPERB
PRESEN
WALL
miss
mod
volcom
HUF
BIG
ANG

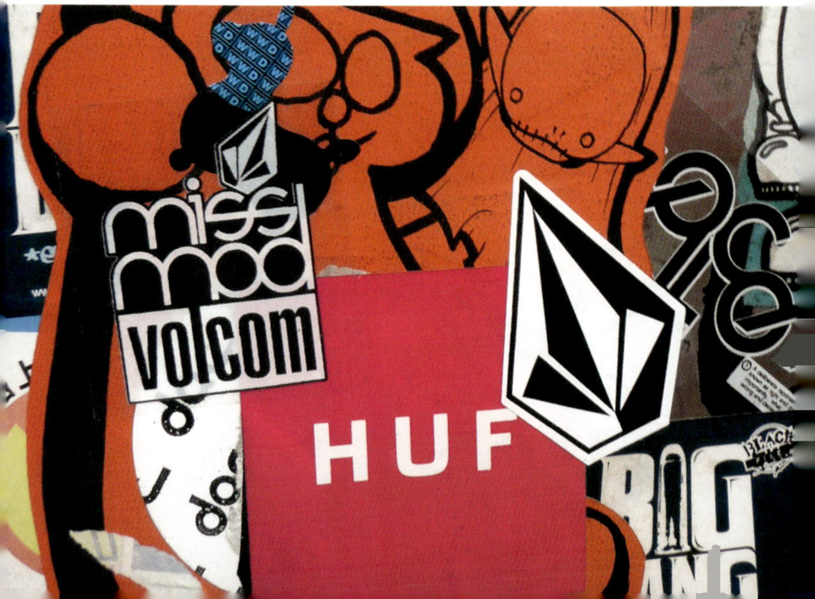

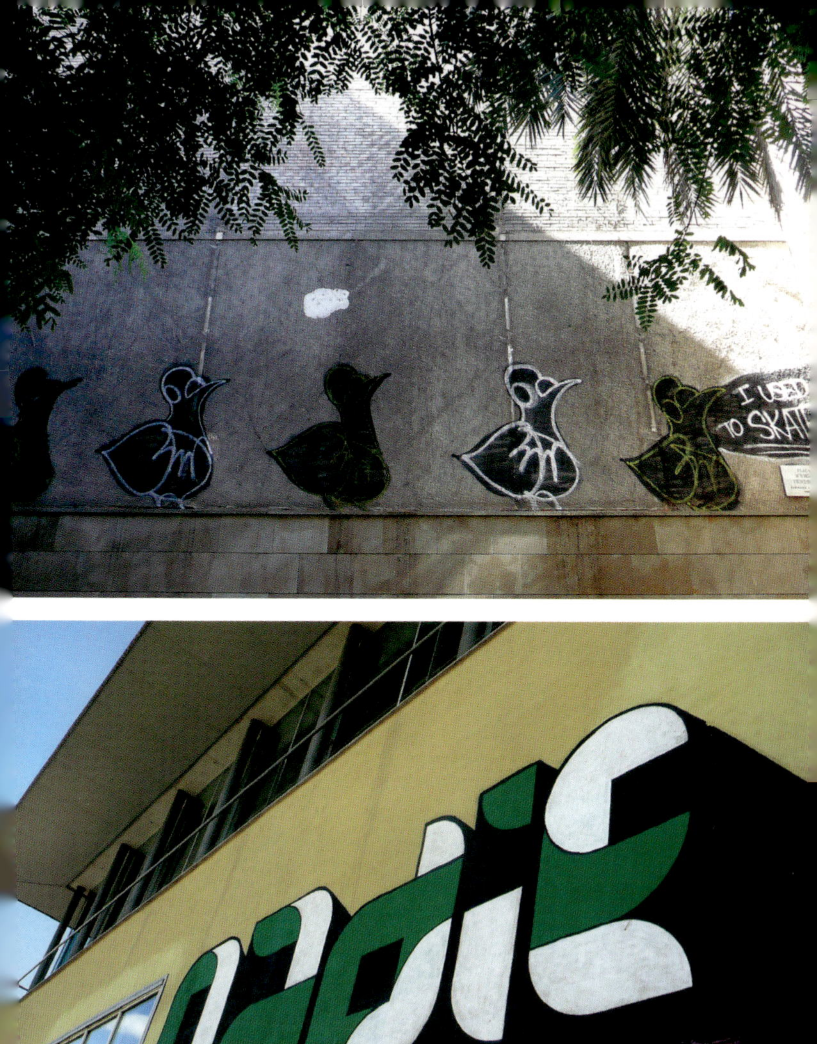

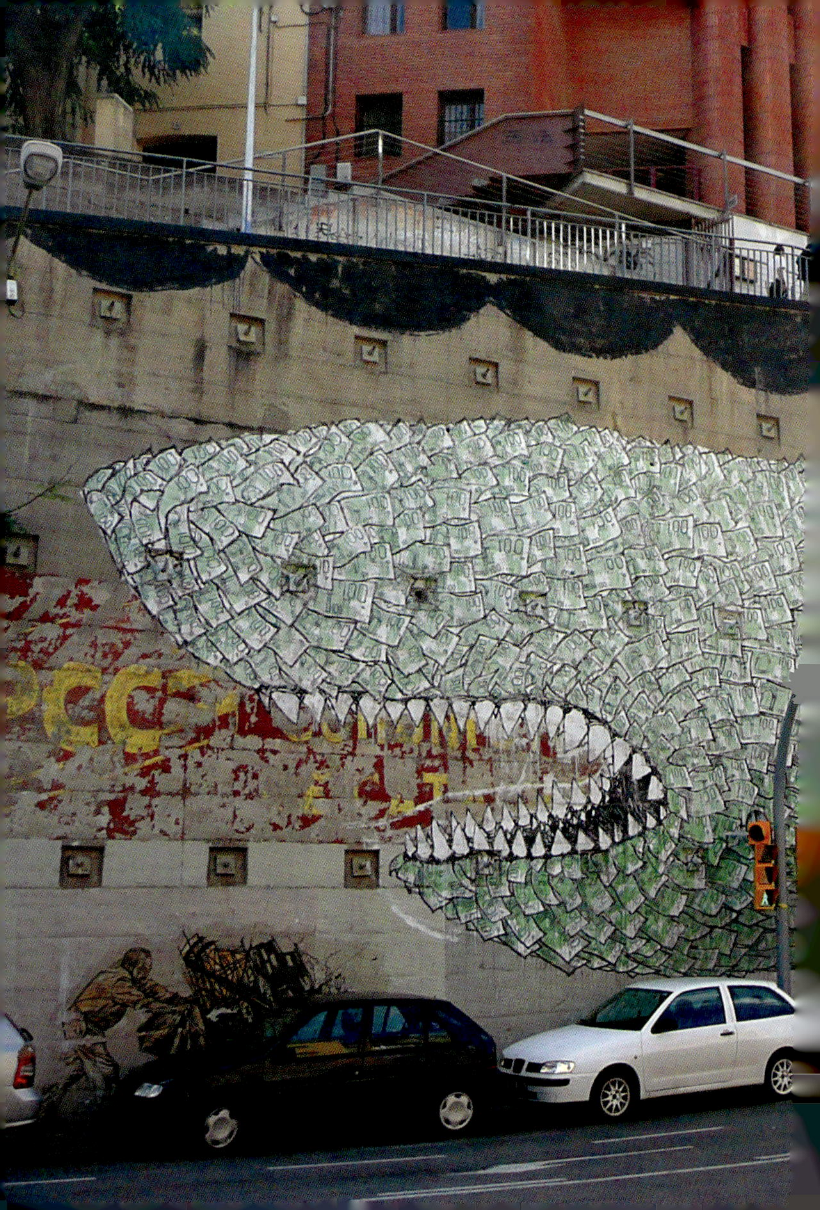

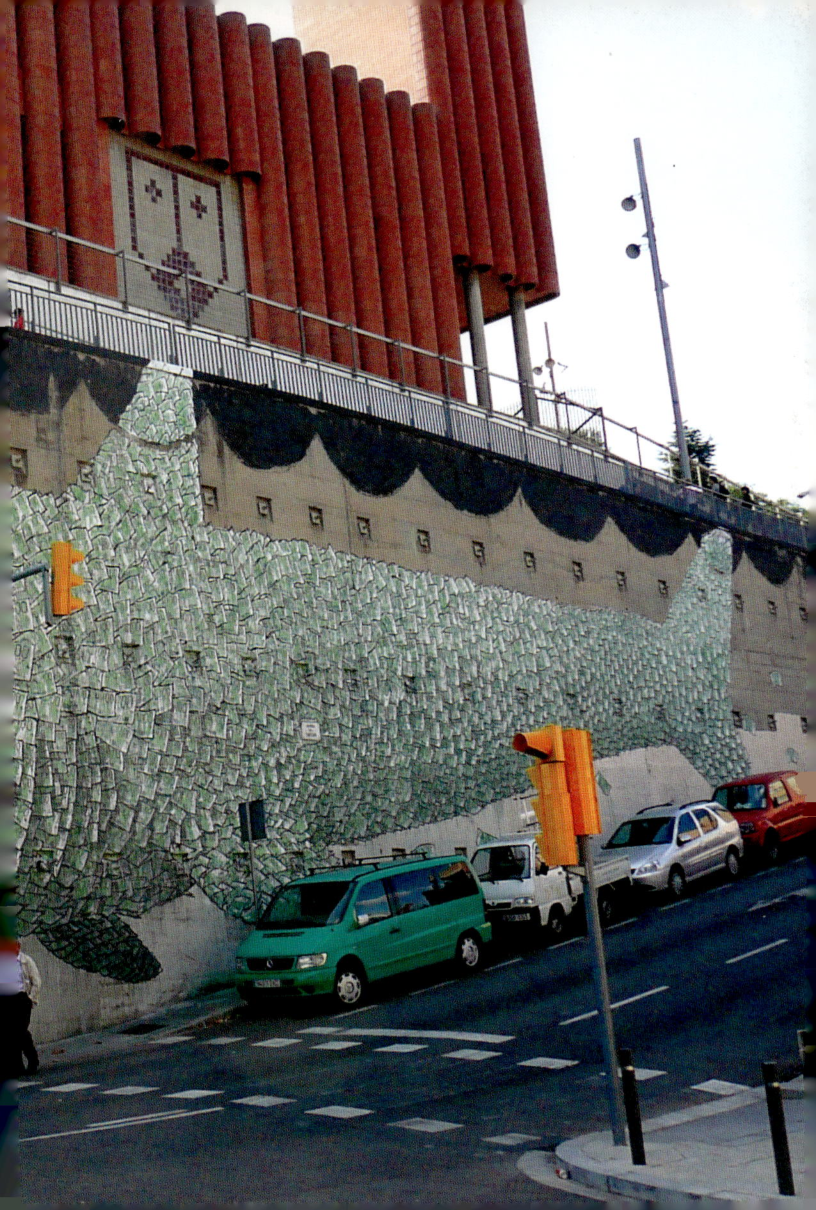

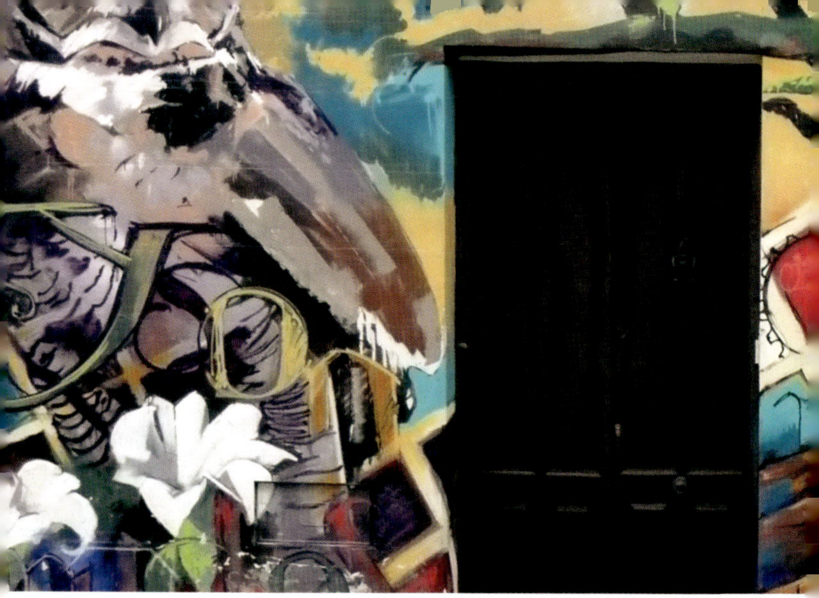

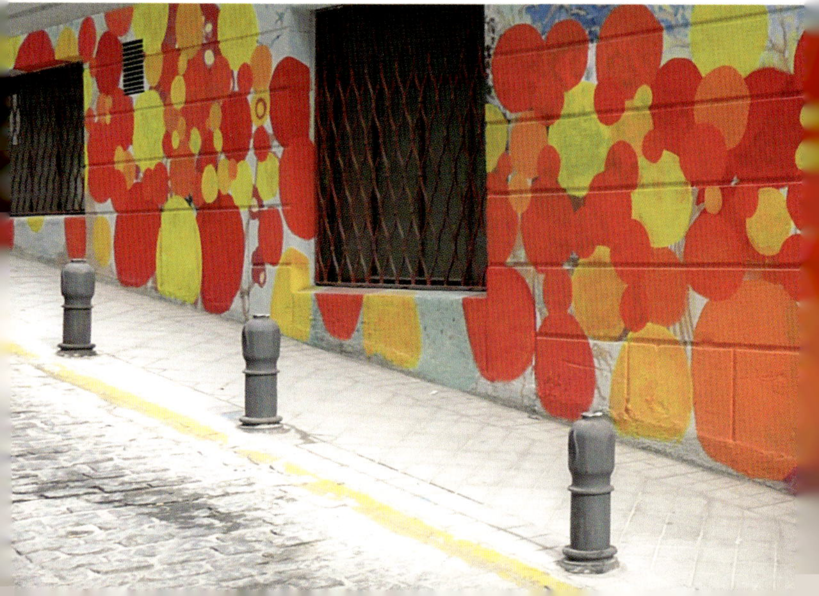

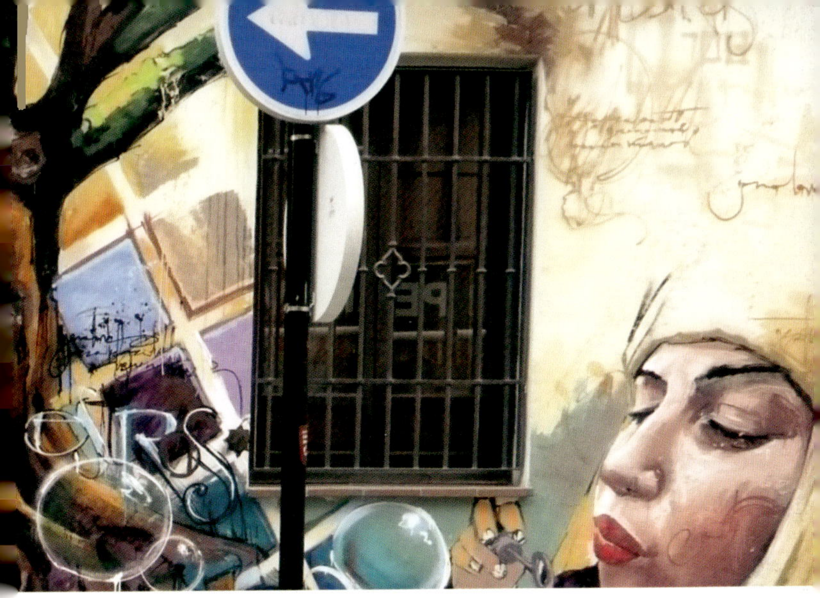

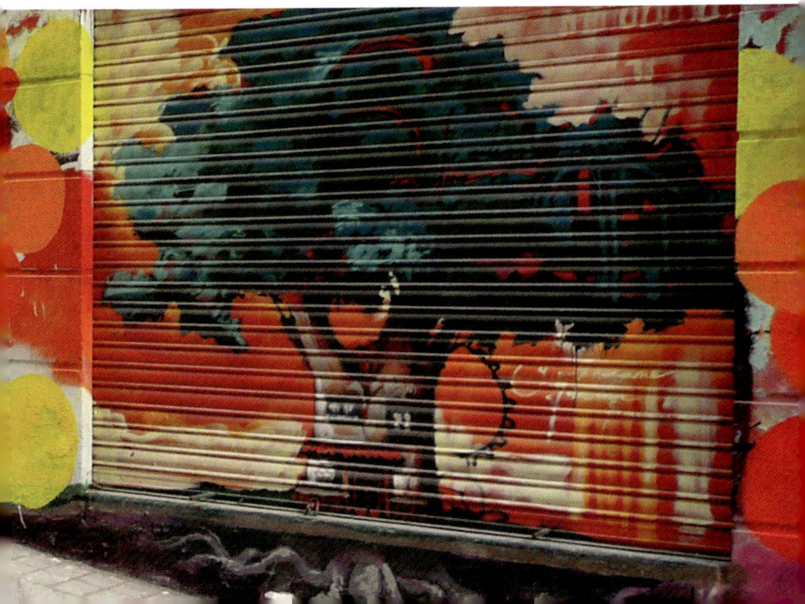

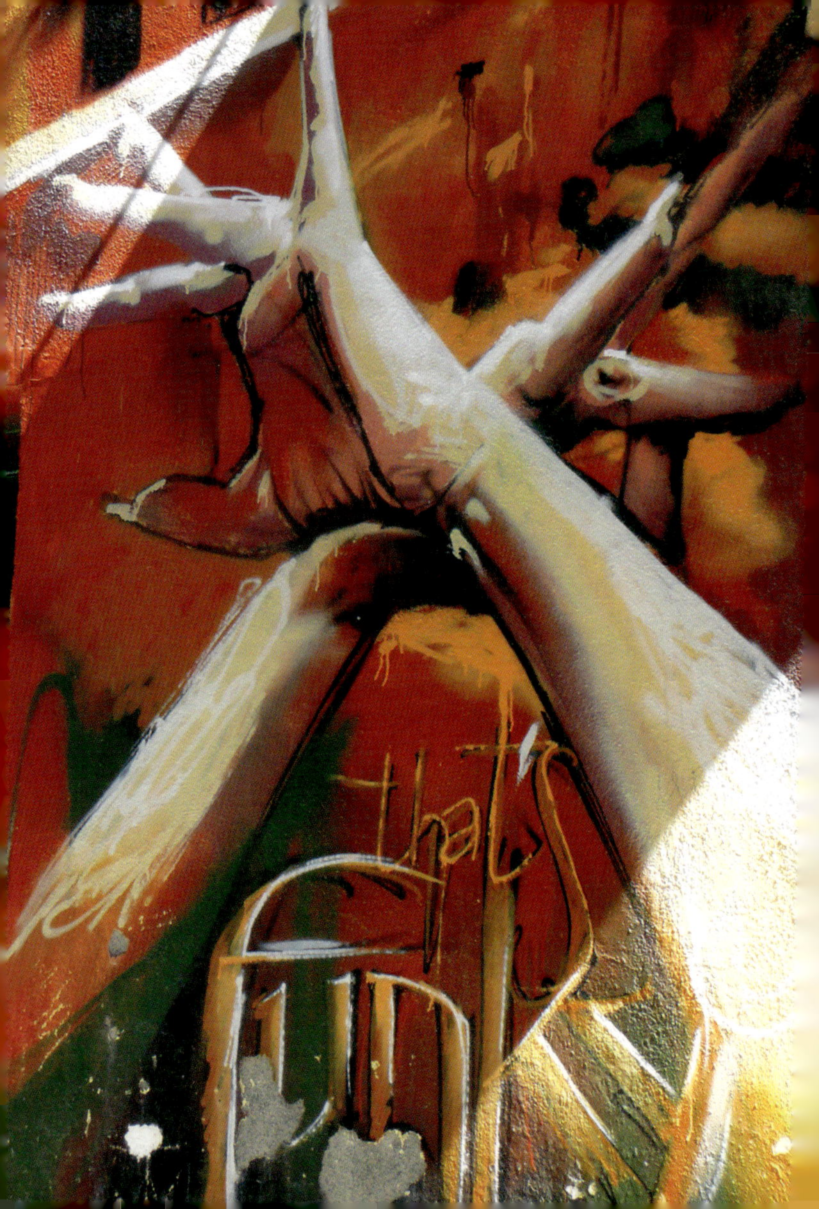
that's

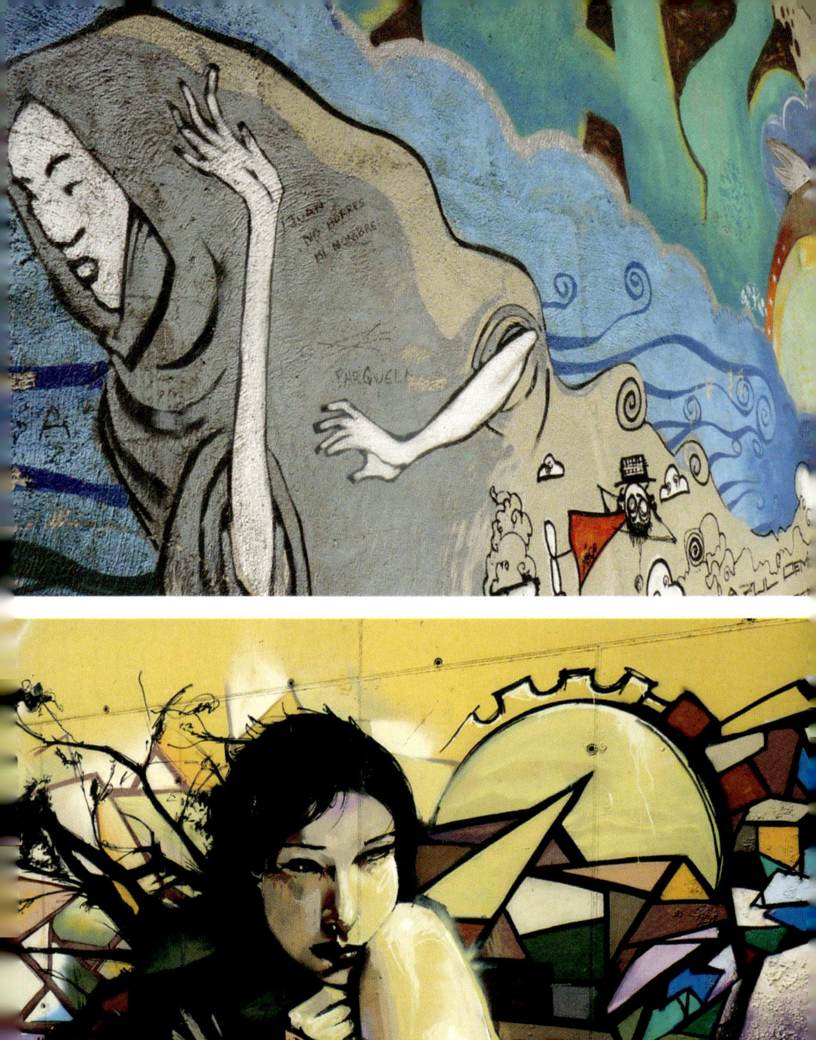
¡JUAN
NO BORRES
MI NOMBRE!
PARQUELA
SEGUIRA

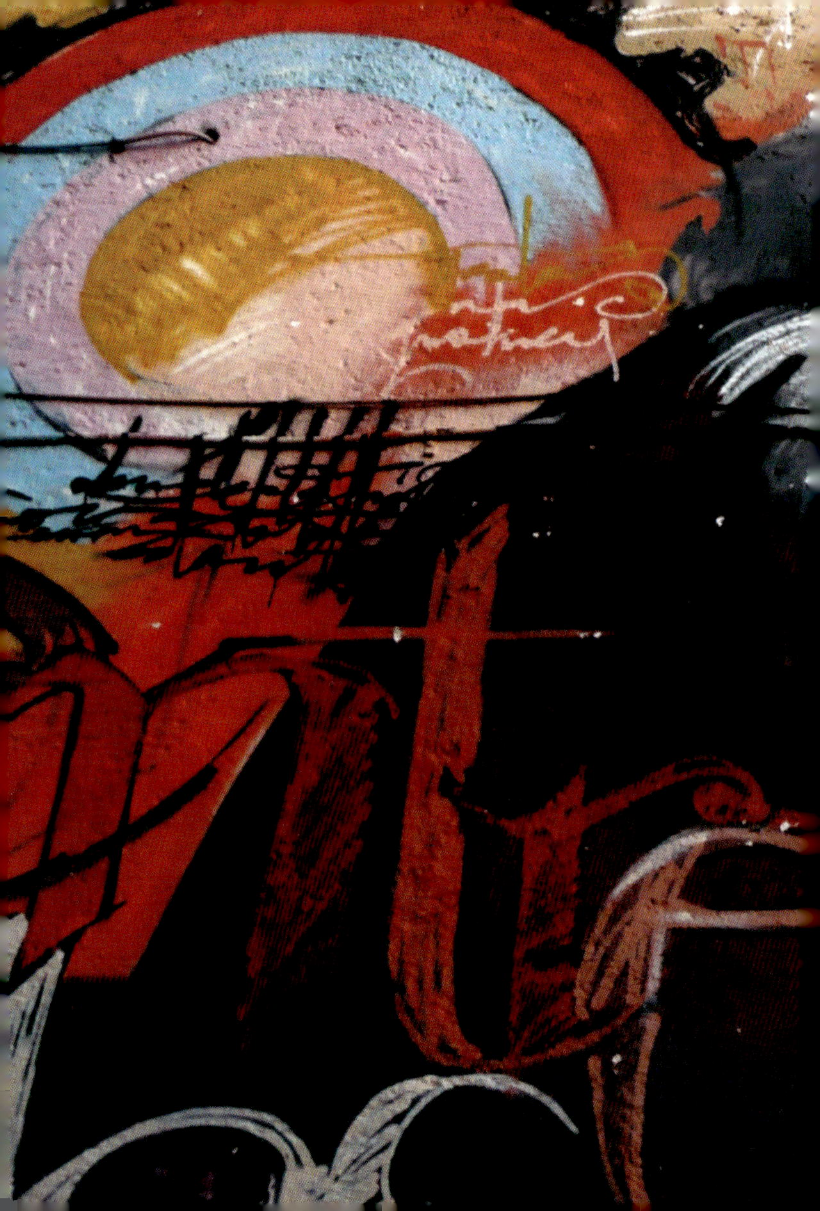

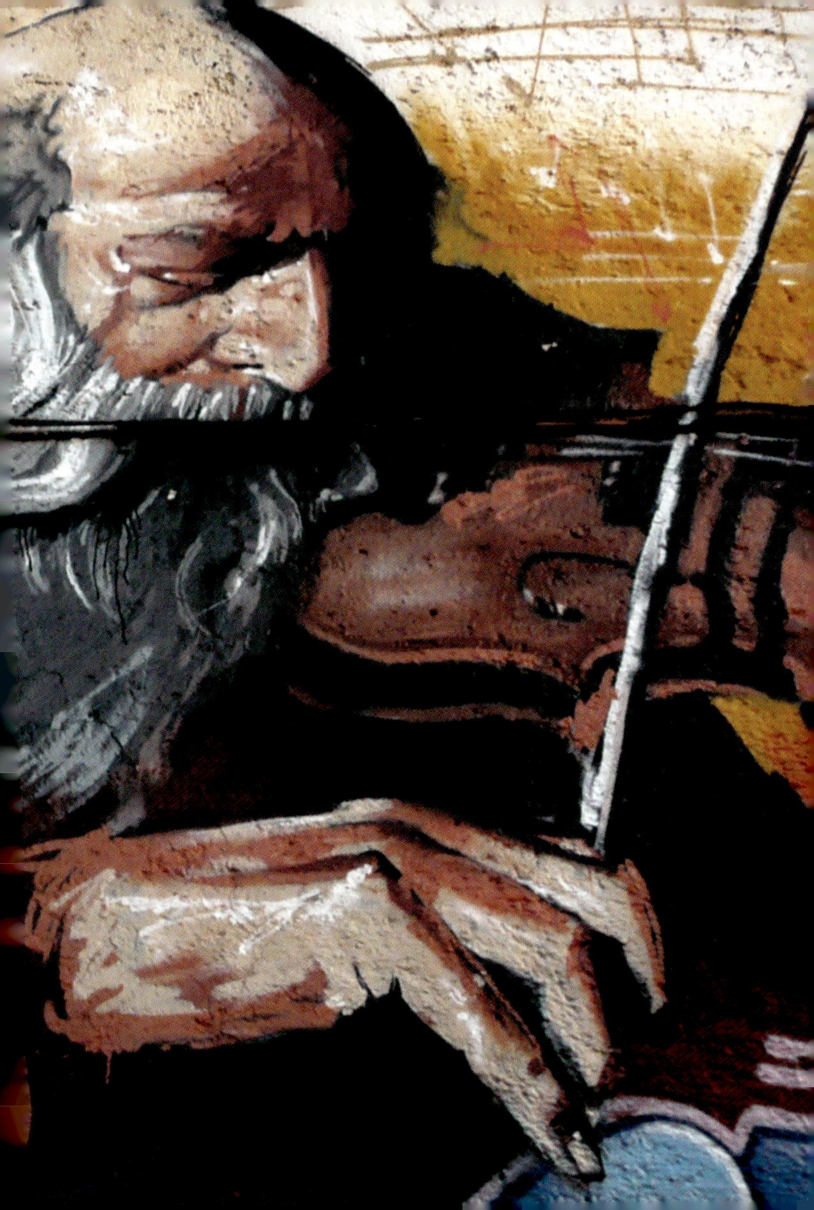

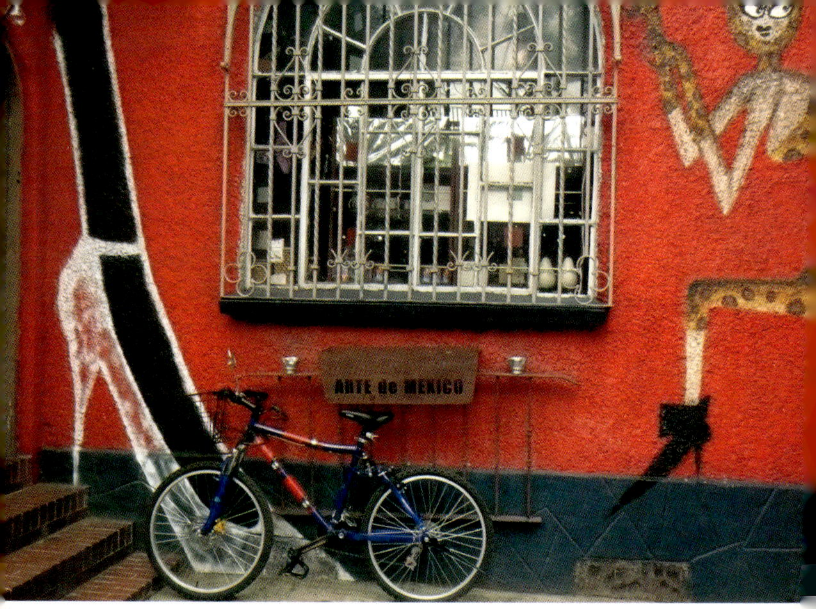

ARTE de MEXICO

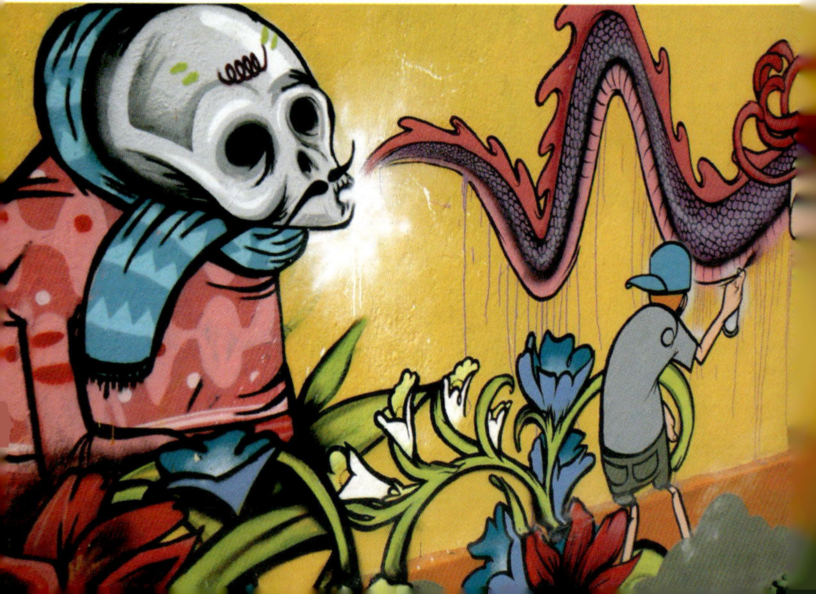

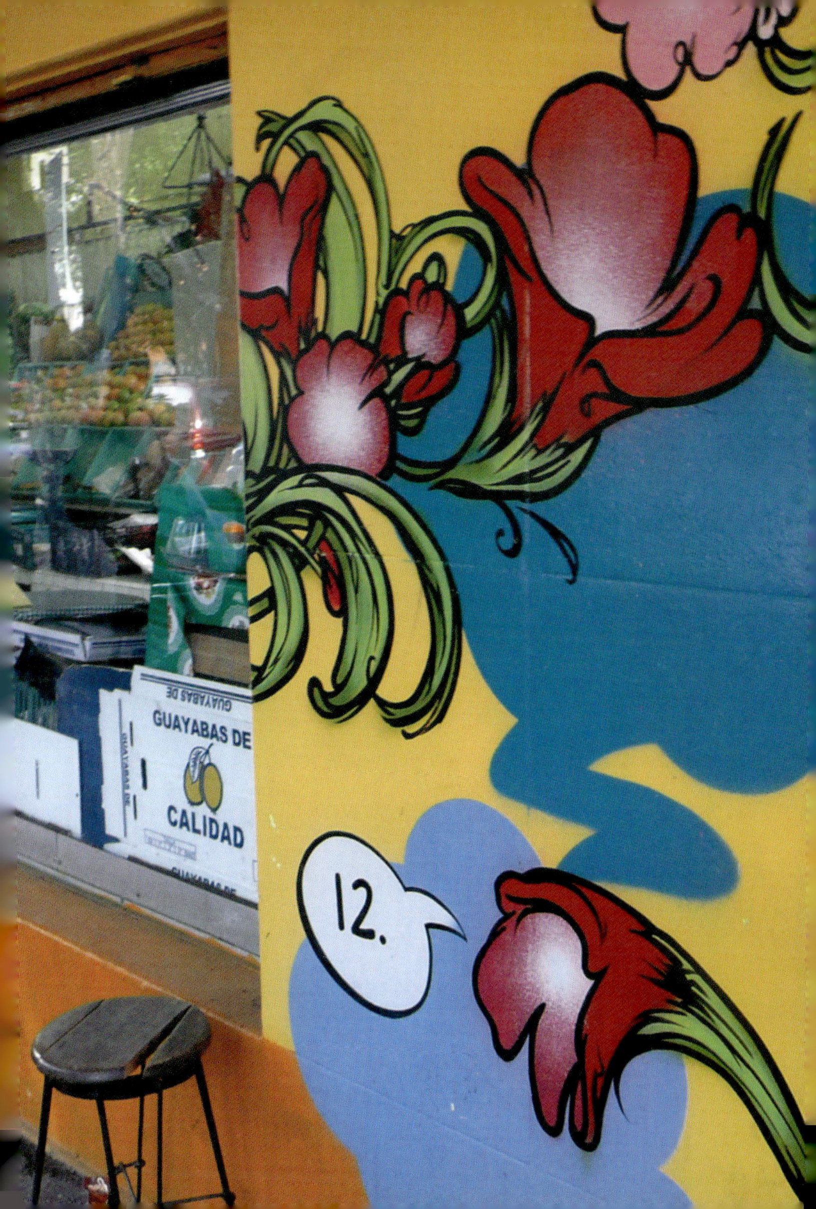
GUAYABAS DE
CALIDAD
12.

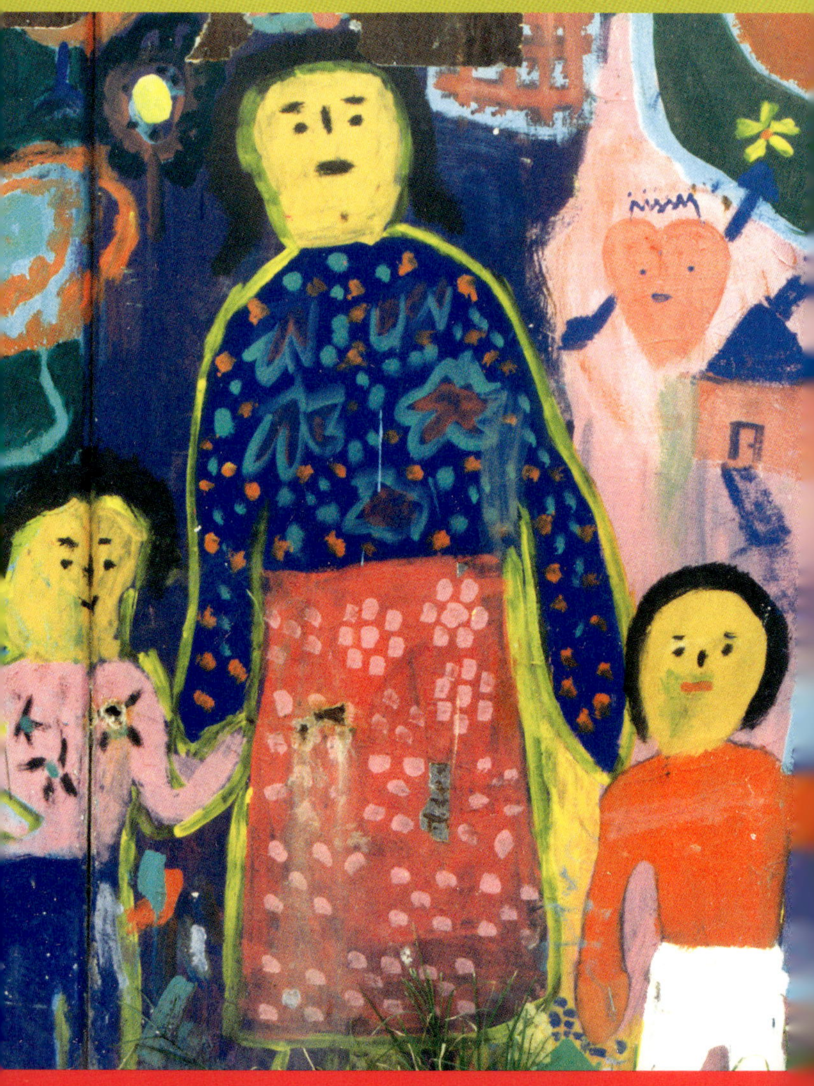

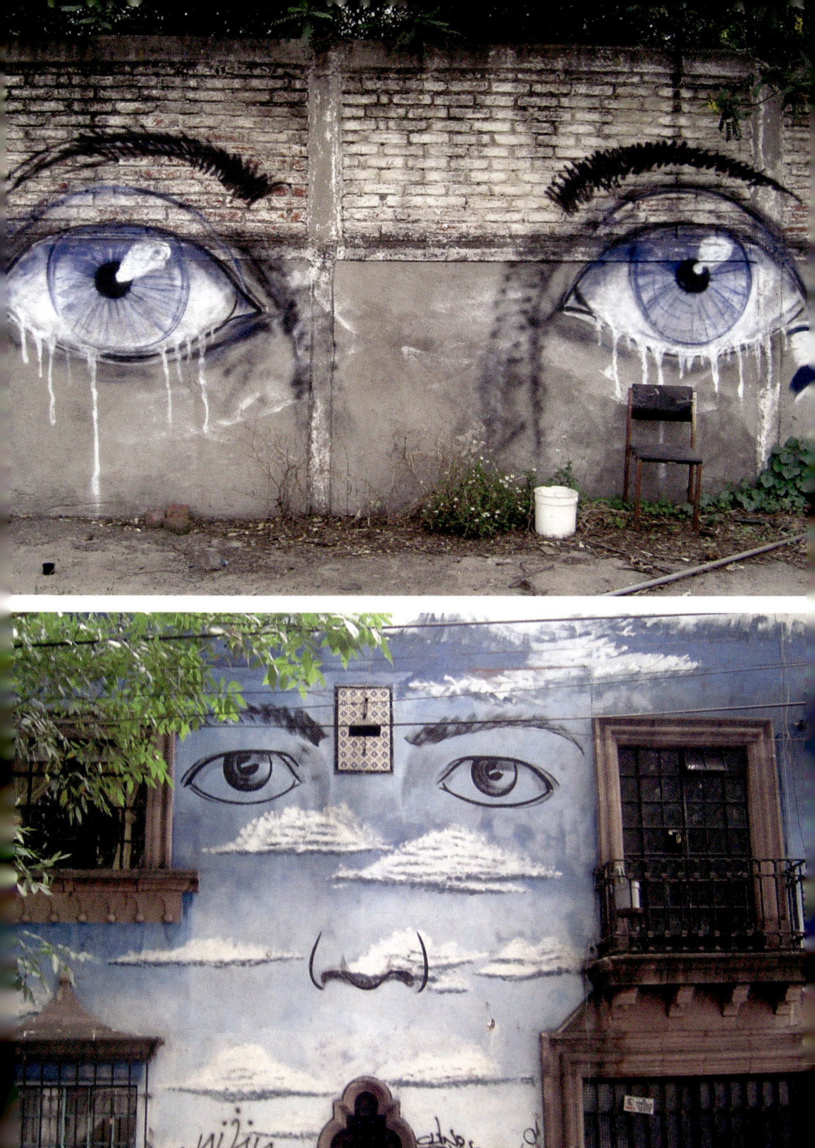

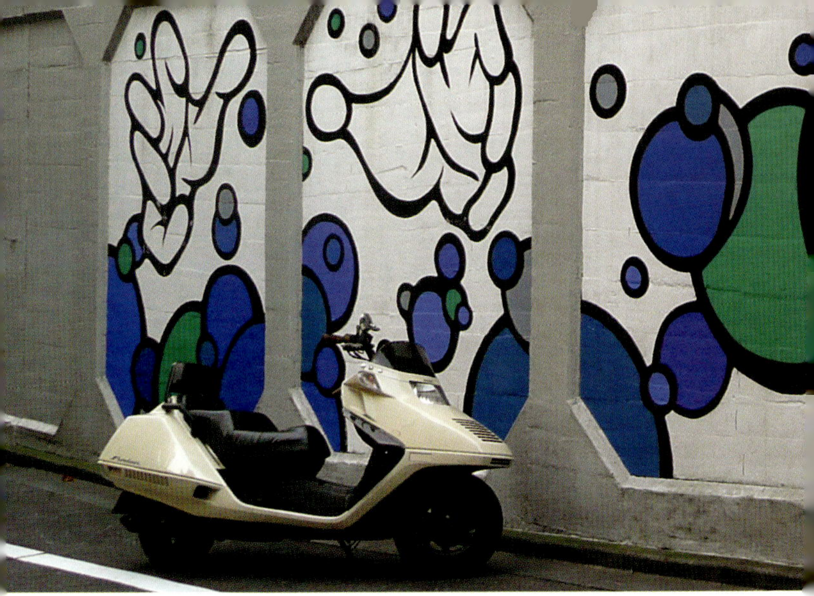

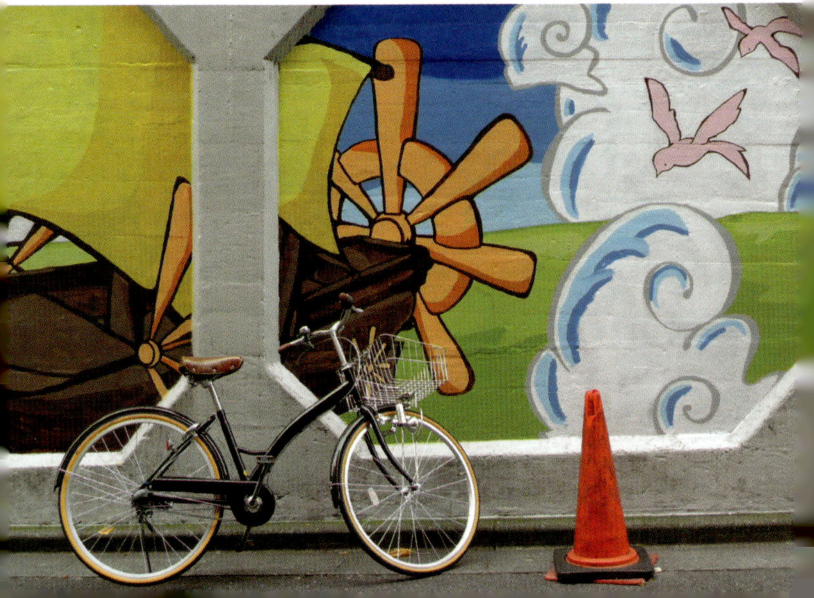

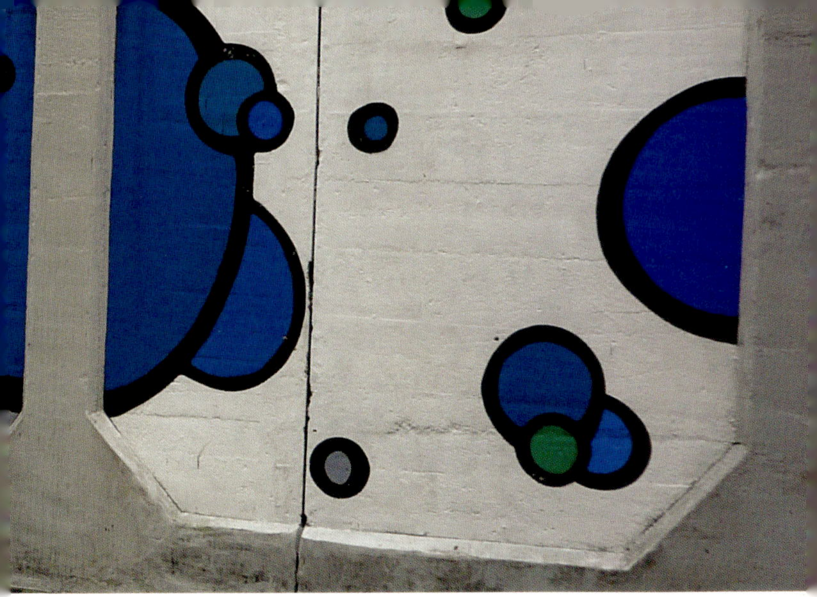

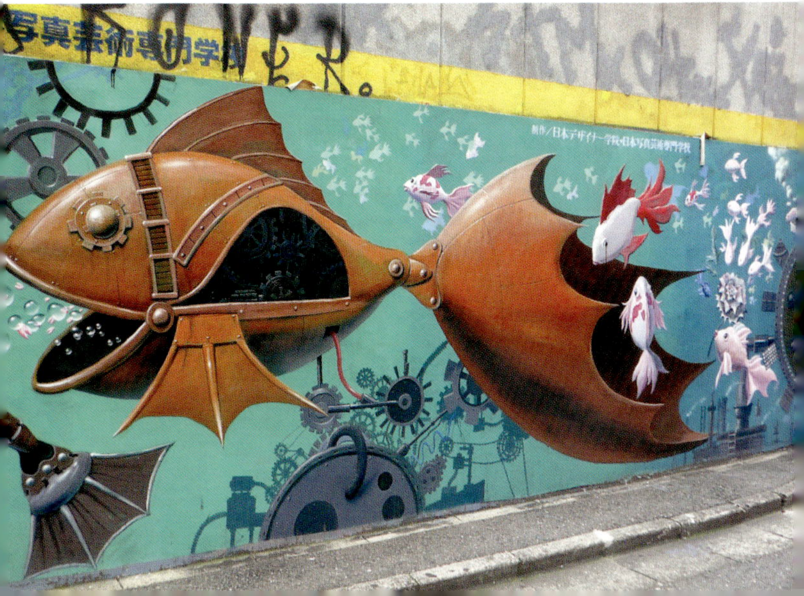

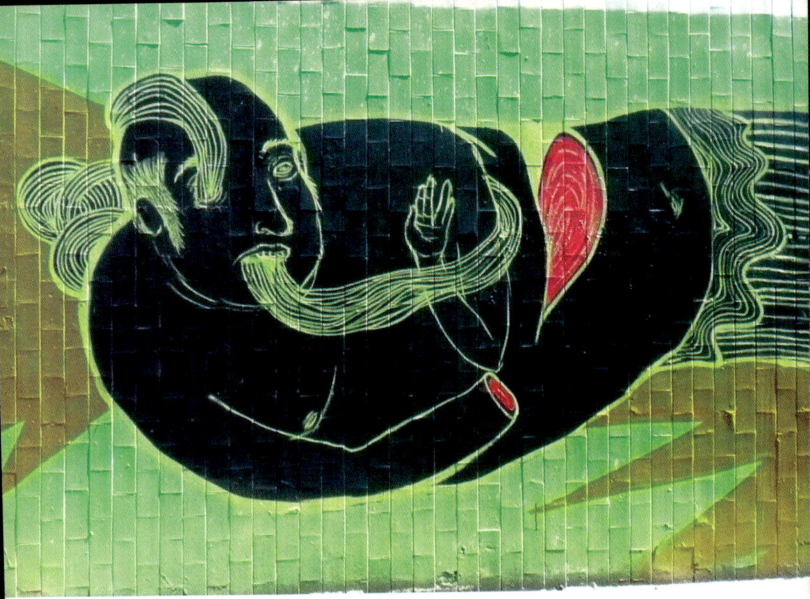

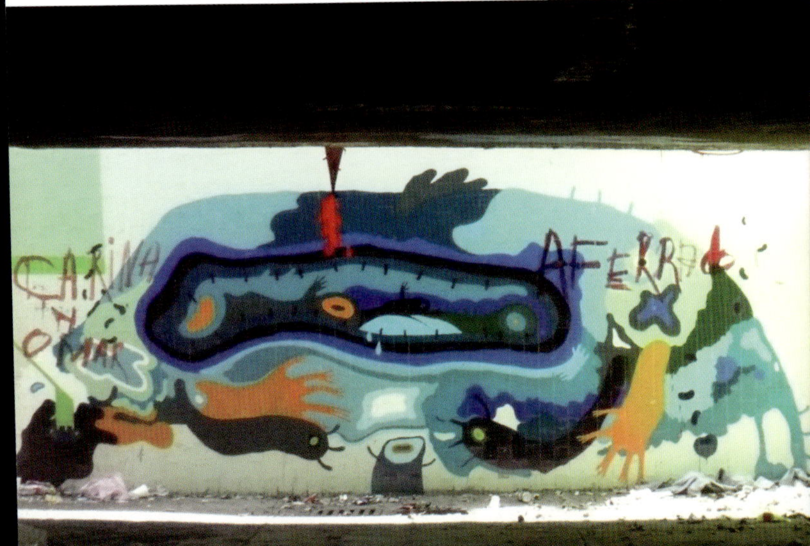

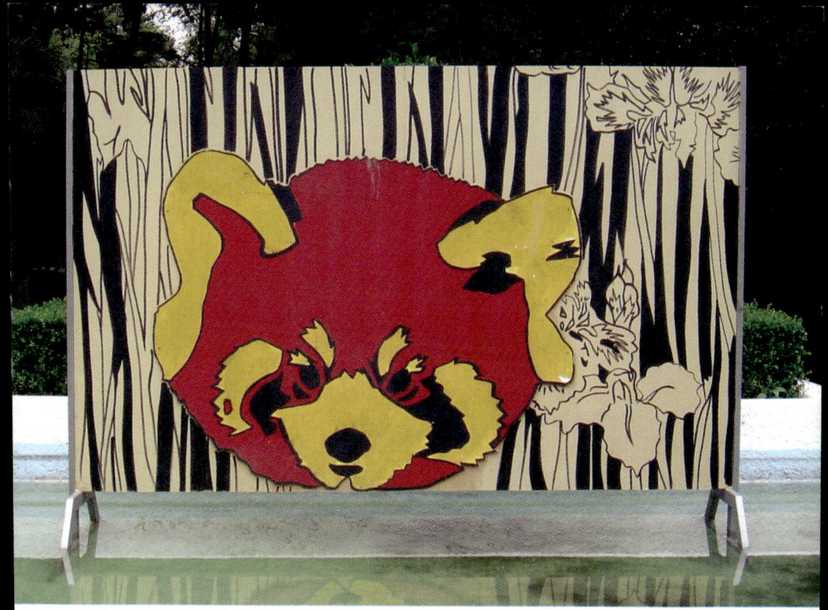

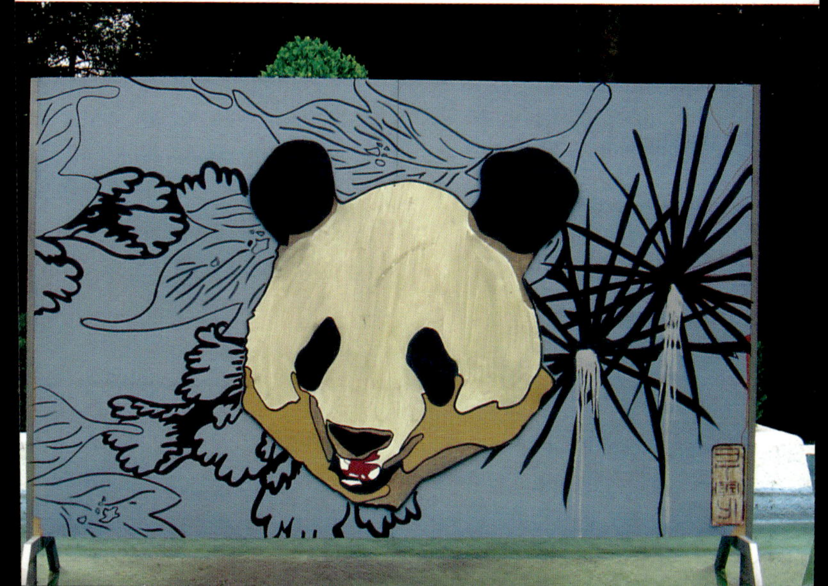

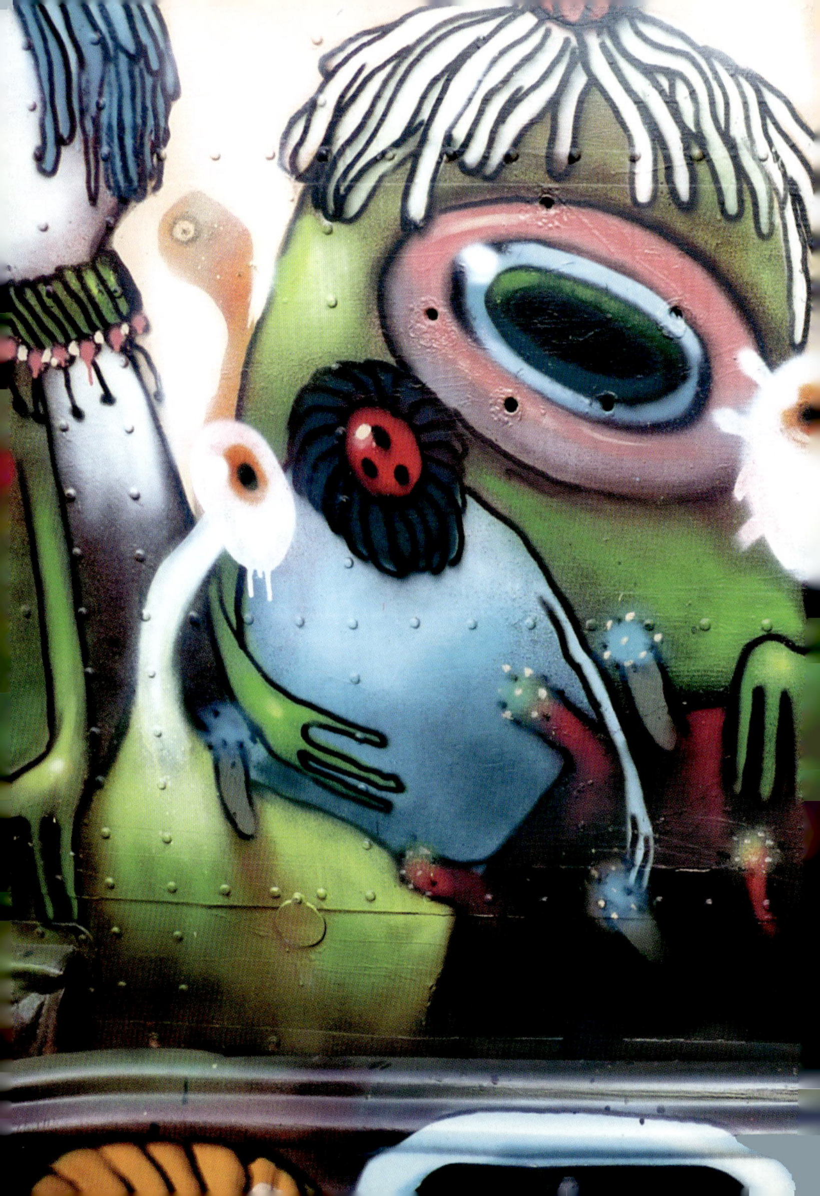

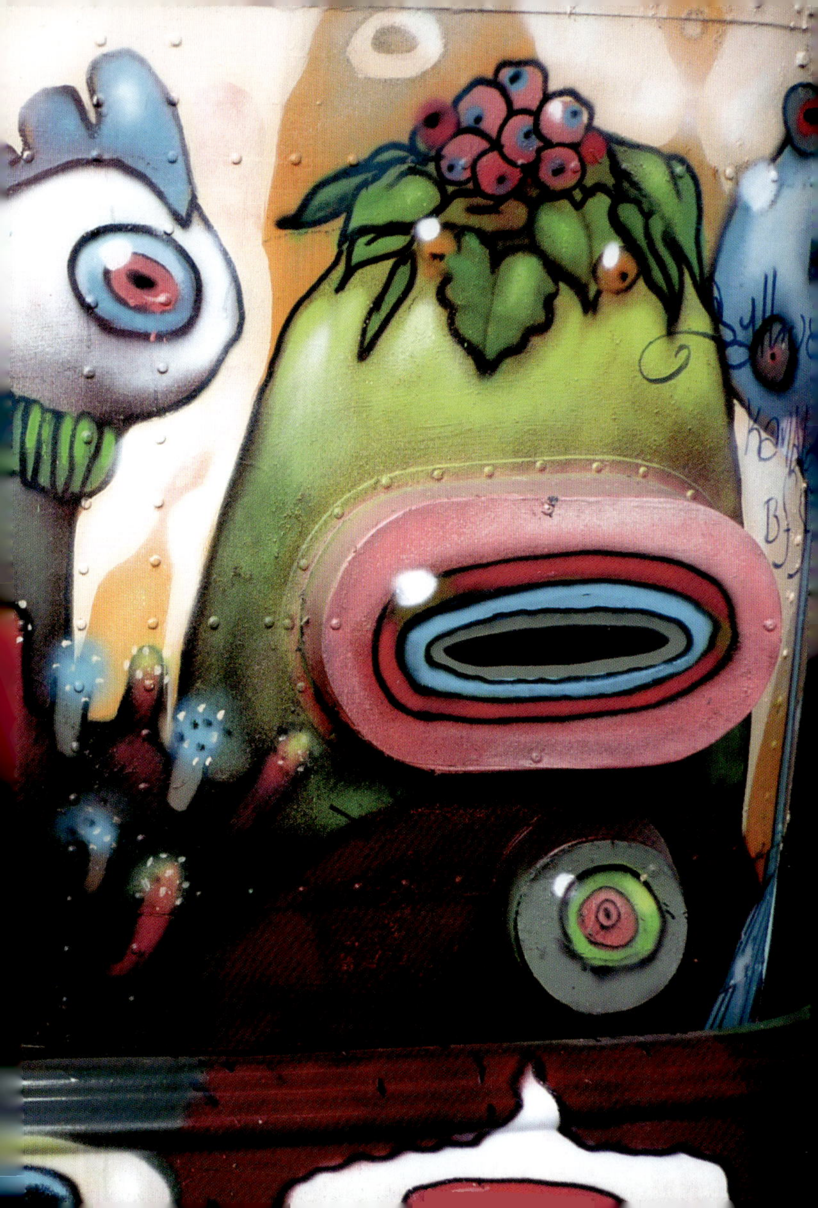

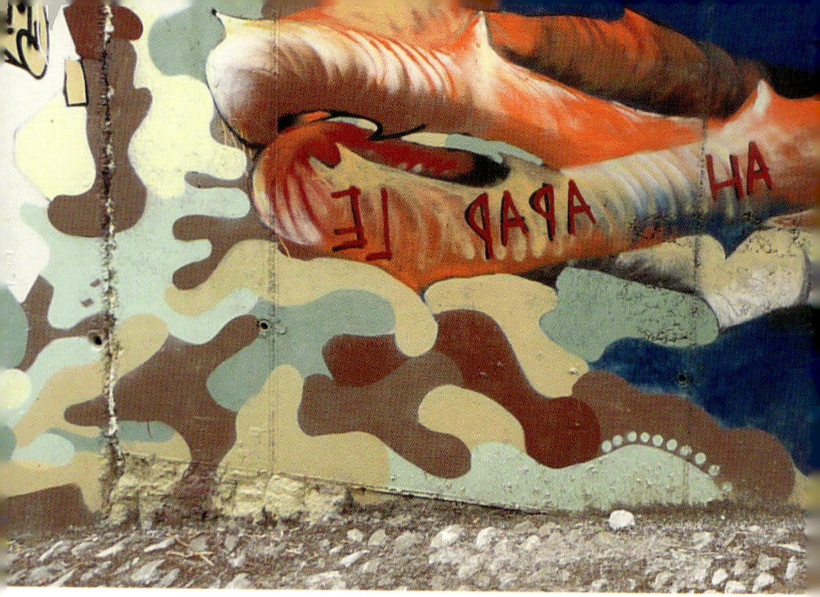

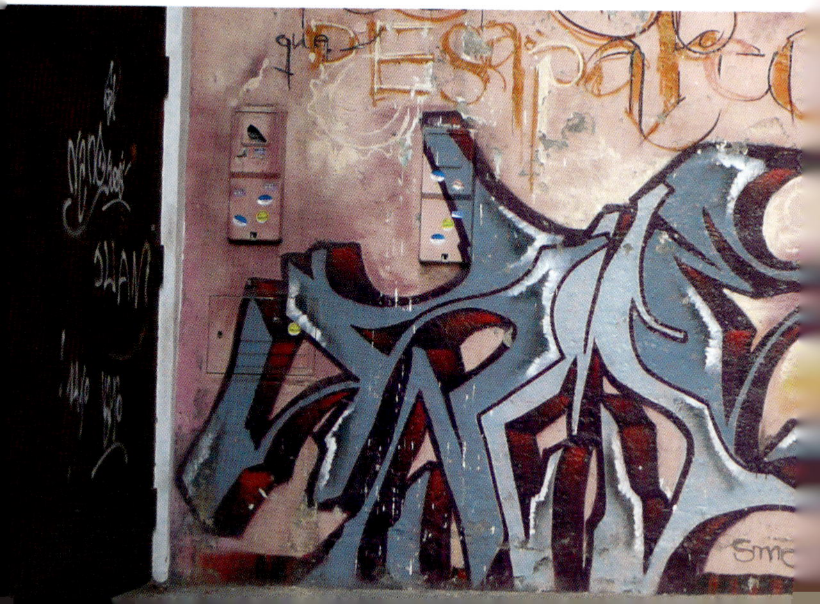

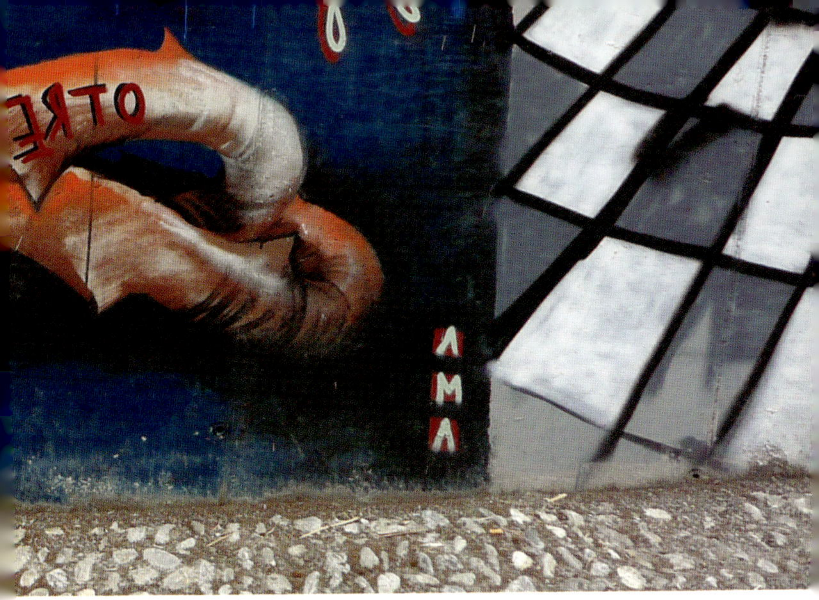

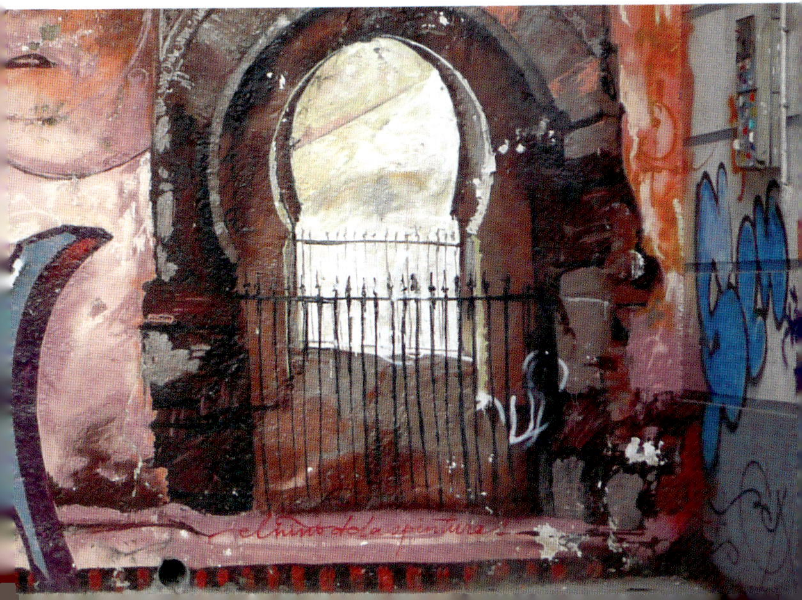

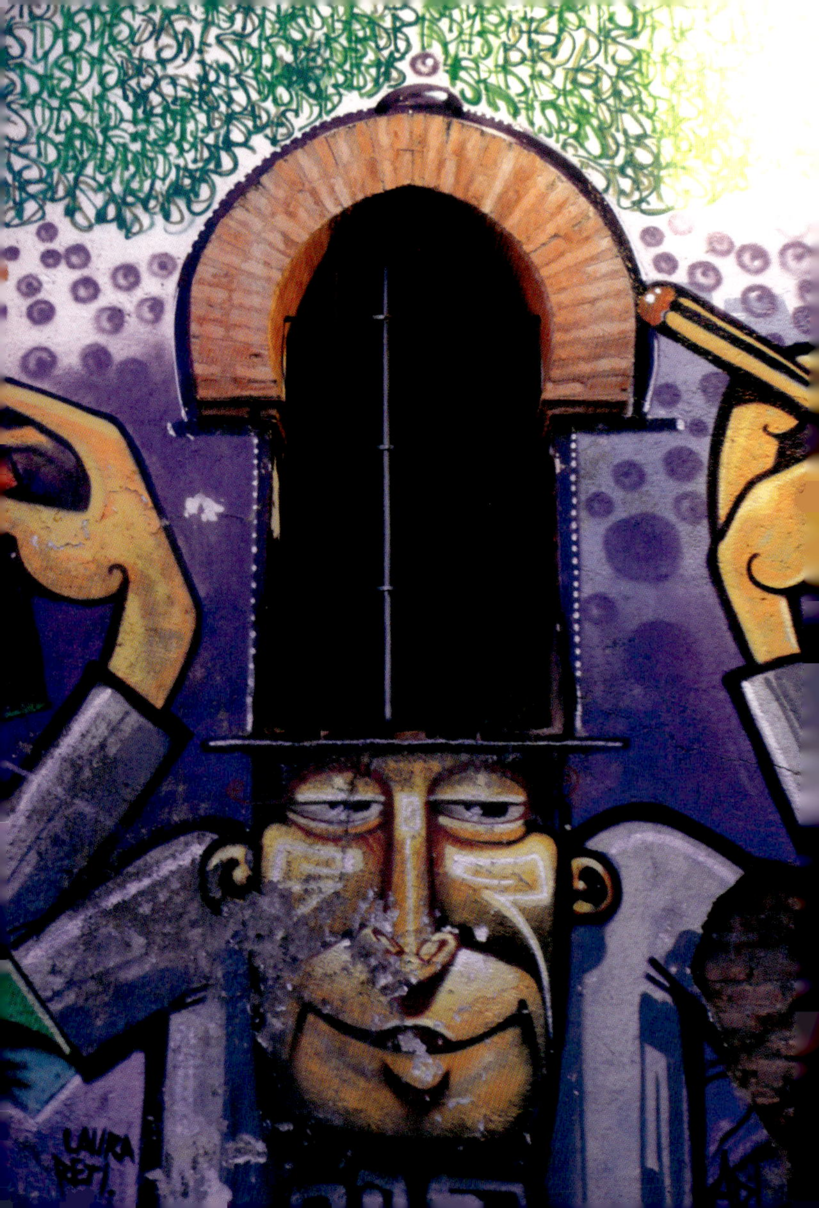

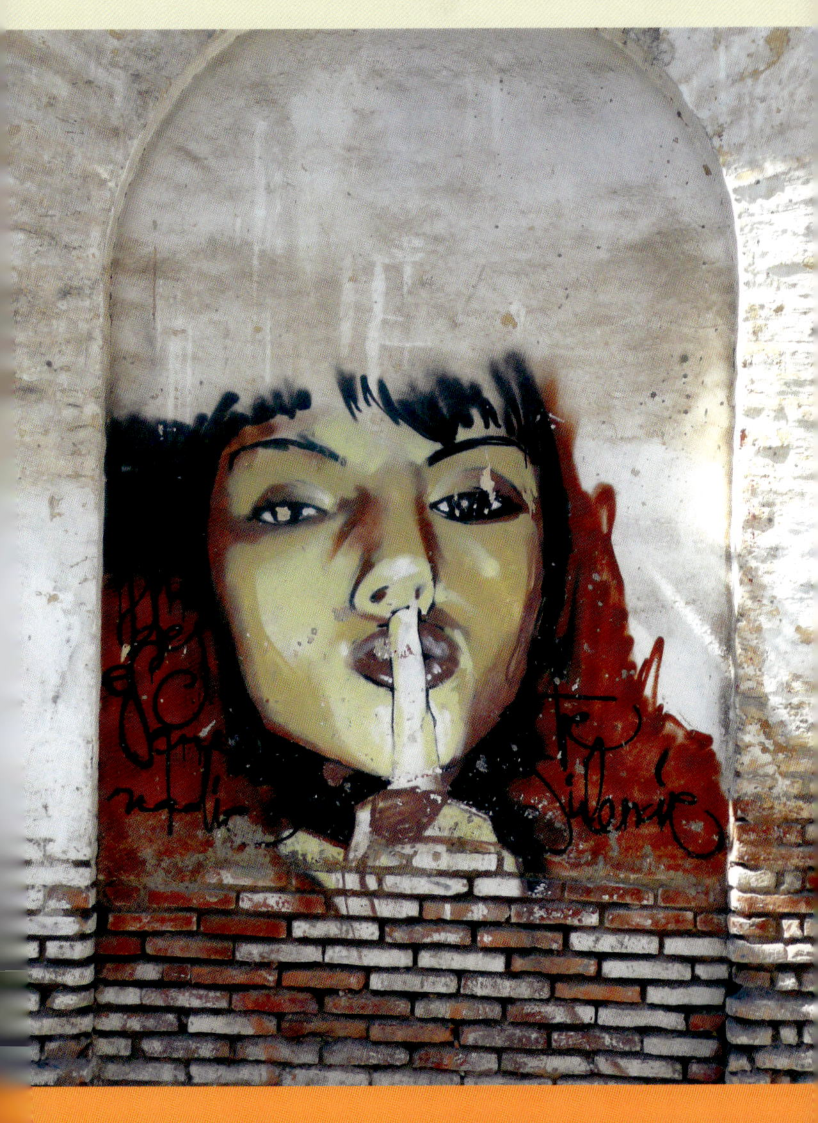

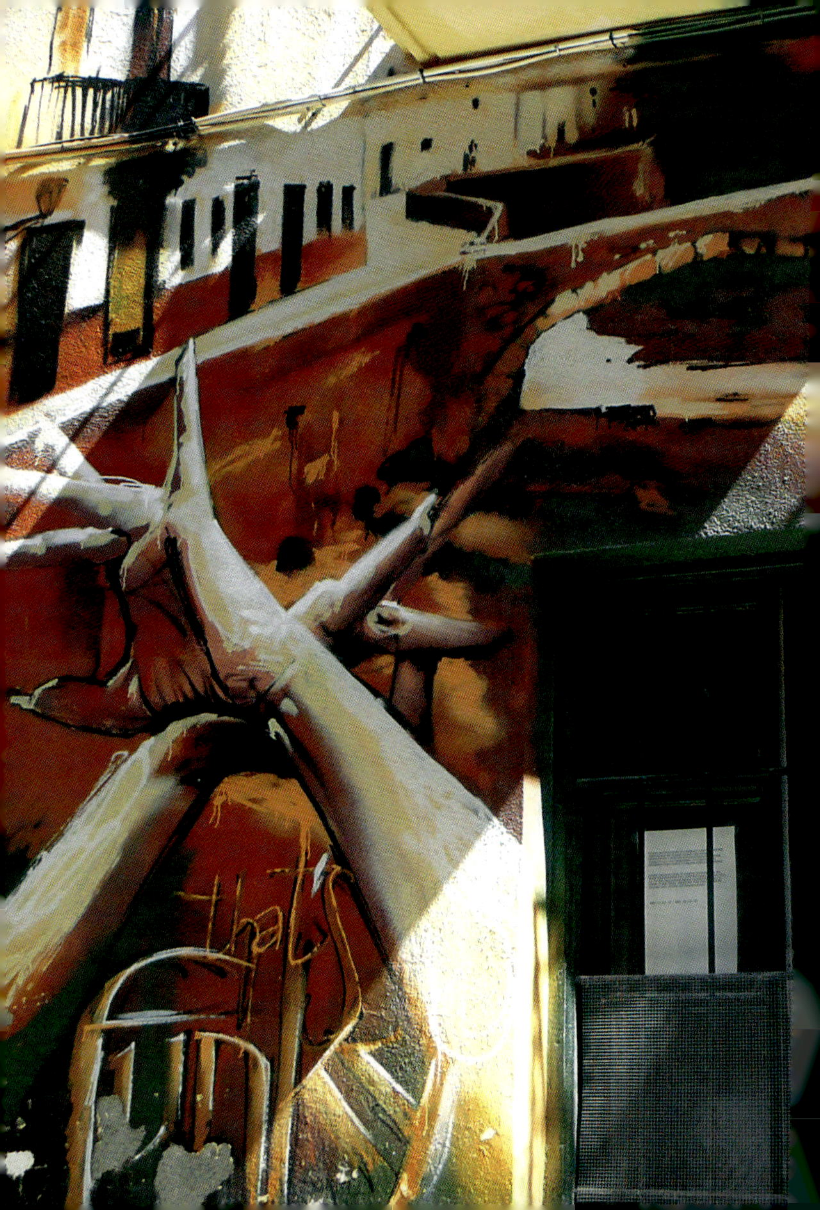
that's

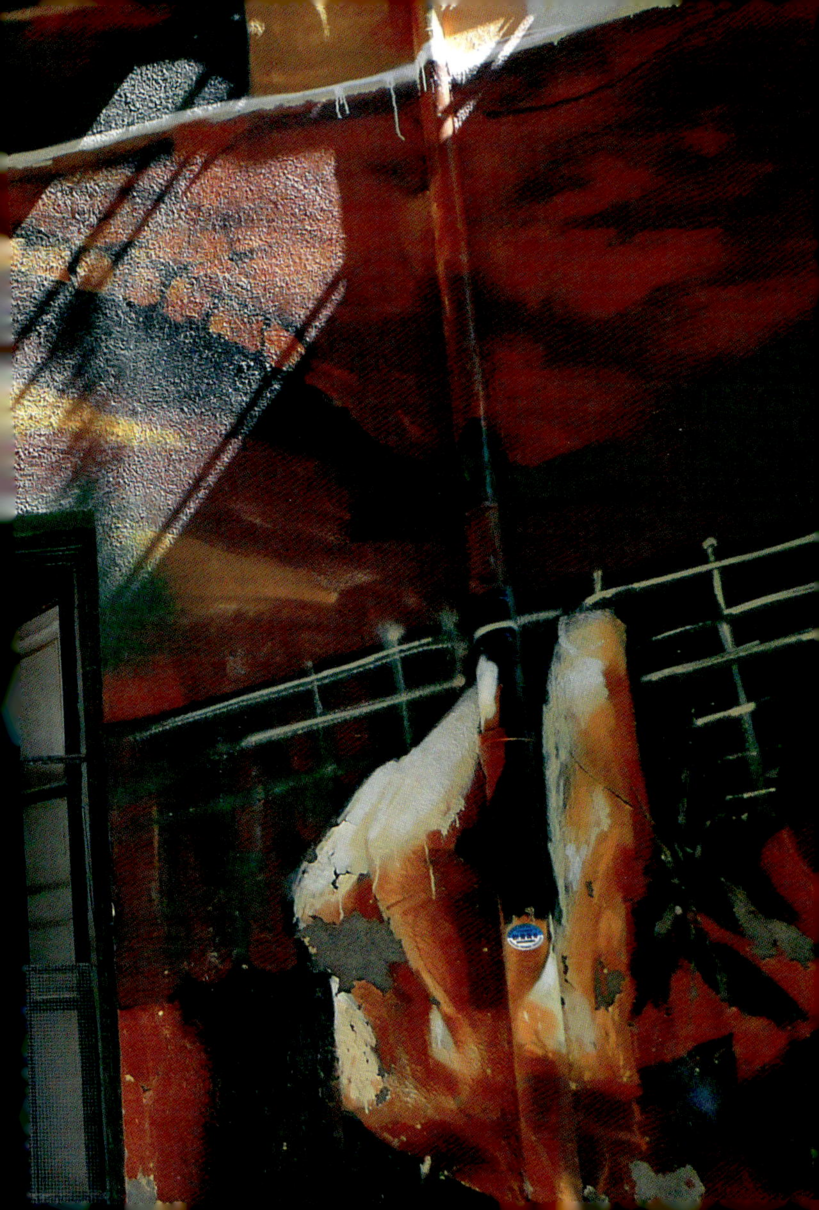

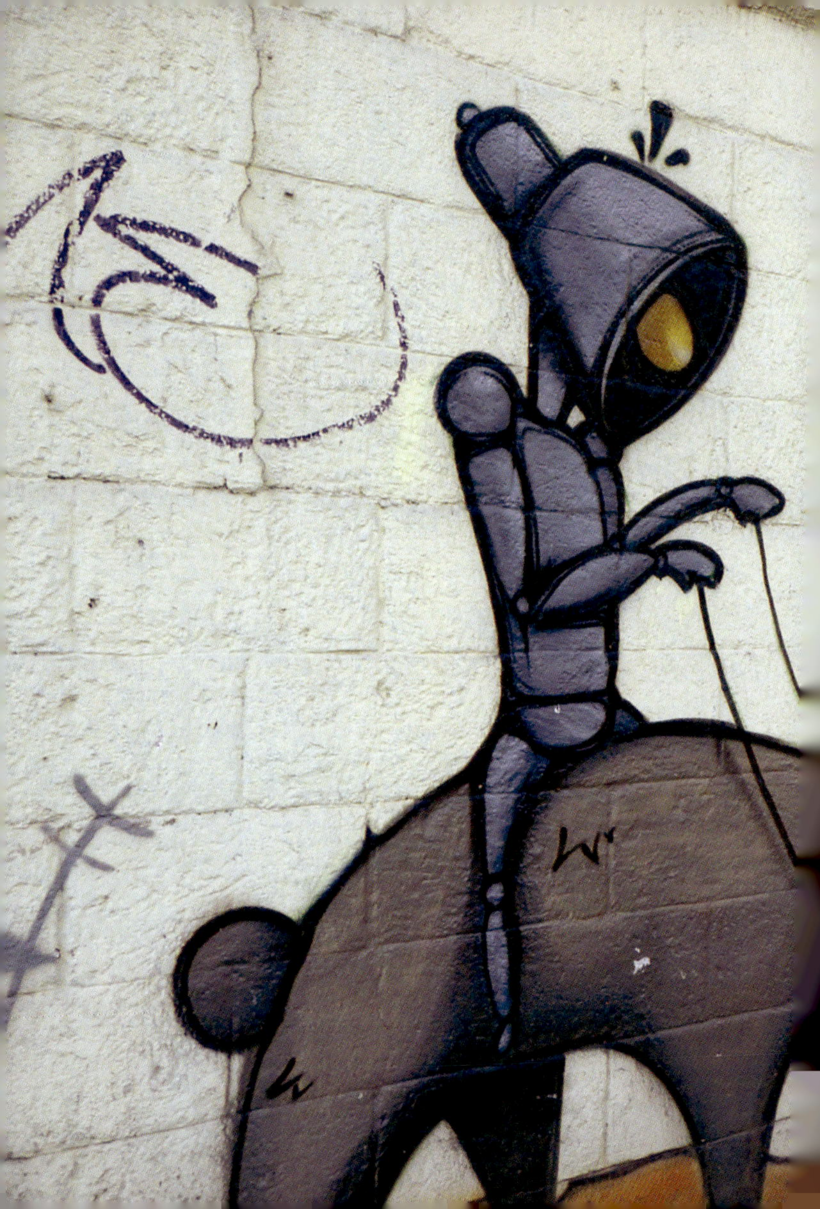

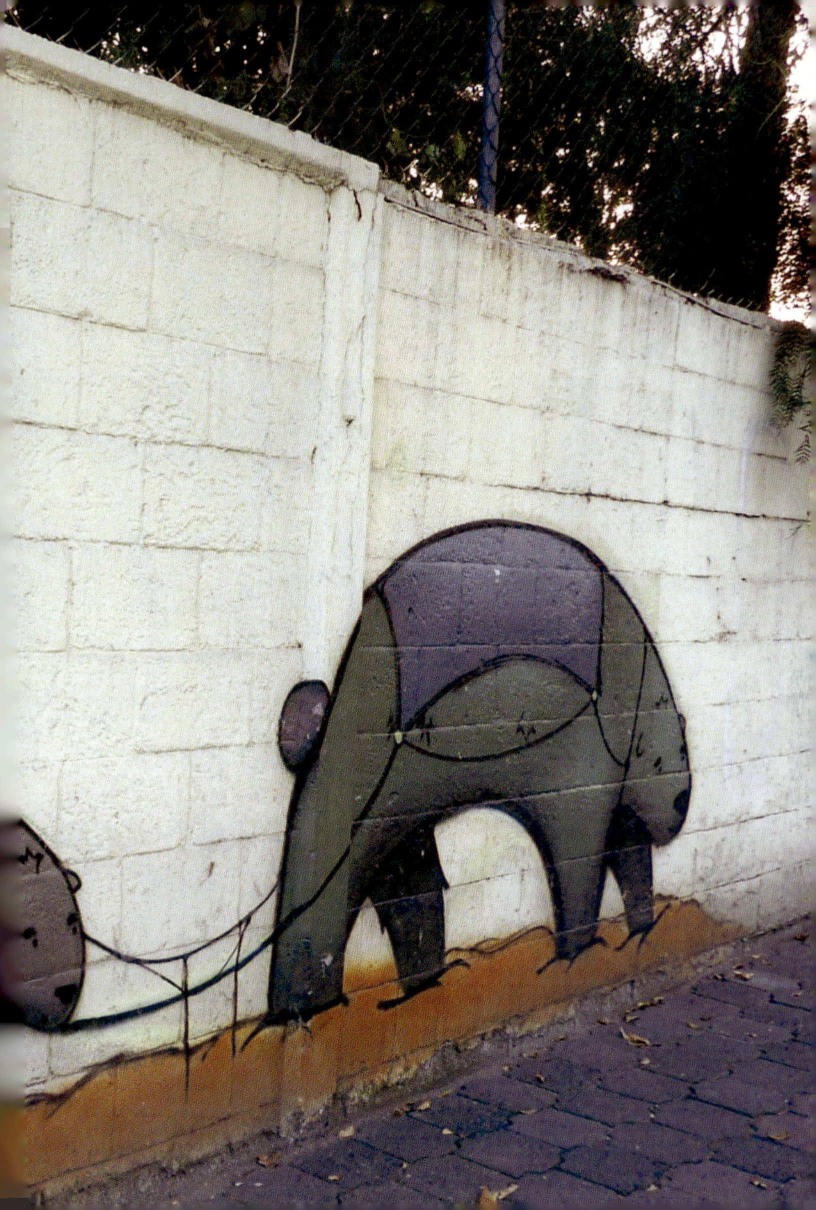

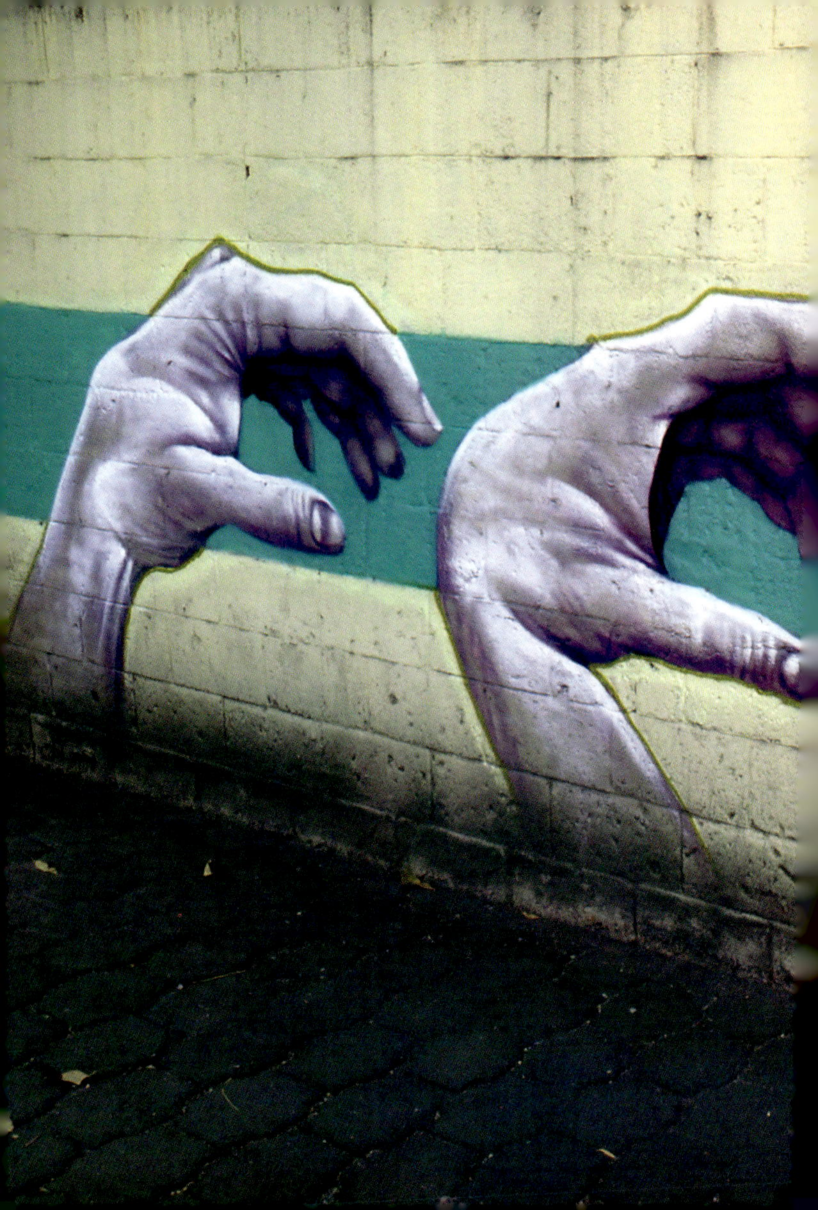

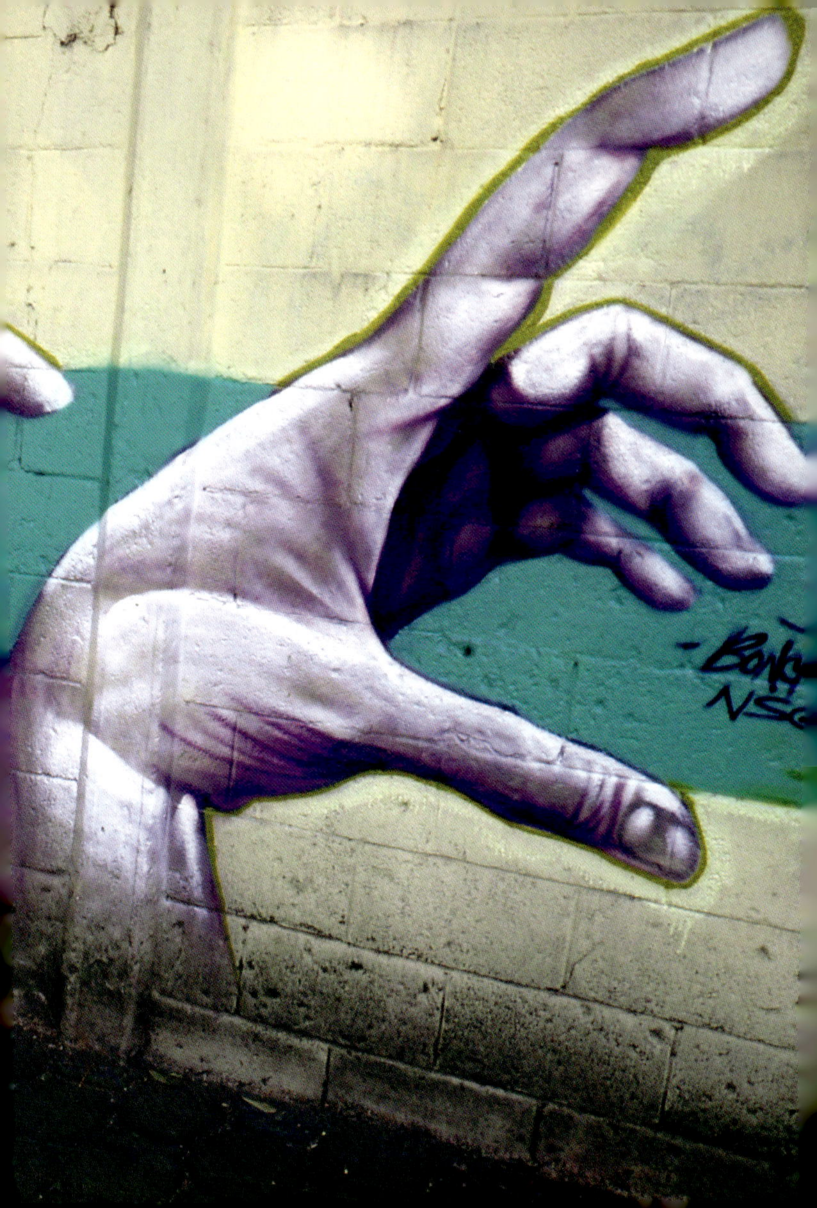

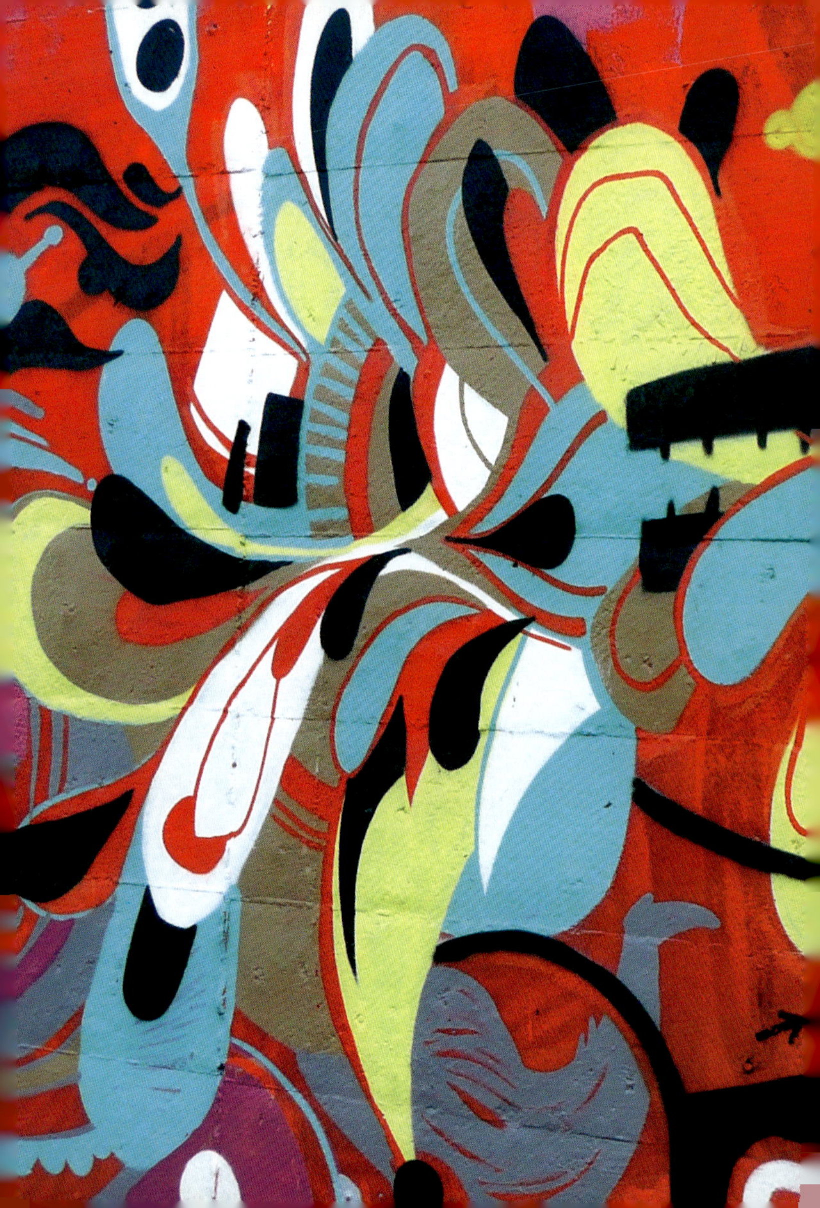

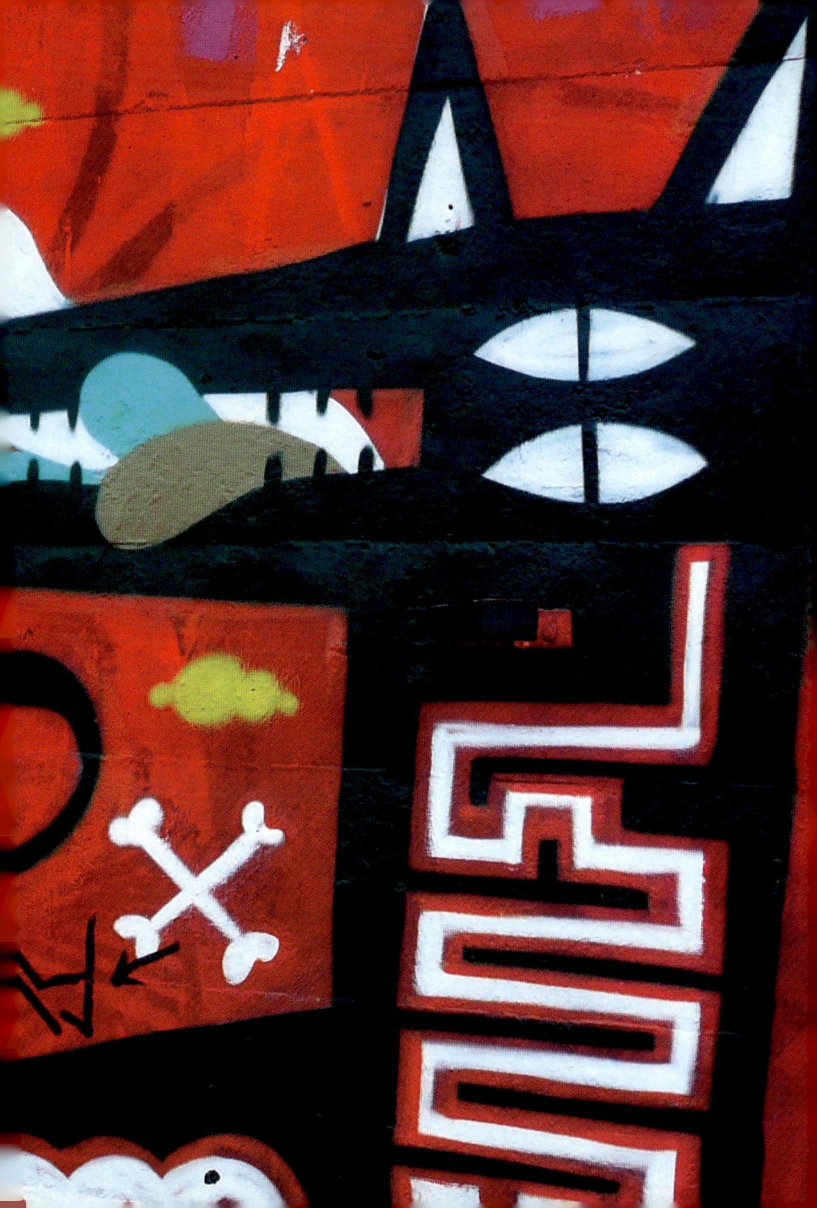

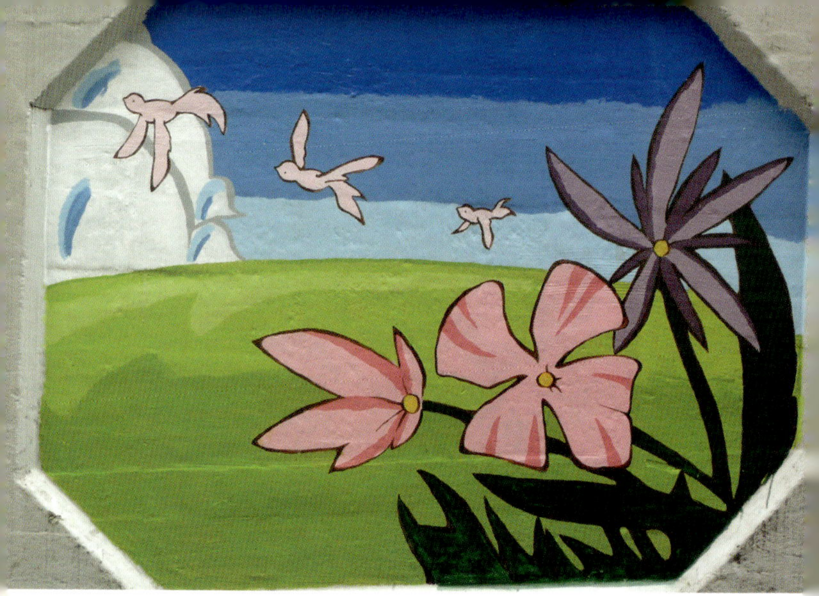

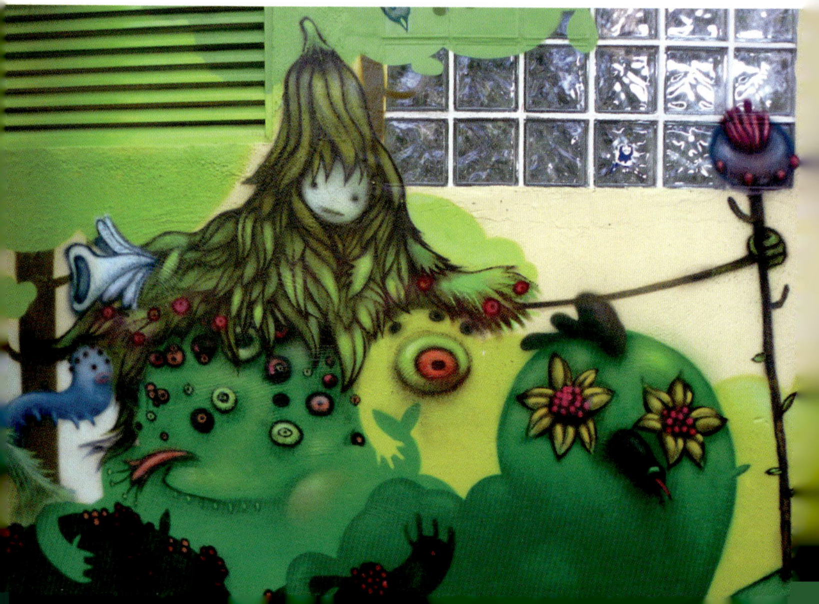

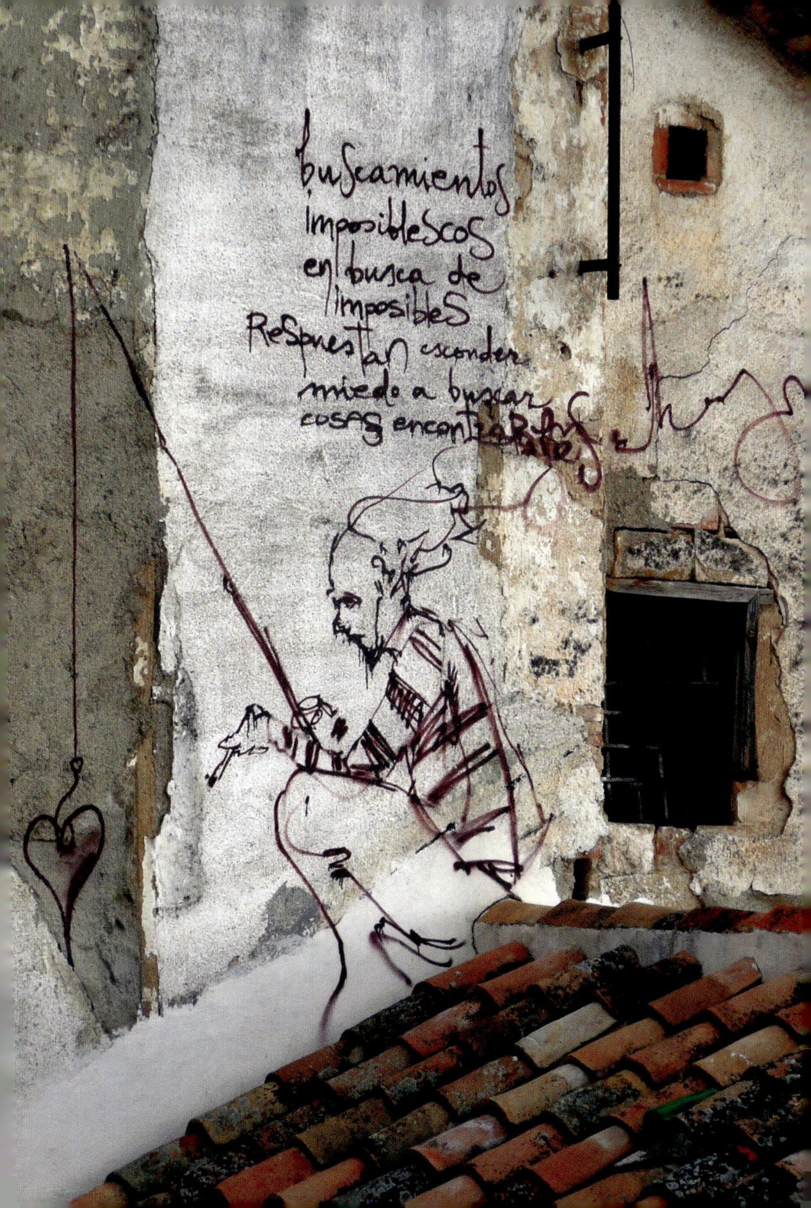

buscamientos
imposiblescos
en busca de
imposibles
Respuestan esconder
miedo a buscar
cosas encont

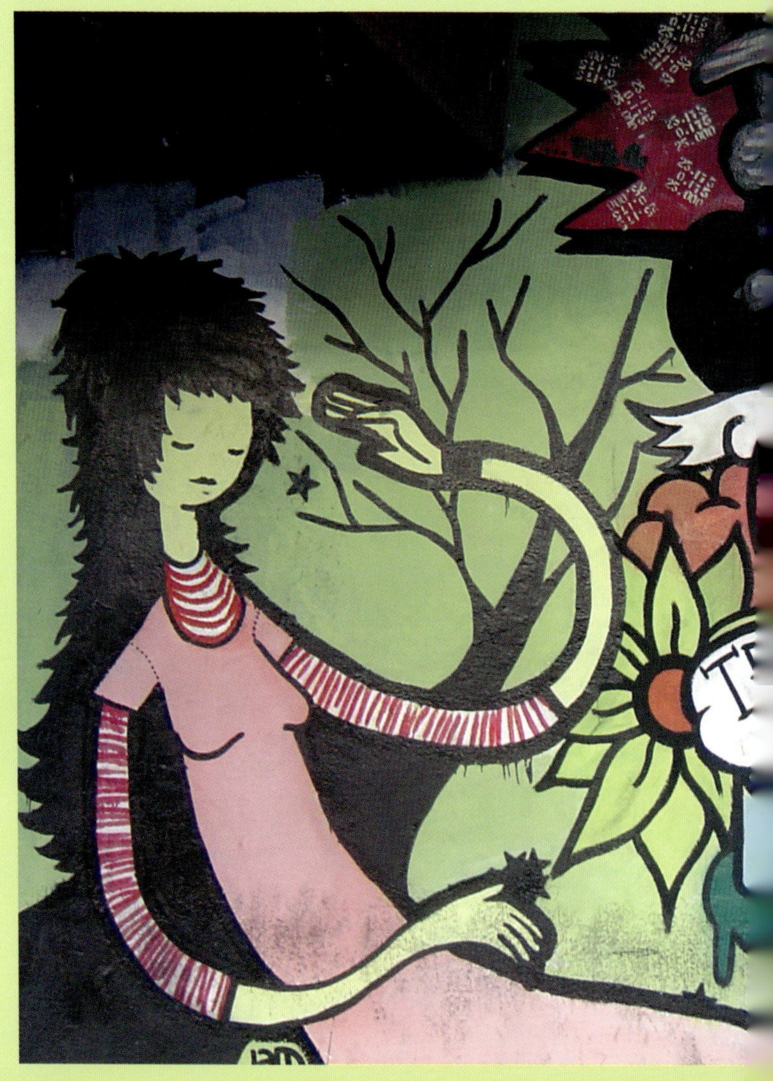

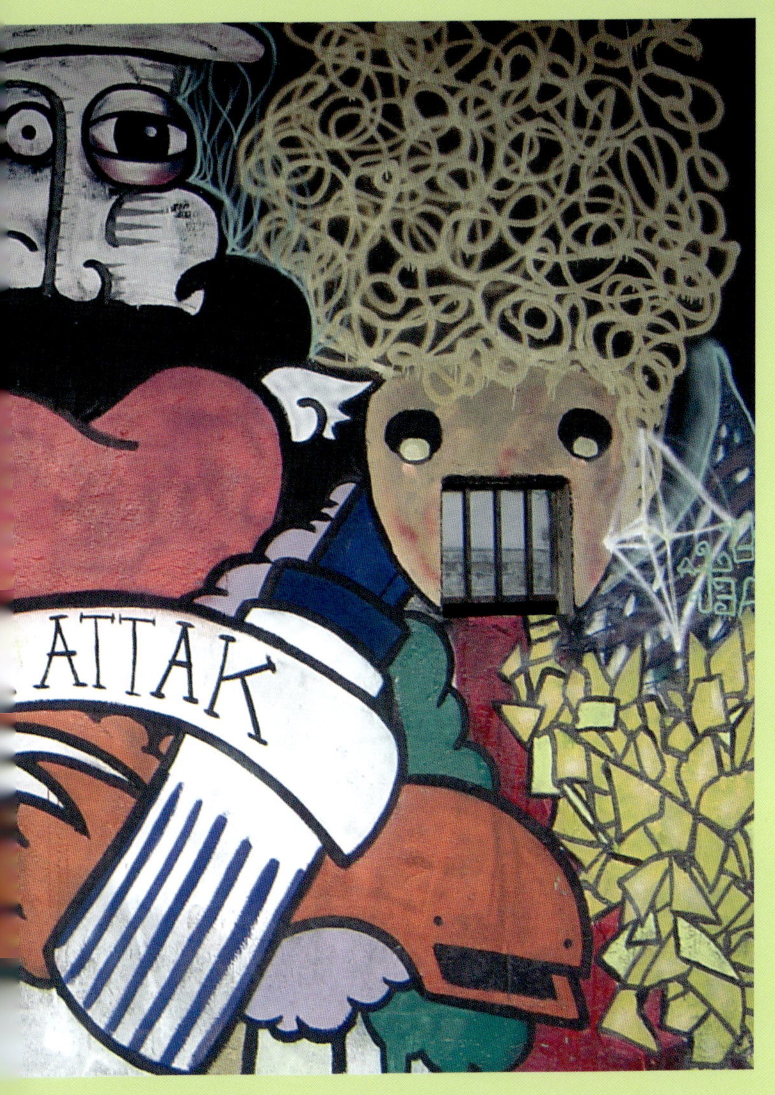
ATTAK

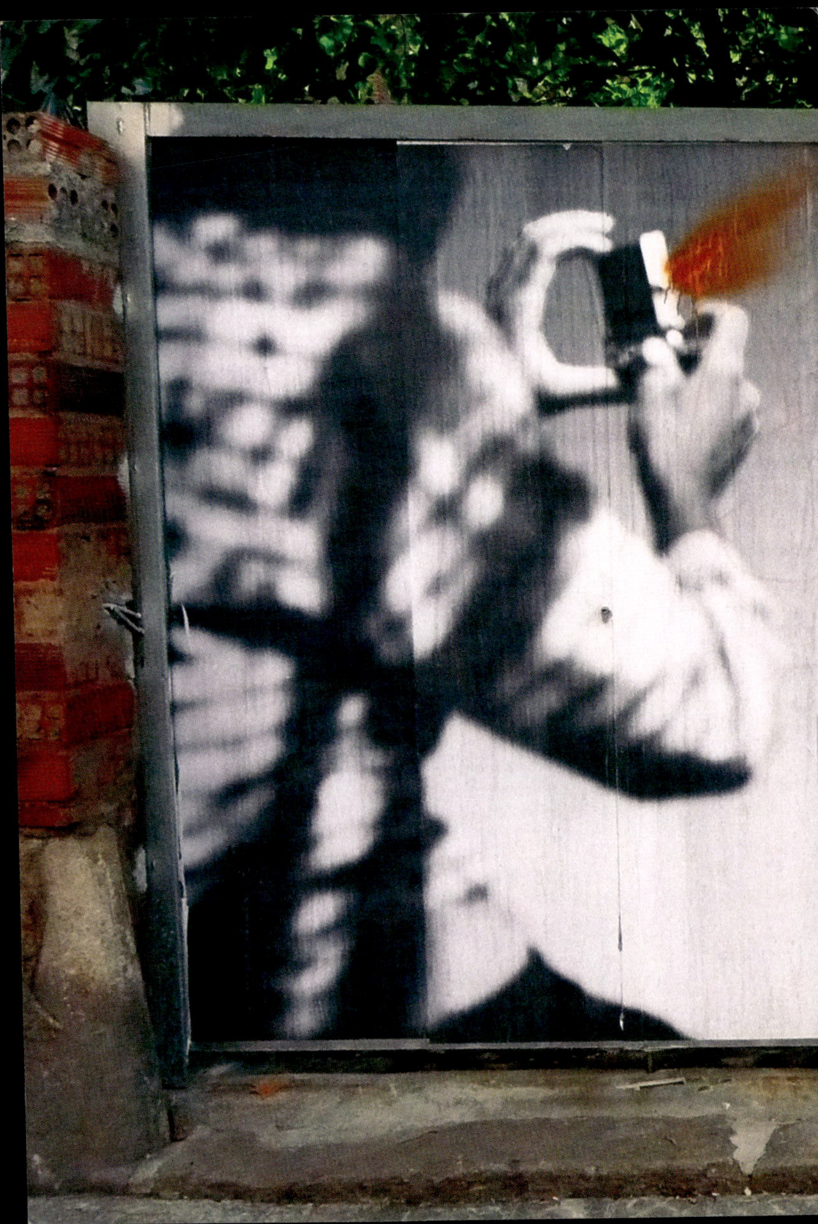

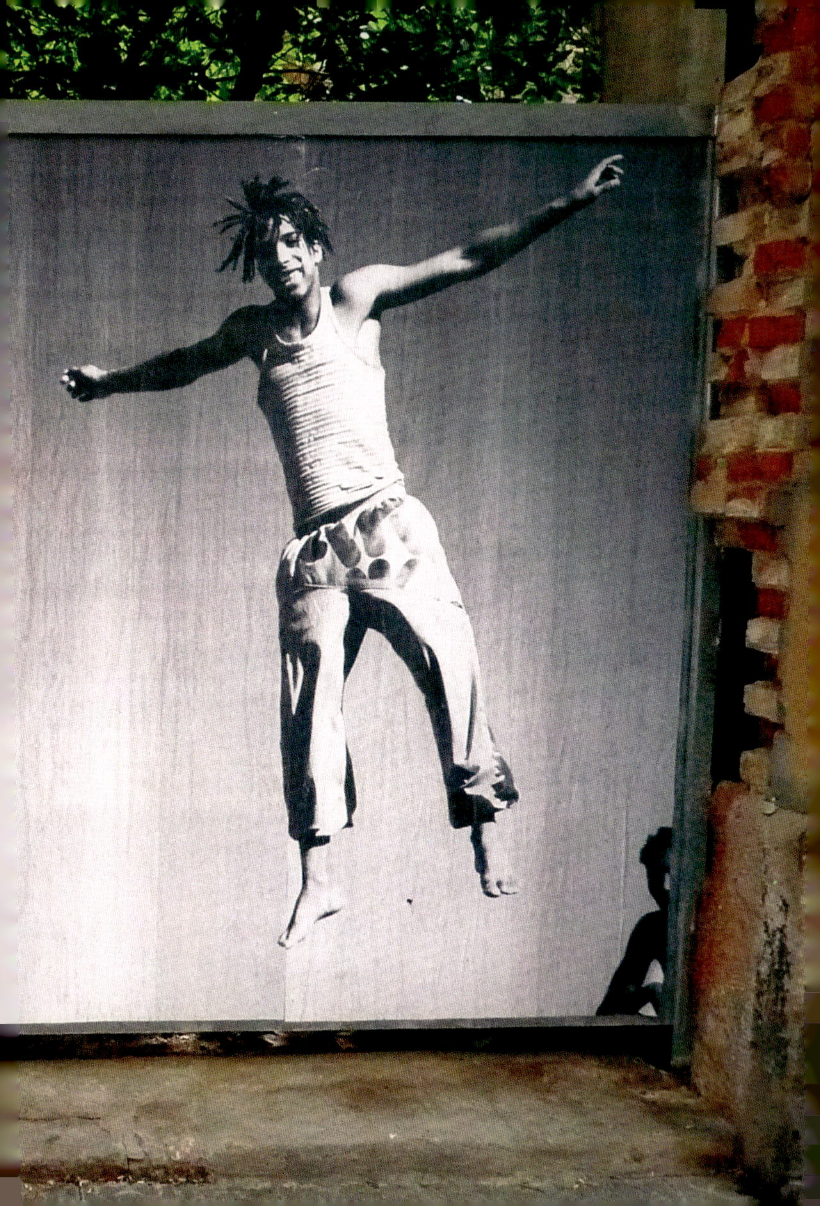

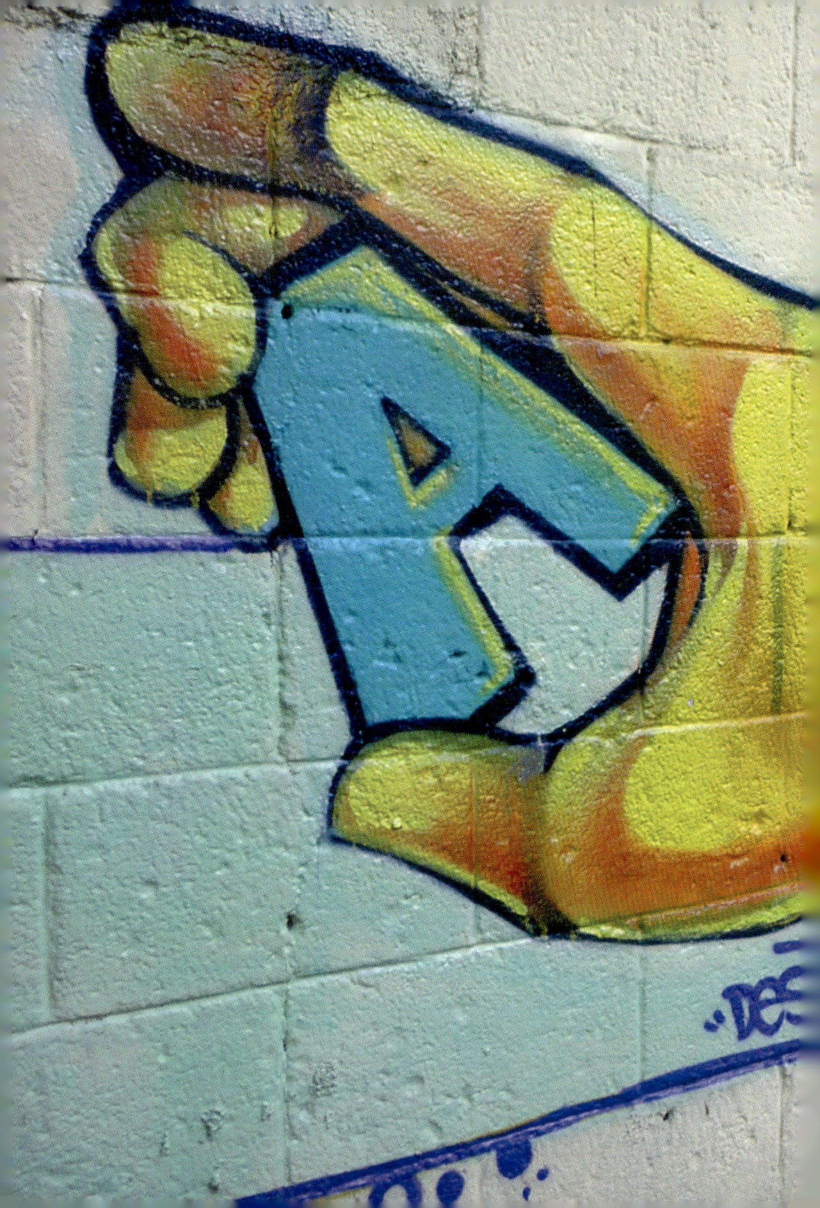

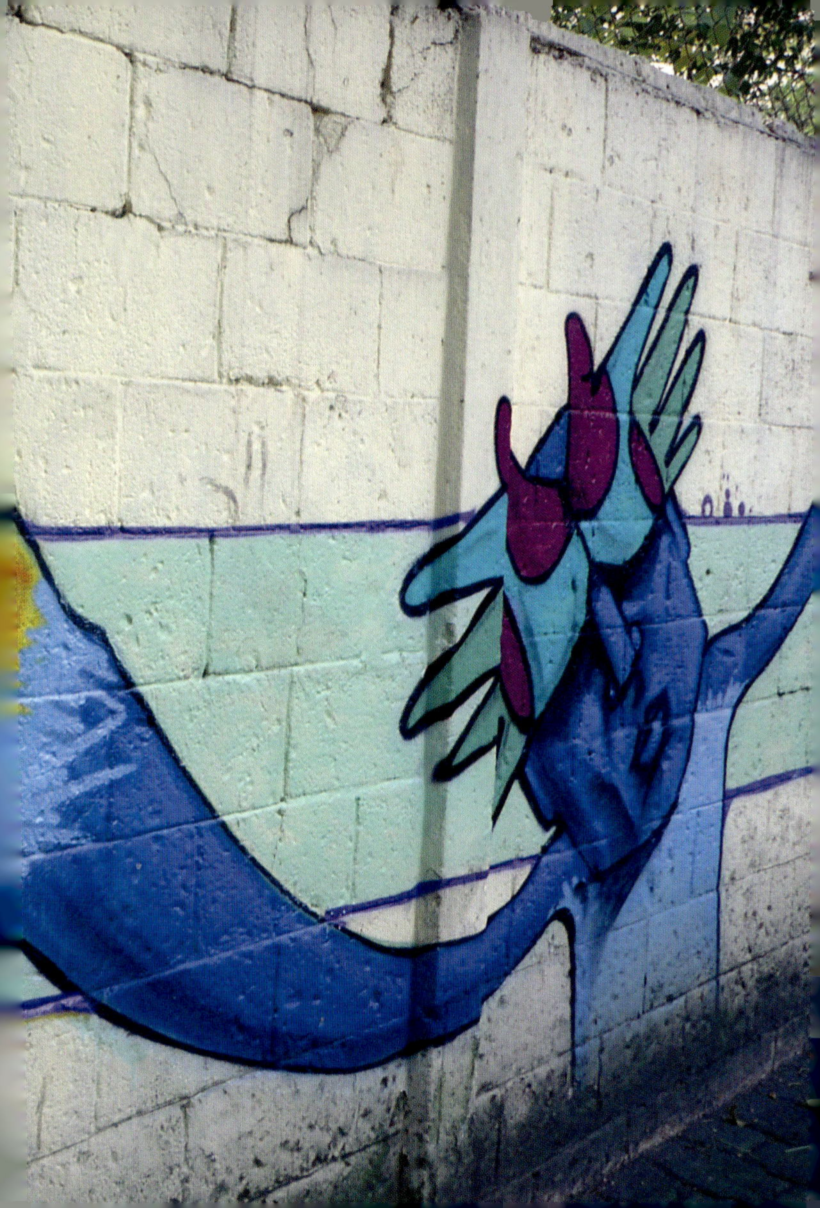

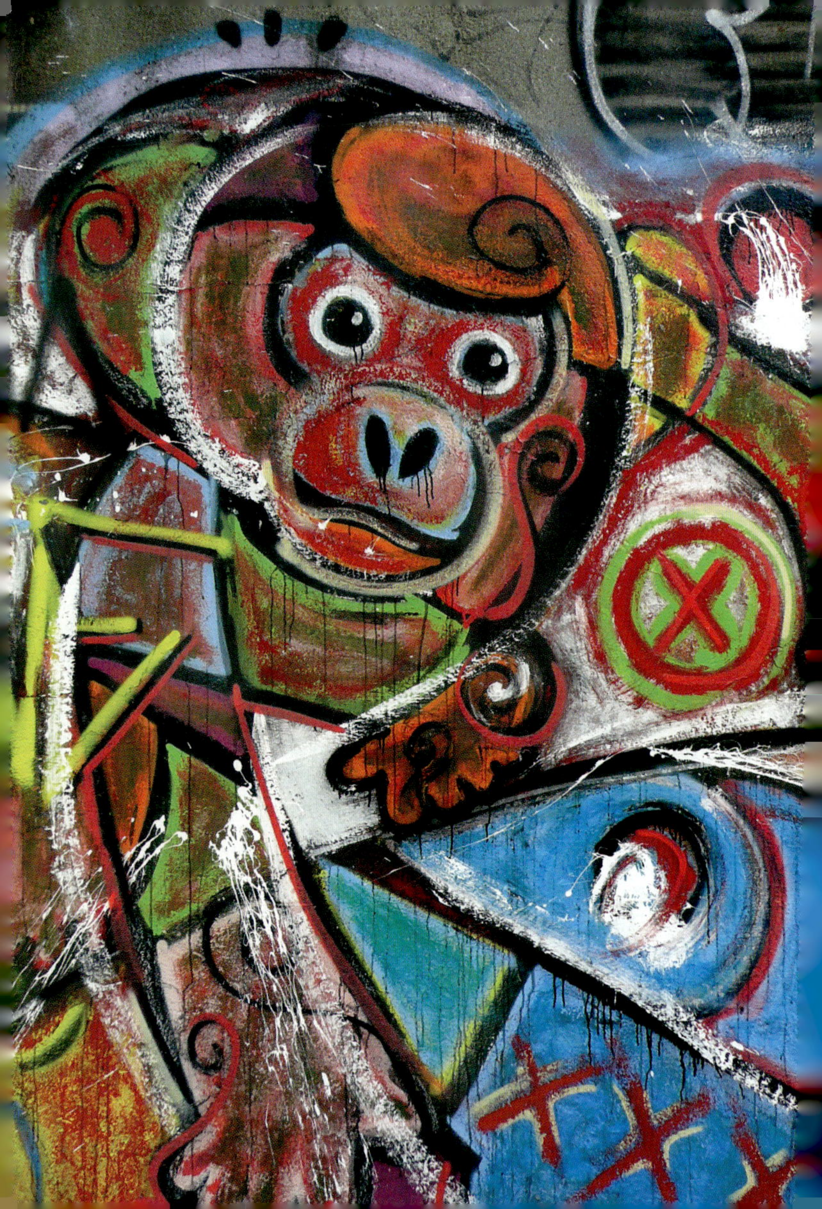

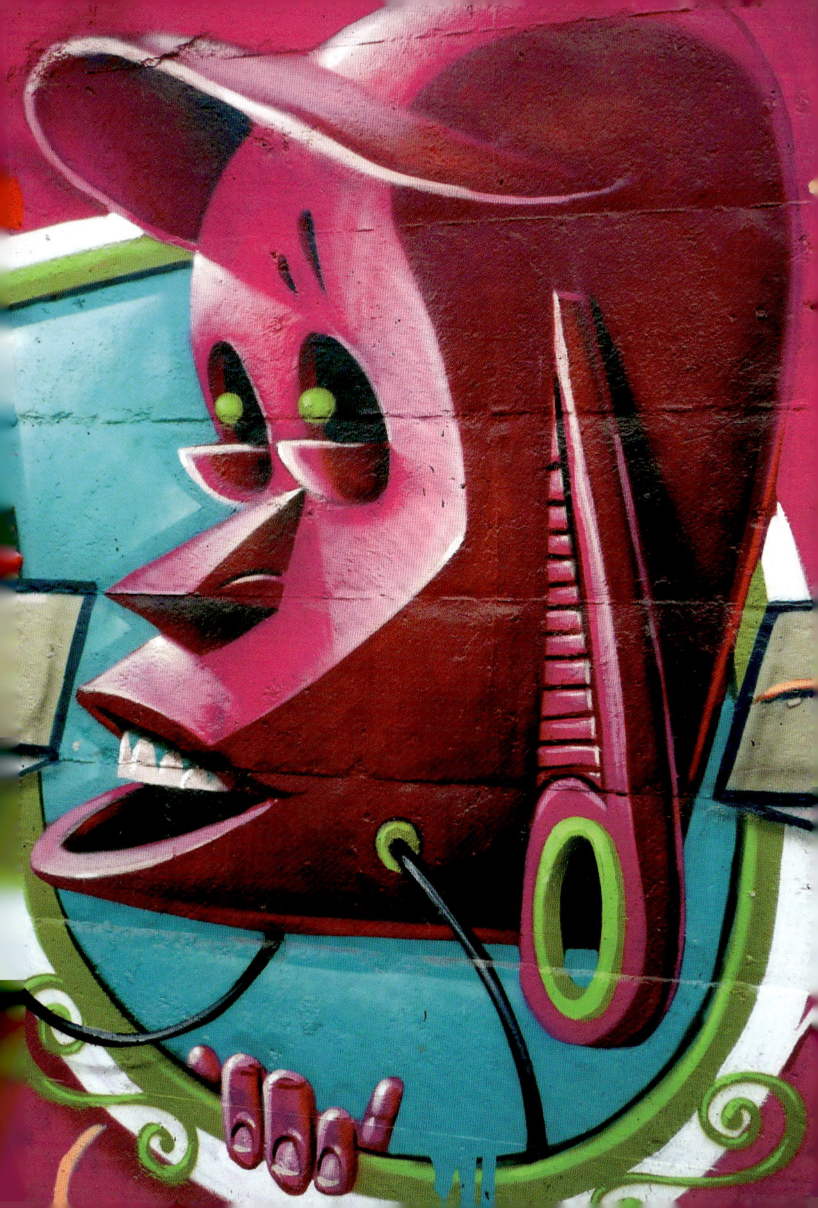

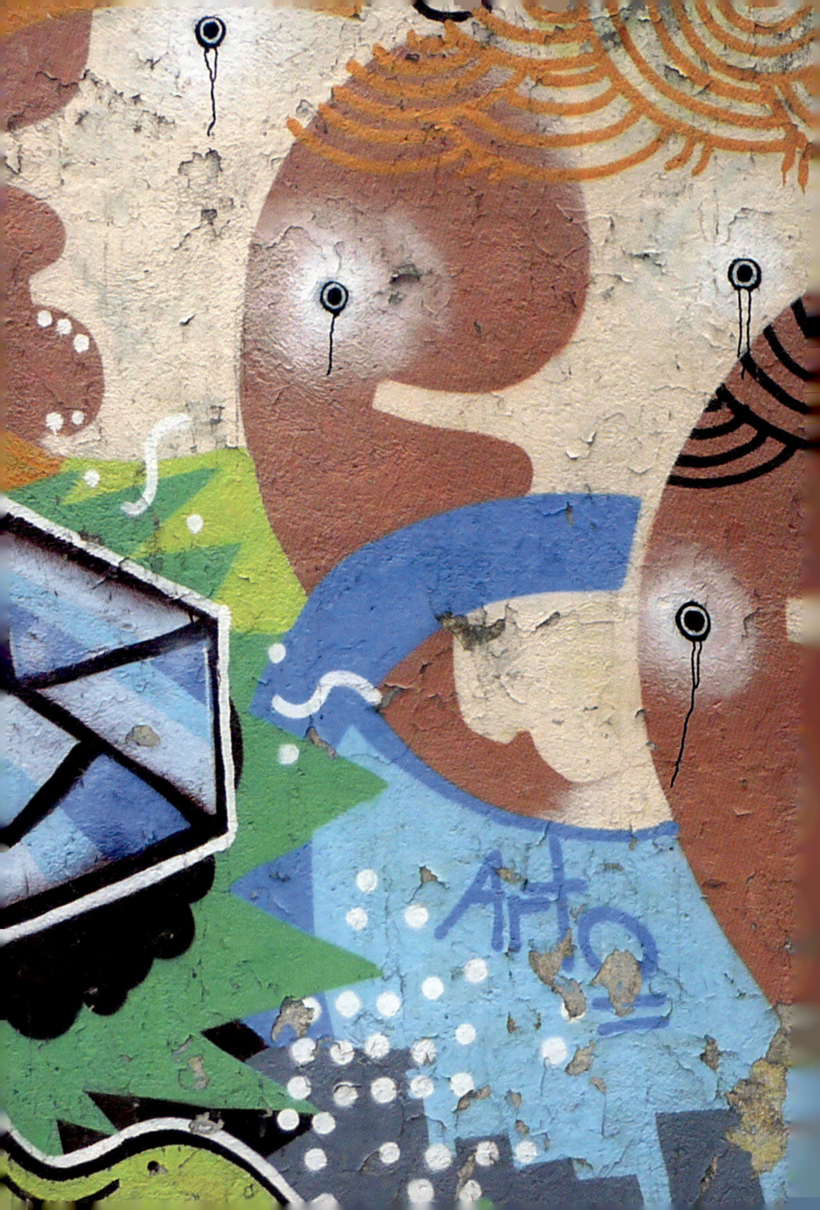

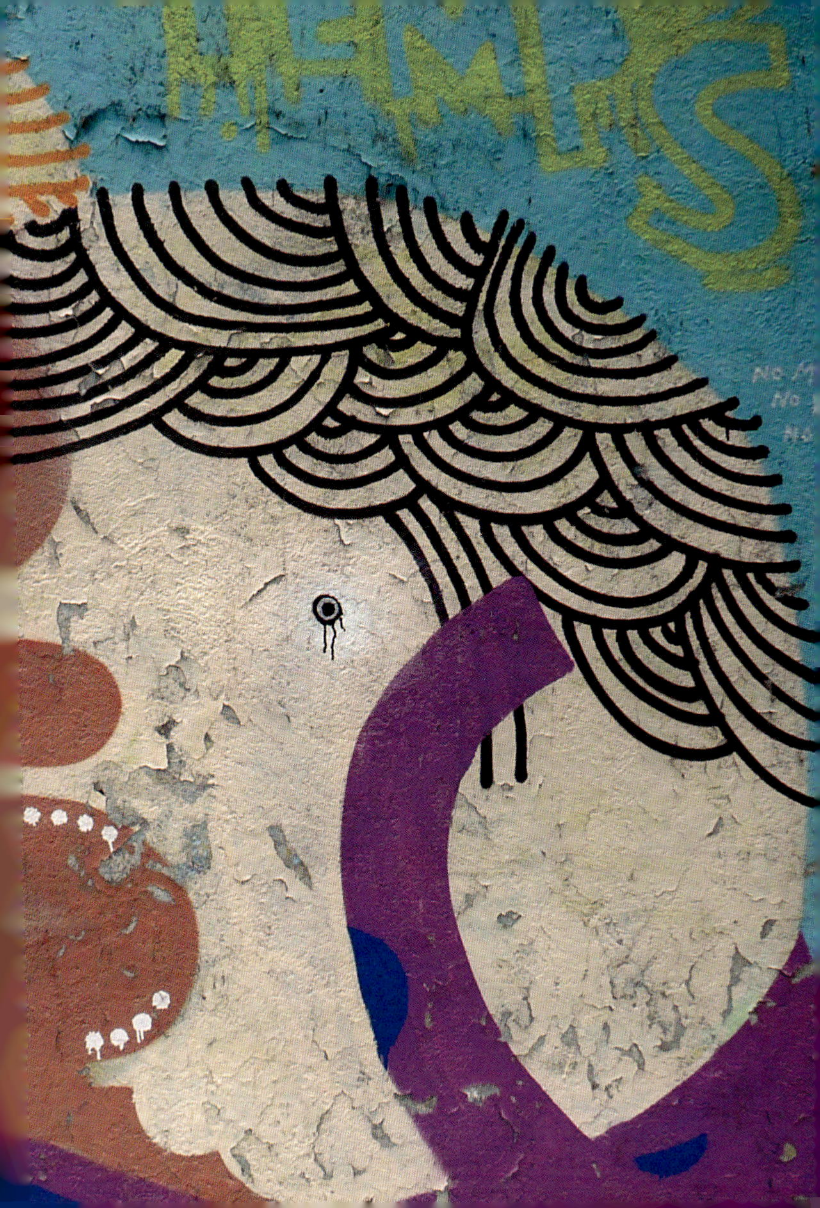

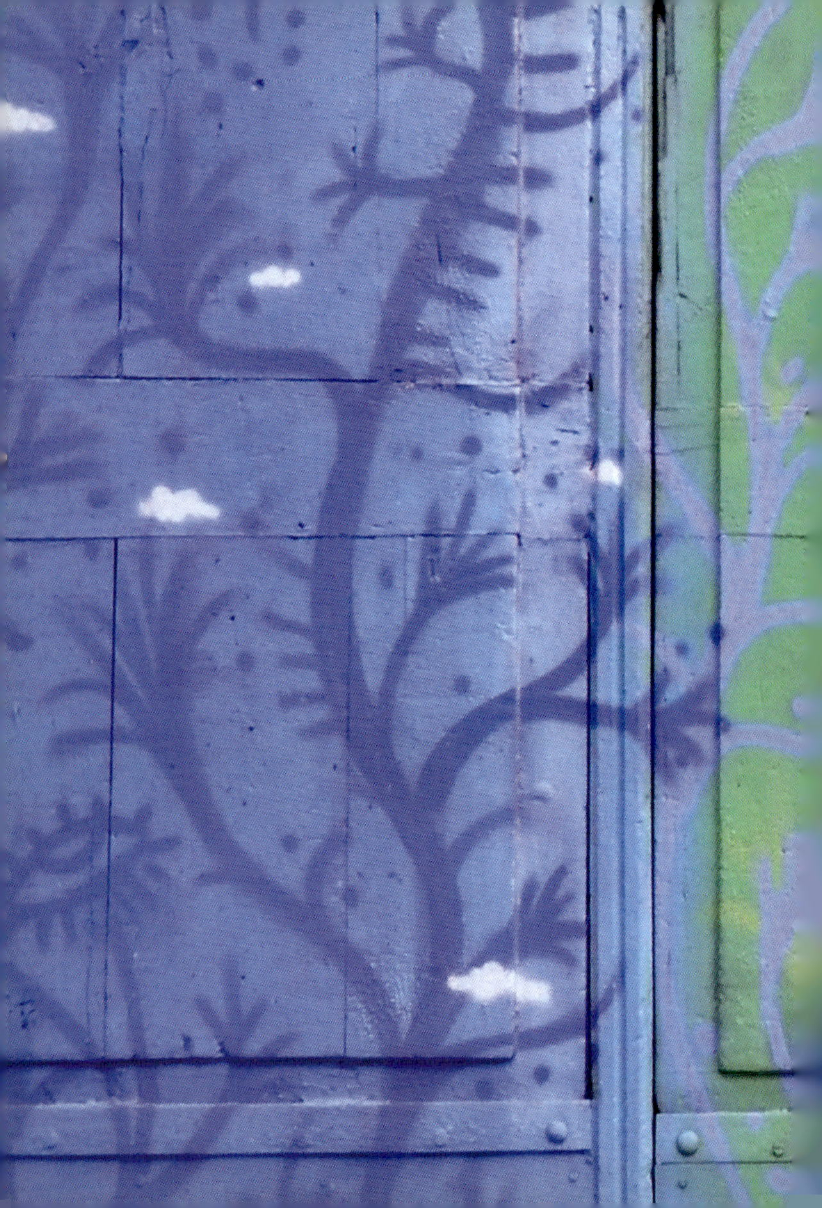

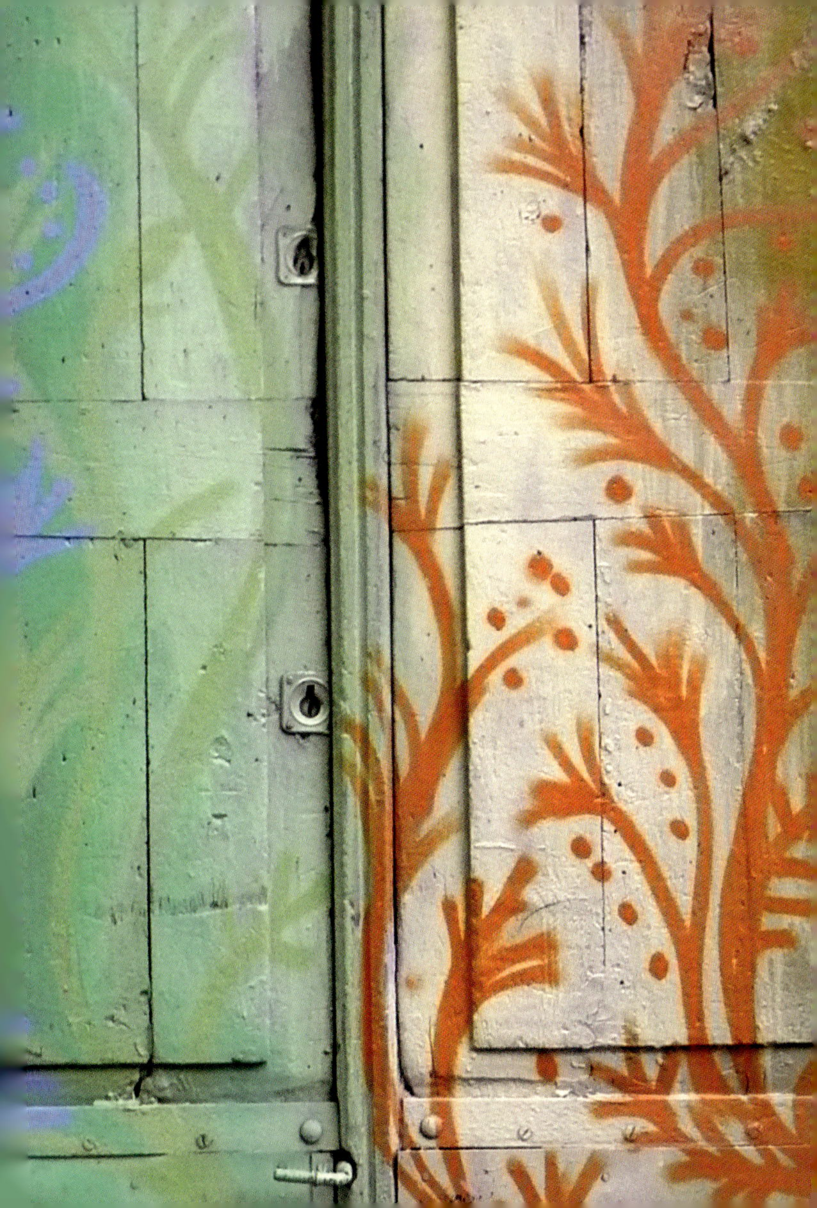

Acknowledgements:
Atl, Búho, Eren, Hobbita, Kiba, Ludger, Mutti, Olli, Repo, Rom, Shing02, Thares1, Xirawe, Zoochi.
Those who fill the concrete jungle with colour.

Graffiti art credits:
Black window, Btoy, Chicle verde, Chu doma, Colectivo Rompecabezas, Dunedain, Eelus, E.P.A, Fizeone, Juarjuar, Juno, Lolo, Mean, Natsue, News, Saner, Seher, Sex, Smithe, Stnk, Thares, Tres mas, Zona norte.